D. H. Lawrence Today

american
university
studies

Series IV
English Language and Literature

Vol. 196

PETER LANG
New York • Washington, D.C./Baltimore • Bern
Frankfurt am Main • Berlin • Brussels • Vienna • Oxford

Barry J. Scherr

D. H. Lawrence Today

Literature, Culture, Politics

PETER LANG
New York • Washington, D.C./Baltimore • Bern
Frankfurt am Main • Berlin • Brussels • Vienna • Oxford

Library of Congress Cataloging-in-Publication Data

Scherr, Barry J. (Barry Jeffrey).
D.H. Lawrence today: literature, culture, politics / Barry J. Scherr.
p. cm. — (American university studies. Series IV, English
language and literature; vol. 196)
Includes bibliographical references and index.
1. Lawrence, D. H. (David Herbert), 1885–1930—Criticism and
interpretation. I. Title. II. Series: American university studies.
Series IV, English language and literature; vol. 196.
PR6023 .A93Z86545   823'.912—dc22   2003022437
ISBN 0-8204-5833-3
ISSN 0741-0700

Bibliographic information published by **Die Deutsche Bibliothek**.
Die Deutsche Bibliothek lists this publication in the "Deutsche
Nationalbibliografie"; detailed bibliographic data is available
on the Internet at http://dnb.ddb.de/.

The paper in this book meets the guidelines for permanence and durability
of the Committee on Production Guidelines for Book Longevity
of the Council of Library Resources.

© 2004 Peter Lang Publishing, Inc., New York
275 Seventh Avenue, 28th Floor, New York, NY 10001
www.peterlangusa.com

All rights reserved.
Reprint or reproduction, even partially, in all forms such as microfilm,
xerography, microfiche, microcard, and offset strictly prohibited.

Printed in Germany

In memory of Leslie Fiedler (1917-2003)

TABLE OF CONTENTS

CHAPTER ONE
Introduction: Lawrence At "The Bloody Crossroads" 1

CHAPTER TWO
Lawrence's Quarrel with the Jews: A Bloomian Reading 97

CHAPTER THREE
"A Matter of Life and Death":
Lawrence, Homosexuality, and "Poetic Immortality" 171

CHAPTER FOUR
Sex, Selfhood, Literature and Politics:
The Left-Wing Attack on D. H. Lawrence—Part One 319

CHAPTER FIVE
Sex, Selfhood, Literature and Politics:
The Left-Wing Attack on D. H. Lawrence—Part Two 343

CHAPTER SIX
Conclusion: Lawrence's "Poetic Immortality" Today 373

Index 447

CHAPTER ONE

Introduction
Lawrence At "The Bloody Crossroads"

Some fifty years ago, in his major work *The Liberal Imagination*, Lionel Trilling astutely observed that "the liberal ideology" had nothing to offer those writers who are "the monumental figures of our time":

> if...we name those writers who...are to be thought of as the monumental figures of our time, we see that to these writers the liberal ideology has been at best a matter of indifference. Proust, Joyce, Lawrence, Eliot, Yeats,...—all have their own love of justice and the good life, but in not one of them does it take the form of a love of the ideas and emotions which liberal democracy, as known by our educated class, has declared respectable. So that we can say that no connection exists between our liberal educated class and the best of the literary minds of our time. And this is to say that there is no connection between the political ideas of our educated class and the deep places of the imagination.

Thus, for the "monumental" literary "figures of our time," the "love of justice and the good life" runs counter to "the liberal ideology"; but what is the reason that "there is no connection between ["the liberal ideology"] and the deep places of the imagination"? In *The Liberal Imagination* Trilling indeed provides the answer; according to Trilling, the fact that "no connection exists" between the political left wing and "the best of the literary minds of our time" is due to the emotional-passional inadequacy of the left wing: for, Trilling tells us, the paradoxical fact is that

> liberalism is concerned with the emotions above all else,...but in its effort to establish the emotions, or certain among them, in some

sort of freedom, liberalism somehow tends to deny them in their full possibility. (*Liberal Imagination*, pp. 94, x)

Indeed, left-wing ideology ("liberalism") is the enemy of "emotions and the imagination":

> Contemporary liberalism does not depreciate *emotion in the abstract*, and in the abstract it sets great store by variousness and possibility. Yet...the conscious and the unconscious life of liberalism are not always in accord. So far as liberalism is active and positive, so far, that is, as it moves toward organization, it tends to select the emotions and qualities that are most susceptible of organization. As it carries out its active and positive ends it unconsciously limits its view of the world to what it can deal with, and it unconsciously tends to develop theories and principles, particularly in relation to the nature of the human mind, that justify its limitation. Its characteristic paradox appears again, and in another form, for in the very interests of its great primal act of imagination by which it establishes its essence and existence—in the interests, that is, of its vision of a general enlargement and freedom and rational direction of human life—it drifts toward a denial of the emotions and the imagination. (Ibid., p. xi; italics mine)

For all its good intentions, then, liberalism ultimately is characterized by "a denial of the emotions and the imagination."

Thus *The Liberal Imagination* is essentially an oxymoronic title; in his critique of "liberal ideology," Trilling decries the left wing's deficiencies—and praises great literature's strengths:

> To the carrying out of the job of criticizing the liberal imagination, literature has a unique relevance,...because literature is the human activity that takes the fullest and most precise account of variousness, possibility, complexity, and difficulty. (Ibid., pp. xii-xiii)

Thus Trilling concludes that literature, with its privileging of "variousness, possibility, complexity, and difficulty," is virtually antithetical to the narrow, oversimplified, stale, sterile, abstract pieties and dogmas of "liberal ideology" ("the liberal imagination," for what it is worth). The extreme limitations of "the liberal imagination" in relation to the evaluation of literature, Trilling tells us, are starkly exemplified by the left wing's privileging of Theodore Dreiser over Henry James—a privileging in which "politics" vanquishes "literature" at "the bloody crossroads": Trilling deplores the doctrinaire indulgence which liberal intellectuals have always displayed toward Theodore Dreiser, an indulgence which becomes the worthier of remark when it is contrasted with the liberal severity toward Henry James. Dreiser and James: with that juxtaposition we are immediately at the dark and bloody crossroads where literature and politics meet. One does not go there gladly, but nowadays it is not exactly a matter of free choice whether one does or does not go. (Ibid., p. 10)

"[At] the dark and bloody crossroads where literature and politics meet": if this is where literary criticism (deplorably) was situated in 1950 (when Trilling wrote), how much worse is the situation today, some fifty years later—today, when "politics" constantly trumps "literature," thanks to "the new academic establishment of tenured radicals" (Kimball 166) who have made "politically inspired criticism" (Ellis 49) hegemonic; this "politically inspired criticism" of literature is indeed *anti*-literature:

> The sad fact is that politically inspired criticism never speaks of the enjoyment or intellectual excitement of literature, and certainly not of the love of it. (Ellis 49)

In place of any great fondness for literature, the "tenured radicals" in their "politically inspired criticism" indeed manifest a great fondness for "political correctness," "the enforced orthodoxy of leftism" (Will 1994, p. 119), "marked by or adhering to a typically progressive [i.e., leftwing] orthodoxy on issues involving esp. race, gender, sexual affinity" (1996 *Random House Compact Unabridged Dictionary, Special Second Edition*). Under the regime of political correctness, Robert Bork tells us,

> Works of literature are read for their subtexts, usually existing only in the mind of the politically correct reader, about the oppression of women, Western imperialism, colonialism, and racism. (Bork 54)

For the politically correct, politically inspired critic, great literature is an object of denigration and even hated since

> In this [politically correct] view, the canon of Western literature is the record and the instrument of the sexism, racism, and class oppression of Western civilization....(Ellis 51)

But of course the reality is that (as Robert Bork recently observed)

> It is ironic that racism and sexism have been discovered to be the deep, almost ineradicable, sicknesses of this [Western] culture at

> precisely the time when they have been successfully overcome. If they have not entirely disappeared, they are mere wisps of their former selves, except when it comes to white, heterosexual males. That discrimination is now so acceptable that it applies not only to matters like college admissions, hiring and promotion..., but even to the design of the curriculum. (Bork 1996, 247)

Of all "the monumental [literary] figures of our time" (to use Trilling's phrase), none, it seems to me, has suffered so much from left-wing academia's "discrimination" against "white, heterosexual males" as has D. H. Lawrence. With the indubitable triumph of left-wing "politics"—i.e., "political correctness"—over "literature" at "the bloody crossroads" of the academy in the 1990's, Lawrence's reputation appears to be in permanent eclipse. As one scholar of "Left Eclecticism" (Crews 1986, 138) in literary theory recently noted, for left-wing literary critics "literary value coincides with the presence of politically acceptable [i.e., politically correct] notions in a text" (Crews 1992, p. xxi)—and indeed the most essential notion and definition of "political correctness" is

> the replacement of excellence...with "diversity," i.e., with gender and racial preference....(Wildavsky, "Politically Correct," *Academic Questions*, Winter 1993-1994, p. 77)

With "excellence" being replaced by "diversity" in academia, D. H. Lawrence as "heterosexual white male" does not stand a chance, as is illustrated in the shocking data presented in the latest (1996) MLA International Bibliography which shows "racial and gender preferences" disturbingly at work against Lawrence, as the bibliography informs us that in 1996 the number of items of literary criticism published on Toni Morrison (fifty) was nearly twice that of the items published on D. H. Lawrence (thirty-one); thus today, thanks to "racial-gender preferences," "the greatest creative writer in English of our time" (Leavis, *D. H. Lawrence: Novelist*, p. 18) receives far less academic-scholarly attention than

> Toni Morrison,...[an author who]...limit[s] her writing to group grievances of race-gender-class issues, which results in a poverty of content that will make her work seem badly dated within a few decades and that will bring contempt on the Nobel committee that so foolishly allowed its mental horizons to be narrowed by the fads of our time. (Ellis 234)

But what of Lawrence's great rival James Joyce? Some five decades ago F. R. Leavis, speaking of Lawrence and Joyce, authoritatively stated that

> he [Lawrence] demanded much further study—...he would repay endless frequentation as Joyce would not. (Those two, it seems to me, were pre-eminently the testing, the crucial authors: if you took Joyce for a major creative writer, then...you had no use for Lawrence, and if you judged Lawrence a great writer, then you could hardly take a sustained interest in Joyce.) (Leavis 10)

Thus half a century ago Leavis realized that Lawrence and Joyce were "the testing, the crucial authors" and a choice had to be made between them. Leavis of course chose Lawrence; indeed, it was in large part due to Leavis' strenuous pro-Lawrence efforts that for many years the consensus among literary critics was that Lawrence and Joyce were very different but equally great literary figures; as one student-practitioner of the novel explained:

> Lawrence exists at the opposite pole of the creative impulse to Joyce; he is a great romantic poet who used the form of the novel, short stories, verse, travel books, and essays to express his criticism of modern civilization and his vision of the good life. Of his contemporaries, Joyce...is the only writer who is his peer, though they are so removed from each other that comparison is impossible. (Allen 431)

Thus, in the 1950s and the 1960s the case was made that Lawrence and Joyce were incomparable in both senses of the word:

> Joyce and Lawrence: in the history of the English novel they stand in curious and uneasy juxtaposition....As artists they are eternal opposites. But in their opposed ways they took the English novel as far as it has yet gone....They are still the advance guard. (Allen 439)

Indeed, in those days the case was often made that Lawrence was superior to Joyce; even a major Joycean scholar opined that

> Lawrence's treatment [of sexual relationships] makes Joyce's treatment of sex seem simple and abstract....Lawrence serves to underline...fundamental limitation[s] in Joyce...as a *novelist*.... (Goldberg, pp. 305-306, 310)

But today the situation is completely different: today it is surely evident that, as one student of both Joyce and Lawrence has remarked, "the work of Joyce is being privileged over Lawrence's" (Ingersoll 1996, 263); indeed, while Lawrence's status in academia is in great decline, "Joyce's reputation is as high as it ever was" (Donoghue, *Joyce in Context*, p. 19)—if not higher: in the 1996 MLA International Bibliography Joyce had far more entries (one hundred and thirty-seven) than Lawrence (thirty-one) and Morrison (fifty) combined (and more also than the supremely trendy Virginia Woolf [120 entries], whom the perspicuous Lionel Trilling considered to be "very far removed from greatness" ["Culture and the Present Moment," *Commentary*, December 1974, p. 38]). Of course Joyce is a great writer, but Lawrence (it seems to me, and to the late F. R. Leavis) was greater: so why the great discrepancy today between Lawrence's "ratings" and those of his arch rival James Joyce?

The answer, it seems to me, can be found in the fact that the "polysemous" Joyce can be made to appear "politically correct," whereas

> Lawrence's [works] do not lend themselves to interpretation at different levels: the personality behind them is too strong for that, too mercurially complex. (Bayley 11)

The "strong," "complex" Lawrence cannot be successfully misrepresented to serve any social-political agenda; the comparatively (philosophically-metaphysically) "simple and abstract" James Joyce (Goldberg 305-306), on the other hand, has been manipulated by major left-wing Joyceans in their aim of

> recuperating a leftist or socialist version of...the heroicized artist. (Norris 8)

Accordingly, one major left-wing Joycean forthrightly—and rather patronizingly—states that

> I am privileging him [Joyce] among the high modernists, as the "social artist"...[and] the "good boy" of modernism. (Norris 21)

Recently one neophyte left-wing Joycean succinctly presented a case for "the [left-wing] political heroicizing of Joyce" (Norris 21):

> Joyce ought to be seen as a political liberal: tolerant, democratic, pacific;...supportive of social and political reform; protective of individual liberties yet, in his own life, committed to social and familial responsibilities. (Segall 14)

While Segall's Joyce is somewhat tepid in his political correctness, more extreme left-wing Joyceans would connect Joyce with more extreme varieties of PC. Thus one radical feminist left-wing Joycean celebrates what she perceives to be

> Joyce's anti-patriarchal obsession (Henke 7)

and happily considers Joyce to be an enemy of "Virility":

> Joyce clearly eschews the literary fraternity that [radical feminist] Shulamith Firestone labels "Virility, Inc." when he challenges an authoritarian power-structure and satirizes patriarchal privilege. By comically deflating sex-role stereotypes of masculine prowess and feminine passivity, Joyce tends to advocate more enlightened principles of androgynous behavior in the complex politics of desire that govern sexual transactions. (Henke, *James Joyce and the Politics of Desire*, "Introduction: Defusing the Patriarchal Can(n)on," p. 4)

In place of "Virility," Henke—and apparently Joyce, her "political hero"—valorize "Polymorphous perversity":

> Joyce deliberately problematizes gender and interrogates sexual practice....Sexual identity [in Joyce] is at once ambiguous and polymorphous, a state to be achieved through the textual exploration of a series of ostensibly perverse psychological drives. Characters are radically decentered by erotic fantasy and attempt to uncover new identities latent in residual needs that overflow the boundaries of sex-role expectations. Polymorphous perversity [in Joyce], translated into the bisexual drives of the unconscious, yields a curious and perplexed dissemination of sexual signifiers that challenge culturally embedded scripts of Oedipal [i.e., patriarchal] triangulation. (Henke 6)

Applauding her "political hero" Joyce's "interrogation" of "[hetero]sexual practice," radical feminist (probably lesbian) Suzette Henke finds Joyce to be much preferable to his great rival

> D. H. Lawrence,...[who] attempts...to compose literary guidebooks to successful heterosexuality. (Henke 212)

Certainly "successful heterosexuality" is not a major part of Henke's agenda; nor does "successful heterosexuality" have priority on the agenda of another left-wing critic, a recent neophyte student of both Lawrence and Joyce who privileges Joyce over Lawrence because

> Lawrence...preserves his ambivalence to patriarchy....[But] Joyce...approaches the postmodern, celebrating liberation [from patriarchy]....(Lewiecki-Wilson, p. 5)

Furthermore,

> The psychostructural relations in both early and late [Lawrence] texts depend upon patriarchy. (Ibid., p. 25)

"Depend[ing] upon patriarchy," Lawrence can never be a true friend to the left wing, whose members "work in whatever small ways we can toward the end of capitalist patriarchy" (Ohmann, p. 13); even worse (in Lewiecki-Wilson's left-wing view),

> Lawrence is a political conservative on broad national-political issues, preferring the individual "great man" and natural aristocrat to the masses. He also appears to endorse a conservative view of gender: men should be manly, women should follow men....(Lewiecki-Wilson, p. 58)

As for "Lawrence's texts,"

> At bottom each is partially conservative in that each relies on a fixed, polar sex/gender system to make its point. (Lewiecki-Wilson, p. 60)

Finally, and worst of all (for Lewiecki-Wilson),

> Lawrence upholds patriarchy (Lewiecki-Wilson, p. 60)

and indeed advocates "a conservative sexual ideology" (ibid., p. 61). On the other hand (according to Lewiecki-Wilson),

> Joyce is more revolutionary (Ibid., p. 61)

—that is to say, more "against patriarchy," than Lawrence is, for

> [A]s Joyce begins to deconstruct received systems, he moves progressively beyond the ground of patriarchy (Ibid., p. 116)

—and consequently moves beyond "the unequal power relations of patriarchy" (ibid., p. 94) which Lewiecki-Wilson deplores; Lewiecki-Wilson, in her abhorrence of "patriarchy," valorizes in its place

> alternative family forms that already exist: for example, the blended families of divorce, gay and lesbian families, African American matriarchal, extended families, Native American clans and tribal families. (*Writing Against the Family*, p. 64)

What is noteworthy about Lewiecki-Wilson's words above, it seems to me, is not only the wrongheadedness of Lewiecki-Wilson's statements (it being common knowledge today that Lewiecki-Wilson's "alternative family forms" are more conducive to crime, poverty, illiteracy, and mental illness than are "patriarchal," traditional "family forms"), but also the blatantly political nature of Lewiecki-Wilson's statements,—their comparatively lengthy, explicitly sociopolitical character and content, which would have been totally out of place in literary criticism—particularly literary criticism dealing with D. H. Lawrence—until extremely recently, in our present day of "the politicization of literary studies" (Sykes 1990, p. 29)—a "politicization" (in Lewiecki-Wilson's case) which replaces "close reading" with tendentious plot summary that is reductive, simplistic, distorted, politically correct; in Lewiecki-Wilson's sketchy discussion of *Women in Love*, for instance, we find the following:

> *Women in Love* links all these elements—the mechanical reproduction of human relations in late industrialism, the spiritual malaise of the modern era, and the impossibility of deep relation with another—with the structure of patriarchy. The images of coldness, whiteness, and snow convey its [i.e., patriarchy's] killing properties. Patriarchy spawns a deathly ideology, exemplified by Gerald's state of mind, a hyperconsciousness based on the need to control and dominate. (Lewiecki-Wilson, p. 107)

Of course, the fact is that "patriarchy" is not to blame for Gerald's death; it is not "the structure of patriarchy" whose "killing properties" are manifested in *Women in Love*—it is those of Gerald's lover Gudrun: it is she, of course, rather than Gerald, who ultimately manifests "hyperconsciousness" and "the need to control and dominate" which makes her the victor in her "love battle" with the finally hapless Gerald; as one authentic Lawrentian critic-scholar observes,

> the message...of Lawrence's *Women in Love* [is]: The man without selfhood, without a strong sense of identity, is doomed to disaster in "love battle" with the domineering, self-centered female. (Scherr 1986, 15)

The above conclusion, politically incorrect though it may be, is certainly supported by several major statements in the novel concerning the relationship of Gerald and Gudrun:

> A strange rent had been torn in him [Gerald]; like a *victim* that is torn open and given to the heavens, so he had been torn apart and given to Gudrun. How should he close again? This wound, this strange, infinitely-sensitive opening of his soul, where he was exposed, like an open flower, to all the universe, and in which he

> was given to his complement, the other, the unknown, this wound, this disclosure, this unfolding of his own covering, leaving him incomplete, limited, unfinished, like an open flower under the sky, this was his cruelest joy....
>
> ...Knowing him [Gerald] finally she [Gudrun] was the Alexander seeking new worlds....
>
> ...[I]n Gerald's soul there still lingered some attachment to the rest, to the whole. And this was his limitation. He was limited, borné, subject to his necessity, in the last issue, for goodness, for righteousness, for oneness with the ultimate purpose. That the ultimate purpose might be the perfect and subtle experiencing of the process of death, the will being kept unimpaired, that was not allowed in him. And this was his limitation [according to Gudrun's point of view]....(*Women in Love*, Chapter XXXI, "Snowed Up"; italics mine)

Thus it is evident that, pace feminist political correctness, Gerald the man is *the "victim"* here, the victim of Gudrun the woman; indeed, Gerald at this point is "sensitive," "exposed," "open,"—certainly not full of "the need to control and dominate" as Lewiecki-Wilson would have us believe (Lewiecki-Wilson 107); furthermore, it is finally revealed that Gerald's ultimate commitment is "for goodness, for righteousness, for oneness with the ultimate purpose"—and for this (evidently moral) commitment the "artistic," avant-garde, ultimately unstable Gudrun holds Gerald in contempt. In addition to her contempt for Gerald, "the mind-dominated Gudrun has a cold integrity of self and cruel survival-capacity, making her a far stronger figure than...Gerald" (Ben-Ephraim 180); consequently "[the Gerald-Gudrun] 'romance'...ends in the death of the male: all along, the novel shows, the love affair of Gerald and Gudrun was one of sado-masochistic submission by Gerald to the woman who does not want him physically and who finally drives him to what is tantamount to suicide" (Butler 118-119); finally, to put it simply, "she [Gudrun] destroys him [Gerald]" (Ben-Ephraim 197)—but of course to say this is to fail to make the woman the *victim*—so, if this (as Butler says) is what "the novel shows" (i.e., that the *man* is the victim), then in today's politically correct academic climate the novel must not be "shown" by the politically correct literary critic at all—and this is what Lewiecki-Wilson does: she fails to *show* the novel *Women in Love* at all; she does no close reading of Lawrence whatsoever—but in politically correct academia today it does not matter whether she actually proves her case, for in academe

> Making the expected charges against patriarchal white Eurocentric culture virtually ensures that one's work will be greeted with universal approbation, for the converted *need no proof* and the doubters dare not reveal their apostasy. (Heather Mac Donald, "Toni Morrison as Literary Critic," *Academic Questions*, Summer 1994, p. 26; italics mine)

For the left-wing literary-cultural critics that predominate in academia today, when it comes to Lawrence the "proof" of "close reading" is not necessary, since Lawrence has been definitively "placed" as the man of letters that the left wing loves to hate, with left-wing critics decrying what they consider to be

> The repressive character [of Lawrence's art]...[which] is evident not only in the misogynist depiction of the [Lawrentian] heroine but in the extensive denial of any specifically social dimension where political conflict might take place. (R.A. Berman 1989, 32)

Refusing to valorize "any specifically social dimension where political conflict might take place," the "repressive" Lawrence instead privileges "the feelings" over "the social system":

> Change in the whole social system is inevitable not merely because conditions change—though partly for this reason—but because people themselves change. We change, you and I, we change and change vitally, as the years go on. New feelings arise in us, old values depreciate, new values arise....
>
> As a novelist, I feel it is the change inside the individual which is my real concern. The great social change interests me and troubles me, but it is not my field. I know a change is coming—and I know we must have a more generous, more human system based on the *life values* and not on the *money values*. That I know. But what steps to take I don't know. Other men know better.
>
> My field is to know the feelings inside a man, and to make new feelings conscious. ("The State of Funk," *Phoenix II*, p 567; italics mine)

The "new feelings" of which Lawrence wishes to "make...[us] conscious" pertain mainly to

> The great relationship, for humanity, [which] will always be the relation between man and woman....And the relation between man and woman will change for ever, and will for ever be the new central clue to human life. It is the *relation itself* which is the quick and the central clue to life....("Morality and the Novel," *Phoenix*, p. 531)

As "*the* novelist" of "the feelings," Lawrence privileges the "life values" of emotional fulfillment over the "money values" which are the simplistic obsession of the left-wing cultural-political elite, from Jane Fonda to Teddy Kennedy, who, wealthy themselves, believe that the only way to be happy is by having welfare state social security from cradle to grave; whether from their own guilt over their own wealth (Bork 1996, 25, 93), or out of their own shallow self-righteousness (Bork 80), or just because of their own lack of passional imagination—their "denial of the emotions and the imagination" (as Trilling powerfully suggests in the "Preface" to *The Liberal Imagination* [p. xi]), the political-cultural left is possessed by materialistic "money values" that are antithetical to Lawrentian "life values"; as the great Lawrentian F. R. Leavis sagaciously noted some seventy years ago, the political-cultural left is, *au fond*, supremely "bourgeois" and "capitalistic" (i.e., materialistic):

> to aim [as the political left does] at solving the problems of civilisation in terms of the "class war" is to aim, whether wittingly or not, at completing the work of capitalism and its products, the cheap car, the wireless and the cinema. (Leavis, *For Continuity*, p. 172)

Seeing human life and human happiness "in terms of...capitalism and its products," the political-cultural left is too "bourgeois," too materialistic, to be capable of recognizing Lawrence's "human values":

> it is a bourgeois incapacity [in the political-cultural left] that cannot recognize the human values that...Lawrence...[is] asserting against the [materialistic] environment....[The Lawrentian values] are not generated in the modern economic process. Indeed, this is our criticism [of the Left], that in the matter of "values" the Marxist is too bourgeois, too much the product of the material environment. (Leavis, *For Continuity*, p. 186)

Thus the political-cultural left adheres to "money values" rather than to Lawrentian-Leavisite "life values" and "human values"; Lawrence, on the other hand, never abandoned his "life values" in favor of "money values," no matter how dire his personal financial circumstances. Indeed, the poverty-stricken Lawrence even in the midst of the Great War fervently believes that "The great relationship...between man and woman" supremely serves the "life values" and surely transcends the "money values" ("money values" which so obsess the socio-political left); he writes, in a letter of 1916:

> I feel...established in my soul—really strong and single. I have finished a novel [*Women in Love*]....*I* think very highly of it, but I don't suppose anybody will publish it—at least for some years to come. We [Lawrence and Frieda his wife] are hopelessly badly off as far as money goes, though it never troubles me, so long as one is strong in one's soul....As far as material things go, one can drift as necessity impels one....
>
> ...The whole crux of life now lies in the relation between man and woman, between Adam and Eve. In this relation we live or die....A man who has a living connection with a woman is, *ipso facto*,...an essential creator. (D. H. Lawrence letter to Cynthia Asquith, 11 November 1916)

"Strong and single" in his soul after having finished his great novel *Women in Love*, Lawrence is unfazed by being "hopelessly badly off as far as money goes"—surely more "badly off" than today's "inner city poor" (notorious for their "Welfare Cadillacs," VCRs, TVs, drugs and guns); indeed, in February 1918 Lawrence found himself to be in such a difficult financial situation that he could say:

> it doesn't bother me much, the poverty—perhaps it ought to bother me more, and I should provide better. For the time has come when I shall have to turn beggar, or something. I find we have got exactly six pounds nineteen shillings in the world: and not a penny due. (D. H. Lawrence letter to Cynthia Asquith, 12 February 1918)

Unlike today's materialistic, consumerist "inner city poor," Lawrence finds that "it doesn't bother me much, the poverty"; but Lawrence of course had something that today's "poor," so "beloved" by the political left millionaires (from Ted Kennedy to Ted Koppel), do not have: Lawrence had strength and greatness "in [his] soul": this strength and greatness of soul enabled Lawrence "never" to be "trouble[d]" by "the poverty" with which he was afflicted for most of his life; and of course Lawrence's strength and greatness of soul was based on Lawrence's belief that "The whole crux of life...lies in the relation between man and woman....In this relation we live or die." Lawrence in late 1916, in the midst of his *Women in Love* period, certainly sees himself as "A man who has a living connection with a woman [his wife Frieda]," and thus as "an essential creator" even in the midst of the Great War. Indeed, Lawrence of course built his reputation—his legacy, one might say—on "sticking up for the love between man and woman":

> God help us [i.e., Lawrence and Frieda]. Once you've known what love *can* be, there's no disappointment any more, and no despair. If the skies tumble down like a smashed saucer, it couldn't break what's between Frieda and me. I think folk have got sceptic about love—that's because nearly everybody fails. But if they fail, they needn't doubt *love*. It's their own fault. I'll do my life work, sticking up for the love between man and woman....I shall always be a priest of love, and...a glad one....(D. H. Lawrence letter to Sallie Hopkin, 25 December 1912)

"Sticking up for the love between man and woman," Lawrence did indeed make it "my life work,"—to the point where he is indeed today regarded as the "priest of love": as one left-wing feminist "Lawrentian" recently put it,

> Lawrence...[is] known so well as the writer of heterosexuality *par excellence*....(Williams 72)

But, lest we think that the feminist Williams intends this as a compliment, she soon makes it clear that for her Lawrence's status as "writer of heterosexuality *par excellence*" simply makes

> Lawrence-the-arch-MCP ["MCP" meaning "male chauvinist pig"]...(Williams 100)

Thus what at one time and in one context would surely be considered praise for Lawrence ("priest of love," "writer of heterosexuality *par excellence*") is today seen as being part and parcel of what for many "intellectuals" is Lawrence's supremely reprehensible identity and reputation as "arch male chauvinist pig"; this extreme denigration of Lawrence's status can indeed be traced to the domination of academia by the politically correct Left, the cultural-intellectual Left which today is so "powerful in the control of [literary] reputations" (Leavis, *D. H. Lawrence: Novelist*, p. 15),—the Left which, rather than deal with the psychological-intellectual-emotional-philosophicoreligious complexities which Lawrence presents, instead chose

> To see him [Lawrence] as fostering the spirit of something akin to Nazism—that was an easy way of dismissing the complications he would have introduced into the simple scheme of salvation adopted on the Left. (Leavis, *D. H. Lawrence: Novelist*, p. 20)

For the Left, with its "denial of the emotions and the imagination" (Trilling, *Liberal Imagination*, p. xi), Lawrence has assumed the role of supremely unmitigated right-wing villain; thus one major left-wing Ivy League professor (Schwarz of Cornell) in a recent review-essay contrasts Lawrence unfavorably with the politically correct E. M. Forster, finding Lawrence to be "hyperbolic" and "intemperate" while Forster is "understated, civilized, liberal, humanist" (Schwarz 1995, 191); Schwarz goes on to deplore what he calls "Lawrence's moral irresponsibility," "violence" and "fascism" (ibid.); he also attacks Lawrence as "vatic" and "hubristic" (ibid., p. 192); finally, Schwarz grandiloquently and self-righteously asserts that

> I have always been troubled by Lawrence's misanthropy, anti-Semitism, and penchant for violent political solutions....(Schwarz 1995, 207)

—yet, when it comes to presenting evidence in support of his accusations, Schwarz, like a left-wing Clinton spinmeister, takes liberties with the truth (to say the least); as evidence of "Lawrence's...anti-Semitism," indeed, Schwarz cites two Lawrence letters to Dr. David Eder, a major leader of the Zionist movement—evidently Schwarz does not even realize that the sheer fact that Lawrence is friendlily writing to a Zionist leader can indeed serve to refute Schwarz's charges of anti-Semitism; furthermore, and what is even worse, Schwarz merely quotes one sentence from each of these two Lawrence letters, and he (Schwarz) seems to be deliberately misleading the majority of his (Schwarz's) readers who will most likely not bother to look up the entire actual Lawrence letters. From the first cited letter to Eder (D. H. Lawrence letter of 24 August 1917), Schwarz quotes only (and indeed out of context) these few words of Lawrence to Eder (who was already a major Jewish leader; see Hobman 71):

> Best cease to be a Jew, and let Jewry disappear—much best...(Quoted in Schwarz 1995, 192)

—but if Schwarz (or any other "Lawrentian," for that matter) wished to present a true account of "Lawrence's...anti-Semitism," he need only have quoted the cited sentence in context:

> I have thought about you often since I saw you in London....[L]ife seemed at a crisis with you—as it is with me....[Y]ou think of going to Palestine with the [Zionist] Jewish Contingent. One must go somewhere, I suppose—it is abominable to keep still in nothingness. Yet it is no good running about either. One has got to live

> through, or die through, this crisis [of World War I]. Why do you go with the Jews? They will only be a mill-stone round your neck. Best cease to be a Jew, and let Jewry disappear—much best...(D. H. Lawrence letter to David Eder, 24 August 1917)

In context the above letter to Eder makes it clear that here Lawrence is in fact trying to persuade one of his (several) close Jewish friends ("I have thought about you often")—with whom he feels considerable psychical kinship ("Life seemed at a crisis with you—as it is with me")—not to leave him to start a new community in a new land (i.e., "Palestine")—especially at a time when he (Lawrence), as everybody knows, was envisioning his very own utopian community, "Rananim"; as he wrote to his closest (and Jewish) friend Koteliansky a few months before his letter to Eder:

> I feel perfectly hopeless and disgusted with the world here. My dear Kot, when we can but set sail for our Rananim, we shall have our first day of happiness. But it will come one day—before very long....That is the living dream. We will have our Rananim yet. (D. H. Lawrence letter to Koteliansky, 8 January 1917)

And again:

> Everything seems to have gone to pot in the world. And still I hope...we can find our Rananim....Hope is a great thing. We are not beaten yet, in spirit, but it is a critical moment. We must pray to the good unknown. I think we shall come out all right, even against so many millions....
>
> ...We shall all come to our Rananim before many years are out—only believe me—an Isle of the Blest, here on earth....(D. H. Lawrence letter to Koteliansky, 9 February 1917)

Indeed, Lawrence's "living dream," "our Rananim" is essentially a "Jewish" dream, for Lawrence evidently derived the word "Rananim" from the Hebrew word for "Rejoice" as used in the opening line of Psalm 33, "Rannani Zadikim, Zadikim l'Adonoi" ("Rejoice in the Lord, O ye righteous"); indeed, it was from his closest (and Jewish) friend Koteliansky that Lawrence learned the Hebrew words to the Psalm employed in the Lawrentian coinage "Rananim," for Koteliansky frequently sang the psalmic phrase ("Rannani Zadikim, Zadikim l'Adonoi") to Lawrence during the early days of their friendship (begun in 1914). (See Zytaruk 1970, pp. xxxiii-xxxiv; Frieda Lawrence, p. 81; Kinkead-Weekes 1996, pp. 148, 791.) Furthermore, as for Lawrence's friendship with David Eder,

Eder's biographer authoritatively concludes that

> the [Lawrence-Eder] correspondence published indicates how constantly he [Lawrence] longed for Eder's trustworthy companionship. What little talk I had with Eder about Lawrence was revealing in its understanding of that most highly sensitive of modern spirits [i.e., D. H. Lawrence] who needed so much more understanding than he usually got or still gets. (Hobman, p. 26)

And Frieda Lawrence confirms Hobman's assessment of the Lawrence-Eder friendship:

> I know Lawrence always felt that the Eders understood him and gave him his due. (Frieda Lawrence, quoted in Hobman, p. 123)

As the Zionist Hobman noted, "that most highly sensitive of modern spirits" D. H. Lawrence still gets very little "understanding" and still does not get "his due"; this is indeed true today, when trendy influential left-wing academics like Schwarz of Cornell (and also recently Judith Ruderman of Duke; see Ruderman 1991) persist in superficial, tendentious, reductive treatments of "Lawrence's anti-Semitism." Surely the complexity of "Lawrence's anti-Semitism" (which is not in fact anti-Semitic) is revealed in the other letter that Schwarz cites in support of his contention that Lawrence is anti-Semitic, Lawrence's letter of 25 April 1919 to David Eder, from which Schwarz quotes only the sentence

> I have a horror of the dreadful hosts of people, "with noses"...(quoted in Schwarz 192)

When we look at that one sentence in context, however, we see that, far from being anti-Semitic, Lawrence longed for "Palestine" (i.e., Israel) and the joyful contact with "the heavens" which he evidently felt went with it; Lawrence fervently wanted to be part of "the Blessed" company that he believed the Jews to be—a "Blessed" company which he indeed wished to imbue with his own Lawrentian values,—Lawrentian "magic" so to speak; as he earnestly expresses it in his letter to Eder:

> Oh, do take me to Palestine, and I will love you for ever. Let me come and spy out the land with you—it would rejoice my heart to the heavens. And I will write you such a beautiful little book, "The Entry of the Blessed into Palestine." Can't I come and do the writing up? Because...I have a hot little interest in Palestine. But I have a horror of the dreadful hosts of people, "with noses," as your sister said. It needs kindling with a spark of [Lawrentian] magic, your Palestine—it will be a dead failure otherwise....

> I wish you would take me to Palestine. I don't believe you'll pull it off, as a *vital* reality, without me....I seriously want to go to Palestine. (D. H. Lawrence letter to David Eder, 25 April 1919)

Thus Lawrence, with his "seriously want[ing] to go to Palestine," indeed can be seen as wanting to be a Jew, as he envisions himself as in fact being needed by the Jews to make their dream (of Palestine) "a *vital* reality"—that is to say, a Lawrentian reality, a "reality" with the unique stamp of D. H. Lawrence upon it; a reality which indeed can be seen as part of Lawrence's scheme (unconscious in nature) to attain "Jewishness" by making himself (in his imagination at least) a vital part of the Jewish "reality." For the fact is that Lawrence as "religious" philosopher-poet was placed in the extremely difficult situation of having as his precursors the ancient Jews, thus placing himself in an "anxiety of influence" relation to them; it is this "anxiety of influence" relation which is a major focus of discussion in the first big chapter of the present volume, a chapter which deals with the true nature of Lawrence's response to the Jews,—a response that was rooted, not in anti-Semitism, but rather in "the immense anxieties of indebtedness" as described by literary theorist Harold Bloom:

> My concern is only with strong poets, major figures with the persistence to wrestle with their strong precursors, even to the death. Weaker talents idealize; figures of capable imagination appropriate for themselves. But nothing is got for nothing, and self-appropriation involves the immense anxieties of indebtedness, for what strong maker desires the realization that he has failed to create himself? (Bloom, *Anxiety of Influence*, p. 5)

According to Bloomian theory, "strong poets, major figures"—such as Lawrence—perforce must have "the persistence to wrestle with their strong precursors, even to the death,"—in view of the fact that a "strong maker" (such as Lawrence) must "appropriate" his "precursors" rather than "idealize" them, for if he idealized his precursors he could not succeed in "self-appropriation" in relation to them—that is to say, he could not use them for his own aims of self-aggrandizement and indeed self-creation, since his idealizing of his precursors would lead him to feel indebted to them for his very poetic identity; thus the strong poet must repress his indebtedness to his precursors so that he can feel that he is "the father of himself" (Bloom, *Anxiety*, p. 64)—of his own "poetic self" (ibid., p. 121), that is. In order that the "strong maker"-"strong poet" believe that he is "the [poetic] father of himself," Bloom tells us, the strong poet needs to believe that he is not influenced, for to be influenced means (for the strong poet) to be

> suffering the anxieties of obligation...(Bloom *Anxiety* 31)

—"obligation" that results from his being influenced by strong precursors, indebted to them and their influence in forming his poetic self. Indeed, for the strong poet,

> The prayer...is to be an influence, and *not to be influenced*....
> (Bloom *Anxiety* 126; italics mine)

One major way in which the strong poet obtains

> strength to overcome his anxiety of influence (Bloom *Anxiety* 6)

is by "denying [his] obligation" (ibid.) to his precursor(s) in such a way as to make them (his precursors) indeed seem to be his very antithesis, even his foe(s): this, it seems to me, is how Lawrence deals with the influence of Plato upon him, as I go to great lengths to demonstrate in my book *D. H. Lawrence's Response to Plato: A Bloomian Interpretation* (Scherr 1996):

> As a "strong poet" and a "strong maker," Lawrence perforce had to quarrel with his "strong precursor" Plato. Lawrence's quarrel with Plato was an essential part of his defense against "the immense anxieties of indebtedness." In his intense hostility toward Plato, Lawrence repressed his indebtedness to Plato and his work, and thus Lawrence was able to "overcome his anxiety of influence." (Scherr 1996, 43)

Similarly, "Lawrence's anti-Semitism" is rooted in his "anxiety of influence" in relation to the Jews (as I go on to discuss at great length in the next chapter of the present volume); thus what left-wing "Lawrentian" academics describe as "Lawrence's anti-Semitism" is in fact evidence of Lawrence's admiration for, and indeed "indebtedness" and "obligation" to, the Jewish way as displayed from Biblical times to his (Lawrence's) own. As somebody who is proud to be a Jew and a Lawrentian as well, I am glad to take issue with those who would make Lawrence out to be an anti-Semite.

But why should Schwarz and others wish to portray Lawrence as an anti-Semite? One clue, it seems to me, is provided by Schwarz's recent statements in favor of

> the field of cultural studies—a field that stresses power relationships among genders, races and classes. (Schwarz 1994, 121)

As everybody knows,

> Characteristic of cultural studies in English-speaking universities is a leftist political orientation....(Leitch, "Cultural Studies," *Johns Hopkins* 180)

—and Schwarz, with his valorization of "genders, races and classes" in relation to literature, is today evidently representative of the academic group that "subordinates lit. to politics, esp. liberal and leftist politics" (Leitch, *New Princeton Encyclopedia*, p. 264). Furthermore, even as he manifests enthusiasm for "the field of cultural studies,...genders, races and classes," Schwarz denigrates the transcendent; he proudly declares that

> we [the academic left] have learned in recent years to be wary of locating essential or transcendent themes [in literature]....(Schwarz 1994, 121)

Schwarz is evidently not very keen on Lawrentian "essential or transcendent themes"—but he does proudly announce his support of trendy left-wing developments, stating that his latest work

> takes part in the exciting dialogue within the profession about the possibilities of cultural criticism....I enthusiastically embrace...cultural studies,...a dialogue with Marxist and poststructural cultural studies. (Schwarz 1994, 122)

In "enthusiastically embrac[ing]" a kind of "dialogue with Marxist and poststructural cultural studies," in "stress[ing] power relationships among genders, races and classes," Schwarz perforce prefers the "liberal" Forster to Lawrence, not only because he (Forster) is politically correct, "liberal" (Schwarz 1994, 191),—but, perhaps most important of all, because he (Forster) is homosexual—*Queer Forster* (Martin 1997), as he is celebrated today in academia, where being "queer," "gay" (homosexual) is as good as being black—that is to say, as good as gold. As Harold Bloom recently (and melancholily) noted, in academia today

> sexual orientation [i.e., homosexuality] is...placed with race, ethnic group and gender as sources of aesthetic and cognitive values (Bloom 1998, *Best*, p. 17)

—and Bloom sardonically alludes to a course called

> "Sado-Masochistic Studies," in particular honor of the god of [left-wing] resentment, the late [homosexual sado-masochist intellectual] Michel Foucault....(Bloom 1998, 17)

And Bloom rhetorically asks,

> If there is a Homosexual Poetic, then why not a Poetics of Pain? (Ibid.)

Thus Bloom, with his references to "Sado-Masochistic," "Homosexual," and "Pain," explicitly attacks "the late Michel Foucault," who is indeed regarded by the intellectual-academic Left as "the best-known intellectual in the West" (Edmundson 1995, 153); as one left-wing literary theorist recently and enthusiastically expressed it:

> When Michel Foucault died of illnesses stemming from AIDS in 1984 he was...the best-known intellectual in the West. Since that time his influence has only grown....And no discipline has grappled with Foucault as fervently as literary studies. His thought is central to much of the most intelligent work that has come out of American English departments over the past two decades. It's been said that literary studies have entered the Age of Michel Foucault. (Ibid.)

Fighting against "the Age of Michel Foucault," Harold Bloom battles against (among other things) the Foucautian dictim that, in the configuration of this our human life,

> things work at the level of on-going subjugation, at the level of those continuous and uninterrupted processes which subject our bodies, govern our gestures, dictate our behaviours etc....[S]ubjects are gradually, progressively, really and materially constituted through a multiplicity of organisms, forces, energies, materials, desires, thoughts etc....
>
> The individual...is an effect of power, and at the same time,...is the element of its [i.e., power's] articulation. The individual which power has constituted is at the same time its vehicle. (Foucault, *Power/Knowledge*, pp. 97-98)

Rather than adhere to the Foucaultian notion that the human self is nothing more than "a subject" (i.e., one that is subjected to, governed by, and constituted through "continuous and uninterrupted processes...[and] a multiplicity of...forces")—"a subject" whose individuality is bogus, since his/her individuality is only "an effect of power...[and] its [i.e., power's] vehicle," Harold Bloom, with his emphasis on "poetic strength" and poetic "self-creation," valorizes "Selfhood"; as one student of literary theory, Art Berman, succinctly notes:

> Selfhood in Bloom...is paramount....Bloom['s]...dominant motivation...is...the preservation of the self so threatened in modern times....(Berman, pp. 6, 270)

But Berman evidently has mixed feelings about Bloom's "motivation" and Bloom's "theory of influence":

> [Bloom's] theory of influence is one of a self-absorbed competitiveness, a competitiveness that bears a resemblance to the ambition of an American self-made man forging his own success, a self-interest...saturated with an egocentricity that, in Bloom's unique recipe for achievement, contains the residue of a modernized reconception of the personality of the nineteenth-century [Romantic] artist: egoist and genius, tormented and struggling, the "isolate selfhood" in what is for Bloom its most compelling manifestation. (Berman, p. 274)

Deploring the "self-absorbed competitiveness," "the ambition," the "self-interest" and "egocentricity" of the Bloomian strong poet, Berman's hostility towards Bloom is mild when compared with that of the major left-wing academic star from which it (Berman's hostility toward Bloom) may indeed derive, Frank Lentricchia, the megabucks Marxist literary critic (one among many) who vehemently attacks Bloom's theory as being guilty of

> the sin against community...(Lentricchia, *After the New Criticism*, p. 329);

according to Lentricchia,

> Bloom...describe[s] a willful drive deeper into the self, toward solipsistic discontinuity—a drive away from community and toward increasing lyric inwardness that will purchase the romantic's *sine qua non*, the unique self....(Ibid.)

For Lentricchia and his followers, the Bloomian strong poet's "drive deeper into the self,...drive away from community and toward increasing lyric inwardness" is the ultimate "sin" against the left-wing political orthodoxy that is the "religion" of many "Lentricchians," for whom "the self" must be denounced so that the "community" may be privileged above the individual self, the "community" for the left wing being nothing less than the replacement for God; indeed, one disciple of Lentricchia recently (and self-righteously) concluded that

> Once God goes, one is tempted to say, only the self remains. But it is more accurate to say that, once the belief in a permanent, divinely sanctioned system of real universals goes, then all value tends to collapse into the human subject's powers of creative invention and its endless project of satisfying its desires whatever they are thought to be. This is fine so far as it goes, I suppose, but self-creation must have more of an ethical end for me than the perfection of the process. If this makes me a modern intellectual nostalgic for some "higher," more-than-human ideal of perfection, so be it....
>
> What is needed, I believe, is a broadly transhistorical (but not God-like) perspective on the practice of interpretation and the interpretive self. No one can hope to reverse the loss of essential values and universal norms. They [i.e., essential values and universal norms] have their own inherent dangers as we know from Foucault's work, anyway....(O'Hara, *Radical Parody*, pp. 7-8)

Happily noting that "God goes...and only the self remains," left-wing Daniel T. O'Hara is glad to be rid of "the belief in a permanent, divinely sanctioned system" while he at the same time asserts his moral ("ethical") superiority by claiming that he is altruistically concerned about matters other than his own "desires" and his own "self-creation"; concerned about matters "higher" than the sublime "poetic immortality" aspirations of the Bloomian strong poets in "Bloom's...world of resentful competition" (*Radical Parody*, p. 146); yet, paradoxically, O'Hara's "higher" aspirations reveal themselves to be nothing more than his own self-aggrandizement as a left-wing Foucaultian-Lentricchian literary-cultural critic valorizing "a broadly transhistorical...perspective" that replaces "the loss of essential values and universal norms" (such as "God"),—"values" and "norms" which O'Hara is happy to see go in view of the fact that (for him and Foucault at least) these universal and essential "norms" and "values" are full of "inherent dangers." (For Foucault, as we shall later see, the greatest danger is evidently from the "universal norm" of heterosexuality ["heterosexism"] which "marginalizes" and condemns homosexuality, sado-masochism and other "perverse" Foucaultian practises as "unnatural" and "abnormal" and immoral.) In positing the "inherent dangers" of "essential values and universal norms," O'Hara cites Foucault; but for the more utopian aspect of his critique O'Hara goes to the left-wing Lentricchian idealization of community. In his Lentricchian definition of "community" O'Hara tendentiously concludes that "community" today is best exemplified

> in the relations between representative members of formerly subaltern groups now making their way upon the world-historical stage, such as women, people of color, and postcolonial peoples. (*Radical Parody*, p. 141)

For O'Hara, then, "community" is tantamount to nothing more or less than political-power "relations" as enacted by "representative members of formerly subaltern groups now making their way upon the world-historical stage"—those "groups," that is to say, which are so privileged by the left wing in the academy; groups ("women, people of color, postcolonial peoples") whose members are the beneficiaries of left-wing policies such as reverse discrimination—policies which deny "the individual" and valorize "the group"; as one right-wing observer recently (and sardonically) explained, the political-cultural Left

> relocated human problems in the dark region of the human psyche where light can only be shed by the healing sciences through the beneficence of the therapeutic state. With enough money and the restructuring of society, we are assured that all will be well with the individual when fitted into the proper group from which he receives his social identity. In the variegated activities imposed on him by the state, the individual has been absorbed into a logos of self-abdication that is the consequence of...[left-wing] ontology. He [the individual] is no longer free, therefore bound to his own choices,...[rather] he is the cipher of the disparate loyalties that now define him (race, sex, and class). (Wayne Allen, "The Principles of Right," *Modern Age*, Summer 1998, p. 245)

In its (the Left's) obsession with maintaining social-political power over "the individual" so as to make sure "that all will be well with the individual" thanks to its (the Left's) engineering of the individual in society ("social engineering"), the Left asserts that the panacea for the troubled individual will be enacted when he (the individual) is "fitted into the proper group from which he [the individual] receives his social identity"; thus for the Left "salvation" for the individual is to be found in his "self-abdication,"—"self-abdication" that leads him (the individual) to be "no longer free," but rather "the cipher of the disparate loyalties that now define him (race, sex, and class)"—"loyalties" that denigrate individual strength and coherence and being, making the "empowerment" of the individual extremely unlikely; indeed, left-wing intellectuals such as O'Hara, in their quest for social-political power put their confidence, not in themselves as individuals, but rather only in themselves as part of a mass "apparatus":

> Our [i.e., left-wing intellectuals'] empowerment in a mass culture is significant en masse as part of the educational apparatus of the modern state, but *individually* it is not usually very significant at all. (O'Hara, *Radical Parody*, p. 15; italics mine)

Lacking confidence in his "empowerment" as an individual, O'Hara comforts himself (as do many left-wing intellectuals) with the Lentricchian belief that the literary-cultural critic can gain power (psychical, socio-political, professional and financial power) in the academy via his/her advocacy of the favored ("preferred" by the academic and governmental Left) groups—i.e., "women, people of color, and postcolonial peoples." Lentricchia evidently relishes this "political" role of the literary-cultural critic:

> Is there culture that is not covert politics? I can conceive of cultural effects apparently not political, but such effects seem to me to be of little interest....
>
> ...it is the task of the oppositional [i.e., left-wing] critic to reread culture so as to amplify and strategically position the marginalized voices of the ruled, exploited, oppressed, and excluded. (Lentricchia, *Criticism and Social Change*, pp. 14-15)

Bored by "culture that is not...politics," Lentricchia aspires to "amplify and strategically position the marginalized voices of the ruled, exploited, oppressed, and excluded" (i.e., "women, people of color," etc.); but what Lentricchia conveniently, reductively and sanctimoniously forgets is that the "exploited, oppressed, and excluded" in present-day society change from place to place, decade to decade, context to context; as Joseph Epstein, discussing the effects of reverse discrimination ("affirmative action") in the academy, poignantly noted in a recent essay:

> the cynicism of young African-Americans must be as nothing compared with the young white males who know that [thanks to reverse discrimination]...they and their intellectual ambitions have been put permanently on the sidelines....What a discouragement of scholarly passion, what a denial of merit, what a shuck and a sham, a hustle and a scam, affirmative action must seem to them! (Epstein, *Commentary*, March 1998, p. 28)

Thus today a very strong case can be made that (especially in left-wing-dominated academia) it is the "white males" that are "exploited, oppressed, and excluded," their "scholarly passion" sorely discouraged, their "merit" ignored and denigrated; indeed, my own "scholarly passion" for Lawrence ("discouraged" though it has been) brings to mind the fact that Lawrence himself would surely have been opposed to reverse discrimination ("affirmative action") and the ideology behind it—an ideology based on the "mongrel, currish desire" that "no man [should be] better than another,"—an ideology based not on equality of opportunity but rather on equality of result in a society where there is no "merit," no "fineness," no "excellence"; a society in which "nothing must be better than anything else"; and, consequently, a society in which standards "all come down to the level of the lowest"—as Lawrence powerfully expressed it in a letter of his *Women in Love* period (also of course the period of World War I):

> we [i.e., the English] need a republic. But heavens, not a republic based on the idea of Equality and Fraternity. We want a republic based on the idea of extrinsic equality, and intrinsic inequality. When we can give precedence to our betters in spirit, and take precedence of our inferiors in spirit, we are true people. We are only equal in so far as that every man should have equal opportunity to come to his own fulfilment. But that every man should come to the same fulfilment is mere rubbish, and that every fulfilment is equal to every other is mere meaningless words.—What the world needs to learn, today, is to give due honor to those who are finer in spirit, and to know the inferiority of those who are mean and paltry in spirit....But people want equality, and if nothing must be better than anything else, and no man better than another, then we must all come down to the level of the lowest, there is no bedrock of humanity but the bottom dog. And this is our actual aim now.—Oh dear, it makes my arms ache with weariness, even to write it.—*When* will people cease from this mongrel, currish desire? (D. H. Lawrence letter to Dollie Radford, 20 December 1916)

Thus Lawrence, like the Right in America today, supports equality of opportunity—"the idea of extrinsic equality"—but acknowledges, indeed welcomes and valorizes, the fact and reality of "intrinsic inequality,"—the fact that some people are more creative, more intelligent, more gifted than others—a fact and reality that affirmative action (reverse discrimination) today seeks to negate; in a Lawrentian world of "true people," on the other hand, "we can give precedence to our betters in spirit, and take precedence of our inferiors in spirit": that is to say, the ontologically superior Lawrentian individual is to be recognized and honoured—which is far from the case today, for "the world needs to learn, today,...to give due honor to those who are finer in spirit, and to know the inferiority of those who are mean and paltry in spirit"; thus, unlike people in "the world...today," Lawrentian "true people" recognize, admire and respect "merit," and acknowledge "intrinsic inequality,"—contra the Left today which through reverse discrimination and other "politically correct" sociocultural measures (e.g., advocacy of multiculturalism, "the abolition of the traditional canon of literary study" [Sykes, *Profscam*, p. 187]) has enacted a sociocultural-political regime which demands that "we must all come down to the level of the lowest," "the lowest" in terms of creative potential and imaginative-intellectual achievement and moral-ethical intensity and seriousness, "the level" of "the bottom dog." This state of affairs certainly pains Lawrence ("Oh dear, it makes my arms ache with weariness, even to write [about] it")—but, in view of the fact that our "world today" has few "true people," and is afflicted with "this mongrel, currish desire" for a state of "equality,...[a state in which] nothing must be better than anything else, and no man better than another," it is extremely unlikely that a better, more "Lawrentian" state of affairs will emerge, one in which "those who are finer in spirit" are "give[n] due honor" and "those who are mean and paltry in spirit" are "known" for what they are; indeed, today (i.e., at the time of this writing, 1998), the situation is that the "mean and paltry in spirit" are in the saddle (as is dramatically demonstrated in the case of the current occupants of the White House), with the evident blessing of "the community,"—a community which (especially in left-wing academia) has come to

> condemn quality as anti-democratic (Elizabeth Fox-Genovese, "The Claims of a Common Culture: Gender, Race, Class and the Canon," *Salmagundi*, Fall 1986, p. 143)

Indeed, in recent years various noxious "anti-democratic" events have taken place that cast doubt upon the left-wing valorization and idealization of "the community": the savage actions of the African-American "community" in the Rodney King riots and the Crown Heights (Brooklyn) pogrom (resulting in the murder of a holy man—Yankel Rosenbaum—simply because he was Jewish); the murderous actions of "the community" in Rwanda, Somalia, Bosnia and other sites; and of course the uniquely evil genocide perpetrated by the Nazi German "community" upon the Jews in the Holocaust—all these atrocities (among many others) suggest that "the community" may indeed be morally inferior to the individual. Lawrence's letter of 20 December 1916, just discussed above, surely demonstrates Lawrence's keen awareness that it is the individual himself who has the potential to be "finer in spirit," while "the community" (indeed, the "democratic" community) inevitably "come[s] down to the level of the lowest,...the bottom dog": this Lawrentian privileging of the individual over "the community" was elucidated by Lawrence during the apocalyptic time of the Great War,—also the time of Lawrence's great *Rainbow-Women in Love* period,—when Lawrence's intrinsic psychic-ontological power and "poetic strength," and Lawrence's quest for "poetic immortality," were at their apex. Indeed, one of Lawrence's most incisive demystifications of the left-wing idealization of "the community" takes place in a pivotal chapter of *The Rainbow*, "First Love" (Chapter XI), where Lawrence as omniscient narrator-philosopher authoritatively declares that

> No highest good of the community would...give him [the individual] the vital fulfilment of his soul....
> ...the highest good of the community as it stands is no longer the highest good of even the average individual....[Some people] thought that, because the community represents millions of people, therefore it must be millions of times more important than any individual, forgetting that the community is an abstraction from the many, and is not the many themselves. Now when the statement of the abstract good for the community has become a formula lacking in all inspiration or value to the average intelligence, then the "common good" becomes a general nuisance, representing the vulgar, conservative materialism at a low level.
> And by the highest good of the greatest number is chiefly meant the material prosperity of all classes....we know what the community wants; it wants something solid, it wants good wages, equal opportunities, good conditions of living, that's what the community wants. It doesn't want anything subtle or difficult. Duty [in "community" terms] is very plain—keep in mind the material, the immediate welfare of every man, that's all.

In *The Rainbow* Lawrence forthrightly declares that the "highest good of the community" indeed militates against "the vital fulfilment" of the "soul," the inner being and ontological potentiality of the individual; indeed, even "the average individual" cannot find his "vital fulfilment" in "the community," in view of the fact that "the highest good of the community as it stands is no longer the highest good of even the average individual." Deploring the concept of "the community" as a sterile "abstraction" that "has become a formula lacking in all inspiration or value," Lawrence concludes that the notion of the "common good" of "the community" is merely an excuse for "vulgar, conservative materialism at a low level"; thus for Lawrence all bosh about "community" and "common good" is just a pretext for "vulgar...materialism"—"vulgar" *Marxist* "materialism" in fact: for Lawrence, Marxism is synonymous with materialism: indeed, Lawrence emphatically deplores what he sees as

> The dead materialism of Marx...(D. H. Lawrence letter to Charles Wilson, 28 December 1928),

—evidently the same "materialism" to which he (Lawrence) alludes in *The Rainbow* (Chapter XI) as "vulgar *conservative* materialism" (my italics)—for, according to Lawrence, "The dead materialism of Marx," rather than being excitingly revolutionary, is indeed essentially cautious ("conservative")—and common and ordinary ("vulgar")—in its obsession with "the material, the immediate [economic] welfare of every man," even at the price of individual freedom and creativity. For surely Lawrence finds that the left-wing version of "the community" and "the common good" goes hand in hand with "the material prosperity of all classes," "prosperity" which has as its price the community's rejection of and incapacity for "anything subtle or difficult": "anything," that is, which "the highest...individual" is capable of aspiring to and indeed attaining. For, in contradistinction to the aversion of "the [left-wing] community" to "anything subtle or difficult" is the aspiration of the great individual—such as Lawrence—to make a real change in society and civilisation; as one pro-Lawrence scholar-critic sympathetically notes:

> Lawrence had...the belief...that one man [i.e., D. H. Lawrence himself] could perhaps start a whole new way of thinking and feeling and living....(Zytaruk, *Spirit of D. H. Lawrence*, p. 292)

Aspiring to "start a whole new way of thinking and feeling and living," Lawrence himself was most keenly aware of the binarism between Lawrence the "fulfilled and happy" individual and Lawrence the frustrated philosopher-poet-prophet thwarted by "the community" in his endeavour to save "the whole race," "the whole body of mankind,"—which Lawrence has "a gnawing craving" to represent; as he poignantly expressed it in a letter written when the Great War was at its height:

> I feel all right in myself: it is the social part of me that feels dragged down. My individual self is all right, but it seems quite cut off and isolated, as if it had no connection and no relations with anybody, beyond Frieda. It is all right for myself: that side of myself which is single is fulfilled and happy. But there *is* a gnawing craving in myself, to move and live not only as a single, satisfied *individual* [italics mine], but as a real representative of the whole race. I am a pure self, and fulfilled in that. But I have *no connection* with the rest of people, I am only at war with them, at war with the whole body of mankind. (D. H. Lawrence letter to Gordon Campbell, 23 December 1916)

Aware of being supremely "satisfied" as "a single...individual,...a pure self," Lawrence nevertheless longs to have an impact upon "the whole race,...the whole body of mankind"—and, as all who read know, Lawrence's apiration is to have his impact as

> the man who...presumes to counsel others on their sexuality[,]...a man who...was [indeed]...prepared to lay down the law for other people [about sex]. (Ellis, "Lawrence and Forster," *Cambridge Quarterly* 27 [1998]: 9)

A major part of my present study deals with Lawrence's heterosexual "presumption"—a "presumption" that prompted him to "lay down the [heterosexual] law for other people" in such a way that he made some of the most important homosexual artists and intellectuals of his day quite angry with him; indeed, even the "understated, civilized" homosexual E. M. Forster (Schwarz 191) viciously attacked Lawrence, denouncing Lawrence as

> the...impercipient fanatic who has nosed over his own little [hetero]sexual round until he believes that there is no other path for others to take....(E. M. Forster letter to D. H. Lawrence, 12 February 1915, in Lago and Furbank, p. 219)

Indeed, the "immortal" image of Lawrence as heterosexual "fanatic" has taken hold to such an extent that

> Lawrence...[is] now notoriously associated, in the public mind at least, with the outspoken celebration of heterosexual union. (Ellis, "Lawrence and Forster," p. 1)

My own interpretation of Lawrence's "fanatic" heterosexual agenda and the strategy he deployed to enact it takes up the longest chapter in this book (Chapter III), a chapter which employs both Bloomian and Foucaultian theories to present a picture of both a "poetical" Lawrence and a "political" Lawrence,—a Lawrence who both lives in

> my own inner world [of the poetic imagination], which is real...(D. H. Lawrence letter to Ottoline Morrell, 15 March 1916),

and at the same time places great importance upon the external sociopolitical-cultural world, which he aspires to impact and to "alter":

> I do write because I want folk—English folk—to alter, and have more sense (D. H. Lawrence letter to Arthur McLeod, 23 April 1913)

—and in particular, to "have more sense" about sex:

> I do so break my heart over England....And I am so sure that only through a readjustment between men and women, and a making free and healthy of the sex, will she get out of her present atrophy. (Ibid.)

Lawrence did indeed strive for "poetic immortality" and (at least in his imagination) for sociopolitical influence as well; these dual energies in Lawrence—the drive for poetic immortality and the urge to sociopolitical influence—reached their apogee in what is still generally recognized as his greatest work, *Women in Love*, in which Lawrence aspired to "alter" society and make sex "free and healthy" by (among other things) eliminating homosexuality,—homosexuality which he regarded as a major threat to his own poetic immortality—for Lawrence's poetic immortality is indeed grounded in the valorization of heterosex, a valorization exemplified in Lawrentian scenes such as this one from *Lady Chatterley's Lover*:

> "Eh! what it is to touch thee!" he said, as his fingers caressed the delicate, warm, secret skin of her waist and hips. He put his face down and rubbed his cheek against her belly and against her thighs, again and again. And again she wondered a little over the sort of rapture it was to him. She did not understand the beauty he found in her, through touch upon her living secret body, almost the ecstasy of beauty. For passion alone is awake to it. And when passion is dead, or absent, then the magnificent throb of beauty is incomprehensible and even a little despicable: warm, live beauty of contact, so much deeper than the beauty of vision....(*Lady Chatterley's Lover*, Chapter Ten)

"And when passion is dead, or absent, then the magnificent throb of [heterosex] beauty is incomprehensible and even a little despicable":

this Lawrentian insight may indeed well explain the recent hostility of certain left-wing "gay affirming" critics towards Lawrence; these critics evidently do indeed find "the magnificent...beauty" of heterosexual love, passion and pleasure to be "incomprehensible and even a little despicable." One recent notable instance of this left-wing-academic attitude towards sex leading to hostility against Lawrence in academic literary criticism can be found in such "Lawrentian" critics as Christopher Craft, who does indeed find that

> his [i.e., Craft's] own sexual practice (Craft, p. xv)

has been far from satisfactory,

> especially since the insistently heterosexual modalities to which he [i.e., Craft, who is talking about himself] has submitted his [i.e., Craft's] body so obviously fail to correspond to the rhythms of [his, i.e., Craft's] desire. (Craft, p. xv)

In other words, Craft's sex life is lousy.

But Craft consoles himself with his belief that nobody practising "normative male heterosexuality" is having any fun:

> I take it as axiomatic...that this disjunctive relation between [homosexual] desire and [heterosexual] practice itself constitutes one of the crucial pivots around which normative male heterosexuality has historically been taught to dance its ugly sidestep. (Craft, p. xv)

Finding "normative male heterosexuality" to be little more than an "ugly" chore, priding himself on his "gay-affirmative thinking and feeling" (Craft xvii), Craft is extremely uncomfortable with "Lawrence's hypercharged emotion, [and] overwrought [hetero]sexuality" (Craft 141), which Craft deems to be "infuriating" and deserving of "violen[t]...repudiation" (ibid.): for Craft finds that the "normative male heterosexuality" so privileged by Lawrence is essentially a baneful "performance":

> The routine performative exertions...of being "masculine" and staying straight can be staggering in their destructiveness and duplicity, as the violent tortuosities of [Lawrence's] *Women in Love*—and of my reading of them—should help make clear. (Craft, pp. 144-145)

In any event, Barry J. Scherr's reading of *Women in Love* in the present volume (Chapter Three) reveals Lawrence's strategy there of promoting his heterosexual agenda by proselytizing for heterosexuality in such a way as to make heterosex more attractive to homosexuals such as the character Loerke while at the same time making possible a sublation of homoerotic interest by means of a Lawrentian gambit in which the spiritual-intellectual-metaphysical-political elements in male-male relationships are privileged over any physical aspect, and the whole domain of male-male association is subordinated to the Lawrentian realm of male-female love, passion and desire; to put it in "colloquial"-Hegelian terms, homoerotic cathexis is "raised" and "annulled," "lifted up" and "cancelled"—"kicked upstairs" (Inwood, *Hegel Dictionary*, pp. 283-284) in the service of the male-female relationship; but all Lawrentian aspirations to "sublation" are, evidently, reductively denigrated by left-wing "Lawrentians" such as Craft, who concludes that all this Lawrentian "metaphysics" is merely a brutal Lawrentian "formula" in which

> after all the metaphysical huffing and puffing, [there remains only] a formula of sufficient brutality: cunt for cock's sake. (Craft 172)

"Cunt for cock's sake": Craft's crude, sophomoric reduction of the Lawrentian ethos is part and parcel of Craft's failure to appreciate Lawrentian heterosex in *Women in Love* and elsewhere; indeed, Craft derides

> *Women in Love*['s]...fundamental heterosexuality, that heavy and funless sexuality...(Craft 175)

Describing "heterosexuality" as "heavy and funless," Craft is evidently no genuine Lawrentian; finally, Craft condemns

> a heterosexuality whose promises of satisfaction, however hard the sell or obsessive the pursuit, nonetheless always leave something to be desired. (Craft 187)

With anti-heterosexual, "gay-affirmative" critics of Lawrence such as Craft in the saddle (getting their books published by "prestigious" presses like University of California Press), it is no wonder that Lawrence is in trouble in academe today.

Furthermore, together with the left-wing denigration and deprecation of Lawrentian heterosex exemplified by Craft, there is the left-wing attack on Lawrence's aspiration to "save" Western civilization, an aspiration which (the left wing claims) is rooted in Lawrence's "radical individualism" (Dollimore 1998, p. 259), an individualism that is anathema to left-wing "collective social praxis" (ibid.). Ridiculing the figure of

> D. H. Lawrence struggling to reinterpret and redirect Western culture in the direction of a wholesome sexuality resolutely on the side of life (Dollimore 1998, 265),

left-wing "Lawrentians" like Jonathan Dollimore condemn

> the [Lawrentian] mystery of being (Dollimore 1998, 269)

as one which is

> only ever imagined from within the universe of a megalomaniac and paranoid individualism. (Ibid.)

What left-wing intellectuals today see as Lawrence's "heterosexis[m]" (Craft 179) and "megalomaniac and paranoid individualism" (Dollimore 1998, 269) is seen by the right wing today as genuine heroism. Right-wing Lawrentian George A. Panichas decisively asserts that Lawrence is "a hero" (Panichas 1992, p. 77), full of "heroic effort":

> In his own life, heroic effort characterized Lawrence's struggle "for more life to come into being."...[In Lawrence's work], it is the heroic impulse that remains evident. This heroism...[is] at once personal and critical. (Panichas 1992, p. 77)

Unlike Dollimore, who derides Lawrence's "prophetic" aspiration to "save" Western civilization as the aim of "a megalomaniac and paranoid" (Dollimore 1998, p. 269), Panichas praises

> Lawrence's heroic impulse, personal and prophetic as well as literary and cultural, or what F. R. Leavis sums up as "the life-courage in the product of his creativity." (Panichas 1992, p. 78)

According to Panichas, "Lawrence's heroism" is

> a living and discriminating heroism. In its critical honesty, too, there reside its sympathy and generosity. Its openness...[is] the attempt of the writer to give of himself as authentically as he can, without any attitudinizing or moralizing, without the sham of mechanical or politic pieties....(Panichas 1992, p. 78)

Thus, while the left-wing Dollimore's Lawrence is "megalomaniac and paranoid," the right-wing Panichas' Lawrence is characterized by "life-courage," "living...heroism," "critical honesty," "sympathy and generosity"; certainly today's right-wing Lawrentians as exemplified by Panichas (among others) demonstrate a greater appreciation of Lawrence

than do the politically correct "Lawrentians" of the Left.
Panichas further observes that

> Lawrence...speaks that language of honesty and courage which he demands not only of [art] but also of one's spiritual being. In the face of the persistent attempts of [anti-Lawrence] critical revisionists [such as Dollimore and Craft, perhaps] to [cast aspersions on] Lawrence..., it needs to be insisted that...[Lawrence experienced] an innately religious vision and search, conveyed and conducted with...[Lawrentian] endemic moral strength....(Panichas 1992, p. 79)

Endorsing Lawrence's "religious vision and search," right-wing Lawrentian Panichas is indeed even able to applaud the fervent heterosexuality of Lawrence (contra left-wing claims of right-wing prudery); for Panichas finds Lawrentian heterosex to be part and parcel of "a presiding reverence in Lawrence's life and art" (Panichas 1992, p. 80):

> Reverence embodies a disciplined fusion of passion and principle, the two most active energies that, for Lawrence, create a delicate equilibrium and that belong to and embody the life of virtue and the idea of value. The possession of this quality of reverence is for Lawrence a precondition to the religious search for meaning....
> ...A metaphysic of virtue and value, however, remains dangerously one-dimensional, incomplete, and unconsummated without due attention to what Lawrence called "the phallic consciousness." His adjectival emphasis here undoubtedly troubled even some of his most ardent supporters as his experiment with the language of emotions became increasingly radical, to judge especially by late writings like *Lady Chatterley's Lover* (1928) and *The Man Who Died* (1931). But critical irritability should not be allowed to distort Lawrence's heroic vision, anchored as it is in concern and commitment. His art is his heroic vision insofar as Lawrence also creates there his phallic conception of heroism and embodies heroic qualities appropriate to the modern age. Lawrence's is a heroism of possibility; eventually it is even an apocalyptic heroism, to be viewed against the background of the great crisis of civilization that announced itself with the Great War of 1914-1918. (Panichas 1992, p. 80)

Thus Panichas finds that Lawrentian heterosex and Lawrentian "reverence" go hand in hand, with Lawrentian heterosex embodying "a disciplined fusion of passion and principle," ensuing "virtue and...value,"—all sine qua nons of Lawrence's "religious search for meaning," a search which necessitates "A metaphysic of virtue and value": and Panichas appreciates the fact that such a metaphysic needs the Lawrentian "phallic consciousness" in order to avoid being "incomplete and unconsummated." Thus the right-wing Panichas in the early 1990s—the very time when left-wing gay extremists like Dollimore were proclaiming Lawrence to be washed-up, "increasingly disregarded and often despised" (Dollimore 1991, p. 268)—the right-wing Panichas clearly realized that Lawrence's explicit valorization of Lawrentian heterosex is essentially the base of "Lawrence's heroic vision": Lawrence's "concern and commitment" to save "the modern age" from destruction makes "his phallic conception of heroism" uniquely "appropriate to the modern age," the age of "the great crisis of civilization that announced itself with the Great War of 1914-18." In Lawrence's "apocalyptic heroism," Panichas tells us, Lawrence supremely demonstrates that

> Strength and greatness of soul, at their depths heroic in the full sense of the word, are at the heart of Lawrence's vision. (Panichas 1992, p. 81)

But Panichas painfully observes that Lawrence's heroic "Strength and greatness of soul" are indeed out of place today:

> Heroism has been increasingly technicalized or collectivized....A devalued and desanctified heroism, lacking promise of greatness and assimilating common and pluralistic habits of mind, fabricates modern forms of the heroic. Heroism has also been robbed of its intrinsically divine element....(Panichas 1992, p. 90)

Today, in contradistinction to Lawrentian "Strength and greatness of soul," there is the predominance of the "technical," the "collective," the anti-divine—all of which can indeed be traced to the dominance of the Left in cultural-intellectual-academic matters at the present time, a dominance which has had (and continues to have) extremely negative consequences for Lawrence's place in Western civilization today. Furthermore, and indeed perhaps most important of all for the decline of Lawrence in academe today, there is the fact that

> Lawrence's [heroism]...is a moral heroism, rooted in *individual* heroic effort....(Panichas 1992, p. 90; italics mine)

"[R]ooted in *individual* heroic [moral] effort," the Lawrentian way is in danger of being completely extirpated by the left-wing intellectual elite that dominates academia, an elite which indeed celebrates the "death of the subject" or, to say it in more conventional language, the end of individualism as such. (Jameson 1983, p. 114)

Decrying "the conception of a unique self and private identity, a unique personality and individuality" as a "construct [which] is merely a philosophical and cultural mystification" (Jameson 1983, pp. 114-115) at best and a manifestation of megalomania and paranoia (Dollimore 1998, p. 269) at worst, the anti-individual, anti-heroic literary-cultural-academic Left today, led by such as Fredric Jameson, Terry Eagleton, and Jonathan Dollimore, is, it seems to me, as much (or indeed more) of an enemy to the appreciation of Lawrence and his greatness as was the Eliotic Right some seven decades ago. The right-wing Eliot deplored Lawrence's "private religion" (Eliot 1931, p. 771), a "private religion" which greatly offends Eliot by "using the terminology of Christian faith to set forth some philosophy or religion which is fundamentally non-Christian or anti-Christian" (Ibid.). But, for the left-wing intellectuals, "the political" is "religion"; thus the left-wing literary-cultural critics who dominate today (such as Jameson, Eagleton and Dollimore) are characterized by

> [their] confident privileging of the political as the ultimate horizon of value, or of the ideological as the basic criterion of criticism....(Bell 1997, p. 222)

The trendy, influential left-wing intellectuals' "confident privileging of the political" has impacted Lawrence criticism today to such an extent that even Mark Spilka, once one of Lawrence's better and more sympathetic critics, has recently yielded to the temptation to turn hard left; in a recent piece on Lawrence, Spilka, apropos of nothing, asserts:

> That women and blacks share a subordinate status in our culture comes as no surprise in these days of raised consciousness about ethnic and gender differences. (Spilka 1996, p. 93)

Prattling about "raised consciousness," "ethnic and gender differences," and "the subordinate status" of "women and blacks...in our culture...in these days" (the days of superstars Hillary Clinton and Oprah Winfrey, Colin Powell and O. J. Simpson!), Spilka in his old age has evidently succumbed to political correctness and trendiness; indeed, the very title of his reductive recent essay on Lawrence—"Domestic Violence in 'The White Stocking': A Lawrencean Case Study"—screams out its political correctness at the reader; it is no wonder, then, that Spilka in this article goes on to attack "[male] chauvinist" Lawrence (Spilka 1996, p. 99), condemning what he (Spilka) sees as

> [Lawrence's] dominance-submission ethos, with its essentially abusive posture toward women....(Spilka 1996, p. 99)

Finally, Spilka here sanctimoniously and tendentiously cites

> his [Lawrence's] own deadly propensities, his own cycle of violence...(ibid., p. 100)

—all this as if the academic opportunist Spilka were morally superior to Lawrence!

Ironically enough, it was in his speech to the D. H. Lawrence Society of North America (December 1988) upon receiving the Harry T. Moore Distinguished Scholar Award in recognition of his "lifelong contribution to and encouragement of D. H. Lawrence studies," that Spilka plainly indicated his intention to turn against Lawrence in favor of the "privileging of the political" (Bell 1997, p. 222); in his speech Spilka complains that

> Whatever Lawrence has done for the sexual liberation of men and women, he has not done enough to save them from each other's *politics*. As *political* institutions, for instance, modern marriage is now on the rocks; male friendship is just another form of male bonding; and the phallic mysteries are passé...evidence of that [Lawrentian] patriarchal outlook....(Spilka 1988, p. 312; italics mine)

Evidently privileging "politics" and "political institutions" over "Whatever Lawrence has done" (a rather condescending phrase, it seems to me), Spilka kvetches that he rather resents "Defending Lawrence" these days:

> Since the 1920s, then, but more especially since the 1950s, the values espoused by the normative Lawrence have been under siege; and as the last remaining refugee from the normative '50s, I have been increasingly hard put to defend them. (Spilka 1988, p. 312)

Self-pitying and self-indulgent, Spilka would have us believe that he is the only one who has been "Defending Lawrence,"—a job that Spilka now evidently finds too difficult and too vexatious to do; in other words, according to Spilka here, "the values espoused by...Lawrence" are today not really worth defending ("I have been increasingly hard put to defend them")—perhaps because today "Defending Lawrence" and gaining an Ivy League professorship (such as Spilka enjoyed at Brown

University for over thirty years, beginning in 1963) are indeed virtually mutually exclusive: that is to say, being a D. H. Lawrence defender today makes one something of a pariah in left-wing politically correct academia. Confessing his reluctance concerning "Defending Lawrence" today, Spilka admits that "the mounting pressures" of the political-intellectual-academic left wing make it extremely difficult for him to continue to be a Lawrence defender:

> my own arguments [in defense of Lawrence] have become more and more convoluted and ingenious, as if the mounting pressures of new perspectives on literature, from the anarchical nihilism of the 1960s through the wilder swings of the advancing sexual revolution to the grim convictions and devastating insights of recent feminism, had pretty much wiped out the possibilities for normative claims on Lawrence's behalf of any kind.
> Indeed, a year ago this September [in 1987] I shaved off my emulative beard in barefaced shame at my previous allegiances to hirsute literary heroes like Lawrence....(Spilka 1988, p. 313)

Thus we have Spilka's "barefaced shame at my previous allegiances to...Lawrence"; the Laodicean Spilka is no Leavis, that is clear; indeed, even as he (Spilka) theatrically declares in his 1988 speech that he has "decided to grow the beard back again for this...occasion [the Harry T. Moore Award for "D. H. Lawrence studies"]," we do not put too much stock in his professed desire "to give myself as well as Lawrence just one more chance of being a *mensch* one might be proud of"—especially since he (Spilka) concludes his speech by self-pityingly (and self-aggrandizingly) referring to the "hardpressed and shaky spirit" (Spilka 1988, p. 313) in which he ostensibly will resume his "precarious defense of Lawrence" (ibid.), sounding almost as if the most important thing about D. H. Lawrence is that he is being "defended" by Mark Spilka. In his latest "defense" of Lawrence (Spilka 1996), already cited here, Spilka concludes by (rather mean-spiritedly) remarking that when "he [Lawrence] became impotent himself from the inroads of tuberculosis" (Spilka 1996, p. 100) in the last years of his life it was a definitely good thing, since (in Spilka's weird and reductive view) Lawrence's "impotence" led to a state of affairs in which "In these last years [of Lawrence], at least, his own deadly propensities, his own cycle of violence, had finally been broken" (Spilka 1996, p. 100). Spilka, with his palaver about Lawrence's "domestic violence," "deadly propensities," and "cycle of violence," at this point makes Lawrence sound more like an O. J. Simpson manqué (Lawrence of course didn't *murder* his wife; moreover, as every Lawrentian knows, Frieda Lawrence gave as good as she got where "domestic violence" was concerned) than like a great creative writer. Furthermore, Spilka's apparent gladness at Lawrence's "impotence" hardly seems sympathetic (With friends like that, who needs enemies?). The aging Spilka (he is in his seventies), with his politically correct hostility to Lawrentian sexuality, is indeed a significant representative of the current hostility toward Lawrence in the left-wing academy; indeed, in all this, it seems to me, it is difficult to make a case that Spilka at this late date remains a genuine Lawrentian.

One major insight, it seems to me, concerning why the left-wing Spilka may no longer be considered a genuine Lawrentian, is provided in a statement made by British Lawrentian Keith Sagar in an essay published around the same time as Spilka was getting rid of his "Lawrentian" beard (1987); in his pro-Lawrence essay Sagar reaches the conclusion that Lawrence must "be fought for":

> If criticism is to count for anything, the job of the critic is to proselytize for all he is worth on behalf of every great writer who ever lived, and there will never be a great writer who does not need to be fought for again and again, every generation, against those who, afraid to meet his challenge, deny his greatness....
>
> Lawrence's enemies are still numerous, perhaps even still a majority in the literary establishment. They kept a low profile in the sixties and seventies. Perhaps the death of F. R. Leavis gave them the courage to come into the open again....
>
> ...In reality it is only the brave few who keep up the great adventure. And they must fight for survival against the majority who have sold out or chickened out of the struggle toward consciousness and creativity in favor of power or possessions or comfort, or who, inadvertently, through loss of vision, are living without faith or in bad faith....
>
> ...the more effectively art is doing its job, the more hostility it will arouse in the defenders of the status quo, the Establishment, the social beings, the ideologists, the lâches, and the salauds—that is, in the great majority which is always wrong. It is a measure of the extent to which Lawrence is still alive as man and artist that he can still offend and sting....They ["the great majority"] are against Lawrence not just as a quirky individual with obsessions and blind spots, but against him as archetypal artist and truthteller. The fight for Lawrence is the fight for art, for the life of the imagination, which is our only hope of redemption. (Sagar 1987, pp. 115, 118, 125)

Rather than criticize Lawrence with the dogmas of political correctness as Spilka does, Sagar here recommends that Lawrentians should "proselytize for all [they are] worth" on behalf of Lawrence and his greatness, for the status of a great writer such as Lawrence is always extremely precarious in view of the fact that in "every generation" there exists a myriad of critics "who, afraid to meet his [i.e., the great writer's] challenge, deny his greatness." Of those genuine Lawrentians who "fought for" Lawrence against all odds, of course, F. R. Leavis was the greatest; and, significantly, "the death of F. R. Leavis" gave "Lawrence's enemies...the courage to come into the open again"; these enemies, interestingly enough—enemies of both Lawrence and Leavis—are today mainly left-wing intelligentsia. Even in 1963, when Lawrence and Leavis were at their peak, left-wing critic Harold Rosenberg demonized Leavis' Lawrentian journal *Scrutiny*:

> It was plain from the start that *Scrutiny* had set itself against Progress, democracy, and political liberalism....(Rosenberg, "Insurrection," *The New Yorker*, March 14, 1964, p. 169)

But the left-wing privileging of "Progress, democracy, and political liberalism" today is essentially the valorization of materialism, mediocrity,—and perverse/perverted multiculturalism. Thus we see, more recently (some thirty years after Rosenberg),—and even more vehemently—the left-wing homosexual theorist Jonathan Dollimore savaging Lawrence as "This increasingly disregarded and often despised writer" (Dollimore 1991, p. 268)—and self-righteously condemning "the Lawrence-Leavis" metaphysic as one which fears "difference and otherness":

> Lawrence takes pride of place in the Great Tradition [of Leavis], about which I can only afford the space to remark that what it excludes is the most significant thing about it. Indeed, what is so striking now is just how much...the Lawrence-Leavis [metaphysic]...wanted to actively exclude and deny; "tradition," "essential humanity," "spontaneous fullness of being" [all Lawrentian-Leavisite watchwords], far from being affirmations of "life" seem now more like a fear of it—in particular a fear of contamination by difference and otherness, a fear of disintegration through democracy and change. (Dollimore, *Radical Tragedy*, p. 267)

Yet in recent years it has become clear that, for Dollimore and many other left-wing Lawrence haters, there is a political-homosexual agenda at work in their denigration of Lawrence; for Dollimore, "difference and otherness" means the valorization of "homosexual desire" (Dollimore, "Sex and death," *Textual Practice* 9 [1995]: 30), even vindicating promiscuous gay sex:

> we [gay men] turn to casual promiscuous sex, hoping to escape from a hostile world into the bars and clubs (Dollimore, "Sex and death," p. 30)

—and celebrating anonymous gay sex as "the most memorable of all fleeting experiences" (Ibid., p. 35); furthermore, Dollimore proudly includes himself among the victims of homophobic "oppression":

> Identity for the homosexual is always conflicted: at once ascribed, proscribed and internalized, it is in terms of identities that we [homosexuals] have experienced self-hatred, violence, mutilation and death. [Dollimore is evidently oblivious of gay-on-gay violence and murder.] (Ibid., p. 46)

Dollimore goes on to privilege promiscuous casual homosexual encounters as the epitome of left-wing politically correct "difference":

> such [casual, promiscuous homosexual] encounters can...be the occasion of identification and empathy across differences of many kinds, including those of class, age, and race. (Ibid., p. 47)

Thus it becomes evident that, when Dollimore cites and condemns what he considers the Lawrentian-Leavisite "fear of contamination by difference," his conception of "difference" is rooted in his advocacy of "deviant [gay] desire" (Ibid., p. 47)—i.e., promiscuous homosex—which for Dollimore is the source of liberation and elation:

> ["Deviant"] Desire can unfix identity in ways that are liberating; it may compel me as a gay person to come out, and to experience that incomparable elation which derives from swopping an inauthentic straight identity for an authentic gay one. (Dollimore, "Bisexuality," *Textual Practice* 10 [1996]: 531)

Finally, it should come as no surprise that Dollimore valorizes/idealizes what he calls "the paradoxical wisdom of the casual [homo]sexual encounter" (Dollimore 1995, p. 49). Indeed, Dollimore even goes so far as to fantasize about the "overthrow" of "evil" heterosex:

> Let us assume...that heterosexuality is a monolithic evil and that the most urgent task in the late twentieth century is to secure its overthrow. (Dollimore 1996, p. 534)

Surely the fact is that many of those left-wing intellectuals that are most hostile to Lawrence—from Kate Millett to Jonathan Dollimore to Christopher Craft to (of course) Michel Foucault—are in fact gays and lesbians who believe that "heterosexuality is...evil,"—and who would like to "secure its [i.e., heterosexuality's] overthrow"; thus the last chapters of my book (in particular the penultimate chapter) contain and present a provocative demystification of the sanctimonious, self-righteous left-wing intellectual-cultural-literary critical elite and their politically correct attack on Lawrence,—an attack which is ultimately not much more than an idealization, defense and glorification of their own frequently psycho-pathological "Foucaultian" (homo)sexual practises (e.g., sado-masochism, fist-fucking, rampant promiscuity leading to AIDS). With his left-wing homosexual agenda Dollimore (for example) is happy to think of Lawrence as "This increasingly disregarded and often despised writer" (Dollimore 1991, p. 268)—but I myself of course completely disagree with Dollimore's rabid attack on Lawrence—and I deny its ultimate "literary-political" viability; thus the final chapters of my book (particularly the last hundred pages or so) are devoted, not only to defending Lawrence against the left wing, but also to demonstrating that Lawrentian thought itself is the enemy of—and a viable weapon against—the politically correct Left.

Thus in the concluding pages of my book there is a culmination of my discussion of the political aspect involved which, it seems to me, perforce involves Lawrentians in certain "political" decisions—decisions which, it seems to me at this point in time at least, should involve a swerve to the right by Lawrentians both inside academia and out.

Thus, having here discussed at some length Jonathan Dollimore's malicious left-wing assault on Lawrence, it is with some sense of relief that in conclusion here I turn once more to the "right-wing" George A. Panichas, of whom it has recently been said that

> he [Panichas] is the most forceful, articulate, and erudite critic writing in America today on the side of critical conservatism. (Aldridge 1994, pp. 390-391)

But not only is Panichas "a conservative" (Panichas 1982, p. ix), he is also a *Leavisite* conservative Lawrentian:

> My concept of literary criticism as a discipline owes a great deal to the thought and influence of the work of Dr. Leavis, especially as it is vigorously set forth in...*D. H. Lawrence: Novelist*

> (1955). The consistency of his critical theory is marked by a sustained devotion and courage of purpose which few other critics can ever hope to equal. His work, particularly as it is expressed in ceaseless concern for critical standards *and* for relevant attention to the problems of contemporary civilization, has helped to stimulate the movement of my own critical thinking. (Panichas, *Reverent Discipline*, p. xviii)

With his "concept of literary criticism" greatly influenced by Leavis' Lawrencean "sustained devotion and courage of purpose" as well as by Leavis' Lawrencean "relevant attention to the problems of contemporary civilization," Panichas is indeed ultimately a more authentic and astute Lawrentian than is (for instance) the politically correct, somewhat opportunistic Mark Spilka. For the right-wing Panichas is finally guided by the following Leavisite directive regarding Lawrence:

> Lawrence stood for life, and shows...an extraordinarily quick and sure sense for the difference between that which makes for life and that which makes against it. (F. R. Leavis, *Scrutiny* 15 [December 1947]: 61)

Fully appreciating "[Lawrence's] extraordinarily quick and sure sense for the difference between that which makes for life and that which makes against it," Panichas is far more generous, helpful and intelligent about Lawrence than are most other Lawrentians; indeed, Panichas' Leavisite-Lawrentian awareness leads him even to have a better comprehension of "the intense sexual scenes" in *Women in Love* than does the Ivy League Lawrentian Mark Spilka, who—unsuccessfully, it seems to me (see Scherr 1996, pp. 65-105)—vehemently attempts to deflate the Lawrencean *Women in Love* sex scenes between Birkin and Ursula that take place in the chapter "Excurse"; Spilka contemptuously states that

> Lawrence...presents...an inflated, opaque, puzzling mystique in [the Birkin-Ursula love scenes of] "Excurse"...(Spilka, "On 'Lawrence Up-Tight'," *Novel* 5 [Fall 1971]: 67)

The left-wing Spilka vehemently depreciates Lawrence's "intense...sexual scenes" in *Women in Love*'s "Excurse"; but the right-wing Panichas (who evidently possesses a more authentically Lawrentian sensibility than Spilka's) wisely sees the "intense" Lawrencean "sexual scenes" as indeed a matter of "that which makes for life and that which makes against it":

> Some of the intense (and unwarrantably criticized) sexual scenes in the novel [*Women in Love*] are frantic attempts to defy the power that nihilates; to attain some moment of permanence, some viable experience of otherness that resists the finality of ending. (Panichas, *Courage*, p. 174)

For Panichas, the "intense" Lawrentian heterosex engaged in by some of the major characters in *Women in Love* leads them "to attain some moment of permanence, some viable experience of otherness,"—an experience which indeed generates a kind of apotropaic power that acts as a defense against death; an apotropaic power which defies "the power that nihilates"; an apotropaic power which "resists the finality of ending,"—resists death, indeed, in those very "intense...sexual scenes" in "Excurse,"—those very scenes that Spilka sees as "inflated" and "opaque," but which Panichas indeed deems to be successful "attempts...to attain...some viable experience of otherness"—an "experience of otherness" that takes place most notably in the "intense...sexual scenes" at the end of "Excurse," in which the "experience of otherness"—"living otherness"—is achieved by Birkin and Ursula by means of Lawrencean sex ("the maximum of unspeakable communication in touch"):

> They [Ursula and Birkin] threw off their clothes and he gathered her to him, and found her, found the pure lambent reality of her forever invisible flesh. Quenched, inhuman, his fingers upon her unrevealed nudity were the fingers of silence upon silence, the body of mysterious night upon the body of mysterious night, the night masculine and feminine, never to be seen with the eye, or known with the mind, only known as the palpable revelation of living otherness.
>
> She had her desire of him, she touched, she received the maximum of unspeakable communication in touch, dark, subtle, positively silent, a magnificent gift and give again, a perfect acceptance and yielding, a mystery, the reality of that which can never be known, vital sensual reality that can never be transmuted into mind content, but remains outside, living body of darkness and silence and subtlety, the mystic body of reality. She had her desire fulfilled, he had his desire fulfilled. For she was to him what he was to her, the immemorial magnificence of mystic, palpable, real otherness.

Thus Panichas' right-wing Leavisite perspective provides insight into the "mysterious," the "vital sensual reality," "the mystic body of reality"—

the Lawrencean reality; insight that the conventional left-wing Spilka is evidently incapable of providing today—today, when, in contradistinction to the Lawrentian valorization of the "mysterious," the "vital," the "sensual," and "the mystic body of reality," there is the left-wing intelligentsia's "progressivist" valorization of the "material" and "sheer material measurement"; this left-wing weltanschauung ultimately results in a reduction of life that is antithetical to the authentic Lawrentian vision of life—indeed, the right-wing Lawrentian Panichas, like his great precursor Leavis, vigorously condemns

> the heralds of modern progressivist enlightenment who reduce life to sheer material measurement, whether as a "New Deal" or as a "Great Society." (Panichas, *Reverent Discipline*, p. 390)

A world in which "life" is reduced to "sheer mechanical measurement"—a world of Big Government, the Welfare State, the "Great Society," racial/gender quotas, the Clintons and the Jesse Jacksons—is a world in which "inert safety"—the "inert safety" of the left-wing Establishment, measured in sheerly material terms—is privileged above vital Lawrencean "life itself": this left-wing materialist world of "inert safety" is the antithesis of the Lawrencean world, for the Lawrentian world is one in which

> life itself, and not inert safety, is the reason for living. (D. H. Lawrence, "Why the Novel Matters")

Surely academia today, with its craven craving for "inert safety," is the obverse of Lawrentian "life"; for in academia today what is sorely lacking is courage—"the courage of judgment" (Panichas 1982, p. 15)—indeed, what ultimately sets right-wing Panichas apart from left-wing Spilka may be the fact that Panichas' praise of Lawrence even in this anti-Lawrentian day and age is praise that is rooted in *courage*,—"the courage of judgment":

> The courage of judgment is the prime virtue of the critic; his *unum necessarium*. To criticize is to take a stand,—it is not necessarily to damn or to deride...; much of the best criticism is considered and selective celebration....
>
> ...In an age given over to all manner of polls, so that one can discover the "trend" and, lest one prove eccentric, follow it, the critic must judge for himself, and then be possessed of the final courage to utter his judgment. (Panichas, *Courage*, pp. xii-xiii)

"The courage of judgment" entails "tak[ing] a stand"—even if that stand goes against the polls and the trends; furthermore, "the courage of judgment" can indeed lead to "celebration,"—the celebration of greatness in writers and in texts; thus, when Panichas recently and forthrightly judged that

> A poetry of genius, of a Shakespearian magnitude, triumphs [in Lawrence's *Women in Love*] (Panichas, *Courage*, p. 174),

he (Panichas) was indeed demonstrating "the courage of judgment"— "courage of judgment" that leads Panichas wisely to suggest that Lawrence at his best—in *Women in Love*, for instance, which Panichas further praises for "The greatness of this prose creation [*Women in Love*] in all its breadth in exploring human sensibility" (Panichas, *Reverent Discipline*, p. 149)—Lawrence at his best is indeed the equal of Shakespeare in his greatest works.

Yet the right-wing privileging of "genius," "courage of judgment" and "celebration" of "greatness" is indeed antithetical to the politically correct academic left-wing privileging of "social justice" (i.e., "quotas"); as Harold Bloom recently (and astutely) noted:

> We [in the academy] are destroying all intellectual and aesthetic standards in the humanities and social sciences, in the name of social justice. Our [academic] institutions show bad faith in this: no [racial-gender-sexual orientation] quotas are imposed upon brain surgeons [thanks to the defeat of the Clinton Health Care Plan]....What has been devalued is learning as such, as though erudition were irrelevant in the realms of judgment and misjudgment. (Bloom, *Western Canon*, p. 35)

Harold Bloom, with wisdom and sadness and indignation, realizes that "social justice" is simply left-wing euphemistic-strategic (Clintonesque) spin for reverse discrimination ("quotas"), of which the left-wing political base is the main beneficiary—and of which literary-cultural-intellectual "greatness" is the main victim.

But Harold Bloom himself is not afraid to valorize politically incorrect "greatness" and "confronting greatness":

> Traditions tell us that the free and solitary self writes in order to overcome mortality. I think that the self, in its quest to be free and solitary, ultimately reads with one aim only: to confront greatness. That confrontation scarcely masks the desire to join greatness, which is the basis of the aesthetic experience once called the Sub-

> lime: the quest for a transcendence of limits....
> Confronting greatness as we read is an intimate and expensive process and has never been much in critical vogue. Now, more than ever, it is out of fashion, when the quest for [psychic-ontological] freedom and solitude is being condemned as politically incorrect, selfish, and not appropriate to our anguished society. (Bloom, *Western Canon*, pp. 523-524)

Privileging "intellectual and aesthetic standards" (Bloom 1994, p. 35), "the free and solitary self" (Bloom 1994, p. 523), "greatness" and "Confronting greatness" (Bloom 1994, p. 524) over whatever "political responsibilities...[a] critic may have" (Bloom 1994, p. 35), Bloom today is indeed hated by the left-wing literary-cultural-sociopolitical-academic intelligentsia-Establishment:

> It is by now *de rigueur*...to dismiss him [Bloom] as one more example of the reactionary right. (Weisman, "Birthing an Ecstatic Anxiety: Harold Bloom's *Western Canon* and its Readers," *Salmagundi*, Fall 1996, p. 221)

As "one more example of the reactionary right," Harold Bloom has received considerable abuse from the academic left; indeed, recently one left-wing extremist actually went so far as to liken Harold Bloom to Rush Limbaugh, grotesquely equating "Bloomian authoritarianism" (i.e., the celebration of "greatness," the advocacy of "intellectual and aesthetic standards") with "Limbaughian authoritarianism," whatever that is (Berube 1998, p. 92):

> it would not be hard to imagine a future [Bloom] book entitled *The Western Canon the Way It Ought to Be* [Berube's sophomoric takeoff on Bloom's *The Western Canon* and Limbaugh's *The Way Things Ought to Be*]. (Ibid.)

Thus it is no surprise that Bloom (like Ken Starr, perhaps!) is a victim of left-wing character assassination: Berube condemns "the arrogance of Blooms [sic]" (Berube 1998, p. 109); queer theorist Eve Kosofsky Sedgwick puerilely refers to the "Harold Bloom buffoon" (*Epistemology*, p. 146) suffering from "heterosexual male self-pity" (*Epistemology*, p. 145); and yet another trendy left-wing theorist-critic, Daniel T. O'Hara, decries what he regards as "Bloom's...rearguard, elitist, and [selfhood-individualism affirming] humanistic recuperation of...literature and literary study" (*Radical Parody*, p. 131)—and this time Bloom is likened to "William Bennett, Reagan's former Secretary of Education" (ibid.)—

yet another figure demonized by the extreme left wing.

Thus it is evident that the literary-cultural-academic left wing today, with its extreme politicization of literary criticism-theory, will not tolerate any diversity of opinion: they will only viciously attack any literary critic or theorist that does not serve their social-political agendas; thus Harold Bloom, who recently concluded that

> [academia's] modish multiculturalism is a lie, a mask for mediocrity and for the thought-control academic police, the Gestapo of our campuses....
>
> ...a literary critic has no political responsibilities, as a critic....
>
> The [left-wing academic] Resenters [of "Greatness" in literature] prate of [sociopolitical] power, as they do of race and gender: these are careerist stratagems and have nothing to do with the insulted and injured, whose lives will not be improved by our reading the bad verses of those who assert that they are the oppressed (Bloom 1998, *Best of the Best*, pp. 21, 24)

—thus Harold Bloom, with his keen demystification of "modish multiculturalism" (multiculturalism being both sham-"lie" and left-fascist "Gestapo" menace), his strong condemnation of left-wing literary-cultural "mediocrity," and his supreme celebration of literary-cultural "Sublime" "Greatness" and "the self" (in *The Western Canon*), remains to this day a major bete noir of the academic-literary-cultural left.

Harold Bloom, of course, is indeed the last "reactionary" (i.e., politically incorrect) literary theorist left who has any substantial status at all in academia—an academia that today is dominated by left-wing phonies; as Bloom himself recently noted:

> They [left-wing literary theorists] ought to become social and political and economic activists and devote their lives to serving the poor....But the truth is that they could not care less. I am one of the few professors from Yale from a working-class background. And I believe that I can smell a hypocrite in these matters from a considerable distance....
>
> They [the hypocrites] are pseudo-Marxists, pseudo-feminists, watery disciples of Foucault....And they are transparently at work propagating themselves in our universities, making sure that only those who hold their precise views receive appointments and advancement. I would say that there is no future for literary studies as such in the United States....I am aware that I am fighting a rear-guard action, and that the war is over and we have lost. (Harold Bloom interview, "Bloom and Doom," *Newsweek*, October 10, 1994, p. 75.)

Thus even Harold Bloom, who (fortunately) was born too early in the century (1930) to have his career ruined by political correctness, multiculturalism and reverse discrimination—even Harold Bloom must come to the conclusion that "we have lost"—"we" being those students, scholars and critics of literature who celebrate "Greatness," "the Sublime," and "the self" that aspires "to confront greatness...[and] to join greatness" by means of a supremely meaningful, creative encounter with the greatest writers and the greatest literature our civilization has produced; yet if the aging Bloom (he is now around seventy years old) has not been too severely penalized by academia for his valorization of "Greatness" and "the self," for those few Lawrentians brave/foolhardy enough to utilize "Bloomian literary theory" (Scherr 1996, p. 22) as

> the source of much insight into the great selfhood of Lawrence, selfhood which brought Lawrence great "poetic strength" and indeed even "poetic immortality" (Scherr 1996, p. 10),

"poetic immortality" which

> makes him [Lawrence] a major force in Western civilization (Scherr 1996, p. 22)

and

> certainly entitles him to a permanent place among creative writers and imaginative thinkers of the highest rank (Scherr 1996, p. 181);

for those few Lawrentians brave/foolhardy enough to practise

> The illumination of Lawrence's greatness by the application of Bloomian theory to Lawrence (Scherr 1996, p. 147),

punishment from the left-wing academic-literary-cultural Establishment is sure, harsh, vehement and wrong-headed, with "[Lawrence's] Bloomian expositor" (Clarke 1998, p. 246) Barry J. Scherr being condemned by politically correct "Lawrentians" as an "extreme masculinis[t]" (Clarke 1998, p. 244), and Scherr's Bloomian study being damned as

> a retrograde attempt, by means of an already fading critical system, to ignore several decades of trenchant [left-wing, politically correct] gender criticism. (Clarke 1998, p. 244)

At around the same time that Scherr's "retrograde" Lawrentian-Bloomian study appeared and was attacked, Bloom's oeuvre itself was indeed being similarly condemned by left-wing literary-cultural critics as "rearguard, [and] elitist" (O'Hara, *Radical Parody*, p. 131), with "the Bloomian stance" (Perloff, p. 161) being denigrated by these left-wingers as a "critical system" which, they presumptuously believe, is "already fading" (Clarke 1998, p. 244) thanks to

> The rapidity of the shift from Bloom's Romantic and Freudian humanism to the more politicized ethos of the 1980s [and later]...(Perloff, p. 161)

—an "ethos" which is antithetical to "the canonical sublime" (Clarke 1998, p. 245) valorized by Bloom (and by Barry J. Scherr, for that matter); for the politically correct left-wing literary-cultural intelligentsia, "the canonical sublime" is merely a site of "masculinist patriarchalism" (Clarke 1998, p. 245) rather than of "Greatness" and the confrontation with greatness—greatness and the confrontation with greatness evidently being beyond the ken of the political-literary-cultural-academic left these days, as they devote most of their time and energy to singing the praises of the "clever adolescent rogue in the White House" (Decter, *Commentary*, January 1999, p. 26), a shrewd yet immature man who represents the quintessence of mediocrity and is antithetical to any sort of mature moral leadership or psychic-ontological-creative greatness, instead fabricating "the Clinton Left...the party of hate, vituperation, and race-baiting" (Novak, *Commentary*, January 1999, pp. 38-39)—in which greatness is trumped by vehement political correctness that reaches its "literary"-"cultural" culmination in "the installation of race, gender, and class perspectives at the center of the college curriculum" (Ellis, *Literature Lost*, p. 3); with the hegemony of race-class-gender criticism and theory in academia, it is no wonder that Harold Bloom, with his "deeply conservative...cultural politics" (Leitch, *Cultural Criticism*, p. 33), is hated and derided by the left-wing politically correct intelligentsia who mock him as "Harold Bloom, self-appointed last man on the Western-canonical barricades" (Pollitt 1998, p. 9).

But indeed, for all the left-wing attacks on Harold Bloom, the fact is that, as left-wing "Lawrentian" and Bloomian ephebe Sandra Gilbert recently (and ruefully) reminded her politically correct MLA audience,

> I told you Bloom would come back again (Gilbert 1997, p. 371)

—and indeed "Bloom would come back again"—not only in *The Western Canon* (1994), but also in *Shakespeare: The Invention of the Human*

(1998), both major bestselling books of literary criticism that celebrate greatness and exemplify "[Bloom's] heroic disregard for academic fashion" (Kerrigan 1998, p. 29)—"academic fashion" that includes political correctness, multiculturalism, and reverse discrimination.

Yet the fact is that Harold Bloom's "heroic disregard for academic fashion" has done little to benefit D. H. Lawrence, whose own "heroic disregard for...fashion" (academic or otherwise) indeed dwarfs that of Bloom. Unfortunately for "Lawrence[,]...[the] all too embarrassingly sincere anthropologist of what have since become politically incorrect emotions [such as heterosexual passion]" (Gilbert 1998, p. 10), Bloom in his *Western Canon* gives short shrift to "The Priest of Love" (Moore 1974), instead devoting laudatory chapters to his (Lawrence's) rivals Joyce, Proust, and even Virginia Woolf. It seems to me that the reason Bloom neglected Lawrence in *The Western Canon* is that Bloom's great precursor canonizer F. R. Leavis had based a major part of his (Leavis') own "strong" critical identity and reputation—indeed, *his* (Leavis') literary-cultural "immortality,"—on his (Leavis') canonizing *Lawrence*, his placing Lawrence in the canon at the top of *his* (Leavis') *Great Tradition* (1948), valorizing Lawrence as "our last great writer," "the great writer of our own phase of civilization" (Leavis, *D. H. Lawrence: Novelist*, p. 9), "the great creative genius of our age, and one of the greatest figures in English literature" (Ibid., p. 303), and enthusiastically concluding that

> Lawrence is incomparably the greatest creative writer in English of our time...; he is one of the greatest English writers of any time...(Ibid., p. 18)

—and thus, in view of Leavis' unique trademark identity as supreme champion of Lawrence, Bloom, in order to overcome his anxiety of influence in relation to his precursor canonizer Leavis, perforce had to repress his (Bloom's) awareness of Lawrence's unique importance as a novelist: he practically avoids mentioning Lawrence at all in *The Western Canon*, simply consigning Lawrence to an omnibus list at the end of *The Western Canon* (along with such worthies as Toni Morrison!), while lavishing considerable attention upon Lawrence's competitors (Proust, Joyce, Woolf); consequently we have a situation in which it may be said that Lawrence is conspicuous by his absence in *The Western Canon*; and thus it evidently must fall to less "established" Leavisite-Bloomian-Lawrentian critics to defend and promote Lawrence,—indeed even using Bloom's controversial, politically incorrect yet evidently enduring theories as assists in the vindication of Lawrence in the midst of the inhospitable literary-cultural-academic world of today, a leftist-dominated world which hates and denigrates the Lawrentian "mystery of being" as the creation of "[Lawrence's] megalomaniac and paranoid individualism" (Dollimore 1998, p. 269), an "individualism" which (according to Dollimore) privileges

> the self-obsessed individual's pursuit of redemption (ibid.),

—"redemption" being antithetical to the "values" and "morality" of the left-wing intelligentsia today, in the Age of Clinton, in which both "the individual" and "redemption" are frowned upon by left-wing nihilists from semi-sociopathic serial adulterer-perjurer King William Jefferson Clinton ("Slick Willie," "The Big Creep") to sacrilegious "Reverend" Jesse Jackson (with his anti-Semitism, his casting aspersions on Jesus' birth, his blasphemous interpretation of the story of King David, his greedy manipulation-extortion of Wall Street, his flacking/shilling for Bill Clinton) to "Congressman" Barney Frank (with his coterie of homosexual prostitutes) to scholar Jonathan Dollimore (with his valorization of gay promiscuity in bars, clubs and baths). These left-wing nihilists, right-wing Lawrentian George Panichas tells us, have

> an instinctive antagonism to the moral sense; to the moral view of the universe as a spiritual cosmos rooted in...*some* [transcendent] principle...grounded in a higher law and higher reality beyond human manipulation or [politically correct] control. (Panichas 1992, p. 99)

Furthermore, Panichas explains,

> The nihilistic forms of...[leftist-dominated, politically correct] society obviate the moral standards that define and inform the concepts of *humanitas* and *humanus religiosus*. (Panichas 1992, p. 130)

In opposition to this left-wing nihilism is

> [the] dissident critic,...[who] is a partisan in the unceasing struggle between moral relativism and moral truth, between the absence and the presence of the moral sense. (Panichas 1992, p. 141)

Representatives of "the absence...of the moral sense," "the entrenched [left-wing] liberal and radical watchers of culture...are in reality, consciously or unconsciously, both purveyors and apologists for nihilism"

(Panichas 1992, p. 232); but these leftist nihilists can be fought by the "dissident critic," Panichas tells us, if we only have courage:

> Ultimately, of course, it [the fight against nihilism] is...a matter of courage: the opportune, and requisite, courage to challenge the [left-wing cultural-sociopolitical] powers that dismiss the inherent idea of value,...of virtue, in short, of first causes and ultimate ends. (Panichas 1992, p. 232)

These left-wing nihilist "powers" in contemporary culture, politics and society have ensconced "desanctifying attitudes and habits" (Panichas 1992, p. 232) as part and parcel of the veritable Establishment in today's literary-cultural-political world, a world in which "the nihilistic traits that are the inevitable consequence of the liberal-radical view" (Panichas 1992, p. 232) reign supreme as "Moral and metaphysical principles...yield to mechanico-materialistic demands" (Panichas 1992, p. 232), "demands" that recently led to the outrageous triumph of the most morally bankrupt president in U. S. history on the grounds that "the economy is good" and "it [Clinton's "misconduct"] is just about sex,"—thus strongly suggesting that, in the USA today at least, "the economy" (i.e., money) is a lot more important than male-female, heterosexual love ("just...sex").

Yet in opposition to these "mechanico-materialistic demands" is "the conservation of transcending principles and commitments, in short, a devotion to higher loyalties and a recognition of higher powers" (Panichas 1992, p. 233)—"a devotion" and "a recognition" that are antithetical to the trendy left-wing literary-cultural-intellectual "circle of mediocrity" (ibid.); and indeed it is surely D. H. Lawrence himself who can be seen as a supreme exemplar of "transcending principles and commitments,...a devotion to higher loyalties and...higher powers" beyond politically correct "mediocrity."

In contradistinction to the left-wing "circle of mediocrity" is the Lawrentian "man of real individuality":

> Any man of real individuality tries to know and to understand what is happening, even in himself, as he goes along. This struggle for verbal consciousness should not be left out in art. It is a very great part of life. It is not superimposition of a theory. It is the passionate struggle into conscious being. (D. H. Lawrence, "Foreword to *Women in Love*")

While the left-wing "circle of mediocrity" encourages and indeed enforces robotic conformity and herd mentality (as the recent Clinton impeachment trial so vividly and blatantly demonstrated), the Lawrentian "man of real individuality" is supremely, self-reliantly capable of and desirous of self-inwardness as he vigorously enacts a journey within in quest of self-knowledge and self-discovery as he "tries to know and to understand what is happening...in himself, as he goes along." The greatest cultural figures such as Lawrence are capable, not only of supreme inwardness and self-understanding, but also of expressing their consciousness through their artistic medium after agonistically experiencing "This struggle for verbal consciousness" which consists of self-understanding and self-expression together in tandem, in a union which for Lawrence is "a very great part of life" since in its power, uniqueness and originality this combination of self-awareness and communicative greatness leads Lawrence ultimately to achieve the great "poetic strength" that is the sine qua non of the "poetic immortality" to which he aspires at the same time that he ardently seeks the truth which will save himself (in his search for the meaning of life) and his civilization (the Western civilization of the Great War)—as Lawrence-Birkin articulates these preoccupations in *Women in Love*:

> What do you think is the aim and object of your life....? ...I find that one needs some one *really* pure single activity—I should call love a single pure activity. (*Women in Love,* Chapter V, "In the Train")

For Lawrence, "love"—heterosexual love and his inimitable discussion of it in his fiction and expository writings—would guarantee his unique identity as a "man of real individuality" who had achieved "verbal consciousness" and consequently/subsequently succeeded in "the passionate struggle into conscious being"—the Lawrentian "conscious being" that ensues in the wisdom about life that distinguishes Lawrence from many another major novelist, thus giving him his eternal life, his "poetic immortality,"—thanks to his "verbal consciousness," "verbal consciousness" which consequently for Lawrence is "a very great part of life,"—*his* (poetic) life, as he "passionate[ly] struggle[s] into conscious being" about his subject, "the aim and the object of [his] life," "the *really* pure single activity" he engages in,—an activity rooted in "The finality of love"—as Lawrence-Birkin explains:

> I want the finality of love....[O]ne woman....[T]he centre and core of [life]...[is] the love between [Birkin-Lawrence] and a woman....It seems to me there remains only this perfect union with a woman—sort of ultimate marriage—and there isn't anything else. (D. H. Lawrence, *Women in Love*, Chapter V, "In the Train")

Lawrence-Birkin's ardent belief in "the finality of love...one woman" provides "the centre and core" of Lawrence's "life" as the novelist-poet-prophet-celebrator of "this perfect union with a woman—sort of ultimate marriage"—Lawrentian male-female "union" and "ultimate marriage" which ultimately and laboriously always valorizes "the same thing" (as Lawrence of course explains in one of his many great letters):

> I always labour at the same thing, to make the sex relation valid and precious, instead of shameful. (D. H. Lawrence letter to Nancy Pearn, 12 April 1927)

This Lawrentian "labour" takes *courage*, what Lawrence in *Lady Chatterley's Lover* calls "the courage of...tenderness" (*Lady Chatterley's Lover*, Chapter XVIII),—courageous tenderness that for Lawrence makes coition between man and woman "the creative act that is far more than procreative" (*Lady Chatterley's Lover*, Chapter XVIII) by virtue of the fact that, for Lawrence, the heterosexual act is "the creative act" that leads to *his literary creations* (such as *Lady Chatterley's Lover*), while for most other human beings the heterosexual act, if it creates anything, can only do it in the context of "procreation" (i.e., physical reproduction, begetting of children). Yet prerequisite to this Lawrentian "creative act that is far more than procreative" which revolves around and has its origins in the sexual act between man and woman,—prerequisite to the Lawrentian "creative act" is the peculiar Lawrentian sexual metaphysic that includes the fervent Lawrentian belief in "warm-hearted...fucking" (as expressed by Lawrence-Mellors in *Lady Chatterley's Lover*):

> I believe in being warm-hearted. I believe especially in being warm-hearted in love, in fucking with a warm heart. I believe if men could fuck with warm hearts, and the women take it warm-heartedly, everything would come all right. (*Lady Chatterley's Lover*, Chapter XIV)

Surely in this politically correct day and age, when "fucking" is regarded by the left-wing academic-intellectual elite as anything but "warm-hearted" but rather as a manifestation of male heterosexist oppression and male chauvinist (macho) harassment (unless the harasser happens to be King William Jefferson Clinton, whose "sex" with Monica Lewinsky—for all her boasts about their "sensuality"—was indeed neither "warm-hearted" nor "fucking" but rather a heterosexual version of Marcuse's immature-bisexual "polymorphous perversity"), Lawrence's ethic of "warm-hearted fucking" is hateful to the anti-heterosex left-wing literary-cultural intelligentsia: in the words of one extreme left-wing anti-Lawrence "Lawrentian," the Lawrentian hero (specifically Mellors in *Lady Chatterley's Lover*) enacts "The aggression of the Phallic Man" with his "deadly and insatiable penetration" (Williams 1993, p. 64). Yet Lawrence-Mellors in fact sees his "Phallic...penetration" of "the woman," not in terms of "aggression," but rather (vice versa) in terms of "pure peace":

> And he had to come in to her at once, to enter the peace on earth of her soft, quiescent body. It was the moment of pure peace for him, the entry into the body of the woman....
> ...[H]e came in to her, with an intensification of relief and consummation that was pure peace to him....(*Lady Chatterley's Lover*, Chapter X)

Thus Lawrence-Mellors sees heterosexual coitus as the way to "pure peace" via the "intensification of relief and consummation" in "the body of the woman." Yet for all the Lawrentian valorization of heterosexual "perfect union with a woman—sort of ultimate marriage" (*Women in Love*, Chapter V, "In the Train"), "warm-hearted fucking" (*Lady Chatterley's Lover*, Chapter XIV), and the "pure peace" of heterosex (*Lady Chatterley's Lover*, Chapter X), the anti-heterosex politically correct left-wing literary-cultural-academic intelligentsia's attacks on Lawrence in recent years have become even more extreme, vehement and absurd. One neophyte left-wing "Lawrentian" critic recently (and outrageously) judged Lawrence's best work, for all its ostensible "tenderness," to be comprised of "a pose of male domination" (Clifford, *Beyond the Heroic*, p. 94) and "the phallocentrism that has become a given for many readers of Lawrence" (Clifford 1998, p. 96), as evidenced (according to Dr. Clifford) in *Women in Love*, for instance, by "[Lawrence-] Birkin's desire for...male supremacy and phallicism [i.e., the macho power of the phallus]" (Clifford 1998, p. 95); as if these extreme (and unproven) assertions were not outrageous enough, Clifford goes on to maintain that

Lady Chatterley's Lover is in fact *au fond* a repository of male chauvinist-heterosexist "idealized rape fantasies in which the subject of the fantasy [i.e., Lady Chatterley] is herself desirous of the violent sexuality that is imposed upon her [by Mellors]" (Clifford 1998, p. 273). Like a typical radical left-wing extremist feminist true believer, Clifford outrageously concludes that

> When Lawrence writes about sexual domination,...he is...employing rape fantasies which suggest that the subject of forced sex, women such as...[Lady] Connie Chatterley, should actually *like* it and even *unconsciously desire* rape. (Clifford 1998, p. 274)

Positing "the rape fantasies of [Lawrence's] fiction" (Clifford 1998, p. 275) as a given fact, Clifford with his politically correct left-wing "New Puritanism" is most likely one of the left-wing multitude who recently and vehemently (and ironically) came to the defense of the first rapist American President (if we are to believe Juanita Broaddrick); he is also probably one of the many politically correct who ignore the fact that the majority of rapes in the United States are committed by black males. Yet, where Lawrence is concerned, Clifford has no qualms about pronouncing that

> This failure to achieve tenderness and communion [in *Lady Chatterley's Lover*] is...indicative of the problem of domination and sexuality in *every* instance of sexual intercourse between Mellors and Connie in the novel....(Clifford 1998, p. 319)

Clifford's postulating of "the problem of domination and sexuality in *every* instance of sexual intercourse" plainly aligns him with the radical left-wing lesbian-feminist ideology of Andrea Dworkin, which holds

> the extraordinary view that normal heterosexual relations are tantamount to rape....[F]or [Dworkin] all sex is rape because women are powerless, and therefore even their consent cannot be a free act....
> ...Many observers imagine that Dworkin's views consign her to the lunatic fringe of feminism, but her writings are in fact a staple of Women's Studies courses. (Ellis 1997, p. 78)

Indeed, the "Lawrentian" Dr. Clifford surely takes his "Women's Studies courses" seriously, as he sings the praises of lesbian-feminist theorist Teresa de Lauretis; he tells us that "My readings [of Lawrence]...rely largely on the theories proposed by Teresa de Lauretis" (Clifford 1998, p. 17), theories that denigrate "male [hetero]sexuality" (ibid.) and "normative heterosexuality" (de Lauretis 1994, *The Practice of Love: Lesbian Sexuality and Perverse Desire*, p. xiii). It is grotesquely ironic that the "Lawrentian" Clifford, in his "Lawrentian" study, should be so dependent on Dr. de Lauretis, Professor of the History of Consciousness at the notoriously left-wing University of California at Santa Cruz (whose leader is the notorious black militant and accused cop killer of the 1970s, Angela Davis!),—Dr. de Lauretis, who proudly declares her quest for

> a model of perverse desire that may account for the representation of lesbianism in texts of fiction, film, poetry, and drama, as well as in the interactions and conversations of many years in my own life [as a lesbian] (de Lauretis 1994, p. xii)

—and who haughtily aims in her work to

> look at...passionate fictions and scenarios of desire that, in representing lesbian sexuality, not only resonate with my own [lesbian desires]...but closely approximate them. (Ibid.)

And de Lauretis proudly confesses that

> Some women have "always" been lesbians. Others, like myself, have "become" one. (Ibid., p. xix)

In view of de Lauretis' substantial influence upon Clifford, it is no wonder that he earnestly enacts his politically correct attack on Lawrentian "male [hetero]sexuality" as being rooted in "phallocentric rigidity" (Clifford 1998, p. 19), the "domination and force" (Clifford 1998, p. 289) of "masculinity[,]...[which is] necessarily limited and essentially destructive" (Clifford 1998, p. 125)—at least according to the anti-heterosex, politically correct literary-cultural left-wing academic elites; furthermore, like most politically-obsessed left-wing literary-cultural-academic critics, Clifford is evidently oblivious of the reverent religious nature of Lawrentian heterosex, far transcending any mundane considerations of quotidian "domination and force,"—a reverent religious nature that is indeed evidenced even in *Lady Chatterley's Lover*, in Lawrence-Mellors' humble and grateful meditation to God, thanking God for Lady Chatterley:

> Thank God I've got a woman! Thank God I've got a woman who is with me, and tender and aware of me. Thank God she's not a bully, nor a fool. Thank God she's a tender, aware woman. (*Lady Chatterley's Lover*, Chapter XVIII)

Rather than being ego-/phallo-centric (as Dr. Clifford would have us believe, positing "[Lawrence-Birkin's] egocentric experience of sexual pleasure" and "[Lawrence-Birkin's] phallocentric desire" [Clifford 1998, p. 107]), Lawrence-Mellors is keenly aware of his debt to God for giving him "a woman who is...tender and aware"—and Lawrence-Mellors' humble and fervent gratitude to and belief in God are even more in evidence in Lawrence's even more metaphysical novel *Women in Love* when Lawrence-Birkin, meditating on all-powerful, all-important God, reaches the religious conclusion that, for all man's egocentric and anthropomorphic self-importance, the fact is that "God can do without man":

> "God cannot do without man." It was a saying of some great French religious teacher.—But surely this is false. God can do without man. God could do without the ichthyosauri and the mastodon. These monsters failed creatively to develop, so God, the creative mystery, dispensed with them. In the same way the mystery could dispense with man, should he too fail creatively to change and develop. The eternal creative mystery could dispose of man, and replace him with a finer created being: just as the horse has taken the place of the mastodon.
>
> It was very consoling to Birkin, to think this. If humanity ran into a cul de sac, and expended itself, the timeless creative mystery would bring forth some other being, finer, more wonderful, some new, more lovely race, to carry on the embodiment of creation. The game was never up. The mystery of creation was fathomless, infallible, inexhaustible forever. Races came and went, species passed away, but ever new species arose, more lovely, or equally lovely, always surpassing wonder. The fountain-head was incorruptible and unsearchable. It had no limits. It could bring forth miracles, create utter new races and new species, in its hour, new forms of consciousness, new forms of body, new units of being. To be man was as nothing compared to the possibilities of the creative mystery....(*Women in Love*, Chapter XXXII, "Exeunt")

In his reverence for "God, the creative mystery," Lawrence-Birkin finds consolation ("It was very consoling") even in "the trauma of the Great War" (Kinkead-Weekes 1998, p. 155)—yet anti-God, anti-religious bias in academia today leads even a fine Lawrence scholar like Keith Sagar to forget this important Lawrentian-Birkinian meditation on God towards the end of *Women in Love*; thus Sagar mistakenly states that

> The only mention of God in *Women in Love* [is]...Birkin's casual phrase "—seeing there's no God." (Sagar, *D. H. Lawrence: Life into Art*, p. 153)

Sagar here is of course referring to the scene in *Women in Love* in which Birkin tells Gerald that "It seems to me there remains only this perfect union with a woman—sort of ultimate marriage—and there isn't anything else," and Gerald proceeds to question him:

> "And you mean if there isn't the woman, there's nothing?" said Gerald.
> "Pretty well that—seeing there's no God." (*Women in Love*, Chapter V, "In the Train")

Far from being a "casual phrase," Birkin's expression "—seeing there's no God" surely indicates the seriousness of his quest for meaning in life in a world in which (for him at this point) "there's no God." But obviously by the end of the book Birkin, having achieved (at least to a certain extent) his "perfect union with a woman—sort of ultimate marriage" with Ursula, is ready to embark upon a quest for God. Indeed, surely Birkin-Lawrence's meditation on God in the last chapter of *Women in Love* (Chapter XXXII, "Exeunt") can be seen as the concluding movement of one major theme of *Women in Love*: Birkin's spiritual-metaphysical odyssey, culminating in a kind of mystical revelation that God does indeed exist, God "the mystery which has brought forth man and the universe," God the "non-human mystery,...[Who] has its own great ends, man is not the criterion. Best leave it all to the vast, creative, non-human mystery" (*Women in Love*, Chapter XXXII, "Exeunt"). Indeed, Lawrence himself surely shares the reverent feelings and longings of his character Birkin towards God and for connexion with God; in the very midst of his *Women in Love* period, in his metaphysical essay "Love" (published in January 1918; most likely written in 1916; see Sagar 1979, p. 72) Lawrence fervently made a declaration of faith that

> there is the love of God; we become whole with God....[T]he Holy Spirit, the unknowable, is single and perfect for us. ("Love")

Birkin-Lawrence humbly and reverently valorizes "the love of God," "becom[ing] whole with God," God "the Holy Spirit, the unknowable,...single and perfect"; today's politically correct left-wing literary-cultural elite, on the other hand, proudly/arrogantly aspires to create "a human culture without God or God substitutes (without God or his doubles)" (House 1994, p. 6); prominent among these left-wing literary-cultural intellectuals is philosopher Richard Rorty, who complacently, patronizingly, and sophomorically dismisses God:

> It isn't that we believe in God, or don't believe in God, or have suspended judgment about God, or consider that the God of theism is an inadequate symbol of our ultimate concern; it is just that we wish we didn't have to have a view about God. It isn't that we know that "God" is a cognitively meaningless expression,...or whatever. We just regret the fact that the word is used so much. (Rorty, *Consequences*, pp. 97-98)

Proudly designating himself a "freeloading atheist" (Rorty 1985, p. 220),—that is to say, an atheist who appropriates from the "Jewish and Christian element in our tradition" (ibid.) whatever he regards as "ethical" in it—Rorty, with his "denial of God" (Goodheart 1997, *Reign of Ideology*, p. 47) considers himself to be morally superior to Judeo-Christianity merely because he valorizes "diversity,"—"diversity" which denigrates Judeo-Christianity's "moral calls to greatness" (Rorty 1991, *Essays on Heidegger*, p. 81) as the major part of a Western civilization and culture which is (according to Rorty)

> often said, with excellent reason, to be racist, sexist and imperialist (Ibid.)

as well as

> Eurocentric, parochial, and intellectually intolerant. (Ibid.)

Rorty declares that he wants "tolerance and comfortable togetherness" rather than "world-historical greatness" (ibid.) for Western civilization: accordingly, Rorty deprecates the strenuous Judeo-Christian "moral...greatness" (ibid.) and instead valorizes

> a [left-wing] culture [that] would have no room for the notion that there are nonhuman forces to which human beings should be responsible. It would drop, or drastically reinterpret, not only the idea of holiness but those [ideas] of "devotion to truth" and of "fulfillment of the deepest needs of the spirit." (*Contingency*, p. 45)

Finally, Rorty in his "implacable antitheism" (Dickstein 1999, p. 14) tells us that all "religious intuitions" should be eliminated, "weeded out" (*Consequences*, p. xxxviii); in place of these "religious intuitions" Rorty with his "atheistic values" (Goodheart 1997, p. 49) sets up "political correctness" as our moral foundation, as he outrageously asserts that

"American leftist academics have a lot to be proud of" because "...Encouraging students to be what mocking neoconservatives call 'politically correct' has made our country a far better place" by "[putting] together such academic disciplines as women's history, black history, gay studies, Hispanic-American studies, and migrant studies" (Rorty 1998, pp. 79-82). (Rorty evidently has no interest in the increase in black racists and anti-Semites on elite American campuses such as the Ivy League; nor is he concerned about the damage done by left-wing black racist leaders like Al Sharpton, Jesse Jackson and Farrakhan; Rorty's desire for "tolerance and comfortable togetherness" evidently extends only as far as the left-wing constituency.) Rorty proceeds to praise left-wing academia for the fact that

> By favoring women in academic hiring and preferment [i.e., reverse discrimination, racial/gender preferences],...colleges and universities have helped change the relations between men and women throughout American society....(Ibid.)

Thus indeed, "For Rorty,...God is dead" (House 1994, p. 7); but for Rorty there is nonetheless the "god" of "political correctness," worshipped in such wise as the practise of reverse discrimination in academia which Rorty valorizes; grotesquely enough, this extremism over "favoring women [and blacks, homosexuals, etc.] in academic hiring and preferment" is as close as left-wing academics such as Rorty (and their patron saint King William Jefferson Clinton) can come to God; but many people are of course totally alienated by the left-wing "religion," the "pieties" of "political correctness"—as one philosopher notes:

> a well-qualified white, [heterosexual] male college professor who has spent twenty years in effectively terminal positions is unlikely to take seriously the pieties of the [left-wing] academic community, especially when they are invoked to support the affirmative action [i.e., reverse discrimination] programs that are...responsible for his situation. (Devine, *Human Diversity*, p. 96)

Lawrence of course is indeed antithetical to the prevailing left-wing literary-cultural academic elite's "pieties," with their belief in political correctness and their "disbelief in the absolute" (Goodheart 1997, p. 52). Indeed, Lawrence even in the midst of the worst days of the Great War asserted his enthusiastic belief in the "Absolute":

> It is an Absolute we are all after,...making unchangeable eternity. (D. H. Lawrence letter to Ottoline Morrell, 27 January 1915)

Indeed, while Rorty and his ilk advocate "proscribing god talk" (Goodheart 1997, p. 52), Lawrence definitively sees God as "the Absolute":

> When everything else is gone,...there is always the sense of God, of the Absolute. Our sense of the Absolute is the only sense left to us [when everything else is gone]. (D. H. Lawrence letter to Bertrand Russell, 29 May 1915)

Declaring that "there is always the sense of God," Lawrence surely stands in contradistinction to "[Rorty's] implacable antitheism" (Dickstein, p. 14); furthermore, while Rorty, with "his [Rorty's] aversion to religion and metaphysics" (Goodheart, p. 55) wishes to eliminate ("weed out") "religious intuitions" (*Consequences*, p. xxxviii), Lawrence valorizes "The true religious faculty":

> The true religious faculty is the most powerful and the highest faculty in man, once he exercises it. And by the religious faculty we mean the inward worship of the creative life-mystery: the implicit knowledge that life is unfathomable and unsearchable in its motives,...[and] that new creative being and impulse surges up all the time in the deep fountains of the soul, from some great source which the world has known as God....("Education of the People," Chapter IV)

Valorizing and defining God as the "great source," Lawrence with his powerful "religious faculty" inimitably perceives humanity's need for God:

> each man according to his need must have a God...that shall compel him to the movement of his own being....
> ...And he must at last always call God the unutterable and the inexpressible, the unknowable....
> ...[God is] the unexpressed Absolute: eternal, infinite, unchanging. Eternal, Infinite, Unchanging: the High God of all Humanity is this. (*Study of Thomas Hardy*, Chapter VII, "Of Being and Not-Being")

In order for man to successfully execute "the movement of his own being," Lawrence tells us, he needs God, "the unexpressed Absolute:...Eternal, Infinite, Unchanging: the High God of all Humanity"; furthermore, Lawrence believes that "the human heart" needs God in order to be capable of vital, salubrious Lawrencean love:

> the human heart must have an absolute. It is one of the conditions of being human. The only thing is the God who is the source of all passion. Once go down before the God-passion, and human passions take their right rhythm....
> Any more love is a hopeless thing, till we have found again, each of us for himself, the great dark God who alone will sustain us in our loving one another. (*Kangaroo*, Chapter XI)

Thus Lawrence fervently sings the praises of "the human heart," "human passions" and "God who is the source of all passion": a far more vital and meaningful trinity, it seems to me, than the left-wing politically correct trinity of "race-gender-class orthodoxy" (Ellis, *Literature Lost*, p. 212) espoused by literary-cultural-political academia.

Valorizing individuality, heterosexual love, "the true religious faculty" and God, D. H. Lawrence today is certainly suffering the slings and arrows of outrageously PC ("politically correct") literary-cultural academia where, today more than ever before, left-wing political considerations dominate in matters of literary judgement, value, merit and attention; as one student of politics and literature recently noted: "[T]he tendency to substitute...political readings for...[literary] interpretation...[has] hurt D. H. Lawrence's reputation more than any other" (Wexler 1999, p. 63).

Themselves in their greatness attempting to transcend politics, Lawrence and his works today have instead become victims of left-wing political agendas; Lawrence today is customarily characterized as a "reactionary" (Shaffer 1993, p. 8)—and in this day and age Lawrence is indeed "the reactionary" who (in academe) is "a somewhat unpopular author" (*YWES* 1994, p. 504)—"a somewhat unpopular author" who is moreover "increasingly disregarded and often despised" (Dollimore 1991, p. 268). Thus the left-wing literary critic's preoccupation with political correctness rather than literary-creative greatness has done Lawrence's reputation great harm; thanks to the left-wing "political indictment of Lawrence" (Wexler 1999, p. 65), it is evidently up to a small but increasingly politically savvy group of moderate-right wing ("culturally conservative") literary critics to restore Lawrence's reputation by recognizing, exposing and demystifying the left wing's politically obsessed literary-cultural agenda in relation to Lawrence and elsewhere.

Prominent among these politically astute "reactionary" literary-cultural conservatives is indeed Harold Bloom, who recently and astutely observed that "current political stances" in academia have resulted in the hegemony of Virginia Woolf over D. H. Lawrence in the academy even though he is a far greater writer than she is; Bloom astutely notes that

> It is difficult, at this time, to maintain any kind of balance or sense of proportion in writing about Woolf. Joyce's *Ulysses* and Lawrence's *Women in Love*...[are] achievements well beyond even [Woolf's] *To The Lighthouse*...(Bloom 1994, *The Western Canon*, p. 436)

—but, because of the political correctness of left-wing literary-cultural academia's "current political stances" (Ibid., p. 446), Virginia Woolf today is supremely celebrated due to her latest role and status as supreme "prophet" and "political theorist" of "feminism" (Ibid., pp. 439, 438, 440)—and as a result she today receives more attention from literary critics and scholars than even James Joyce.

It seems to me to be significant and revealing that in the above block quotation Bloom concedes at least that Lawrence (*Women in Love*) and Joyce (*Ulysses*) may be of equal rank and greatness as writers—yet, interestingly enough, this laudatory Bloomian mention of Lawrence is not even cited in the index listing for Lawrence—perhaps because of Bloom's "anxiety of influence" in relation to Lawrence's greatest champion, F. R. Leavis, from whom Bloom surely wished to distance himself so as to maintain his (Bloom's) uniqueness; indeed, in private conversations with me, Bloom manifested vehement hostility towards Leavis that can certainly be ascribed to the anxiety of influence; at one point Bloom passionately denounced Leavis in a story he (Bloom) told me about when he (Bloom) was Leavis' student in England (at Cambridge) and one day Leavis commented that the weather was pleasant when in fact (in Bloom's vivid recollection), to Bloom's horror and disgust at Leavis' lack of judgement, it was indeed a *cloudy* day; Bloom's hyperbolic denunciation of Leavis' weather report certainly impressed me with Bloom's anxiety of influence in relation to Leavis—an anxiety which resulted in a hostility to Leavis that was, it seems to me, extremely unfortunate for Lawrence, since, had a great major critic such as Bloom succeeded Leavis as Lawrence's champion, Lawrence's reputation would not have suffered so much as it has in recent years in the literary-cultural-academic world. Yet nevertheless surely Bloom in his pro-Lawrence heart of hearts would not disapprove of his theories being used in support of

Lawrence by such minions as myself—and certainly Lawrence needs all the friends he can get at this stage, with the latest *MLA International Bibliography* (1997) placing Lawrence (47 listings) far behind both James Joyce (180 listings) and Toni Morrison (124 listings)—and Virginia Woolf now the supremely attended figure in twentieth-century British literature (214 entries).

Thus, with this left-wing political approach to literature having such a harmful effect on Lawrence,

> "Lawrence"...the creature of cultural production—a cultural *figure*, rather than merely "a writer" (Widdowson, pp.2-3),

—with the left-wing literary-cultural elite "Lawrentians" cynically concluding that

> the different constructions of Lawrence...are productions of cultural *politics* (Widdowson, p. 18; italics mine),

it is time for a right-wing Lawrentian literary-cultural criticism to emerge which will act on the left-wing political "wisdom" that

> "Lawrence" [i.e., Lawrence as "the creature of cultural production"] becomes more complex, more unstable,...as the range and sophistication of the attention paid to him increases. In other words,...the vast, and vastly differentiated, cultural reproduction of Lawrence's work means that we can make less and less sense of it in any absolute way....All we can do is reconstruct it, temporarily and partially, in our own image and for our own ends. (Widdowson, p. 24)

It seems to me that now is the right time for moderate-right wing Lawrentians to step forward and make their presence felt in the academy,—the left-wing politically correct elite literary-cultural academy which has evidently caused Lawrence to come to be "increasingly disregarded" (Dollimore 1991, p. 268) by academic-literary critics and scholars (as the latest [1997] MLA Bibliography so shockingly and indubitably demonstrates); indeed, the ways and means to revive "Lawrence" may well most likely materialize in a moderate-right "political" approach to Lawrence that utilizes a "political" literary-cultural awareness both to defend Lawrence against politically motivated criticism/attacks and at the same time to attempt to create and promote a new image of Lawrence that may well serve to sustain him in these dangerous political times; an approach essentially rooted in a moderate-right literary criticism that would "never let politics overwhelm the fineness of [its] literary and moral discriminations" (Seaton 1996, *Cultural Conservatism*, p. 6), yet at the same time will be keenly aware of political elements and how they factor in various dubious discussions of "Lawrence" today,—discussions of Lawrence that have indeed taken place recently and in which, wittingly or unwittingly, "Lawrentians" have let their "literary and moral discriminations" be "overwhelm[ed]" by "politics"— and these "Lawrentians" should indeed be taken to task for this privileging of the "political" over the literary-moral Lawrencean realm; indeed, recently there have been a few intimations that the moderate-right political awareness may someday be felt in Lawrence studies as a corrective to the current left-wing privileging of "politics" and its concommitant political "abuse" of Lawrence.

In a recent book review, Weldon Thornton, valorizing "creativity and religious feeling in Lawrence," took Paul Poplawski to task for privileging "modernist skepticism," "political correctness," and "contemporary [left-wing] critics" over "spontaneous creativity and the reality of religious experience":

> While Poplawski sometimes explores creativity and religious feeling in Lawrence with sympathy and understanding, he does not do so consistently. The problem is that Poplawski does not himself sufficiently believe in these dimensions of experience to present this material from the sympathetic perspective that it deserves. His presentation suggests that he would *like* to believe in spontaneous creativity and the reality of religious experience, but he can never resist glancing over his shoulder at those contemporary [left-wing] critics whose skepticism [regarding religious experience, creative greatness, etc.] has so much authority for him....
>
> Poplawski...claims to understand and appreciate these [religious] dimensions of Lawrence's thought, and yet he constantly defers to those in our intellectual milieu who dismiss these aspects of experience as illusory and self-indulgent. Given the nature of these [Lawrentian religious-creative] ideas, to write about them with real understanding rather than simply to echo the skepticism of our age, does require some participation in their reality....
>
> ...Poplawski's critique of Lawrence...sometimes involves a standard close to mere "political correctness."...
>
> Poplawski...fails to recognize the radically exploratory nature of Lawrence's writing....Lawrence had...audacity and courage...in

> his writings...about creativity and the religious impulse....[But Poplawski's] book falls short of doing justice to these dimensions of Lawrence's mind and work. (Thornton 1996, pp. 213-214)

Deploring Poplawski's conventional, rather timid and unoriginal "political correctness" and "skepticism," Weldon Thornton here manifests a rather astute moderate-right political awareness,—an awareness of the deleterious effect which left-wing "political correctness" with its obsessive social-political agendas has had on literary criticism: political correctness, as Leslie Fiedler recently pointed out, political correctness makes literary criticism

> an act of conformity and submission to established authority (Fiedler 1993, p. 30),

—the "established authority" of left-wing literary-cultural academia, an "authority" which substitutes left-wing pc dogmas for the genuine moral authority of (say) such a great Lawrentian as F. R. Leavis, who in his classic *The Great Tradition* celebrates the great novelists who are

> all distinguished by a vital capacity for experience, a kind of reverent openness before life, and a marked moral intensity. (Leavis, *The Great Tradition*, p. 9)

Supreme among these great novelists in terms of "vital capacity for experience," "reverent openness before life," and "marked moral intensity" is of course D. H. Lawrence, who with his religious sense remained all-important for Leavis even to the very end as the source of his (Leavis') hope, inspiration and values; indeed, in his very last book Leavis intensely studies Lawrence and finds "religious" wisdom and strength in Lawrence with which to fight the left-wing pseudoreligion of political correctness and reverse discrimination which Leavis presciently realized was thriving even in the early 1970s; in his last book, *Thought, Words and Creativity: Art and Thought in Lawrence*, Leavis portrays Lawrence as the supreme exemplar of genuine religion and transcendence,—which may "sustain a civilization,"—in contradistinction to left-wing political correctness, which is indeed rooted in "egoistic satisfaction and aims": Lawrence, Leavis tells us,

> Lawrence...is convinced that no positive acceptance, no "belief," however strongly based in cultural habit, can be adequate to sustain a civilization, or even an individual being, that is not at bottom essentially religious—that doesn't, that is, keep unforgettably

> present for recognition the need to transcend all egoistic satisfactions and aims. (Leavis, *Thought*, p. 79)

The Lawrentian valorization of religion and transcendence to sustain Western civilization is indeed antithetical to the "egoistic satisfactions and aims" of the left-wing intelligentsia, who believe that their "intellectual and moral superiority [is] self-evident" (Goodheart 1997, *Reign*, p. 4), and whose public policy is "suffused with arrogance" (Andrew J. Bacevich, "The World According to Clinton," *First Things*, June/July 1999, p. 29); in academia, indeed, the "egoistic satisfactions and aims" of the left-wing intellectual literary-cultural elite are perhaps most pronounced—as John Ellis recently noted:

> Oddly enough, it is the intellectual snobbery and elitism of many of the [left-wing] literati that politically correct [dogma] appeals to; their partiality to literary [PC] is based...on its hostility to...the middle class. The character of this [politically correct] anti-bourgeois sentiment...has...its origin in aristocratic disdain for the lower orders [of society]....
>
> ...Many [PC literary-cultural academics] are attracted to the field because they have literary ambitions of their own, and because very few achieve those ambitions, the failed poets among them are impatient with their secondary role as interpreters of the great. They would have preferred to be subjects of critical attention rather than critics. This explains, at least in part, the otherwise baffling fact that [left-wing] literature professors now denigrate literature and replace it with [politically correct] theory, for that new emphasis shifts the professor from secondary to primary status. [These left-wing PC professors]...[are] anxious to be recognized for [their] own performance rather than as...explicator[s] of someone else's. (Ellis, *Literature Lost*, pp. 214-215)

In their lust for "egoistic satisfactions," the left-wing literary-cultural critics desperately seek to aggrandize themselves by promoting politically correct sociocultural-political agendas at the expense of authentic interpretation of "the great"—and few among "the great" (Ellis 1997, p. 214) have suffered from them so much as has Lawrence.

Over eight decades ago Lawrence vehemently and astutely described and analyzed left-wing egoism as manifested in particular by his erstwhile friend Bertrand Russell:

> They [the left-wing activists like Bertrand Russell] all want the same thing: a continuing in this state of disintegration wherein each separate little ego is an independent little principality by itself. What does [Bertrand] Russell really want? He wants to keep

> his own little established ego, his finite and ready-defined self intact, free from contact and connection....That's what they [the left wingers] all want, ultimately....[T]hey want an outward system of nullity, which they call peace and goodwill, so that in their own souls they can be independent little gods, referred nowhere and to nothing: little mortal Absolutes, secure from question. That is at the back of all [left-wing] liberalism, Fabianism, and democracy. It stinks. It is the will of the louse. (D. H. Lawrence letter to Cynthia Asquith, 16 August 1915)

Deploring the left-wing privileging of a "state of disintegration" and supreme egoism in which the left-winger's "little established ego...[is] free from contact and connection" with (say) the Lawrentian religious Unknown, Lawrence attacks the left wing elitist ambition to be "in their own souls...independent little gods...little mortal Absolutes, secure from question"—an elitist ambition which they cover up by protesting their desire for "peace and goodwill," an ostensible desire that in fact masks the left wing's actual "will of the louse." (This reads like a description of Queen Hillary Clinton.)

Transcending left-wing politics, transcending "the will of the louse," Lawrence-Leavis and their genuine readers and devotees can indeed be the corrective to the myriad "left-wing extremists" in our midst, "left-wing extremists" whose "supreme anti-human triumph"—the triumph of politically correct race-gender-class dogma—goes against God-given, natural, "completely human humanity"—as the essential(ist) Lawrentian F. R. Leavis presciently and superbly put it over twenty years ago, in his last book, perhaps his best, a book about Lawrence and, indeed, about politics as well; Leavis here asserts, fervently invoking Lawrence, that the "modern religion" of political correctness is perverting humanity:

> Lawrence remarked half-a-century ago [in *Women in Love*, Chapter XVII, "The Industrial Magnate"] that the passion for equality was now the only religion left. The "passion for equality" is the religion of egalitarianism; and no one more or less grown up expects the religion you profess and the life you actually lead to be wholly consistent with one another: the advanced development of democracy we have achieved...has brought home to us that unqualified equality is hard to establish, and would be, even if we restricted the ideal to terms of money, power and privilege. *Even left-wing extremists* know that you can't do without differentials....

> Nevertheless, the ubiquity of egalitarianism as the modern "religion" means that few people seem to be disturbed at the supreme anti-human triumph of the [left-wing, anti-individualist] technologico-Benthamite spirit: the proclaimed (and enforceable) "equality" of women and men [and today, of course, black and white, etc., etc.]; whereas difference [between women and men, black and white, individual and individual, etc., etc.] is the essential fact, and it is not a matter of inequality or "underprivilege"; difference, without which there could be no completely human humanity....it [difference] can by no means be completely abolished, merely impoverished, frustrated and perverted—effects which our democratic civilization [through reverse discrimination] ensures....(Leavis, *Thought*, pp. 141-142; italics mine)

In this Godless age, where "religion" is made meaningless by such facts as that Bill Clinton goes to church virtually every Sunday,—in this Godless age, the left-wing "passion for equality"—*equality of result* (which demands quotas, racial/gender preferences, etc.)—is taken to the limit by "left-wing extremists" (among them President Clinton himself, in his "heart of hearts"), who choose to ignore God and Nature (and the fact that "unqualified equality" is unnatural and "anti-human"), and who indeed enact "the supreme anti-human triumph of...the proclaimed (and enforceable) 'equality'" of men and women, white and black, etc., etc.—an "equality" rigorously enforced in the United States today (for instance) by the Clinton Administration's corrupt Justice and Education Departments, which ignore the will of the people (as expressed recently [1996] in California's Proposition 209, for example) and instead advocate and institute "the proclaimed (and enforceable) 'equality' of women and men [and blacks and whites, etc.]" by State dictate,—a dictate of the left-wing State, enforced via reverse discrimination, a dictate which contravenes "completely human humanity" (Leavis 1976, p. 142) and thwarts us in our attempts to become "fully human" (Leavis 1962, p. 26), to attain "our spontaneous-creative fullness of being" (Lawrence, *Psychoanalysis*, p. 48),—thwarts us by "impoverish[ing]" and "frustrat[ing]" "difference,...the essential fact,...[which] is not a matter of inequality or 'underprivilege' [as the Left would have it]," but is rather "difference, without which there could be no completely human humanity" (Leavis 1976, p. 142); in one of his great meditations in *Women in Love*, Birkin-Lawrence envisions "the new day"—the "day" in which "difference" is vindicated:

> There is now to come the new day, where we are beings each of us, *fulfilled in difference*. (D. H. Lawrence, Women in Love, Chapter XVI, "Man to Man"; italics mine)

"Fulfilled in difference": Lawrence insists that the fulfillment of the individual being ("each of us") can only be attained in "the new day" not yet arrived, a "day" in which

> The highest Collectivity has for its true goal the purest individualism, pure individual spontaneity (Lawrence, "Democracy," Chapter I)

and

> the first great purpose of Democracy...[will be] that each man shall be spontaneously himself—each man himself, each woman herself, without any question of equality or unequality entering in at all; and...no man shall try to determine the being of any other man, or of any other woman. ("Democracy," Chapter IV ["Individualism"])

Thus, even in the midst of his pessimistic post-World War I period (during which he wrote "Democracy" [1919]), Lawrence envisaged a Lawrentian "State" that would advocate and promote "the purest individualism" so that ultimately "each man shall be spontaneously himself—each man himself, each woman herself, without any question of *equality* or unequality entering in at all" (italics mine); Lawrentian liberation requires "individualism" and "spontaneity"—"individualism" and "spontaneity" unhindered by the left-wing canard of "equality,"— a canard which has led to the deplorable state in which we find ourselves today, a state (State) in which a "left-fascist" government and academy do indeed "try to determine the being" of men and women (through reverse discrimination, political correctness, multiculturalism, etc.), a state of governmental-academic affairs so bad that it leads even an old left-wing literary-cultural critic like Russell Jacoby to decry the left-wing canard of "equality":

> That people are equal and should be treated equally is one matter; that their thoughts and activities are equal is another. The second does not follow from the first....
>
> Scholars and critics have surrendered to an inexorable logic of equality. "Since all people are equal, then everything they do must be equal" goes the reasoning....
>
> These [left-wing] approaches [to "equality"]...[succeed in]

casting aside...truth, individuality and perfection....(Jacoby 1999, p. 69)

"Truth, individuality and perfection": all Lawrentian values—

> Art-speech is the only truth. (D. H. Lawrence, *Studies in Classic American Literature*, Chapter I, "The Spirit of Place")
>
> [M]y work...is true and unlying, and will last out all the other stuff. (D. H. Lawrence letter to J. B. Pinker, 9 January 1917)
>
> And...the more I am singled out into utter individuality, the more [the] intrinsic me rejoices....
>
> Could I then, being my perfect self, be selfish?...
>
> And necessarily accompanying this more perfect being of myself is the more extended knowledge of that which is not myself. That is, the finer, more distinct the individual, the more finely and distinctly is he aware of all other individuality....(D. H. Lawrence, *Study of Thomas Hardy*, Chapter V, "Work and the Angel and the Unbegotten Hero")
>
> This dark, subtle reality of him [Birkin]...liberated her [Ursula] into perfection, her own perfected being....(*Women in Love*, Chapter XXIII, "Excurse")
>
> To touch...his [Birkin's] suave perfect loins and thighs of darkness, this was her [Ursula's] sustaining anticipation. (Ibid.)
>
> "It isn't really a locality, though," he [Birkin] said [to Ursula]. "It's a perfected relation between you and me, and others—the perfection relation—so that we are free together." (Ibid.)

Yet, instead of being under the sway of the Lawrentian "perfection relation" rooted in sublime "utter individuality," "truth," and being "free together," Western culture today—thanks to the left-wing literary-cultural-academic Establishment—Western culture today is dominated by "the dictatorship of virtue":

> We are subject to the tyranny of political correctness, the dictatorship of virtue, because we have granted the forces of the [left-wing, anti-Western] New Consciousness the right to determine what virtue is....
>
> ...The bearers of the New Consciousness have, quite simply, arrived at the point of critical mass. They have become capable of determining the moral agenda, of establishing which subjects will get attention, of drawing the iconography of the culture, of getting the new programs and foundation grants, starting the new journals and attracting the graduate students, and, perhaps most important, of exerting just enough intimidation so that certain opinions that run counter to the left-liberal orthodoxy have become virtually

> taboo....[T]he threat of ideological tyranny...comes from the left, and it now has to do with collective guilt, an overweening moralism, and multiculturalism. The danger to such things as free speech and genuine diversity of opinion is...due to the triumph of a modish, leftish, moralistic liberalism. (Bernstein 1994, *Dictatorship of Virtue*, pp. 229-230)

Ironically, soon after the appearance of Leavis' great last book on Lawrence (*Thought, Words and Creativity*, 1976), one left-wing literary-cultural reviewer suggested that Lawrence and Leavis were oblivious of the threat to "freedom of the spirit" posed by "dictatorship":

> Both Lawrence and Dr. Leavis inveigh against mechanistically imposed egalitarianism [e.g., quotas, racial/gender preferences, reverse discrimination], but this is not the only enemy to freedom of the spirit in the twentieth century. There is also dictatorship. (Smith 1978, *Review of English Studies*, p. 112)

But of course the fact is that both of the "enem[ies] to freedom of the spirit in the twentieth century" today—"mechanistically imposed egalitarianism" as well as "dictatorship"—emanate from the literary-cultural-political-academic Left, with its "tyranny of political correctness" and its "dictatorship of virtue": these must be fought by the devotees of Lawrence and Leavis, who today necessarily must be on the moderate-right politically (it seems to me). Indeed, the literary-cultural right wing itself is coming to see that it has and should make common cause with Lawrence and Leavis. In the context of today's inchoate but growing political awareness among the literary-cultural moderate right Leavis is approvingly identified by right-wing intellectuals as a "paleoconservative" (Winchell 1991, *Neoconservative Criticism*, p. 48) as well as "an indispensable critic" (ibid.) with an extraordinary "breadth of knowledge and courage of conviction" (ibid.); furthermore, Leavis' master collection of literary criticism, his journal *Scrutiny* (1932-1953), which includes many of his most important essays on Lawrence, was recently hailed by the literary-cultural right-wing *National Review* as being "Enormously important," one of "The 100 Best Non-Fiction Books of the Century" (Jeffrey Hart, *National Review*, May 3, 1999, p. 47). Indeed, one of the leading members of the literary-cultural moderate-right is none other than Norman Podhoretz, "F. R. Leavis's most gifted living disciple" (Winchell, p. 150). Podhoretz proudly identifies himself as "a Leavisian" (Podhoretz, *Making It*, p. 79); and he enthusiastically praises Leavis' "powerful" intelligence, "puritanical ferocity," and "exquisite" sensibility:

> it was precisely this quality of puritanical ferocity...informing the workings of an intelligence as powerful and a sensibility as exquisite as any I have ever encountered, which gave Leavis a hold over me such as no one had previously been able to exert or ever would again. (Ibid.)

Much of Leavis' "hold" on Podhoretz was due to "Leavis's own moral intensity" (Podhoretz 1986, *Bloody Crossroads*, p. 84), a moral intensity which indeed is quintessentially Lawrencean, the moral intensity of

> the moral artist, who is the truthteller,...*D. H. Lawrence*,...condemned out of hand...in the United States (until only the other day). (Leslie Fiedler, *No! in Thunder*, p.3 [italics mine]).

In 1960, Leslie Fiedler was a bit overly optimistic when he suggested that Lawrence "the moral artist,...the truthteller" would no longer be "condemned out of hand"; similarly, F. R. Leavis in 1976 was evidently a bit excessively hopeful regarding the "inevitable" perseverance of the Lawrencean "creative effort," and the "final victory" of Lawrence and "the clear truth he conveys"—as Leavis authoritatively stated:

> What we know is that the Lawrentian genius, as we have it, is convincing—is irresistible...[for] those who have recognized in his [i.e., Lawrence's] a voice pre-eminently demanding our attention and found the clear truth he [Lawrence] conveys truth to live with and to ponder....
>
> ...I felt the courage grow in me as I met more and more people who shared my conviction about him [Lawrence] and the nature of his genius: he has readers who understand him. I now see grounds for believing that they begin to form a public, and that we should be thinking about the ways of making it more effectively and consciously a public. It is in numbers very small, and, at its largest, will inevitably remain numerically very small. But influence is not a matter of numerical impressiveness. Civilization's belief in what it stands for has broken down, and humanity has a desperate sense of the vacuum. Lawrence...is himself a force of life bursting through....[W]e too are life....
>
> ...[W]e have the incitement, which is irresistible, of the life-courage in the product of his creativity, and that makes it inevitable for us to carry on the creative effort with all our intelligence, courage and resource. Who can be sure? Logic and automatism, impossible as it now seems, may yet be robbed of their final

victory; the decisively new and unforeseen may yet reward us.
(Leavis 1976, pp. 145-146, 156)

Leavis' optimism concerning the impending formation of an influential Lawrentian "public" was indeed misplaced. Leavis in 1976 did not anticipate the complete hegemony of PC in literary-cultural academia; he did not foresee the wholesale victory of those academics-intellectuals who replace Lawrentian-Leavisian "moral intensity" with PC—indeed, Leavis in 1976 was most likely heartened by the appearance, in 1973, of *D. H. Lawrence: A Critical Anthology*, a collection of literary criticism about Lawrence edited by one of Leavis' most devoted students, H. Coombes, an ardent Leavisite and Lawrentian. Harry Coombes, "a Leavisian enthusiast" (MacKillop 1995, p. 285) who furthermore believed that "Lawrence was marvellous" (Coombes 1973, p. 38) and that of course "It can hardly be disputed that Leavis has written the most important criticism of Lawrence's work" (Ibid., p. 39), did indeed produce an anthology that glorified Leavis—and Leavis' approach to Lawrence (Leavis' "irresistible truths" about Lawrence [Coombes, p. 40], Leavis' "feast of perception and reflection" about Lawrence [Ibid., p. 55])—in such a way that Leavis may indeed have felt encouraged to see the ultimate triumph of "the life-courage...[which is] the product of his [Lawrence's] creativity": "I felt the courage grow in me," Leavis fervently tells us; the courage "to carry on" the Lawrentian struggle for "life" "with all our intelligence, courage and resource" even in the midst of politically correct "Logic and automatism."

Thus Leavis in 1976; he died two years later, in 1978—the same year, ironically, in which Foucault's *History of Sexuality* appeared; I say "ironically" because, shortly after the appearance of *History of Sexuality, Volume I: An Introduction*, "Foucault, the most influential figure among race-gender-class scholars" (Ellis 1997, p. 27)—Foucault veritably achieved hegemony in literary-cultural academia, so that before long it could easily be said that "the most influential form of criticism currently active descends from Michel Foucault" (Edmundson 1995, p. 3), and furthermore, "Since his death [in 1984], Foucault's academic stock has only risen" (Miller 1993, *Passion*, p. 17).

But of course, while the "academic stock" of Foucault has surely risen, that of Lawrence (and Leavis) has correspondingly fallen, until of course by 1991 Jonathan Dollimore can confidently, complacently and maliciously refer to Lawrence as "This increasingly disregarded and often despised writer" (Dollimore 1991, p. 268). Thus, how can Lawrentians and Leavisians hope to "carry on" the Lawrencean "creative effort" in the midst of such a dispiriting state of affairs? How can Lawrentians and Leavisites regain some of their previous literary-cultural influence, in this power-obsessed, politically-obsessed "Age of Foucault"? For the answer here perhaps it is best to turn once more to Leavis' protege Norman Podhoretz, for, in addition to his appreciation of Leavis' "moral intensity," Podhoretz had a keen appreciation of the political astuteness of his other major mentor, Lionel Trilling:

> his [Trilling's] work was drenched in politics....
> ...his [literary-cultural] essays...resonated with political meaning and carried a political charge. It was this very quality, indeed, that made Trilling so much more exciting to read than most literary critics....
> ...[T]he political resonance of his writings made Trilling stand out with a salience no other American critic of his time managed to achieve....In the case of Trilling's critical essays, the political charge was strong enough to electrify the mind and yet so subtle and muted that it never overwhelmed their independent value as literary criticism. (Podhoretz, *Breaking Ranks*, pp. 279-280)

Full of "political meaning," "political charge," and "political resonance," Trilling's literary-cultural criticism—as, indeed, significantly discussed at the very beginning of the present chapter with reference to his classic *The Liberal Imagination*—Trilling's literary-cultural criticism provides an exceedingly helpful example for genuine Lawrentians as they confront the politically savvy left-wing literary-cultural critics who continue to attack Lawrence as "pathologically sexist" (Eagleton 1992, p. 36), "megalomaniac and paranoid" (Dollimore 1998, p. 269); with such vitriol coming from the literary-cultural left, "Lawrence" the cultural product (Widdowson 1992, pp. 3, 11, 19, 24) today may have no choice but to look for assistance to the literary-cultural moderate-right as personified these days by such as Trilling and his "neoconservative" followers, for Trilling today is indeed recognized as moderate-right: one major member of the black left-wing academic elite establishment recently (and indeed hostilely) characterized Lionel Trilling as "Godfather of Neo-Conservatism" (West, p. 233); and moreover, Trilling's "neoconservative" student-disciples such as right-wing literary-cultural critic Jeffrey Hart delightedly and affectionately conclude that

"Lionel was astute and highly political, his literary criticism from the beginning had political bearings, and...was political at that juncture where politics bears upon culture....his work moved far to the right" (Hart, "Lionel Trilling in the Classroom," *New Criterion*, May 1998, p. 75). Indeed, Hart named Trilling's *The Liberal Imagination* (discussed at the very beginning of the present volume) as one of "The 100 Best Non-Fiction Books of the Century" (*National Review*, May 3, 1999, p. 46).

Lawrence, too, is beginning to be (favorably) perceived and appreciated as having an affiliation with the literary-cultural-political Right; indeed, Trilling's right-wing disciple Norman Podhoretz very recently characterized Lawrence as a "man of the Right" (Podhoretz 1999, p. 14)—and coming from Podhoretz these days, this can certainly be considered a compliment. Furthermore, even more recently, Lawrence today is evidently being deployed by moderate-right literary-cultural critics to help promote the right-wing issue of "family values." One moderately young, moderate-right literary-cultural critic quite recently wrote expressing a rather keen sociopolitical awareness in an article on Lawrence and the family crisis/situation today:

> A century ago, when the socialist tide was rising, writers like Friedrich Engels...called for the state to abolish the family as a relic of the patriarchal age. Now...arguments for or against [this] call have become moot: families are being abolished by the behavior of individuals. To speak only of America, one-third of all births occur outside of marriage (60 percent in black neighborhoods, 35 percent in white), and the children growing up in fatherless households have difficulty staying in school, staying out of jail, or, as Robert Bly in two popular books has convincingly argued, just understanding what it might mean to draw on the masculine and feminine energies within themselves, and to mature as male or female persons. (Jeffers, Summer 1999, p. 191)

Referring to "fatherless households" and "Robert Bly['s] two popular books," Professor Jeffers here shows his awareness of the latest trends in sociological research and in "New Age" psychocultural-mythopoeic studies of "masculinity" and fatherhood; furthermore, Jeffers here succinctly and relevantly expresses the neoconservative (and paleoconservative) concern that "families are being abolished [in the Western world] by the behavior of individuals"; he then proceeds to cite appropriate sociocultural-political statistics about "births...outside of marriage." But of course, even far more important (from my perspective at least), after manifesting this kind of "neoconservative" sociocultural-political awareness of the deplorable state of the family and "family values" today, Professor Jeffers rather interestingly contends that none other than D. H. Lawrence may provide some of the solution to "the current crisis" of the family:

> he [Lawrence] is...the author whose work can...reinvigorate those principles that stable family life is based on. (Jeffers, Summer 1999, p. 191)

As "a man of the Right," then, Lawrence today is presented as the vindicator and reinvigorator of "stable family life"; further, Jeffers presents Lawrence as the basis of an "educational project" (Jeffers 1999, p. 192) which may indeed exercise a salvational impact on the life values of all those persons that are mature enough and literate enough to understand Lawrence:

> High school students are too young and often too subliterate, but college students and adults generally can, if they read at all, learn from Lawrence to value nothing less than heterosexual love, stable marriage, and the two-parent family. (Jeffers 1999, p. 192)

A "man of the Right," a champion of all-important ("nothing less than") "heterosexual love, stable marriage, and the two-parent family," "Lawrence" today may ultimately find that his salvation and revival surely lies, *not* in tendentious left-wing treatments that *attack* Lawrence's writing—

> At its worst, the writing [of Lawrence] is the voice of conservative resistance itself...[in] the moments containing the unqualified defense of...heterosexual morality....(Kelsey 185),

—attack Lawrence's writing as "the voice of conservative resistance," "resistance" to left-wing-"polymorphous desire" (Kelsey 179) anti-heterosex initiatives, activism and theories; and *condemn* Lawrence as the supreme defender of "heterosexual morality" (as if both "heterosexuality" and "morality" were reprehensible); rather, "Lawrence" today ultimately finds that his "literary-cultural" salvation and renewal lies indeed in the moderate-right sociopolitical-literary-cultural awareness which certainly celebrates "a sense of the power and variety of literature" (Ellis 1997, p. 230).

Jeffers' recent article is a short (fourteen pages) but promising indication that such a moderate-right sociopolitical-literary-cultural awareness may soon make itself felt in Lawrence criticism/studies; but, with the exception of the present volume, it seems to me that there exists no book-length study by a student/scholar of Lawrence that demonstrates "the courage to correct situations that need correction" (Ellis 1997, p. 230); yet there is one book, I would say, which has of late appeared, that manifests the moderate-right sociopolitical awareness as meaningfully applied to the dire situation generally existing in literary-cultural academia today, a situation which can succinctly be described as

> "*Literature Lost*: Social Agendas and the Corruption of the Humanities" (Ellis 1997, p. iii).

Indeed, it is this John Ellis book, *Literature Lost*, it seems to me, which distinctively takes a political stand in relation to the literary-cultural-academic situation today, and makes some extremely astute (and controversial) sociopolitical observations about the crisis in the study of literature today—observations such as the following:

> affirmative action [i.e., reverse discrimination]...provides both the content of this new [left-wing, politically correct] intellectual fashion and the means to implement it. Most of the key ideas of race-gender-class scholarship (oppression, discrimination, and so on) are carried over from affirmative action. (The difference is that whereas affirmative action ostensibly asks for some admissions and appointments, the race-gender-class transformation wants the entire curriculum.) The intellectual catastrophe that has overtaken the humanities is not just a by-product of affirmative action. It *is* affirmative action transformed into a curricular and intellectual climate. In literary studies, what began as a program for social justice in hiring has long since developed into hiring to service a teaching program that is *about* the themes of affirmative action. A vicious circle ensues, as changed hiring patterns drive changes in the curriculum and those curriculum changes then intensify the need for more skewed hiring. Even if affirmative action on behalf of faculty diversity were to be abandoned tomorrow, much of the same kind of hiring would have to take place to service the new curriculum....
>
> What can be done to reverse or at least halt the deterioration [of literature departments in academia]?...[T]he most obvious step that could be taken is to stop the mechanism that continues to make the situation worse day by day: affirmative action. (Ellis 1997, *Literature Lost*, pp. 216, 226)

"The intellectual catastrophe that has overtaken the humanities" has indeed, alas, overtaken D. H. Lawrence Studies as well—and if, in attempting to redress the balance in Lawrence's favour, it is necessary for intrepid Lawrentians (such as myself) to take on reverse discrimination-affirmative action, then so be it,—especially in view of the fact that "The intellectual catastrophe that has overtaken the humanities...*is* affirmative action transformed into a curricular and intellectual climate." Professor Ellis forthrightly states that "the most obvious step that could be taken" in order to "reverse...the deterioration" of the study of literature in academia is "to stop...affirmative action [i.e., racial/gender preferences]"; for this (and other moderate-right sociopolitical-cultural suggestions) Ellis has been vilified as "brutal" and "loathsome" (Ross, pp. 434, 435); his book has been derided by one left-wing Ivy League professor as "reductive," "nasty," "whiny," a "shrill polemic" (Schwarz 1998, pp. 570, 571).

Yet it seems likely that at least a few members of the literary-cultural Left are beginning to open their eyes to the truth about political correctness, affirmative action, and other sociopolitical-intellectual issues; one old left-wing literary-cultural critic recently went so far as actually to admit that, when "institutions of higher learning" use the phrase "equal opportunity employer," what they really mean is

> "No white heterosexual males need apply." (Pinsker 1999, p. 12)

"No white heterosexual males need apply": no other major author, it seems to me, has suffered as much from this left-wing sociocultural-political dictum as has D. H. Lawrence. What is to be done? It seems to me that it is only by means of a return to the celebration/valorization of "greatness" and "the great," as delineated some years ago by W. J. Bate, that we can (re)gain the inner strength that will enable us to be genuine Lawrentians, privileging the creative "vision of greatness" over sterile, repressive "political correctness"; as Bate so fervently adumbrated it some three decades ago:

> ...in and through the personal rediscovery of the great, we find that we need not be the passive victims of what we deterministically call "circumstances" (social, cultural, or reductively psychological-personal), but that by linking ourselves...with the great we can become freer—freer to be ourselves, to be what we most want and value....
> But always available to man, if he hopes to rise above "cultural

> declines" and fatigues from whatever cause—or to rise above anything else that threatens to imprison or deflect him personally—is the companionship, the support to the heart and spirit, of a direct and frank turning to the great....[T]ime after time, whatever the sinking of spirit,...the vision of greatness can operate suddenly as a release as well as an incentive to the creative initiative of the spirit. (Bate, pp. 129-130)

Transcending sociocultural-psychological "circumstances" by "linking ourselves" with D. H. Lawrence, we genuine Lawrentians can indeed gain the Lawrentian freedom "to be ourselves," rather than to be mere flunkies of the race-class-gender "political correctness" persuasion of literary-cultural criticism. The "direct and frank turning" to the Lawrencean "vision of greatness" is thus strongly advocated throughout the present volume, in the hope that the promulgation of this vision will in fact act as "an incentive to the creative initiative of the spirit," this creative spirit indeed serving as a veritable counter to the sterile, malignant dogmas of political correctness,—political correctness which, as has become so clear in this the Age of Bill Clinton, is indeed antithetical to "the vision of greatness" and "Moral education" as well; as Bate declares, citing his mentor Alfred North Whitehead:

> "Moral education," said Whitehead—a fundamental education of the whole self into action or being—"is impossible apart from the habitual vision of greatness. If we are not great, it does not matter what we do or what is the issue. Now the sense of greatness is an immediate intuition and not the conclusion of an argument...The sense of greatness is the groundwork of morals"—of what one really does and *is*. (Bate, p. 128)

Surely Lawrence himself in his writings brings us both "Moral education" and "the vision of greatness"—as he himself was keenly aware:

> [I] don't write for anybody; [I] rather write from a deep moral sense—for the race, as it were. (D. H. Lawrence interview with Kyle S. Crichton, *New York World*, 11 October 1925, in *D. H. Lawrence: A Composite Biography, Volume II*, ed. Nehls, p. 414)

Writing from "a deep moral sense—for the race," Lawrence with his "moral intensity" does indeed "have inside me a sort of answer to the *want* of today" (D. H. Lawrence letter to Edward Garnett, 1 February 1913), "today" being our own present age: an age unfortunately characterized by (among other ills) the drastic decline of "the sense of greatness," or what George A. Panichas recently referred to as "the eclipse of the idea of excellence" (Panichas 1999, p. 187),—an "eclipse" which leads to social-political "decadence"—as Panichas explains:

> Clearly, the eclipse of the idea of excellence is directly reflected in the eclipse of the quality of leaders—and, too, of a people's perception of representatives of leadership. This perception increasingly becomes a decadent one....
>
> Any diminution of the moral sense and the discriminating faculty is bound to be pernicious to one's capacity for the recognition, analysis, and measurement of leadership and of its representatives in all areas of human endeavor. And any detrition of standards of leadership must be accompanied by a confluent detrition of the character of leadership and in turn of our estimation of leader-types. Pseudo-leadership and pseudo-leaders characterize current conditions as more and more citizens confuse leadership with the cult of personality and the world of celebrities. Immoral and amoral conditions breed immoral and amoral tendencies. And the leveling or the absence of standards influences one's view of leaders and of the qualities that they project and that, ostensibly, satisfy one's hopes and desires. (Panichas 1999, pp. 187, 189)

Thus today "the eclipse of the idea of excellence" has enormous implications and ramifications, not only of course for the field of literary-cultural endeavours, but also in the realm of social-political "leadership," which today is indeed characterized by "Pseudo-leadership and pseudo-leaders" (as inimitably exemplified by the current occupant of the White House, Boy President Liar-in-Chief Bill Clinton); furthermore, in tandem with this deplorable state of "Pseudo-leadership and pseudo-leaders" is the concomitant situation of "the eclipse...of a people's perception of representatives of leadership": that is to say, today "we begin to accept inferior qualities, inferior leaders, inferior aspirations, inferior choices" (Panichas 1999, pp. 187-188), and consequently people today lack the "capacity for the recognition, analysis, and measurement of leadership and of its representatives in all areas of human endeavor." This "absence of standards" is ultimately "immoral and amoral," and comes to dominate "our estimation of leader-types" and "the qualities that they project and that, ostensibly, satisfy one's hopes and desires"—"hopes and desires" that today are indeed essentially grounded in the decline of greatness and "the eclipse of excellence"—the characteristic "conditions of our situation" (Panichas 1999, p. 189), "our present predicament" (Panichas 1999, p. 190).

Lawrence's "answer," in part, to this dire situation of "the eclipse of excellence" can indeed be found in the notion of Lawrencean democracy, "The true democracy," which he adumbrates at the end of *Studies in Classic American Literature*:

> The true democracy, where soul meets soul, in the open road. Democracy...where all journey down the open road, and where a soul is known at once in its going....The soul passing unenhanced, passing on foot and being no more than itself. And recognized, and passed by or greeted according to the soul's dictate. If it be a great soul, it will be worshipped in the road.
>
> The love of man and woman: a recognition of souls, and a communion of worship. The love of comrades: a recognition of souls, and a communion of worship. Democracy: a recognition of souls, all down the open road, and a great soul seen in its greatness, as it travels on foot among the rest, down the common way of the living. A glad recognition of souls, and a gladder worship of great and greater souls, because they are the only riches....
>
> ...souls in the Open Road, full of glad recognition, full of fierce readiness, full of the joy of worship, when one soul sees a greater soul.
>
> The only riches, the great souls. (D. H. Lawrence, *Studies in Classic American Literature*, Chapter 12)

The Lawrencean definition of "The true democracy" entails the recognition of the "great soul" by the ordinary or mediocre "soul" or self, and valorizes the ensuing "worship" of that "great soul"—"the heroic soul in a greater man" (*Aaron's Rod*, Chapter XXI, "Words")—"worship" by the average, "unheroic" "souls" (i.e., selves) that encounter and acknowledge this "great soul"; by "worship" Lawrence here means "respect, admiration or devotion" for "anyone or anything to whom [one] attributes an esp. exalted character" (*Webster's Third International Dictionary*)—but today (in the "Age of Clinton"), rather than perceive and praise "a great soul...in its greatness," people in their "hopes and desires" aspire, not to the appreciation, "recognition...[and] worship of great and greater souls, because they are the only riches," but instead find "riches," not in greatness of character and achievement, but rather in the narcissistic-materialistic satisfaction of their own selfish conventional mediocre "hopes and desires"—"hopes and desires" which are indeed embodied in the behavior of the self-indulgent, irresponsible American President Clinton, who, far from manifesting the "true classic dignity and self-responsibility" so admired by Lawrence (D. H. Lawrence letter to Lady Ottoline Morrell, 7 April 1916), instead represents a sort of postmodern immaturity, amorality and moral relativism, with this entire Clinton situation serving to demonstrate the validity of Lawrence's contention that

> the willingness to give the response to the heroic, the true aristocratic call, gets weaker and weaker in every democracy, as time goes on....Then men turn against the heroic appeal, with a sort of venom. They will only listen to the call of mediocrity wielding the insentient bullying power of mediocrity: which is evil. Hence the success of painfully [morally] inferior and [morally] base [e.g., Clintonesque] politicians. (D. H. Lawrence, *Apocalypse*, Chapter IV)

Yet, even in the midst of the "evil mediocrity" characteristic of this "Age of Clinton,"—mediocrity which on the literary-cultural level manifests itself in multiculturalism, reverse discrimination, the politically correct assault on the Western canon—even in the midst of all this there remains the fact that, in contradistinction to all this "bullying power of mediocrity" there still exists the literary-cultural example of "Lawrence,"—Lawrence, who with his extraordinary moral intensity and courage is even today seen as "a nonconformist of heroic stature" (Siegel 1999, p. 165). As a "heroic" nonconformist, Lawrence is indeed "a great soul" who deserves to be "worshipped in the road"—that is to say, he is worthy of being praised as a "heroic soul,...a greater man" than most other human beings; as for Lawrence, he himself in his religious sense is "eager to worship" God Himself:

> God, Almighty God....: strength and glory and honour and might and beauty and wisdom. These are the continual attributes of Almighty God,...who enters us and imbues us with his strength and glory and might and honour and beauty and wisdom, this is a god we are eager to worship....
> ...Almighty God, the God of strength and glory and might and wisdom:...a vital and magnificent God. (D. H. Lawrence, "Book Review of *Art Nonsense and Other Essays* by Eric Gill," *Phoenix*, p. 396)

Votary of "a vital and magnificent God," Lawrence attributes his own psychic-poetic strength to God's intervention and influence, as God "enters [Lawrence] and imbues [Lawrence and Lawrence's works] with his [God's] strength and glory and might and honour and beauty and wisdom," just as in the Old Testament story of Samson, for example, "the spirit of the Lord came mightily upon him [Samson] (Judges 14:6, 14:19, 15:14)," giving him the strength to do his great deeds, deeds in which

"Out of the strong came forth sweetness" (Judges 14:14)—the "strength" and "sweetness," in Lawrence's case, of great art.

Alluding to the story of Samson, Harold Bloom in one of his major works of literary theory concludes that "Out of the strong comes forth strength,...and when strength has imposed itself long enough, then we learn to call it tradition, whether we like it or not" (Bloom, *Map*, p. 200). Based on "long," "imposed," enduring strength, the Lawrence "tradition" in the coming years will certainly derive in part from Lawrence's being recognized as a vital force against political correctness, multiculturalism and anti-individualism in the literary-cultural-academic world today; the ensuing regeneration of "Lawrence" will be, it seems to me, a (politically and culturally) moderate-right regeneration of Lawrence proceeding from a kind of neoconservative/paleoconservative synthesis and stance that spits in the eye of the left-wing literary-cultural-academic elite, an elite which would have Lawrence eliminated as a force in "our civilization" (Leavis 1955, p. 15); yet in the long run it would seem that "Lawrence" cannot help but have the supreme victory in terms of "tradition," in view of the fact that, as Harold Bloom maintains,

> Tradition is...a conflict between past genius and present aspiration, in which the prize is literary survival....That conflict cannot be settled by social concerns, or by the judgment of any particular generation of impatient idealists, or by Marxists....(Bloom 1994, *Western Canon*, pp. 8-9)

Ardently practising "conflict" with "past genius" in his agons (creative struggles) with great precursors from Plato (see Scherr 1996) to the Jewish race (see the next chapter in the present volume) to numerous novelists and poets, Lawrence in his "aspiration" to poetic immortality is a supreme example of a great writer whose "depth of inwardness" was stronger, surely, than that of practically all other writers. Harold Bloom tells us that

> [The] depth of inwardness in a strong writer constitutes the strength that wards off the massive weight of past achievement [of his precursors], lest every originality be crushed before it becomes manifest (Bloom, *Western Canon*, p. 11),

—and with this Bloomian criterion in mind, we can surely conclude that Lawrence is among those few who possess more than enough "depth of inwardness" to guarantee them "the strength that wards off the massive weight of past achievement"—as the present study demonstrates in its treatment of Lawrence's response to the Jews as well as of Lawrence's response to the "massive weight" of the left-wing literary-cultural elite of his own day, whose sociocultural-intellectual-political "achievement" indeed had the potential to impede Lawrence's attempts to attain poetic immortality by means of his (Lawrence's) valorization of heterosexuality,—heterosex which, in the midst of the heyday of the Bloomsbury left-wing literary-cultural elite (led by such luminaries as Lytton Strachey and John Maynard Keynes), was being denigrated and besmirched, as it (heterosex) indeed is today by the left-wing gay-lesbian heirs of Michel Foucault (Leo Bersani, David Halperin, Jonathan Dollimore, Judith Butler, Eve Kosofsky Sedgwick, and on and on), who today easily dominate the literary-cultural-academic world as much as the "Bloomsbuggers" (i.e., the homosexual members of Bloomsbury; Delany, p. 89) ever did. Of course, such a politically incorrect study as the present one always runs the risk of being condemned as "retrograde" (Clarke 1998, p. 244)—or worse—by the left-wing literary-cultural establishment that dominates academia today, today being indeed "the worst of all times for literary criticism" (Bloom 1994, *Western Canon*, p. 22), a time when—as Harold Bloom astutely observes—politically incorrect literary-cultural critics face situations in which "even our own universities would feel compelled to indict us as racists and sexists" (Ibid., p. 16) for saying/doing the politically incorrect thing,—for standing up against left-wing "political correctness." Yet, as for myself and the present work,—if anything I say or have said here in this chapter (or anywhere else in the present volume) prompts accusations of "political incorrectness"—or, indeed, of "a megalomaniac and paranoid individualism" (Dollimore 1998, p. 269),—then I am proud to share the honour of these distinguishing characteristics with Lawrence; as a marginalized white heterosexual male Lawrentian in academia I can do no more; as a genuine Lawrentian I can do no less.

WORKS CITED

Aldridge, A. Owen. "Review of George A. Panichas, *The Critic as Conservator: Essays in Literature, Society, and Culture*." *Comparative Literature Studies* 31 (1994): 390-393.

Allen, Walter. *The English Novel*. New York: Dutton, 1954.

Allen, Wayne. "The Principles of Right." *Modern Age* 40 (Summer 1998): 243-249.

Bate, W. Jackson. *The Burden of the Past and the English Poet*. Cambridge: Harvard University Press, 1970.

Bayley, John. "Lawrence's comedy, and the war of superiorities." In *Rethinking Lawrence*. Ed. Keith Brown. Philadelphia: Open University Press, 1990.

Bell, Michael. *Literature, Modernism and Myth: Belief and responsibility in the twentieth century*. Cambridge: Cambridge University Press, 1997.

Ben-Ephraim, Gavriel. *The Moon's Dominion: Narrative Dichotomy and Female Dominance in Lawrence's Earlier Novels*. Rutherford: Fairleigh Dickinson University Press, 1981.

Berman, Art. *From The New Criticism to Deconstruction*. Urbana: University of Illinois Press, 1988.

Berman, Russell A. *Modern Culture and Critical Theory*. Madison: University of Wisconsin Press, 1989.

Bernstein, Richard. *Dictatorship of Virtue*. New York: Knopf, 1994.

Berube, Michael. *The Employment of English: Theory, Jobs, and the Future of Literary Studies*. New York: New York University Press, 1998.

Bloom, Harold. *The Anxiety of Influence: A Theory of Poetry*. New York: Oxford University Press, 1973.

Bloom, Harold. *A Map of Misreading*. New York: Oxford University Press, 1975.

Bloom, Harold. *The Western Canon*. New York: Harcourt Brace, 1994.

Bloom, Harold. "Introduction." *The Best of the Best*. Ed. Harold Bloom. New York: Scribner, 1998.

Bloom, Harold. "Bloom and Doom." *Newsweek*, October 10, 1994.

Bork, Robert H. *Slouching Towards Gomorrah: Modern Liberalism and American Decline*. New York: Regan Books, 1996.

Butler, Gerald J. *This Is Carbon*. Seattle: Genitron Press, 1986.

Clarke, Bruce. "Lawrence, Plato, Bloom." Review of Barry J. Scherr, *D. H. Lawrence's Response to Plato: A Bloomian Interpretation*. *English Literature in Transition* 41 (1998): 243-246.

Clifford, Stephen P. *Beyond the Heroic "I": Reading Lawrence, Hemingway, and "Masculinity"*. Lewisburg: Bucknell University Press, 1998.

Coombes, H. *D. H. Lawrence: A Critical Anthology*. Harmondsworth: Penguin, 1973.

Craft, Christopher. *Another Kind of Love: Male Homosexual Desire in English Discourse, 1850-1920*. Berkeley: University of California Press, 1994.

Crews, Frederick. *Skeptical Engagements*. New York: Oxford University Press, 1986.

Crews, Frederick. *The Critics Bear It Away*. New York: Random House, 1992.

Delany, Paul. *D. H. Lawrence's Nightmare: The Writer and His Circle in the Years of the Great War*. New York: Basic Books, 1978.

de Lauretis, Teresa. *The Practice of Love: Lesbian Sexuality and Perverse Desire*. Bloomington: Indiana University Press, 1994.

Devine, Philip E. *Human Diversity and the Culture Wars: A Philosophical Perspective on Contemporary Cultural Conflict*. Westport: Praeger, 1996.

Dickstein, Morris. *The Revival of Pragmatism: New Essays on Social Thought, Law, and Culture*. Durham: Duke University Press, 1998.

Dollimore, Jonathan. *Death, Desire and Loss in Western Culture*. New York: Routledge, 1998.

Dollimore, Jonathan. "Bisexuality, heterosexuality, and wishful theory." *Textual Practice* 10 (1996): 523-539.

Dollimore, Jonathan. "Sex and death." *Textual Practice* 9 (1995): 27-53.

Dollimore, Jonathan. *Sexual Dissidence*. Oxford: Clarendon, 1991.

Dollimore, Jonathan. *Radical Tragedy*. Brighton: Harvester Press, 1984.

Donoghue, Denis. "Is There a Case against *Ulysses*?" In *Joyce in Context*. Ed. Vincent Cheng and Timothy Martin. Cambridge: Cambridge University Press, 1992.

Edmundson, Mark. *Literature Against Philosophy, Plato to Derrida*. Cambridge: Cambridge University Press, 1995.

Eliot, T. S. "Review of *Son of Woman: The Story of D. H. Lawrence*." *The Criterion* 10 (1931): 768-774.

Ellis, David. "Lawrence and Forster in 1915." *Cambridge Quarterly* 27 (1998): 1-14.

Ellis, John M. *Literature Lost: Social Agendas and the Corruption of the Humanities*. New Haven: Yale University Press, 1997.

Epstein, Joseph. "Is Affirmative Action on the Way Out? Should It Be?" *Commentary*, March 1998, pp. 27-29.

Fiedler, Leslie. "The Canon and the Classroom: A Caveat." In *English Inside and Out*. Ed. Susan Gubar and Jonathan Kamholtz. New York: Routledge, 1993.

Fiedler, Leslie. *No! in Thunder: Essays on Myth and Literature*. Boston: Beacon Press, 1960.

Foucault, Michel. *Power/Knowledge: Selected Interviews and Other Writings, 1972-1977*. Ed. Colin Gordon. New York: Pantheon Books, 1980.

Gilbert, Sandra. "Shadows of Futurity: The Literary Imagination, the MLA, and the Twenty-First Century." *PMLA* 112 (1997): 370-379.

Gilbert, Sandra. "Leave off saying I want you to be savages." Review of David Ellis, *D. H. Lawrence: Dying Game*. *London Review of Books*, 19 March 1998, pp. 9-10.

Goldberg, S. L. *The Classical Temper: A Study of James Joyce's "Ulysses"*. New York: Barnes & Noble, 1969.

Goodheart, Eugene. *The Reign of Ideology*. New York: Columbia University Press, 1997.

Hobman, J. B. *David Eder*. London: Victor Gollancz, 1945.

Henke, Suzette. *James Joyce and the Politics of Desire*. New York: Routledge, 1990.

House, D. Vaden. *Without God or His Doubles: Realism, Relativism and Rorty*. New York: E. J. Brill, 1994.

Ingersoll, Earl G. "Review of Cynthia Lewiecki-Wilson, *Writing Against the Family: Gender in Lawrence and Joyce.*" *Studies in the Novel* 28 (1996): 263-266.

Inwood, Michael. *A Hegel Dictionary*. Oxford: Blackwell, 1992.

Jacoby, Russell. *The End of Utopia: Politics and Culture in an Age of Apathy*. New York: Basic Books, 1999.

Jeffers, Thomas L. "Lawrence, *Sons and Lovers*, and the End of Sex." *Hudson Review* 52 (1999): 191-204.

Kelsey, Nigel. *D.H. Lawrence: Sexual Crisis*. New York: St. Martin's, 1991.

Kerrigan, William. "The Case for Bardolatry: Harold Bloom Rescues Shakespeare From The Critics." *Lingua Franca*, November 1998, pp. 28-35.

Kimball, Roger. *Tenured Radicals: How Politics Has Corrupted Our Higher Education*. New York: Harper & Row, 1990.

Kinkead-Weekes, Mark. *D.H. Lawrence: Triumph to Exile 1912-1922*. Cambridge: Cambridge University Press, 1996.

Kinkead-Weekes, Mark. "The Genesis of Lawrence's Psychology Books: An Overview." *D.H. Lawrence Review* 27 (1997-1998): 153-170.

Lago, Mary, and Furbank, P. N., eds. *Selected Letters of E. M. Forster: Volume One*. Cambridge: Harvard University Press, 1983.

Lawrence. D.H. *Aaron's Rod*. Ed. Mara Kalnins. Cambridge: Cambridge University Press, 1994.

Lawrence. D.H. *"Apocalypse" and the Writings on Revelation*. Ed. Mara Kalnins. Cambridge: Cambridge University Press, 1980.

Lawrence. D.H. *Kangaroo*. Ed. Bruce Steele. Cambridge: Cambridge University Press, 1994.

Lawrence. D.H. *Lady Chatterley's Lover*. Ed. Michael Squires. Cambridge: Cambridge University Press, 1993.

Lawrence. D.H. "Democracy." In *"Reflections on the Death of a Porcupine" and Other Essays*. Ed. Michael Herbert. Cambridge: Cambridge University Press, 1988.

Lawrence. D.H. "Education of the People." In *"Reflections on the Death of a Porcupine" and Other Essays*. Ed. Michael Herbert. Cambridge: Cambridge University Press, 1988.

Lawrence. D.H. "Study of Thomas Hardy." In *"Study of Thomas Hardy" and Other Essays*. Ed. Bruce Steele. Cambridge: Cambridge University Press, 1985.

Lawrence. D.H. *Women in Love*. Ed. David Farmer, Lindeth Vasey, and John Worthen. Cambridge: Cambridge University Press, 1987.

Lawrence. D.H. "Love." In *"Reflections on the Death of a Porcupine" and Other Essays*. Cambridge: Cambridge University Press, 1988.

Lawrence, D. H. "Why the Novel Matters." *Phoenix: The Posthumous Papers of D. H Lawrence*. Ed. Edward D. McDonald. New York: Viking, 1936.

Lawrence, D. H. *Studies in Classic American Literature*. New York: Viking, 1975.

Lawrence, D. H. *The Letters of D. H. Lawrence: Volume I: September 1901-May 1913*. Ed. James T. Boulton. Cambridge: Cambridge University Press, 1979.

Lawrence, D. H. *The Letters of D. H. Lawrence: Volume II: June 1913-October 1916*. Ed. George J. Zytaruk. Cambridge: Cambridge University Press, 1981.

Lawrence, D. H. *The Letters of D. H. Lawrence: Volume III: October 1916-June 1921*. Ed. James T. Boulton and Andrew Robertson. Cambridge: Cambridge University Press, 1984.

Lawrence, D. H. *The Letters of D. H. Lawrence: Volume VI: March 1927-November 1928*. Ed. James T. Boulton, Margaret H. Boulton, and Gerald M. Lacy. Cambridge: Cambridge University Press, 1991.

Lawrence, D. H. *The Letters of D. H. Lawrence: Volume VII: November 1928-February 1930*. Ed. Keith Sagar. Cambridge: Cambridge University Press, 1993.

Lawrence, D. H. "Morality and the Novel." *Phoenix: The Posthumous Papers of D. H Lawrence*. Ed. Edward D. McDonald. New York: Viking, 1936.

Lawrence, D. H. "The State of Funk." *Phoenix II: Uncollected, Unpublished and Other Prose Works by D. H Lawrence*. Ed. Warren Roberts and Harry T. Moore. New York: Viking, 1970.

Lawrence, Frieda. *"Not I, But the Wind..."* New York: Viking, 1934.

Leavis, F.R. "Approaches to T.S. Eliot." *Scrutiny* 15 (1947): 56-67.

Leavis, F.R. *D.H. Lawrence Novelist*. New York: Simon & Schuster, 1969.

Leavis, F.R. *For Continuity*. Cambridge: Minority Press, 1933.

Leavis, F.R. *The Great Tradition*. New York University Press, 1964.

Leavis, F.R. *Thought, Words and Creativity: Art and Thought in Lawrence*. New York: Oxford University Press, 1976.

Leavis, F.R. *Two Cultures? The Significance of C. P. Snow*. London: Chatto & Windus, 1962.

Leitch, Vincent B. "Cultural Criticism." In *The New Princeton Encycolpedia of Poetry and Poetics*. Ed. Alex Preminger and T.V.F. Brogan. Princeton: Princeton University Press, 1993.

Leitch, Vincent B. *Cultural Criticism, Literary Theory, Poststructuralism*. New York: Columbia University Press, 1992.

Leitch, Vincent B. "Cultural Studies: 2. United States." In *The Johns Hopkins Guide to Literary Theory & Criticism*. Ed. Michael Groden and Martin Kreiswirth. Baltimore: Johns Hopkins University Press, 1994.

Lentricchia, Frank. *After the New Criticism*. Chicago: University of Chicago Press, 1980.

Lentricchia, Frank. *Criticism and Social Change*. Chicago: University of Chicago Press, 1983.

Lewiecki-Wilson, Cynthia. *Writing Against the Family: Gender in Lawrence and Joyce*. Caronbdale: Southern Illinois University Press, 1994.

Martin, Robert K., ed. *Queer Forster*. Chicago: University of Chicago Press, 1997.

Moore, Harry T. *The Priest of Love: A Life of D. H. Lawrence*. New York: Farrar, 1974.

Nehls, Edward, ed. *D.H. Lawrence: A Composite Biography: Volume II, 1919-1925*. Madison: Unviersity of Wisconsin Press, 1958.

Norris, Margot. *Joyce's Web: The Social Unraveling of Modernism*. Austin: University of Texas Press, 1992.

O'Hara, Daniel T. *Radical Parody: American Culture and Critical Agency After Foucault*. New York: Columbia University Press, 1992.

Ohmann, Richard. "On P.C. and Related Matters." In *PC Wars: Politics and Theory in the Academy*. Ed. Jeffrey Williams. New York: Routledge, 1995.

Panichas, George A. *The Critic as Conservator: Essays in Literature, Society, and Culture*. Washington, D.C.: Catholic University of America Press, 1992.

Panichas, George A. *The Courage of Judgment: Essays in Criticism, Culture, and Society*. Knoxville: University of Tennessee Press, 1982.

Panichas, George A. *The Reverent Discipline: Essays in Literary Criticism and Culture*. Knoxville: University of Tennessee Press, 1974.

Panichas, George A. *The Critical Legacy of Irving Babbitt: An Appreciation*. Wilmington: ISI Books, 1999.

Perloff, Marjorie. "Modernist Studies." In *Redrawing the Boundaries: The Transformation of English and American Literary Studies*. Ed. Stephen Greenblatt and Giles Gunn. New York: Modern Language Association of America, 1992.

Pinsker, Sanford. "Are Some Job Candidates 'More Equal' than Others?" *Academic Questions*, Winter 1998-99, Vol. 12, No. 1, pp. 10-13.

Podhoretz, Norman. *Making It*. New York: Random House, 1967.

Podhoretz, Norman. *The Bloody Crossroads: Where Literature and Politics Meet*. New York: Simon and Schuster, 1986.

Podhoretz, Norman. *Breaking Ranks: A Political Memoir*. New York: Harper & Row, 1979.

Podhoretz, Norman. *Ex-Friends: Falling Out with Allen Ginsberg, Lionel & Diana Trilling, Lillian Hellman, Hannah Arendt, and Norman Mailer*. New York: Free Press, 1999.

Pollitt, Katha. "The Best and the Rest." *The Nation*, May 11, 1998, p. 9.

Rorty, Richard. *Achieving Our Country: Leftist Thought in Twentieth-Century America*. Cambridge: Harvard University Press, 1998.

Rorty, Richard. *Consequences of Pragmatism*. Minneapolis: University of Minnesota Press, 1982.

Rorty, Richard. *Contingency, Irony, and Solidarity.* Cambridge: Cambridge University Press, 1989.

Rorty, Richard. *Essays on Heidegger and Others*. Cambridge: Cambridge University Press, 1991.

Rorty, Richard. "Postmodern Bourgeois Liberalism." In *Hermeneutics and Praxis*. Ed. Robert Holliger. Notre Dame: University of Notre Dame Press, 1985.

Ross, Trevor. "After the Canon Wars." *Dalhousie Review* 76 (1996): 431-443.

Ruderman, Judith. "D.H. Lawrence and the 'Jewish Problem': Reflections on a Self-confessed 'Hebrophobe'." *D.H. Lawrence Review* 23 (1991): 99-109.

Sagar, Keith. "D. H. Lawrence: The Man and the Artist." In *The Modernists: Studies in a Literary Phenomenon*. Ed. Lawrence B. Gamache and Ian S. MacNiven. Rutherford: Fairleigh Dickinson University Press, 1987.

Sagar, Keith. *D. H. Lawrence: Life into Art*. New York: Viking, 1985.

Sagar, Keith. *D. H. Lawrence: A Calendar of His Works*. Austin: University of Texas Press, 1979.

Scherr, Barry J. *D.H. Lawrence's Response to Plato: A Bloomian Interpretation*. New York: Peter Lang, 1996.

Scherr, Barry J. "Lawrence, Keats and *Tender is the Night*: Loss of Self and 'Love Battle' Motifs." *Recovering Literature* 14 (1986): 7-17.

Schwarz, Daniel R. *The Transformation of the English Novel, 1890-1930: Studies in Hardy, Conrad, Joyce, Lawrence, Forster and Woolf*. Basingstoke: Macmillan, 1995.

Schwarz, Daniel R. "Ellis's Complaint." *Journal of English and Germanic Philology* 97 (1998): 568-578.

Schwarz, Daniel R. "'Thirteen Ways of Looking at a Blackbird': Wallace Stevens's Cubist Narrative." In *Narrative and Culture*. Ed. Janice Carlisle and Daniel R. Schwarz. Athens: University of Georgia Press, 1994.

Seaton, James. *Cultural Conservatism, Political Liberalism: From Criticism to Cultural Studies*. Ann Arbor: University of Michigan Press, 1996.

Sedgwick, Eve Kosofsky. *Epistemology of the Closet*. Berkeley: University of California Press, 1990.

Segall, Jeffrey. *Joyce in America*. Berkeley: University of California Press, 1993.

Shaffer, Brian W. *The Blinding Torch: Modern British Fiction and the Discourse of Civilization*. Amherst: Univeristy of Massachusetts Press, 1993.

Siegel, Carol. "Reappraising Lawrence's Later Years." *D. H. Lawrence Review* 28 (1999): 161-165.

Smith, Shelia M. "Review of F.R. Leavis, *Thought, Words and Creativity: Art and Thought in Lawrence.*" *The Review of English Studies* 29 (1978): 110-112.

Spilka, Mark. "Domestic Violence in 'The White Stocking': A Lawrentian Case Study." In *D.H. Lawrence: The Cosmic Adventure: Studies in his Ideas, Works, and Literary Relationships*. Ed. Lawrence Gamache. Nepean, Ontario: Borealis Press, 1996.

Spilka, Mark. "Defending Lawrence." *D.H. Lawrence Review* 20 (1988): 311-313.

Sykes, Charles J. *ProfScam: Professors and the Demise of Higher Education*. Washington, D. C. : Regnery, 1988.

Sykes, Charles J. *The Hollow Men: Politics and Corruption in Higher Education*. Washington, D. C. : Regnery, 1990.

Thornton, Weldon. "Review of Paul Poplawski, *Promptings of Desire: Creativity and the Religious Impulse in the Works of D.H. Lawrence*." *D.H. Lawrence Review* 25 (1993-1994): 212-214.

Trilling, Lionel. *The Liberal Imagination: Essays on Literature and Society*. New York: Harcourt Brace Jovanovich, 1979.

West, Cornel. "Lionel Trilling: Godfather of Neo-Conservatism." *New Politics* 1 (Summer 1986): 233-242.

Wexler, Joyce. "Realism and Modernists' Bad Reputation." *Studies in the Novel* 31 (1999): 60-73.

Widdowson, Peter. "Introduction: Post-modernising D.H. Lawrence." In *D.H. Lawrence*. Ed. Peter Widdowson. New York: Longman, 1992.

Will, George. *The Leveling Wind: Politics, the Culture and Other News, 1990-1994*. New York: Viking, 1994.

Williams, Linda Ruth. *Sex in the Head: Visions of Femininity and Film in D.H. Lawrence*. New York: Harvester Wheatsheaf, 1993.

Winchell, Mark Royden. *Neoconservative Criticism*. Boston: Twayne, 1991.

Year's Work in English Studies 1994, Volume 75. Oxford: Blackwell, 1997.

Zytaruk, George J. "Rananim: D.H. Lawrence's Failed Utopia." In *The Spirit of D.H. Lawrence: Centenary Studies*. Ed.Gamini Salgado. London: Macmillan, 1988.

Zytaruk, George J. *The Quest for Rananim: D.H. Lawrence's Letters to S.S. Koteliansky*. Montreal: McGill-Queen's University Press, 1970.

CHAPTER TWO

Lawrence's Quarrel with the Jews
A Bloomian Reading

Leslie Fiedler, "an American Lawrentian" (Stoll 16), in a recent essay describes the emotional-religious superiority of the Jews to the Christians, who "are inadvertent matricides simply for having abandoned the Synagogue, and [who] compound their primal crime by murdering, or advocating the murder of those who still remain faithful to the maternal cult [i.e., the Jews]. Having thus killed Rachel, they [the Christians] are forever impotent, capable perhaps of imagining the ultimate mystery, of seeing in the mind's eye the Grail, borne typically in the legend, I remind you, by a woman, who represents typically, I suggest, what is feminine in the Divine, the Great Mother: but not of touching it, possessing it" (Fiedler 101). Thus in Lawrentian terms the Jews with their ability to "touch the quick of the mystery" (*Women in Love* 314)—they can "touch" and therefore "possess" the "ultimate mystery" (Fiedler 101)—are superior to the Christians, who in quasi-Platonic fashion are "capable perhaps of imagining the ultimate mystery" with "the mind's eye" of mental-consciousness (like the Platonic wise men of the *Symposium* and the *Phaedrus*, who with "the mind's eye" behold "absolute beauty" and "true Being" respectively). But, in the Fiedleresque-Lawrentian sense, the Christians in their (Platonic) privileging of mental-visual capacity are "forever impotent," forever incapable of attaining the tactile-religious ultimate experience of the Jews, "God's Chosen People"

(Fiedler 102), with their tactile superiority that results in religious superiority.

Tactile superiority taken together with religious superiority: such a combination surely indicates that the Jewish people are *the* Lawrentian people—and indeed, the terms of praise that Fiedler applies to the Jewish people in his essay are virtually identical to those used by Lawrence some seventy years earlier in his essay "Study of Thomas Hardy." Can it be that the ultra-Jewish Fiedler feels the same way about the Jews as does the "anti-Semitic" Lawrence? The fact is that, far from being anti-Semitic, Lawrence actually conceived the Jewish people to be the heroes of the supreme Lawrentian religious mystery. This Lawrentian affinity with the Jews—this Lawrentian conception of the Jews as sensual-religious heroes—is given powerful presentment in his "Study of Thomas Hardy," and indeed serves as Lawrence's last word in *Apocalypse* and other writings. Thus Lawrence's feelings about the Jews were extraordinarily rich, extraordinarily complex, and a far cry from anti-Semitism.

The complexity—and indeed the extraordinary admiration—contained in Lawrence's view of the Jews is evident in one of the first works of his philosophical-poetic maturity, "Study of Thomas Hardy"(which he wrote at the age of twenty-nine)—a work which Lawrence scholars have praised as "[a] major pronouncement" (Daleski 24) and "[a] most brilliant and...most individual essay (Kinkead-Weekes 90). Here Lawrence makes clear his great admiration for "the Jewish cycle" of male-female union, a cycle exemplified by the Jewish heroes David and Solomon:

> In the Jewish cycle, David, with his hand stretched forth, cannot recognize the woman, the female. He can only recognize some likeness of himself. For both he and she have not danced very far from the source and origin where they were both one. Though she is in the gross utterly other than he, yet she is not very distinct from him. And he hails her Father, Almighty, God, Beloved, Strength, hails her in his own image. And with hand outstretched, fearful and passionate, he reaches to her. But it is Solomon who touches her hand, with rapture and joy, and cries out his gladness in the Song of Songs. Who is the Shulamite but God come close, for a moment, into physical contact? . . .
>
> ...David, when he lay with a woman, lay also with God; Solomon, when he lay with a woman, knew God and possessed Him and was possessed by Him. (*Phoenix* 449-50)

Like Fiedler in his essay, Lawrence in "Hardy" connects the Jewish "possession" of God with the superior Jewish tactual sense—a superior tactual sense that is indeed presented by Lawrence as tantamount to a sort of Jewish sexual superiority: "David, when he lay with a woman, lay also with God; Solomon, when he lay with a woman, knew God and possessed Him and was possessed by Him." Thus, through the woman—who (as Fiedler remarks) "represents...what is feminine in the Divine"—the Jewish-Lawrentian heroes David and Solomon touch and possess God, "the ultimate mystery." Surely the Jewish people themselves are indeed the Lawrentian people; as Lawrence himself tells us in "Hardy":

> For centuries, the Jew knew God as David had perceived Him, as Solomon had known Him. It was the God of the body....The Jew lived on in physical contact with God....His [the Jew's] religion had become a physical morality, deep and fundamental....Its living element was...physical voluptuousness, wonderful and satisfying in a large measure. (*Phoenix* 450-51)

With its "wonderful and satisfying" element of "physical voluptuousness," the Jewish religion as portrayed by Lawrence in "Hardy" certainly corresponds to the Lawrentian religion enunciated by Lawrence in his "great religion" letter written the year before he began "Hardy":

> My great religion is a belief in the blood, the flesh, as being wiser than the intellect. We can go wrong in our minds. But what our blood feels and believes and says, is always true....All I want is to answer to my blood, direct, without fribbling intervention of mind, or moral, or what not. I conveive a [human] body as a kind of flame.... [I am] concerned with the mystery of the [bodily] flame.... (*Letters I* 503)

In his concern with "the mystery of the [bodily] flame," Lawrence is like the Lawrentian verson of the Jews that he presents in "Hardy": here Lawrence sings the praises of

> The Jewish tradition, with its great physical God. (*Phoenix* 462)

Like the Lawrentian God, "the Jewish God [announces] the magnificence and eternality of the physical law" (*Phoenix* 462), "the [Jewish] Law [which] is the immediate law of the body" (*Phoenix* 466).

According to the Lawrentian interpretation of "Jewish Law," the way of the fleshly body is the way of human identity and self-knowledge:

> Now in the Law, no man shall know himself, save in the Law. And the Law is the immediate law of the body. And the necessity of each man to know himself, to achieve his own consummation, shall be satisfied and fulfilled in the body. (*Phoenix* 466)

This Lawrentian interpretation of the Jewish "bodily" way of identity is indeed virtually synonymous with Lawrence's conception of "bodily" identity in his "great religion" letter:

> I conceive a [human] body as a kind of flame....I am... concerned with...the mystery of the flame forever flowing, coming God knows how from out of practically nowhere, and being *itself*.... We have got so ridiculously mindful, that we never know that we ourselves [in our bodies] are anything....[We] ought to look at ourselves [in the body] and say 'My God, I am myself!'... [W]e have forgotten ourselves [i..e. our bodies]. We are Hamlet without the Prince of Denmark. We cannot *be*. 'To be or not to be'—it is the question with us now.... And nearly every Englishman says 'Not to be.'... The real way of living is to answer to one's [bodily] wants. (*Letters I* 503)

Similarly, the way in which the Jewish heroes (according to the Lawrentian version of them in "Hardy") knew God "when [they] lay with a woman" is indeed reminiscent of Lawrence's declaration—made about two years before he finished "Hardy"—in his unpublished Foreword to *Sons and Lovers* (January 1913)—that

> God the Father,... we [i.e. D.H. Lawrence] know in the Flesh, in Woman.... In her [woman, during sex] we go back to the Father: but...blind and unconscious. (Huxley 102)

Thus, like his Jewish heroes, Lawrence knows God through fleshly sexual contact with "Woman"—contact during which Lawrence is "blind and unconscious," as indeed the heroic David and Solomon must have been in Lawrence's vision-version of them. Indeed, for Lawrence (in "Hardy") "God the Father" is "the God of the ancient Jew" (*Phoenix* 454): the Jewish God being indeed "the bodily father" (*Phoenix* 455). Furthermore, in their "blind and unconscious" state during sexual contact with Woman, Lawrence and his Jewish heroes are surely "blood-conscious" adventurers, for, as Lawrence describes it in his great "blood-consciousness" letter to Bertrand Russell (8 December 1915),

> [the] blood-consciousness...exists in us independently of the ordinary mental consciousness, which depends on the eye as its

> source or connector. There is the blood-consciousness, with the sexual connection holding the same relation as the eye, in seeing, holds to the mental consciousness. One lives, knows, and has one's being in the blood, without any reference to nerves and brain....[W]hen I *see*, there is a connection between my mental-conssciousness and an outside body, forming a percept; but at the same time, there is a transmission through the darkness which is never absent from the light, into my blood-consciousness: but in seeing, the blood-percept is... not strong. On the other hand, when I take a woman, then the blood-percept is supreme, my blood-knowing is overwhelming. There is a transmission... between her blood and mine, in the act of connection. So that afterwards, even if she goes away, the blood-consciousness persists between us, when the mental consciousness is suspended; and I am formed then by my blood-consciousness, not by my nerves at all.

Blood-consciousness, being anti-mind and anti-nerves, is indeed a kind of religious consciousness/experience in the context of a living reality of darkness—as Lawrence told Lady Cynthia Asquith a few days before his blood-consciousness letter (28 November 1915):

> the conscious life...is no more than a masquerade of death: there is a living *unconscious* life. If only... we were all struck *blind*, and things vanished from our sight:...We should find reality in the darkness. (my italics)

This "blind, unconscious life," this "dark reality," is of course the reality adumbrated by Lawrence in his Foreword to *Sons and Lovers* (1913) – the reality that leads us "blind and unconscious" back to "God the Father," "the God of the body," the Jewish God. The way to God the Father, Lawrence tells us, is through Woman—in the way taken by Lawrence's Jewish heroes David and Solomon. This "blind, unconscious" way to God is indeed the way of Lawrentian blood-consciousness; and surely Lawrence's heroes David and Solomon are "blood-conscious" heroes; thus the Jewish people are Lawrentian people of "blood-consciousness"; and Bertrand Russell is indeed "grotesque" (Delany 180) when he accuses Lawrence's blood-consciousness letter of "[leading] straight to Auschwitz" (Delany 180). For, on the contrary, the Lawrence of the "Hardy" and "blood-consciousness" letter period (1914-1915) did surely view the Jews as archetypal exemplars of Lawrentian values of "blood-consciousness," "religious" (God-contacting) sex, and reverence for the body.

Yet the Lawrentian affinity to the Jews placed Lawrence in an extremely difficult position as a great creative artist striving for supreme originality and uniqueness. Lawrence's difficulty with respect to "The Jewish Tradition, with its great physical God" (*Phoenix* 462) is greatly illuminated by Harold Bloom's theory of "the anxiety of influence." Harold Bloom tells us that the greatest poets must believe that they are "unique and irreplaceable" (*Anxiety of Influence* 63)—that they have create[d] [themselves]" (*Anxiety* 5); it is a matter of life and death for the poetic self:

> [A] poet's stance, his Word, his imaginative identity, his whole being, *must* be unique to him, and remain unique, or he will perish, as a poet.... (*Anxiety* 71)

In his quest for uniqueness the supremely great poet "must persuade himself" (*Anxiety* 72) that he possesses "imaginative priority" (*Anxiety* 72)—"imaginative priority" being "the authority [resulting from the great poet's true originality and supremely strong imagination]... of having named something first" (*Anxiety* 78). Yet, instead of enjoying the "absolute firstness" (*Map of Misreading* 51) of priority, the modern poet is generally afflicted by "a psychology of belatedness" (*Map* 35)—he knows that "we...*are* latecomers" (*Map* 27), and "He has come late in the story" (*Anxiety* 61)—the "story" of Western civilization.

Lawrence's keen awareness of his belatedness in relation to the priority of the Jews is poignantly expressed in a remarkable letter of 9 October 1916 to the Jewish artist Mark Gertler—a letter in which Lawrence gives fervent praise to Gertler's painting and Gertler's race:

> It would take a Jew to paint this picture [Gertler's "The Merry-Go-Round"]. It would need your national history to get you here, without disintegrating you first. You are of an older race than I, and in these ultimate processes, you are beyond me, older than I am. But I think I am sufficiently the same, to be able to understand.

Here Lawrence makes clear his awareness of the unique nature of the Jewish race, a race which he knows holds priority over him ("an older race than I")—a race which he feels is "beyond" him, but which he nevertheless presumes himself to be comparable to ("I think I am sufficiently the same").

Lawrence believes that he is "sufficiently the same" as the Jewish race in his ability "to understand" the "ultimate processes"; yet throughout his letter to Gertler, Lawrence indicates that he is haunted by a sense of belatedness:

> And it will be left for the Jews to utter the final and great death-cry of this epoch.... I must say, I have, for you, in your work, reverence, the reverence for the great articulate extremity of art....
>
> You are twenty-five, and have painted this picture—I tell you, it takes three thousand years to get where your picture is—and we Christians haven't got two thousand years behind us yet.
>
> I feel I write stupidly and stiltedly, but I am upset....

But what is Lawrence "upset" about? A few days before his letter to Gertler, in a letter to Ottoline Morrell (3 October 1916), Lawrence is full of enthusiasm and self-esteem as he speaks about "my novel" (which he would soon name *Women in Love*):

> I know it is true, the book [*Women in Love*]. And it is another world, in which I can live apart from this foul world.... The world of my novel is big and fearless.... I love it [*Women in Love*], and love it passionately....

Only two days after his letter to Gertler, in a letter to Catherine Carswell (11 October 1916), Lawrence actually says that

> I feel pretty happy inside....I believe we shall see some desired things come to pass, before we die....

Thus it is only in his letter to Gertler that Lawrence is "upset." Indeed, a few days earlier (in his letter to Ottoline Morrell), he is extremely proud and happy about his novel; a couple of days after his letter to Gertler, Lawrence explicitly says that he is "happy inside." Thus it seems likely that it was indeed Lawrence's thoughts of Gertler's "older" Jewish race and "the great articulate extremity of art" of that race—the "older race" than Lawrence's "we Christians"—that made Lawrence feel "upset"—"upset" and indeed inferior, for he writes of his great letter—one of the most eloquent, poignant statements of belatedness ever written—that it is "stupid" and "stilted." Ironically—and extremely poignantly—it was when Lawrence was at the height of his greatness as a writer—in the very midst of his *Women in Love* period—that Lawrence made these rare self-denigrating remarks—remarks that stand in contrast to the many self-congratulatory comments he made in the letters of his *Rainbow-Women in Love* period: for surely Lawrence did indeed find himself to be far superior to "this foul [modern] world";

as he told Bertrand Russell: "Where are my peers? I acknowledge no more than five or six—not so many—in the [modern] world" (2 June 1915). Indeed, in October 1916 Lawrence declared that "I can live apart from this foul world which I will not accept or acknowledge or even enter." Thus in October 1916 Lawrence certainly felt superior to the "foul" modern world in which he lived—and to the people in it.

But then why did Lawrence denigrate himself in his letter to Gertler? The answer, it seems to me, becomes evident even as we read the first letter Lawrence wrote almost immediately after his letter to Gertler—a letter to John Middleton Murry (11 October 1916): writing about his relation with his wife Frieda, Lawrence proudly tells Murry that

> Frieda and I have finished the long and bloody fight at last, and are at one. It is a fight one has to fight—*the old Adam* to be killed in me, *the old Eve* in her—then *a new Adam and a new Eve*. (my italics)

That same day (11 October 1916), in his letter to Catherine Carswell, Lawrence writes happily that

> I do really think we shall see this old order collapsing....I want to have some seed of a new spirit ready....We shall be like *Noah*, taking all the precious things into the ark, when the flood comes, and disembarking on a new world. (my italics)

Adam, Eve, Noah—all these intense, subjective references to Old Testament figures in Lawrence's letters during this period do indeed indicate that, rather than living in the "foul" modern world of the Great War and the British persecution of *The Rainbow*, Lawrence was living and feeling and thinking in another, much "older" world—the "Jewish" world of the Old Testament. As Lawrence tells us in his last book, *Apocalypse*, for him the Bible is essentially a "Jewish" (not Christian) book:

> the *Jewish* poetry [of the Bible] penetrates the emotions and the imagination, and the *Jewish* morality penetrates the instincts....(my italics)

"Emotions," "imagination," "morality [which] penetrates the instincts": this emotional-imaginative-instinctive-moral phenomenon is a hallmark not only of the Jewish-Biblical way but also of the Lawrentian way—a way the religious nature of which was explicitly posited by Lawrence some sixteen years before he wrote *Apocalypse*.

> But primarily I am a passionately religious man, and my novels must be written from the depth of my religious experience. (22 April 1914)

But what was Lawrence's "religion"? Certainly not Christianity—indeed, by the age of twenty-two Lawrence had concluded that

> I do not, cannot believe in the divinity of Jesus. (D.H. Lawrence letter to Reverend Robert Reid, 3 December 1907)

As he matured Lawrence became ever more assertive in his rejection of Christianity; when he was at the height of his powers, during his *Rainbow-Women in Love* period, he wrote emphatically to Bertrand Russell (7 July 1915) that

> I am rid of all my Christian religiosity.

A year later, in a letter to Catherine Carswell (16 July 1916), Lawrence bluntly stated:

> I am not a Christian.

Thus, by the time Lawrence wrote his letter of 9 October 1916 to his Jewish friend Mark Gertler, Lawrence surely did not think of himself as a Christian—yet in his letter to Gertler he does indeed self-pityingly refer to himself as one of "[us] Christians," "we Christians [that] haven't got [even] two thousand years behind us yet" and who are thus, Lawrence here tells us, for the most part incapable of "get[ting] where" the Jews are in terms of "articulate extremity."

It seems to me to be no exaggeration to say that here Lawrence actually feels ashamed of being a belated "Christian" inferior to the "older race," the Jews—whom Lawrence nonetheless aspires to equal, despite his misfortune/handicap of not being born a Jew.

Surely Lawrence felt it was his great misfortune as an artist not to have been born a Jew; nonetheless, he hopes that he is "sufficiently the same" to be uniquely capable (even though a "Christian") of attaining "the great articulate extremity of art"; here indeed Lawrence perceives himself as "unique and irreplaceable" (Bloom *Anxiety* 63)—a non-Jew capable of achieving the "great articulate extremity" exemplified (so Lawrence felt) by the Jewish Gertler.

Yet in his desire to be "a Jew" full of great "articulate extremity" Lawrence had to be confronted with "the anxiety of influence": because of his "belatedness" even Lawrence's greatest most Lawrentian creations had their metaphysical roots in the "Jewish" way (or at least in Lawrence's view of the Jew). To see this it is again extremely illuminating to look at "Hardy"; here Lawrence makes it clear that his "metaphysic" is Jewish not Christian: as Lawrence contrasts them in "Hardy":

> For centuries, the Jew knew God as David had perceived him, as Solomon had known him. It was the God of the body....The Jew lived on in physical contact with God. Each of his physical functions he shared with God....His [the Jew's] religion had become a physical morality, deep and fundamental....Its living element was this...physical voluptuousness, wonderful and satisfying in large measure. (*Phoenix* 450-451)

On the other hand,

> Christianity...went on in...[a] fight against the body, against the senses.... (*Phoenix* 453-454)

Later in "Hardy" Lawrence asserts that

> in Christ we abjure flesh, there is no flesh. A man must lose his life to save it. All the natural desires of the body, these a man must be able to deny [in Christianity].... (*Phoenix* 465)

Thus for Lawrence in "Hardy" the Jewish religion is a living, Lawrentian "physical morality," while Christianity is anti-body, anti-life, anti-natural. In "Hardy" Lawrence contrasts Jewish "Law" with Christian "Love":

> the [Jewish] Law is the immediate law of the body. And the necessity of each man to know himself, to achieve his own consummation, shall be satisfied and fulfilled in the body. God, Almighty God, is the father, and in fatherhood man draws nearest to him. In the act of [sexual] love, in the act of begetting, Man is with God and of God. Such is the Law....
>
> This is the old [Jewish] religious leap.... It is the [Jewish] Law [of the body]. But through Christ it was at last declared that in the physical act of love...man does not necessarily know himself, nor become Godlike, nor satisfy his deep, innate desire to BE. The physical act of love may be...a nothing. (*Phoenix* 466)

According to the Lawrentian interpretation of Christianity in "Hardy,"

> A man [according to the Christian religion] shall find his consummation [in] the crucifixion of the body.... (*Phoenix* 467)

Lawrence, of course, prefers "the [Jewish] Law...of the body" with its privileging of "the act of [sexual] love" in which (according to Lawrence's version of Jewish "Law") "man [Man] become[s] Godlike" and "satisf[ies] his deep, innate desire to BE"—this, for Lawrence, is indeed preferable to the Christian privileging of "the crucifixion of the body."

Obviously Lawrence found the "anti-body" religion of Christianity repugnant to his religion of sexual love; yet, despite his rejection of Christianity, Lawrence as "a passionately religious man" desired religious support for his metaphysic—and, as the Hardy essay indicates, Lawrence during his great *Rainbow-Women in Love* period derived that support from his vision of the "old" Jewish "Law"—which he saw as the natural law of the body, in opposition to Christian "Love"—which, unlike "the act of love," is exclusively spiritual, anti-body and anti-nature. Lawrence of course prefers "The Old [Jewish] Law":

> The Old Law bids us live [in the body]....So that the...Christian preaching...is indeed against the Law....For by the Law, Man shall in no wise injure or deny or desecrate his living body of flesh. (*Phoenix* 467)

Thus the Lawrence of the "Hardy"-*Rainbow-Women in Love* period surely regarded his metaphysic's valorization of the sexual body as rooted in the pro-"living body of flesh" Jewish "Law."

So Lawrence wanted religious roots and he found them in his vision of Jewish "Law"; but at the same time he did also find "the anxiety of influence"—for, as Harold Bloom tells us,

> the commodity in which poets deal, their authority, their property, turns upon priority. They own, they are, what they become first in naming. (*Anxiety* 54)

How could Lawrence "own" the phenomenon of "the living body of flesh" if that phenomenon had been first named (indeed according to Lawrence's own version of things), not by Lawrence, but long before him, by Jewish "Law"?

Lawrence's "anxiety of influence" in relation to the Jews was indeed exacerbated by his association with Gertler. For Lawrence, Gertler epitomized not only the "priority" of the "old" Jewish race, with its "great articulate extremity," but also the unique ability of the Jewish race to portray "the end of the world":

> And it will be left for the Jews to utter the final and great death-cry of this epoch....I must say, I have, for you, in your work, reverence, the reverence for the great articulate extremity of art.
> (D. H. Lawrence letter to Gertler, 9 October 1916)

Yet of course, at the very same time that Lawrence was praising the ability of the Jewish race to portray "the final and great death-cry of this epoch," he himself was in the midst of completing his own "great death-cry" utterance; indeed, a month after praising Gertler's "articulate extremity," Lawrence said of his own "utterance,"

> *Women in Love.*—The book frightens me: it is so end-of-the-world.
> (D. H. Lawrence letter to Catherine Carswell, 7 November 1916)

In his remarkable letter to Gertler (9 October 1916), Lawrence praises Gertler's painting as "great, and true,...horrible and terrifying"; and two weeks later Lawrence praises his own *Women in Love*, saying

> It [*Women in Love*] is a terrible and horrible and wonderful novel.
> (D. H. Lawrence letter to J.B. Pinker, 25 October 1916)

Thus Lawrence praised his own *Women in Love* using virtually the same gigantic-apocalyptic terms he had applied in his praise of Gertler's painting. Surely the Lawrence of *Women in Love* viewed himself as doing virtually the same kind of "death-cry" art as the Jewish Gertler. Furthermore, Lawrence clearly saw himself as a supreme "death-cry" artist. Yet Lawrence certainly labored under a poignant sense of his belatedness in relation to the priority of the Jews. Nonetheless, it can surely be said that by the time Lawrence finsished his final work on revising *Women in Love* (September 1919) Lawrence was no longer overawed by the "priority" of the Jews; indeed, *Women in Love* can be seen as Lawrence's supreme imaginative triumph over his feelings of "belatedness" in relation to the Jewish race.

Women in Love: Lawrence's "Jewish" Novel

Women in Love, it seems to me, can surely be viewed as Lawrence's "Jewish" novel: in *Women in Love* Lawrence subsumes the character of both the ancient Jewish race, with its valorization of "the living body of flesh" emblematized by such Old Testament heroes as David and Solomon, and the modern Jewish race (epitomized by Gertler), with its unique "articulate extremity" and "death-cry" utterance.

Even before the novel proper begins, Lawrence in his "Foreword" to *Women in Love* (written on 12 September 1919) makes clear the "Jewishness" of his novel—this "Jewishness" being that which he described in "Hardy" as the Jewish reverence for "the living [sexual] body of flesh." In his "Foreword" Lawrence declares that *Women in Love* is a manifestation and revelation of "Eros of the sacred mysteries"—sexual "mysteries" which should be "venerate[d]"; but Lawrence's "sacred" Eros is actually a metonymy for the Jewish "physical voluptuousness" and "physical morality" which Lawrence praised so fervently in "Hardy"—the "physical voluptuousness" and "physical morality" of David and Solomon, who are, of course, in Lawrence's vision/version of them, supreme appreciators of the "sacred" nature of sex ("In the act of [sexual] love,...Man is with God and of God. Such is the [Jewish] Law [according to Lawrence's vision of Solomon and David in "Hardy," *Phoenix* 466]"). Of course Lawrence himself surely shared their appreciation of "sacred" sex: "I shall always be a priest of love," Lawrence had emphatically declared on Christmas Day 1912—and of course the "love" he is speaking of is not "Christian"-spiritual love but fleshly-sexual love; seven years later, in his Foreword to *Women in Love*, Lawrence reiterates his "sacred" belief in "the sensual passions and mysteries":

> Let us hesitate no longer to announce that the sensual passions and mysteries are equally sacred with the spiritual mysteries and passions.

Thus the Lawrence of *Women in Love* immediately declares that the purpose of his novel is to demonstrate the "sacred" nature of "the sensual passions and mysteries"—the life of the "living body of flesh." In advocating the "living body of flesh" Lawrence is in fact acting as a "Jew," a champion of the ancient Jewish "Law" of the body; accordingly, it is the Lawrence figure in *Women in Love*, Rupert Birkin, who is indeed the modern spokesman for the ancient Jewish "law of the [sacred-sexual] body."

Birkin-Lawrence makes clear his ancient "Jewish" status starting in Chapter III of *Women in Love*, "Class-room," in which Birkin attacks his mistress Hermione for not being authentically "Jewish":

> [Y]our passion is a lie [Birkin tells Hermione]. It isn't passion at all, it is your *will*. It's your bullying will. You want to clutch things and have them in your power. You want to have things in your power. And why? Because you haven't got any real body, any dark

sensual body of life. You have no sensuality. You have only your will and your conceit of consciousness, and your lust for power, to *know*.

In contradistinction to the bogus sensuality of Hermione rooted in mind and will is the authentic, religious sensuality of the "Jewish" Law,

> the Old [Jewish] Law, which says, "In the life of the body we [i.e., the Jews] are one with the Father [i.e., the Jewish God]." The Old [Jewish] Law bids us live: it is the old, original [Jewish] commandment, that we shall live in the Law, and not die....For by the [Jewish] Law, Man shall in no wise injure or deny or desecrate his living body of flesh....("Hardy," *Phoenix* 467)

The "dark sensual body of life" in *Women in Love* is Birkin-Lawrence's equivalent of the Lawrentian-Jewish "living body of flesh" in "Study of Thomas Hardy." By advocating the "dark sensual body of life," Birkin-Lawrence in *Women in Love* takes over the Jewish "physical morality" values (attributed to the Jews by Lawrence himself in "Hardy") as if he (Birkin-Lawrence) were the first person ever to discover these sexual-moral phenomena. Birkin-Lawrence goes on in "Class-room" to elaborate his "dark sensual body of life" philosophy in terms of "great...knowledge":

> It [real sensuality] is a fulfilment—the great dark knowledge you can't have in your head....

The source of Birkin's "dark knowledge" philosophy is none other than the Lawrentian Jew; in "Hardy" Lawrence declares that

> the God of Knowledge...[is] the Father, the God of the Ancient Jew. ("Hardy," *Phoenix* 454)

The kind of unique "Knowledge" which "the God of the Ancient Jew"—with His rule of "the magnificence and eternality of the physical law" ("Hardy" 462)—possesses, is powerfully defined by Lawrence in his great "blood-consciousness" letter to Bertrand Russell, written in the period between "Hardy" and *Women in Love*; here Lawrence tells Russell about another kind of knowledge, "another seat of consciousness than the brain and the nerve system." This new kind of knowledge is "blood-knowledge," "blood-consciousness":

> there is a blood-consciousness which exists in us independently of the ordinary mental consciousness....There is the blood-consciousness, with the sexual connection....One lives, knows, and

> has one's being in the blood, without any reference to nerves and brain....[W]hen I take a woman [sexually], then...my blood-knowing is overwhelming. There is a transmission, I don't know of what, between her blood and mine, in the act of [sexual] connection. So that afterwards, even if she goes away, the blood-consciousness persists between us, when the mental consciousness is suspended; and I am formed then by my blood-consciousness, not by my mind or nerves at all....
>
> ...All living things...have a blood-being....And blood-knowledge [in human beings] comes...through the sex [relation]....

"Blood-knowledge"—so different from mundane "mental"-brain knowledge—is the extraordinary knowledge which has its origin in "the God of Knowledge,...the God of the Ancient Jew"—He, it would seem, allows human beings to partake of this knowledge: it is contained in the "transmission" that can take place between male and female "in the act of [sexual] connection" when they are overwhelmed by "blood-knowledge" experience. But clearly only certain individuals are capable of receiving this divine "transmission," this marvelous "blood-consciousness" experience; for, as Lawrence tells us in "Hardy,"

> Usually, sex is only functional, a matter of relief or sensation, equivalent to eating or drinking or passing of excrement. (*Phoenix* 445)

But for the "Jewish" Birkin-Lawrence, the sexual act is indeed sacred, religious in the best Biblical (Old Testament) sense, as the chapter "Excurse" powerfully demonstrates.

In "Excurse" Lawrence-Birkin becomes an Old Testament hero—so "old" in fact, that he attains priority over his Jewish precursors; for Birkin is presented as one of "the Sons of God" who existed before the Flood, before Noah—and before Abraham and the establishment of the Jewish religion:

> She [Ursula, Birkin's future wife] looked at him [Birkin]....New eyes were opened in her soul, she saw a strange creature from another world, in him. It was as if she were enchanted, and everything were metamorphosed. She recalled again the old magic of the Book of Genesis, where the Sons of God saw the daughters of men, that they were fair. And he was one of these, one of these strange creatures from the beyond, looking down at her, and seeing she was fair. (312)

By being "metamorphosed" into one of "the Sons of God" of the early part of the Book of Genesis (Genesis 6:2), Birkin-Lawrence imaginatively becomes the precursor of the Jews; indeed, he is presented as

> one of the Sons of God such as were *in the beginning of the world*, not a man, something other, something more. (313; italics mine)

By becoming "one of the Sons of God such as were in the beginning of the world," Birkin-Lawrence imaginatively places himself prior to the formation of the Jewish race and the Jewish religion—thus here in "Excurse" Lawrence deploys the Bloomian "anxiety of influence" strategy of "daemonization," which Bloom describes this way:

> Turning against the precursor's Sublime, the newly strong poet undergoes *daemonization*, a Counter-Sublime whose function suggests *the precursor's relative weakness*. (*Anxiety of Influence*, p. 100)

In the case of Lawrence and the Jews in "Excurse," the precursor is none other than the first Jew, whom Lawrence manages to precede by placing himself "in the beginning of the world"; furthermore, the first Jew was evidently a man—but Lawrence in "Excurse," through his persona Birkin creatively-imaginatively manages to outdo this human condition by making himself "one of the Sons of God,...*not a man*, something other, something more": this more-than-human state is Lawrence's "daemonization," his "Counter-Sublime" which suggests that, since he is "something more" than human, then he must be "something more" than his "human" Jewish precursors, who even as The Chosen People were still "People." Then, once again, in his insistent drive for priority Lawrence tells us:

> She [Ursula] had had lovers, she had known passion. But this was neither love nor passion. It was the daughters of men coming back to the Sons of God, the strange inhuman Sons of God who are in the beginning. (313)

Thus Lawrence-Birkin is definitively placed "in the beginning," removing any doubt as to his priority: he is, in short,

> one of the Sons of God from the Beginning....(313)

As "one of the Sons of God from the Beginning," Birkin-Lawrence certainly attains supreme priority—as indeed the supreme "Jew," that is to say, the supreme adherent of God's Law, the "law" of "the body." Accordingly, Lawrence-Birkin's "body" in "Excurse" is sublimely portrayed as his strange, whole *body*,...like the bodies of the Sons of God who were in the beginning. (314; italics mine)

But not only does Birkin-Lawrence manage to assert his sublime "Jewish"-Old Testament priority in *Women in Love*, he also succeeds in surpassing the "Jewish" "death-cry utterance" of the contemporary Jewish artist Gertler; Lawrence does this by having his persona Birkin propound a Lawrentian apocalyptic quite early in the novel. Indeed, even in Chapter II Birkin is already "thinking about race or national *death*" (30; italics mine) and in Chapter V Lawrence-Birkin goes so far as to meditate: "Well, if mankind is destroyed, if our race is destroyed like Sodom, and there is this beautiful evening with the luminous land and trees, I am satisfied. That which informs it all is there, and can never be lost. After all, what is mankind but just one expression of the incomprehensible. And if mankind passes away, it will only mean that this particular expression is completed and done. That which is expressed, and that which is to be expressed, cannot be diminished....Let mankind pass away—time it did. The creative utterances will not cease, they will only be there. Humanity doesn't embody the utterance of the incomprehensible any more. Humanity is a dead letter. There will be a new embodiment, in a new way. Let humanity disappear as quick as possible." Even here at this early point in *Women in Love* Lawrence manages to outdo—to be more "Jewish" than—Gertler's "death-cry utterance" by presenting his "end-of-the-world" vision in "Jewish" religious terms resonant and reminiscent of the Old Testament ("if our race is destroyed like Sodom") and the humble reverence of the prophet before God ("the incomprehensible"). But of course Birkin-Lawrence, in his aspiration to complete uniqueness and individuality cannot admit his "Jewishness"; thus we have the "religious"-apocalyptic Birkin asserting in the same Chapter V that "there's no God" even as he does in fact believe (as his meditations in Chapter V indicate) in "That which informs it all,...the incomprehensible"—God.

And soon Lawrence-Birkin is definitively verbalizing his "death-cry" meditations of Chapter V to Ursula: "Humanity itself is dry-rotten, really. There are myriads of human beings hanging on the bush—and they look very nice and rosy, your healthy young men and women. But they are apples of Sodom, as a matter of fact, Dead Sea fruit, gall-apples....their insides are full of bitter, corrupt ash....[M]ankind is a dead tree, covered with fine brilliant galls of people" (126). And he adds, employing Old Testament prophet terms: "I abhor humanity, I wish it was swept away. It could go, and there would be no *absolute* loss, if every human being perished tomorrow. The reality would be untouched. Nay, it would be better. The real tree of life would then be rid of the most ghastly heavy crop of Dead Sea Fruit, the intolerable burden of myriad simulacra of people, an infinite weight of mortal lies" (127). Here Birkin sounds much like Jeremiah 9, which laments the fact that "Every one deceives his neighbour, and no one speaks the truth; they have taught their tongue to speak lies;...Their tongue is a deadly arrow; it speaks deceitfully; with his mouth each speaks peaceably to his neighbour, but in his heart each plans an ambush for him." In his "articulate extremity" Lawrence-Birkin has the "end-of-the-world" contemporary "Jewish" quality of Gertler, but he also has the ancient "Jewish" quality of "the body"; as Ursula notes: "the moulding of him [Birkin] was so quick and attractive, it gave such a great sense of freedom: the moulding of his brows, his chin, his whole physique, something so alive, somewhere, in spite of the look of sickness" (129)—"sickness" which comes from Birkin's other "Jewish" aspect—the aspect of the didactic prophet who detests the corrupt world around him and is at the same time without honor in his own country: like Jeremiah, who was ridiculed and persecuted by his own homeland (as is Birkin-Lawrence) and died in a foreign country (as did D. H. Lawrence). But predominant in Birkin is his other "Jewish" aspect, "his wonderful, desirable life-rapidity, the rare quality of an utterly desirable man" (129-130), a "rare quality" emblematic of "the Jew,...[whose] religion had become a physical morality, deep and fundamental,...[whose] living element was...scrupulous physical voluptuousness, wonderful and satisfying in a large measure."

Birkin's "physical voluptuousness" is emphasized in Chapter 14, the "Water-Party" chapter: here Birkin experiences

> the rushing of passion that came up his limbs and over his face as she [Ursula] drew him. And soon he was a perfect hard flame of passionate desire for her.... he only wanted her, with an extreme desire that seemed inevitable as death, beyond question....
> ...What did anything matter save this ultimate and triumphant experience of physical passion, that had blazed up anew like a new spell of life. (187-188)

With his experiencing "ultimate and triumphant...physical passion," Birkin in "Water-Party" attains his ultimate "Jewish" aspect insofar as his "physical voluptuousness" with Ursula reaches its consummate peak: he fully appreciates the religious nature of his "perfect...passionate desire" for Ursula; similarly, Birkin in "Water-Party" provides consummate Lawrentian expression of the "great death-cry of this epoch" (as Lawrence terms it in his letter to Gertler), as he tells Ursula about "our real reality":

> Dissolution rolls on, just as production does [Birkin tells Ursula]. It is a progressive process—and it ends in universal nothing—the end of the world, if you like. (173)

In discussing Gertler's picture Lawrence refers to "sensational extremity" and "lurid processes of inner decomposition" as part and parcel of his "death-cry" utterance—and in "Water-Party" Lawrence-Birkin postulates that "When the stream of synthetic creation lapses, we find ourselves part of the inverse process, the blood of *destructive creation*" (172; italics mine). This is Lawrence's equivalent of the "sensational...inner decomposition" portrayed by Gertler—"decomposition" which is leading to the "death" of "this epoch." But in *Women in Love* Lawrence swerves away from Gertler's "death-cry" utterance by making Birkin postulate a movement of death and rebirth in relation to "the end of the world": "But why isn't the end of the world as good as the beginning?" Birkin rhetorically asks Ursula; and he goes on to maintain that

> It [the end of the world] means a new cycle of creation after—but not for us. If it is the end, then we are of the end—.... (173)

By asserting that he and Ursula are "of the end," Birkin-Lawrence once again places himself as a member of the Jewish race; for of course in his letter to Gertler, Lawrence had asserted: "At last your race is at *an end* (my italics)—"your race" being the Jewish race. As a "Jew," Birkin-Lawrence can regard himself as one who was able to experience and endure "a violent maelstrom of destruction and horror" in his "inner soul," to get "here, without disintegrating...first." Like the Lawrentian Jew as portrayed in Lawrence's letter to Gertler, Birkin-Lawrence has experienced "the fire of ultimate expression" without completely "disintegrating." Consequently Birkin is capable of prognosticating the "death" of Western civilization even while he is still alive; imaginatively foreseeing the future, Birkin tells Gerald (in Chapter XVI, "Man to Man") that "There's a long way to go, after the point of intrinsic death, before we [Western civilization] disappear....Right down the slopes of degeneration—mystic, universal degeneration. There are many stages of pure degradation to go through: age-long. We live on long after our death, and progressively, in progressive devolution." The "Jewish" Birkin can contemplate this "degeneration" of Western civilization without himself suffering complete "disintegration," despair and cynicism; indeed, it is the named Jew Loerke who possesses

> sinister knowledge, devoid of illusions and hopes.
> To Gudrun, there was in Loerke the rock bottom of all life. Everybody else had their illusion, must have their illusion, their before and after. But he...did without any before and after, dispensed with all illusion. He did not deceive himself in the last issue. In the last issue he cared about nothing, he was troubled about nothing, he made not the slightest attempt to be at one with anything....
> ...He seemed to be the very stuff of the underworld of life. There was no going beyond him. (427)

Birkin tells Gerald that there is "no going beyond" Loerke when it comes to "social hatred":

> "And what *is* the end?" he [Gerald] asked [Birkin].
> Birkin shook his head.
> "I've not got there yet, so I don't know. Ask Loerke, he's pretty near. He is a good many stages further than either you or I can go."
> "Yes, but stages further in what?" cried Gerald, irritated.
> Birkin sighed, and gathered his brows into a knot of anger.
> "Stages further in social hatred," he said. (428)

And Birkin adds significantly:

> I expect he is a Jew....

The nexus between "Jew" and "social hatred" is prominently mentioned by Lawrence in a letter of his *Women in Love* period (the letter is dated 7 May 1918):

> I feel queer and desolate in my soul....And the world is such a useless place....I am reading Gibbon. He says the Jews are the great *haters* of the human race—and the great *anti-social* principle.—Strikes me that is true—for the last 2,500 years, at least.—I feel such profound hatred myself, of the human race, I almost know what it is to be a Jew. (*Letters* III 242-243)

Thus even in the midst of revising *Women in Love*, Lawrence was intensely misanthropic and "anti-social"—and he associates these characteristics with the Jews; indeed, he happily identifies himself with the Jews in these "anti-social" respects.

In *Women in Love* of course Birkin has the Lawrentian-"Jewish" misanthropy: "I abhor humanity, I wish it was swept away," he tells Ursula (Chapter 11), and he adds: "I don't believe in the humanity I pretend to be part of, I don't care a straw for the social ideals I live by, I hate...social mankind" (Chapter 11)—certainly Birkin-Lawrence is as "anti-social" as any "Jew." Indeed, early on (Chapter 5) in *Women in Love* Lawrence as omniscient narrator states of Birkin:

> His dislike of mankind...amounted *almost* to an illness. (my italics)

The key word here of course is "almost." Whereas Loerke's "social hatred" is noxious, Birkin"s never reaches that insalubrious level—thus Birkin, in the best "Jewish" tradition, can indeed attain the consummate vision of "articulate extremity"—but "without disintegrating...first." The reason that Birkin can do this, is capable of this, is that Birkin possesses the ancient "Jewish" quality of David and Solomon, a "religious" quality which brings them (David and Solomon) and him (Birkin) in contact with "the source and origin" (*Study of Thomas Hardy*, Chapter VII) through "lay[ing] with a woman"—in Birkin's case, this "Jewish" characteristic saves him (Chapter 27):

> And he [Birkin] went across to her [Ursula] and gathered her like a belonging in his arms. She was so tenderly beautiful, he could not bear to see her, he could only bear to hide her against himself. Now, washed all clean by her tears, she was new and frail like a flower just unfolded, a flower so new, so tender, so made perfect by inner light, that he could not bear to look at her, he must hide her against himself, cover his eyes against her. She had the perfect candour of creation, something translucent and simple, like a radiant, shining flower that moment unfolded in primal blessedness. She was so new, so wonder-clear, so undimmed. And he was so old, so steeped in heavy memories. Her soul was new, undefined and glimmering with the unseen. And his soul was dark and gloomy, it had only one grain of living hope, like a grain of mustard seed. But this one living grain in him matched the perfect youth in her.
>
> "I love you," he whispered as he kissed her, and trembled with pure hope, like a man who is born again to a wonderful, lively hope far exceeding the bounds of death.

> She could not know how much it meant to him, how much he meant by the few words. Almost childish, she wanted proof, and statement, even over-statement, for everything seemed still uncertain, unfixed to her.
>
> But the passion of gratitude with which he received her into his soul, the extreme, unthinkable gladness of knowing himself living and fit to unite with her, he, who was so nearly dead, who was so near to being gone with the rest of his race down the slope of mechanical death, could never be understood by her. He worshipped her as age worships youth, he gloried in her because, in his one grain of faith, he was young as she, he was her proper mate. This marriage with her was his resurrection and his life.

Thus Birkin is the true Lawrentian Jew, embodying both "Jewish" components—the misanthropic-"end of the world" aspect (a la Loerke) and the saving contact with woman in the "Flitting" chapter. Birkin, even though he possesses the "Jewish" misanthropy and "end of the world" knowledge of Loerke, does not have the "illness" of Loerke (Birkin's "dislike of mankind...amounted *almost* to an illness"). The reason for this is that Birkin's sexual love for Ursula nurtures Birkin's soul's "one grain of living hope," causes Birkin to experience "a wonderful, lively hope far exceeding the bounds of death"—a hope rooted in Birkin's "knowing himself living and fit to unite [sexually] with her [Ursula]" even though "he [Birkin]...was so nearly dead,...so near to being gone with the rest of his race down the slope of mechanical death"—but now, Birkin's race is the true Lawrentian "Jewish" race, so he does not suffer the fate of "mechanical death" that is surely the lot of the "end-of-the world" Jew Loerke, who

> laughed out some mocking dream of the destruction of the world by a ridiculous catastrophe of man's invention: a man invented such a perfect explosive that it blew the earth in two, and the two halves set off in different directions through space, to the dismay of the inhabitants: or else the people of the world divided into two halves, and each half decided *it* was perfect and right, the other half was wrong and must be destroyed; so another *end of the world* [italics mine]. Or else, Loerke's dream of fear, the world went cold, and snow fell everywhere, and only white creatures, polar-bears, white foxes, and men like awful white snow-birds, persisted in ice cruelty. (453)

The true Lawrentian Jew (i.e., Birkin) can "get...here"—"here" being the site of the knowledge of death and disintegration of individual and civilization—"without disintegrating...first"—that is, without disintegrating before he has imaginatively experienced the "end of the world." But Loerke, the titular Jew, has been so reduced in significance and power by Lawrence that his meaning is contracted to that of a signifier of

> the perfect and subtle experiencing of the process of death. (452)

Birkin, on the other hand, as Keith Sagar concludes,

> moves freely through all the levels of hell, but is not himself one of the damned. He is in perpetual danger of being sucked into the whirlpool, but struggles to hang onto a vision so large that it contains the whirlpool. (Sagar 191)

The reason why Birkin is "not himself one of the damned"—the reason why he can experience "a violent maelstrom of destruction and horror...[in his] inner soul" (to use a phrase from Lawrence's letter to Gertler) without his "disintegrating...first"—is that he is a Lawrentian "Jew."

LAWRENCE AS WANDERING JEW

At the end of *Women in Love*, the "Jewish" Birkin-Lawrence proudly and humbly asserts his belief in God:

> Whatever the mystery which has brought forth man and the universe ["mystery"=God], it is a non-human mystery, it has its own great ends, man is not the criterion. Best leave it all to the vast, creative, non-human mystery....
> "God cannot do without man." It was a saying of some great French religious teacher. But surely this is false. God can do without man. God could do without the ichthyosauri and the mastodon. These monsters failed creatively to develop, so God, the creative mystery, dispensed with them. In the same way the mystery could dispense with man, should he too fail creatively to change and develop. The eternal creative mystery could dispose of man, and replace him with a finer created being. Just as the horse has taken the place of the mastodon.
> It was very consoling to Birkin to think this. If humanity ran into a cul-de-sac, and expended itself, the timeless creative mystery would bring forth some other being, finer, more wonderful,...to carry on the embodiment of creation....The mystery of creation was fathomless, infallible, inexhaustible, for ever....The fountain-head was incorruptible and unsearchable. It had no limits. It could bring forth miracles, create...new forms of con-

> sciousness, new forms of body, new units of being. To be man was as nothing compared to the possibilities of the creative mystery. To have one's pulse beating direct from the mystery, this was perfection, unutterable satisfaction....The perfect pulse throbbed with indescribable being, miraculous unborn species. (478-479)

In search of the miraculous, Lawrence towards the end of his *Women in Love* period concludes that

> I *must get out*. I must get out of England, of Europe. There will never be anything here but increasing rottenness, generally slow, sometimes quick, but always rottenness. I want to know about Palestine [Israel]....I'll go to Palestine....(2 January 1919)

Lawrence did not get to Palestine; but in his mind he soon became the "wandering Jew":

> I am turned into a wandering Jew. (18 December 1919)

Furthermore,

> What ails me I don't know....(Ibid.)

One thing that "ailed" Lawrence was his continued "Jewish" obsession:

> What is there at the bottom of the soul of a Jew which makes him a Jew? That's what I want to know....[I]s there a basic consciousness of difference—radical difference between Jew and Gentile? Is there or isn't there? If there is, then it must be something important indeed....I sort of feel there is a gulf: but always hidden and bridged over....I am tired of sympathy and universality—I prefer the sacred and ineradicable *differences* between men and races: the sacred gulfs. (23 March 1921)

In fact, of course, what Lawrence "want[ed] to know" was a way out of his "anxiety of influence" in relation to the Jews; he was hoping that, even as he conducted his "Jewish" search for the miraculous, he might find "the sacred and ineradicable *differences*" between him and his precursors the Jews. Thus during the period 1919-1921, Lawrence continued to wrestle with his "Jewish problem": that is to say, he made great use of the Jewish tradition in Western civilization but at the same time did not want to feel any of the "immense anxieties of indebtedness" (Bloom, *Anxiety of Influence*, p. 5) to which he could certainly be liable. To deal with his quandary during this period—in which he wrote *Aaron's Rod* and *Kangaroo*, two novels full of "Jewish" elements and influence—Lawrence in an almost schizoid manner manifested a degree of anti-Semitism while at the same time his works became more and more obviously "Jewish."

The "Jewish" nature of *Aaron's Rod* (1922) is made quite evident and quite specific even in its very, unmistakably "Jewish" title. Aaron, the main character, is essentially looking for his "Moses"—his "brother" and "leader"—throughout the novel. Furthermore, "Aaron's rod"—like that of his namesake—possesses magical powers; but of course in the Old Testament Aaron's rod is his staff, while in Lawrence's novel "Aaron's rod" is his flute—and his penis. Lawrence's explicit phallicizing here is his creative swerve away from the "Jewish" way, the Old Testament. By making "Aaron's rod" both artistic (flute) and sexual (phallus) Lawrence here shows that for him art and sex are both full of religious, sacred resonance comparable to the Jewish belief in Jehovah. The musical-sexual power of "Aaron's rod" (in *Aaron's Rod*) come together in Aaron's relation with the Marchesa. Aaron with his flute ("Aaron's rod") "miraculously" restores the Marchesa's singing voice:

> He did as she wished....he went into the big music-room to play. And the stream of sound came out with the quick wild imperiousness of the pipe. It had an immediate effect on her. She seemed to relax the peculiar, drug-like tension which was upon her at all ordinary times. She seemed to go still, and yielding. Her red mouth looked as if it might moan with relief. She sat with her chin dropped on her breast, listening. And she did not move. But she sat softly, breathing rather quick, like one who has been hurt, and is soothed. A certain womanly naturalness seemed to soften her.
>
> And the music of the flute came quick, rather brilliant like a call-note, or like a long quick message, half command. To her it was like a pure male voice—...a pure male voice, not only calling, but telling her something, telling her something, and soothing her soul to sleep....It [Aaron's "rod"] seemed to cause a natural relaxation in her soul, a peace....
>
> When Aaron came in, she looked at him with a gentle, fresh smile....
>
> She said nothing to him, only just smiled. And the look of knowledge in her eyes seemed, for the moment, to be contained in another look: a look of faith, and at last happiness....
>
> She had a beautiful, strong, sweet voice.
>
> ...His [Aaron's] flute was at his mouth, he was watching her....[H]e sounded the note, a challenge....And...she began to sing....[H]er soul and her voice got free, and she sang—she sang as

> she wanted to sing, as she had always wanted to sing, without that awful scotch, that impediment inside her own soul, which prevented her.
>
> She sang free, with the flute gliding along with her. And oh, how beautiful it was for her!...Her soul seemed to breathe as a butterfly breathes, as it rests on a leaf....For the first time! For the first time her soul drew its own deep breath. All her life, the breath had caught half-way. And now she breathed full, deep, to the deepest extent of her being.

Aaron's magic rod here serves to liberate the Marchesa's "soul," her being; while the Old Testament Aaron had sacred authority over all the people of Israel, Lawrence's Aaron has power—extremely brief power—over just this one woman; furthermore, Moses-Lilly doesn't even have power over his own wife, who scolds him in public: "[Y]ou're so beastly ungrateful....Because I hold you safe enough all the time you like to pretend you're doing it all yourself [she tells him]"—and, when Lilly's visitor Jim gives Lilly "A Punch in the Wind" (Chapter VIII), she takes the side of the assailant: "But...you must admit it was your own fault," she tells her husband. Indeed, it seems to me that Lilly-Moses, ironically enough, can be seen to be less powerful than Lawrence's Aaron, who at least has and uses his "rod" (flute, penis), and feels—albeit briefly—

> his desire...strong, fierce....Like the strength of an eagle with the lightning in his talons. Something to glory in, something overweening, the powerful male passion, arrogant, royal, *Jove's thunderbolt* [my italics]....He had got it back, the male godliness, the male godhead.

The fugacity of Aaron's phallic power is soon made evident, however; and so is Lawrence's lack of strong "Jewish" quality in *Aaron's Rod*. Even in the above quote, with its conspicuous mention of "Jove's thunderbolt," we see the inconsistency of Lawrence's "Jewishness" in *Aaron's Rod*: he is not capable of sustaining it, just as Aaron is not capable of sustaining his phallic power in his encounter with the Marchesa: after his sex with her, Aaron

> felt withered. Curiously he felt blasted. (Chapter XVIII)

However, not only is Aaron "blasted," but, before long, his "rod" is as well: his flute is "smashed" (conveniently) by a bomb towards the end of the book: and by smashing "Aaron's rod" Lawrence also smashed any hope he may have had of rising to the "Jewish" occasion of *Aaron's Rod*:

as a strong (creative) misinterpretation/ misreading/ response to the "Jewish" precursor, *Aaron's Rod* is a mishmash, a failure—even though, as a novel, it does manage to have some very great Lawrentian moments in it.

Thus, despite the strength of such episodes as that of "Aaron's rod" with the Marchesa, the fact is that for the most part *Aaron's Rod* is a rather weak appropriation of its Old Testament precursor: the Aaron-Lilly relationship is not quite compelling; Lilly is no charismatic Moses, yet he is essentially treated with the utmost seriousness by Lawrence. At the end of the novel Aaron decisively concludes:

> Lilly...was something incomprehensible, which had dominion over him [Aaron], if he chose to allow it. (Chapter XXI)

Lawrence's claims for Lilly are not really powerful or convincing; nor is his appropriation of the Old Testament, the "Jewish" way in *Aaron's Rod*. Lawrence himself surely realized this; in "The Evening Land" (1922), published at about the same time as *Aaron's Rod*, Lawrence with characteristic self-awareness expressed his sense of his failure to attain "Jewishness": but he displaces his feelings for "Jewishness," making America the object of his frustration—on the surface; addressing America, Lawrence litotically writes of America's

> dark, unfathomed will, that is *not un-Jewish* [italics mine] (*Complete Poems*, p. 292)

—thus making America—"dark, unfathomed" America—a substitute for "Jewishness," the "Jewishness" that Lawrence has failed to attain:

> Dark, elvish
> Modern, unissued, uncanny America,
> Your nascent demon people
> Lurking among the deeps...
> Alure me till I am beside myself,
> A nympholepht,... (*Complete Poems*, p. 293)

"A nympholepht," Lawrence here admits he has been seized by demoniac desire for the unattainable: that unattainable in fact being the unattainable "Jewishness" Lawrence sought for himself; to realize this we need only notice that Lawrence's description of America here— "Dark, elvish/ Modern, uncanny...,/...demon . . ./ Lurking among the deeps"—is indeed a description of the Jew Loerke in *Women in Love*!

Lawrence wrote "The Evening Land" in Baden-Baden in spring

1921; he also finished *Aaron's Rod* in Baden-Baden, in spring (June) 1921; also in Baden-Baden during this period (spring 1921) Lawrence makes some blatantly anti-Semitic remarks, referring to "money hogs in motorcars, mostly Jews" (letter of 11 June 1921) and remarking:

> It is nice to be in a country [i.e., Germany] where people are not so disgustingly full of money as they are everywhere else. Nobody has any money any more except the profiteers, chiefly Jews, with which Baden Baden is swarming. (16 June 1921)

But, strangely enough, a few months later Lawrence in his mind and in his letters is once again stressing the priority of the Jews; on the way to Ceylon from Italy, Lawrence on shipboard writes of seeing Mount Sinai:

> There stood Mount Sinai, red as old, dried blood, naked as a knife, and so sharp, so unnaturally sharp,...and always there, like something dreadful, between man and his lost Paradise. All is Semitic and cruel—naked, sharp, no tree, no leaf, no life....It is a strange exit, through this Red Sea—Bitter. Behind lies at last Jerusalem, Greece, Rome and Europe—fulfilled and past, a great terrible dream. *With Jews it began, with Jews it ends* [italics mine]. You ought to see Sinai, then you could know it. The ideal has been wicked to man: and Jahveh [Jehovah] is father of the ideal, and Zeus and Jupiter and Christ are only sons. And thank God Sinai and Red Sea are past and fulfilled. (7 March 1922)

Desperately seeking fully to confront and overcome his failure to attain "Jewishness" in *Aaron's Rod*, Lawrence in March 1922 no longer indulges in the trite, conventional anti-Semitism of his day (about "rich Jews"), but instead he returns to his serious, awe-stricken consideration of the archetypal-historical priority of the Jews: "With Jews it began," Lawrence here profoundly admits. But here, realizing his lack of priority, Lawrence is surely, sorely hurt; emblematized by Mount Sinai for Lawrence, the Jewish precursor is "so sharp,...and always there, like something dreadful, between man [i.e., Lawrence] and his lost Paradise [the "lost Paradise" of "priority"]." Realizing that the Jews have priority over "Greece, Rome and Europe"—all of Western civilization—Lawrence feels that to him the "Semitic" is "cruel," since he at this point cannot sustain for himself the illusion of priority, and it is "strange" and "Bitter" for him; but he takes consolation in his belief (at this point anyway) that "Jerusalem [i.e., Jewish priority and authority and influence]...[is] fulfilled and past, a great terrible dream"—a dream whose "terrible"-sublime quality has been "wicked" to Lawrence, who in his wisdom knows that "With Jews it began, with Jews it ends"—for both classical civilization ("Greece," "Rome," "Zeus," "Jupiter") and Christian civilization ("Europe," "Christ") are only ephebes—"only sons": the Jewish God ("Jahveh," "Jehovah") is the source, the "father," the reason Lawrence experiences "the anxiety of influence."

Since the Jewish God is the source of Western civilization—and of Lawrence's "anxiety of influence"—Lawrence realizes that he must consign that source to the past since he cannot attain priority over it: thus Lawrence in his 7 March 1922 letter keeps repeating that "Jerusalem...[is] fulfilled and past,...past and fulfilled."

Trying to convince himself that he rejects the past and the West, Lawrence is plainly attempting to deal with his "anxiety of influence"; but after a couple of weeks in Ceylon Lawrence stops trying to fool himself: with characteristic self-knowledge he admits that

> I do think, still more now I am out here, that we make a mistake forsaking England and moving out into the periphery of life. After all, Taormina, Ceylon, Africa, America—as far as *we* go, they are only the negation of what we ourselves stand for and are: and we're rather like Jonahs running away from the place we belong. That is the conclusion that is forced on me....I really think that the most living clue of life is in us Englishmen in England, and the great mistake we make is in not uniting together in the strength of this real living clue—religious in the most vital sense—uniting together in England and so carrying the vital spark through. Because as far as we are concerned it is in danger of being quenched....It is in ourselves, or nowhere,...[to] be invaluable for *saving Europe* [my italics here]. (letter of 30 March 1922)

Failing to forget Europe, Lawrence once more aspired to save it as he had during his "Messianic phase"; as Paul Delany tells us: "Lawrence's Messianic phase—the time when he imagined himself a prophet called to save England, and to build *a new Jerusalem* [my italics] on the ruins of the old—lasted nine months, from late January to late October 1915" (Delany, p. 64). Lawrence in this "Messianic" frame of mind wrote some of his greatest work; for in seeing himself as "a prophet...[who could] build a new Jerusalem," Lawrence was able to overcome his "anxiety of influence" and imaginatively attain "priority" with a "Salvator Mundi" like the "Jewish" Lawrence-Birkin.

That Lawrence *au fond* still saw himself in 1922 as "Jewish" is evident in the above letter when he describes himself as a "Jonah" who commits the sin of "forsaking England"—"England" really being (in the Lawrentian mind) "Jerusalem." Thus Lawrence once more decided to save Europe rather than forget it: he felt better—more "Jewish"—that way.

"I don't like the east. It makes me feel sick in my stomach: seems sort of unmanly," Lawrence concluded (letter of 3 April 1922); and indeed it was "unmanly" for Lawrence, like "Jonah," to run away from the "Jewish" challenge. And Lawrence concludes: "Europe is, I fancy, the most satisfactory place in the end" (letter of 3 April 1922). Furthermore, Lawrence writes to his Jewish friend Koteliansky that

> One learns to value what one actually knows and possesses, and to have a wholesome indifference to strange gods. (17 April 1922)

One thing that Lawrence has certainly learned to value is the "Jewish" way—which he "knows and possesses," unfortunately for him and his anxiety of influence: for in knowing the Jewish way rather than creating it Lawrence cannot claim priority, and while as a Western philosopher-poet he "possesses" Jewish tradition, it also (even more) possesses him. But the "strange gods" of the east are useless and insalubrious:

> The east is queer....[I]t seems to bleed ones energy and make one indifferent to everything....(17 April 1922)

Lawrence, of course, could not be "indifferent"; finally, he could never feel "indifferent" about being "Jewish" (i.e., part of Western civilization)—or, to use his terms, "English":

> I break my heart over England when I am out here [in Ceylon]. Those natives are *back* of us—in the living sense *lower* than we are. But they're going to swarm over us and suffocate us. We are, have been for five centuries, the growing tip. Now we're going to fall. But you don't catch me going back on my whiteness and Englishness and myself. English in the teeth of all the world, even in the teeth of England. (30 April 1922)

Proud of his "Jewishness" ("whiteness and Englishness and myself"), Lawrence finally could not deny his fondness for, his connection with, Western civilization; thus his "anxiety of influence" about "Jewishness" persisted—for indeed after his Ceylon experience Lawrence once again strongly identified himself with the "Jewish" way; reaching Australia, he wrote to his mother-in-law:

> So, the *new Jews* [my italics] shall wander on (15 May 1922)

—"the new Jews" being he and his wife Frieda.

Once again thinking himself "Jewish," Lawrence once again was inevitably confronted by his "anxiety of influence"; but in Australia he had a new way of dealing with it, a new solution to his problem: rather than reject his privileging of "priority," Lawrence would valorize the "old":

> I've got a bitter burning nostalgia for Europe,...for old civilisation and for real human understanding.... (30 May 1922)

Full of enthusiasm "for old [Western] civilisation"—"Jewish" civilization—which for him now is hand in glove with "real human understanding," Lawrence was surely as much as ever a prey to the "anxiety of influence"—once again he calls himself and Frieda "wandering Jews" (letter of 9 June 1922); to deal with all this—or rather, to try to deal with it—Lawrence in June-July 1922 wrote *Kangaroo*. In his creative mind Lawrence came to imagine that Australia itself has "priority." In a letter of his *Kangaroo* period, Lawrence writes:

> [Australia] has an extraordinary hoary, weird attraction. As you get used to it, it seems so *old*, as if it has missed all this Semite-Egyptian-Indo-European vast era of history, and was coal age, the age of great ferns and mosses. It hasn't got a consciousness—just none—*too far back* [my italics]. A strange effect it has on one....I can't quite explain it: as if one resolved back almost to the plant kingdom, before souls, spirits and minds were grown at all....(22 June 1922)

A few weeks later, on the verge of completing *Kangaroo*, Lawrence states that

> I love Australia: its weird, far-away natural beauty and its remote, almost coal-age pristine quality. Only it's too far for me....Further than Egypt....It [Australia] eludes me, and always would. It is *too far back* [my italics]. It seems to me that generation after generation must people it with ghosts, and catastrophes water it with blood, before it will come alive with a new day of its own. Too far for me: strains my heart, reaching. But I am very glad to have glimpsed it....But nobody has *seen* Australia yet: can't be done....Oh there is a great magic here....
>
> Australia seems to me a most marvellous country to disappear into. When one has had enough of the world—when one doesn't want to wrestle with another single thing, humanly—then to come

> to Australia and...drift away, and live and forget and expire in Australia. (3 July 1922)

Now valorizing Australia as "extraordinary" and "old," Lawrence conceives it to be a place that is "so *old*" that it is indeed prior to "all this Semite-...European [i.e., "Jewish"] vast era of history"—a continent that "hasn't got a consciousness"—or a "Jewish" way—because it is "too far back" in time, way before Judaism—way before human beings: back to the time of "the plant kingdom, before souls, spirits and minds"—and of course before "the anxiety of influence." Thus now Lawrence "love[s] Australia"; for "nobody has *seen* Australia yet"—for Australia has priority over the ways of seeing of "this...vast era of history": for Australia (in Lawrence's imagination and mind at least) is supremely prehistorical ("too far back," "coal-age," "pristine"); and, with its "pristine quality," its "priority," Australia certainly fits Geoffrey Hartman's concept of "priority," as Harold Bloom explains it:

> A Wordsworthian critic, even one as loyal to Wordsworth as Geoffrey Hartman, can insist upon clearly distinguishing between *priority*, as a concept from the *natural order* [my italics], and *authority*, from the spiritual order...."By seeking to overcome priority," Hartman wisely says, "art fights nature on nature's own ground, and is bound to lose." (*Anxiety of Influence*, p. 9)

Yet Lawrence, perhaps even wiser than Hartman, Wordsworth and Bloom, uses the *"priority...*[of] the natural order"—as manifested in Australia—to aid *him* in attaining "priority." Bloom, of course, tells us that

> the commodity in which poets deal, their authority, their property, turns upon priority. They own, they are, what they become first in naming. (*Anxiety*, p. 64)

In *Kangaroo* Lawrence makes it clear that Australia is the locale of priority:

> he [Somers-Lawrence] was looking mostly straight below him, at the massed foliage of the cliff-slope. Down into the centre of the great, dull-green whorls of the tree-ferns, and on to the shaggy mops of the cabbage-palms. In one place a long fall of creeper was yellowish with damp flowers. Gum-trees came up in tufts. *The previous world!* [italics mine]—the world of the coal age. The lonely, lonely world that had waited, it seemed, since the coal age. (177-178)

Nobody had seen Australia before, according to Lawrence ("But nobody has seen Australia yet," Lawrence said in his letter of 3 July 1922)—but now, as Lawrence completes his novel *Kangaroo* in late July 1922, Lawrence can feel that he has seen it. The tree-ferns, the gum-trees, the cabbage-palms: all these serve as an objective correlative for the feeling of *natural priority* possessed by Australia—and of *poetic priority* possessed by Lawrence, who conceives himself to be the "first in naming" Australia's "coal age" essence—a "coal age" character which is, of course, prior to the "Jewish" way of Lawrence's great precursors. Furthermore, in Australia, Somers-Lawrence tells us,

> What was the good of trying to be an alert conscious man here? You couldn't. Drift, drift into a sort of obscurity, *backwards into a nameless* [i.e., pre-Jewish] *past* [my italics], hoary as the country is hoary. Strange old feelings wake in the soul: *old, non-human feelings*. (178; my italics)

By seeing Australia as the source of "old, non-human feelings"—*pre-human* feelings—Lawrence could confidently give himself priority over his Jewish precursors (in his psyche at least), for his Jewish precursors were not so "old" as to be pre-historic and "non-human." On 3 July 1922 Lawrence made his comment about Australia not being "seen"; but now, a few days later, in *Kangaroo* (finished in mid-late July) he sees the primeval "fern-world" influence of Australia that supersedes the "anxiety of influence":

> Worlds come, and worlds go: even worlds. And when the *old, old influence* [my italics] of the fern-world comes over a man, how can he care? He breathes the fern seed and drifts back, becomes darkly half-vegetable, devoid of pre-occupations....The dark world *before conscious responsibility was born*. (178; my italics)

"Before conscious responsibility": and before "the anxiety of influence." Thus, with its Australian setting, *Kangaroo* gave Lawrence the illusion of priority over his Jewish precursors; "the old, old influence of the fern-world" came before the "Jewish" way—and Lawrence makes hay of this.

But it is not just the Australian location that Lawrence uses to create, maintain and strengthen his sense of his poetic priority in *Kangaroo*. Almost at once Lawrence-Somers is presented to the reader by the omniscient narrator as an avatar of

> the magic of the old world,...the old culture, the old glamour (19)

"The old world," "the old culture": the "Jewish" way—this is what Lawrence-Somers really represents in *Kangaroo*, Lawrence will say; and he represents it better than the actual Jew in the book, the title character Kangaroo!

In the chapter "Kangaroo" (Chapter VI), Lawrence first introduces the title character Kangaroo, Ben Cooley, a Jewish lawyer and political leader in Australia. Soon after introducing Kangaroo, Lawrence-Somers gives away his admiration for the "Jewish" way:

> And surely, thought Somers [looking at Kangaroo's face], it is Jewish blood. The very best that is in the Jewish blood: a faculty for pure disinterestedness, and warm, physically warm love, that seems to make the corpuscles of the blood glow....The man had decidedly Jewish blood. And he was almost purely *kind* [italics Lawrence's], essential kindliness, embodied in an *ancient* [italics mine], unscrupulous shrewdness. He was so shrewd, so clever. And with a rogue or a mean man, absolutely unscrupulous. But for any human being who showed himself sincere and vulnerable, his heart was pure in kindness. An extraordinary man. This pure kindliness had something Jehovah-like in it. And in every difficulty and every stress, he would remember it, his kindly love for real, vulnerable human beings. It had given his soul an absolute direction....Yet once he felt any man or woman was cold, mean, barren of this warmth which was in him, then he became at once utterly unscrupulous in defeating the creature. He was not angry or indignant. He was more like a real Jehovah. He had only to turn on all the levers and forces of his clever, almost fiendishly subtle will, and he could triumph. And he knew it. Somers had once had a Jewish friend with this wonderful, *Jehovah-like kindliness* [my italics], but alas , without the shrewd fiendish subtlety of will. But it helped him to understand Cooley. (110-111)

Here in *Kangaroo* Lawrence-Somers delineates the characteristics of "the Jewish blood," the Jewish race; chief among these characteristics is "a faculty for...warm, physically warm love"—but what kind of love? About this Lawrence is unclear at first, but soon enough we see that it is not the sexual-sensual "Jewish" love of David and Solomon that Lawrence celebrated in his *Study of Thomas Hardy*, but rather it is a love that is rooted in asexual philanthropy— "essential kindliness"—*agape*, not Eros. Lawrence-Somers apparently admires this "pure kindliness": he praises it as having "something Jehovah-like in it"—yet when did Lawrence ever think of Jehovah as philanthropic? And what about Lawrence's view of the Jews in his letter of 7 May 1918?

> the Jews are the great *haters* [Lawrence's italics] of the human race....

In May 1918 Lawrence had praised the Jews as "the great haters of the human race" and he had happily identified himself with them in this role ("I feel such profound hatred myself, of the human race, I almost know what it is to be a Jew"). But in *Kangaroo* the Jewish character (Kangaroo) is veritably obsessed with Love, love of "the human race": "'I *love* them [the human race],' he shouted, in a voice suddenly become loud and passionate. 'I love them. I *love* you [Mrs. Somers], you woman born of man, I do, and I defy you to prevent me....I know I love you, and I know that...you love me....'" (121-122). Kangaroo here sounds rather ridiculous and hysterical, and his tone continues throughout the novel; in the next chapter (Chapter 7) he passionately (and absurdly) expresses his love for the Australian people:

> "They're generous—generous to recklessness," shouted Kangaroo. "And I love them [the Australian people]. I love them. Don't you come here carping to me about them. They are my children, I love them...." (131)

Kangaroo goes on to make it clear that he devotes his "mental consciousness" to the service of love:

> Kangaroo sat up and adjusted his eyeglasses.
> "Don't you run away with the idea, though," he said, "that I am just an emotional fool." His voice was almost menacing, and with a strange cold, intellectual quality that Somers had never heard before.
> "I believe in the one fire of love. I believe it is the one inspiration of all creative activity. I trust myself entirely to the fire of love. This I do with my reason also. I don't discard my reason. I use it at the service of love, like a sharp weapon. I try to keep it very sharp—and very dangerous. Where I don't love, I use only my will and my wits. Where I love, I trust to love alone." The voice came cold and static.(133)

Thus this Kangaroo, far from being the Lawrentian Jew valorized in "Hardy," is indeed yet another Lawrentian "creative misinterpretation": for Kangaroo is the exemplar of the "mental"-"love will" that Lawrence attacked—for all his "Jehovah-like kindness," Kangaroo exemplifies

> the plaintive bullying of love,...the benevolent bullying of love

—to use a phrase from Lawrence's *Fantasia of the Unconscious* (Chapter III, "Plexuses, Planes, and So On"), written shortly before *Kangaroo*. This "love-will" (the phrase is from *Fantasia*, Chapter X) is represented by Kangaroo's belief that "love is the one and only exclusive force or mystery of living inspiration" (*Kangaroo*, "The Battle of Tongues," Chapter VII).

Somers-Lawrence, now more "Jewish" than Kangaroo, attacks the "Christian" nature of Kangaroo's "love": "I know your love, Kangaroo. Working everything from the spirit, from the head....Now it is time for the spirit to leave us again; it is time for the *Son of Man* [italics mine] to depart" (Chapter 7)—"the Son of Man" being an appellation of that ultimate Christian hero, Jesus, whose Christianity privileged the

> deliberate mentally directed love-will,...the beautiful, benevolent, idealistic,...and finally obscene love-will....Always the *will* [Lawrence's italics], the will, the love-will, the ideal will, directed from the ideal mind. ("The Vicious Circle," *Fantasia of the Unconscious*, Chapter XI)

Like Jesus ("the Son of Man"), Kangaroo exemplifies "the mental-conscious love-will" (*Fantasia*, "The Vicious Circle"); but Somers-Lawrence wants to get rid of Jesus, replace him with "The god you can never see or visualise, who stands dark on the threshold of the phallic me" (*Kangaroo*, Chapter 7)—this invisible god being the Lawrentian equivalent or version of the Jewish god, Jehovah, who, rather than being philanthropic, "is a great God on the threshold of my lower self, *whom I fear while he is my glory*" (my italics)—as the "Jewish" Somers-Lawrence says ("The Battle of Tongues").

Thus the "Christian" Kangaroo, with his advocacy of "the Son of Man," is opposed by Somers-Lawrence, who advocates the fearful Jehovah of the Old Testament. Evidence of Somers' "Jewishness" appears further as *Kangaroo* continues. At the end of Chapter 9 ("Harriet and Lovat at Sea in Marriage"), Lawrence as omniscient narrator tells us that Somers must submit to the one God:

> He [Somers] did not yet submit to the fact which he *half* knew: that before mankind would accept any man for a king,...he, this selfsame Richard who was so strong on kingship, must open the doors of his soul and let in a dark *Lord and Master* [italics mine] for himself.

In Chapter XI of *Kangaroo* ("Willie Struthers and Kangaroo") Lawrence-Somers goes on to delineate the nature of his "Lord and Master":

> the human heart must have an absolute. It is one of the conditions of being human. The only thing is the God who is *the source of all passion*. Once go down before the God-passion and human passions take their right rhythm....[Humans need the] deep *God who is source of all passion and life*....
>
> Any more love is a hopeless thing, till we have found again, each of us for himself, the great dark God who alone will sustain us....
>
> Richard [Lovat Somers] knew this....(*Kangaroo*, Chapter 11; italics mine)

—and of course Lawrence knew this: in a letter written during his *Study of Thomas Hardy* period, Lawrence authoritatively stated that

> passion is not in heat, but in deep, deep strength and profundity of source. *The source of passion* is the *burning darkness* which quickens the whole ball of this earth, from the centre, it is...the dark fire, the hidden, invisible passion,...(1 March 1915; italics mine)

To the knowledgeable reader, it is clear that Lawrence-Somers' "deep God who is the source of all passion and life," "the great dark God who alone will sustain us"—is the 1915 Lawrence's "dark fire, the hidden invisible passion"—"the burning darkness": and that this Lawrentian version of God is tantamount to the Jewish God of the Old Testament as explicitly presented in Exodus 3, the story of the Burning Bush. As Louis Ginzberg tells us (*Legends of the Jews, Volume II*):

> The first thing Moses noticed was the wonderful burning bush, the upper part of which was a blazing flame, neither consuming the bush, nor preventing it from bearing blossoms as it burnt, for the celestial fire has three peculiar qualities: it produces blossoms, it does not consume the object around which it plays, and it is *black of color*. (my italics)

With the Old Testament "Jewish" Burning Bush as a precursor of Lawrence's "burning darkness," "dark fire," "great dark God," it is not surprising to find Lawrence-Somers, surrounded by Australian politicos (of the left and of the right), sadly remarking of the situation that

> It all seemed so far from the dark God he [Somers-Lawrence] wished to serve, the God from whom the dark, sensual passion of

> love emanates, not only the spiritual love of Christ. (*Kangaroo*, Chapter 11)

The "it" that is "so far from the dark God he [Somers-Lawrence] wished to serve" is the hodgepodge of Christianity and politics represented by Kangaroo on the right and Struthers on the left. The leftist Struthers, after a fashion, is "Christian":

> Struthers didn't mind Christ. Christ could easily be made to subserve his egoistic purpose. But the first, dark, ithyphallic God whom men had once known so tremendous—Struthers had no use for Him (Chapter 11)

—"Him" being in fact, when all is said and done, the Jehovah of the Jews; or, rather, the Lawrentian version of Jehovah: for "the first, dark, ithyphallic God" is surely reminiscent of the Jewish "God of the body" Lawrence presented in *Study of Thomas Hardy*. As for "the spiritual love of Christ," this is okay with Struthers, whose manipulative socialism can appropriate Christianity easily enough, as Lawrence-Somers realizes:

> "It [Australia] *does* [Lawrence's italics] need some sort of religion" [Somers tells Struthers].
> "Well then—well then—the religious question is ticklish, especially here in Australia. But all the churches are established on Christ. And Christ says Love one another."
> Richard laughed suddenly.
> "That makes Christ into another political agent," he said. (Chapter 11)

Somers-Lawrence is surely skeptical of Christianity and its god; but as *Kangaroo* continues, Somers-Lawrence becomes more and more committed to the "Jewish" God. Early in Chapter 15, Somers cites the "jealous God":

> "For I, the Lord thy God, am a jealous God." So true. A jealous God, and a vengeful. (*Kangaroo*, Chapter 15)

This, of course, is the same "Jewish" God Lawrence praised in *Study of Thomas Hardy* (Chapter VII):

> It was the female [i.e., Jewish] spirit which conceived the saying:
> "For I, the Lord thy God, am a jealous God...."

Of course, the ultimate source of Lawrence's "jealous God" is the Jewish Old Testament: in the Book of Exodus, Chapter 20, Jehovah tells Moses:

> I am the Lord thy God, which have brought thee out of the land of Egypt, out of the house of bondage.
> Thou shalt have no other gods before me.
> Thou shalt not make unto thee any graven image, or any likeness of any thing that is in heaven above, or that is in the earth beneath, or that is in the water under the earth:
> Thou shalt not bow down thyself to them, nor serve them: for I the Lord thy God am a jealous God....

Lawrence in *Kangaroo* feels extremely comfortable with the "jealous God"; indeed, Lawrence goes on to link the "jealous God" of the Jews with the anti-Victorian Lawrentian God:

> "The Lord thy God am a jealous God."
> So He is. The Lord thy God is the invisible stranger at the gate in the night, knocking. He is the mysterious life-suggestion, tapping for admission. And the wondrous Victorian Age managed to fasten the door so tight, and light up the compound so brilliantly with electric light, that really, there *was* no outside, it was all in. The unknown became a joke: is still a joke.
> Yet there it [i.e., God, the unknown] is, outside the gate, getting angry. "Behold I stand at the gate and knock." "Knock away," said complacent, benevolent humanity, which had just discovered its own monkey origin [i.e., Darwinism] to account for its own monkey tricks. "Knock away, nobody will hinder you from knocking."
> ...But whoever it is that's knocking [i.e., God]...[has] got sick of it. He'll be kicking the door in just now.
> "For I the Lord thy God am a jealous God."

Lawrence's constant representation of the "jealous God" in *Kangaroo* makes it clear that Lawrence-Somers is the true Jew in *Kangaroo*; the Jew that knows and upholds the one jealous "Jewish" God in all His supreme power and irrationality and incomprehensibility while the rest of the rational Victorian world ignores and mocks Him at its own peril. As Lawrence goes on to insist:

> ...outside the gate it is one dark God, the Unknown. And the Unknown is a terribly jealous God, and vengeful....(*Kangaroo*, Chapter 15)

As *Kangaroo* reaches its conclusion, it becomes clear that the "Jewish" Lawrence-Somers is in intense conflict with the "Christian" Ben Cooley, who is the nominal Jew in *Kangaroo* but in fact is a megalomaniacal-philanthropic perversion of Christianity—as Lawrence-Somers concludes in Chapter 16:

> "Now, Kangaroo," said Richard [Lovat Somers], "is in a false position. He wants to save property for the property owners, and he wants to save Labour from itself and from the capitalist and the politician and all. In fact, he wants to save everything as we have it, and it can't be done....Kangaroo wants to be God Himself, and save everybody, which is just irritating, at last. Kangaroo as God Himself...is worse than Struthers' [Bolshevist] absolute of the People. Though it's a choice of evils, and I choose neither. I choose the Lord Almighty." (*Kangaroo*, Chapter 16)

Choosing "the Lord Almighty" over the "Christian" Kangaroo, Somers-Lawrence in Chapter 17 rejects Ben Cooley's directive that Somers should

> Teach them [the Australian working classes] the beauty of love between men, Richard, teach them the highest—greater love than this hath no man—teach them how to love their own mate,...

The famous phrase "greater love than this hath no man" gives away the "Christian" nature of Kangaroo *au fond*—for this phrase of course comes from the Christian New Testament: in John 15:13, Jesus says: "Greater love hath no man than this, that a man lay down his life for his friends"—which Kangaroo, the "Christian," ultimately does. The "Jewish" Lovat-Lawrence, on the other hand, privileges

> Man's isolation [which] was always a supreme truth and fact, not to be forsworn. And the mystery of apartness. And the greater mystery of the dark God beyond a man, the God that gives a man passion, and the dark, unexplained blood-tenderness that is *deeper than love* [italics mine], but so much more obscure, impersonal, and the brave, silent blood-pride, knowing his own separateness, and the sword-strength of his derivation from the dark God. This dark, passionate religiousness and inward sense of an inwelling magnificence, direct flow from the unknowable God, this filled Richard's heart first, and *human love seemed such a fighting for candle-light, when the dark is so much better*....(*Kangaroo*, Chapter 17; italics mine)

Privileging "the dark God" above "human love," Lawrence-Somers is surely "Jewish" here; for in the Old Testament the Jewish hero-patriarch Abraham is quite ready to obey God when He tells him to "Take now thy son, thine only son Issac, whom thou lovest, and get thee into the land of Moriah; and offer him there for a burnt offering upon one of the mountains which I will tell thee of" (Genesis 22:2); similarly, Lawrence-Somers is ready to sacrifice Harriet-Frieda in favor of "the dark God":

> Back to Harriet....Harriet?...If only she wouldn't speak, talk, feel....
>
> Harriet and he? It was time they both agreed that nothing has any meaning.

At this point ("Kangaroo is Killed," Chapter 17), Somers sees the desirability of sacrificing the "human" Harriet—the one who can "speak, talk, feel"—because he is totally overwhelmed by the phenomenon of "Man's isolation," "the mystery of apartness"—a mystery which is also ultimately "Jewish." Lilly in *Aaron's Rod* declares that man is "alone,"

> Essentially, at the very core..., alone. Eternally alone. And choosing to be alone, because by one's own nature one is alone....
>
> In so far as he is a single individual soul, he *is* [Lawrence's italics] alone—ipso facto. In so far as I am I, and only I am I, and I am only I, in so far, I am inevitably and eternally alone, and it is my last blessedness to know it, and to accept it, and to live with this as the core of my self-knowledge. (*Aaron's Rod*, Chapter XVII)

This principle stated by Lilly has its ultimate source, indeed, in the "Jewish" God of the Old Testament in His talk with Moses in Exodus 3:13-14:

> And Moses said unto God, Behold, when I come unto the children of Israel, and shall say unto them, The God of your fathers hath sent me unto you; and they shall say to me, What is his name? what shall I say unto them?
>
> And God said unto Moses, I AM THAT I AM: and he said, Thus shalt thou say unto the children of Israel, I AM hath sent me unto you.

Thus the ultimate source of Lawrentian individuality is the Jewish God of the Old Testament; and this Lawrentian "Jewish" emphasis on supreme individuality—even opposed to "Christian" love—reaches its peak in *Kangaroo*, where Lawrence-Somers goes so far as to say he loves nobody:

> "No," said Richard to himself, thinking of Kangaroo. "I don't love him—I detest him. He can die. I'm glad he is dying. And I don't like Jack either. Not a bit. In fact I like nobody. I love nobody and I like nobody, and there's the end of it, as far as I'm concerned. And if I go around "loving" anybody else, or even "liking" them, I deserve a kick in the guts like Kangaroo."

At this point in *Kangaroo* (Chapter 17, "Kangaroo is Killed"), Lawrence-Somers' rejection of love and privileging of "the dark God" of supreme individuality ("the God that gives a man...the brave, silent blood-pride, *knowing his own separateness* [italics mine]") surely makes him a supreme Jew: even his Lawrentian "separateness" is caused by "his derivation from the dark God," "the unknowable God"—the "Jewish" God of Abraham and Moses, among other Jews. The two Lawrentian "religious" phenomena—"aloneness" and "the dark God"—go hand in hand; as the "Jewish" Somers-Lawrence says:

> "The only thing one can stick to is one's own isolate being, and *the God in whom it is rooted* [my italics]. And the only thing to look to is the God who fulfils one from the dark. And the only thing to wait for is for men *to find their aloneness and their God in the darkness*...." (*Kangaroo*, Chapter 17, "Kangaroo is Killed"; my italics)

By the end of *Kangaroo* it is obvious that Lawrence-Somers is the true "Jew" and Kangaroo, with his emphasis on "love," the true "Christian." Thus "Kangaroo is Killed" in two ways: he is physically killed through assassination, and his "Jewishness" threat is killed off by making him more of a "Christian" than Somers-Lawrence. Insofar as in *Kangaroo* Lawrence makes lucid and coherent use of his Jewish precursors and at the same time manages to promote his own unique "Jewish" way, *Kangaroo* is a greater, stronger novel than *Aaron's Rod*, for in *Aaron's Rod* Lawrence merely adumbrated some of his major insights and themes concerning "Jewish" separateness and individuality, and furthermore in *Aaron's Rod* Lawrence ended up in a mythopoeic muddle involving Judaic and pagan with no consistent reference to his "Jewish" topos, while in *Kangaroo* Lawrence's agon with the "Jewish" influence is prominent, compelling, authentic.

The pseudo-"Jewish" Kangaroo dies from "a kick in the guts" (gunshot to stomach) as the upshot of his "Christian" love; but the "Jewish" Lawrence-Somers survives, even finally overcoming his lack of enthusiasm for love, instead evincing "the dark, unexplained blood-tenderness that is deeper than love"—he experiences this feeling for a couple of kangaroos at the zoo:

> And yet, when he went over to the Zoo,...and he saw the animals, the tenderness came back....And one golden brown old-man kangaroo, with his great earth-cleaving tail and his little hanging hands, hopped up to the fence and lifted his sensitive nose quivering, and gently nibbled the sweet between Richard's fingers. So

gently, so determinedly nibbled the sweet, but never hurting the fingers that held it. And looking up with the big, dark, prominent Australian eyes, *so aged in consciousness, with a fathomless, dark, fern-age gentleness and gloom.* The female wouldn't come near to eat. She only sat up and watched, and her little one hung its tiny fawn's head and one long ear and one fore-leg out of her pouch, in the middle of her soft, big, grey belly.

Such a married couple! Two kangaroos. And the blood in Richard's veins all gone dark with a sort of sad tenderness. The gentle kangaroos, with their weight in heavy blood on the ground, in their great tail! It wasn't love he felt for them, but a *dark,* animal tenderness, and another sort of consciousness, *deeper than human.*
(*Kangaroo,* Chapter 17, "Kangaroo is Killed"; my italics)

Finally, after experiencing the "dark" emotion of "sad tenderness" for the kangaroos—a "Jewish" emotion rooted in "the dark God beyond a man,...the unknowable God"—Lawrence-Somers is possessed of "another sort of consciousness, deeper than human"—a kind of "Jewish," "Chosen People" consciousness—a "blood-consciousness" that is anything but fascistic, for it is surely a feeling of "deeper than human" tenderness felt for—in this case—"gentle kangaroos," who also possess "heavy blood" (i.e., "blood-consciousness").

Lawrence-Somers' "Jewishness" continues even to the end of the climactic "Kangaroo is Killed" chapter (Chapter 17), as, in the final paragraph, Somers senses "The call, call!" from "God without feet or knees or face"—the invisible God of the Jews.

Of course, the sudden appearance of the "fern-age" kangaroo towards the end of Chapter 17 can serve to remind us that at one point at least Lawrence in *Kangaroo* had sought to fool himself about his "priority" to the Jews by portraying Australia as the supremely ancient, primeval "fern-age" land; but in the final chapter of *Kangaroo* Lawrence rejects this solution to his "Jewish" problem. Leaving Australia, Somers-Lawrence realizes that staying there would be the easy way out:

"Then why am I going [away from Australia]?" he [Somers] asked himself.

"Wait! Wait!" he answered himself. "You have got to go through the mistakes. You've got to go all round the world, and then half way round again, till you get back. Go on, go on, the world is round, and it will bring you back. Draw your ring round the world, the ring of your consciousness. Draw it round until it is complete."

So he prepared with a quiet heart to depart.

Leaving Australia, Lawrence-Somers will continue to be "The Wandering Jew"—and of course he will continue his *agon* with his Jewish precursors.

Lest there be any doubt about Lawrence's "Jewishness" in *Kangaroo*, it is re-affirmed even to the very end of the last chapter. The Australian Jaz tries to persuade Somers to stay in Australia, telling him to "give in" to it:

> "Why, Mr. Somers!" laughed Jaz, "seems to me you just go round the world looking for things you're not going to give in to...."
> "Maybe," said Richard. "But I'll give in to the Lord Almighty, which is more than you'll do—"
> "Oh, well, now—we'd give in to Him if we saw Him," said Jaz, smiling with an odd winsomeness he sometimes had.
> "All right. Well I prefer not to see, and yet to give in," said Richard.

Like the ancient Jews Lawrence valorized in his *Study of Thomas Hardy*, Somers wants to "give in to the Lord Almighty," the invisible God. Furthermore, as a "Jew," Lawrence-Somers decides he will not reject Western civilization after all; on the contrary, says Somers-Lawrence,

> I won't give up the flag of our real civilised consciousness....the aware, self-responsible, deep consciousness that we've gained. I won't go back on that....

Demonstrating how "deep" and "aware" and "self-responsible" his "Jewish" consciousness is, Lawrence-Somers towards the very end of the last chapter of *Kangaroo* is vehemently preaching at his non-"Jewish" wife, who tries to ignore the power of the Lord:

> You must be under the hand of the Lord. You can't escape the dark hand of the Lord, not even in free Australia.

It soon becomes clear that "the Lord" whom Somers' wife tries to ignore is the Jewish God:

> She [Somers' wife] was black, sick with chagrin. And she hated that barking white dog of a Richard, with his yap-yap-yapping about control and authority and the hand of the Lord. She had left Europe with her teeth set in hatred of Europe's ancient encumbrance of authority and of the withered, repulsive weight of the Hand of *the Lord, that old Jew*, upon it....(*Kangaroo*, Chapter 18, "Adieu Australia"; italics mine)

Thus the preachy Lawrence-Somers champions the "Jewish" cause of "the Lord, that old Jew"—even against his own wife. Indeed, at this point in his life (late 1922) Lawrence almost seems resigned to his "Jewishness" and Judaic "priority" over him—he does not seem to want "freedom" from this:

> Thank God I am not free, any more than a rooted tree is free,

Lawrence writes from America, "The Land of the Free" (letter of 23 September 1922 to Harriet Monroe). And, as if chiding himself for his own stubborn resistance to the "Jewish," Lawrence writes an elaborate attack on the American "will":

> Everything in America goes by *will*. A great negative *will* seems to be turned against all spontaneous life—there seems to be no *feeling* at all—no genuine bowels of compassion and sympathy; all this gripped, iron, *benevolent* will, which in the end is diabolic....Frieda, like you, always secretly hankered after America and its freedom: it's very freedom *not* to feel. But now she is just beginning to taste the iron ugliness of what it means, to live by this will *against* the spontaneous inner life, superimposing the individual, egoistic will over the real genuine sacred life. Of course I know that you will jeer when I say there is any such thing as sacred spontaneous life, with its pride and its sacred power. I know you too believe in the screwed-up human will *dominating* life. But I don't. And that's why I think America is neither free nor brave, but a land of tight, iron-clanking little *wills*, everybody trying to put it over everybody else, and a land of men absolutely devoid of the real courage of trust, trust in life's sacred spontaneity. They can't *trust* life until they can *control* it. So much for them—cowards! You can have the Land of the Free—as much as I know of it. — In the spring I want to come back to Europe. (D. H. Lawrence letter to Else Jaffe, 27 September 1922)

Here, at the same time that he denounces "the...human will *dominating* life," Lawrence privileges "life's sacred spontaneity"; meanwhile, like Harriet Somers in *Kangaroo*, anti-"Jewish" Frieda Lawrence "hankered after freedom:...[the] freedom *not* to feel"; but the "Jewish" Lawrence, like the Jews David and Solomon of the *Study of Thomas Hardy*, is the votary of "sacred spontaneous life" and "trust in life's sacred spontaneity"—and Lawrence apparently (in September 1922) finds Europe to be most hospitable to this "life": "In the spring I want to come back to Europe." As for his travels away from Europe, Lawrence at this point concludes that

> perhaps it is my destiny to know the world....It is all a form of *running away from oneself and the great problems*: all this wild west [of America] and the strange Australia. (letter of 29 September 1922; italics mine)

One thing Lawrence was running away from was his Jewish precursors; even in New Mexico Lawrence thinks of the Old Testament:

> [American] *resistance* to the divinity...always resistance. Reminds me of the great cries of the Old Testament: "How long will ye harden your hearts against me." But who is Jehovah in this case....An Almighty, not a Dove! (letter of 4 October 1922)

Still singing the praises of Almighty Jehovah, Lawrence in America longs for the "Jewish" origin, Europe:

> Truly I prefer Europe. (17 December 1922)

One interesting indication of Lawrence's growing acceptance of his "Jewishness" is his strong (for him) affection for his Jewish publisher Thomas Seltzer:

> My publisher Thomas Seltzer was here for a week: such a tiny little Jew: but nice, one of the *believing* sort. (letter of 24 January 1923)

It is rare for Lawrence to call any man "nice," but here Lawrence—evidently weakening in his agon with his Jewish precursors—certainly wants to feel fond of the Jews: and unthreatened by them (as in that redundant description "tiny little..."). Lawrence also managed to assuage his anxiety, it would seem, by perceiving Seltzer as "one of the *believing* sort"—that is, one who *believed* in Lawrence's work. Indeed, Lawrence was so sure of Seltzer's good will and friendship that Lawrence went so far as to end his friendship with his literary agent Robert Mountsier, whom he had known since 1916; Lawrence had always disliked Mountsier's anti-Semitism:

> Mountsier...is one of those irritating people who have generalised detestations: his particular ones being Jews, Germans, and Bolshevists. So unoriginal. He got on my nerves badly....(D. H. Lawrence letter to Koteliansky, 10 November 1921)

By February 1923 Lawrence could tell Seltzer that

> Whatever friendship I felt for him [Mountsier] before, I don't feel now. (1 February 1923)

Two days later Lawrence dismissed Mountsier:

> I wish now to break the connection between you and me. (DHL letter to Mountsier, 3 February 1923)

That very same day, Lawrence wrote Seltzer that

> I do agree with you. I have this minute written to him—Mountsier—that I wish to break my agreement with him....

It is evident that Lawrence stood with "the Jew" Seltzer against the anti-Semitic Mountsier:

> We won't worry about Mountsier any more. He has a bad will, I have done with him....Enough. (DHL to Seltzer, 10 February 1923)

And a few days later Lawrence humbly wrote:

> I seem to give you a great deal of trouble. But everything is coming straight. And we will make a success of things.
> Thank you so much for all...the trouble you have taken. (DHL to Seltzer, 22 February 1923)

Interestingly enough, during this period of Lawrence's great friendship with Seltzer—the period of early 1923—Lawrence did little writing, even complaining about this fact to Seltzer's wife Adele:

> I should never be able to write on this continent [North America]—something in the spirit opposes one's going forth....(21 April 1923)

What perhaps "oppose[d]" Lawrence's "going forth" at this time was his relaxed attitude towards his anxiety of influence; away from the greatest site of "Jewish" civilization—Europe—Lawrence's poetic imagination may have become tranquil, lazy; indeed, even a month later (22 May 1923), Lawrence again complained to "Jewish" Adele Seltzer about his writer's block:

> The enemy almost gets us down, sometimes. Am having a hard fight myself. The enemy of all the world. Doesn't want me to write my novel either. (22 May 1923)

Lawrence's "enemy" may indeed have been his anxiety of influence about the Jews—and his failure at this time to engage in an agon with his great precursors. Lawrence did vent his spleen at this time, not on his Jewish precursors, but rather on his contemporary "Mr. Joyce" (among others) in his essay "Surgery for the Novel—Or a Bomb" (April 1923); according to Lawrence here, Joyce is guilty of practising (in *Ulysses*)

> self-consciousness picked into such fine bits that the bits are most of them invisible, and you have to go by smell. Through thousands and thousands of pages Mr. Joyce and Miss [Dorothy] Richardson tear themselves to pieces, strip their smallest emotions to the finest threads, till you feel you are sewed inside a wool mattress that is being slowly shaken up, and you are turning to wool along with the rest of the woollyness.
>
> It's awful. And it's childish. It really is childish, after a certain age, to be absorbedly self-conscious. One has to be self-conscious at seventeen: still a little self-conscious at twenty-seven; but if we are going it strong at thirty-seven, then it is a sign of arrested development, nothing else. And if it is still continuing at forty-seven, it is obvious senile precocity.
>
> And there's the serious novel: senile precocious.

Attacking his great contemporary rival James Joyce for immaturity, Lawrence could for the time being forget the far more formidable "Jewish" rival he faced; yet in this same essay ("Surgery for the Novel," now known as "The Future of the Novel") there occurs a passage which gives some strong indication of Lawrence's future response to his "Jewish" problem:

> *What next?* That's what interests me. *What now!* is no fun anymore.
>
> If you like to look in the past for *What-next?* books, you can find the little early novels by Saint Matthew, Saint Mark, Saint Luke and Saint John, called the Gospels. But these are novels with a clue for the future, a new impulse, a new motive, a new inspiration. They don't care about how it *is* [Lawrence's italics] just now, or how it *was* [Lawrence's italics] in the past....What they want is to put a new impulse into the world.
>
> And they [the Gospels] are *little novels* [my italics], in the highest sense. You can't deny it. ("The Future of the Novel," in *"Study of Thomas Hardy" and Other Essays*)

The fact is that the publishers of this essay (published in 1923 as "Surgery for the Novel—Or a Bomb") *did* deny Lawrence's assertion that "the Gospels...are little novels"—as Lawrence scholar Bruce Steele tells us:

> there is evidence of censorship [in the essay "Surgery for the Novel" as published], most notably the removal of the passages making reference to the Gospels as novels. (Bruce Steele, "Introduction" to *"Study of Thomas Hardy" and Other Essays*)

Steele tells us that "some readers [of Lawrence's essay "Surgery for the Novel," now known as "The Future of the Novel" in its unexpurgated text as printed for the first time in the Cambridge edition of *Study of Thomas Hardy and Other Essays* (1985)] might have construed [Lawrence's references to the Gospels] as sacrilegious" (Steele, p. 280).

Lawrence's "sacrilegious" approach to the Gospels occurs throughout his essay "The Future of the Novel" (1923, but not published in unexpurgated form until 1985):

> You've got to find a new impulse for new things, in mankind. And it's really fatal to find it through abstraction. Even in the Gospels there is rather too much sermon. Blessed are X, Y, and Z.—I don't care about X, Y, and Z. Let me see Tom, Dick, and Harry, each *in propria persona*, being blessed. Let me see if Tom is blessed when he's being meek, or whether he's more blessed when he's being haughty. Those X's in the Beatitudes won't do. X may be all right when he's poor in spirit, but Jack is detestable in the same shoes....
>
> [I]t's only the novels like the four Gospels, or the picaresque Acts of the Apostles, or Augustine's Confessions,...that really try to make a great change in feeling, to get on into something really new. *And these do stumble a bit among X's, Y's, and Z's.* [my italics]
>
> The novel has got a future. Its future is to take the place of gospels....

Lawrence's condescending, irreverent attitude to the Gospels, the New Testament, Christianity, seemed greatly to mitigate his anxiety of influence in relation to the Jews.

Surely Lawrence at this time regarded the Christian Gospels as simply Lawrentian novels manqués, incapable of doing what the Lawrentian novel can do:

> The novel has got a future. It's got to have *the courage* to tackle new propositions without using abstractions; it's got to present us with new, really new feelings, a whole new line of emotion, which will get us out of the old emotional rut. Instead of snivelling about what is and has been, or inventing new sensations in the old line, it's got to break a way through, like a hole in the wall.

> And the public will scream....("The Future of the Novel"; italics mine)

—as, of course, the public had already "scream[ed]" at Lawrence's *The Rainbow* and *Women in Love*. The Christian Gospels, on the other hand, despite having a "clue for the future, a new motive, a new inspiration," despite their desire "to put a new impulse into the world," are ultimately too full of "abstraction,...rather too much sermon," "too far on the algebraical tack," "stumbl[ing] a bit among X's, Y's, and Z's" ("Future of the Novel"). Thus Christianity, for all its aspiration to transmit "a new impulse into the world," is too unvital, too weak to succeed. As for the greatest "Christian" of them all, Lawrence during this period came to see "Christ" as only a mere child: complaining about his wife Frieda, Lawrence writes:

> Frieda doesn't understand that today a man needs to be a hero, and more than a husband. Husband yes, also. But more. I must go back and forth, through the world....I do not come for peace....F. must always think and write and say and ponder *how* she loves me. It's stupidity. I am after all no *Christ lying on his mother's lap*. (letter of 10 November 1923; first italics Lawrence's; second italics mine)

Sneering at his version of an infantile "Christ lying on his mother's lap," Lawrence obviously considers himself far superior to the chief "Christian": he (Lawrence) is the real "hero," with a hero's need for "strength":

> the man does not need, does not ask for love from his wife, but strength, strength, strength. It is fighting, fighting, fighting and still fighting. And one needs strength and courage and weapons....Give me strength, only battle-strength, weapon-strength, fighting-strength. (10 November 1923)

The "strength" that "the man" needs in this case is indeed "Poetic strength"; as Bloom tells us,

> Poetic strength comes only from a triumphant wrestling with the greatest of the dead,...(*A Map of Misreading*, p. 9)

But at this time (November 1923) Lawrence was not engaged in "wrestling with the greatest of the dead"—that is, he was not "wrestling" with his great Jewish precursors; instead, Lawrence displaced his aggression, attacking not his Jewish precursors but rather the belated, not-so-great Christians. This displacement of aggression reached its consummation in *The Plumed Serpent*.

To get some sense of Lawrence's pro-"Jewish" feeling during his *Plumed Serpent* period (1923-1925), it is beneficial to look at some important passages from his book *The Boy in the Bush*, which he wrote during the early part of his *Plumed Serpent* period (September-November 1923). Here Lawrence as omniscient narrator describes his own relation to the bible (even though he is ostensibly talking about the protagonist, Jack Grant):

> [He] knew the bible....it supplied his imagination with a chief stock of images, his ear with the greatest solemn pleasure of words, and his soul with a queer heterogeneous ethic. He never really connected the bible with christianity proper....He had no use for christianity proper: just dismissed it. But *the bible* [my italics] was perhaps the foundation of his consciousness. Do what seems good to you in the sight of the Lord. This was the moral he always drew from bible lore. And since the Lord, for him, was always the *Lord Almighty, Almighty God, Maker of Heaven and Earth, Jesus being only a side issue* [my italics]; since the Lord was always *Jehovah the great and dark* [my italics], for him, one might do as David did, in the sight of the Lord, or as Jacob, or as Abraham or Moses or Joshua or Isaiah, in the sight of the Lord....(*The Boy in the Bush*, Chapter X)

Here Lawrence makes the God of the Jews—"Jehovah the great and dark"—his God, the Lawrentian God of the *Study of Thomas Hardy* and of the "great religion" letter written over ten years before *Boy in the Bush*:

> My great religion is a belief in the blood, the flesh, as being wiser than the intellect....[W]hat our blood feels and believes and says, is always true....All I want is to answer to my blood, direct,...The real way of living is to answer to one's wants...."For the living of my full flame—I want that liberty, I want that woman, I want that pound of peaches, I want to go to sleep, I want to go to the pub. and have a good time, I want to look a beastly swell today, I want to kiss that girl, I want to insult that man." (17 January 1913)

Thus it is evident that there is remarkable continuity between the Lawrence of the "great religion" letter ("I want . . ."), the Lawrence of the *Hardy* ("the Jew knew God as David had perceived him, as Solomon had known him. It was the God of the body" [Chapter VII]) and the Lawrence of *The Boy in the Bush* ("Do what seems *good to you* in the sight of the Lord....[O]ne might do as David did, in the sight of the Lord, or as Jacob, or as Abraham or Moses or Joshua or Isaiah, in the sight of the Lord" [my italics]). The Lawrentian-Jewish God is clearly the God of desire, of the "great religion" of "answer[ing] to one's wants," "the body," and "do[ing] what seems good to you." The Lawrentian approach to desire and its fulfillment as a subject of religious urgency, seriousness and import and imperative clearly looks for kinship with the Jewish God, "Jehovah the great and dark"; it is only the Jewish heroes (Moses, Jacob, David, Abraham, Joshua, Isaiah) whom Lawrence celebrates as those who found it sacred and imperative to follow their urgent desire, their "deeper, fiercer, untamed sort of goodness,...the old heroic goodness of untamed [Jewish] men, with the wild great God who was for ever too unknown to be a paragon" (*Boy in the Bush*, Chapter XXIV). Here Lawrence in his "Jewish" zealousness creatively misreads the "great" Jewish God as being exclusively "wild"—the God of "Thou shalt" (i.e., desire and fulfillment) without "Thou shalt not" (i.e., prohibition).

Indeed, in 1923 Lawrence seems to reach a peak of "Jewishness"; yet, furthermore, in his "Jewish" fervor Lawrence reaches the peak of his anti-Christian feeling, forcefully and significantly distinguishing between the "Jewish" way which he adores—and the "Christian" way which he abhors. In *The Boy in the Bush*, in addition to the unmistakable enthusiasm for the Jewish heroes, there is a vehemently anti-Christian, anti-Jesus thrust: for Lawrence-Jack Grant, "Jesus [is] only a side issue" (Chapter X); and

> The Christian goodness had gone bad, decayed almost into poison.
> (Chapter XXIV)

But *The Boy in the Bush* is a mere foreshadowing of the Lawrentian attack on Christianity in *The Plumed Serpent*.

Don Ramon, the Lawrence persona in *The Plumed Serpent*, makes clear that Christian Jesus is certainly no greater a god than the Mexican Quetzalcoatl; indeed, according to Lawrence-Ramon, Quetzalcoatl is none other than Jesus' "brother." Jesus, according to the myth created by Ramon-Lawrence, is tired of performing the role of a god and wishes to return to "the Father" and let Quetzalcoatl take over (*Plumed Serpent*, Chapter VII). This Lawrentian notion of parity between Jesus and Quetzalcoatl soon redounds to Quetzalcoatl's advantage: for it soon becomes clear that Jesus has failed to be the savior, as Lawrence the omniscient narrator states that

> Jesus is no Saviour....He is a dead god....
> ...[Indeed] the white men...find themselves at last shut in the tomb along with their dead god. (*Plumed Serpent*, Chapter VIII)

The reason that Jesus is "a dead god," Lawrence tells us, is that Jesus is the lord of only "one way," while Quetzalcoatl-Ramon-Lawrence is "lord of the two ways" (*Plumed Serpent*, Chapter XI); thus the Quetzalcoatl religion is presented as superior to Christianity, which lacks the comprehensiveness and inclusiveness of the Quetzalcoatl religion, which encompasses both "Flesh" and "Spirit" (*Plumed Serpent*, Chapter XI):

> But I, I am lord of two ways [Quetzalcoatl tells Jesus]. I am master of up and down....Lo! I am I! the lord of both ways. Thou wert lord of the one way....Farewell! (*Plumed Serpent*, Chapter XV)

Saying "Farewell!" to Jesus, Quetzalcoatl-Ramon-Lawrence, "lord of *both* ways" (*Plumed Serpent*, Chapter XV; my italics), supersedes Jesus, "lord of the one way." Having averred the superiority of Quetzalcoatl to Jesus, Lawrence-Ramon thinks nothing of "Burn[ing] the images of Our Lord [Jesus] and Our Lady [Mary]" (*Plumed Serpent*, Chapter XVII). In the chapter "Auto-da-Fe" (Chapter XVIII), in fact, this is exactly what happens. The title of the chapter ("Auto da Fe," trans. "act of the faith") indicates that the religion of Quetzalcoatl is surely as valid a "faith" in its burning of Christian images as the religion of Christianity was with its Spanish Inquisition (where the term "auto da fe" originated) which burned actual people as punishment for heresy.

But, to Lawrence in *The Plumed Serpent*, the "Christian" religion is indeed the reprehensible one, for, Lawrence vehemently states, its main figure is

> the god of death, the Crucified [Jesus] streaked with blood (*Plumed Serpent*, Chapter XVIII)

Yet, if Jesus and Christianity are associated with death, Ramon and the religion of Quetzalcoatl are connected with vital life: "I am the living Quetzalcoatl," Ramon declares, and adds that "My Father [i.e., Almighty God]...sends the eagle of silence down on wide wings／To lean over my head and my neck and my breast／And fill them *strong* with *strength* of wings.／He sends the serpent of *power* up my feet and my loins／So that *strength* wells up in me like water in hot springs" (*Plumed Serpent*, Chapter XXI; italics mine). Thus, in contradistinction to the "dead" Jesus, Quetzalcoatl-Ramon is full of "strength" and "power"—

"strength" and "power" that is mental-spiritual ("the eagle," "wide wings," "my head and my neck and my breast," "strength of wings") and bodily-sexual ("the serpent of power," "my feet and my loins"): not merely "one way" (i.e., spiritual) power like that of "dead" Jesus. And Ramon concludes insistently: "I am the Living Quetzalcoatl..../ I am Quetzalcoatl of the eagle and the snake./ The earth and air..../ I am Lord of the *Two Ways*" (*The Plumed Serpent*, Chapter XXI, italics mine). And Lawrence-Ramon makes it clear that, unlike the enervated Jesus of Christianity, he is allied with the God of Power—not the God of spiritual love:

> the Unknown God pours His Spirit over my head and His fire into my heart, and sends His *power* like a fountain of oil into my belly, and His lightning like a hot spring into my loins,

Ramon proudly asserts (Chapter XXI; italics mine)—and he aspires to

> take the wine of *my spirit* and the red of *my heart*, the strength of *my belly* and the power of *my loins*, and mingle them all together, and kindle them to...my God who is Unknown. (Chapter XXI, italics mine)

Thus Lawrence-Ramon glories in the spiritual ("my spirit")—emotional ("my heart")—physical ("my belly")—sexual ("my loins") power he receives "all together" from "the Unknown God"—a power against which "Lord Jesus!" (*Plumed Serpent*, Chapter XXI) is inefficacious.

The inefficacy of "Lord Jesus" is made exceedingly manifest in the very center of Chapter XXI of *The Plumed Serpent* ("The Opening of the Church"), where, in the midst of the ceremonies opening the Church of Quetzalcoatl, Ramon's wife Carlota, a rabid Christian indeed, prays that "Lord Jesus!" kill her husband Ramon at once:

> "Lord! Lord!" she cried, in a strange ecstatic voice that froze [the main character] Kate's bowels with horror: "Jesus! Jesus! Jesus! Jesus! Jesus! Jesus!"
>
> Carlota strangled in her ecstasy. And all the while, Ramon, the *living* Quetzalcoatl, stood before the flickering altar with naked arm upraised, looking with dark, inalterable eyes down upon the woman.
>
> Throes and convulsions tortured the body of Carlota. She gazed sightlessly upwards. Then came her voice, in the mysterious rhapsody of prayer:
>
> "Lord! Lord! Forgive!"
>
> "God of love, forgive! He knows not what he does.

> "Lord! Lord Jesus! Make an end. Make an end, Lord of the world, Christ of the cross, make an end. Have mercy on him, Father. Have pity on him!
> Oh, take his life from him now, now, that his soul may not die."
> Her voice had gathered strength till it rang out metallic and terrible.
> "Almighty God, take his life from him, and save his soul."
> And in the silence after that cry her hands seemed to flicker in the air like flames of death.
> "The Omnipotent," came the voice of Ramon, speaking quietly, as if to her, "is with me, and I serve Omnipotence!"

Here Jesus, far from being in fact the "God of [spiritual] love," is summoned as a god of destruction ("Make an end. Make an end,...Christ of the cross, make an end") and murderous death ("take his life from him now..."). Fortunately for Ramon, the "Christian" Jesus called on by Carlota to fulfill such death-dealing intentions is not so powerful as she had hoped; indeed, Ramon confidently asserts that "Almighty God" is connected, not with Jesus and Christianity, but with Ramon himself: "The Omnipotent [God] is with me, and I serve Omnipotence!" Ramon declares. Thus the Christian Jesus is connected with maliciousness, death and weakness, while "The Omnipotent" God of Ramon is connected with strength and life.

The deathly nature of Jesus and Christianity is made evident in the fate of Carlota, whose Christian fanaticism leads her to die a hysterical death:

> She remained with her white clasped hands upraised, her white arms and her white face showing mystical, like onyx, from her thin black dress. She was absolutely rigid....
> A strong convulsion seized her body. She became tense again, making inarticulate noises. Then another convulsion seized her. Once more she recovered herself, and thrust up her clenched hands in frenzy. A third convulsion seized her as if from below, and she fell with a strangling moan in a heap on the altar steps.
> Kate had risen suddenly and run to her, to lift her up. She found her stiff, with a little froth on her discoloured lips, and fixed, glazed eyes.

Grotesque and psychotic in death, Carlota is rabid ("froth on her discoloured lips"), rigid, frenzied; she has been foiled in her desire to have Ramon killed by Jesus—for Ramon is "the Living Quetzalcoatl," while

Jesus as "god" is now dead: Jesus, who only knew one way, while Ramon-Lawrence can say "I am Quetzalcoatl, of the Two Ways"—"Two Ways" which "serve Omnipotence!" and make for a "religious" situation in which "The Omnipotent is with me," as Ramon-Lawrence says (Chapter XXI).

But who is "The Omnipotent" of Ramon-Lawrence? First of all, in contradistinction to the "Christian" Jesus who is connected with death—as here, in the death of Carlota—"The Omnipotent" privileges life—as Lawrence-Ramon says:

> "It is life," he [Ramon-Lawrence] said, "which is the mystery. Death is hardly mysterious in comparison." (Chapter XXI)

The sacred Lawrentian religious mystery is oriented towards life, not death: it is Lawrentian life, not death, which "serve[s] Omnipotence!"

But what is the nature of "The Omnipotent" that Ramon-Lawrence so proudly serves? To answer this question we can indeed go to the very last thing Lawrence wrote, a book review in which he declares that

> the "service of God" is only that condition in which we feel ourselves most truly alive and vital, and the "will of God" is the inrush of pure life to which we gladly yield ourselves.
>
> It all depends what you make of the word God....*It is not a question of Jesus* [my italics]. It is a question of God, Almighty God....*Almighty God—the old vital meaning*: strength and glory and honour and might and beauty and wisdom. These are the continual attributes of Almighty God, *in the far past* [my italics]. And the same today, the god who enters us and imbues us with his strength and glory and might and honour and beauty and wisdom, this is a god we are eager to worship....
>
> ...you must give men back their belief in God,...Almighty God, the God of strength and glory and might and wisdom:...a vital and magnificent God....[W]e no longer any of us *really* believe in an exclusively "good" God....[But the Lawrentian belief is] some living, instinctive "faith" in the God of Life. (*Phoenix* 396)

Thus Lawrence on his deathbed indeed clarifies the nature of "The Omnipotent" God that he celebrates in *The Plumed Serpent* to the definite exclusion of Christianity and Jesus. "The Omnipotent" God can make Lawrence feel "most truly alive and vital," full of "pure life," unlike Jesus ("It is not a question of Jesus. It is a question of God, Almighty God"). Thus for Lawrence, Jesus has *nothing* to do with Almighty God, "old [and] vital" Almighty God. Indeed, it soon becomes evident that Almighty God, "old," "vital," strong, glorious, "in the far past," "vital and magnificent," is none other than the "Jewish" Jehovah—Jehovah about Whom Lawrence wrote frequently in his last days, most memorably in *Apocalypse*.

Not, however, in *Apocalypse* as it was finally published (posthumously) in 1931—but rather in its original version, written in November 1929 (now available as "*Apocalypse*, Fragment One," in *Apocalypse and the Writings on Revelation*, ed. Mara Kalnins [New York: Cambridge University Press, 1980]), when Lawrence was nearing the end of all his agons (he died 2 March 1930). In "*Apocalypse*, Fragment 1," Lawrence sings the praises of the Jews and Jehovah:

> The Jews did a wonderful thing when they focussed the whole religious feeling of man upon One God....But surely the Jehovah of Genesis and Numbers, Samuel, Psalms, Isaiah, Ezekiel, surely he is all the gods....You can't make an idol to Jehovah because he has all the qualities of all the ancient gods in turn....He is One because he is all of them....He is himself all the gods . . ., savage and fertile, and even he is all the unknown gods that are yet to come....For all the gods are only "sides" of the One God. (156)

Dying Lawrence in November 1929 surely privileges the Jewish "One God" Who, according to Lawrence, is all-powerful and all-inclusive as well. But, if in his last months Lawrence gave in to his enthusiasm for the Jewish God rather than engage in an agon with Judaism, Lawrence in his last great burst of creative energy (in July 1928) made the Jewish God less all-encompassing, less "bodily," less "phallic"—less "Lawrentian"—and for good reason: for Lawrence needed to overcome his anxiety of influence in order to complete his last great work of fiction, *The Escaped Cock*.

In *The Escaped Cock*, Jehovah—rather than being prized by Lawrence as "the God of the [sexual] body" as He had been in the *Hardy* study—is instead chided by Jesus-Lawrence for deliberately hiding from Jesus the joy of sex:

> He [Jesus] untied the string on the linen tunic, and slipped the garment down, till he saw the white glow of her white-gold breasts. And he touched them, and he felt his life go molten. "Father!" he said, "why did you hide this from me?" And he touched her with the poignancy of wonder, and the marvellous piercing transcendence of desire. "Lo!" he said, "this is beyond prayer." (57)

Here Jesus-Lawrence's statement, "Father! why did you hide this from me?" is of course exceedingly reminiscent of Jesus' New Testament statement (on the cross), "My God, my God, why hast thou forsaken me?" In both cases—*The Escaped Cock* and the New Testament—Jesus feels his "Father"—Jehovah—has betrayed him; and in a very real sense in *The Escaped Cock*, "The Father"—the Lawrentian God—the Jewish "God of the body" so praised in *Study of Thomas Hardy*—has forsaken Lawrence-Jesus: for the "Father" in Lawrence's *Escaped Cock* no longer privileges the body and instead hides its joys from his "Son" Jesus-Lawrence; yet ultimately of course this betrayal of Lawrence by Jehovah, "the Father," the Jewish "god of the body"—is rooted in Lawrence's own imagination and its defense against the anxiety of influence.

In the *Hardy* study (*Phoenix* 476) "the Father" is synecdochical of "the Flesh," and the Father is indeed Jehovah; but in *The Escaped Cock* the Jewish God is apparently antithetical to "the marvellous piercing transcendence of desire" that Jesus experiences, not as a Jew, or with a Jew, but as an impostor: a *pagan* impostor (he impersonates the god Osiris)—with a *pagan* priestess. Of course, the only reason Jesus has his great sexual awakening is that he has the good fortune to be mistaken for the pagan god Osiris; the Jewish Jehovah has no part in it: it is thanks to the pagans that Jesus-Lawrence has the experience that is "beyond prayer."

Indeed, Jesus-Lawrence's identity as "pagan" is emphasized quite early on in *The Escaped Cock*. Towards the end of Part I, Jesus-Lawrence

> set out into the phenomenal world, to be fulfilled in his own aloneness in the midst of it.... Yet even now he did not go quite alone, for under his arm, as he went, he carried the cock, whose tail fluttered gaily behind, and who craned his head excitedly, for he too was adventuring out for the first time into the wider phenomenal world, which is the stirring of the body of cocks also.... (31)

As Part I goes on, it becomes evident that the Lawrence-Jesus of *The Escaped Cock* finds more value in that which is emblematized by the escaped cock that he carries with him than he does in the legendary-conventional figure of Jesus Christ:

> he [Jesus-Lawrence] overtook two men going slowly, and talking.... he [Jesus-Lawrence] heard they were speaking of himself. And he remembered them, for he had known them in his life, the life of his mission. So he greeted them, but did not disclose himself in

the dusk, and they did not know him. He said to them:

"What then of him who would be king, and was put to death for it?"

They answered suspiciously:

"Why ask you of him?"

"I have known him, and thought much about him," he [Jesus-Lawrence] said.

So they replied:

"He is risen."

"Yea! And where is he, and how does he live?" [Jesus-Lawrence ironically asks].

"We know not, for it is not revealed. Yet he is risen, and in a little while will ascend unto the Father."

"Yea! And where then is his Father?"

"Know ye not?...The Father is in heaven, above the cloud and the firmament."

"Truly? How then will he ascend?"

"As Elijah the prophet, he shall go up in a glory."

"Even into the sky?"

"Into the sky."

"Then he is not risen in the flesh?"

"He is risen in the flesh."

"And will he take flesh up into the sky?"

"The Father in Heaven will take him up."

The man who had died [Jesus-Lawrence] said no more, for his say was over, and words beget words, even as gnats. But the men asked him:

"Why do you carry a cock?"

"I am a healer," he said, "and the bird hath virtue."

"You are not a believer?"

"Yea! I believe the bird is full of life and virtue." (32-33)

Ironically, Jesus-Lawrence is "not a believer" in Christianity; instead he believes in the phallic-healing power of "the bird"—"the cock": "the bird is full of life and virtue"—that is to say, the cock is "full of life and virtue"—"virtue" meaning goodness as well as power. In singing the praises of the cock as "full of life and virtue" for "a healer" who "carr[ies] a cock," Lawrence-Jesus is symbolically transformed into the pagan god of healing, Asclepius; as Lawrence scholars Evelyn J. Hinz and John J. Teunissen tell us:

> Asclepius was the god of healing and the patron of medicine in the pagan world. As the divine healer, he was the classical counterpart to the Christian Savior....

> ...[Jesus-Lawrence's] cure is symbolized in his assumption of the Asclepian role as the "healer" associated with the cock,

for

> The cock was the common sacrifice made to Asclepius by those whom he had cured....the cock was viewed as an appropriate sacrifice because it was the herald of the dawn, and Asclepius was the god who restored to the ill "the light of day." ("Savior and Cock," *Journal of Modern Literature* 5 [1976]: 283, 289)

As a pagan "healer," Lawrence-Jesus in *The Escaped Cock* manifests great enthusiasm for the pre-Christian ways of the classical world: an enthusiasm which puts him at odds with the "Jewish" way and Jehovah.

Lawrence-Jesus' enthusiasm for the pagan way becomes even more apparent in Part II of *The Escaped Cock*. Finding refuge in the temple of Isis, Jesus feels that here is where he is really at home:

> here at the temple [of Isis] he felt peace, the hard, bright *pagan* peace....(44; my italics)

Lawrence-Jesus shows he is even more at home in the pagan world in *The Escaped Cock* Part II when he goes to "look on Isis" in "the inner shrine" of the temple, "the almost darkness"; here Jesus-Lawrence is overwhelmed with enthusiasm for her:

> "Great is Isis!" he [Jesus-Lawrence] said. "In her search [for Osiris] she is greater than death. Wonderful is such...a woman, wonderful the goal. All men praise thee, Isis, thou greater than the mother unto man." (45)

Forgetting about Jehovah the Father, Jesus-Lawrence finds solace in Isis; indeed, he is so intense in his enthusiasm that the priestess of Isis believes him to be Osiris himself:

> The woman of Isis heard [Jesus' praise of Isis]....Then she looked at [Jesus].
> "Is it well with thee here?" she asked him. "Has Isis brought thee home to herself?"
> He looked at the priestess in wonder and trouble.
> "I know not," he said.
> But the woman was pondering, that this was the lost Osiris. She felt it in the quick of her soul. And her agitation was intense. (45)

Full of "wonder and trouble" at the priestess' suggestion that he belongs with Isis, Jesus-Lawrence is confused: "I know not"; but "the woman" is certain that Jesus-Lawrence is "the lost Osiris": and before long Jesus-Lawrence is glad to go along with her, glad to forget and reject his "Jewish" roots.

The priestess of Isis gives Jesus-Lawrence good reason to forget the "Jewish" way and instead impersonate the great pagan Osiris: "He [Jesus-Lawrence] looked at her....[and] his loins stirred." The young "naive" woman pleads with him to stay because he is Osiris, and he finds no problem with this impersonation:

> "Would you detain me, girl of Isis?" he said.
> "Stay! I am sure you are Osiris!" she said.
> He laughed suddenly.
> "Not yet!" he said....(46)

"Not yet!"—by that Jesus-Lawrence means that he is not yet "pagan" enough to be Osiris.

Jesus-Lawrence does not have long to wait, however; for the priestess of Isis is eager to find "Osiris"; and in her eagerness she will gladly give Jesus-Lawrence the "pagan" fulfillment "of the body" that he needs—a fulfillment with which the Jewish God is no longer connected. As it turns out, only the pagan priestess can give Jesus-Lawrence what he needs now:

> "And art thou not Osiris?" she asked.
> He [Jesus-Lawrence] flushed suddenly.
> "Yea, if thou wilt heal me!" he said. (47)

The "healing" of Jesus-Lawrence clearly will take place in a pagan context. Alone and thinking of the "woman of Isis," Jesus-Lawrence declares a kind of allegiance to her:

> He [Jesus-Lawrence] was absorbed and enmeshed in new sensations. The woman of Isis was lovely to him....Best of all was her tender desire for him....
> "She is like sunshine upon me," he said to himself, stretching his limbs. "I have never before stretched my limbs in such sunshine as her desire for me. The greatest of all gods granted me this."(52)

Lawrence gives us no clue as to who is "The greatest of all gods" (according to Jesus-Lawrence) in *The Escaped Cock*; but it is evident that in *The Escaped Cock* "The greatest of all gods" is not the Jewish Jehovah, for here Jehovah is not affiliated with the "sunshine" of "desire." Indeed, here it seems that Jesus-Lawrence is trying hard to convince himself that there is some "greater power" of which he has hitherto been ignorant:

> "There are destinies of splendour," he [Jesus-Lawrence] said to the night, "after all our doom of littleness and meanness and pain." (52)

Obviously for Lawrence-Jesus "our doom of littleness and meanness and pain"—the crucifixion—is quite inferior to the "destinies of splendour" he looks forward to; Christianity is no competition for "The greatest of all gods." But what of Judaism? Jesus-Lawrence continues to commune with himself:

> So he went up silently to the temple, and waited in darkness against the inner wall, looking out on a grey darkness....And he said again to himself: "There are destinies of splendour, and *there is a greater power*." [my italics]

Here Jesus-Lawrence alludes to, not only "destinies of splendour," but also "a greater power": a power certainly beyond Christianity and, perhaps, it would seem, beyond Judaism. Yet Lawrence's failure lucidly to elucidate the nature of this "greater power" indicates that he himself does not completely believe in and/or understand it; nor is it clear whom he means to be "The greatest of all gods" at this point; indeed, it seems likely that this mention of "the greatest of all gods" by Jesus-Lawrence is merely a means, an unconscious device by which he may estrange/separate himself from "The Father," "The One God," "Jehovah" (to use Lawrence's terms in "*Apocalypse*, Fragment 1").

It soon becomes clear that, for "The greatest of all gods" and the "greater power" with its "splendour," both Christianity and paganism alike are merely instrumental. The priestess of Isis, readying herself for sexual relations with Jesus-Lawrence, is poignantly presented at this point:

> He [Jesus-Lawrence] watched the strange rapt woman, and he said to himself: I must leave her alone in her rapture, her female mysteries....And as he watched her, he saw her soul in its aloneness, and its female difference. He said to himself: How different she is from me, how strangely different! She is afraid of me, and my male difference. She is getting herself naked and clear of her fear. How sensitive and softly alive she is, with a life so different from mine!...What a beautiful thing,...She is making herself com-

pletely penetrable. Ah! how terrible to fail her, or to trespass on her! (53)

This emphasis on sexual penetration and its desirability leads to the climactic scene in which the priestess of Isis brings about the "resurrection" of Jesus-Lawrence—or, perhaps we should say, Osiris-Lawrence:

> She turned to him [Jesus-Lawrence], her face glowing from the goddess [Isis].
> "You are Osiris, aren't you?" she said *naively* [my italics].
> "If you will," he [Jesus-Lawrence] said.
> "Will you let Isis discover you? Will you take off your things [i.e., in preparation for sex], and come to Isis?"
> He looked at the woman, and lost his breath....

Breathless from passion, Jesus-Lawrence gladly (and with a straight face) impersonates Osiris so that he can have his sexual experience with the sexy, "naive" priestess. Indeed, at this point in *The Escaped Cock* it can perhaps be said that the joke is on both Christianity (which Jesus-Lawrence renounces for sex with "Isis") and the pagan way (which, as personified by the "naive" priestess, is duped by the wily Jesus-Lawrence). Yet of course underneath all this apparent chicanery is the quintessential Lawrentian reverence—for life, for sex, for "the religious sense." An eloquent gloss on this Lawrentian "religious" attitude—which is indeed part and parcel of his "anxiety of influence" in relation to Judaism—can be found in a letter of October 1922 to Willard Johnson:

> the great gods pulse in the dark....There are different dark gods, different passions....*The god of gods* [my italics] is unknowable, unutterable, but all the more terrible: and from the unutterable god step forth the mysteries of our prompting in different mysterious forms:...different promptings, different mysterious forms....[T]urn again to the dark gods, which are the dark promptings and passion-motions inside you, and have a reverence for life. (*Collected Letters* Moore II 726)

In *The Escaped Cock* at this point, "reverence for life" is connected with the "Goddess," Isis, to whom Jesus-Lawrence prays: "Ah Goddess, I would be so glad to live, if you would give me my clue again." And now all religious differences are transcended (temporarily) as the priestess of Isis heals Jesus-Lawrence:

> And he could not help smiling at her, in her naif priestess' absorption. This was her dream, and he was only a dream-object to her.

> She would never know or understand what he was....But what did it matter? She was different. She was woman....Only she was good to him. (54)

Because "Only she was good to him," here Jesus-Lawrence connects "Life" with the pagan woman and the pagan goddess:

> I want so much to live [Jesus-Lawrence says to himself]. Life has brought me to this woman with warm hands. And her touch is more to me now than all my words. For I want to live—
> "Go then to the Goddess!" she said softly, gently pushing him towards Isis. And as he stood there dazed and naked as an unborn thing, he heard the woman murmuring to the goddess, murmuring, murmuring with a plaintive appeal....The woman was trembling softly and murmuring in Greek. (55)

And finally Jesus-Lawrence realizes that

> I am going to be flushed warm again, I am going to be whole! I shall be warm like the morning. I shall be *a man*. It doesn't need understanding. It needs *newness*. She brings me newness— (56; my italics)

The "newness" that the priestess brings Jesus-Lawrence is also the "newness"—and the "manly" strength—of originality, "poetic strength."

The "newness" surely shows up in Lawrence-Jesus' use of biblical language, as Jesus begins to make love to the priestess of Isis:

> He stooped beside her and caressed her softly, blindly, murmuring inarticulate things. And...he knew only the crouching fulness of the woman there, the soft white rock of life.
> "On this rock I build my life!"
> The deep-folded, penetrable rock of the living woman! the woman, hiding her face. Himself bending over, powerful and new like dawn. He crouched to her, and he felt the blaze of his manhood and his power rise up in his loins, magnificent.
> "I am risen!" (57)

The "rock" for Lawrence-Jesus is of course not "Peter, the Rock; and on this rock I will build my church" (Matthew 16:18)—but rather the body of woman ("soft white rock of life"): on the body of woman Lawrence-Jesus declares that he "build[s] my life" as man and creative writer. For the woman of Isis makes Lawrence-Jesus feel "powerful and new like dawn"—the dawn of a new (poetic) world in which he has priority—or at least the illusion of priority. For Lawrence-Jesus, "I am risen!" means not only that he has achieved phallic erection, but also that he has attained "poetic immortality" by virtue of his sexual experience with the priestess of Isis: the sort of experience which his "Father"—the Jewish God Jehovah—had kept hidden from him; thus Jesus-Lawrence's sexual act with the priestess of Isis is "beyond prayer," for it is beyond anything that his "religious" experience with Jehovah the "Father" had ever acquainted him with. Yet of course the fact is that many years before *The Escaped Cock* (during Lawrence's *Hardy* period) "the Father" (Jehovah) in Lawrence's mind had indeed been connected with the flesh, the body, the sexual experience ("lying with a woman"). But, some dozen years after the *Hardy* study, dying Lawrence (unconsciously) forgets (represses the memory of) his earlier alliance with the Jewish God: forgets so that in *The Escaped Cock* he can create a unique tale in which the "Jewish" Jesus-Lawrence is initiated into sex by a pagan priestess, representative of a pagan way that at this point valorizes a sexuality which the Jewish Jehovah ("the Father") apparently does not; thus *The Escaped Cock*, far from being the pro-Christian tale some Lawrentians (e.g., Spilka, Cowan) make it out to be, evidently privileges the pagan way: Jesus-Lawrence makes this apparent preference clear when, after his sex with the pagan priestess he declares:

> "Lo, Isis is a kindly goddess, and full of tenderness. Great gods are warm-hearted and have tender goddesses." (58)

Jesus-Lawrence's valorization of the pagan "kindly goddess" Isis, who is "full of tenderness"—his praise for "warm-hearted," "Great gods"—seems clear enough, but it assumes another meaning when we remember that in *Lady Chatterley's Lover* Lawrence-Mellors, when asked what he believes in, answers that

> I believe in being warm-hearted. I believe especially in being warm-hearted in love, in fucking with a warm heart (*Lady Chatterley's Lover*, Chapter Fourteen)

—thus making Mellors too one of the "warm-hearted" "Great gods" of Jesus-Lawrence, as is Jesus-Lawrence himself, after he has his "warm-hearted fucking" with "Isis": afterwards, looking at the universe, Jesus-Lawrence concludes:

> How full it is, and *great beyond all gods*. How it leans *around me*, and *I am part of it*, the great rose of space....(58; my italics)

Here we have, neither paganism nor Christianity nor Judaism, but rather the "triumphant solipsism" of the strong poet Jesus-Lawrence, who at this point fancies himself to be a major "part of it" ("it leans around *me*")—*it* being infinite space "great beyond all gods" ("gods" here having no capital letter). The pagan sexual initiation, ultimately, has been merely instrumental for Jesus-Lawrence: instrumental to his attaining "the absolute stillness and fulness of touch"(*Escaped Cock*, p. 58)—a unique Lawrentian "absolute" which is part and parcel of the uniqueness of Lawrence, his "poetic strength." Of course, to create this unique tale (*The Escaped Cock*) dying Lawrence had to forget that the younger Lawrence had already attributed great sexuality to Judaism and the Jewish God—for the "strong" dying Lawrence, no less than the "strong" younger Lawrence of the *Women in Love* period, had to rest secure in the poetic consummation of victorious isolation, triumphant solipsism which, in "an unconsciously purposeful forgetting" (Bloom's phrase, *Map of Misreading*, p. 73), now neglects to remember, not only the sexual aspect of the Jewish Jehovah, but also the fact that another being—a woman—was actively involved in Jesus-Lawrence's attainment of "newness," consummation.

The ultimate evidence of Jesus-Lawrence's triumphant solipsism in *The Escaped Cock* appears in the very last paragraph of *The Escaped Cock*, after Jesus-Lawrence has escaped from the Romans—and from the priestess of Isis as well:

> the priestess came no more at night. The man who had died [Jesus-Lawrence] rowed slowly on, with the current, and laughed to himself: *I have sowed the seed of my life and my resurrection, and put my touch forever upon the choice woman of this day*....(61; my italics)

In his "triumphant solipsism" (Bloom, *Map of Misreading*, p. 9), "the splendor of an ultimate isolation" (Bloom, *Anxiety of Influence*, p. 128), Jesus-Lawrence has become the father of himself ("I have sowed the seed of my life")—thanks to his sex with "the choice woman of *this day*" (my italics): yet in his description of his relation with "the choice woman," Jesus-Lawrence in "laugh[ing] to himself" at the memory of his great achievement (of sexual and poetic strength), evidently treats the pagan priestess as a mere object: he is categorical subject ("I," "my life," "my resurrection," "my touch")—surely an outrage to feminists. Thus Jesus-Lawrence has apparently used the priestess: she has served her purpose, "this day,"—and for the time being "golden," "splendid" phallic-sexual activity is unnecessary for Jesus-Lawrence: "But the gold and flowing serpent is coiling up again, to sleep at the root of my tree," Jesus-Lawrence says to himself as he "rowed slowly on," away from sex, the priestess of Isis, and paganism—paganism which has served its purpose as an aid to Lawrence's attainment of "poetic strength," but which ultimately the dying Lawrence could not embrace as he would, finally, the Jewish God Whom he had had to forget in order to create his great unique tale of a "pagan" sexy Jesus.

Unfortunately, even major Lawrence critics such as James C. Cowan see *The Escaped Cock* idealistically:

> Written as a parable for contemporary Christian society, the novella [*Escaped Cock*] sets forth one of D. H. Lawrence's major themes: rebirth of the whole man through tenderness in the sexual relationship. (Cowan, *D. H. Lawrence and the Trembling Balance*, p. 253)

To idealize *The Escaped Cock* as "a parable for contemporary Christian society" takes away from the great drama and courage and strength of Lawrence's agon with the "Jewish" way—an agon he needed for his attainment of "poetic strength."

So Cowan is also mistaken when he concludes that "The question [about *The Escaped Cock*]...is whether Lawrence seeks to revitalize the established Christian religion or to substitute in its place a pre-Socratic religion founded on pagan vitalism" (p. 250). In fact Lawrence in *The Escaped Cock* does not seek to do either of these things: what he seeks is "poetic immortality."

"Tomorrow is another day," Jesus-Lawrence concludes in the very last sentence of *The Escaped Cock*; the "tomorrow" that concerns Lawrence here is the "tomorrow" of poetic strength and immortality; poetic strength and immortality that was further insured by *The Escaped Cock* and its unique naming of a "pagan" Jesus. But as Lawrence came nearer and nearer to death, he searched his soul for what he sincerely felt about the Jews and the "Jewish" way. Thus in November 1929 Lawrence wrote "*Apocalypse*, Fragment 1," a great philosophical work which tells us of Lawrence's ultimate reverence and enthusiasm for "the Jewish mind" and "the Jewish soul" and "Jehovah":

> The Jews were able to make a One God because they came into contact with so many peoples and so many civilisations, so many alien gods, each of which lent something to the Jewish mind, and to the Jewish soul. All the old Jewish poetry is the poetry of adven-

ture with strange peoples and strange gods, and the Bible is perhaps more profoundly a book of roaming than is...the Odyssey. (157)

In 1930 Lawrence (in his "Introduction to *The Dragon of the Apocalypse* by Frederick Carter") clearly privileges the Jews over the Greeks, the Bible over Homer:

> the Bible...is splendid:...a fascinating account of the adventure of the Jewish—or Hebrew or Israelite nation, among the great old civilized nations of the past....Reading the Bible...is more fascinating than reading Homer, for the adventure goes even deeper into time and into the soul....(55)

In "*Apocalypse*, Fragment 1" Lawrence attributes supreme powers of creative synthesis to the "roaming" Jews, who assimilated the cultures of others for their own purposes, transforming the "influence" of other cultures and making it part of their own:

> the influence...is dual. The Jews *loved* roaming, they loved meeting strange peoples, learning from strange cultures, which meant strange religions....In a sense, they are a people that always has lived and always will live on the culture of other races. The Jewish mind is simply an amalgam of all the cultures of the ages. (157)

In a remarkable "creative misreading" of the Jewish way, Lawrence here makes the Jews the supreme "strong poets" triumphing over the "anxiety of influence" in relation to their neighbors and predecessors. Indeed, according to Lawrence in "*Apocalypse*, Fragment 1," the Jews to this day are still masters at soaking up "influence":

> The Jew has such a curious duality. His real delight is centrifugal: he *loves* to go to strange peoples and to assimilate strange cultures: he always did. But his fear of losing himself in slavery made him, after Egypt, react savagely against all strange peoples, and pivot himself on his *One God*, whose *Chosen People* he belonged to [157; first italics Lawrence's; second italics mine].

Here it is evident that Lawrence wishes to see the Jews as going through the same psychological-creative dilemma in relation to their neighbors as he is in relation to *them*. Indeed, Lawrence here obviously envies the Jews their "One God" and "Chosen People" role. And, of course, Lawrence is talking about his own feelings in relation to the Jews when he states of his precursors that

> The Jewish prophets hated their neighbours so bitterly because the Jewish people were all too prone to like their neighbours over-

> much, and merge too easily....And the splendid thing about the Bible is the wideness of its contact and the bigness of its intelligence and its secret sympathy. (157-158)

Of course, what Lawrence is really talking about is his "secret sympathy" for the Jews, with their "splendid" Bible and "wideness of contact" and "bigness of intelligence." Indeed, in his enthusiasm for the Jewish way Lawrence even has it subsume pagan culture:

> the Old Testament...is a strange and fascinating Odyssey of a whole race wandering among strange races that attracted them intensely, and threatened to absorb them, would have absorbed them but for the violent, frenzied resistance of the prophets, from Moses onwards. (158)

According to Lawrence, the Jews outdo Homer's Odyssey; furthermore, they are the supreme example of the "anxiety of influence" and the triumph over it, for, according to Lawrence,

> The [Jewish] Bible evolved from centuries of vivid contact with strange races and strange gods. Even Jehovah himself was so evolved. (158)

The Jews, "fascinated" by their pagan neighbors, nonetheless managed to "assimilate" the "strange" pagan beliefs, managed to "transume" them and utilize them to strengthen Judaism and give it "priority." The Jews themselves, in Lawrence's vision (or "re-vision") of them, are "[i]n a sense,...a people that always has lived and always will live on the culture of other races" (157).

By attributing the anxiety of influence to his Jewish precursors, Lawrence alleviated his own anxiety of influence in relation to the Jews; thus in "*Apocalypse*, Fragment 1," Lawrence is able to praise the Jewish God with great enthusiasm (since Lawrence no longer feels quite so insecure in relation to Jehovah's "Chosen People"):

> Jesus was very careful, really, *not* to assume power, and not to destroy power. The great God of Power, of Might, was the Father....the kingdom is the Father's, it belongs to the Lord Almighty, the Lord of Hosts, the God of power, to him who gives life and strength and potency....
>
> ...There is a great and terrible Ruler of the cosmos, who gives forth life, and takes back life....But if we refuse the Almighty, the Ruler, we refuse the life. And whoever cuts us off from the Almighty cuts us off from life. Whoever gets between me and the Lord of Life,...Lord of Hosts and giver of might, source of our

> strength and power and our glory as far as we can be glorious, whoever gets between me and this, or Him, if you like, is my enemy, and *hates* me....(*Apocalypse*, Fragment 1"; 165-166)

and Lawrence concludes "*Apocalypse*, Fragment 1" with a remarkable "Jewish" declaration of faith:

> Dionysos and Isis, also Mithras and Attis, they are all mediator gods,...; they are not Almighty God himself....
>
> Now lest there seem an element of sentimentality or falsity in this feeling, let us ask ourselves again, do we really *believe* in Almighty God, anyhow?...
>
> From the last far corner of the soul comes the confession: There is Almighty God....[There is that] in the universe which contains the potentiality of all things, contains the potency also of thought and act and feeling and will, along with the rest. And this terrific and frightening and delighted potency I call Almighty God. I think of it, and am filled with fear—fear of my own crass presumptuousness,—and filled with a sense of delight and liberation. If there is Almighty God, I care about nothing else. There is Almighty God, and I am delighted, the whole burden of my fear shifts over. (175)

Thus it is evident that in *The Escaped Cock*, when Jesus-Lawrence refers to "gods," he really only means the "mediator gods": Almighty God, the Jewish Jehovah, is *sui generis*, in a class by Himself—and Lawrence is ultimately a "Jewish" monotheist.

As a "Jewish" monotheist, dying Lawrence in November 1929 feels "delight and liberation" in his "Jewishness"—"Jewishness" which has overcome his "fear of my own crass presumptuousness"—"presumptuousness" which has been replaced by

> *the Jewish feeling* of the Chosen People, watched over by God....("*Apocalypse*, Fragment 2,"p. 178; italics mine)

Surely Lawrence at this time (November 1929) had this "Jewish feeling" of being "watched over by God"; at the same time that Lawrence wrote his *Apocalypse* fragments, Lawrence wrote his essay "The Real Thing" in which he expresses his belief that the Jewish "God" is looking after him:

> What *is* the real thing? Ah, there's the rub. There are millions of ways of living, and it's all life. But what is the real thing in life? What is it that makes you *feel* right, makes life really feel good?
>
> It is the great question. And the answers are old answers....

> What makes life good to me is the sense that, even if I am sick and ill, I am alive, alive to the depths of my soul, and in touch somewhere in touch with the vivid life of the cosmos. Somehow my life draws strength from the depths of the universe, from the depths among the stars, from the great "world." Out of the great world comes my strength and my reassurance. One could say "God," but the word "God" is somehow tainted. But there *is* a flame or a Life Everlasting wreathing through the cosmos for ever and giving us our renewal, once we can get in touch with it. (*Phoenix* 202)

In "The Real Thing" Lawrence was writing for publication: "I wrote ["The Real Thing"] with an eye to *Vanity Fair*" (Letter to Nancy Pearn, 4 November 1929); but in the discarded *Apocalypse* Fragments 1 and 2 Lawrence is writing for himself and throws reticence to the winds; thus Lawrence uses the word "God" more definitively in the discarded *Apocalypse* Fragments 1 and 2; for here Lawrence is eager to give himself away, to commune with himself—and with God: in the communion of his *Apocalypse* fragments Lawrence recognizes his need for the Jewish God, the unique Jewish God Who (according to Lawrence) is "all the gods," "One and Eternal," "the One God," "the Almighty, the Ruler," "the Lord of Life," "Lord of Hosts and giver of might," "Almighty God." Indeed, Lawrence also needed Judaism itself, the religion which (for him) uniquely contains both "Almighty God" and the "pagan" glorification of power and the self:

> The pagan religions, the Jewish religion never got beyond the great conception of power. In the beginning, the cosmos itself was the great Power that Is. The cosmos was alive, and its power was a great living effluence. Looking into the sky was like looking into the eyes of some mighty living creature, or being: and even today, we cannot look into the eyes even of a cat or a baby without quivering from the naked contact with life and the power of life. The universe was all power, and man derived power from the cosmos. At his maximum, he was full of power, and like a bridegroom, vivid with potency. (*Apocalypse*, Fragment 1, p. 171)

Here, in the idea of man as "bridegroom, vivid with potency" we have Lawrence's return to his notion, expressed in the *Hardy*, that man—the Jewish man, who (according to Lawrence in *Hardy*)

> knew God as David had perceived Him, as Solomon had known Him. It was the God of the body, the rudimentary God of physical laws and physical functions. The Jew lived on in physical contact with God. Each of his physical functions he shared with God;

> he kept his body always like the body of a bride ready to serve the bridegroom. (*Phoenix* 450)

—yet now in *Apocalypse* the dying Lawrence lowers his defenses to the extent that the Jew is now "bridegroom," not "bride." Now that the dying Lawrence is ready to accept and realize his identification with his Jewish precursor, he sees and portrays the Jews as potent, "pagan" "bridegrooms" full of "the power of life"—"the power of life" that goes hand in hand with

> the self-glorification consummated in the pagan and Jewish ritual....(*Apocalypse*, Fragment 1, p. 172))

As a supremely strong poet, Lawrence required both "self-glorification" and "naked contact with life and the *power* of life" (my italics)—both of which he finds in "*Apocalypse*, Fragment 1" in his new version (or vision) of the "pagan" Jews, who possess the powerful conception of "Almighty God" together with "the naked contact with life and the power of life" that the pagans enjoyed.

Thus Lawrence's enthusiasm for the "Jewish" way and his aspiration to "poetic immortality" go hand in hand; for in his heart of hearts Lawrence knew that only in Judaism could he find at one and the same time "Almighty God" and a glorious and heroic stance for himself as well; indeed, Lawrence's glory, like that of Jesus towards the end of *The Escaped Cock*, when he (Jesus) beholds the cosmos and contemplates his place in it—

> How full it is,...How it leans around me, and *I am part of it*,...(*The Escaped Cock*)

—Lawrence's glory, as he explains in the penultimate paragraph of *Apocalypse*, is based on the fact that

> I am a part of the great whole, and I can never escape

—"the great whole" of which Lawrence is a great part being not only the cosmos: for not only is the dying Lawrence of *Apocalypse* a part of the universe, but also of the pantheon of the strong poets, "the mighty dead," in whose company Lawrence would find himself soon after finishing *Apocalypse* (Lawrence finished *Apocalypse* on 9 January 1930; he died on 2 March 1930).

WORKS CITED

Bloom, Harold. *The Anxiety of Influence: A Theory of Poetry*. New York: Oxford University Press, 1973.

Cowan, James C. *D. H. Lawrence and the Trembling Balance*. University Park: Pennsylvania State University Press, 1990.

Daleski, H. M. *The Forked Flame: A Study of D. H. Lawrence*. Evanston: Northwestern University Press, 1965.

Fiedler, Leslie. *Fiedler on the Roof: Essays on Literature and Jewish Identity*. Boston: David R. Godine, 1991.

Huxley, Aldous, ed. *The Letters of D. H. Lawrence*. New York: Viking, 1932.

Kinkead-Weekes, Mark. "Lawrence on Hardy." In *Thomas Hardy after Fifty Years*. Ed. Lance St. John Butler. London: Macmillan, 1977.

Lawrence, D. H. *The Escaped Cock*. Ed. Gerald M. Lacy. Los Angeles: Black Sparrow, 1973.

Lawrence, D. H. *Women in Love*. Ed. David Farmer, Lindeth Vasey, and John Worthen. Cambridge: Cambridge University Press, 1987.

Lawrence, D. H. *The Boy in the Bush*. Ed. Paul Eggert. Cambridge: Cambridge University Press, 1990.

Lawrence, D. H. "Foreword to *Sons and Lovers*." In *The Letters of D. H. Lawrence*. Ed. Aldous Huxley. New York: Viking, 1932.

Lawrence, D. H. *The Complete Poems of D. H. Lawrence*. Ed. Vivian de Sola Pinto and F. Warren Roberts. New York: Viking, 1964.

Lawrence, D. H. *Phoenix: The Posthumous Papers of D. H. Lawrence*. Ed. Edward D. McDonald. New York: Viking, 1936.

Lawrence, D. H. "The Future of the Novel." *Study of Thomas Hardy and Other Essays*. Ed. Bruce Steele. Cambridge: Cambridge University Press, 1985.

Lawrence, D. H. *The Letters of D. H. Lawrence: Volume I: September 1901-May 1913*. Ed. James T. Boulton. Cambridge: Cambridge University Press, 1979.

Lawrence, D. H. *The Letters of D. H. Lawrence: Volume II: June 1913-October 1916*. Ed. George J. Zytaruk. Cambridge: Cambridge University Press, 1981.

Lawrence, D. H. *The Letters of D. H. Lawrence: Volume III: October 1916-June 1921*. Ed. James T. Boulton and Andrew Robertson. Cambridge: Cambridge University Press, 1984.

Lawrence, D. H. *The Letters of D. H. Lawrence: Volume IV: June 1921-March 1924*. Ed. Warren Roberts, James T. Boulton, and Elizabeth Mansfield. Cambridge: Cambridge University Press, 1987.

Lawrence, D. H. *Kangaroo*. Ed. Bruce Steele. Cambridge: Cambridge University Press, 1994.

Lawrence, D. H. *Kangaroo*. New York: Viking, 1960.

Lawrence, D. H. *The Plumed Serpent.* Ed. L. D. Clark. Cambridge: Cambridge University Press, 1987.

Moore, Harry T., ed. *The Collected Letters of D. H. Lawrence.* New York: Viking, 1962.

Sagar, Keith. *D. H. Lawrence: Life into Art.* Athens: University of Georgia Press, 1985.

Spilka, Mark. *The Love Ethic of D. H. Lawrence.* Bloomington: Indiana University Press, 1955.

Stoll, John E. *D. H. Lawrence: A Bibliography, 1911–1975.* Troy: Whitston Publishing Company, 1977.

CHAPTER THREE

"A Matter of Life and Death"
Lawrence, Homosexuality, and "Poetic Immortality"

Lawrence's attitude towards homosexuality was part and parcel of his attitude towards his own originality and uniqueness; in a world where homosexuality was predominant among the elite, Lawrence stood alone in championing the male-female relationship; in a letter of 2 December 1913, young D. H. Lawrence (not yet even legally married to Frieda) declares that he alone is capable of being "re-born, re-constructed" from the relation with "a woman":

> I should like to know why *nearly every man that approaches greatness* tends to homosexuality, whether he admits it or not: so that he loves the *body* [Lawrence's italics] of a man better than the body of a woman—as I believe the Greeks did,...by far. I believe a man projects his own image on another man, like on a mirror. But from a woman he wants himself re-born, re-constructed. So he can always get satisfaction from a man, but *it is the hardest thing in life to get ones soul and body satisfied from a woman, so that one is free from oneself.* (D. H. Lawrence letter to Henry Savage, 2 December 1913; italics mine)

"[N]early every man that approaches greatness tends to homosexuality": such is the sad state of Western civilization, says D. H. Lawrence; "nearly every man"—but not I, is Lawrence's unmistakable implication; and, to emphasize the historical magnitude of his uniqueness in this respect, Lawrence cites the ancient Greeks as classic examples of "great men" who "love[d] the *body* of a man better than the body of a woman"—of course, they also loved the mind and soul of a man better than the mind and soul of a woman (as any reader of Plato may surmise). Lawrence, who was well versed in Plato (see Scherr 1996), knew of the ancient Greek elite males' admiration for one another in the gymnasium and elsewhere—an admiration based on (according to Lawrence) the fact that "a man projects his own image on another man, like on a mirror"; this self-regarding, narcissistic element in homosexuality has recently been emphasized by Eve Kosofsky Sedgwick:

> any given man must be assumed to have more in common with any other given man than he can possibly have in common with any given woman....these *are* the assumptions that underlie...the definitional invention of "homosexuality." (*Epistemology of the Closet*, p. 159)

Sedgwick goes on to discourse upon the "love of the same":

> How does a man's love of *other* men become a love of the *same*? The process is graphic in *Dorian Gray*, in the way the plot of the novel facilitates the transition back and forth between "men's desire for men" and something that looks a lot like what a tradition will soon call "narcissism."...[In *Dorian Gray* there occurs] the linguistically unappealable classification of anyone who shares one's gender as being "the same" as oneself, and anyone who does not share one's gender as being one's Other. (p. 160)

Lawrence pits himself against this privileging of "the same" elucidated by Sedgwick; in a letter of June 1914, when he was at the beginning of his supreme *Rainbow-Women in Love* period, Lawrence authoritatively declares that

> *the* one thing to do, is for men to have courage to draw nearer to women, expose themselves to them, and be altered by them: and for women to accept and admit men. That is the only way for art and civilisation to get a new life, a new start—by bringing themselves together, men and women—revealing themselves each to the other, gaining great blind knowledge and suffering and joy, which it will take a big further lapse of civilisation to exploit and work out. Because the source of all life and knowledge is in man and woman, and *the source of all living is in the interchange and the meeting and mingling of these two: man-life and woman-life, man-knowledge and woman-knowledge, man-being and woman-being.* (D. H. Lawrence letter to Arthur McLeod, 2 June 1914; my italics)

For Lawrence, the valorization of "the same" is antithetical to Lawrence's main concern: "a new life" for "art and civilisation"; this "new life" can only be attained, Lawrence says, through the love of the other, the privileging of otherness rather than "the same"—a privileging which is a Herculean endeavor for "nearly every man," for "it is the hardest thing in *life* [my italics] to get...satisfied [body and soul] from a woman": "the hardest thing," but the all-important thing as well, if "civilisation" is to be renewed at a time when "art" is "unwholesome," "stale," and "despise[s] life." The "art" of which Lawrence here speaks is Thomas Mann's *Death in Venice*, which Lawrence reviewed in July 1913 (see *Phoenix* 840)—only a few months before his letter to Savage on "greatness" and "homosexuality." Clearly Lawrence, after reading Mann's "unwholesome," homoerotic *Death in Venice*, was angered by this "aesthetic" idealization of homosexual-pederastic lust in which formal perfection disguises "decadent" homosexual desires. An extraordinarily astute and intuitive literary critic, Lawrence perspicaciously equates Mann with Aschenbach in *Death in Venice*:

> It [*Death in Venice*] is absolutely, almost intentionally, unwholesome. The man [Mann] is sick, body and soul. He [Mann] portrays himself as he is, with wonderful skill and art, portrays his sickness. And since any genuine portrait is valuable, this book [*Death in Venice*] has its place. It portrays one man, one atmosphere, one sick vision. (*Phoenix* 312)

As Lawrence sensed, a considerable part of Mann's "sickness" was his homosexuality (which has been discussed at length in recent Thomas Mann scholarship; see Feuerlicht 1982; Heilbut 1996; Dollimore 1998, pp. 275-293); Mann's homosexuality, according to Lawrence, went hand in hand with his "craving for form" which is "the outcome of a certain attitude to life"—an "attitude to life," Lawrence asserts, that is indeed anti-life:

> Thomas Mann...feels vaguely that he has in him something finer than ever physical life revealed. Physical life is a disordered corruption, against which he can fight with only one weapon, his fine aesthetic sense, his feeling for beauty, for perfection, for a certain fitness which soothes him, and gives him an inner pleasure, however corrupt the stuff of life may be. There he [Mann] is,...full of disgusts and loathing of himself....And so,...he [Mann] sits,...reducing himself grain by grain to the statement of his own disgust, patiently, self-destructively, so that his statement at least may be perfect in a world of corruption. (*Phoenix* 312)

Mann, "loathing himself" for his "corrupt" homosexuality, "soothes him[self]" by "reducing himself...to the statement of his own disgust" with himself, his artistic "statement" manifesting "his fine aesthetic sense" in its "perfection" which (in Mann's view) overcomes the "disordered corruption" of "physical life," "the stuff of life"—and Mann's art/life binarism is abhorrent to Lawrence, who opposes it with his Lawrentian belief that "a new life" for "art and civilisation" is possible only if "men and women" succeed in "bringing themselves together." "Men and women...bringing themselves together": this is the main theme of Lawrence's major work in the period after his "greatness" and "homosexuality" letter of 2 December 1913. Fighting to save high culture from homosexuality, Lawrence pitted his own unique Lawrentian form against the "unwholesome" perfection of form he decried in Thomas Mann.

First of all, Lawrence declares that the artistic form of his great work of this period—*The Rainbow*—is rooted in his own heterosexual nature: Lawrentian artistic form, he maintains, is the creation produced by Lawrence as a great heterosexual deeply involved with his wife:

> I am so sure of this now, this novel [*The Rainbow*]. It is a big and beautiful work. Before, I could not get my soul into it. That was because of the struggle and the resistance between Frieda and me. Now you will find her and me in the novel, I think, and *the work is of both of us*. (D. H. Lawrence letter to Edward Garnett, 22 April 1914; my italics)

Thus, according to Lawrence in April 1914, his self-concept at this point in his life as man and writer is intertwined with, part and parcel of, his intensely heterosexual identity: an identity which, he says, has resulted in "a big and beautiful work" which is the product of "Frieda and me."

But, as Harold Bloom says, "the poet-in-a-poet *cannot marry*, whatever the person-in-a-poet chooses to have done" (*A Map of Misreading*, p. 19); and, indeed, in the same letter to Garnett (22 April 1914), Lawrence gives himself away:

> I am not after all a child working erratically. All the time, underneath, there is something deep evolving itself out in me. And it is *hard* to express a new thing, in sincerity. And you should understand, and help me to the new thing, not get angry and say it is *common*....You see—you tell me I am half a Frenchman and one-eighth a Cockney. But that isn't it. I have very often the vulgarity and disagreeableness of the common people, as you say

> Cockney, and I may be a [lecherous] Frenchman. *But primarily I am a passionately religious man, and my novels must be written from the depth of my religious* experience [italics mine]. That I must keep to, because I can only work like that....But you should see the religious, earnest, suffering man in me first....Mrs. Garnett says I have no true nobility—with all my cleverness and charm. But that is not true. It [nobility] is there [in Lawrence and his work]....

Here Lawrence makes it clear that "there is something deep...*in me* [my italics]"—not "in me and Frieda"—that is responsible for Lawrence's creative art and form: and this "something" evidently is both erotic ("a Frenchman") and "common" ("a Cockney"); but most important of all, this "something" is "passionately religious." Without this unique Lawrentian religious sense, Lawrence could not write: "my novels must be written from the depth of my religious experience. That I must keep to, because I can only work like that"—and Lawrence's singular religious sense is unique to him alone: he is "the religious, earnest, suffering man" who is doing the writing—Frieda is not.

But Frieda as Woman and Wife to Lawrence The Supremely Heterosexual Writer is all-important, essential: without her and his heterosexual relation to her, Lawrence the "passionately religious man" would not have that which to be "passionate" and "religious" about. Out of this Lawrentian "religious" passion came the Lawrentian "moral scheme" which he placed against "the moral scheme" of Tolstoi and Dostoievski—a "dull, old, dead" moral scheme (as Lawrence calls it in his letter of 5 June 1914 to Edward Garnett) that leads to decadence and homosexuality like that of Mann in *Death in Venice,* which Lawrence had already read and reviewed (1913); in contradistinction to "unwholesome" Mann and *Death in Venice,* Lawrence in his *Rainbow* period presents a vision of "vital love":

> One must learn to love, and go through a good deal of suffering to get to it, like any knight of the Grail, and the journey is always *towards* the other soul, not away from it. Do you think love is an accomplished thing, the day it is recognised. It isn't. To love, you have to learn to understand the other, more than she understands herself, and to submit to her understanding of you. It is damnably difficult and painful, but it is the only thing which endures. You mustn't think that your desire or your fundamental need is to make a good career, or to fill your life with activity, or even to provide for your family materially. It isn't. Your most vital necessity

> in this life is that you shall *love your wife completely and implicitly and in entire nakedness of body and spirit.* Then you will have peace and inner security, no matter how many things go wrong. And this peace and security will leave you free to act and to produce your own work, a real independent workman. (D. H. Lawrence letter to Thomas Dunlop, 7 July 1914)

Thus, according to the supremely heterosexual creative writer Lawrence of 1914, it is of the uniquely heterosexual creative artist that much is expected: "learn[ing] to love," "go[ing] through a good deal of suffering," "journey[ing] *towards* the other soul," "learn[ing] to understand the [heterosexual] other, more than she understands herself," "submit[ting] to her understanding of you," "lov[ing] your wife completely and implicitly and in entire nakedness of body and spirit"—and it is also to him (the uniquely heterosexual creative artist) that much is given: "peace and inner security, no matter how many things go wrong": the "peace and inner security" that are vital aids for the aspiring artist, for "this peace and security will leave [the artist] free to act and to produce [his] own work, a real independent workman." Here as in his earlier letter (2 December 1913) on "greatness" and "homosexuality," Lawrence valorizes heterosexuality as the hard way to go, the arduous road to take, for "it is the hardest thing in life to get ones soul and body satisfied from a woman, so that one is *free from oneself*" (Lawrence to Savage, 2 December 1913); it is being "free from oneself" that the heterosexual Lawrence valorizes, in opposition to the homosexual man who in his immature narcissism "projects his own image on another man, like on a mirror" (Lawrence letter to Savage, 2 December 1913) rather than accept the challenge of vital heterosexuality—vital heterosexuality which is characteristic of the best of Western civilization (according to Lawrence):

> And one is kept by all tradition and instinct from loving men, or a man—for it means just extinction of all the purposive influences. (D. H. Lawrence letter to Henry Savage, 2 December 1913)

Here by "tradition" Lawrence clearly means the Hebraic, not Hellenic, "tradition"; by "instinct" he means his own natural-poetic-religious "instinct" of vital heterosexuality—an instinct that goes against "[men] loving men" in a sexual way: for this "loving" (says Lawrence) is synonymous with "extinction of all the purposive [creative] influences," "the purposive influences" that keep Western civilization going.

These "purposive influences" were obviously under siege in 1913—the year Lawrence wrote his "greatness" and "homosexuality" letter (December 1913), and also the year he wrote his review of Mann's "unwholesome" *Death in Venice* (May 1913); furthermore, in June 1913 Lawrence wrote his classic short story "The Prussian Officer": a story in which Lawrence delineates the relation between "unwholesome" homosexuality and "extinction of all the purposive influences"—this "extinction" being tantamount to death. Surely it is no coincidence that "The Prussian Officer" is contemporaneous with Lawrence's review-essay on Thomas Mann's *Death in Venice*: both Lawrence texts make the connexion between homosexuality and "unwholesome" death.

In "The Prussian Officer" Lawrence memorably presents his two main characters: the orderly, Schoner, and "the Prussian officer," "Herr Hauptmann." Schoner is presented early on in the story as a Lawrentian heterosexual, who is on his way to attaining "peace and inner security" as a result of "vital love":

> The soldier [Schoner] had a sweetheart....The two walked together, rather silently. He went with her, not to talk, but to have his arm round her, and for the physical contact. This eased him,...; for he could rest with her held fast against his chest. And she, in some unspoken fashion, was there for him. They loved each other.

But Schoner, with his "vital love" for his "sweetheart" and his "physical contact" with her, is placed in definitive—and fatal—opposition to Herr Hauptmann, a (closet) homosexual whose only passion is his homosexual-sadistic feeling for Schoner; Herr Hauptmann the Captain has never enjoyed heterosexuality:

> He [the Captain] went away for some days with a woman.
> It was a mockery of pleasure. He simply did not want the woman. But he stayed on for his time. At the end of it, he came back in an agony of irritation, torment, and misery.

The only pleasure the Captain gets is from torturing Schoner; he is full of "unwholesome" passion for Schoner, unwholesome passion which Lawrence does not try to idealize or glamorize as Mann did in *Death in Venice*. Instead, Lawrence makes it clear that the Captain, who is "almost unliving" in his closet homosexuality, is incapable of appreciating the living heterosexuality and vital Lawrentian power of Schoner, who is (early in the story) "so free and self-contained" that he seems to be a true Lawrentian hero like Mellors in *Lady Chatterley's*

Lover; yet, instead of being influenced by Schoner's presence to follow the Lawrentian way of "vital love" and life-saving heterosexuality, the Captain is overwhelmed by sadistic and hateful lust for Schoner and his qualities:

> He [the Captain] did not choose to be touched into life by his servant....To see [Schoner's] young, brown, shapely peasants' hands grasp the loaf or the wine-bottle sent a flash of hate or of anger through the elder man's blood. It was...[Schoner's] blind, instinctive sureness of movement of an unhampered young animal that irritated the officer to such a degree.

Thus the Prussian officer, rather than "be touched into life"—the life of heterosexual Lawrentian joy—by the influence and example of Lawrentian Schoner, instead is overwhelmed by his "unwholesome" (repressed) homosexual attraction and passion—which lead (as Lawrence declares in his "homosexuality" and "greatness" letter) to "extinction"— that is, to death, for both the Prussian officer and the Lawrentian orderly Schoner.

But why does the Lawrentian Schoner have to die? The reason for this is that, alas, it turns out that Schoner is no Mellors: he lacks inner strength and secure being. When the Prussian officer first expresses his "unwholesome" passion for Schoner by violently staring at him, the young soldier is overwhelmed and afraid:

> Once, when a bottle of wine had gone over, and the red gushed out onto the table-cloth, the officer had started up with an oath, and his eyes, bluey like fire, had held those of the confused youth for a moment. It was a shock for the young soldier. He felt something sink deeper, deeper into his soul, where nothing had ever gone before. It left him rather blank and wondering. Some of his natural completeness in himself was gone, a little uneasiness took its place....
>
> Henceforward the orderly was afraid of really meeting his master.

Rather than stand up to the perverse, anti-Lawrentian Captain, Schoner is "confused," "blank and wondering," "uneasy," "afraid"; indeed, he has lost "[s]ome of his natural completeness in himself"—the "natural completeness" that had come from his Lawrentian contact with his sweetheart. As it turns out, Schoner does not possess enough "peace and inner security, no matter how many things go wrong" (as Lawrence phrases it in his letter of 7 July 1914 to Dunlop) to save himself in his encounter with the Captain; instead, Schoner too becomes emotionally involved:

> All his [Schoner's] instinct was to avoid personal contact, even definite hate. But in spite of himself the hate grew, responsive to the officer's passion.

"Responsive to the officer's passion," Schoner finally finds that even his Lawrentian sweetheart has become unimportant to him: after the Prussian officer gives Schoner a severe beating for being "insubordinate," Schoner is overwhelmed by the feeling that

> No one should ever know [what the Captain had done to him]. It was between him and the captain. There were only the two people in the world now—himself and the captain.

"There were only the two people in the world now—himself and the captain": thus Lawrence tells us that, for Schoner now, his Lawrentian "sweetheart" has ceased to exist: all his heart and soul, passion and thoughts, are devoted to the Prussian officer. Thus, at this turning point in "The Prussian Officer," the forces of heterosexuality represented by Schoner have indeed been contaminated and overwhelmed by the "unwholesome" homosexual force of the Prussian officer, thus causing the Lawrentian Schoner to forget his heterosexual life in favor of being "responsive to the officer's passion"—a "passion" which, Lawrence tells us, can only lead to "extinction of all the purposive influences" (D. H. Lawrence letter to Savage, 2 December 1913)—that is to say, death.

And so it goes in "The Prussian Officer." Forgetting Lawrentian Eros, Schoner is overcome by "unwholesome" Thanatotic feelings of "passion" for the Captain—"passion" which leads to the Captain's death; a death which is presented in sexual terms:

> all the force of his [Schoner's] blood exulting in his [hands'] thrust, he shoved back the head of the other man [the Prussian officer], till there was a little "cluck" and a crunching sensation....Heavy convulsions shook the body of the officer, frightening and horrifying the young soldier. Yet it pleased him too....It pleased him to keep his hands pressing back the [Captain's] chin,... to feel the hard twitchings of the prostrate body jerking his own whole frame, which was pressed down on it.

Thus Schoner brings about the "extinction" of the Captain; but for Schoner this is a Pyrrhic victory, for

> Here his own life also ended.

But why is it that "his own life also ended?" Why is it that Schoner's murder of the "homosexual" Captain cannot be considered a triumph of Lawrentian life over "homosexual" death? The reason for this is evident: it is that Schoner, in forgetting his sweetheart and becoming obsessed with the "homosexual" Captain, has himself become tainted by deathly homosexuality. Having lost his Lawrentian heterosexual identity, proven himself to be only a Lawrentian manqué, Schoner is overwhelmed by the deathly, "unwholesome," "homosexual" passion of the Captain; he fails to remain true to "the physical contact" with his "sweetheart," the contact of vital Lawrentian heterosexual love: instead he ultimately opts for the death-dealing, "unwholesome"-"homosexual" "physical contact" with the Captain.

It did not have to end that way; as Lawrence scholar Michael Black notes:

> the orderly [Schoner], who has a reason for killing the captain, has better reasons for not killing him; and nothing compels him to kill the captain with enjoyment. (Black, *D. H. Lawrence: The Early Fiction*, p. 223)

By having Schoner kill the Prussian officer "with enjoyment," Lawrence the prophet issues a prediction and a warning: the "unwholesome" male-male "physical contact" will lead only to death. (In "The Thorn in the Flesh," which Lawrence wrote contemporaneously with "The Prussian Officer," Lawrence has the Lawrentian soldier escape from the army into the arms of a Lawrentian woman with whom he has great "physical contact" and who finally rescues him.) Indeed, later events proved Lawrence to be totally right about the deathly nature of "unwholesome" "physical contact" between men: World War I broke out only a year after Lawrence wrote "The Prussian Officer."

In response to the war, Lawrence wrote "my book about Thomas Hardy":

> What a miserable world. What colossal idiocy, this war. Out of sheer rage I've begun my book about Thomas Hardy. It will be about anything but Thomas Hardy I am afraid....(D. H. Lawrence letter to J. B. Pinker, 5 September 1914)

Later Lawrence called his *Study of Thomas Hardy* "a sort of Confessions of my Heart" (D. H. Lawrence letter to Amy Lowell, 18 November 1914);

essentially what Lawrence here "confesses" (once again) is the importance of heterosexuality to him as man and artist:

> the first and chiefest factor [in "the struggle into being"] is the struggle into love and the struggle with love; *by love meaning the love of a man for a woman and a woman for a man.* The via media to being, for man or woman, is love, and love alone. (*Study of Thomas Hardy*, Chapter III; my italics)

Thus in *Study of Thomas Hardy*, Lawrence's definition of "love" is completely rooted in heterosexuality ("love meaning the love of a man for a woman and a woman for a man"); furthermore, according to Lawrence here, the only way ("via media") to achieve "being" is "love, and love alone"; and it is heterosexual "love" which Lawrence places in opposition to the sexually perverted "sensationalism" which (according to Lawrence) led to World War I:

> Where is...the origin of all the sex-perversion?...It lies in the heart of man....No wonder there is a war. No wonder there is a great waste and squandering of life....we go to war to show that we can throw our lives away. Indeed, they have become of so little value to us. We cannot live, we cannot *be*. Then...let us rush throwing our lives away. Then at any rate we shall have *a sensation*....(*Study of Thomas Hardy*, Chapter II; first italics Lawrence's; second italics mine)

While Europe in 1914 wallows in "sensationalism" as a result of its Thanatotic (Death Wish) impulse, Lawrence wishes to cure Europe of its longing for death, a longing rooted in Europe's boredom with its own "Conceit, conceit of self-preservation and of race-preservation, conceit!" (*Study of Thomas Hardy*, Chapter I): that is to say, Europe's own "rage of self-preservation" has led it to believe that "life is the great struggle for self-preservation, that this struggle for the means of life is the essence and whole of life. As if it [life] would be anything so futile" (*Study of Thomas Hardy*, Chapter I)—and this obsession with "self-preservation," Lawrence wisely tells us, this obsession is the result of "our own self-love and caution[,]...our own cowardice and sluggish greed of security and well-being" (*Hardy*, Chapter II)—part and parcel of the European failure of heterosexual courage—a failure of the heterosexual courage that is essential to the achievement of being: lacking this courage,

> We [i.e., Western civilization] cannot live, we cannot *be*....
> ...All that matters is that each human being shall *be* in his

> own fulness. If something obstruct us we break it or put it aside, as the shoots of the trees break even through the London pavements. That is, if life is strong enough in us. (*Study of Thomas Hardy*, Chapter II; italics Lawrence's)

But in Western civilization today, Lawrence tells us, "life is [*not*] strong enough in us"—so, instead of achieving "*be*[ing] in [our] own fulness,"

> we are glad to fight with [i.e., on the side of] death (*Hardy*, Chapter II)

—for "the war shows us how little, under all our carefulness, we count human life and human suffering, how little we value ourselves at bottom, how we hate our own security....we send ourselves to be killed and torn and tortured, we spread grief and desolation, and then, only then, we are somewhat satisfied. For have we not proved that we can transcend our own self-preservation, that we do not care so much for ourselves after all. Indeed, we almost hate ourselves" (*Study of Thomas Hardy*, Chapter II).

This European self-"hate" is based on the European "self-love and caution," the European "cowardice,"—the failure of European courage to accept the challenge to *be* through heterosexuality; because Europe is afraid to be, "We [i.e., Western civilization] can only *die*" (*Hardy*, Chapter II; italics mine).

Speaking of European "death," Eve Kosofsky Sedgwick ruefully remarks that

> From at least the biblical story of Sodom and Gomorrah, scenarios of same-sex desire have had a privileged...relation in Western culture to scenarios of both genocide and omnicide....[O]ne of the few areas of agreement among modern Marxist, Nazi, and liberal capitalist ideologies is that there is a peculiarly close...affinity between same-sex desire and some historical condition of moribundity...to which...whole civilizations are subject. (*Epistemology of the Closet*, pp. 127-128)

It was not long before Lawrence was face to face with "scenarios of same-sex desire" among the British elite; in November 1914 Lawrence was "just finishing a book [*Study of Thomas Hardy*], supposed to be on Thomas Hardy, but in reality a sort of Confessions of my Heart" (D. H. Lawrence letter to Amy Lowell, 18 November 1914)—and three months later Lawrence was meeting with that great closet homosexual E. M. Forster. As Forster's biographer P. N. Furbank explains:

> [At this time] Lawrence was in the process of systematizing his "philosophy." He had also...drawn up the constitution of his Utopia, Rananim, and was on the look-out for recruits (*E. M. Forster: A Life, Volume Two*, p. 5)

—and at first Lawrence thought that Forster might be one of these "recruits"; but it was not long before Lawrence realized that there was something "bodily" wrong with Forster:

> there never was a free soul in a chained body....The freedom of the soul within the denied body is a sheer conceit.
> Forster is not [financially] poor, but he is bound hand and foot bodily....
> But why can't he act? Why can't he take a woman and fight clear to his own basic, primal being? (D. H. Lawrence letter to Bertrand Russell, 12 February 1915)

Only weeks earlier, Lawrence in his *Study of Thomas Hardy* had categorically declared that male-female interaction is indeed responsible for all creation and being:

> In life...no new thing has ever arisen, or can arise, save out of the impulse of the male upon the female, the female upon the male. The interaction of the male and female spirit begot the wheel, the plough, and the first utterance that was made on the face of the earth. (*Study of Thomas Hardy*, Chapter VII)

In *Study of Thomas Hardy* Lawrence makes it clear that for him the *only* sexuality is heterosexuality:

> normally, the centre, the turning pivot of a man's life is his sex life, the centre and swivel of his being is the sexual act. Upon this turns the whole rest of his life, from this emanates every motion he betrays. And that this should be so, every man makes his effort....The supreme desire of *every man* is for mating with a woman, such that the sexual act be the closest, most concentrated motion in his life,...the prime movement of himself....(*Study of Thomas Hardy*, Chapter VII, "Of Being and Not-Being"; italics mine)

Thus Forster, who cannot "take a woman and fight clear to his own basic, primal being," is certainly inadequate and inappropriate according to Lawrentian standards. Thus for Lawrence, Forster, in completely failing to "take a woman and fight clear to his own basic, primal being," is a dreadful disappointment, yet at the same time Forster's failure gives Lawrence reason to rejoice in his (Lawrence's) own vital-sexual superiority; for, as one scholar of Lawrence and Forster notes of Forster at this time (1915):

> Forster himself [in 1915] had achieved [sexual—i.e., homosexual] fulfillment only in [his] imagination; for a man of thirty-five his actual experience of sex was pathetically meager. (Paul Delany, *D. H. Lawrence's Nightmare: The Writer and His Circle in the Years of the Great War*, p. 54)

Indeed, Lawrence surely felt superior to the (closet) homosexual Forster, whom Lawrence intuited to be totally incapable of meeting the heterosexual challenge: Lawrence's question, "Why can't he [Forster] take a woman and fight clear to his own basic, primal being?" is essentially rhetorical: the answer of course is that the closet homosexual Forster is deficient in life-vitality and is utterly inferior to the heterosexual prophet D. H. Lawrence, who in his first long letter to Forster (28 January 1915) went so far as to brag that

> I do feel every man must have the devil of a struggle before he can have stuffed himself full enough to have satisfied all his immediate needs, and can...yield himself up to his metamorphosis, his crucifixion, and so come to his new issuing, his wings, his resurrection, his whole flesh shining like a mote in the sunshine, fulfilled....
>
> ...perhaps my own resurrection is too new, one must feel if the scars are not there, and wince—and one must see the other people all writhing and struggling and unable to [be resurrected]. (D. H. Lawrence letter to E. M. Forster, 28 January 1915)

Thus Lawrence sees himself as "resurrected"—and alone in his resurrection, for the rest of Western civilization ("the other people all writhing and struggling and unable . . .") is engaged in "sensationalism"—as he tells Bertrand Russell:

> That is sensationalism—that I go to a woman to feel myself only. Love is, that I go to a woman to know myself, and knowing myself, to go further, to explore in to the unknown, which is the woman, venture in upon the coasts of the unknown, and open my discovery to all humanity. But if I know that humanity is lame and cannot move,...my offering it discoveries is only a cynicism. (D. H. Lawrence letter to Bertrand Russell, 12 February 1915)

Thus the "resurrected" Lawrence sees himself as superior to "lame" Western civilization, which is incapable of appreciating his supreme heterosexual "discoveries" resulting from his "explor[ing] in to the unknown, which is the woman"; "lame" humanity prefers to engage in "sensationalism":

> The repeating of a *known* reaction upon myself is sensationalism [my italics]. This is what nearly *all* English people now do [italics Lawrence's]. When a man takes a woman, he is *merely* repeating a known reaction upon himself, not seeking a new reaction, a discovery [italics Lawrence's]. And this is like self-abuse or masterbation. The *ordinary* Englishman of the educated class goes to a woman now to masterbate himself [my italics]. Because he is not going for discovery or new connection or progression, but only to repeat upon himself a known reaction. (D. H. Lawrence to Russell, 12 February 1915)

This Lawrentian definition of the "sensationalism" of "ordinary" heterosexuality in which the "[sexual] reaction" is always "a known reaction," makes "ordinary" heterosexuality sound a lot like homosexuality; as one moral philosopher of "the erotic" explains:

> The homosexual unites with an individual who does not lie beyond the divide which separates the world of men from the world of women. Hence the homosexual has a peculiar inward *familiarity* [my italics] with what his partner feels. His discovery of his partner's sexual nature is the discovery of *what he knows* [italics mine]. (Roger Scruton, *Sexual Desire: A Moral Philosophy of the Erotic*, p. 283)

This "familiarity," this "known" quality, is a major characteristic of both homosexuality and "ordinary" heterosexuality according to Lawrence—indeed, Lawrence maintains that this "known reaction" kind of "ordinary" heterosexuality inevitably leads to "Sodomy":

> When this condition [of "ordinary" heterosexuality] arrives, there is always Sodomy. The man goes to the man to repeat this ["known"] reaction upon himself. It is a nearer form of masterbation. But still it has some *object*—there are still two bodies instead of one. A man of strong soul has too much honour for the other body—man or woman—to use it as a means of masterbation. So he remains neutral, inactive. That is Forster. (D. H. Lawrence letter to Bertrand Russell, 12 February 1915)

Thus the Lawrentian definition of homosexuality ("Sodomy") here is that it (homosexuality) is "a nearer [i.e., closer] form of masterbation" than the "ordinary" heterosexuality that Lawrence decries as well: both homosexuality and "ordinary" heterosexuality are against "discovery or new connection or progression": thus for Lawrence they are both undesirable and reprehensible. Lawrence wants "the unknown," the exploration of the unknown, as embodied in woman:

> Any man who takes a woman is up against the unknown. (D. H. Lawrence letter to Bertrand Russell, 12 February 1915)

Lawrence finds himself to be uniquely capable of "tak[ing] a woman [and being] up against the unknown"; indeed, he seems rather condescending when he praises Forster merely for being "neutral, inactive,"—for refraining from "sodomy" and "masterbation." Perceiving Forster to be sexually "inactive," Lawrence could feel comfortably superior to him: "I liked him [Forster], but his life is so ridiculously inane, the man is *dying* of inanition" (D. H. Lawrence letter to Mary Cannan, 24 February 1915; italics mine): the "inanition" of (closet) homosexuality.

While the closet homosexual Forster is "dying of inanition," Lawrence the vigorous prophet of heterosexual love feels at this time that he is at his peak: on the same day that Lawrence dismisses Forster as "dying of inanition" (24 February 1915), Lawrence authoritatively declares to Bertrand Russell that

> the great *living* experience for every man is his adventure into the woman....*The man embraces in the woman all that is not himself*, and from that one resultant, from that embrace, comes every new action. (D. H. Lawrence letter to Bertrand Russell, 24 February 1915; italics mine)

Thus here Lawrence is boldly (and perhaps naively) making Lawrentian (anti-"ordinary") heterosexuality the prerequisite and basis for sociopolitical efficacy: for Lawrence makes it clear that the "new action" he is speaking of is "a revolution of society," "a new movement, a new combination," "a campaign for this freer life" (D. H. Lawrence letter to Bertrand Russell, 24 February 1915; D. H. Lawrence letter to Mary Cannan, 24 February 1915). Surely at this time Lawrence's optimism and self-confidence were at their peak; in the same letter to Mary Cannan (24 February 1915) in which he dismisses Forster as "ridiculously inane," Lawrence proudly announces that

> We must form a revolutionary party. I have talked about it with various people—also Bertrand Russell. I am going to stay with him in Cambridge, March 6th-8th. Then we shall go into it more thoroughly....We must create an idea of a new, freer life, where men and women can really meet on *natural* terms....(24 February 1915; italics mine)

Hoping to secure some sort of political power base at Cambridge in March, Lawrence looked forward to the success of his "revolution"—as well as of his new novel *The Rainbow*, which he finished right before his fateful Cambridge visit; clearly Lawrence felt that the "revolutionary" power of his great new novel *The Rainbow* entitled him to "revolutionary" political power as well:

> I have finished my *Rainbow*, bended it and set it firm. Now off and away to find the pots of gold at its feet....
> ...I am *frightfully excited* over this novel now it is done.
> I am going to begin a book about Life—more rainbows, but in different skies—...my initiation of the great and happy revolution. (D. H. Lawrence letter to Viola Meynell, 2 March 1915)

Indeed, at this point in his life Lawrence is actually "happy":

> I have finished my novel so am very glad. I am also very excited about my novel. I feel like a bird in spring that is amazed at the colours of its own coat.
> Also, I feel very profound about my book....It is my revolutionary utterance. I take on a very important attitude of profundity to it, and so feel happy.
> Also I feel frightfully important coming to Cambridge—quite momentous the occasion is to me....I only care about the revolution we shall have. (D. H. Lawrence letter to Bertrand Russell, 2 March 1915)

The Lawrentian "revolution" is to be "great and happy"; its aspiration is to achieve "a new, freer life" based on the "natural" meeting of man and woman. Indeed, Lawrence's pride in his "natural" "revolution" through vital heterosexuality was so great that his own wife Frieda accused him of being conceited:

> I want...instant social revolution....
> ...I know that *I* am the English nation—that *I* am the European race....L'Etat c'est moi....La race c'*est* moi—La race humaine, c'est *moi*....
> Frieda says I am vain—but it isn't true....
> I can see nothing to begin on, but a social revolution. For I write my novels, and I write my book of philosophy, and I must also see the social revolution set going. (D. H. Lawrence letter to Gordon Campbell, 3 March 1915)

But Lawrence soon received a rude awakening from his dream of a "natural" "social revolution" for "the English nation," "the European race" of which he believed himself to be the supreme representative—a "natural" revolution rooted in Lawrentian vital heterosexuality. Instead of "natural" heterosexuality at Cambridge, Lawerence found there a left-wing homosexual elite headed by John Maynard Keynes, "the foremost economist of the twentieth century" (Chura, "Bloomsbury: A Gay Perspective," *Gay Roots*, p. 346). Thus at Cambridge Lawrence to his horror witnessed linkage between homosexuality—the antithesis of Lawrentian heterosexual salvation—and socioeconomic power. "I went to Cambridge and hated it beyond expression," Lawrence bitterly concluded (D. H. Lawrence letter to Barbara Low, 10 March 1915).

Lawrence's ineffable hatred for Cambridge went hand in hand with severe depression:

> Cambridge made me very black and down. I cannot bear its smell of rottenness, marsh-stagnancy. I get a melancholic malaria. How can so sick people rise up? They must die first. (D. H. Lawrence letter to Bertrand Russell, 19 March 1915)

Lawrence was "very black and down" from his realization at Cambridge that the people he had been counting on for his "natural" "revolution" were themselves essentially "unnatural," and "so sick" in their blatant homosexuality that they made D. H. Lawrence, the prophet of heterosexual salvation, feel

> too sad to write my "philosophy" (forgive the word) any more. I can't write it when I am depressed or hopeless. (D. H. Lawrence letter to Bertrand Russell, 19 March 1915)

"Depressed" and "hopeless" due to his meeting with the elite Cambridge homosexuals, Lawrence at this point believed that these "sick people"—supposedly the best and brightest of British civilization—would have to psychosexually-ontologically "die first"—and be "resurrected"—if Western civilization was to have any hope of survival. The psychosexual-ontological "resurrection" would, of course, have to be a Lawrentian one, based on the Lawrentian faith in creative, vital heterosexuality—a faith that Lawrence even now would not abandon:

> But it comes back all right, the philosophy and the belief. God help us, and give us endurance. (D. H. Lawrence letter to Bertrand Russell, 19 March 1915)

For Lawrence in 1915, his "philosophy" and "belief" of vital heterosexuality were all that stood against the homosexual "evil" he saw at Cambridge—"evil" which depressed him throughout the month of March:

> I get depressed by the sense of evil in the world. (D. H. Lawrence letter to Koteliansky, 24 March 1915)

Lawrence, "depressed by the sense of evil in the world," rejected the urbane tolerance of his friends in the liberal elite such as Lady Ottoline Morrell; in matters of the life and death of Western civilization, Lawrence felt that he could not afford to be tolerant:

> The feeling that comes out of your letter is like a scent of flowers, so generous and reassuring. It is no good now, thinking that to understand a man from his own point of view is to be happy about him. I can imagine the mind of a rat, as it slithers along in the dark, pointing its sharp nose. But I can never feel happy about it, I must always want to kill it. It contains a principle of evil. There *is* a principle of evil. Let us acknowledge it once and for all. I saw it so plainly in Keynes at Cambridge, it made me sick. I am sick with the knowledge of the prevalence of evil, as if it were some insidious disease. (D. H. Lawrence letter to Lady Ottoline Morrell, 24 March 1915)

Rejecting the liberal bromide that "to understand a man from his own point of view is to be happy about him," Lawrence concludes that he cannot "be happy about" unmitigated homosexuals such as John Maynard Keynes and his friends at Cambridge who, instead of being the source of hope for the future of England and the West, were full of the "principle of evil," and in their elite power manifested to Lawrence "the prevalence of evil"—"evil," which in the Lawrentian definition, is "anti-life":

> The real principle of Evil is not anti-Christ or anti-Jehovah, but anti-life. (D. H. Lawrence letter to Else Jaffe, 12 June 1929)

For Lawrence, "evil" homosexuality was "anti-life"—and the homosexuality of the Cambridge-Bloomsbury group was as "anti-life" as the First World War. Indeed, the "anti-life" "evil" of the elite homosexual Cambridge-Bloomsbury group made Lawrence feel extremely frustrated and angry as he sensed that without any political power base his Messianic dreams were doomed to failure; consequently he fell prey to fantasies of violence:

> Sometimes I wish I could let go, and be really wicked—kill and murder—but kill chiefly. I do want to kill. But I want to select whom I shall kill. Then I shall enjoy it. The war is no good. It is this black desire [to kill and murder] I have become conscious of. We cant so much about goodness—it is canting. Tell [Bertrand]

> Russell he does the same—let him recognise the powerful malignant will in him. This is the very worst wickedness, that we refuse to acknowledge the passionate evil that is in us. This makes us secret and rotten. (D. H. Lawrence letter to Lady Ottoline Morrell, 8 April 1915)

At this point Lawrence felt that his very poetic identity as "the priest of love" was direly threatened both by the war and the homosexual Cambridge-Bloomsbury intelligentsia. Indeed, he had at this point the temptation (in his imagination) to kill them: "this black desire I have become conscious of" that Lawrence has is of course not homosexual—it is homicidal. Indeed, the fact is that at this point Lawrence's greatest passion was beyond the sexual—it was the passion for poetic immortality as the poet-prophet of heterosexual love; and, as a threat to Lawrence's attainment of poetic immortality via the theme of valorized vital heterosexuality, the homosexual Cambridge-Bloomsbury set and its influence had to be eliminated—in Lawrence's creative imagination as "The Priest of Love," at least. Indeed, Lawrence's hatred of the homosexual threat to his greatness led him again intensely to question the liberal-philanthropic pieties of his friend Lady Ottoline Morrell:

> I believe you, that love is all. But it is not easy. If I love a man, and a dog bites him, I must hate the dog. But if I must love the dog? And if I love my fellow-men, how must I feel, say, about [the homosexuality of] Cambridge? Must I take hope and faith? [Lawrence asks with bitter sarcasm.] But if I have a toothache I don't depend on hope nor faith nor love, but on surgery. And surgery is pure hate of the defect in the loved thing. And it is surgery we want, Cambridge wants, England wants, I want. (D. H. Lawrence letter to Lady Ottoline Morrell, 15 April 1915)

Full of hate for the Cambridge homosexuals who had frustrated his plans for sociopolitical-philosophical greatness and power, "Messianic" power, Lawrence at first feels guilty about his "pure hate"—he wants at first to be cured of his misanthropy by "surgery"—but before long he accepts and understands his unmitigated hate:

> To hear these young [homosexual] people talking really fills me with black fury: they talk endlessly, but endlessly—and never, never a good or a real thing said. Their attitude is so irreverent and blatant. They are cased each in a hard little shell of his own and out of this they talk words. There is never for one second any outgoing of feeling, and no reverence—not a crumb or grain of reverence. I cannot stand it. I *will not* have people like this—I had rather

> be alone. They [the young homosexuals] made me dream in the night of a beetle that bites like a scorpion. But I killed it—a very large beetle. I scotched it—and it ran off—but I came upon it again and killed it. It is this horror of little swarming selves that I can't stand: Birrells, D. Grants, and Keynses [all homosexuals]....(D.H. Lawrence letter to Lady Ottoline Morrell, 19 April 1915)

These young homosexuals, lacking in the "good" and the "real," lacking reverence for the natural ("so irreverent"), full of narcissistic character armor ("cased each in a hard little shell of his own"), are Lawrence's bêtes noires—they have "no reverence—not a crumb or grain of reverence" for the Lawrentian heterosexual salvation over which Lawrence was so enthusiastic. In his extreme aversion to these young homosexuals that were antithetical to Lawrence's poetic strength as poet-prophet of heterosexuality, Lawrence realized that he would rather do without human society entirely than deal with the young homosexual intelligentsia: "I cannot stand it. I *will not* have people like this—I had rather be alone"—and in his intense desire to "be alone," Lawrence here manifests the "triumphant solipsism" of the supremely strong poet; as Harold Bloom authoritatively states,

> Poetic strength comes only from a triumphant wrestling with the greatest of the dead, and from an even more triumphant solipsism.
> (*Map of Misreading*, p. 9)

At this time (1915) Lawrence had already begun his agon ("triumphant wrestling") with "the greatest of the dead," the philosopher-poet Plato among them (see Scherr 1996); but in pitting himself against the homosexual elite society of his day Lawrence further assures his "poetic strength," his uniqueness as he presents himself triumphantly alone ("triumphant solipsism") as the sole defender of heterosexuality in an "irreverent," talky, pseudo-intellectual elite society of homosexuals ("they talk endlessly, but...never a good or a real thing said"). As the great intellectual-philosopher-poet defending heterosexuality, Lawrence conceives himself to be uniquely qualified to fight the homosexual "beetle-scorpion"; indeed, Lawrence's "scorpion" dream ("They [the homosexuals] made me dream in the night of a beetle that bites like a scorpion. But I killed it") is surely an unconscious reference to his early days of passionately heterosexual love with Frieda, when he did indeed kill a scorpion: in a letter of 15 October 1912, written from romantic Italy, Lawrence tells his friend Edward Garnett that

> We [Lawrence and Frieda] found a scorpion in the spittoon—I don't know *why* we have a spittoon—it stands on F's side of the bed, because she smokes. We found a scorpion in the spittoon. F. fled for her life and I tackled the beast with a toothbrush. Instead of calling me St. Lawrence or St. George, she said it had come because birds of a feather flock together. As if I could bite with my tail [here "tail" is slang for penis]. (15 October 1912)

Rescuing Frieda from a scorpion, young "priest of love" Lawrence in 1912 proudly refers to his "tail" (i.e., penis) and already conceives himself to be "St. Lawrence or St. George"—a "saintly" defender of sacred heterosexuality; and in 1915 Lawrence surely persists in his "saintly," Messianic impulse—he will not be deterred or dismayed by the homosexual elite; instead he will fight for the souls of such young men as (the bisexual) David Garnett, son of Lawrence's friend Edward Garnett:

> I like David Garnett—but there is something wrong with him. Is he also [homosexual] like Keynes and [his lover] Grant. It is enough to drive one frantic....Sometimes I think I can't stand this England any more: it is too wicked and perverse. (D. H. Lawrence letter to Lady Ottoline Morrell, 19 April 1915)

But Lawrence as heterosexual messiah and supremely strong poet decides against despair and surrender to the "wicked and perverse" homosexual elite:

> But we must fight this Baal [of homosexuality], and keep the other flag [i.e., of heterosexuality] flying. Dear Lady Ottoline, remember we must stick together. It really seems to me a matter of life and death....(19 April 1915)

"A matter of life and death": this is how Lawrence felt about the homosexual threat not only to the "life" of Western civilization, but also of course to the "life" of Lawrence the supremely strong poet aspiring to "poetic immortality" through his treatment of the motif of vital male-female relationships; fighting "Baal," the false god of homosexuality amongst the Cambridge-Bloomsbury elite, Lawrence sees himself alone "flying" "the other flag" of "living," "religious" heterosexuality. Indeed, Lawrence sees no alternative—his very poetic life, he believes, depends on the maintenance and promotion of vital Lawrentian heterosexuality and its defense against the homosexual onslaught.

Accordingly, when Lawrence intuitively sensed that "there is something wrong with" David Garnett (Garnett was in fact homosexually involved with Keynes' lover Duncan Grant; see Angelica Garnett, *Deceived with Kindness: A Story of Bloomsbury*), Lawrence felt compelled to dissuade David Garnett from his "wicked and perverse" ways (even though David Garnett did not admit to homosexual affairs); thus the "frantic" Lawrence "priest of [heterosexual] love" desperately warns David Garnett to mend his "wicked" (bisexual) ways:

> I can't bear to think of you, David, so wretched as you are—and your hand shaky—and everything wrong. It is foolish of you to say that it doesn't matter either way—the men loving men. It doesn't matter in the public way. But it matters so much, David, to the man himself—at any rate to us northern nations—that it is like a blow of triumphant decay, when I meet [David Garnett's homosexual friend] Birrell or the others. (D. H. Lawrence letter to David Garnett, 19 April 1915)

Believing young Garnett to be "wretched" and "shaky" and "wrong" because of his bisexuality, Lawrence desperately wants to save the "foolish" David Garnett from his proclivity for "the men loving men." Lawrence recognizes the social power of the homosexual Cambridge-Bloomsbury elite—he knows that "in the public way" they have not been hurt by their homosexuality; but the British Romantic Lawrence knows that the inner self—"the [inner] man himself"—suffers irreparable damage to his being as a result of "the men loving men"; indeed, this ontological damage is so great that it is tantamount to "triumphant decay"—the triumph of decadent homosexuality over Lawrentian heterosexual salvation. Lawrence the prophet of heterosexual love, like Elijah the prophet of the Lord God against Baal and his priests, feels a visceral revulsion towards his "wicked" opponents,—in this case the homosexuals John Maynard Keynes, Francis Birrell, and Duncan Grant:

> I simply can't bear it [to meet the "triumphantly decadent" homosexuals]. It [homosexuality] is so wrong, it is unbearable. It [homosexuality] makes a form of inward corruption which truly *makes me scarce able to live*. Why is there this horrible sense of frowstiness, so repulsive, as if it came from deep inward dirt—a sort of sewer—deep in men like K[eynes] and B[irrell] and D[uncan] G[rant]. It is something almost unbearable to me (D. H. Lawrence letter to David Garnett, 19 April 1915; italics mine)

—"unbearable" to Lawrence precisely because "It [homosexuality]...makes me scarce able to live"—"to live" as a man and—even more important—as a supremely strong poet of heterosexuality: for Lawrence knew that his achievement of "poetic immortality" would be placed in jeopardy by the hegemony of "the men loving men"; thus the practitioners of "it" (i.e., homosexuality) are "horrible" and "repulsive" and "almost unbearable" to Lawrence: "horrible" and "repulsive" for they (the homosexuals) are antithetical to his goals and aspirations as immortal poet-prophet of vital heterosexuality; "almost unbearable" because he does not know if he can deploy a strategy to defeat their oppositional mode of being. Indeed, Lawrence makes it clear that his aversion to homosexuality is not simplistically moralistic or puritanical or prudish:

> [Homosexuality] is something almost unbearable to me. And not from any moral disapprobation. I myself never considered Plato very wrong, or Oscar Wilde. I never knew what it [homosexuality] meant till I saw K[eynes], till I saw him at Cambridge. We went into his rooms at midday, and it was very sunny. He was not there, so [Bertrand] Russell was writing a note. Then suddenly a door opened and K[eynes] was there, blinking from sleep, standing in his pyjamas. And as he stood there gradually a knowledge passed into me, which has been like a little madness to me ever since. And it was carried along with the most dreadful sense of repulsiveness—something like carrion—a vulture gives me the same feeling. I begin to feel mad as I think of it—insane. (D. H. Lawrence letter to David Garnett, 19 April 1915)

Here Lawrence makes it clear that he does not distinguish between the austere, philosophical homosexuality of Plato and the flamboyant, dandyish homosexuality of Oscar Wilde; thus Paul Delany is wrong when he asserts that Lawrence "felt a violent repugnance for the particular style of upper-class homosexuality he encountered at Cambridge and in Bloomsbury" (Delany, *D. H. Lawrence's Nightmare*, p. 88); for the fact is that all modes of homosexuality are "almost unbearable" to Lawrence, "not from any moral disapprobation"—that is to say, not from any kind of high Victorian "moral scheme" which Lawrence hated (D. H. Lawrence letter to Edward Garnett, 5 June 1914)—but from Lawrence's sense of his own unique Lawrentian morality, which defined Evil as that which is "anti-life": thus, by connecting homosexuality (as personified by Keynes in pyjamas at Cambridge) with "carrion" and "a vulture," Lawrence lucidly delineates his conception of homosexuality as evil because it is tantamount to dead flesh ("carrion") and feeding on death (as does "a vulture"). Furthermore, of course Lawrence at this point as the "priest of [heterosexual] love" could say of homosexuality, as Keats did of Milton, "Life to him would be Death to me" (quoted in Bloom, *Anxiety of Influence*, p. 32): that is to say, the predominance of homosexuality in his civilization would make it impossible for Lawrence to attain poetic immortality. Thus, seeing his battle against homosexuality as "a matter of life and death" for himself as a supremely strong poet, Lawrence feels "mad" and "insane" in his desperation to turn the tide against the homosexuals. Consequently he severely reproves David Garnett, whom he wishes to save from a life of "men loving men":

> Never bring [David Garnett's homosexual friend] B[irrell] to see me any more. There is something nasty about him, like black-beetles [who eat carrion]. He is horrible and unclean. I feel as if I should go mad, if I think of your set, D. G. and K. and B....Somehow, I can't bear it. It is wrong beyond all bounds of wrongness....(19 April 1915)

Assuming a rather peremptory tone with young Garnett, Lawrence here becomes rather patriarchal in his expostulations, invoking the elder Garnett in an attempt to persuade David to reject his "friends" and their "repulsive" ways:

> David, my dear, I love your father and I love your mother....And I feel, because I love your father, that you must leave these 'friends', these beetles. You must wrench away [from homosexuality] and start a new life....you can be all right. You can come away, and grow whole, and love a woman, and marry her, and make life good, and be happy.

Like an Old Testament prophet (i.e., Elijah), Lawrence encourages David Garnett to leave "the false god" ("Baal") of elite homosexuality and make an effort to "start a new life...[and] be all right" with "the true god" of Lawrentian vital heterosexuality, which involves "grow[ing] whole," "lov[ing] a woman," "marry[ing] her," "mak[ing] life good," and "be[ing] happy"; in opposition to the Lawrentian way of wholeness and happiness through heterosexuality is the "blasphemy against love" (i.e., homosexuality) practised by David Garnett and his "friends":

> Now David, in the name of everything that is called love, leave this [homosexual] set and stop this blasphemy against love. (19 April 1915)

Once again Lawrence explains that his hatred of homosexuality is not based on provincial or prudish Victorian morality:

> It isn't that I speak from a moral code. Truly I didn't know it [homosexuality] was wrong, till I saw K. that morning in Cambridge. It was one of the crises in my life. It sent me mad with misery and hostility and rage (19 April 1915)

—"mad with misery and hostility and rage" at the fact that such important and powerful members of the British intelligentsia were practising homosexuals. Conceiving himself to be fighting the homosexual elite for the soul of young David Garnett, Lawrence makes a final desperate appeal to him:

> Go away, David, and try to love a woman. (19 April 1915)

But, fearing that young David Garnett (he was 23 years old) will be intimidated and irritated by his insistence on love and marriage, Lawrence offers him another option in opposition to homosexuality:

> Go right away and be alone and work, and come to your real self. But do leave this group of 'friends'....Do go right away, right away, and be by yourself. (19 April 1915)

To "be by [my]self" is certainly what Lawrence wants for himself at this time; for of course he would rather be alone than surrounded by homosexuals:

> These horrible little frowsty people, men lovers of men, they give me such a sense of corruption, almost putrescence....It is abominable. To escape from visitors, I must go to Italy again. (D. H. Lawrence letter to S. S. Koteliansky, 20 April 1915)

But Lawrence didn't leave; for he knew that he was needed:

> One must speak for life and growth, amid all this mass of destruction and disintegration. (D. H. Lawrence letter to Harriet Monroe, 15 September 1915)

One way in which Lawrence was "speak[ing] for life and growth," he believed, was by developing a strategy to deal with homosexuality.

In his fight for "life and growth," Lawrence finds homosexual E. M. Forster to be "dead":

> It is a great struggle now, whether the whole tree of life dies now, in Europe, and crumbles down to dust....[T]hat is the most wretched form of undying death. One must try to save the quick, to send up the new shoots of a new era: a great, utter revolution, and the dawn of a new historical epoch: either that, or the vast amorphous dust.—I can make nothing of the men, they are all

without involving the male members of the species. Furthermore, Lawrence in his vision of "the world that is to be,...the new life that shall be," feels that it is extremely necessary to possess

> endless courage to reject false dead things and false, killing processes (DHL letter to Ottoline Morrell, 12 December 1915)

One of the "false, killing processes" that Lawrence was concerned with at this time was homosexuality; we know that in February 1916, Lawrence wrote "Goats and Compasses," another work of "my philosophy"—and apparently one of its major subjects was homosexuality (the manuscript of "Goats and Compasses" has not survived; see Delany, *D. H. Lawrence's Nightmare*, p. 197). According to Lawrence's erstwhile friend Cecil Gray, writing some twenty years after the event, "Goats and Compasses" dealt at length with homosexuality:

> It ["Goats and Compasses"] struck me, even at that time [1916] when I was under the spell of [Lawrence] the prophet, as being Lawrence at his very worst: a bombastic, pseudo-mystical, psycho-philosophical treatise dealing largely with homosexuality—a subject, by the way, in which Lawrence displayed a suspiciously lively interest at that time. (Cecil Gray, quoted in Delany, *D. H. Lawrence's Nightmare*, p. 198)

But, if Lawrence in "Goats and Compasses" did indeed deal with homosexuality, he dealt with it as its antagonist—an antagonist whose weapon is heterosexual love; as Lady Ottoline tells us in her diary:

> It ["Goats and Compasses"] seems to me deplorable tosh....A gospel of hate and violent individualism. He [Lawrence] attacks the will, love and sympathy. Indeed, the only thing that he [Lawrence] doesn't revile and condemn is love between men and women. (Quoted in Delany, *D. H. Lawrence's Nightmare*, p. 197)

Thus, by putting together the information provided by Ottoline Morrell and Cecil Gray, we can see that at the time of "Goats and Compasses" (early 1916) Lawrence's major concerns included "homosexuality," "individualism," and "love between men and women." The manuscript of "Goats and Compasses" is gone; but, a few months before writing "Goats and Compasses," Lawrence wrote "The Crown"; and here we can find some of Lawrence's insights about "homosexuality" at this time. Clearly thinking of E. M. Forster and other Cambridge-Bloomsbury intellectual-homosexuals, Lawrence writes of the "sensitive man" who is homosexual; this "sensitive man," while of course incapable of attaining the salubrious Lawrentian relation with woman, is at the same time "too subtle" to use the woman as a tool with which to "obtain the prime gratification of reduction in physical connection":

> It is only coarse, insensitive men who can obtain the prime gratification of reduction in physical connection with a woman. A sensitive man is too subtle, he cannot come like a perverse animal, straight to the reduction of the self in the sex. Many many processes intervene. There are all the complexities of the mind and the consciousness to reduce first....
>
> The sensitive man, caught within the flux of reduction, seeking a woman, knows the destruction of some basic self in him, while the complexity and unity of his consciousness remains intact above the reduction. Which gives him jangled horror. He is too conscious, too complete. Instead of obtaining the gratification of reduction, he has got only a wound in his unified soul, a sort of maiming. He is horrified at his own mangled, maimed condition, of which he is painfully aware in his complete consciousness. So that a woman becomes repulsive to him, in the thought of connection with her. It is too gross, almost horrible. (*Reflections on the Death of a Porcupine*, p. 472)

The "sensitive man," says Lawrence, needs to reduce "all the complexities of the mind and the consciousness" before he can "obtain the prime gratification of reduction"—a "gratification" which is anathema to Lawrence here; furthermore, "the sensitive man" in his hyper-intellectuality finds he is "too conscious," "too complete" in his "mental consciousness" to succeed in "obtaining the gratification of reduction with a woman": trapped in "the flux of reduction" which (according to Lawrence in "The Crown" in 1915) is the ontological reality for virtually all men of the modern Western world in general and the world of the Great War in particular, "the sensitive man" seeks total self-reduction, complete psychic-ontological disintegration: in sexual relation with a woman, the excessively "mental" conscious "sensitive man" experiences merely "the destruction of *some* [i.e., not all] basic self in him"—this partial self-destruction is not complete enough—it does not produce "the jouissance of self-loss" (to use a term from gay theory; see Bersani, *Homos*, p. 96) that the "sensitive" cerebral homosexual is seeking, for "the complexity and unity of his consciousness remains intact above the [partial] reduction" of self that he can experience with the woman. Being "too conscious, too complete [in mental-consciousness]," the "sensitive man" receives no "jouissance" from sex relation with the woman; this partial loss of self, this incomplete self-disintegration, provides no "gratification of reduction" but "only a [psychic] wound": this "wound in [the "sensitive" man's] unified soul" is a psychic-ontological "maiming" which is mentally painful for the hyper-cerebral sensitive man "in his complete consciousness." Associating woman with his psychic pain resulting from his failure to obtain "the gratification of reduction," the "sensitive man"—who is incapable of Lawrentian desire for woman in the first place—now finds "woman [to be] repulsive to him, in the thought of [sexual] connection with her." Here Lawrence, telling us that the "sensitive man" finds even "the thought of [sexual] connection with [woman]" to be "too gross, almost horrible," is obliquely expressing his contempt for and opposition to "sensitive" men of the Cambridge-Bloomsbury-E. M. Forster ilk, who, for all their intellectual sophistication, were exceedingly immature in psychosexual matters; as Paul Delany notes:

> the emotional atmosphere he [Lawrence] encountered at Cambridge ranged from the celibate to the frankly homoerotic. [G. E.] Moore married late, and [G. H.] Hardy never; Moore's ethics...were held by his disciples to be consistent with homosexuality. Another leading figure at Cambridge, included in Russell's list of "contacts" for Lawrence, was the political scientist Goldsworthy Lowes Dickinson, who in 1915 was already planning a postwar league of nations. Dickinson's tender feelings were mainly directed toward young men; following Plato, he held that love between persons of the same sex was a higher, because more disinterested, relationship than marriage. He disliked having female students at his lectures, remarking, with what passed for wit in donnish circles, that he could never tell them apart because they all resembled cows. (*D. H. Lawrence's Nightmare*, p. 79)

Lytton Strachey, one of the major gay Bloomsburies, met Lawrence once (in November 1915) at a party in London and observed that

> He [Lawrence] behaved to everyone with the greatest cordiality, but I noticed for a second a look of intense disgust and hatred flash into his face...caused by [Lytton Strachey]....(Lytton Strachey, letter to David Garnett, 10 November 1915, in Michael Holroyd, *Lytton Strachey: The New Biography* [New York, 1995], p.334)

Strachey's biographer Holroyd remarks that

> What caused Lawrence this intense disgust on seeing Lytton [in November 1915]...was the Bloomsbury cult of "higher sodomy." (ibid.)

The cult of "higher sodomy" had been celebrated by Strachey as early as 1906, when Strachey told fellow homosexual John Maynard Keynes that

> we must tell the whole truth; and the whole truth is the Devil....It's madness of us to dream of making dowagers understand that feelings are good, when we say in the same breath that the best ones are sodomitical. If we were crafty and careful, I dare say we'd pull it off. But why should we take the trouble? On the whole I believe that our time will come about a hundred years hence, when preparations will have been made, and compromises come to, so that, at the publication of our letters, everyone will be, finally, *converted* (Lytton Strachey letter to John Maynard Keynes, 8 April 1906, in Michael Holroyd, *Lytton Strachey: The New Biography* [New York: Farrar, 1995], p. 92; italics mine)

—"converted," that is, to the belief that homosexual (i.e., "sodomitical") feelings are "the best ones."

But Lawrence of course did not believe in the "higher sodomy"—indeed, on the contrary Lawrence sees homosexuality as a means of becoming "a lower type of man":

> What he [the homosexual intellectual] loves is a man who is to a certain degree less developed than himself. Then he can proceed to reduce himself to this level.... It may be he wishes to reduce himself only to the level of a lower type of man. In which case he will love boy or man, as it may be. His ideal, his basic desire, will be to get *back* to a state which he has long surpassed. And the getting back, the reduction, is a sort of progress to infinite nullity, to the beginnings. So that his progression has some sort of satisfaction ("'The Crown': 1915 Variants," in *Reflections on the Death of a Porcupine and Other Essays* [Cambridge University Press, 1988], p. 472)

—"satisfaction," however, that is anything but "higher"; as Lawrence goes on:

> He [the homosexual] is given up to the flux of reduction, his mouth is upon the mouth of corruption. *This* is the reason of homosexuality, and of connection with animals.

Thus the Lawrence of "The Crown" of 1915—the year of Lawrence's meeting such intellectual-aesthetic homosexuals as Keynes and Strachey—felt intense repugnance and hostility toward homosexuality, equating "homosexuality" with bestiality ("connection with animals")—for, according to Lawrence, in both homosexuality and bestiality,

> This is always the higher, more developed type seeking to revert to the lower. (Ibid.)

Yet, for all his antipathy toward homosexuality, Lawrence in his "Messianic" phase wanted to "save" the homosexual cultural elite from "reduction,...corruption"; for Lawrence believed that this homosexuality was simply caused by "the envelope of nullity within which *all* mankind is enclosed":

> And all this [homosexuality among the "sensitive" cultural elite] comes because of the envelope of nullity within which mankind is enclosed, the envelope of the achieved self, the womb of the past era. Within this envelope, this enclosure, nothing but reduction, disintegration can take place. For the envelope [of the achieved self] is completely impermeable, it is conceived as the outer nullity, and all that *is*, is within. (Ibid., pp. 472-473)

In 1915 Lawrence evidently believed that the homosexual cultural elite were incapable of being permeated within the "enclosed envelope" of their collective, self-centered "nullity"—the "nullity" of their "achieved self" which is incapable of and repulsed by the "connection" with the unknown (i.e., "a woman")—a "connection" which would make it possible for them to be saved via psychic rebirth; but, if the homosexual elite were incapable of this rebirth, Lawrence was certain that he and a few of his best friends were capable of a better fate; as he told Katherine Mansfield:

> Do not be sad. It is one life which is passing away from us, one "I" is dying; but there is another coming into being, which is the happy, creative you....[For] us there is a rising from the grave, there is a resurrection, and a clean life to begin from the start, new, and happy. Don't be afraid, don't doubt it, it is so.
>   You have gone further into your death than [Katherine's lover and later husband John Middleton] Murry has. He runs away. But one day he too will submit, he will dare to go down, and be killed, to die in this self which he is. Then he will become a man: not till. He is not a man yet....
>   ...From the old life, all is gone....We must not look back....We must look forward into the unknown that is to be, like flowers that come up in the spring. Because we really *are* born again. (D. H. Lawrence letter to Katherine Mansfield, 20 December 1915)

In late 1915 Lawrence believed that he and a few others were in the process of achieving psychic "resurrection" after a death of their "old" selves; this "resurrection," asserts Lawrence, leads to "a clean life..., new and happy"—but only after one (such as Murry) "will dare...to die in this self which he is"; Katherine's (heterosexual) lover Murry had not done this yet; neither had the homosexual elite: thus both were "not a man [or men] yet"; they were not able to "look forward into the unknown."

Of course, one reason why Lawrence felt that the "sensitive" homosexual elite could not reach the unknown was that they were too chock-full of "all the complexities of the mind and the consciousness"—that is to say, they have too much "mental consciousness" to be saved, resurrected; yet by the end of 1915 Lawrence, visiting Derbyshire, the land of his boyhood, found the coal-mining proletariat to be far more hopeless than the homosexual cultural elite:

> Altogether the life here [in Derbyshire] is so dark and violent: it all happens in the senses, powerful and rather destructive: no mind nor mental consciousness, unintellectual. These men are passionate enough, sensuous, dark—God, how all my boyhood comes back—so violent, so dark, the mind always dark and without understanding, the senses violently alive. It makes me sad beyond words. These men, whom I love so much—and the life has such a power over me—they *understand* mentally so horribly: only industrialism, only wages and money and machinery. They can't *think* anything else....They are utterly unable to appreciate any pure, ulterior truth: only this industrial-mechanical-wage idea. This they will act from—nothing else....Which is a reduction to the lowest terms—nothing higher than that which now is, only lower....It is necessary to get the germ of a new developement *towards the highest,* not a reduction to the lowest....
>
> The strange, dark, sensual life, so violent, and hopeless at the bottom, combined with this horrible paucity and materialism of mental consciousness, makes me so sad, I could scream....I love them [the miners] like brothers—but my God, I hate them too: I don't intend to own them as masters—not while the world stands. One must conquer them also....
>
> At last, at last, one will be able to set forth from it all, into the uncreated future, the unborn, unconceived era. One must leave all this to finish itself: the new unanimity, the new complete happiness beyond—one must be strong enough to create this....(D. H. Lawrence letter to Ottoline Morrell, 27 December 1915)

While Lawrence loved these "passionate,...sensuous, dark" men "like brothers," he finally found that the fact that they had "no mind nor mental consciousness" made "these men" ultimately repulsive to him: their "unintellectual" nature made them "utterly unable to appreciate any pure, ulterior truth: only this industrial-mechanical wage idea"—the "industrial-mechanical wage idea" being even more antithetical to the Lawrentian way than the "higher sodomy" of the Cambridge-Bloomsbury intelligentsia. For Lawrence believed that "this industrial-mechanical-wage idea" was "a reduction to the lowest terms," while the "higher sodomy" of Cambridge-Bloomsbury could be transmuted into something essentially Lawrentian in nature. Lawrence imagined that, once he converted the powerful homosexual intellectual-political elite to his ideas on male-male and male-female relationships, this elite would help him to succeed in his own quest (in his imaginative mind) for sociopolitical power:

> I don't intend to own them as masters—not while the world stands.
> One must *conquer them* also (my italics)

—and, to help him "conquer" all those of "lower" consciousness who would seek to be his "masters," Lawrence needed the support of the elites—elites whom he would lead (or so he imagined)

> into the uncreated future, the unborn, unconceived era

—an "unconceived era" in which Lawrentian values would prevail despite all their enemies, after Lawrence would "conquer" his would-be masters. It is, of course, entirely understandable that Lawrence in December 1915 would want to "conquer" those who might seek to "master" him; only a month earlier Lawrence's great novel *The Rainbow* had been condemned as obscene and ordered destroyed by the court. Feeling betrayed and deserted by the civilization he had sought to save, Lawrence takes consolation in his creative imagination:

> There is my intimate art, and my thoughts....It is enough, more than enough, if they will only leave me alone.
> ...There is another world, a sort of rarer reality....There is another world, which I prefer....(D. H. Lawrence letter to Kotelian-sky, 6 January 1916)

In contradistinction to Lawrence's "intimate art" and "thoughts" and "another world" was

> the horrible hopelessness of life! We've got to face it out. I feel now pushed to the brink of existence, and there remains only to fall off into oblivion, or to give in, and accept the ruck: or some way out, as yet undiscovered....I don't know what to do nor how to go on....What good is it all. There is nothing but betrayal and denial, nothing at all: no trust, no faith, no hope from anybody, only betrayal and denial.
>
> ...there's only...this England, which nauseates my soul, nauseates my spirit and my body—this England....this banquet of vomit, this life, this England, this Europe. Out of the disciples, there was one Judas. In modern life, there are twelve Judases in the twelve disciples. They are all Judases, one and all, all Judases. Where is one to turn one's face?...
>
> ...It seems to be now a case of death, or a miracle. I still believe in miracles—supernatural. I don't believe in human life any more. And failing the miracle, I am finished. (D. H. Lawrence letter to John Middleton Murry, 9 January 1916)

The "miracle" that Lawrence would find—the "way out" in the midst of his alienation and the "betrayal and denial" of *The Rainbow* by "this England"—the "way out" was through the "miracle" of the Lawrentian creation (in his imagination) of "another world, a sort of rarer reality"—the "world" and "reality" of *Women in Love*.

Indeed, in 1916 the main characteristic of the quintessential Lawrentian reality continued to be the "love between a man and a woman":

> That is the right way to be happy—a nucleus of love between a man and a woman, and let the world look after itself. It is the last folly, to bother about the world. One should be in love, and be happy—no more. (D. H. Lawrence letter to John Middleton Murry and Katherine Mansfield, 17 January 1916)

As for "another world," Lawrence in 1916, in his imaginative strength feels that he has found that world in Cornwall:

> I love Cornwall. It is bare and desolate and like the beginning of the world, the old promethean powers. (D. H. Lawrence letter to Hopkin, 25 January 1916)

Conceiving Cornwall to be "like the beginning of the world," Lawrence living in Cornwall could conceive himself to be uniquely original, the first creative artist ever to write—at "the beginning of the world": accordingly, Lawrence could easily feel himself to be imbued with the "primeval" "promethean powers":

> I should like to stay in Cornwall....
> ...the shore is absolutely primeval: those heavy, black rocks, like solid darkness, and the heavy water like a sort of first twilight breaking against them, and not changing them. It is really like the first craggy breaking of dawn in the world, a sense of the primeval darkness just behind, before the Creation. That is a very great and comforting thing to feel, I think: after all this whirlwind of dust and grit and dirty paper of a modern Europe....I love to see those terrifying rocks, like solid lumps of the original darkness....(D. H. Lawrence letter to J. D. Beresford, 1 February 1916)

Thus in February 1916 Lawrence conceived himself to be full of "promethean powers"—"primeval," like Cornwall itself ("the shore is absolutely primeval"); "primeval," originating in the "solid darkness" and the "*first* twilight," "like the *first*...breaking of dawn in the world, a sense of the primeval darkness just behind, *before the Creation*" (italics mine). This feeling of priority, of being first, is "a very great and comforting thing to feel" for Lawrence, indeed making him feel far superior to "dirty...modern Europe" which has rejected and betrayed him and his *Rainbow*.

Earnestly desiring to fight "dirty...modern Europe" with his creative-imaginative mind and being, Lawrence hopes to find allies in the earthy population of Cornwall: Cornwall, where, Lawrence believes,

> the old race is still revealed, a race which believed in the darkness, in magic, and in the magic transcendency of one man over another, which is fascinating (Ibid.)

—so "fascinating" to Lawrence for the reason that he conceives himself to be their "magic[al]" leader, since he sees them as believing in "the magic transcendency of one man over another"—with himself in his imaginative priority as the supreme "magic...man" with the power of the original, originating "darkness." Yet ultimately for Lawrence, the "Cornish people," like those of Derbyshire, were too lacking in Lawrentian virtues:

> But curse them, they are entirely mindless, and yet they are living purely for social advancement. They ought to be living in the darkness and warmth and passionateness of the blood, sudden, incalculable. Whereas they are like insects gone cold, living only for money, for *dirt*. They are foul in this. They ought all to die. (ibid.)

With their materialism ("living only for money"), their lack of creative mind ("entirely mindless"), and their lack of Lawrentian "darkness and warmth and passionateness of the blood," the Cornish people are not capable of sustaining Lawrence's enthusiasm; he will not save them ("They ought all to die").

But of course with his Messiah complex Lawrence longed to save Western civilization from self-destruction: yet in this endeavor Lawrence—in February 1916 at least—rejected the "mindless," money-hungry lower classes of Cornwall and Derbyshire as a source of savable people ("They ought all to die") and instead determined to save the apparently less materialistic, less "foul" artistic-aesthetic-intellectual classes—including, indeed, the homosexual-intellectual elite that he formerly had scorned so vehemently less than a year earlier (in March 1915, after meeting Keynes at Cambridge). In February 1916 Lawrence begins to form an imaginative connection between saving Western civilization and somehow making homosexuality redeemable. In early February 1916 Lawrence is intensely contemplating homosexual Sodom and Gomorrah as a simile for the world today:

> The world is a bad place...; there are a few good people, but like Sodom and Gomorrah, not ten to each city—not enough to save the ship, I am afraid. (D. H. Lawrence letter to Katherine Clayton, 2 February 1916)

Thus in February 1916 Lawrence in his vision of "the world" likened it to Sodom and Gomorrah, Biblical cities famed for "decadence" and "sin" in general and homosexuality in particular—and most famous of all for the absolute destruction ("brimstone and fire") with which they were punished by God for their wickedness. In his intense private religious-mystical-Biblical imagination Lawrence searched for a saving vision which could be applied to the modern world to remedy its powerful tendency to self-destruction as manifested by the Great War. Going back in time in his imagination for his saving vision, Lawrence envisions a "primeval" world prior to the sins and decadence of Sodom and Gomorrah:

> The war, the whole world, has gone out of my imagination. I feel like a Sleeper of Ephesus who has waked up, not a 100 years after, but about 5000 years before. This Cornwall is very primeval: great, black, jutting cliffs and rocks, like the original darkness, and a pale sea breaking in, like dawn. It is like the beginning of the world, wonderful: and so free and strong. I feel as if all that Europe were so long ago and so disremembered. It does not exist in me any

more. (D. H. Lawrence letter to Lady Cynthia Asquith, 7 February 1916)

"[F]eel[ing] like a Sleeper who has waked up...about 5000 years before," Lawrence in "my imagination" can transcend the decadence and deathliness of "The war, the whole world" and can instead conceive himself to be "free and strong"—"free and strong" in another world, a world which, paradoxically, is "like the beginning of the world" and is at the same time a world which makes "Europe [seem] so long ago and so disremembered." In February 1916 "the whole world" in Lawrence's imagination is indeed "free and strong" and complex: here the Lawrentian world is at one and the same time "primeval" (i.e., *older* than Europe), "original," "wonderful," "free and strong"; and yet at the same time is much *newer* than Europe—"Europe,...so long ago and so disremembered." This "world," archetypal yet new, is indeed the Lawrentian vision, not just of the old ("primeval") world of Cornwall, but of the "new world" of America—a world in which Lawrence's imagination was deeply immersed via Lawrence's reading of Melville's *Moby Dick* in February 1916. Unlike "the others," Lawrence greatly appreciates *Moby Dick*:

> I am reading *Moby Dick*. It is a very odd, interesting book: to me interesting, the others can't bear it. (D. H. Lawrence letter to Lady Ottoline Morrell, 7 February 1916)

One major reason why Lawrence finds *Moby Dick* "very...interesting" is that, as one important gay critic, Robert K. Martin, avers,

> The radical vision of *Moby Dick*...arises from...its demonstration that...it is love alone, as manifested in the marriage of Ishmael and Queequeg, that can offer an alternative to the impending apocalypse of destructive, and ultimately self-destructive, fury. (Robert K. Martin, *Hero, Captain, and Stranger: Male Friendships, Social Critique, and Literary Form in the Sea Novels of Herman Melville*, p. 70)

"[T]he impending apocalypse of destructive, and ultimately self-destructive, fury": this phrase is certainly reminiscent of the situation faced by Lawrence and indeed all Western civilization in February 1916, when Lawrence reading *Moby Dick* reached the conclusion (as we shall soon see) that male-male "love" needed to be re-created in such a way as to contribute to the preservation, rather than the destruction, of Western civilization; but of course the actual nature of this male-male "love" is the most important thing about it; and Robert K. Martin's great (exceedingly heterosexual) precursor Leslie Fiedler sagaciously explains the nature of male-male "love" in *Moby Dick*:

> *Moby Dick* can be read...not only as an account of a whale-hunt, but also as a love story, perhaps the greatest love story in our [American] fiction, cast in the peculiar American form of innocent homosexuality. (Leslie Fiedler, *Love and Death in the American Novel* [1960; repr. New York: Doubleday, 1992], p. 370)

Leslie Fiedler goes on to say that

> It will not do to sentimentalize or Christianize Melville's pagan concept of love. It is not *caritas* which he celebrates; and his symbol for the redeeming passion is Priapus rather than the cross. Perhaps it is least misleading to think of the love which redeems Ishmael as Platonic, in the authentic historical sense of the word. Rising from the particular object to the universal, it remains suspect nonetheless; for like the ideal Eros of *The Symposium*, it is grounded in a relationship unequivocally rejected by the Judaeo-Christian tradition. Genteel or orthodox advocates of love should look hard at Melville's text before deciding to applaud the conquest of death he celebrates in *Moby Dick*. Yet it is love in the fullest sense which that book makes its center; not a brutal or casual relationship, but one which develops on the pattern of a marriage: achieving in the course of a single voyage the shape of a whole lifetime shared, and symbolizing a spiritual education. (Ibid., p. 372)

And Fiedler concludes that

> This is Platonism without sodomy, which is to say, marriage without copulation: the vain dream of genteel ladies fulfilled in a sailor's rooming-house by two men. (Ibid., p. 375)

According to Fiedler, the "love story" of *Moby Dick*—a "love story" rooted in "innocent homosexuality"—is "suspect," "grounded in a relationship unequivocally rejected by the Judaeo-Christian tradition": even though the "innocent homosexuality" of *Moby Dick* "is Platonism *without sodomy*,...[homosexual] marriage without copulation" (my italics), it is still ultimately quite objectionable; thus Fiedler's seminal-classic interpretation of *Moby Dick* is ultimately censured by his ephebe Robert K. Martin (who is gay):

> Fiedler's analysis...is coupled with a strong sense of judgment from a heterosexual point of view. As he wrote in the preface to the first edition [of *Love and Death in the American Novel*], his subject is "the failure of the American fictionist to deal with adult hetero-

D. H. LAWRENCE TODAY

> sexual love and his consequent obsession with death, incest and innocent homosexuality." The language of Fiedler's comment speaks for itself: he is studying a "failure" and a subsequent "obsession."...Fiedler's phrase "adult heterosexual love" is a telling one, since it indeed suggests that all heterosexual love is adult (and, by implication, that all homosexual love is childish, or more pertinently, adolescent)....
>
> ...Fiedler's book [*Love and Death*] has had enormous importance..., and it is in fact unlikely that I should be writing the present study had it [i.e., *Love and Death*] not led the way for such discussions of sexuality. But recognizing my own substantial debt to Fiedler's work, and to his identification of a homosexual strain in American literature in general and in Melville in particular, cannot prevent me from saying how painful it has been to see homosexuals' lives and artistic creations so abused, so turned to other purposes, so insistently read as failed versions of something else. *Love and Death* was important for gay people in the same way that the Kinsey Report was; it announced that we were there. At the same time, though, it [*Love and Death*] said, in effect, that we must be cured, just as American literature was to come to its senses and to create mature heterosexual novels. (Martin, pp. 8-9)

With his valorization of "a strong...heterosexual point of view" privileging "adult heterosexual love," Leslie Fiedler in his "analysis" is evidently a Lawrentian; as he himself tells us:

> Of all the literary critics who have written about American books, the one who has seemed to me closest to the truth,...and who has brought to his subject an appropriate passion and style, is, of course, D. H. Lawrence. His *Studies in Classic American Literature* attempted for the first time the kind of explication which does not betray the complexity or perilousness of its theme....(*Love and Death in the American Novel*, p. 14)

With his "truth,...passion and style" that bravely confront "the complexity [and] perilousness" of "American books" such as *Moby Dick*, Lawrence like his disciple Leslie Fiedler did of course also say, "in effect," as Robert K. Martin puts it, that "[homosexuals] must be cured" via a "mature heterosexual" dispensation and deployment. As agent of the "adult heterosexual love" dispensation and deployment, Lawrence in February 1916, in the midst of his reading *Moby Dick*, is peculiarly full of poetic-creative strength; indeed, it certainly appears that reading *Moby Dick* had quite a salubrious effect on Lawrence:

> Soon I shall be a Hercules, a Samson (D. H. Lawrence letter to Koteliansky, 9 February 1916),

he announces, while in the midst of reading *Moby Dick*; and, on the very same day that he mentions reading *Moby Dick*, Lawrence announces that

> I feel my old strength coming back, like a pulse that begins to beat and sounds very deep and strong, as if it went to the very heart of the uncreated darkness [i.e., the origin of the cosmos]. I am glad. (D. H. Lawrence letter to Cynthia Asquith, 7 February 1916)

And, in the very letter in which he praises *Moby Dick* ("a very odd, interesting book"), Lawrence declares that

> I feel the strength striking back into me, like a new strong pulse, with all the power of the uncreated darkness behind. (D. H. Lawrence letter to Lady Ottoline Morrell, 7 February 1916)

And Lawrence in his great "strength" would soon make an attempt to "cure" the homosexual elite.

Lawrence's greatest attempt to "cure" homosexuality takes place in *Women in Love*, which he began writing shortly after finishing his reading of *Moby Dick*, which Lawrence "loved" ("I loved Melville's *Moby Dick*"; D. H. Lawrence letter to Barbara Low, 30 May 1916); furthermore, Lawrence asserted,

> Melville's *Moby Dick*...is a *real* masterpiece....(D. H. Lawrence letter to Koteliansky, 12 June 1916)

—a "masterpiece" which surely influenced Lawrence's writing of his "philosophy," which he wrote while reading *Moby Dick*:

> I have nearly done the first, the destructive, half of my philosophy. At last it can stand. It is the last word. I am sure it marks the end of a great epoch: at least for me. (D. H. Lawrence letter to Lady Ottoline Morrell, 15 February 1916)

This philosophy, entitled "Goats and Compasses," was soon destroyed by Lawrence and was never published; but, as mentioned earlier, "Goats and Compasses" has been described as "a bombastic, pseudo-mystical, psycho-philosophical treatise dealing largely with homosexuality" (according to Cecil Gray)—a "treatise" in which "the only thing that he [Lawrence] doesn't revile and condemn is love between men and women" (according to Lady Ottoline Morrell). This was in February

1916; at this time, Lawrence in "Goats and Compasses" most likely launched an attack on homosexuality with a view to abolishing it or converting it into something Lawrentian which he could use to further the fantasies of his Christ-Messiah complex as well as to make him feel more socio-politically powerful in the hostile world which had destroyed his *Rainbow*; but the tolerant, very urbane Lady Ottoline Morrell did not appreciate Lawrence's anti-homosexual "philosophy"; yet Lawrence remained undeterred:

> Never mind that you don't like my philosophy: it doesn't matter....
>
> The world will go its own way, and I shall go mine: if only it will let me alone. What I write now I write for the gods. I am useless to this mankind, and this mankind is useless to me. It is no good pretending any more that there is a relation between it and me. If only it will let me alone, and not try to destroy my own inner world, which is real, I don't mind. But my life is not any more of this world, this world of this humanity, and I won't pretend it is. (D. H. Lawrence letter to Lady Ottoline Morrell, 15 March 1916)

Feeling extremely alienated from and "useless to this mankind," "this mankind" which "is useless to me," Lawrence went about creating a *new* mankind in his imagination—"my own inner world, which is real"—an "inner world" which was greatly influenced by Lawrence's reading of Melville and other classics: soon after reading *Moby Dick*, Lawrence immersed himself in reading the ancient Greek historian Thucydides, whom Lawrence enthusiastically praised:

> Thucydides...is a very splendid and noble writer, with the simplicity and the directness of *the most complete culture and the widest consciousness*. I salute him. More and more I admire this true classic dignity and self-responsibility. (D. H. Lawrence letter to Lady Ottoline Morrell, 7 April 1916; italics mine)

Inspired by the "true classic dignity and self-responsibility" of ancient Greek civilization—"the most complete culture and the widest consciousness" according to Lawrence in April 1916—Lawrence in his "inner world" determined to create a new world, a new humanity:

> One must live quite apart,...having another world, a world as yet uncreated (Ibid.)

—a "world" which Lawrence soon proceeded to create in *Women in Love*; a world in which Lawrence, like the great ancient Greek contemporaries of Thucydides—namely, Plato and Socrates—would attempt to save Western civilization from total moral and social decay; and a major part of that Lawrentian salvation for civilization lay in his (Lawrence's) prescriptions for re-creating the "world" of male-male relationships in such a way that "another world"—a more vital, life-affirming, salubrious Lawrentian world—would take shape.

Thus, in late April 1916, when Lawrence announced that "I began a novel" (D. H. Lawrence letter to Mark Gertler, 26 April 1916), Lawrence surely was thinking of Thucydides as well as of Melville; indeed, a few weeks later he linked their names together:

> I loved Melville's *Moby Dick*. I read Thucydides too, when I have the courage to face the fact of these wars of a collapsing era, of a dying idea. He is very good, and very present to one's soul. (D. H. Lawrence letter to Barbara Low, 30 May 1916)

Like Thucydides with his *Peloponnesian War*, Lawrence in the midst of the Great War conceived himself to be witness to "wars of a collapsing era, of a dying idea"—and in response to this overwhelming state of affairs Lawrence aspired to manifest the "true classic dignity and self-responsibility" he so admired in Thucydides. Indeed, Lawrence continued to read Thucydides throughout his *Women in Love* period:

> The Peloponnesian war was the death agony of Greece....I am just reading Thucydides—when I can bear to—it is too horrible to see a people, adhering to traditions, fling itself down the abyss of the past, and disappear.
>
> We must have the courage to cast off the old symbols, the old traditions: at least, put them aside, like a plant in growing surpasses its crowning leaves with higher leaves and buds. There is something beyond the past. The past is no justification. Unless from us the future takes place, we are death only. (D. H. Lawrence letter to Catherine Carswell, 16 July 1916)

Thus Lawrence, admiring Thucydides' "classic dignity and self-responsibility," hoped himself to possess these qualities in even greater abundance than did Thucydides—and, furthermore, to use these great attributes of the classic past—"dignity and self-responsibility"—to go "beyond the past," to transcend "the abyss of the past," and so to succeed where Thucydides and the other ancient Greeks had failed: for they had indeed failed to prevent their great civilization from "collapsing" and "dying." Lawrence, on the other hand, believed that the salvation of modern Western civilization was indeed attainable: this Lawrentian salvation lay in the application of "classic dignity and self-responsibility" to the "establishing of pure relationships" between man and woman—and between man and the universe:

> I shall find my deepest desire to be a wish for pure, unadulterated relationship with the universe, for truth in being. My pure relationship with one woman is marriage, physical and spiritual: with another, is another form of happiness, according to our nature. And so on for ever.
>
> It is this establishing of pure relationships which makes heaven, wherein we are immortal, like the angels, and mortal, like men, both. And the way to immortality is in the fulfilment of desire. (D. H. Lawrence letter to Catherine Carswell, 16 July 1916)

By "pure relationships" Lawrence means authentic, intense relationships; in July 1916, after working on *Women in Love* for a couple of months, Lawrence's main quest was for "pure relationships" with the universe and with women: there he aspired to find "the way to immortality,...the fulfilment of desire"; and of course, by portraying the cosmic nature of male-female relationships in *Women in Love*, Lawrence hoped to achieve

> the largest of desires for a poet, poetic immortality....(Bloom, *Map of Misreading*, p. 186)

Yet when Lawrence first began writing *Women in Love* (late April 1916), the first relationship that Lawrence hoped to make "pure," evidently, was the male-male relationship; fresh from Ottoline's rejection of his anti-homosexual "Goats and Compasses," still remembering the Cambridge-Bloomsbury homosexual elite, inspired by Melville's "masterpiece" *Moby Dick* and Thucydides' "classic dignity and self-discipline," Lawrence in late April 1916 felt that he could make the attempt to save the male-male relationship, to make it "pure": this he essayed to do in the "Prologue" chapter for *Women in Love*.

Lawrence scholar George H. Ford tells us that

> In April 1916,...it is probable that this Prologue chapter [of *Women in Love*] was written. It is also probable that the discarding of this chapter occurred three months later, in July 1916, when he [Lawrence] himself began typing out a copy of the novel to send to his publishers. (Ford, "An Introductory Note to D. H. Lawrence's

Prologue to *Women in Love,*" in Colin Clarke, *D. H. Lawrence: The Rainbow and Women in Love: A Casebook*, pp. 38-39)

Lawrence critic Frank Kermode concludes that "the real importance of the Prologue is precisely that Lawrence struck it out" (Kermode, *D. H. Lawrence*, p. 64).

But why did Lawrence reject the Prologue to *Women in Love*? To answer this question it is necessary to look at the Prologue with a view to drawing some conclusions about the artistic power and poetic strength of that text. For the fact is that the Prologue to *Women in Love* is quite inferior to virtually all of Lawrence's mature work; indeed, in the "Prologue" Rupert Birkin, far from being a genuine and mature Lawrentian character, is merely an inferior version of Paul Morel—a Paul Morel manqué. Like Paul Morel in *Sons and Lovers*, the Ur-Birkin of the "Prologue" to *Women in Love* mistreats "the spiritual woman" with whom he is involved:

> Birkin knew what she was feeling and thinking. Yet he continued almost spitefully against her. He *did* want to betray the heights and depths of nearly religious intercourse which he had with her. He, the God, turned round upon his priestess, and became the common, vulgar man who turned her to scorn. He performed some strange metamorphosis of soul, and from being a pure, incandescent spirit burning intense with the presence of God, he became a lustful, shallow, insignificant fellow running in all the common ruts. Even there was some vindictiveness in him now, something jeering and spiteful and low, unendurable. It drove her mad. She had given him all her trembling, naked soul, and now, he turned mongrel, and triumphed in his own degeneration. It was his deep desire, to be common, vulgar, a little gross. She could not bear the look of almost sordid jeering with which he turned on her, when she reached out her hand, imploring. It was as if some rat bit her, she felt she was going insane. And he jeered at her, at the spiritual woman....He jeered at her horribly...(492)

The Ur-Birkin of the "Prologue," like Paul Morel in relation to Miriam in *Sons and Lovers*, "spitefully...want[s] to betray" the relationship he has with "spiritual" Hermione by becoming "lustful" and "shallow" (in Miriam-Hermione's view) and "jeering" at her; but this aspect of Lawrence's portrayal of the Ur-Birkin in the "Prologue" is little more than an expository repetition of Lawrence's classic depiction of Paul Morel in *Sons and Lovers* some four years earlier: indeed, compared to the vital portrait of the Paul Morel-Miriam relationship in the earlier work, the Ur-Birkin-Hermione relationship is depicted in an abstract and uninspired fashion: it is a mere shell of the Paul Morel-Miriam relationship. One reason for the relative failure of the portrayal of the Ur-Birkin-Hermione relationship is that the Ur-Birkin is scarcely autobiographical at all; let us look at this description of the Ur-Birkin's "love for Hermione":

> There was his love for Hermione....He *knew* he did not love her with any living, creative love. He did not even desire her: he had no passion for her....(496-497)

The Ur-Birkin's feelings for Hermione lack the complexity of Paul Morel's feelings for Miriam; Ur-Birkin is essentially unattracted to Hermione ("He *knew* he did not love her....He did not even desire her"); in the more autobiographical *Sons and Lovers*, on the other hand, Lawrence-Paul Morel feels both love and desire for Miriam:

> He never forgot seeing her as she lay on the bed....First he saw only her beauty, and was blind with it. She had the most beautiful body he had ever imagined. He stood unable to move or speak, looking at her, his face half smiling with wonder. And then he wanted her....
> And afterwards [i.e., after the sex] he loved her—loved her to the last fibre of his being. He loved her.

But the Ur-Birkin of the "Prologue" is evidently incapable of love:

> He did not love any woman. He *wanted* to love. But between wanting to love, and loving, is the whole difference between life and death. (497)

Here Lawrence the great heterosexual "priest of love" fervently declares his belief that "between wanting to love [a woman], and loving [a woman], is the whole difference between life and death." As everybody knows from reading Lawrence's letters, Lawrence believed himself to be one of the few human beings capable of genuine heterosexual love in the sick modern world; furthermore, we know that Lawrence felt that his unique capability in this psychosexual-passional realm guaranteed him his "poetic immortality"—a matter of life and death for the great creative writer. Harold Bloom notes that, for the strong poet,

> poetic immortality...[is] the only eternal happiness that is relevant...(*Map of Misreading*, p. 57)

Thus when confronted with the fact of rampant homosexuality among England's socio-intellectual elite at Cambridge-Bloomsbury, Lawrence sensed this as a major threat to his "poetic immortality"—"a matter of life and death" for him as the strong poet who posits that "the whole difference between life and death" is the difference between being able to love a woman and *not* being able to (and merely wanting to); indeed, even on the very verge of his *Women in Love* period Lawrence is enthusiastically reaffirming his psychic-ontological strength and its capabilities in true, genuine heterosexual marriage:

> For myself, thank God, I feel myself becoming more and more unified, more and more a oneness. And Frieda and I become more and more truly married—for which I thank heaven....(D. H. Lawrence letter to Lady Ottoline Morrell, 15 February 1916)

Surely the "unified" Lawrence of February 1916 is a far cry from the "divided" Ur-Birkin of the "Prologue" to *Women in Love*:

> To be spiritual, he [Birkin] must have a Hermione, completely without desire: to be sensual, he must have a slightly bestial woman, the very scent of whose skin soon disgusted him, whose manners nauseated him beyond bearing....
>
> He [Birkin] knew he obtained no real fulfilment in sensuality, he became disgusted and despised the whole process as if it were dirty. And he knew that he had no real fulfilment in his spiritual and aesthetic intercourse with Hermione. That process he also despised, with considerable cynicism.
>
> And he recognized that he was on the point either of breaking, becoming a thing, losing his integral being, or else of becoming insane. He was now nothing but a series of reactions from dark to light, from light to dark, almost mechanical, *without unity* or meaning.
>
> This was the most insufferable bondage, the most tormenting affliction, that he could not save himself from these extreme reactions, the vibration between two poles, one of which was Hermione,...the other of which was a prostitute, anti-social, almost criminal. He knew that in the end, subject to this extreme vibration, he would be shattered, would die, or else, worse still, would become a mere disordered set of processes, without purpose or integral being. He knew this, and dreaded it. Yet he could not save himself.
>
> To save himself, he must *unite* the two halves of himself, spiritual and sensual. And this is what no man can do at once, deliberately. It must happen to him. (500; my italics)

The Ur-Birkin of the "Prologue" is "without unity": in his being there is no unity between "the two halves of himself, spiritual and sensual"; Lawrence in 1916, on the other hand, enjoys a state in which "I feel myself becoming more and more unified." This Lawrentian unity of being is virtually a religious state (*"thank God*, I feel myself becoming more and more unified") and leads to Lawrence's "becoming more and more truly married"—another Lawrentian religious state ("Frieda and I becoming more and more truly married—for which *I thank heaven*"). But of the Ur-Birkin, Lawrence can only conclude that

> he went on, month after month, year after year, *divided* against himself....
> ...But to be so divided against oneself, this is terrible, a nullification of all being. (504; my italics)

In contradistinction to the "divided" Ur-Birkin's "nullification of all being" is Lawrence's vital, live *"new being"* with Frieda:

> Frieda and I have a kind of *new being*, for each other, which is *life*.
> (D. H. Lawrence letter to Lady Ottoline Morrell, 25 February 1916; my italics)

Thus, in the Lawrentian ethos, "loving a woman" (i.e., loving his wife Frieda) is tantamount to "life," with Lawrence being the supreme exemplar of "life"; and the Ur-Birkin, with his failure at "loving a woman," being the deathly exemplar of "nullification of all being."

Thus even a cursory review of Lawrence's letters at this time (i.e., early 1916) makes it evident that the Ur-Birkin of the "Prologue" is not D. H. Lawrence; indeed, the exceedingly judgemental, even condescending, tone of Lawrence the omniscient narrator in relation to the Ur-Birkin makes it extremely likely that the Ur-Birkin character is a composite of several of Lawrence's friends and associates of this period—friends and associates that bitterly disappointed Lawrence. Thus let us look at Lawrence's description of his young friend Heseltine in early 1916:

> About Heseltine....It is queer. He declares he does not like this one, the Puma, but he does really....he is really attached to her in the senses, in the unconsciousness, in the blood. He is always fighting away from this. But in doing so he is a fool. She is very nice and very real and simple, we like her. His affection for Mlle. [the other woman, not the Puma] is a desire for the light because he is in the dark. If he were in the light he would want the dark. He

> wants Mlle. for *companionship*, not for the blood connection, the dark, sensuous relation. With Puma he has this second, dark relation, but not the first. She is quite intelligent, in her way, but no mental consciousness; no white consciousness, if you understand, all intuition, in the dark, the consciousness of the senses. But she is quite fine and subtle in that way....
>
> Perhaps he [Heseltine] is *very split*, and would always have the two things separate, the real blood connection, and the real conscious or spiritual connection, always separate. (D. H. Lawrence letter to Ottoline Morrell, 15 February 1916)

Thus, a couple of months before Lawrence depicted the "split" character of the Ur-Birkin in the "Prologue" to *Women in Love* ("he went on, month after month, year after year, divided against himself"), Lawrence was describing Heseltine as "very split"; furthermore, it is in this very same letter about the "split" Heseltine that Lawrence celebrates his own "unified" state ("thank God, I feel myself becoming more and more unified, more and more a oneness"; D. H. Lawrence letter to Ottoline Morrell, 15 February 1916): thus it is evident that, in contrast to Ur-Birkin-Heseltine, Lawrence finds himself to be full of psychic-ontological superiority—a superiority which makes it very unlikely that the Ur-Birkin of the "Prologue" is supposed to be Lawrence himself. Indeed, in another letter of February 1916 (25 February 1916) on Heseltine, Lawrence once again makes it clear that there are remarkable parallels between young Heseltine and the Ur-Birkin:

> Heseltine is in a great state of (unjustly) hating the Puma, and looking on Mlle [the other woman]...as a white star. He will swing from dark to light till he comes to rest. I believe if he stayed long enough with Mlle *exclusively*, he would hate her: but perhaps not. We can but let him oscillate violently....But he is exasperating because he is always in such a state of mad *reaction against* things, all mad reactions. (D. H. Lawrence letter to Lady Ottoline Morrell, 25 February 1916)

These words of Lawrence, describing Heseltine's "state of mad reaction" and his "swing from dark to light," are extremely reminiscent of Lawrence's description of the Ur-Birkin in the "Prologue":

> He [the Ur-Birkin] was now nothing but a series of *reactions from dark to light, from light to dark,*...without unity or meaning. (my italics)

Like Heseltine, but unlike Lawrence, the Ur-Birkin "is always in such a state of mad *reaction,*...all mad reactions" (as Lawrence said of Heseltine; D. H. Lawrence letter of 25 February 1916); similarly, the Ur-Birkin, like Heseltine, goes "from dark to light, from light to dark" ("Prologue"); and both Heseltine and the Ur-Birkin are "very split" (D. H. Lawrence letter of 15 February 1916), "divided against [themselves]" ("Prologue"), "without unity or meaning" ("Prologue").

In contrast to Heseltine-Ur-Birkin, Lawrence is "becoming more and more unified, more and more a oneness" (D. H. Lawrence letter of 15 February 1916); and he, together with his wife Frieda, "have a kind of new being, *for each other*, which is life." Obviously Lawrence in his psychic-ontological vitality and his emotional-marital maturity felt far superior to both Heseltine and the Ur-Birkin; yet of course Lawrence did for a time consider Heseltine a true friend and candidate for Lawrence's "new world ahead":

> ...in our retreat we will make the bombs to smite the Philistine. Oh, to *bust* up the Philistine—only that.
> I feel a new life, a new world ahead—for us....We will be a centre of a new life, a centre of destruction of the old. I believe in the "Rainbow books and music," quite gaily. (D. H. Lawrence letter to Philip Heseltine, 24 February 1916)

The "Philistine" host of whom Lawrence here speaks so hostilely to Heseltine are of course all those who had frustrated and suppressed his *Rainbow* a few months before; and young Heseltine, significantly enough, had enthusiastically offered (in February 1916) to arrange for the private publication of *The Rainbow* (in a business venture called "Rainbow books and music"); this business venture failed, but it earned Heseltine the friendship of Lawrence—but only for a little while; by 22 April 1916 Lawrence could write of their friendship that

> I shall be glad when...this affair is finished. It has become ludicrous and rather shameful. I only wish that you and Puma [Heseltine's mistress, later his wife] should not talk about us [i.e., Lawrence and his wife], for decency's sake. I assure you I shall have nothing to say of you and her....
> ...we will let the whole relation cease entirely, and remove the indecency of it. (D. H. Lawrence letter to Philip Heseltine, ante 22 April 1916)

"[T]his affair" evidently concerns "Lawrence's meddlesomeness" concerning "two of Heseltine's girls" (Harry T. Moore, *The Priest of Love: A Life of D. H. Lawrence*, p. 256); the details of "this affair" are not important for the purposes of this study: what is important is the fact that Lawrence around 22 April 1916 ended his friendship with Heseltine—and at this very same time he wrote the "Prologue" to *Women in Love* ("This last week...I began a novel [*Women in Love*]." D. H. Lawrence letter to Mark Gertler, 26 April 1916)—a "Prologue" in which the Ur-Birkin, rather than being a quintessential Lawrentian figure (as the actual Birkin of *Women in Love* turns out to be), is instead partially based on Lawrence's perception of his young ex-friend Heseltine—Heseltine, who, like the Ur-Birkin, is "divided against himself" ("Prologue"), "a series of reactions...without unity or meaning" ("Prologue"), "in...a state of...all mad reactions" (D. H. Lawrence on Heseltine, letter of 25 February 1916), "very split" (D. H. Lawrence on Heseltine, letter of 15 February 1916).

Thus it is evident that the Ur-Birkin, with his "divided"-"split" nature, is based to a considerable extent upon Heseltine; but there is another aspect of the Ur-Birkin character that does not derive from Heseltine: this is "his [i.e., the Ur-Birkin's] latent homosexuality" (Langbaum, *Mysteries of Identity*, p. 348). This "latent homosexuality" of the Ur-Birkin is rather suddenly discussed towards the end of the "Prologue":

> All the time, he [the Ur-Birkin] recognized that, although he was always drawn to women, feeling more at home with a woman than with a man, yet it was for men that he felt the hot, flushing, roused attraction which a man is supposed to feel for the other sex....[T]he male physique had a fascination for him, and for the female physique he felt only a fondness, a sort of sacred love, as for a sister.
>
> In the street, it was the men who roused him by their flesh and their manly, vigorous movement, quite apart from all individual character, whilst he studied the women as sisters, *knowing their meaning and their intents*. It was the men's physique which held *the passion and the mystery* to him. The women he seemed to be kin to, he looked for the soul in them. *The soul of a woman and the physique of a man*, these were the two things he watched for, in the street. (501-502; italics mine)

"The soul of a woman and the physique of a man": this phrase indicates the derivative, inauthentic nature of Lawrence's portrayal of the Ur-Birkin in the "Prologue"; and it was this inauthenticity and derivativeness—this lack of originality, uniqueness and sincerity—in his presentment of the Ur-Birkin character which led Lawrence to cancel the "Prologue" to *Women in Love*.

But, if the portrait of the Ur-Birkin is derivative, where is it derived from? To answer this question, we need only read this passage from Edward Carpenter's *The Intermediate Sex* (1908):

> More than thirty years ago...an Austrian writer, K. H. Ulrichs, drew attention in a series of pamphlets...to the existence of a class of people who...while belonging distinctly to one sex as far as their bodies are concerned they may be said to belong *mentally* and *emotionally* to the other; that there were men, for instance, who might be described as *of feminine soul enclosed in a male body* (*anima muliebris in corpore virili inclusa*)....(Edward Carpenter, "The Intermediate Sex," in Edward Carpenter, *Selected Writings, Volume 1: Sex*, p. 190)

Edward Carpenter, a major left-wing-feminist-homosexual intellectual of the early twentieth century, was quite influential with some of the young Lawrence's older friends, among them William E. Hopkin and Alice Dax, the young Lawrence's mistress; both Hopkin and Dax were active in feminist-socialist circles; indeed, it is evident that Lawrence must have read Carpenter's work; as Lawrence-Carpenter biographer Emile Delavenay informs us:

> the evidence is there; [the young Lawrence's sweetheart] Jessie Chambers...assured us in 1935 that their mutual friend Alice Dax [the young Lawrence's mistress]...owned most of Carpenter's works. Jessie was sure that Lawrence had read *all the books* on Mrs Dax's shelves, being a frequent visitor to her house....(Emile Delavenay, *D. H. Lawrence and Edward Carpenter*, p. 21)

Delavenay also remarks that

> It is important to note that Lawrence does not appear anywhere in his writings to have *named* Carpenter....(Ibid., pp. 10-11)

—but we now know that here Delavenay is mistaken. In a (recently published) letter to William Hopkin in September 1915, Lawrence asks Hopkin to send Edward Carpenter a leaflet promoting Lawrence's magazine *The Signature* (in which Lawrence published "The Crown"):

> If you will send Edward Carpenter a leaflet, I shall be glad: though he is not in my line. But he may give the paper to some young creature. (D. H. Lawrence letter to William and Sallie Hopkin, 25 September 1915)

Here Lawrence asserts his definite difference from—and opposition to—Edward Carpenter ("he is not in my line"); indeed, recently, one major homosexual historian-theorist actually makes mention of "the sexual dialectic of D. H. Lawrence, whose influence was quite oppositional to Carpenter's" (Jeffrey Weeks, *Sex, Politics and Society*, p. 174). Furthermore, Lawrence in his letter to Hopkin exhibits a bit of contempt for Carpenter's sexual orientation; as one Lawrence scholar tells us, Lawrence's suggestion of Carpenter's giving his (Lawrence's) "paper to some young creature" is "a sardonic reference to Carpenter's entourage of homosexual young men" (Delany, *D. H. Lawrence's Nightmare*, p. 143). Thus, *pace* Delavenay, we now know that Lawrence had a degree of contempt for Edward Carpenter; but the "political" Lawrence was keenly aware of the power and influence of the left-wing, pro-homosexual elite; and it was this "political" Lawrence, in tandem with the "Messianic" Lawrence, that desired both to save the homosexual elite from themselves in their "blasphemy against love" (as Lawrence called homosexuality, "the men loving men," in his letter of 19 April 1915 to David Garnett) and to engage the aid of that same elite in order to save his *Rainbow* and other literary-philosophical works from the public enemies that would permanently defeat them; this, it seems to me, was Lawrence's frame of mind in April 1916, a frame of mind which motivated him to write the "Prologue" to *Women in Love*. A few days before he began writing the "Prologue" Lawrence was full of anger and despair over the way his "art" was being "degraded" by "the public":

> Thank you very much for offering to help us with money [he wrote to a wealthy friend]. For the present, we can manage. I wish I could always be sure of earning enough to keep us, but I can't. At the Renaissance, Art was holy....Now art is degraded beneath mention, really trampled under the choice of...public opinion. When I think of art, and then of the British public...then a sort of madness comes over me, really as if one were fastened within a mob, and in danger of being trampled to death. I hate the "public," the "people," "society," so much, that a madness possesses me when I think of them....(D. H. Lawrence letter to Lady Ottoline Morrell, 7 April 1916)

In his fear and hatred of "the mob," Lawrence in April 1916 sought the aid of the homosexual elite; thus he made the Ur-Birkin of the "Prologue" to *Women in Love* a latent homosexual, using virtually the exact phrases from Edward Carpenter's gay classic *The Intermediate Sex* to describe the Ur-Birkin's desires: Carpenter's "feminine soul enclosed in a male body" becomes—in the "Prologue"—"The soul of a woman and the physique of a man": this, says Lawrence, is what the Ur-Birkin is "watch[ing] for, in the street."

But why "in the street"? Here again we see the derivative, inauthentic nature of Lawrence's portrayal of the Ur-Birkin in the "Prologue"—a portrayal that was a major tactic in Lawrence's imaginary strategy to secure the support of the cultural homosexual elite against the "public," the "mob"; for Lawrence in April 1916 believed that he needed the political support of the homosexual elite, and at the same time he wanted to save them from their "decadent" ways: accordingly, Lawrence himself, who indeed was not homosexual, needed other, external sources for his depiction of the character of the latent homosexual Ur-Birkin.

One major source for Lawrence's portrayal of the "homosexual" Ur-Birkin in the "Prologue" was evidently Havelock Ellis. According to the latest biography of Lawrence, even the young Lawrence knew the work of Havelock Ellis:

> A sense of the twentieth-century's limitless possibilities filled the pages of *The New Age*, a weekly journal to which Lawrence began subscribing [in 1908] for six shillings a year....Founded in 1907, *The New Age* provided a steady infusion of pungent, stylish essays on politics, medicine, science, art and morals. Its pages were spattered with the names of the social crusaders and secular priests of the day—Beatrice and Sidney Webb, George Bernard Shaw, H. G. Wells and Havelock Ellis....(Brenda Maddox, *The Married Man: A Life of D. H. Lawrence*, p. 16)

Thus, Lawrence even in his early twenties was quite familiar with the work of Havelock Ellis, whose classic psychological study of homosexuality, *Sexual Inversion*, was first published in 1897; thus the young Lawrence was likely to have read it around 1910, when it was in its second edition. Even more important, Lawrence's close friend at the time right before the writing of *Women in Love*, Philip Heseltine, was a big fan of Havelock Ellis; as one Lawrence biographer tells us:

> At Oxford he [Heseltine] immersed himself in the study of the advanced sexual theorists of the day, such as Havelock Ellis, [and] Edward Carpenter....(Delany, *D. H. Lawrence's Nightmare*, p. 168)

Indeed, it was in 1915, the very year of Lawrence's great friendship with Heseltine, that *Sexual Inversion* appeared in its third, revised and enlarged edition; this edition Heseltine must surely have read and talked about to Lawrence in November 1915:

> I hope you didn't mind the holding forth of last night. But do think about what we were saying, of art, and life....
>
> One must fight every minute—at least I must—to overcome this great flux of disintegration,...homosexuality, the reduction process....When men come together, that is immediate reduction..., liberating a conscious knowledge of the component parts....the *knowledge* is always contained and included within the spirit, the process, of reduction, disintegration. (D. H. Lawrence letter to Heseltine, 22 November 1915)

"Holding forth" (i.e., preaching) to Heseltine about fighting against "homosexuality" with its "conscious knowledge of the component parts," its "mental" knowledge which is part and parcel of "the spirit, the process, of reduction, disintegration" of the healthy self and the healthy civilization, Lawrence feared that the Oxford-educated Heseltine himself was involved in (what Lawrence deemed to be) the sordid-cerebral activity of "homosexual love":

> those complex states [of Western civilization], the finest product of generations of synthetic [i.e., creative-heterosexual] living, are *reduced* in homosexual love....(D. H. Lawrence letter to Heseltine, 22 November 1915)

Seeing himself as the defender of "synthetic [heterosexual] living" against reductive "homosexual love," Lawrence determined to save Heseltine from "homosexuality, the reduction process"; as Heseltine's latest biographer tells us:

> Clearly their [i.e, Lawrence and Heseltine's] conversation the previous night [prior to Lawrence's letter of 22 November 1915 to Heseltine] must have included the subject of homosexuality, with Lawrence possibly having suspicions as to Philip's sexual orientation. It is perhaps significant that Lawrence was soon to lend Philip the manuscript of a philosophical work, "Goats and Compasses." (Barry Smith, *Peter Warlock: The Life of Philip Heseltine*, p. 77)

"Goats and Compasses," we know, was a "psycho-philosophical treatise dealing largely with homosexuality" (according to Heseltine's friend Cecil Gray, who claimed to have read the manuscript, which has been lost; see Smith, p. 77, and also Cecil Gray, *Peter Warlock: A Memoir of Philip Heseltine*, p. 114). Thus "Goats and Compasses" (written in February 1916) can be considered to be the Lawrentian metaphysic dealing with homosexuality upon which the fictional attempt—the "Prologue" to *Women in Love* (written in April 1916)—may be based; as Lawrence explained in "Study of Thomas Hardy":

> It is the novelists...who have the hardest task in reconciling their metaphysic, their theory of being and knowing, with their living sense of being. Because a novel is a microcosm, and because man in viewing the universe must view it in the light of a theory, therefore every novel must have the background or the structural skeleton of some theory of being, some metaphysic. ("Study of Thomas Hardy," Chapter IX)

The Lawrentian "metaphysic," as expressed in "Goats and Compasses," must have privileged the "creative synthesis" of heterosexuality and demonized the decadent "disintegration" of homosexuality. We know that "Goats and Compasses" was described by Lady Ottoline Morrell as "A gospel of hate and violent individualism. He [Lawrence] attacks the will, love and sympathy. Indeed, the only thing that he doesn't revile and condemn is love between men and women" (Ottoline Morrell, quoted in Delany, *D. H. Lawrence's Nightmare*, p. 197). The upper-class, liberal Lady Ottoline, with her sympathetic tolerance toward homosexuality, had even argued with her lover Bertrand Russell about it; Russell had written to her (in March 1915):

> Lawrence has the same feeling against sodomy as I have; you had nearly made me believe there is no great harm in it, but I have reverted; and all the examples I know confirm me in thinking it sterilizing. (Quoted in Delany, *D. H. Lawrence's Nightmare*, p. 80)

Lawrence before sending his anti-homosexual "metaphysic" ("Goats and Compasses") to Lady Ottoline had enthusiastically praised it to her:

> I have nearly done...my philosophy. At last it can stand. It is the last word. I am sure it marks the end of a great epoch: at least for me....I feel that probably you won't like it, for a time. But do read it. (D. H. Lawrence letter to Ottoline Morrell, 15 February 1916)

Certainly Ottoline read it and hated it—"deplorable tosh," she called it (Delany, p. 197)—and must have made her feelings about it known to Lawrence, who wrote her:

> Never mind that you don't like my philosophy: it doesn't matter. I am writing nothing just at present....(D. H. Lawrence letter to Ottoline Morrell, 15 March 1916)

But Lawrence could not be "writing nothing" for long; stung by Ottoline's rejection of his "philosophy," Lawrence knew that he would have to develop a new strategy to deal with the problematic of homosexuality; a strategy to win the support of the socially powerful homosexuals and to change them at the same time. Thus, about a month after his letter to Ottoline acknowledging her rejection of his "philosophy," Lawrence, fresh from his rupture with young Heseltine, commenced to write the "Prologue" to *Women in Love* with a view to deploying a new strategy that would utilize the writings of the popular intellectual sexologists, Havelock Ellis and Edward Carpenter, whom Lawrence had discussed at length with Heseltine; these sexologists, extremely sympathetic to homosexuality, gave Lawrence a perspective with which to write about homosexuality from a more understanding point of view. Indeed, Bertrand Russell, too, in 1916 was reading "Havelock Ellis on sex":

> I have read a good deal of Havelock Ellis on sex. It is full of things that everyone ought to know, very scientific and objective, most valuable and interesting....I think almost all civilized people are in some way what would be thought abnormal, and they suffer because they don't know that really ever so many people are just like them. (Bertrand Russell letter to Ottoline Morrell, 30 January 1916, *The Autobiography of Bertrand Russell*, Volume II)

Ellis' major concern was to help homosexuals who "suffer because they don't know that...so many people are just like them." Indeed, Ellis evidently felt the pain of the suffering homosexuals; his own wife was a lesbian. Thus Ellis' strategy, he told (homosexual) sex theorist Edward Carpenter, was even to promote homosexuality as "the highest ideal":

> We want to obtain sympathetic recognition for sexual inversion [i.e., homosexuality] as a psychic abnormality which may be regarded as the highest ideal....Nothing of the kind has yet been published,...and I cannot help feeling that the book [idealizing homosexuality] will do much good. (Quoted in Grosskurth, *Havelock Ellis*, pp. 177-178)

In his book *Sexual Inversion* (1915) Ellis was quick to idealize homosexuality as the characteristic of "men of great ability and...great moral worth":

> Homosexuality seems to have flourished in Rome during the empire, and is well exemplified in the persons of many of the

> emperors. Julius Caesar, Augustus, Tiberius, Caligula, Claudius, Nero, Galba, Titus, Domitian, Nerva, Trajan, Hadrian, Commodus, and Heliogabalus—many of them men of great ability and, from a Roman standpoint, great moral worth—are all charged, on more or less solid evidence, with homosexual practices. (Ellis, *Sexual Inversion*, p. 24)

Furthermore, Ellis attributes homosexuality to "men of exceptional intellect":

> The fact that homosexuality is especially common among men of exceptional intellect was long since noted by Dante....It has often been noted since and remains a remarkable fact....(Ibid., p. 26)

And Ellis goes on to authoritatively declare that:

> There cannot be the slightest doubt that intellectual and artistic abilities of the highest order have frequently been associated with a congenitally inverted sexual temperament. (Ibid.)

Surely it is evident that Ellis' valorization of homosexuality ("congenitally inverted sexual temperament") as a site of "intellectual and artistic abilities of the highest order"—a valorization which Ellis began as early as 1897 (the year of the first version of *Sexual Inversion*)—is that valorization at which Lawrence must be venting his mystified annoyance in his letter of 2 December 1913 (to Henry Savage) when Lawrence says that he "should like to know why nearly every man that approaches greatness tends to homosexuality, whether he admits it or not." It is, of course, the Havelock Ellis paradigm connecting homosexuality with "greatness"—"intellectual and artistic abilities of the highest order"—it is this Ellis paradigm to which Lawrence himself takes exception, with Lawrence himself as *the exception*—the exception who shows that a man can be "great" and heterosexual; unfortunately for Lawrence's present reputation, this exceptional—indeed, extraordinary—Lawrentian quality is connected with what today is hatefully called heterosexism, male chauvinism, etc.; as Lawrence says, in the same letter to Savage (2 December 1913), the reason a man may desperately turn to homosexuality—or suicide—is that he lacks the psychic-ontological power to deal with a woman—to "form" her:

> one doesn't believe in one's power to find and to form the woman in whom one can be free—and one shoots oneself, if one is vital and feels powerfully and down to the core.

Here Lawrence refers to the minor poet Richard Middleton (Henry Savage was a Middleton enthusiast); Middleton committed suicide, and Lawrence believed Middleton did this because he (Middleton) "[did not] believe in [his] power to find and to form the woman in whom one can be free"; consequently, he (Middleton) "would have loved a man, more than a woman: even physically: like the ancients did." Thinking of the "great" "ancients" who were homosexual, Lawrence may very well have been referring to Ellis' long catalogue of classical homosexuals. But Lawrence, unlike the modern Middleton as well as "the ancients," tells Savage that he (Lawrence) has risen to the occasion and has been able "to find and to form the woman in whom [he] can be free"—that woman of course being Frieda. Thus Lawrence sets himself apart from the great ancients, further assuring his originality and uniqueness as one full of "greatness" and heterosexual as well. But recent feminist students of Lawrence do not appreciate Lawrence's remarkable talk of "find[ing] and...form[ing] the woman" who will help him to attain his maximal artistic power and greatness.

If Lawrence could indeed utilize "the woman" for his artistic uniqueness and greatness, he could also utilize Ellis' *Sexual Inversion*. Ellis makes clear that what he has to say does not relate only to "the ancients," but indeed also to "modern Europe":

> In modern Europe we find the strongest evidence of the presence of what may finally be called true sexual inversion when we investigate the men of the Renaissance....
>
> As the Renaissance developed, homosexuality seems to become more prominent among distinguished persons....It is among artists [of the Renaissance]...that homosexuality may most notably be traced....Michelangelo, one of the very chief artists of the Renaissance period, we cannot now doubt, was sexually inverted. (Ellis, *Sexual Inversion*, pp. 30-32)

Rather than see Michelangelo as an example of "sexual inversion," Lawrence in his *Women in Love* period praised Michelangelo as an artist who "turned his eyes to the Great God of Power and Might, whose sons we [i.e., Lawrence and Michelangelo] are" (D. H. Lawrence letter to Ottoline Morrell, 7 April 1916). Thus Lawrence early on in his *Women in Love* period (he began *Women in Love* in April 1916) deployed a strategy one part of which was to view and glorify that which Ellis celebrated as "sexually inverted" as instead a kind of sublime masculinity connected with "the Great God of Power and Might, whose sons we are"—the same "God of Power and Might" Who destroyed Sodom and Gomorrah. Thus Lawrence could fight the Ellisian paradigm by transposing any notion of "sexual inversion" to the quintessentially Lawrentian quasi-divine realm of transcendence; this Lawrence does at the beginning of his "Prologue" to *Women in Love*: here he portrays the intense friendship of Birkin and Gerald as a transcendental experience initiated in the sublime realm of "mountain-climbing":

> The week of mountain-climbing passed like an intense brief lifetime. The three men [Birkin, Gerald, and their mutual friend Hosken] were very close together, and lifted into an abstract isolation, among the upper rocks and the snow. The world that lay below, the whole field of human activity, was sunk and subordinated, they had trespassed into the upper silence and loneliness. The three of them had reached another state of being.

Having attained "another state of being [i.e., transcendent being]," Birkin and Gerald are exempted from Ellis' "sexual inversion"; nevertheless, they ostensibly feel very deeply about one another:

> They knew they loved each other, that each would die for the other. ("Prologue," *Women in Love* 490)

This Birkin-Gerald relationship seems to aspire to be some sort of David-Jonathan friendship; but alas, Lawrence's portrayal of this relationship is not ultimately convincing: it is full of contradictions—on the one hand, "each would die for the other"; but, on the other hand,

> Rupert Birkin...[was] strongly centred in himself, [and] never gave way in his soul, to anyone. He remained in the last issue detached, self-responsible, having no communion with any other soul. (Ibid., p. 490)

The "self-responsible" loner Birkin certainly is unlikely to immerse himself in any intense "love" relationship with Gerald; indeed, in the "Prologue" Birkin is finally described as "callous":

> In the last issue he [Birkin] was callous, and without feeling, [and] confident....(Ibid., p. 491)

If Birkin is "without feeling," how can he have "a passion of desire for Gerald Crich"? (Ibid., p. 493) As the "Prologue" goes on:

> It satisfied him [Birkin] to have to do with Gerald Crich, it fulfilled him to have this other man, this hard-limbed traveller and sportsman, following implicitly, held as it were consummated within the

> spell of a more powerful understanding. Birkin felt a passion of desire for Gerald Crich, for the clumsier, cruder intelligence and the limited soul, and for the striving, unlightened body of his friend. (Ibid., p. 493)

It is clear here that Birkin's "passion of desire for Gerald Crich" is not sexual, but rather political: he wants Gerald to be his follower, "following [him] implicitly" because he (Birkin) possesses "a more powerful understanding" than does Gerald. With Gerald Crich, "a well-set young Englishman of strong conservative temperament, and heir to considerable wealth" (Ibid. 491), as Birkin's follower, Birkin-Lawrence could indeed attain the sociopolitical power he needed to survive (at least in his imagination) in a world afflicted with "Decay and decomposition" (Ibid. 495); yet finally Lawrence knew that he must be less politically manipulative, more psychologically sympathetic, in his delineation of the "homosexual" Ur-Birkin if he were to win the support of the homosexual intelligentsia in England: thus we have, towards the end of the "Prologue" to *Women in Love*, this abrupt disquisition on Birkin's "hot, flushing, roused attraction"—"for men":

> All the time, he recognised that...it was for men that he felt the hot, flushing, roused attraction which a man is supposed to feel for the other sex....[T]he male physique had a fascination for him....
>
> In the street, it was the men who roused him by their flesh and their manly, vigorous movement,...whilst he studied the women as sisters, knowing their meaning and their intents. ("Prologue," pp. 501-502)

Here Lawrence, attempting to make a favorable impression on the pro-homosexual elite, creates a scene which seems to me to be a composite deriving from the writings of both Havelock Ellis and Edward Carpenter. The Ur-Birkin of the "Prologue," as "he studied the women as sisters, knowing their meaning and their intents"—as Lawrence rather vaguely describes it—is extremely reminiscent of Carpenter's "Uranian man":

> If now we come to what may be called the more normal type of the Uranian [i.e., homosexual] man, we find a man who...[possesses] the tenderer and more emotional soul-nature of the woman—and sometimes to a remarkable degree....[E]motionally they [i.e., Uranian-homosexual men] are extremely complex, tender, sensitive, pitiful and loving,...;...intuition is always strong; like women they read characters at a glance, and know, without

knowing how, what is passing in the minds of others....
That men of this kind despise women, though a not uncommon belief, is one which hardly appears to be justified. Indeed, though naturally not inclined to "fall in love" in this direction, such men are by their nature drawn rather near to women, and it would seem that they often feel a singular appreciation and understanding of the emotional needs and destinies of the other sex, leading in many cases to a genuine though what is called a "Platonic" friendship. (Edward Carpenter, "The Intermediate Sex," *Edward Carpenter: Selected Writings, Volume I: Sex*, p. 198)

Thus the character of the Ur-Birkin, who "studied the women as sisters, knowing their meaning and their intents," is essentially derived from Carpenter's "Uranian man" who "feel[s] a singular appreciation and understanding of the emotional needs and destinies of the other sex"; similarly, the "in the street" site of the Ur-Birkin's "roused attraction" to "the men" is evidently derived from various case histories of Havelock Ellis' *Sexual Inversion* (1915); here, for instance, is a bit of "History XXI":

In passing along a side-street one night I was overtaken by a man who began conversation on the weather. He asked me if I were not cold, began passing his hand up and down my back; then came a question about caning at school, whether certain parts of me were not sore, leading to an investigating touch. I put his hand aside shyly, but did not resent the action. Presently he was for exploring my trousers pockets and I began to think him a pickpocket; repulsed in that direction, he returned to rubbing my back. The sensation was pleasant. I now took him for a pimp who wished to take me to a prostitute, and as at that time [early teens] I had begun to realize such pleasures were not to my taste I was glad to find myself at my destination, and said good-bye sharply, leaving him full of astonishment at his failure with one who had taken his advances so pleasantly. I could not bring myself to believe that others had the same feelings as myself. Later I realized my escape, not without a certain amount of regret, and constructed for my own pleasure a different termination to the incident. (Havelock Ellis, *Sexual Inversion* [1915; repr. New York: Random House, 1936], 3rd edition, Chapter III, "Sexual Inversion in Men," History XXI, p. 153)

This "History XXI," with its sordid "in the street" setting, seems to me to be a likely source of some of the material in the "Prologue" to *Women in Love*; Lawrence himself, it seems to me, would have found such encounters grotesque and obscene: thus, in depicting the Ur-Birkin's "in the street" desires, Lawrence is a bit out of his depth, and this results in a treatment which is rather unconvincing and derivative. Similarly, the Ur-Birkin's sense of his attraction to men as "a new torture to him" ("Prologue" 502) is extremely reminiscent of "a very radical case of sexual inversion"—"History XX" in the 1915 edition of *Sexual Inversion*:

> He ["History XX"] has suffered extremely throughout life owing to his sense of the difference between himself and normal human beings. No pleasure he has enjoyed, he declares, can equal a thousandth part of the pain caused by the internal consciousness of pariahdom. The utmost he can plead in his own defense, he admits, is irresponsibility, for he acknowledges that his impulse may be morbid. But he feels absolutely certain that in early life his health was ruined and his moral repose destroyed owing to the perpetual conflict with his own inborn [homosexual] nature, and that relief and strength came with indulgence. (Ellis, *Sexual Inversion*, pp. 143-144)

In relation to "History XX," the Ur-Birkin can be seen as a would-be "History XX"—"History XX" who is described by Ellis as "a successful man of letters who...passed through a long period of mental conflict before he became reconciled to his homosexual instincts" (Ibid., p. 144). The Ur-Birkin, too, has written "essays on Education [that] were brilliant....He wrote also harsh, jarring poetry, very real and painful,...and sometimes, shallower, gentle lyrics" ("Prologue" 491-92). But does the Ur-Birkin "[pass] through a long period of mental conflict" regarding homosexuality? No; for the fact is that further evidence of the inauthentic, half-hearted, derivative nature of Lawrence's portrayal of the Ur-Birkin in the "Prologue" to *Women in Love* can be found in the fickle, the unconvincing nature of the Ur-Birkin's attraction towards men:

> He [the Ur-Birkin] loved his friend [whom we are never told about], the beauty of whose manly limbs made him tremble with pleasure. He wanted to caress him.
> But reserve, which was as strong as a chain of iron in him, kept him from any demonstration. And if he were away for any length of time from the man he loved so hotly, then he forgot him, the flame which invested the beloved like a transfiguration passed away, and Birkin remembered his friend as tedious. He could not go back to him, to talk as tediously as he would have to talk, to take such a level of intelligence as he would have to take. He forgot his men friends completely, as one forgets the candle one has blown out. ("Prologue," pp. 502-503)

Thus the Ur-Birkin, rather than feeling any real intensity of "conflict" concerning his "homoerotic" desires, can easily forget them completely, and can consider the objects of his "desire" to be simply "tedious"; indeed, the fact is that the Ur-Birkin's "men friends" care far more for him than he does for them:

> He forgot his men friends completely, as one forgets the candle one has blown out. They remained as quite extraneous and uninteresting persons living their life in their own sphere, and having not the slightest relation to himself, even though they themselves maintained a real warmth of affection, almost of love for him. He paid not the slightest heed to this love which was constant to him, he felt it sincerely to be just nothing, valueless.
>
> So he left his old friends completely, even those to whom he had been attached passionately, like David to Jonathan. Men whose presence he had waited for cravingly...became to him mere figures, as non-existent as is the waiter who sets the table in a restaurant.
>
> He [the Ur-Birkin] wondered very slightly at this [lack of real homoerotic desire in him], but dismissed it with hardly a thought. ("Prologue," p. 503; my italics)

But why does the Ur-Birkin "[dismiss] it with hardly a thought"? The answer, evidently, is that the Ur-Birkin is not really very "homo-erotic" after all—in the "Prologue" Lawrence does his best to present an intense and convincing picture of a "latent homosexual," but ultimately Lawrence himself does not have enough genuine "homoeroticism" in his own imagination to convey this picture, instead producing a delineation of the "homoerotic" Ur-Birkin that is rife with contradictions and inconsistencies: Lawrence *tells* us, he does not *show* us, that the Ur-Birkin has a

> passionate desire to have near him some man he saw, to exchange intimacy, to unburden himself of love to this new beloved.
>
> It might be any man, a policeman who suddenly looked up at him, as he enquired the way, or a soldier who sat next to him in a railway carriage....
>
> *In his mind* was a small gallery of such men, men whom he had never spoken to, but who had flashed themselves upon his senses unforgettably, men whom he apprehended intoxicatingly in his blood. ("Prologue," p. 503; my italics)

Here Lawrence's portrayal of the Ur-Birkin is indeed full of contradictions: on the one hand, the Ur-Birkin's "passionate desire" for "this new beloved [man]" or "[this] new beloved...small gallery of...men" is rooted "[i]n his [the Ur-Birkin's] mind"—thus making this "desire" a product of "the mental consciousness"—the "mental consciousness" which Lawrence only a few months before the "Prologue" had posited as being antithetical to sexual desire and "connection":

> there is a blood-consciousness which exists in us independently of the ordinary mental consciousness....There is the blood-consciousness, with the sexual connection....One lives, knows, and has one's being in the blood, without any reference to nerves and brain....[W]hen I take a woman, then...my blood-knowing is overwhelming. There is a transmission...between her blood and mine, in the act of connection. So that afterwards, even if she goes away, the blood-consciousness persists between us....(D. H. Lawrence letter to Bertrand Russell, 8 December 1915)

Thus, for Lawrence, the "blood-consciousness"—not "the mind"—is the site of "the sexual connection"; furthermore, according to Lawrence, the "blood-consciousness" dominates "when I take *a woman*" (italics mine). So, in the "Prologue," when the Ur-Birkin's passion "for men" transpires "in his mind," he is not being Lawrentian at all—and when, a little later in this same sentence of the "Prologue" Lawrence says that the Ur-Birkin "apprehends" these men "intoxicatingly in his blood," Lawrence is not only contradicting himself—by mixing "his [the Ur-Birkin's] mind" with "his [the Ur-Birkin's] blood," but he is also contaminating the "blood-consciousness" with the cerebral "apprehensions" of the "mental consciousness" that take place—mistakenly—in the Ur-Birkin's "blood" even though in fact there has been no "sexual connection" at this point with "a woman"—the Lawrentian way set forth in the "blood-consciousness" letter to Russell—nor with "the men" whom the Ur-Birkin ostensibly desires.

Thus, at every level, the Ur-Birkin is no Lawrentian male; and in the portrayal of the Ur-Birkin's desires Lawrence makes a muddle which once again indicates that this configuration of homoerotic desire and frustration came from some external source. Let us look at "History VII" in Havelock Ellis' *Sexual Inversion* (1915):

> In early manhood,...owing, I believe, to the great emotional tension under which I lived, my nervous system was a good deal shattered and exhausted....
>
> ...My own [homo]sexual nature was a mystery to me [as a young adolescent]. I found myself cut off from the understanding

of others, felt myself an outcast, and...was intensely miserable. I thought about my male friends...during the day and dreamed about them at night, but was too convinced that I was a hopeless monstrosity ever to make any effectual advances. Later on...I made a few special friends, and at last it came to me occasionally to sleep with them and to satisfy my imperious need by mutual embraces and emissions. Before this happened, however, I was once or twice on the brink of despair and madnes with repressed passion and torment. ("History VII," in Ellis, *Sexual Inversion* [1915; repr. New York: Random House, 1936], Part Two, Volume II of *Studies in the Psychology of Sex*, pp. 107-108)

"History VII" is in fact written by none other than Edward Carpenter, the very man that Lawrence had ridiculed and described as "not in my line"; though he (Lawrence) would be happy to use Carpenter to disseminate his (Lawrence's) leaflets promoting his (Lawrence's) philosophy (D. H. Lawrence letter to Hopkin, 25 September 1915).

So why did Lawrence use the feelings of someone "not in my line" to describe the emotional state of the Ur-Birkin? The answer, it seems to me, lies in Lawrence's visionary socio-political aspirations, aspirations to which the support of the homosexual elite was essential. Indeed, one thing that the "Prologue" to *Women in Love* does tell us about Lawrence in April 1916 (when he wrote it) is that Lawrence's attitude towards "his men friends" may well have been mainly manipulative; the Ur-Birkin, we are told in the "Prologue," "forgot his *men* friends completely" (my italics), but "they [the Ur-Birkin's men friends] themselves maintained a real warmth of affection, almost of love for him" ("Prologue" 503). After the banning of *The Rainbow*, Lawrence of course became intensely misanthropic; yet he would have welcomed "a real warmth" of support from some powerful political quarter to help him rectify the social injustice which had been done to him. In Lawrence's metaphysical-political fantasy of the "Prologue" to *Women in Love*, the despairing Ur-Birkin concludes that there is

no great philosophic idea,...[;] for the time being, mankind, instead of going through a period of growth, is going through a corresponding process of decay and decomposition....

...What should a man add himself on to?—to science, to social reform, to aestheticism, to sensationalism? The whole world's constructive activity was a fiction, a lie, to hide the great process of decomposition, which had set in. ("Prologue," pp. 495-496)

Of course, part of "the great process of decomposition" that Lawrence was fighting against at this time was homosexuality—as Lawrence had said to Heseltine:

> One must fight every minute—at least I must—to overcome... homosexuality, the reduction process....
> (D. H. Lawrence leter to Heseltine, 22 November 1915)

—and for this fight, Lawrence—who was indeed less despairing than the Ur-Birkin—for this fight Lawrence needed, paradoxically enough, the support of the very homosexual elite he sought to destroy—or, rather, to transform.

In endeavoring to transform the homosexual elite, Lawrence soon realized that the bogusness of the Ur-Birkin's "sexual inversion" desires would redound to the discredit of Lawrence's new novel both as a work of art and as a text of persuasion; thus Lawrence evidently felt that the inauthentic nature of his portrayal of the Ur-Birkin's homoerotic desires would lead to Lawrence's failure in both the private domain of the artistic-creative imagination and the public domain of social-political persuasion. Lawrence at this time surely valorized "desire"—indeed, Lawrence emphasizes the supreme importance of desire at the very same time that he decides to cancel the "Prologue" to *Women in Love*; at about the same time as he deleted the "Prologue," Lawrence wrote a lengthy letter to Catherine Carswell on "the fulfilment of our desires":

> What we want is the fulfilment of our desires, down to the deepest and most spiritual desire....*every* desire, to the very deepest. And I shall find my deepest desire to be a wish for pure, unadulterated relationship with the universe, for *truth in being* [italics mine]. My pure relationship with one woman is marriage, physical and spiritual: with another, is another form of happiness, according to our nature. And so on for ever.
> It is this establishing of pure relationships which makes heaven, wherein we are immortal, like the angels, and mortal, like men, both. And the way to immortality is in the fulfilment of desire....
> Because, you see, what intimation of immortality have we, save our spontaneous wishes? God works in me (if I use the term God) as my desire. He gives me the understanding to discriminate between my desires, to discern between greater and lesser desire....God in me is my desire. (D. H. Lawrence letter to Catherine Carswell, 16 July 1916)

Lawrence scholar George H. Ford tells us that "the discarding of this chapter ["Prologue"] occurred...in July 1916, when he [Lawrence] himself began typing out a copy of the novel to send to his publishers" (Ford, "Introductory Note," p. 39); thus Lawrence at this time realized that he had to cancel the "Prologue" if he was to be true to his own "desires" and achieve "truth in being." Indeed, it is evident to me that the sublime Lawrence here represents a stark contrast to the Ur-Birkin—the Ur-Birkin with his guilt, ambivalence, and sordid ("In the street") aspect. Here Lawrence speaks of "pure relationships," "immortality" and "God"—a far cry from the nihilistic Ur-Birkin who

> ran about from death to death. Work was terrible, horrible because he did not believe in it....Nowhere more than in education [the Ur-Birkin's field] did a man feel the horror of false, rootless, spasmodic activity more acutely. The whole business was like dementia. It created in him a feeling of nausea and horror....
>
> In his private life the same horror of futility and wrongness dogged him....("Prologue," p. 496)

Unlike the Ur-Birkin, Lawrence certainly did believe in his "work" and his "private life"—both of which would, he hoped, lead to his success in attaining "poetic immortality."

Making a "creative synthesis" of "pure relationships," "immortality" and "God," Lawrence in his letter to Catherine Carswell (16 July 1916) here makes it clear that for him the greatest desire is to achieve "immortality"—that is, poetic immortality—with the help of "God"—that is, his heterosexual "desire" ("God in me is my desire")—which will lead to his (Lawrence's) uniquely powerful depictions of "pure relationships"—"relationships" "with the universe,...with one woman [in] marriage,...with another [woman]," all being "form[s] of happiness." It is noteworthy, it seems to me, that in discussing the "form[s] of happiness" that constitute "my deepest desire" Lawrence makes no mention of male-male relationships of any sort (sexual or non-sexual), thus acknowledging that for him any kind of friendship with his own gender was surely a "lesser desire," while relationships with "one woman...[and] another" were clearly a "greater desire"; indeed, in his letter of 16 July 1916 to Catherine Carswell, Lawrence goes on to declare that, without the support of "his women," "man...must die":

> it seems to me, man must find a new expression, give a new value to life, or his women will reject him, and he must die.

Thus in July 1916, at the very time he was rejecting the "Prologue" to *Women in Love*, Lawrence believed that if man was rejected by woman, "he must die"—in other words, the male-female relation was "a matter of life and death," with a vital male-female relation weighing in on the "life" side of the equation; and, evidently, a sexually "inverted" male-to-male relation, on the other hand, conducing to the site of death: for, according to Lawrence, "creative life" can only take place in "the true relationship established between *different* things, different spirits" (D. H. Lawrence letter to Carswell, 16 July 1916; italics mine)—and for Lawrence in July 1916, immersed in his quest for poetic immortality via *Women in Love* and his relation with Frieda, the supreme evidence of "difference" manifests itself in the male-female relationship:

> Frieda...is quite right, about the *difference* between us [Lawrence and Frieda] being the adventure, and the true relationship established between different things, different spirits, this is creative life....[T]here must be an act of love which is a passing of the self into a pure relationship with the other, something new and creative in the coming together of the lovers, in their creative spirit, before a new child can be born, a new *flower* in us before there can be a new seed of a child. (D. H. Lawrence letter to Carswell, 16 July 1916)

Thus it is adventurous heterosexual "difference"—the "true relationship" established between male and female—that is the Lawrentian definition of "creative life"—"creative life" in Nature and in Art, with the (hetero)sexual Lawrentian "act of love which is a passing of the self into a pure relationship with the other" being required for the making of "something new and creative in the coming together of the lovers," whether that "something new" be "a new child...born" in the biological sense, or "a new flower" of art in the literary-cultural sense.

Yet Lawrence as prophetic artist in the midst of the Great War was keenly aware that the omnipresence of death must inevitably and fully be dealt with in art; and the form of art must be rooted in

> the *opposition* of life [against death]....[In art there must be] enough *resistance* of life [against death] to bring that solid equilibrium which is the core of art, an absolute reached by the sheer tension of life stubborn against death, the two in opposition creating the third thing, the pure resultant, absolved, art. (D. H. Lawrence letter to Catherine Carswell, 22 July 1916)

Thus Lawrence valorized "the sheer tension of life stubborn against death" in art as well as in life, with the making of art (according to

Lawrence) originating in the creative conflict between life and death, "the two [i.e., life and death] in opposition creating the third thing, the pure resultant, absolved, art." Furthermore, at the same time that Lawrence postulates art as the product ("resultant") of the tension between life and death ("sheer tension of life stubborn against death"), Lawrence proceeds to define "life" and "death" in terms of heterosexuality ("those who are married") and homosexuality ("men all together, women all together") respectively:

> I think...we [Lawrence and Frieda] will...live the life of contemplation. It is those who are married who should live the life of contemplation; together. In the world, there is the long day of destruction to go by. But let those who are single [i.e., not heterosexual], man torn from woman, woman from man, *men all together, women all together*, separate violent and deathly fragments, each returning and adhering to its own kind, the body of life torn in two, let *these* [homosexuals-lesbians] finish the day of destruction, and those [heterosexuals] who have united go into the wilderness to know a new heaven and a new earth. (D. H. Lawrence letter to Catherine Carswell, 22 July 1916; italics mine)

Considering himself and Frieda to be of the elect, "who should live the life of contemplation; together," Lawrence in July 1916, just as he had decided to reject the "Prologue" with its homosexual subject matter, at the same time definitely asserts his privileging of the heterosexual couple ("those who are married") as the only ones capable of salvation via "the life of contemplation" which will lead to their discovery, in "the wilderness," of "a new heaven and a new earth" of "life," from which will be excluded "those...[homosexual] men all together, [lesbian] women all together" whom Lawrence thinks of as "deathly fragments, each returning and adhering to its own kind" in homosexual connexion which culminates in *the* final "day of destruction." Connecting homosexuality (evidently) with the end of the world, Lawrence at this point (22 July 1916) evidently decides to give up any salvific attempt to treat homosexuals and homosexuality in his novel, which he *now* significantly entitles Women in Love (D. H. Lawrence letter to Catherine Carswell, 10 August 1916) as he decides to make his main objective here the expression of his "deepest...desire"—the desire for "pure" (i.e., ultimate, sublime) marriage; indeed, the actual first chapter of Women in Love makes clear from the very beginning the nature of Lawrence's main concern:

"Ursula," said Gudrun, "don't you *really want* to get married?"

Ursula laid her embroidery in her lap and looked up. Her face was calm and considerate.

"I don't know," she replied. "It depends how you mean."

Gudrun was slightly taken aback. She watched her sister for some moments.

"Well," she said ironically, "it usually means one thing!—But don't you think, anyhow, you'd be—" she darkened slightly—"in a better position than you are in now?"

A shadow came over Ursula's face.

"I might," she said. "But I'm not sure."

Again Gudrun paused, slightly irritated. She wanted to be quite definite....

"You wouldn't consider a good offer?" asked Gudrun.

"I think I've rejected several," said Ursula.

"*Really!*" Gudrun flushed dark.—"But anything really worth while? Have you *really*?"

"A thousand a year, and an awfully nice man. I liked him awfully," said Ursula.

"Really! But weren't you fearfully tempted?"

"In the abstract—but not in the concrete," said Ursula. "When it comes to the point, one isn't even tempted.—Oh, if I were tempted, I'd marry like a shot.—I'm only tempted *not* to." The faces of both sisters suddenly lit up with amusement.

"Isn't it an amazing thing," cried Gudrun, "how strong the temptation is, not to!"

They both laughed, looking at each other. In their hearts they were frightened. (Chapter I, "Sisters")

By beginning *Women in Love* with "Sisters" Ursula and Gudrun and their discussion of marriage, Lawrence makes it clear that the main thrust of his novel is the all-importance of heterosexuality in general and marriage in particular in a modern world in which salvific "pure relationships"—of which marriage is most important—are virtually impossible of attainment. Clearly this is why the sophisticated "Sisters" Ursula and Gudrun are so "frightened" *au fond* "in their hearts": despite their defensive, irreverent laughter regarding the subject of marriage, they in fact fear that they may never achieve "this establishing of pure relationships [in marriage] which makes heaven" (as Lawrence says in his letter of 16 July 1916 to Catherine Carswell)—in other words, they fear that they are damned to their sophisticated feminist isolation.

But, no sexist in his "deepest desire" to save humanity through marriage, Lawrence a bit later on in *Women in Love* (Chapter V, "In the Train") makes it plain that men too must find life meaning through marriage. Thus, at the very beginning of "In the Train" (Chapter V), the two main male characters, Birkin and Gerald, earnestly converse about a newspaper essay which declares that

> "there must arise a man who will give new values to things, give us new truths, a new attitude to life, or else we shall be a crumbling nothingness in a few years, a country in ruin—" (Chapter V, "In the Train")

The "man," of course, is Lawrence himself: the newspaper essay's remarks are extremely reminiscent of Lawrence's letter, at the height of his *Women in Love* period, to Catherine Carswell (16 July 1916), where he declares that "man must find a new expression, give a new value to life"; and the "new value to life" which Lawrence expresses through Birkin in "In the Train" is one that valorizes "[heterosexual] love [as] the be-all and the end-all of life":

> "Do you think love is the be-all and the end-all of life?" Birkin asked, with direct, attentive seriousness.
> "Of my own life?" said Gerald.
> "Yes."
> There was a really puzzled pause.
> "I can't say," said Gerald. "It hasn't been, so far."
> "What has your life been, so far?"
> "Oh—finding out things for myself—and getting experiences—and making things *go*."
> Birkin knitted his brows like sharply moulded steel.
> "I find," he said, "that one needs some one *really* pure single activity—I should call love a single pure activity...."

As in his letters of the *Women in Love* period, Lawrence here in *Women in Love* privileges the quest for the "pure," the vital in a deathly, decadent modern world which is rapidly turning meaningless; as Birkin tells the skeptical Gerald:

> The old ideals are dead as nails—nothing there. It seems to me there remains only this perfect union with a woman—sort of ultimate marriage—and there isn't anything else. (58)

Thus, in the actual *Women in Love*, Lawrence's Rupert Birkin, rather than being implicated in the homosexual desire of the "Prologue," is instead dedicated to the promotion of "perfect union with a woman," "ultimate marriage"—and nothing else ("there isn't anything else").

But Lawrence knew that if his advocacy of "ultimate marriage" were to succeed in the modern world he would need to make a place for all humanity in his vision of life; and here the Lawrence of the Great War-*Women in Love* period is tormented by ambivalence: on the one hand is Lawrence's extreme misanthropy; as he tells his friend Koteliansky:

> I don't believe they will conscript you, in the end....Surely they have got their mouths as full of conscripted England, as they can chew. I must say I hate mankind—talking of hatred, I have got a perfect androphobia. When I see people in the distance,...I want to crouch in the bushes and shoot them silently with invisible arrows of death. I think truly the only righteousness is the destruction of mankind, as in Sodom. Fire and brimstone should fall down. (D. H. Lawrence letter to Koteliansky, 4 September 1916)

Here Lawrence's misanthropy, intensified by the Great War and its threat of conscription for himself and his friends, culminates in his wish for "the...righteous...destruction of mankind, as in Sodom"—with the mention of Sodom a poignant reminder of the Biblical-cultural connexion between homosexuality and the end of the world ("Fire and brimstone"); yet in this same misanthropic letter Lawrence poignantly enough expresses his utopian hope to Koteliansky:

> Where is our Rananim? If only we had the courage to find and create it, two years ago. Perhaps it is not too late. (Ibid.)

Rananim, "the Utopian society Lawrence yearned to establish somewhere in the world" (Zytaruk, *Quest*, p. xxxiii), was indeed deeply on his mind in September 1916; almost two years earlier, he had adumbrated his conception of "Rananim" to his friend Willie Hopkin:

> I want to gather about twenty souls and sail away from this world of war and squalor and found a little colony where there shall be...some real decency. It is to be a colony built up on the real decency which is in each member of the Community—a community which is established upon the assumption of goodness in the members, instead of the assumption of badness. (D. H. Lawrence letter to Willie Hopkin, 18 January 1915)

It should be noted that Willie Hopkin, the recipient of Lawrence's "Rananim" letter, is the same Willie Hopkin to whom Lawrence wrote disparagingly of the homosexual-sexologist Edward Carpenter and his company ("he is not in my line....he may give the paper to some young creature"; D. H. Lawrence letter to Hopkin, 25 September 1915); in his "Rananim" letter to Hopkin, however, Lawrence aspires to a "community" in which will be manifest "some real decency" and "the assumption of goodness in its members"—including, most likely, any possible "members" who might be of Edward Carpenter's "inverted" sexual orientation—E. M. Forster, of course, comes to mind—who nonetheless would demonstrate "real decency"; a "decency," it would certainly seem, that precludes "sodomy" and homosexual practises of all sorts: practises of a decadent, end-of-the-world connexion and signification. By bringing about "real decency" in the "blasphem[ers] against love" (as Lawrence called the homosexuals in his letter of 19 April 1915 to David Garnett), Lawrence could, he felt, save Western civilization—but first he would need a complete and successful hearing regarding his "panacea" of "this perfect union with a woman—sort of ultimate marriage—and there isn't anything else."

But in the "In the Train" chapter of *Women in Love*, Lawrence-Birkin finds that his message falls on deaf ears:

> Birkin...knew that Gerald wanted to be *fond* of him without taking him seriously. And this made him [Birkin] go hard and cold. As the train ran on, he [Birkin] sat looking at the land, and Gerald fell away, became as nothing to him [Birkin]. (*Women in Love*, Chapter V, "In the Train")

With Gerald showing disrespect for Birkin and his vision of "ultimate marriage," Birkin finds that he can easily be oblivious of Gerald ("Gerald fell away, became as nothing to him"); yet as soon as he forgets Gerald, Lawrence-Birkin's thoughts return to the likelihood of the Sodom-like end of the human race:

> Birkin looked at the land, at the evening, and was thinking: "Well, if mankind is destroyed, if our race is destroyed like Sodom, and there is this beautiful evening with the luminous land and trees, I am satisfied. That which informs it all is there, and can never be lost. After all, what is mankind but just one expression of the incomprehensible. And if mankind passes away, it will only mean that this particular expression is completed and done....Let mankind pass away—time it did....Humanity doesn't embody the utterance of the incomprehensible any more. Humanity is a dead letter. There will be a new embodiment, in a new way. Let humanity disappear as quick as possible." (59)

In other words, for Lawrence-Birkin the choice is to either complacently acquiesce in "our race [being] destroyed like Sodom"—or else to save the race with Lawrentian constructs such as "ultimate marriage"; at first Birkin concludes that "Humanity doesn't embody the utterance of the incomprehensible [i.e., God] any more....Let humanity disappear as quick as possible"; but then, like Lawrence in his 4 September 1916 letter to Koteliansky, Birkin is optimistic again—and insisting on his "panacea":

> "That [i.e., "ultimate marriage"] is your panacea," said Gerald [to Birkin]. "But you haven't even tried it on yourself yet, and you are sick enough."
> "I am," said Birkin. "Still, I shall come right."
> "Through marriage?"
> "Yes," Birkin answered obstinately.
> "And no," added Gerald. "No, no, no, my boy."
> There was a silence between them, and a strange tension of hostility. They always kept a gap, a distance between them, they wanted always to be free each of the other. Yet there was a curious heart-straining towards each other.
> "Salvator femininus," said Gerald, satirically.
> "Why not?" said Birkin. (*Women in Love*, Chapter VIII, "Breadalby")

Still attempting to convert Gerald to his "panacea" of salvation through marriage, Birkin confidently ("Why not?") rebuts Gerald's skepticism—but without convincing Gerald that he (Birkin) is right; indeed, it is at this point in *Women in Love* that we begin to see that Lawrence-Birkin, if he is to convince even heterosexual men such as Gerald,—let alone homosexual sorts such as Forster and Carpenter,—of his socio-cultural sagacity—needs to address himself to the male-to-male relation in such a way as to enact/execute a strategy to appeal to *men*—heterosexual and homosexual alike; thus at this juncture in *Women in Love* we see Lawrence abruptly and awkwardly indicate that the Birkin-Gerald relation is indeed extremely significant and complex and rich, containing elements of both "strange...hostility" and "curious heart-straining towards each other"—or so at least Lawrence would have us believe.

Lawrence's manipulation of the male-male relationship as a major part of his strategy to promote his heterosexual-"ultimate marriage" agenda gains momentum towards the end of the "Water-Party" chapter (Chapter XIV) when Gerald tells Birkin that

> "I'd rather come and have a chat with you than—than do anything else, I verily believe. Yes, I would. You mean a lot to me, Rupert, more than you know."

Here we see Lawrence manipulating a situation (in which Gerald's sister has just drowned at a "water-party") in such a way as to insinuate that, for some men (e.g., Gerald Crich) "hav[ing] a chat" with another man (e.g., Rupert Birkin) is preferable to any other form of human activity; this suggestion, it seems to me, is a key part of Lawrence's strategy to wean homosexuals away from sodomy into the "real decency" of exclusively—"purely"—platonic relationships that are intensely intellectually stimulating and thought-provoking to a degree where feelings of (homo)sexual stimulation, inclination and provocation will be successfully transcended, sublimated via cerebral joys such as those that must have been experienced by members of the Cambridge-Bloomsbury set such as Keynes, Forster and Strachey; these homosexual intellects did not abstain from sexual activity, of course, but in Lawrence's utopian vision they would be sufficiently fulfilled in their personal-intellectual relations with other men to refrain from homosexual practises and instead devote all their energies to making another world,

> a new world, where people could be happy together, and pure in spirit....[W]hat does not exist, one can create....(D. H. Lawrence letter to Barbara Low, 29 September 1916)

But, in creating his "new world" including even homosexual "people...happy together, and pure in spirit," Lawrence knew that he would have to accommodate his own Lawrentian dictum—

> My great religion is a belief in the blood, the flesh, as being wiser than the intellect (D. H. Lawrence letter to Ernest Collings, 17 January 1913)

—and in the Rupert Birkin-Gerald Crich relationship in *Women in Love*, Lawrence does indeed deal with "the blood, the flesh" as it pertains to male-male relationships in his utopian vision—in such a way, he must have believed, that the Lawrentian reconstruction and rehabilitation of homosexuality would successfully take into consideration the homosexual need for physical contact; and all this takes place in the context of two major "chat[s]" between Birkin and Gerald.

First, the "blood" aspect of the Lawrentian male-to-male relationship is adumbrated in the "Man to Man" chapter of *Women in Love*

(Chapter XVI); this chapter can be considered central, for it is the exact middle chapter of the novel (chapter 16 out of 32 chapters). In the middle of "Man to Man" Birkin tells Gerald that the two of them together can "make another world":

> "...Instead of chopping yourself down to fit the world, chop the world down to fit yourself.—As a matter of fact, two exceptional people make another world. You and I, we make another, separate world....It's just the special quality you value. Do you *want* to be normal or ordinary?—It's a lie. You want to be free and extraordinary, in an extraordinary world of liberty."

Positing "an extraordinary world of liberty," Lawrence-Birkin surely suggests that such a world will indeed contravene the "normal or ordinary"; yet of course this "extraordinary world of liberty" will not include homosexuality; herein it would appear that Lawrence contradicts himself: yet, on the other hand, the "free and extraordinary" Lawrentian-Birkinian approach to male-male relationships is in its own way far more subversive than mere standard homosexuality. A major part of the unconventionality of Birkin-Lawrence's approach to relationships "between men" lies in that approach's insouciant disregard of queer theorist Eve Kosofsky Sedgwick's "homosexual panic":

> For the elaboration of secular power over male bonds,...it made sense that the molly-house [i.e., house of homosexuality] persecutions [in the late seventeenth century] be pogromlike in nature, that the distinctly homosexual man not know whether or not to expect to be an object of legalized violence. But a subtler, answering strategy was also called for, complementary to this one, to consolidate control over the bonds of men who were not part of the distinctly homosexual subculture. Not only must homosexual men be unable to ascertain whether they are to be the objects of "random" homophobic violence, but no man must be able to ascertain that he is not (that his bonds are not) homosexual. In this way, a relatively small exertion of physical or legal compulsion potentially rules great reaches of behavior and filiation.
> ...what we are describing is a space or mechanism of potential power; the result [of this mechanism of potential power] has been a structural residue of terrorist potential, of *blackmailability*, of Western maleness through the leverage of homophobia.
> So-called "homosexual panic" is the most private, psychological form in which many twentieth-century western men experience their vulnerability to the social pressure of homophobic blackmail....(Eve Kosofsky Sedgwick, *Between Men*, pp. 88-89)

In "homosexual panic," the average heterosexual man (i.e., the man who is "not part of the distinctly homosexual subculture") exists in a constant state of uncertainty as to whether or not he and "his bonds" (i.e., his male-male relationships) are "homosexual"; this state of "insecurity about their own masculinity," says Sedgwick (*Epistemology of the Closet*, p. 20), leads Western men inevitably to experience "homosexual panic," for

> Our culture still sees to its being dangerous enough that women and men who find or fear they are homosexual, or are perceived by others to be so, are physically and mentally terrorized through the institutions of law, religion, psychotherapy, mass culture, medicine, the military, commerce and bureaucracy, and brute violence. (*Epistemology of the Closet*, p. 58)

Thus, according to Sedgwick, "Our culture" is guilty of "terroriz[ing]" anybody who has "insecurity about their own masculinity" and "uncertainty about his own sexual identity" (*Epistemology*, p. 20); but Lawrence-Birkin is evidently so sure in his "Western maleness," so secure about his own "masculinity," so certain about his own "[hetero]sexual identity"—and so invulnerable to "social pressure"—that he is immune to "homophobic blackmail." Thus Birkin can unselfconsciously tell himself that he loves Gerald:

> Suddenly he [Birkin] saw himself confronted with...the problem of love and eternal conjunction between two men. Of course this was necessary—it had been a necessity inside himself all his life—to love a man purely and fully. Of course he had been loving Gerald all along, and all along denying it. (*Women in Love*, Chapter XVI, "Man to Man")

Free from "homosexual panic" and its terror, Birkin-Lawrence can think of "love...between two men" without worrying or caring about whether or not he or "his bonds" are "homosexual"; indeed, he is so oblivious to "the social pressure of homophobic blackmail" (Sedgwick, *Between Men*, p. 89) that he can go so far as to articulate to Gerald the slightly extravagant, essentially archetypal nature of his vision of "love and eternal conjunction between two men":

> "You know how the old German knights used to swear a Blutbrüderschaft," he [Birkin] said to Gerald, with quite a new happy activity in his eyes.
> "Make a little wound in their arms, and rub each other's blood into the cut?" said Gerald.

> "Yes—and swear to be true to each other, of one blood, all their lives.—That is what we ought to do. No wounds, that is obsolete.— But we ought to swear to love each other, you and I, implicitly and perfectly, finally, without any possibility of going back on it." (206-207)

Invulnerable to "homophobic blackmail," Lawrence-Birkin can strongly suggest to Gerald that they "swear to love each other,...implicitly and perfectly, finally, without any possibility of going back on it"; Lawrence-Birkin's gesture, antihomophobic yet heterosexual at the same time, is indeed uniquely Lawrentian, part and parcel of the Lawrentian "wish for pure, unadulterated relationship[s]"—for, according to the Lawrentian valorization of "achieving...pure relationship[s],"

> If we think about it, we find that our life *consists in* this achieving of a pure relationship between ourselves and the living universe about us. This is how I "save my soul," by accomplishing a pure relationship between me and another person....("Morality and the Novel")

By "pure relationship" Lawrence means a relationship which will enhance his "truth in being" (as he puts it in his 16 July 1916 letter to Catherine Carswell), his "spontaneous-creative fullness of being" (as he puts it in *Psychoanalysis and the Unconscious* [1921]) in such a way as to create a psychic-imaginative state in him "which makes heaven" on earth for him—a creative-paradisal state in which he (Lawrence) is "immortal,...and mortal,...both" (D. H. Lawrence letter to Catherine Carswell, 16 July 1916) in the attainment of his "spontaneous wishes" (Ibid.).

Lawrences's greatest "spontaneous wish" during his *Women in Love* period was indeed to "save [his] soul" via the "immortal...mortal" state of "poetic immortality"—the immortality attained only by those creative artists (mortals) who possess the greatest poetic strength leading to poetic immortality; yet we must remember that

> Poetic strength comes only from...triumphant solipsism. (Bloom, *Map of Misreading*, p. 9)

And indeed the fact is that Lawrence in the supreme "poetic strength" of his *Women in Love* period was ultimately too "individual," too "solipsistic," to achieve a "Blutbruderschaft" with another man; indeed, the only kind of "homosocial" relationship which Lawrence in his supreme poetic strength (and solipsism) can tolerate is one which aggrandizes him as man and especially as writer: thus, in the supreme poetic strength of his *Women in Love* period, the only "blood brother" relationship that Lawrence makes is with his typewriter; as Lawrence explains it in a remarkable letter to Amy Lowell:

> Thank God they did not make me a soldier....There is something in military life that would kill me off, as if I were in an asphyxiating chamber. The whole thing is abhorrent to me—even the camaraderie, that is so glamorous—the Achilles and Patroclus business. The spirit, the pure spirit of militarism is sheer death to a nature that is at all constructive or social-creative. And it is not that I am afraid or shy: I can get on with the men [in a "macho" way] like a house on fire. It is simply that the spirit of militarism is essentially destructive, destroying the individual and the constructive social being. It is *bad*....
>
> ...we [Lawrence and Frieda] live very quietly indeed, being far from the world....I am very much better, much stronger, now....I am busy typing out a new novel, to be called *Women in Love*. Every day I bless you for the gift of the type-writer. It runs so glibly, and has at last become a true confrère. I take so unkindly to any sort of machinery. But now I and the type writer have sworn a Blutbruderschaft. (D. H. Lawrence letter to Amy Lowell, 23 August 1916)

According to Eve Kosofsky Sedgwick, "homosocial" relationships (i.e., "social bonds between persons of the same sex" [*Between Men*, p. 1]) when practised "between men" ("male bonding" [Ibid.]) are based on "men promoting men's interests" (*Between Men*, p. 3) and are accompanied by extreme homophobia:

> at least since the eighteenth century in England and America, the continuum of male homosocial bonds has been brutally structured by a secularized and psychologized homophobia, which has excluded certain shiftingly and more or less arbitrarily defined segments of the continuum from participating in the overarching male entitlement—in the complex web of male power over the production, reproduction, and exchange of goods, persons, and meanings. I argue that the historically shifting, and precisely the arbitrary and self-contradictory, nature of the way *homosexuality*...has been defined in relation to the rest of the male homosocial spectrum has been an exceedingly potent and embattled locus of power over the entire range of male bonds, and perhaps especially over those that define themselves, not *as* homosexual, but *as against* the homosexual. Because the paths of male entitlement...required certain *intense male bonds* [my italics] that

> were not readily distinguishable from the most reprobated [homosexual] bonds, an endemic and ineradicable state of what I am calling male homosexual panic became the normal condition of the male heterosexual entitlement. (Eve Kosofsky Sedgwick, *Epistemology of the Closet*, p. 185)

Pace Sedgwick, Lawrence during his *Women in Love* period was so strong in his solipsistic-creative imagination that he had no need for "homosocial" relationships and the "male power" that supposedly came with them; thus Lawrence surely feels no attraction to the "male power" of "military life," with the homosocial "camaraderie" of "the Achilles and Patroclus business" being "abhorrent" to him: for Lawrence finds the homosocial "male power" of "militarism" to be antithetical—and indeed fatal—to the "constructive [and] social-creative" nature of the supremely strong poet such as Lawrence himself, who privileges "the individual and the constructive social being" of the creative-artistic nature, while at the same time decrying the "destructive," anti-individual "spirit of militarism" even as he (Lawrence) boastingly (defensively?) avers that he is not "afraid or shy: I can get on with the men like a house on fire." Assertively secure in his belief that he is macho and masculine even while abhorring the "military life" and its "camaraderie," Lawrence happily declares that he has "a true confrère,...a Blutbruderschaft"—but, remarkably enough, the only "Blutbruderschaft" that Lawrence can see his way clear to making is one with his typewriter, the very typewriter which is aiding him in his quest for supreme poetic strength and immortality via the writing ("typing") of *Women in Love*; thus Lawrence's sole access to homosocial "male power" (to use Sedgwick's phrase [*Epistemology*, p. 185]) at this point (his *Women in Love* period) was by means of his "intense male bonds" (Ibid.) with his typewriter. Indeed, in view of Lawrence's limited affinity for "male homosocial bonds" (Ibid.) during his *Women in Love* period, his sole "male heterosexual entitlement" (Ibid.) at this juncture is, not the "male power over...goods, persons, and meanings" which Sedgwick posits (Ibid.), but rather "the male heterosexual entitlement" of a married man to the erotic body of his wife (provided she is willing, of course); keenly aware of his "male heterosexual entitlement" to his wife together with his "male homosocial bonds" with his typewriter, Lawrence goes on in his "Blutbruderschaft" letter (23 August 1916) to put together wife and typewriter:

> We go down and bathe among the rocks—not the typewriter, but Frieda and I. (D. H. Lawrence letter to Amy Lowell, 23 August 1916)

Lawrence's linkage of the two, Frieda and his typewriter, in the same sentence, is certainly suitable and significant, since both Frieda and Lawrence's typewriter are essential and instrumental to Lawrence's triumphant attainment of poetic strength and poetic immortality, with Frieda as Lawrence's wife providing the experiential basis for Lawrence's claim to the title of "priest of love," and Lawrence's "typewriter" (or pen, as the case may be) providing the writerly means for Lawrence to communicate his vision of "life" and "love" which he has derived in good part from his life with Frieda—as Lawrence himself says, at the height of his *Women in Love* period:

> The novel is the first thing—I feel with mine [i.e., *Women in Love*], that when it is finished, I have knocked the first loop-hole in the prison where we are all shut up. But I shall do it—I feel a bubbling of gladness inside. Frieda and I are in accord—it needs *a man and a woman* to create anything....(D. H. Lawrence letter to Catherine Carswell, 11 October 1916; italics mine)

"The novel is the first thing": in other words, for Lawrence during his *Women in Love* period his novel holds supreme importance for him—it has priority over every other aspect of his life; indeed, Lawrence believes that his novel will have supreme importance for all Western society, since in it he will "have knocked the first loop-hole in the prison where we are all shut up," liberating, via the Lawrentian scheme, all Western civilization ("we"); this makes Lawrence very happy ("I feel a bubbling of gladness inside"). Fundamental to Lawrence's happiness is the fact that "Frieda and I are in accord—it needs a man and a woman to create anything."

"[I]t needs a man and a woman to create anything," Lawrence authoritatively states in the midst of his *Women in Love* period; "a man and a woman": never two *men* (or two *women*, for that matter). It is no wonder, then, that Lawrence named his novel *Women in Love*: it was the love of *women* (i.e., Frieda and others) he needed in order to create *Women in Love*—indeed, in order "to create anything"; furthermore, for the same reason, it is no wonder that the "Man to Man" chapter—and relationship—of Birkin and Gerald ends in failure, with Gerald rejecting Birkin's offer of "Blutbruderschaft":

> He [Birkin] looked at Gerald with clear, happy eyes of discovery. Gerald looked down at him, attracted, so deeply bondaged in fascinated attraction, that he was mistrustful, resenting the bondage, hating the attraction. ("Man to Man," Chapter XVI, *Women in Love*)

Here Lawrence manages to assert Birkin's charisma ("fascinated attraction") while at the same time ensuring Birkin's failure to create a major "man to man" relationship with Gerald, who is "mistrustful,...hating the attraction." But is Gerald right to be "mistrustful"? Indeed, he tells Birkin that "I feel that there is always an element of uncertainty about you....I'm never sure of you. You can go away and change as easily as if you had no soul" (*Women in Love*, Chapter XVI, "Man to Man")—and Gerald proceeds to meditate on his relationship with Birkin:

> He knew Birkin could do without him—could forget, and not suffer. This was always present in Gerald's consciousness, filling him with bitter unbelief: this consciousness of the young, animal-like spontaneity of detachment. It seemed almost like hypocrisy and lying, sometimes, oh, often, on Birkin's part, to talk so deeply and importantly. (*Women in Love*, Chapter XVI, "Man to Man")

It does indeed seem that the fact is that Lawrence-Birkin can do without Gerald; Lawrence-Birkin, with his "animal-like spontaneity of detachment," does indeed demonstrate (as one critic astutely notes) "the nature of Birkin's separateness: his near indifference to the actuality of Gerald" (Donaldson, p. 59) in the "Man to Man" chapter; Lawrence himself, as omniscient narrator, explains to us that Gerald is right to mistrust Birkin ("He *knew* that Birkin could do without him") because Birkin does in fact enjoy "the...animal-like spontaneity of detachment" that would make it possible for him to "forget, and not suffer" if he had to "do without" Gerald.

But, if Birkin is "animal-like" in his "spontaneity of detachment," what animal is it that he is like? The answer to this question is given long before the "Man to Man" chapter (Chapter XVI), in the chapter "Breadalby" (Chapter VIII), when at a party given by his mistress Hermione, Birkin begins spontaneously dancing:

> Birkin, when he could get free from the weight of the people present, whom he disliked, danced rapidly and with a real gaiety. And how Hermione hated him for this irresponsible gaiety.
>
> "Now I see," cried the Contessa [a party guest] excitedly,

> watching his [Birkin's] purely gay motion,which he [Birkin] had all to himself. "Mr. Birkin, he is a changer."
> Hermione looked at her slowly, and shuddered....
> "Cosa vuol dire, Palestra?" she asked, sing-song.
> "Look," said the Contessa, in Italian. "He is not a man, he is a chameleon, a creature of change." (*Women in Love*, Chapter VIII, "Breadalby")

As "a chameleon," Birkin-Lawrence is in good company—the company, indeed, of John Keats, who in a famous letter asserts that

> What shocks the virtuous philosopher, delights the camelion Poet. (John Keats letter to Richard Woodhouse, 27 October 1818)

As "a chameleon, a creature of change," Birkin-Lawrence, like Keats' "camelion Poet," is not bound by the sterile pieties, abstractions and idealisms of "the virtuous philosopher"; indeed, Lawrence-Birkin, like the Yeatsian dancer, enjoys "his purely gay motion, which he had *all to himself*" (italics mine). Of course, the fact is that Birkin-Lawrence is "all to himself" because, in his "triumphant solipsism,"

> He [Birkin] said the individual was *more* than love, or than any relationship. For him, the bright, single soul accepted love as one of its conditions, a condition of its own equilibrium. (*Women in Love*, Chapter XIX, "Moony")

Yet, as a "chameleon" who privileges "the individual" over "any relationship," Birkin-Lawrence will only engage in "any relationship" if it will aggrandize and amplify his own identity and individuality; thus, when Gerald fails to be enthusiastic about Birkin's "Blutbruderschaft" idea—

> "We'll leave it till I understand it better," he [Gerald] said [to Birkin], in a voice of excuse (*Women in Love*, Chapter XVI, "Man to Man")

—Birkin finds Gerald to be less than worthy of his "bloodbrotherhood":

> Birkin was looking at Gerald....He [Birkin] seemed now to see...the man [Gerald] himself, complete, and as if fated, doomed, limited. This strange sense of fatality in Gerald, as if he were limited to one form of existence, one knowledge, one activity, a sort of fatal halfness, which to himself seemed wholeness,...filled him [Birkin] with a sort of contempt, or boredom....(*Women in Love*, Chapter XVI, "Man to Man")

Thus the self-involved, mercurial "chameleon" Birkin, thwarted in his attempt to aggrandize his self through a "Blutbruderschaft" with Gerald in which he (Birkin), with his Olympian "spontaneity of detachment" will evidently be the leader, judges Gerald to be boring, "limited," contemptible ("Gerald...filled him with a sort of contempt, or boredom"); clearly, in relation to Gerald, Birkin is indeed a "chameleon" mainly interested in his own self-serving and self-aggrandizing designs. Thus it is absurd to posit (as "gay-affirming" critics and others do) "Birkin's homosexual longing for Gerald" (Craft, p. 189), when in fact Birkin's "longing" is of a sublime nature, beyond "love, or...any relationship"; furthermore, this sublime "longing" of Birkin's gives pride of place to "the individual": "the individual was *more* than love, or than any relationship"—"*any* relationship": with man or even with woman. Lawrence's privileging of "the individual" here is extremely reminiscent of his statement, at the height of his *Women in Love* period, that

> I do esteem individual liberty above everything. (D. H. Lawrence letter to Thomas Dunlop, 12 July 1916)

This Lawrentian valorization of "the individual" and "individual liberty above everything" is especially relevant to Birkin's potential "relationship" with Gerald: that relationship, as far as it goes, could never be more than a mere adjunct to Birkin's relationship with Ursula; and Birkin's relationship with Ursula, in its turn, would never supersede Birkin-Lawrence's quest for supreme individuality beyond "love,...or any relationship": the supreme individuality of the strong poet—an individuality which, paradoxically enough, was to be achieved by means of a work which was evidently immersed in the subject matter of "love" and "relationship"—with, of course, the "love" relationship between man and woman enjoying supreme importance as the theme of Lawrence's work. Lawrence himself surely was well aware of the intimate connection between his own quest for "individual liberty [as strong poet] above everything" and his need for—and dependence on—"love" and "women"; the day after he wrote his letter of 12 July 1916 "esteem[ing] individual liberty above everything," Lawrence decided to call his novel "*Women in Love*" (D. H. Lawrence letter to J. B. Pinker, 13 July 1916). By naming his novel *Women in Love*, Lawrence essentially acknowledges that, without "women in love" (even perversely in love as are Hermione early in the book and Gudrun later on), he would of course have had no book to title—and finally no opportunity for "poetic immortality." Thus it is no wonder that, as far as the place of male-male relationship in *Women in Love* is concerned, that relation plays a definitely subordinate role in the Lawrentian organization of the novel.

The connection between Birkin-Lawrence's quest for supreme individuality and Birkin-Lawrence's aspiring to implement the male-male relation as a means to achieving that individuality while at the same time experiencing and privileging an extremely intense sexual relation with a woman is made evident when we trace the parallel thematic organization between the "Man to Man" chapter (Chapter XVI) of *Women in Love* and the climactic chapter of *Women in Love* concerning the male-male relation theme, "Gladiatorial" (Chapter XX). At the beginning of "Man to Man," just before Birkin suggests "bloodbrotherhood" ("Blutbruderschaft") to Gerald, he (Birkin) is meditating to himself about the utopian possibility of a world in which individuality reigns supreme:

> There is now to come the new day, where we are beings each of us, fulfilled in difference. The man is pure man, the woman pure woman, they are perfectly polarised. But there is no longer any of the horrible merging, mingling, self-abnegation of love. There is only the pure duality of polarisation, each one free from any contamination of the other. In each, the individual is primal, sex is subordinate, but perfectly polarised. (*Women in Love*, Chapter XVI, "Man to Man")

Here Lawrence-Birkin contemplates the utopian state of "the new day"—a "day" when the "mingling" and "merging" and "self-abnegation of love" are replaced by a state in which "the individual is primal" even while he engages in sex to his complete satisfaction: here "sex is subordinate" to "the individual"; "the individual" is "primal" and at the same time sexually fulfilled; this is precisely what Lawrence-Birkin desires:

> He [Birkin] wanted so much to be free, not under the compulsion of any need for [sexual] unification, or tortured by unsatisfied [sexual] desire. Desire and aspiration [for sex] should find their [sexual] object without all this torture [of sexual-emotional dependence], as now, in a world of plenty of water, simple thirst is inconsiderable, satisfied almost unconsciously. And he wanted to be with Ursula as free as with himself, single and clear and cool, yet balanced, polarised with her. The merging, the clutching, the mingling of love was become madly abhorrent to him. (*Women in Love*, Chapter XVI, "Man to Man")

Envisioning himself "free" in a utopian-psychic state in which he can have his desire for sex satisfied as simply and naturally ("almost unconsciously") as his desire for water, without "mingling and merging" with the woman who satisfies his sexual "thirst," Birkin-Lawrence imagines that in this sublime state of liberation he will be absolutely independent, "free" from "The merging, the clutching, the mingling of [heterosexual] love."

Immediately after Birkin's culminating meditation on "primal" individuality in "Man to Man" ("the individual is primal, sex is subordinate"), Gerald enters the chapter, and he and Birkin have their talk about "Blutbruderschaft" ("bloodbrotherhood") which we have already discussed here; it seems to me that it is significant that, even in the "Man to Man" chapter, it is the man-woman relationship that actually has priority, both in the chronological sense—the chapter opens with Birkin's meditations on the male-female relation—and in the sense of importance: for it seems to me to be more than fortuitous that Gerald appears on the scene just as Birkin is feeling weak and in need of increased psychic strength via self-aggrandizement, which by the end of the chapter is achieved as we recognize that Birkin is clearly the superior of the "limited" Gerald in psychic-ontological strength and "presence": at the end of the "Man to Man" chapter, "Gerald...was held by the presence of the other man [Birkin]. He [Gerald] had not the power to go away" (*Women in Love*, Chapter XVI, "Man to Man"); the mysterious Birkin, on the other hand, "unsounded and unknown" (Ibid.), is full of renewed strength: he subsequently goes to "the south of France for a time" (*Women in Love*, Chapter XIX, "Moony") and when he returns to England he is ready to deal with Ursula—*not* Gerald—once again—and in the center of the "Moony" chapter Birkin, after meeting Ursula again, has another major meditation on "primal individuality":

> There was...the way of freedom. There was the Paradisal entry into pure, single being, the individual soul taking precedence over love and desire for union, stronger than any pangs of emotion, a lovely state of free proud singleness, which accepts the obligation of the permanent connection with others, and with the other, submits to the yoke and leash of love, but never forfeits its own proud individual singleness, even while it loves and yields. (*Women in Love*, Chapter XIX, "Moony")

Invigorated and strengthened by his meditations on "primal individuality" and "free proud singleness," Birkin enthusiastically and impulsively decides to marry Ursula:

> He must go to her at once. He must ask her to marry him. They must marry at once, and so make a definite pledge, enter into a definite communion. He must set out at once and ask her, this moment. There was no moment to spare.
>
> He drifted on swiftly to Beldover [Ursula's hometown], half-unconscious of his own movement. He saw the town on the slope of the hill,...and it looked like Jerusalem to his fancy. The world was all strange and transcendent. (Ibid.)

Confident of the strength of his "individual soul..., stronger than any pangs of emotion," Birkin at this point feels that he is secure enough in his "proud individual singleness" to propose to Ursula, marry her, and subsequently create and sustain a "Paradisal" state of being in which he can experience the pleasures of sexual fulfillment ("love and desire") yet at the same time maintain his "free proud singleness" and great psychic-ontological strength. Here (in "Moony") Lawrence the omniscient narrator makes it plain that Birkin has already attained considerable psychic-ontological strength, enough to make him far superior to Ursula's father, Will Brangwen, who keenly feels a "sense of inferiority in strength" (Ibid.) in relation to Birkin in "Moony." Nevertheless, despite Birkin's psychic-ontological strength—or, rather, because of it—Ursula rejects Birkin's proposal at this point in *Women in Love*, charging that he and her father "want to bully me!" (Ibid.). Birkin, after being rejected by Ursula, is extremely angry:

> she [Ursula] could see Birkin going up the road. He went in such a blithe drift of rage, that her mind wondered over him. He was ridiculous, but she was afraid of him. She was as if escaped from some danger. (Ibid.)

Realizing that Birkin, with his great psychic-ontological strength, "would never abandon himself *finally* to her" (Ibid.), Ursula is "afraid of him" because she senses that he is a "danger" to her insofar as she may be tempted to abandon *herself* to *him* ("she believed in an absolute surrender to love. She believed that love by far surpassed the individual" [Ibid.]) without receiving his "final self-abandonment" in return ("He did not believe in final self-abandonment" [Ibid.]). For Ursula it is a package deal: "Man must render himself up to her....Let him be *her man* utterly, and she in return would be his humble slave—whether he wanted it or not" (Ibid.). In rejecting Birkin's proposal at this point, Ursula is rejecting Birkin's belief that "the individual was *more* than love, or than any relationship"; Birkin, on the other hand, rejects Ursula's possessive love in favor of supreme individuality; accordingly, immediately after Ursula rejects his proposal, Birkin goes to visit Gerald, at the very beginning of the "Gladiatorial" chapter:

> After the fiasco of the proposal, Birkin had hurried blindly away from Beldover, in a whirl of fury. He felt he had been a complete fool....But that did not trouble him at all. He was deeply, mockingly angry that Ursula persisted always in this old cry: "Why do you want to bully me?" and in her bright, insolent abstraction.
> He went straight to Shortlands [Gerald's home]. There he found Gerald....(*Women in Love*, Chapter XX, "Gladiatorial")

The point of all this progression—from Birkin's rejection by Ursula in "Moony" to Birkin's arrival at Gerald's home in "Gladiatorial"—is, it seems to me, that Gerald is supposed to help Birkin achieve the "primal individuality" that will make Birkin much more effective and powerful in his dealings with Ursula, who, with "her bright, insolent abstraction," would do much damage to Birkin's selfhood, and who, indeed, in rejecting Birkin's proposal of marriage has hurt his self-esteem, made him feel a fool, and, most importantly, discouraged him in his quest for supreme individuality and sexual fulfillment together; in order to achieve these twin goals of sexual fulfillment and supreme individuality, Birkin at this point in *Women in Love* needs to be involved in some self-aggrandizing experience which will renew and indeed increase his psychic-ontological strength and so enable him to be victorious in his next encounter with Ursula.

Birkin has his self-aggrandizing, victorious, "conquering" experience in the "Gladiatorial" chapter of *Women in Love* (Chapter XX); indeed, this chapter, significantly enough, was originally entitled "The Conquering" by Lawrence (*Women in Love*, Cambridge edition, eds. David Farmer, Lindeth Vasey and John Worthen, p. 561 n.)—indicating, it seems to me, that the main purpose of the wrestling match in "Gladiatorial" is indeed "gladiatorial": a matter of two men engaged in a fight in which one must "conquer" the other; thus it is absurd to call the Birkin-Gerald wrestling match "a sexual encounter" (Adelman 94) and "an erotic fulfillment" (Adelman 95); it is, rather, a mystical-physical "encounter" in which Birkin *alone* (not Gerald as well) has a sublime psychic-ontological "fulfillment" as a consequence of his "gladiatorial" "conquering" of Gerald.

In his jiu-jitsu wrestling match with Gerald, Birkin manifests "uncanny force" and "a great subtle energy":

> they [Birkin and Gerald] had a real struggle. They seemed to drive their white flesh deeper and deeper against each other, as if they would break into a oneness. Birkin had a great subtle energy, that would press upon the other man with an uncanny force, weigh him like a spell put upon him. (*Women in Love*, Chapter XX, "Gladiatorial")

Here Birkin is presented as definitely Gerald's superior in strength, "uncanny" strength which, while evidently having its source in some numinous field of force, has its definite physical manifestation in his victory over Gerald in the wrestling match:

> He [Birkin] seemed to penetrate into Gerald's more solid, more diffuse bulk, to interfuse his body through the body of the other, as if to bring it subtly into subjection, always seizing with some rapid necromantic foreknowledge every motion of the other flesh, converting and counteracting it....It was as if Birkin's whole physical *intelligence* interpenetrated into Gerald's body, as if his fine, *sublimated* energy entered into the flesh of the fuller man, like some potency, casting a fine net, a prison, through the muscles into the very depths of Gerald's physical being. (*Women in Love*, Chapter XX, "Gladiatorial"; italics mine)

Here the key phrase is "sublimated energy"; indeed, in his "conquering" of Gerald, Birkin surely possesses the power of the sublime moment, as defined by scholar of the sublime, Martin Price:

> The process by which this [sublime] moment...is reached involves some encounter with a presence, some taking into the self or release from within of powerful energies. (Price 213)

In his wrestling match "encounter" with Gerald, Birkin, encountering the "presence" of Gerald—

> He [Gerald] seemed to stand with a proper, rich weight on the face of the earth, whilst Birkin seemed to have the centre of gravitation in his own middle. And Gerald had a rich, frictional kind of strength, rather mechanical, but sudden and invincible, whereas Birkin was abstract as to be almost intangible (*Women in Love*, Chapter XX, "Gladiatorial")

—Birkin, encountering the "presence" of Gerald, releases his (Birkin's) "powerful energies" "from within" and consequently triumphs over Gerald; Birkin's energy is "sublimated energy" in that it is "exalted, noble, elevated" and "impressing the mind with a sense of grandeur or power; inspiring awe, veneration, etc." (*Random House Dictionary*); the "mind" which is "impress[ed]" by Birkin's "power" is none other than that of Gerald:

> "It surprised me," panted Gerald, "what strength you've got. Almost—supernatural."
> "For a moment," said Birkin. (*Women in Love*, Chapter XX, "Gladiatorial")

That "moment" is a "sublime moment"—to use a phrase from Weiskel (p. 1)—for Birkin, a moment in which he impresses and indeed overwhelms Gerald with his (Birkin's) sublime "physical intelligence" and "fine, sublimated energy"; Birkin's "sublime moment" is short-lived, however: for in the very next chapter (Chapter XXI, "Threshold") Gerald ridicules Birkin's aspirations toward "*ultimate* marriage":

> I am no expert on marriage, and degrees of ultimateness [Gerald tells Gudrun behind Rupert Birkin's back]. It seems to be a bee that buzzes loudly in Rupert's bonnet

—and a bit further on, in the same chapter:

> "You think Rupert is off his head a bit?" Gerald asked [Gudrun]

—and Gerald goes on to join Gudrun in attacking Birkin's emphasis on marriage:

> "...He [Birkin] seems to think that if you marry you can get through marriage into a third heaven, or something—all very vague" [Gudrun tells Gerald].
> "Very! And who wants a third heaven?—As a matter of fact, Rupert has a great yearning to be *safe*—to tie himself to the mast."

Throughout the "Threshold" chapter, Gerald continues skeptically to deride Birkin's valorization of marriage; when Gudrun makes fun of Birkin's beliefs about marriage, Gerald gladly complements her mockery:

> "...he [Birkin] says he believes that a man and wife can go further than any other two beings—but *where*, is not explained. They can know each other, heavenly and hellish, but particularly hellish, so perfectly that they go beyond heaven and hell—into—there it all breaks down—into nowhere—"
> "Into Paradise, he says," laughed Gerald.

In "Threshold" (Chapter XXI), Gerald laughs at Birkin; he is full of skepticism about Birkin's privileging of marriage and individuality; but in "Gladiatorial" Gerald shows great respect, even reverence, for Birkin and his "supernatural" strength of being:

> "Of course you," said Gerald [to Birkin], as if he had been thinking; "there's something curious about you. You're curiously strong. One doesn't expect it, it is rather surprising." (*Women in Love*, Chapter XX, "Gladiatorial")

One major reason why Gerald is so impressed by Birkin in "Gladiatorial" is indicated by Lawrence in his description of the wrestling match between Birkin and Gerald in terms of "mindlessness," "headlessness," "sightlessness":

> So they wrestled swiftly, rapturously, intent and *mindless* at last....Often, in the white, interlaced knot of violent living being that swayed silently, *there was no head to be seen*, only the swift, tight limbs, the solid white backs, the physical junction of two bodies clinched into oneness. Then would appear the gleaming, ruffled head of Gerald, as the struggle changed, then for a moment the dun-coloured, shadow-like head of the other man would lift up from the conflict, the eyes wide and dreadful and *sightless*. (*Women in Love*, Chapter XX, "Gladiatorial"; italics mine)

The fact that both Birkin and Gerald are "mindless" during their wrestling match is extremely significant from a Lawrentian perspective: for Gerald's "mindlessness" at this time makes it possible for him to suspend his cerebral "mental-consciousness" skepticism concerning Birkin's aspiration towards the "paradisal" states of "ultimate marriage" and "free proud singleness." Because Gerald is "mindless" during the wrestling match, he like Birkin is (figuratively not literally of course) "headless" ("Often [during the wrestling]...there was no head to be seen"); accordingly, neither he nor Birkin is under the influence of the "mental consciousness": rather, they are both dominated at this point by the Lawrentian "blood-consciousness" which is antithetical to the "mental consciousness"; as Lawrence explains it in his great "blood-consciousness" letter to Bertrand Russell written a few months before he began writing *Women in Love*:

> there is another seat of consciousness than the brain and the nerve system: there is a blood-consciousness which exists in us independently of the ordinary mental consciousness, which depends

> on the eye as its source or connector....One lives, knows, and has one's being in the blood, without any reference to nerves and brain. (D. H. Lawrence letter to Bertrand Russell, 8 December 1915)

During their wrestling match Birkin and Gerald "[have their] being in the blood, without any reference to nerves and brain"; indeed, they constitute a "knot of violent living being": "violent," *not erotic*, "living being" in their wrestling, wrestling in the course of which they temporarily can be seen as "two bodies clinched into oneness"—visual, *not sexual* "oneness," of course: that is to say, the "oneness" between Birkin and Gerald exists only as regards the sense of sight of the hypothetical observer ("Often...there was no head *to be seen*, only...the physical junction of two bodies clinched into oneness" [my italics]), not the sense of touch of the actual participants (i.e., Birkin and Gerald); as for the two wrestlers themselves (Gerald and Birkin), they are evidently "mindless" and "headless," with their mental-visual sense suspended, for the "mental consciousness...depends on the eye as its source or connector" (D. H. Lawrence letter to Bertrand Russell, 8 December 1915). In his "sightless" state Birkin in "Gladiatorial" is overwhelmed by the Lawrentian "blood-consciousness" since the ocular "mental-consciousness" is weak at this "sightless" time for him; indeed, immediately after the wrestling match,

> The earth seemed to tilt and sway [for Birkin], and *a complete darkness was coming over his mind*. (*Women in Love*, Chapter XX, "Gladiatorial"; italics mine)

The "complete darkness...over [Birkin's] mind" is tantamount to the "blood-consciousness," for

> the blood-consciousness...is one half of life, belonging to *the darkness* (D. H. Lawrence letter to Bertrand Russell, 8 December 1915; italics mine)

—and "the darkness" is what triumphs over Birkin's mind ("a complete darkness was coming over his mind") after his wrestling match with Gerald—and, accordingly, with the triumph of "the darkness" and "the blood-consciousness" over Birkin comes his return to thoughts of Ursula:

> But really it was Ursula, it was the woman who was gaining ascendance over Birkin's being, at this moment [immediately following the wrestling match with Gerald]. Gerald was becoming dim again, lapsing out of him.

The reason why "Ursula...[is] gaining ascendance over Birkin's being, at this moment" after the wrestling match is that the wrestling match, by making Birkin "mindless" and "sightless" and overwhelmed by "a complete darkness [which] was coming over his mind," has now placed Birkin in the field of force of the "blood-consciousness"; as Lawrence expounds it:

> there is this other great half of our life active in *the darkness, the blood-relationship*....[W]hen I take a woman,...my blood-knowing is overwhelming. There is a transmission, I don't know of what, between her blood and mine, in the act of [sexual] connection. So that afterwards, *even if she goes away, the blood-consciousness persists between us, when the mental consciousness is suspended*; and I am formed then by my blood-consciousness, not by my mind or nerves at all. (D. H. Lawrence letter to Bertrand Russell, 8 December 1915; italics mine)

During and after the wrestling match with Gerald, Birkin's "mental consciousness is suspended" and consequently he is "formed then [i.e., after the wrestling match] by [his] blood-consciousness, not by [his] mind or nerves at all"; such being the case, "...it was the woman [Ursula] who was gaining ascendance over Birkin's being," since he (Birkin) had "take[n] [the] woman [Ursula]" earlier in *Women in Love*, in the chapter "Water-Party" (Chapter XIV):

> And soon he was a perfect hard flame of passionate desire for her....he only wanted her, with an extreme desire that seemed inevitable as death, beyond question.
>
> Afterwards [i.e., after the sex], satisfied and shattered, fulfilled and destroyed, he went home away from her, drifting vaguely through the darkness, lapsed into the old fire of burning passion....[W]hat did anything matter save this ultimate and triumphant experience of physical passion, that had blazed up anew like a new spell of life....

In "Water-Party" Birkin "takes" Ursula and experiences a vital "transmission" from her "in the act of connection"—"a transmission... between her blood and mine," which is "like a new spell of life"; thus in "Gladiatorial," once Birkin's mental consciousness is suspended, he is overwhelmed in his "being" not by Gerald—even though it is Gerald in whose presence Birkin in "Gladiatorial" experiences "a complete darkness...coming over his mind," and undergoes a "quite unconscious," then "half-conscious" psychic state that is prerequisite to Birkin's immersion in the heterosexual "blood-consciousness" ("...when I take a woman, then...my blood-knowing is overwhelming")—not by Gerald, but by Ursula: having caused Birkin's mental consciousness to be suspended, the wrestling match with Gerald leads Birkin to be "formed...by my blood-consciousness," which in turn brings about that state in which Ursula, the woman he has "take[n]," does indeed "[gain] ascendance over Birkin's being, at this moment," even though she is now separated from him and they are (for the time being) estranged: still she is dominant "over Birkin's being"—thanks to the vital "transmission" he experienced with her earlier in the novel—a "transmission" he has not experienced with Gerald, who is fast fading into insignificance for Birkin: "But really it was Ursula, it was the woman who was gaining ascendance over Birkin's being, at this moment. Gerald was becoming dim again, lapsing out of him."

"Dim *again*": this phrase is indeed significant of the fact that, for Birkin, Gerald has generally been, as a presence, only "dim" (thus: "dim *again*"); it is only in "Gladiatorial" that Gerald assumes a major role as a presence in Birkin's life—and here only because Ursula has just rejected Birkin; and furthermore, Gerald is only to play a major role in reinvigorating Birkin's self-esteem so that he can return to his pursuit of Ursula after suffering the discouragement he experienced in "Moony"; Gerald himself clearly recognizes that Birkin has only come to him because of Ursula: after Birkin tells him of his failed marriage proposal to Ursula, Gerald concludes that Birkin has used him to work through his frustration and resentment concerning Ursula's rejection of his "proposition":

> He [Gerald] leaned back in his chair, filled with delight and amusement.
> "Well, that's good," he said. "And so you came here to wrestle with your good angel, did you?"
> "Did I?" said Birkin.
> "Well it looks like it. Isn't that what you did?"
> Now Birkin could not follow Gerald's meaning.
> "And what's going to happen?" said Gerald. "You're going to keep open the proposition, so to speak?"
> "I suppose so. I vowed to myself I would see them all to the devil. But I suppose I shall ask her again, in a little while."

As Birkin's "good angel," Gerald is instrumental in Birkin's coping with the negative emotions—anger, frustration, doubt—elicited by Ursula's rejection of him at the end of "Moony"; for, after wrestling with Gerald in "Gladiatorial" and "conquering" him, Birkin is once more ready for the challenge of Ursula. Thus once again Birkin's wrestling match with Gerald can indeed be categorized as a sublime encounter, for, as Martin Price tells us,

> The self-division of doubt and despair that disables feeling is the greatest enemy [of transcendent self-fulfillment] (Price 205)

and

> the [sublime] act of transcendence is the winning through (Ibid.)

against such self-subversive doubt and despair; thus after wrestling with Gerald, Birkin's heart and mind return to Ursula: his "feeling" is indeed by no means "disabled"—his feeling for Ursula in particular is exceedingly strengthened, and he goes on to considerable sexual-marital fulfillment with Ursula in subsequent chapters to "Gladiatorial" such as "Excurse" (Chapter XXIII), in which he and Ursula achieve "the marvellous fulness of immediate gratification,...mystically-physically satisfying," and "Flitting" (Chapter XXVII), in which he and Ursula are "married by law." Thus the male-male Birkin-Gerald situation in "Gladiatorial" can easily be seen as being a mere adjunct to Birkin-Lawrence's "sublime" heterosexual aspirations.

Yet in recent years various readers of *Women in Love* strongly suggest that Birkin-Lawrence's aspirations in *Women in Love* are neither sublime nor heterosexual. In 1973 Lawrentian Roger Sale saw the "Gladiatorial" chapter of *Women in Love* as evidence that "Birkin is potentially a murderer in his effort to resolve his incomplete relation with Ursula...by wrestling and conquering Gerald Crich" (Sale 94); according to Sale, "Birkin...feels free after he wrestles, and relaxed, because he has dominated Gerald, subjected him" (Sale 93). Furthermore, according to Sale,

> Birkin has no chance for any positive relation with Gerald because, as we have seen in "Gladiatorial," Gerald is for him a means of controlling someone else and living in a world dominated by his [Birkin's] will. So too with Lawrence. He hates Gerald, he wants to kill him, but in that hate and want is narcissistic and homosexual temptation that becomes in the last third of the book so strong it brushes everything else aside....
>
> He [Lawrence] is of Gerald's civilization at last, infected by it so that he can only express his desire for Gerald and his sick passion

> by hunting him and it down, destroying Gerald, passion, and self at once. History finally has become the monolithic and irreversible motion of dissolution, perversion, and death. (Sale, pp. 104-105)

Thus, rather than finding elements of the sublime in the Birkin-Gerald relation, Sale instead certainly sees the Birkin-Gerald relation as a site of

> Lawrence's...quasi-homosexual and narcissistic urge to dominate

(as Sale phrases it in an earlier version of his Lawrence essay ["D. H. Lawrence, 1912-1916," *Massachusetts Review* 6 (1965): 479]).

A quick look at the historical context of Sale's Lawrence essays helps to place and explain their tone and content. The year of the first Sale essay, 1965, saw the Vietnam War begin in earnest following the Gulf of Tonkin Resolution (August 1964) authorizing the Johnson administration to take "all necessary measures" for the defense of U. S. allies in Southeast Asia. Thus, when in his 1965 essay Sale assails

> [the] aim of Birkin's passion for Gerald [as] a simple world where otherness is destroyed, where domination and therefore destruction and murder are possible (Sale 1965, 476),

he (Sale) is evidently attacking the "domination,...destruction and murder" of American "imperialism" in Vietnam; thus in looking at the political-historical context of Sale's statements we can make some sense of Sale's somewhat grotesque attacks on Birkin-Lawrence, whom Sale goes on to condemn as "solipsistic and narcissistic" (Ibid.). Furthermore, Sale, no doubt equating Gerald with the "military-industrial complex" of America, simplistically asserts that

> Gerald is the villain, to be sure, profound in his need to destroy and be destroyed,...[he is] the final flower of industrial monstrosity. (Sale 479)

Moreover, Lawrence, according to Sale in 1965, redeems himself by destroying "industrial, powerful and dominating" Gerald:

> Lawrence must murder the great phase of life [personified by Gerald] that is industrial, powerful, and dominating....(Ibid.)

According to Sale, Lawrence in destroying Gerald Crich "rid[s] himself [Lawrence] of the quasi-homosexual and narcissistic urge to dominate" (Ibid. 479)—thus the liberal Sale in the 1960s, with his hatred of the "military-industrial complex." Yet there is a difference between the liberal

Sale of 1965 and the liberal Sale of 1973: in 1965 Sale only briefly mentions what he calls Lawrence's "quasi-homosexual" aspect—Sale is more interested in attacking Lawrence's "urge to dominate" and Gerald's "industrial monstrosity"; but in 1973 Sale devotes considerably more attention to Lawrence's "homosexual temptation" in relation to Gerald, his (Lawrence's) "sick passion" for Gerald that (according to Sale) results in Lawrence's need "to kill Gerald" (Sale 1973, 104); here evidently Sale emphasizes Lawrence's "homosexual temptation" in such a way as to censure, not the "temptation" itself, but rather Lawrence's reaction to that temptation by "killing" Gerald instead of "express[ing] his desire for Gerald" in a more nonviolent (erotic?) fashion; thus it appears that the liberal Sale in 1973 not only discusses homosexuality in more detail but also with more sympathy as he inveighs against Lawrence's "murder" of Gerald as a desperate defense against his (Lawrence's) "homosexual temptation," a "temptation" which (according to Sale) becomes a "sick passion" of Lawrentian "dissolution" and "perversion" that culminates in Gerald's "death"; yet in all of this Sale somehow conveniently forgets that the fact is that Gerald's death is indeed indicative of Lawrence's obsessive *heterosexual* "temptation"; as Lawrence scholar Mark Spilka observed:

> Birkin is his [Lawrence's] older self, seeking singleness of being; Gerald, his [Lawrence's] youthful self, seeking annihilation in dependent love....(Spilka 1967, 370)

Gerald of course is not "murdered" by Lawrence to get rid of his (Lawrence's) "homosexual temptation" in relation to him; on the contrary, in "killing" Gerald, Lawrence shows that the sexual power of *woman* over man can be so overwhelming that it can lead to his (i.e., Gerald's) destruction if ever he should be denied the woman's sexual favors or be rejected by her—as Gerald is ultimately rejected by Gudrun at the end of *Women in Love*; thus when, in the final chapter of *Women in Love*, "Exeunt" (Chapter XXXII), Gudrun, upon learning of Gerald's death, goes to Loerke, she expresses Lawrence's view of the matter:

> She found Loerke sitting alone in the lounge. She went straight up to him.
> "It isn't true, is it?" she said.
> He looked up at her. A small smile of misery twisted his face. He shrugged his shoulders.
> "True?" he echoed.
> "We haven't killed him [Gerald]?" she asked. He [Loerke] dis-

liked her coming to him in such a manner. He raised his shoulders wearily.

"It has happened," he said.

Gudrun, together with Loerke, "killed" Gerald; losing her to Loerke, Gerald could not go on: and here we have, not only "A pretty little sample of the eternal triangle!" as Gudrun calls it (*Women in Love*, Chapter XXXII, "Exeunt"), but also a manifestation of Lawrence's strategy in his "temptation" to change the homosexuals of his time; for the fact is that it is Loerke the homosexual who is Gudrun's final conquest and consort; he is instantly attracted to her:

> He [Loerke] wanted very much to dance with Gudrun. From the first moment he had seen her, he wanted to make a connection with her. (*Women in Love*, Chapter XXX, "Snow")

Indeed, Loerke's attraction to Gudrun is so intense that it causes him to hate his young homosexual "love-companion" when he dances with her:

> Because Gudrun had danced with the well-built, soft youth, his [Loerke's] companion, Loerke was more pettish and exasperated than ever....
>
> ...Loerke...felt a sardonic, ruthless hatred for his young love-companion, Leitner....He mocked the youth, with an acid ridicule....(Ibid.)

Gudrun easily prevails over Leitner for Loerke's attention; Loerke is very soon mesmerized by her beauty:

> The professor and Loerke went into a small lounge to drink. They both watched Gudrun go...upstairs.
>
> "Ein schones Frauenzimmer," said the Professor.
>
> "Ja!" assented Loerke, shortly. (*Women in Love*, Chapter XXX, "Snow")

Keenly aware that Gudrun is "A beautiful lady" ("Ein schones Frauenzimmer"), Loerke decides that she is "his mate":

> Loerke was watching [Gudrun] closely, with his uncanny, full, suspicious eyes. Something in Gudrun seemed to accord with him. He was really like one of the "little people" who have no soul, who has found his mate in a human being. (Ibid.)

Thus here Lawrence is telling us that for the "homosexual" Loerke the true "mate" is in fact Gudrun—in other words, then, for Lawrence there is no such thing as homosexuality: according to Lawrence here, homosexuality is a deviation that can be cured once a man finds "his mate"; as Gudrun's "mate," Loerke possesses extraordinary "unconscious" knowledge about her:

> she [Gudrun] knew what he [Loerke] was unconscious of, his tremendous power of understanding, of apprehending her living motion. He did not know his own power. He did not know how, with his full, submerged, watchful eyes, he could look into her and see her, what she was, see her secrets. He would only want her to be herself.—He knew her verily, with a subconscious, sinister knowledge, devoid of illusions and hopes.

Loerke's understanding of Gudrun's "living motion" evidently qualifies him for a heterosexual relationship with her as "his mate"; yet nevertheless Lawrence does not sing the praises of the Gudrun-Loerke relationship; on the contrary, Lawrence tells us that this relationship is based on Loerke's "subconscious, *sinister* knowledge [of Gudrun], [a knowledge] devoid of illusions and hopes" (italics mine). This Loerkean "hopeless knowledge" is indeed antithetical to the kind of knowledge Lawrence does in fact aspire to and valorize in *Women in Love*—the sort of knowledge Lawrence describes in terms of the Birkin-Ursula relationship in the important "Flitting" chapter (Chapter XXVII):

> She [Ursula] was so new, so wonder-clear, so undimmed. And he [Birkin] was so old, so steeped in heavy memories. Her soul was new, undefined and glimmering with the unseen. And his soul was dark and gloomy, it had only one grain of *living hope*, like a grain of mustard seed. But this one living grain in him matched the perfect youth in her.
> "I love you," he whispered as he kissed her, and trembled with *pure hope*, like a man who is born again to *a wonderful, lovely hope* far exceeding the bounds of death.
> She could not know how much it meant to him, how much he meant by the few words....
> But the passion of gratitude with which he received her into his soul, the extreme, unthinkable gladness of knowing himself living and fit to unite with her, he, who was so nearly dead, who was so near to being gone with the rest of his race down the slope of mechanical death, could never be understood by her. He worshipped her as age worships youth, he gloried in her because, in his one grain of *faith*, he was young as she, *he was her proper mate*. This marriage with her was his resurrection and his life....(italics mine)

In contradistinction to Loerke's "hopeless knowledge" which forms the basis of his relation with Gudrun, there is the Lawrentian-Birkinian knowledge which, while fully acknowledging the "dark and gloomy" quality of human life, does nonetheless possess "one grain of living hope,...pure hope,...a wonderful, lovely hope far exceeding the bounds of death." Indeed, Lawrence's mention of "death" here is no accident, for *Women in Love* was of course written in the midst of World War I, a war whose "deathly" influence Lawrence at the height of his *Women in Love* period (1916-1917) yet felt himself supremely able to transcend:

> for *me* the war is utterly wrong, stupid, monstrous and contemptible, and nothing, neither life nor death, makes it any different, for *me*....For me, the war is wrong, and nothing, neither life nor death, can make it right....
>
> ...I *will* not die, in spite of all. There is another life to live, here on earth, a different life. (D. H. Lawrence letter to Lady Cynthia Asquith, 15 November 1916)

So Lawrence, like Birkin, saw himself uniquely as the man who would not be "gone with the rest of his race down the slope of mechanical death"; but, while Birkin ultimately is more or less content to save himself alone by virtue of "This marriage with her [Ursula]...[which] was his resurrection and his life," Lawrence here—never forgetting his Salvator Mundi aspect—aspired to bring "another life to live,...a different life," "a new hope" to all European humanity: during the period in which he was revising *Women in Love*, Lawrence wrote of his contemporaneous metaphysical work, "The Reality of Peace," that

> It may be the initiation of a new state of feeling, or the nucleus of a new hope....it is time something new and good came to pass: therefore we must bring it to pass....now to begin. There must be a new spirit—and then a new world....(D. H. Lawrence letter to Dollie Radford, 31 March 1917)

"[A] new state of feeling," "a new hope," "something new and good," "a new spirit—and then a new world": all this Lawrence sought to bring about by making "us" (i.e., Western civilization) "understand...the death in ourselves" so that we "may go beyond" it:

> The beginning of spring lies in the awakening from winter. For us, to understand is to overcome. We have a winter of death, of destruction, vivid sensationalism of going asunder, the wintry glory of tragical experience to surmount and surpass. Thrusting through these things with the understanding, we come forth in first-flow-

ers of our spring with pale and icy blossoms, like bulb-flowers, the pure understanding of death. When we know the death in ourselves we are merging into the new epoch. For whilst we are in the full flux of death, we can find no bottom of resistance from which to understand [death]. When at last life stands under us we can know what the flood [of death] is, in which we are immersed.

That which is understood by man is surpassed by man. When we understand our extreme being in death, we have surpassed into a new being. Many bitter and fearsome things there are for us to know, that we may go beyond them, they have no power over us any more.

Understanding, however, does not belong to every man, is not incumbent on every man. But it is vital that some men understand, that some few go through this final pain and relief of [the] knowledge [of death]....[F]or the few there is the bitter necessity to understand the death that has been, so that we may pass quite clear of it.

The anguish of this knowledge, the knowledge of what we ourselves, we righteous ones, have been and are within the flux of death, is a death in itself. It is the death of our established belief in ourselves, it is the end of our current self-esteem....

We are not only creatures of light and virtue. We are also alive in corruption and death. It is necessary to balance the dark against the light if we are ever going to be free....

Either we can and will understand the other thing that we are, the flux of darkness and lively decomposition, and so become free and whole, or we fight shy of this half of ourselves, as man has always fought shy of it, and gone under the burden of secret shame and self-abhorrence. For the tide of our own corruption is rising higher, and unless we adjust ourselves, unless we come out of our veiled temples, and see and know, and take the tide as it comes, ride upon it and so escape it, we are lost....

This is the condition of freedom: that in the understanding I fear nothing....("The Reality of Peace," Chapter II, in *Reflections on the Death of a Porcupine and Other Essays*, ed. Michael Herbert)

"For us, to understand is to overcome," Lawrence tells us: by understanding the "winter of death"—whether that "winter" be manifested in the "tragical experience" of world war or the "sensationalism" of certain decadent sexual practices (e.g., homosexuality)—we surpass it, transcend it; for "That which is understood by man is surpassed by man"—but only by "us" life-affirming Lawrentian men who "at last" attain an ontological state in which "life stands under us" as our basis and true foundation even while "we are immersed" for the time being in "the flood" of death: once we are capable "at last" of being rooted in a psychic-ontological state in which "life stands under us" we then have the "bottom of resistance from which to understand...the flood [of death]...in which we are immersed"; thus it is only the truly Lawrentian man who can understand and consequently transcend death, for "That which is *understood* by man is surpassed by man," and Lawrence of course surely believes that, while "*Understanding...does not belong to every man, is not incumbent on every man,*" he indeed is one of the chosen and "incumbent" (i.e., morally obliged) few who "must go through this final...knowledge": "for the few [chosen ones such as Lawrence] there is the bitter necessity to understand the death that has been, so that we [i.e., Western civilization] may pass quite clear of it." Lawrence, having achieved "the understanding," has attained "the condition of freedom" and consequently "I fear nothing," for

> I...have the gift of understanding....(Ibid., p. 37)

Enjoying "the gift of understanding," Lawrence finds that he has no fear of "the desire of death":

> I shall accept all my desires and repudiate none....And then my desire of life will encompass my desire of death, and I shall be quite whole, have fulfilment in both. Death will take its place in me, subordinate but not subjected, I shall be fulfilled of corruption within the strength of creation. (Ibid., pp. 37-38)

In other words, Lawrence, as the representative of Western civilization—

> I know that *I* am the English nation—that *I* am the European race....(D. H. Lawrence letter to Gordon Campbell, 3 March 1915)

—as this representative man Lawrence can say that, despite the European "desire of death" so supremely manifested in World War I—this "desire of death" will not lead to ruination but rather to strengthening once it is "accept[ed]" and not "repudiate[d]"—since when "the desire of death" is accepted it paradoxically becomes less powerful, less threatening, less "fascinating" (Ibid. 38), and then "my desire of life will encompass my desire of death," subordinating it.

Subordinating death, Lawrence here valorizes life, and beyond life, "pure being":

> For there are ultimately only two desires, the desire of life and the
> desire of death. Beyond these is pure being, where I am absolved
> from desire and made perfect. This is when I am like a rose, when
> I balance for a space in pure adjustment and pure understanding.
> The timeless quality of *being* is understanding; when I understand
> fully, flesh and blood and bone, and mind and soul and spirit one
> rose of unison, then I *am*. Then I am unrelated [to time] and perfect [in being]. In true understanding I am always perfect and timeless. In my utterance of that which I have understood I am
> timeless as a jewel. (Ibid., p. 38)

Here Lawrence makes it clear that for him "pure being" essentially means what Harold Bloom has called "poetic immortality" (*Map of Misreading*, p. 57); that is to say, at this point in his poetic life Lawrence as a great creative writer aspires to attain "timeless" poetic immortality, aspires to reach this "perfect" state by virtue of his "pure understanding," "pure understanding" which—according to Lawrence's metaphysic—is part and parcel of "The timeless quality of being": by attributing to himself the ability to "understand fully, flesh and blood and bone, and mind and soul and spirit," Lawrence self-confidently characterizes himself as having "true understanding," "true understanding" which makes him "always perfect and timeless"; and, even more important, Lawrence credits himself with the supreme power of "utterance": "In my utterance of that which I have understood I am timeless as a jewel"—in other words, it is Lawrence's "poetic strength"—his power of "utterance"—in tandem with his power of "true understanding" that makes him poetically immortal, "timeless as a jewel." Indeed, Lawrence here goes on to give a brief definition of the Lawrentian "understanding" that will assure his "poetic immortality":

> In our whole understanding, when sense and spirit and mind are
> consummated into pure unison, then we are free in the world of
> the absolute. (Ibid., p. 38)

Encompassing "sense and mind and spirit," the Lawrentian "understanding" is "whole," including "blood consciousness"-"phallic consciousness" as well as "mental-spiritual consciousness." This all-inclusive Lawrentian understanding is "a transcending into absolution"—"absolution" in the sense that this Lawrentian "understanding" of death enables us to experience a "setting free from...[the] penalty" of death (the latter quoted phrase is from *Webster's Third New International Dictionary* definition of absolution); and "absolution" also in the sense that this "pure understanding" causes us to attain a transcendent state in which "we are free in the world of the absolute" ("Reality of Peace" 38); as Lawrence declares:

> We understand death, and in this there is no death....It is now no mystery, finally. Death is understood in us, and thus we transcend it....Nevertheless, we only transcend death by understanding down to the last ebb the great process of death in us. We can never destroy death. We can only transcend it in pure understanding. We can envelop it and contain it. And then we are free. ("Reality of Peace," pp. 39-40)

Thus the Lawrentian imaginative "understanding" of death makes for a psychic-ontological state in which "there is no death" because death is demystified, there is "now no mystery, finally" about death, and "thus we transcend [death]" by dint of the Lawrentian "understanding down to the last ebb the great process of death in us." "[T]ranscend[ing] [death] in pure understanding [of death]," the Lawrentian way of dealing with death "envelop[s] it and contain[s] it" and consequently "we [Lawrentians] are free" from death's domination.

Lawrence at this point in "The Reality of Peace" proceeds to stress the fact that with his Lawrentian "understanding" he defends life against death with his mind as much as with his senses and spirit:

> our understanding of death in life is an act of living.
> ...in the mind we must understand death. Understanding is not necessarily mental. It is of the senses and the spirit.
> But we live also in the mind. And the first great act of living is to encompass death in the understanding. Therefore the first great activity of the living mind is to understand death in the mind. Without this there is no freedom of the mind, there is no life of the mind, since creative life is the attaining a perfect consummation with death. When in my mind there rises the idea of life, then this idea must encompass the idea of death, and this encompassing is the germination of a new epoch of the mind. (Ibid., p. 40)

Thus the "living" Lawrentian mind in its creativity and originality "encompass[es] the idea of death," and in its encompassing of death the Lawrentian mind gives rise to "a new epoch of the mind"; but this Lawrentian mind, while encompassing death, nevertheless privileges life:

> We long most of all to belong to life. This primal desire, the desire to come into being, the desire to achieve a transcendent state of existence, is all we shall ever know of a *primum mobile*. But it is

> enough....
>   We long most of all for life and creation. That is the final truth. But not all life belongs to life. (Ibid.)

Lawrentian "belong[ing] to life" is synonymous with "com[ing] into being," which in turn is tantamount to "achiev[ing] a transcendent state of existence"; thus Lawrentian "life" leads to "a state of transcendent being." But antithetical to Lawrentian life are "the living dead." "[E]ncompassed" by death, "the living dead" are denied the "Heaven[ly]" Lawrentian "consummation of manhood":

> We long most of all for life and creation. That is the final truth. But not all life belongs to life. Not all life is progressing to a state of transcendent being....
>   The quick can encompass death, but the living dead are encompassed....
>   ...Heaven lies about us in our consummation of manhood, if we are men. If we are men, we attain to heaven in our achieved manhood, our flowering maturity. But if we are like bugs....(Ibid., pp. 40-43)

For Lawrence here in "The Reality of Peace," Lawrentian "Heaven" is tantamount to "our achieved manhood, our flowering maturity." Thus Lawrentian heaven is equivalent to, and can only be attained by, achieving the "flowering maturity" of "our consummation of manhood,...our achieved manhood"—"mature" manhood. A sagacious gloss on Lawrence's "maturity" of "achieved manhood" is provided by Lawrentian Leslie Fiedler in his classic *Love and Death in the American Novel*; discussing the "problem" of "the American writer," Fiedler theorizes that

> He [the American writer] faces...[a serious psychological] problem, which has resulted in a failure of feeling and imagination perceptible at the heart of even our most notable works. Our great novelists, though experts on indignity and assault, on loneliness and terror, tend to avoid treating the passionate encounter of a man and woman, which we expect at the center of a novel. Indeed, they rather shy away from permitting in their fictions the presence of any full-fledged, mature women, giving us instead monsters of virtue or bitchery, symbols of the rejection or fear of sexuality....
>   ...[The American writer has] a desperate need to avoid the facts of wooing, marriage, and child-bearing....
>   ...the typical male protagonist of our [American] fiction has been a man on the run, harried into the forest and out to sea, down

> the river or into combat—anywhere to avoid "civilization," which is to say, the confrontation of a man and woman which leads to the fall to sex, marriage, and responsibility. (*Love and Death*, pp. 24-26)

Fiedler here, in defining the psychosexual "problem" of "the American writer" as "a failure of feeling and imagination" in relation to "the passionate encounter of a man and a woman," begins to explain Lawrentian "maturity" in terms of what it is not: while the American writer's "failure of feeling and imagination" is characterized by "the rejection or fear of sexuality," Lawrentian "flowering maturity" celebrates "the facts" of "wooing, marriage, and child-bearing," "the confrontation of a man and woman which leads to...sex, marriage, and responsibility." Both Fiedler and Lawrence define and valorize "maturity" in sexual terms; as Lionel Trilling astutely remarked in a review of Fiedler's *Love and Death*:

> For Mr. Fiedler the ideal of mature genital sexuality is fixed and firm, the right and proper criterion by which the human condition is to be judged. Whatever historical skepticism he directs upon love as a mere idea, he gives to that idea his entire allegiance. His book is based on the Laurentian belief that a man finds his salvation, or at least the sign of his salvation, in a satisfying relation with a woman....[I]n his view of culture, Mr. Fiedler is conservative....[W]hatever Mr. Fiedler thinks about this or that aspect of our culture, he likes the idea of culture in general and wants to save (conserve) it: it makes trouble but it also makes life. (Lionel Trilling, "Love and Death in the American Novel," *The Mid-Century*, Number 10, March 1960, p. 14)

As Trilling recognizes, both Lawrence and Fiedler privilege "the ideal of mature genital sexuality"; for both Fiedler and Lawrence, "maturity" is synonymous with "genital sexuality," the "Laurentian" sexuality unique to "the passionate encounter of a man and woman," "the confrontation of a man and woman which leads...to sex, marriage, and responsibility."

"[T]he confrontation of a man and woman which leads to...sex, marriage, and responsibility": this is Leslie Fiedler's definition of "civilization" (*Love and Death*, p. 26); when Trilling asserts that Fiedler is "conservative" and "likes the idea of culture...and wants to save (conserve) it" because "it [culture]...makes life," it is "Laurentian" culture and "civilization" of which Trilling speaks; thus Fiedler is "conservative" in the "Laurentian" sense that "finds...salvation" for both "man" and "civilization" in "a satisfying relation with a woman." This "conservative," "mature," heterosexual "culture" is, according to Lawrence and Fiedler and Trilling, a culture that "makes life" via "The love between man and woman"; as Lawrence says:

> There is the love between man and woman, sacred and profane....
> Only in the conjunction of man and woman has love kept a duality of meaning. Sacred love and profane love, they are opposed and yet they are both love. The love between man and woman is the greatest and most complete passion the world will ever see, because it is dual, because it is of two opposing kinds. The love between man and woman is the perfect heart-beat of life, systole, diastole. (D. H. Lawrence, "Love")

Thus, for Lawrence, if "culture" is to "make life" (as Trilling says), then it must also make "The love between man and woman," for "The *love* between man and woman is the perfect heart-beat of *life*" (my italics): the life that encompasses the maturity and responsibility, as well as the joy and fulfillment, of "the greatest and most complete passion the world will ever see."

In contradistinction to the "conservatism," "culture," and "mature genital sexuality" of Lawrence and Fiedler is the "polymorphous perversity" of Norman O. Brown; as Trilling explains, in his review of Brown's *Life Against Death*:

> He [Brown] does not accept the idea...that a crucial test of a successful individual development is the absorption of all the impulses of infantile sexuality into mature genital sexuality. This means, negatively, that he is not in accord with all those (*D. H. Lawrence*, for example) who conceive of the opportunity for freedom of genital sexuality as a therapeutic condition for the individual and as the test of a culture. For Mr. Brown the repression of genital sexuality is not the real issue, which he finds to be the repression, or sublimation, of the "polymorphous-perverse" impulses of the infantile state, at the behest of, among other agencies, the "tyranny" of adult sexuality. (Lionel Trilling, "Paradise Reached For," *The Mid-Century*, Number 5, Fall 1959, p. 20; italics mine)

Leslie Fiedler explains a bit more explicitly than Trilling what Norman O. Brown's "polymorphous perverse" entails:

> But what lies beyond the sexual revolution through which we have lived from the beginning of the Twenties to the verge of the Six-

> ties? On the one hand, a revolt against the orgasm, based on a concept of a universal fleshly love without penetration and consummation; and on the other, an attack on heterosexuality, either frankly homosexual in nature or, more politely, committed to some shadowy ideal of "bisexuality." Norman O. Brown, in his *Life Against Death*,...[is] insisting...that "mankind is unalterably, in the unconscious, in revolt against sexual differentiation and genital organization"; and proposing in their place the "infantile" ideal of the "polymorphous perverse." (Leslie Fiedler, *Waiting for the End*, pp. 160-161)

Thus Lawrentian "manhood," exemplified by "mature genital sexuality," is opposed by Brown and his "polymorphous perversity," which deplores "the orgasm,...[heterosexual] penetration and consummation," and entails "an attack on heterosexuality," heterosexuality which, according to Brown, constitutes a "tyranny," "the tyranny of genital organization" (Brown, *Life against Death*, p. 29); Brown, in pseudo-Freudian mode, postulates that his main enemy and target is none other than D. H. Lawrence:

> In Freud's theory of infantile sexuality there is first of all a critique of the genital function and an implied rejection of genital intercourse—"free love" and the orgasm—as a solution to the sexual problem....[T]here [is] an implied critique of D. H. Lawrence....(Brown, *Life against Death*, p. 29)

The "critique of D. H. Lawrence"—and of Lawrentian "mature genital sexuality"—is, it seems to me, essentially rooted in what philosopher Jean-Francois Lyotard calls the "*postmodern*...incredulity toward metanarratives" (Lyotard xxiv), a "metanarrative" (in Lyotard's jargon) being (as one Lyotard scholar describes it) a narrative which "claims to be the story that can reveal the meaning of all stories, be it the weakness or the progress of mankind" (Readings, *Introducing Lyotard*, p. 63). Lawrence, with his "metanarrative" of "The love between man and woman, the greatest and most complete passion the world will ever see," "mature genital sexuality" leading to "spontaneous-creative fullness of being" (*Psychoanalysis and the Unconscious*, p. 48), was of course deplored by skeptic, left-wing, deconstructionist critics for his authoritative sexual vision; one such anti-"authoritarian" critic concludes that

> with Lawrence the reconciliation in the body has a certain authoritarian ring to it....[Lawrence's "authoritarianism" in his work] stretches at times even to what men and women are supposed to

feel in sex. That Lawrence presumes to know what a woman feels is one thing that women writers since Simone de Beauvoir have rightly attacked him for; and to that must also be added the charge that his illusions of solipsistic grandeur do not adequately represent what a man need feel either. (Gould, *Mythical Intentions*, pp. 223-224)

Thus Lawrence is caustically, self-righteously condemned by mean-spirited left-wing critics for his "authoritarianism"; these left-wing critics fail to appreciate that Lawrence's "authoritarianism" is part and parcel of his prophetic, "Messianic" aspirations as well as of his quest for "poetic strength" and "poetic immortality" with its "triumphant solipsism" (Bloom, *Map*, pp. 9, 57) or "solipsistic grandeur" (Gould 224); instead, such left-wing critics as Gould attack Lawrence's "treatment of sexuality" (Ibid., p. 222) as characterized by

the remarkably arrogant male need to find woman waiting to be opened up to consciousness by the "dark potency" of the phallus. Obviously there can be little defense for a love ethic which is so atavistic, which depends on asserting the pompous imperialism of [Lawrence's "heterosexist"-"authoritarian" heroes] "the sons of God" coming to the "daughters of Men" [in *Women in Love* and other Lawrence works]....(Gould, p. 222)

According to Gould (and many others recently), Lawrence's "love ethic" is "remarkably arrogant" (Ibid.), "atavistic" (Ibid.), "imperialis[tic]" (Ibid.) and "heterosexist" (Ibid. 224) and "authoritarian" (Ibid. 224). Similarly, major liberal Lawrentian Eugene Goodheart recently portrayed the Lawrentian way as the way of the bully:

Lawrence's protagonists from Birkin on are given a bully pulpit to expound their views and to coerce others to change their lives. Lawrence and his heroes affirm the overriding importance of spontaneity, which they then lay as a compulsion on others. Be yourself, but let me tell you what I know to be the true conditions of selfhood. (Goodheart, *Desire*, p. 71)

"[C]oerc[ing] others to change their lives," Lawrence-Birkin is for liberal Eugene Goodheart a menace: for, according to Goodheart,

Desire in Birkin, as in Lawrence, becomes an ungratified will to power. (Ibid., p. 74)

What Goodheart fails to understand, of course, is that Lawrence's "desire" was not "an ungratified will to power," but rather a *gratified* aspiration to "poetic strength" and "poetic immortality"; an aspiration which Lawrence attained in large part by virtue of the authority with which he "tell[s]...what I know to be the true conditions of selfhood" in sexual and social relationships. But the liberal Goodheart, with his excessive political consciousness, cannot fathom that Lawrence's "desire" for "power" is something beyond the conventional, the mundane, the political.

But Goodheart is far from alone in his excessively political attitude toward "power" in Lawrence; in recent years, such "gay-affirmative" critics as Christopher Craft (Craft, p. xvii), full of the vehemence of "identity politics" (Craft xiii), have rather bitchily attacked Lawrence for his "poetic strength" authority in relation to

> women's desire and pleasure, a subject about which Lawrence seemed to believe he knew everything....(Craft, *Another Kind of Love*, p. 172)

Professor Craft is evidently in the process of coming out of the closet in his book *Another Kind of Love*; one recent review of Craft's book concludes that in its "last pages..., Craft...[is] offering what appears to be his own coming-out celebration" (Ingersoll 1993, 154-155). But evidently many gays and lesbians were not as fortunate as Professor Craft—especially "before the 1970s" (Cruikshank 2)—and gay-lesbian liberation activists actually blame the homosexual "self-loathing and...desire to convert to heterosexuality" of the 1950s and 1960s on none other than D. H. Lawrence:

> some homosexuals [before the 1970s] escaped self-loathing and a desire to convert to heterosexuality. They were able to do this even though the few images they found in literature portrayed them as doomed or damned—D. H. Lawrence's [fiction]..., for example. (Margaret Cruikshank, *The Gay and Lesbian Liberation Movement*, p. 8)

Blaming Lawrence as the creative writer most responsible for their plight, gay activist literary critics endeavor to deflate Lawrence's heterosexual authoritativeness—authoritativeness which "portrayed them [homosexuals] as doomed or damned." And what better way to deflate Lawrence's heterosexual authority-authoritativeness, then, than to portray him as gay? Thus lesbian activist literary critic Karla Jay blatantly and tersely states that "D. H. Lawrence...[is] a closet case" (Jay 72); Jay does not elaborate, however. Christopher Craft for his part engages in a lengthy delineation of his psycho-machy in relation to *Women in Love* in general and Gerald Crich in particular:

> [Lawrence in *Women in Love*] refuses to countenance the masculinity of male homosexual desire, a refusal shared, we should note, by Lawrence's title *Women in Love*, which silently ingests, all the better to occlude, the open secret of the novel's secret subject: men in love.
> The gender metathesis embedded within the inversion figure entails a specific violence: the elimination of at least one male, either by murder or "castration."...Only in *Women in Love* does Lawrence adequately calculate the destructiveness of this process, and there only equivocally. In sacrificing the character [Gerald Crich] whose radiant maleness so exacerbates Birkin's nagging "problem" [of "male homosexual desire"], Lawrence unleashes...the implacable death drive that crouches within the inversion trope. From the beginning of the narrative [of *Women in Love*],...[Lawrence] targets Gerald's person and Gerald's body with a sniper's patient calculation....(Craft, pp. 166-167)

Condemning Lawrence's refusal "to countenance the masculinity of male homosexual desire" in *Women in Love*, Craft considers Lawrence to be guilty of duplicity in *Women in Love*, for, according to Craft, the true subject of *Women in Love* is "men in love"; furthermore, since "the novel's secret subject: men in love" must be "occlude[d]," it is necessary for "at least one male" to suffer "elimination..., either by murder or 'castration'"—and, according to Craft, it is this "[destructive] process" which takes place in *Women in Love*, with the "homosexual" temptation of Gerald's "radiant maleness" making "Gerald's person and Gerald's body" Lawrence's inevitable "target"—a "target" that, according to Craft, is the victim of "Lawrence's...psychotic intensity":

> Lawrence's novel [*Women in Love*] works, with a sometimes psychotic intensity, to produce this loss [of Gerald], this corpse [of Gerald], this murder [of Gerald] as its narrative telos, the single definitive event toward which this whole creation [*Women in Love*] moves....(Craft, p. 189)

Turning confessional, Craft declares that he shares "Birkin's homosexual longing for Gerald" (Craft, p. 189)—and Craft goes on to explain "*My* homosexual desire" for Gerald and "my guilt" over Gerald's death:

> I did not merely (like Birkin) want Gerald's superlative maleness, all thrust and drive—I also wanted (like Gudrun) to kill him for the

> extraordinary imposition his desirability entailed. *My homosexual desire...was thus fundamentally linked to a murderous impulsion....*And out of the ferocious conjugation of these desires, one homosexual and one homicidal, a third torsion unfolded itself....Not content (or even able) simply to desire Gerald, I also identified with him, and...[i]n the fantasia of my reading and rereading [*Women in Love*], Gerald's bewildered death sentence had become my own....Whatever "I" I may have had when I entered the text was now thoroughly dispersed among conflicting desires....I could assume all subject-positions and enact the entire drama "myself": I did not merely receive Gudrun's "great downward stroke" of annihilation [i.e., Gerald's "annihilation" by Gudrun]—*I delivered it too*, no doubt with a homicidal relish indistinguishable from suicidal relief. And once done with the killing [of Gerald] and the dying [as Gerald], I could invoke my reader's exemption and (like Birkin) exit the text intact, saved (more accurately, made safe) by the freshness of a grief that occluded, even as it inherited, my guilt....(Craft, pp. 189-190)

Craft's self-indulgent, jargonistic discussion of *Women in Love* is evidently rooted in left-wing ideology and "guilt"—guilt and ideology which lead to a state of affairs in which homosexuality is privileged above "bourgeois" heterosexuality; as Leslie Fiedler astutely noted some four decades ago:

> Implicit in the whole [pro-homosexual] trend is a certain impatience with the customary taboos and restraints; and particularly in its highbrow manifestations the celebrations of homosexual sensibility imply a rejection of the ideal of marriage and the family and of men who are men (i.e., Gary Cooper). It is, perhaps, more than that, too: the last possible protest against bourgeois security and the home in the suburbs in a world where adultery is old hat. But they come so fast, the new homosexuals, queen treading on queen: and we are so ready for them, so eager to prove our own emancipation by understanding and accepting. (Leslie Fiedler, *No! in Thunder*, p. 186)

As Leslie Fiedler notes, at the same time that the left wing valorizes the homosexual in an attack on the "bourgeois," the bourgeois liberal himself is "hopelessly understanding" (*Waiting for the End*, p. 162), "eager to prove [their] own emancipation by understanding and accepting" (*No!*, p. 186).

One such bourgeois liberal is critic Eugene Goodheart, who with his "radical democratic conscience" (*Culture and the Radical Conscience*, p. 85) is extremely disturbed by reactionaries like...D. H. Lawrence (Ibid., p. 80)

—D. H. Lawrence, who (according to Goodheart) is guilty of "political barbarism": discussing "the political claim of the imagination," Goodheart asserts that

> What makes the claim dubious...[is] the unmistakable symptoms of political barbarism in the character of the artist, of the imagination, and of the work of art itself, where one would hope to find anticipations of the ideal polity. Even those who have created works of art...have often lacked nobility not only in their lives but in their imaginations as well. One has only to consider a political order constituted by the imagination of a D. H. Lawrence....(*Culture and the Radical Conscience*, p. 133)

Disturbed by "reactionary" D. H. Lawrence with his "political barbarism" and his lack of "nobility," Goodheart in recent years deploys a strategy by means of which he attempts both to discredit Lawrence the "priest of [heterosexual] love" and to subvert "Lawrence, the political and social anarchist" (*Desire*, p. 74) and the Lawrentian "scheme" in which "life values (rather than merely rational values) are preserved by an elite of the gifted and the imaginative, while the rest of society performs the necessary social and economic functions" (*Culture and the Radical Conscience*, p. 142). Lawrence's "aristocratic anarchism of the cult of imagination" (ibid., p. 145) is anathema to Goodheart, who believes that

> Between Lawrence and every serious reader of him there must be...a permanent tension: a sense of provocation and danger.
> Lawrence is...an artist beyond good and evil who compels our admiration and mistrust....Lawrence enters the human community a stranger and an enemy, possessed by a vision [that is] so subversive and dangerous...(*Utopian Vision*, pp. 172-173)

—"so subversive and dangerous," indeed, that Goodheart feels obliged to deflate and distort that "dangerous fellow" D. H. Lawrence (ibid., p. 170) and his meaning; accordingly, Goodheart tries to make a mockery of Lawrence's claims to authority: Goodheart does this in the first place by attempting to gainsay Lawrence's status as "[heterosexual] priest of love":

> Our most powerful and persistent associations with Lawrence's novels emanate from his portrayal of scenes of sexual passion....In the cultural imagination, Lawrence is the greatest of our modern

> professors of desire. This represents a profound misunderstanding of the significance of Lawrence's achievement....(*Desire*, p. 59)

—and, as for "Lawrence's achievement" in *Women in Love*, Goodheart asserts that Lawrence's main "portrayal of scenes of sexual passion" in that great novel takes place in the "Gladiatorial" chapter:

> In "Gladiatorial" Gerald and Birkin will strip naked and engage in a wrestling match that has an erotic intensity unmatched in the novel [*Women in Love*]....The wrestling, represented as a kind of male bonding (a blood brotherhood), is so charged with homosexual suggestion that it would be sophistical and misleading to deny it, as some critics have done. (Goodheart, *Desire*, pp. 72-73)

Thus, according to Eugene Goodheart who is trying to subvert Lawrence's reputation as "the greatest of our...professors of desire," Lawrence's "erotic intensity" in his greatest work *Women in Love* is supremely manifested, not in "his [Lawrence's]...scenes of [male-female] sexual passion" between Ursula and Birkin and/or Gudrun and Gerald, but rather in "The wrestling" between Birkin and Gerald, wrestling which Goodheart prefers to see as "so charged with homosexual suggestion that it would be sophistical and misleading to deny it"; yet it is Goodheart himself who is "sophistical and misleading" in his treatment of *Women in Love*; he is evidently oblivious of the great "erotic intensity" manifest in such scenes as the famous "sons of God" scene in "Excurse" (Chapter XXIII of *Women in Love*), with its "deeper and deeper physical intensity" (Clark, p. 166) and its portrayal of "oral and anal gratifications" (ibid.)—as illustrated, for instance, in the following passage:

> And she [Ursula] was drawn to him [Birkin] strangely, as in a spell. Kneeling on the hearth-rug before him, she put her arms round his loins, and put her face against his thighs. Riches! Riches! She was overwhelmed with a sense of a heavenful of riches....
>
> Unconsciously, with her sensitive finger-tips, she was tracing the back of his thighs, following some mysterious life-flow there. She had discovered something, something more than wonderful, more wonderful than life itself. It was the strange mystery of his life-motion, there, at the back of the thighs, down the flanks. It was a strange reality of his being, the very stuff of being, there in the straight downflow of the thighs. It was here she discovered him one of the sons of God such as were in the beginning of the world, not a man, something other, something more....

> She closed her hands over the full, rounded body of his loins, as he stooped over her, she seemed to touch the quick of the mystery of darkness that was bodily him. She seemed to faint beneath, and he seemed to faint, stooping over her. It was a perfect passing away for both of them. (*Women in Love*, Chapter XXIII, "Excurse")

Here in "Excurse" Lawrence's compelling eroto-religious "intensity" is surely evident, as "This ["sons of God"] scene [in "Excurse"] contains a brilliant rendering of emotions extremely difficult to translate into language....In this ["sons of God"] scene Lawrence touches on a number of emotional reflexes, some well nigh indefinable" (Clark, p. 166). In "Excurse" we have Ursula, "her arms round [Birkin's] loins,...her face against [Birkin's] thighs"; Birkin and Ursula both attaining "a perfect passing away": indeed, we can certainly agree with Gerald Doherty that "Excurse" enacts "an *Ars Erotica* theory of pleasure, based on transcendent attainment" (Doherty 140); and Doherty rightly characterizes "Excurse" as a site of "transcendent" erotic "pleasure":

> Focused entirely on Birkin and Ursula, and confined to one pivotal episode aptly named "Excurse," this *Ars Erotica* offers the protagonists [Birkin and Ursula] access to a new plane of existence where states of transcendent pleasure [take place]....(Doherty 140)

"Excurse," concludes Doherty, "offers an experiment in erotic narration for which no real precedent exists in the English tradition" (Doherty 148).

But Eugene Goodheart, with his excessively political, and "politically correct," perspective sees the "erotic" Ursula-Birkin scene in "Excurse" as "a fantasy of power, not sexual pleasure" (*Desire*, p. 73), with the real "unmatched" "erotic intensity" of *Women in Love* to be found (according to Goodheart) in the "Gladiatorial" chapter's "homosexual" wrestling match between Birkin and Gerald (*Desire*, p. 73). Yet Goodheart's misreading here of *Women in Love* is merely representative of the kind of "misreading" that is welcomed by the left-wing, politicized academy of today; for, as one scholar of the current critical scene astutely observes:

> For many [left-wing] readers now, willfully misrepresenting one's subject is at worst a critical misdemeanor, and this peccadillo is redeemed by any motive, like that of promoting gay liberation, that can be designated as politically correct. (Carroll, *Evolution and Literary Theory*, p. 165)

Goodheart, with his "liberal guilt" and "radical conscience," aspires to "transform" society:

> I believed with my radical friends that...society should be transformed, and that we should be agents of transformation. (*Pieces*, p. 1)

One major way in which Goodheart aims to be one of the "agents of transformation" of society is by "promoting gay liberation"; the politically correct Goodheart forthrightly states that

> Homosexual desire...belongs to the host of desires that have a right to satisfaction....(*Desire*, p. 55)

Ardently advocating the "right" of "homosexual desire" to "satisfaction," the liberal Goodheart has nothing but contempt for "bourgeois prejudice against homosexuality" (*Desire*, p. 55)—a "prejudice" that he finds egregiously exemplified by his political adversaries the neoconservatives:

> I find them [the neoconservatives] stridently confident, predictable, and even fanatical in their opposition to every liberal or radical tendency (e.g., *homosexual culture*...), in their habit of dividing the world too neatly between good and evil....
> ...I have never been tempted to embrace the conservative position, because of what I have always felt to be a deficiency in social compassion and social justice. (*Pieces*, pp. 4, 6; my italics)

Fancying himself to be fighting for "social compassion and social justice" for "homosexual culture," Goodheart does not find it difficult to deploy literary criticism as "propaganda"—as one scholar of literary criticism-theory today explains:

> From this [politically correct, left-wing] perspective, the main purpose of criticism is not to understand and appreciate works of literature; it is, rather, to use works of literature for the cause of political liberation. Neither a form of objective knowledge nor a form of aesthetic responsiveness, criticism thus is a form of propaganda. (Carroll, *Evolution and Literary Theory*, p. 165)

In his recent attempt to promote "gay liberation" via his discussion of D. H. Lawrence, Goodheart uses the criticism-as-propaganda strategy famously deployed by queer theorist Eve Kosofsky Sedgwick in *Epistemology of the Closet* and elsewhere; Joseph Carroll tells us that

> The work of Eve Kosofsky Sedgwick can be taken to illustrate a...strategy for normativizing homosexuality—[namely,] to rein-

terpret heterosexual relations as covert depictions of homosexual relations and thereby extend homosexuality to the point at which it takes on the appearance of a virtually universal condition. (Carroll, p. 164)

In his discussion of *Women in Love* Goodheart uses the Sedgwick strategy in which homosexuality is "normativized" by "reinterpret[ing] heterosexual relations as covert depictions of homosexual relations": the "heterosexual relations" with which Goodheart deals in his discussion of *Women in Love* are indeed none other than those involved in the wrestling match between Birkin and Gerald, a wrestling match that Goodheart prefers to look at as evidence of "an erotic intensity unmatched in the novel" and "so charged with homosexual suggestion that it would be sophistical and misleading to deny it"; but, *pace* Goodheart, the fact is that the Birkin-Gerald wrestling match is essentially an action undertaken by two incorrigibly heterosexual men who are in a temporary albeit intense state of considerable rage and aggression, Birkin for the specific reason of his recent rejection by Ursula:

> After the fiasco of the proposal, Birkin had hurried blindly away from [Ursula], in a whirl of fury....He was deeply, mockingly angry [with] Ursula....("Gladiatorial")

—and Gerald for the more general reason of aboulia and inertia:

> Gerald...[felt] utterly hollow. He had done all the work he wanted to do—and now there was nothing....He was suspended motionless, in an agony of inertia....
> "...I want something to hit...." [Gerald tells Birkin] ("Gladiatorial")

Insofar as this is the case—that Birkin and Gerald's wrestling is motivated by rage and aggression—then the wrestling match is a site, not of Eros, but rather of Thanatos; thus to say as does Goodheart that the wrestling match is a site of great "erotic intensity" is to ignore the essentially Thanatotic-aggressive origins and elements of the Birkin-Gerald wrestling match and to "misread" the "Gladiatorial" scene in a reductive, misleading manner.

Yet, for all its Thanatotic aspect, the Birkin-Gerald wrestling match does indeed ultimately redound to the benefit of "heterosexual relations"—as Barry J. Scherr clearly explains:

> In the famous chapter "Gladiatorial," of course, there is physical contact between Birkin and his puissant friend Gerald in their

naked wrestling together—but this physical contact is certainly not sexual or erotic: instead, as the chapter title itself tells us, their physical encounter is "gladiatorial" in the sense that Birkin and Gerald engage in physical combat with each other—a combat from which Birkin with his "uncanny force" emerges triumphant. It is Birkin's "fine, sublimated energy" and "almost supernatural" strength that are demonstrated in the wrestling scene; furthermore, it is this "uncanny" power in Birkin that enables him to have his transcendental experience with Ursula in "Excurse." Thus the man-to-man encounter in "Gladiatorial" is merely instrumental, a means by which Birkin's strength is tested and affirmed to ensure his sexual-transcendental success with Ursula....

...[Thus] in "Gladiatorial" Lawrence has nonsexual physical contact between two men lead the hero (Birkin) to his triumphant heterosexual encounter....Lawrence, of course, gives heterosexuality top priority in *Women in Love*: the meeting between his two male characters (Birkin and Gerald) in "Gladiatorial" surely does service to the male-female relationship (of Birkin and Ursula) in the novel. (Scherr, *D. H. Lawrence's Response*, pp. 93-94)

Indeed, we know for a fact that, no sooner does Birkin prove his "Almost-supernatural" strength in his wrestling match with Gerald—

> "It surprised me," panted Gerald, "what strength you've got. Almost—supernatural" [Gerald tells Birkin after the wrestling]

—no sooner does Birkin prove his "strength" than

> His [Birkin's] mind had reverted to Ursula. She seemed to return again into his consciousness....
> ...But really it was Ursula, it was the woman who was gaining ascendance over Birkin's being, at this moment. Gerald was becoming dim again, lapsing out of him. ("Gladiatorial")

Like Birkin, Lawrence's "consciousness" and "being" too return to "the woman"—and to "The love between man and woman,...the greatest and most complete passion the world will ever see" ("Love"): the subject that is the source of Lawrence's great poetic strength; thus Lawrence-Birkin goes on to his heterosexual triumph with Ursula in "Excurse"; yet despite this triumph there is still a problem which continues to preoccupy Lawrence in his plan for Western civilization and for his own poetic strength and immortality: the problem of what to do with homosexuality; and here Eugene Goodheart, for all his left-of-center tendentiousness, is capable of providing us with significant insight which will assist us in understanding Lawrence's agenda and strategy in relation to homosexuality; discussing "Lawrence's adversarial role as an artist" (*Desire*, p. 77), Goodheart concludes that

> In their combat with modern life, Lawrence and his protagonists perform deliberate acts of self-alienation from family, community, society, "real life." Lawrence was as much the alienated artist as any formalist modernist. In this fashion, he conceived his task as the reconception of the whole world in his consciousness. (*Desire*, p. 77)

What Goodheart does not perceive is the fact that a major part of Lawrence's "combat with modern life," a major part of Lawrence's "task" of "the reconception of the whole world in his consciousness" was creating in his imagination—and, he hoped, in "real life" as well—creating a "modern life" in which homosexuality would be benevolently eliminated by means of a unique Lawrentian strategy which deals with the "bodies and pleasures" issues of homosexuality while at the same time weaning homosexuals away from the practise of "this blasphemy against love" (as Lawrence calls homosexuality—"the men loving men"—in his letter of 19 April 1915 to David Garnett).

"Bodies and pleasures" is in fact a periphrastic Foucaultian euphemism for the practise of a sadomasochistic sexual economy. As one major Foucauldian disciple (weirdly) explains: "Of course, the classic case of the strategic use of power differentials to produce effects of pleasure instead of effects of domination is sadomasochistic eroticism....S/M is a strategy for creating pleasure...." (Halperin, *Saint Foucault*, pp. 85-86). Foucault himself authoritatively states that

> the S/M game is very interesting because it is a strategic relation, but it is always fluid. Of course, there are roles, but everyone knows very well that those roles can be reversed....Or, even when the roles are stabilized, you know very well that it is always a game....This strategic game as a source of *bodily pleasure* is very interesting....It is an acting out of power structures by a strategic game that is able to give sexual pleasure or bodily pleasure. (Foucault, quoted in *Saint Foucault*, p. 86; italics mine)

On the Foucauldian relation between S/M and "bodily pleasure," Halperin concludes that

> S/M represented to Foucault "a process of invention," insofar as it detaches sexual pleasure from sexuality (in an S/M scene, the precise gender and sexual orientation of one's sexual partner may lose some of their importance as prerequisites of sexual excite-

> ment) and insofar as it frees bodily pleasure from organ specificity, from exclusive localization in the genitals. S/M thereby makes possible a new relation between the body and pleasure....(Halperin, *Saint Foucault*, p. 87)

Like Foucault, Lawrence in "Gladiatorial" valorizes "a process...[which] detaches sexual pleasure from sexuality...and...frees bodily pleasure from organ specificity, from exclusive localization in the genitals"; Lawrence in "Gladiatorial" "makes possible a new relation between the body and pleasure"; but, while Foucault's "bodies and pleasures" strategy serves S/M and can be seen as making the body a site of psychosociopathy, Lawrence's strategy in "Gladiatorial" can indeed be seen as "Platonizing" the male body in the most essential sense of the word: making the male body a site of Platonic pleasure—as Birkin indeed explains to Gerald after the wrestling match:

> "It [the wrestling match] was a real set-to, wasn't it?" said Birkin, looking at Gerald with darkened eyes.
> "God, yes," said Gerald. He looked at the delicate body of the other man, and added: "It wasn't too much for you, was it?"
> "No. One ought to wrestle and strive and be physically close. It makes one sane."

Here Birkin emphasizes the Greek ideal, of Plato's day, of a sound mind in a sound body. And Birkin goes on to make it evident that he is so secure in his heterosexuality that "homosexual panic" in relation to himself is an absurd notion, the product of a homophobic society that he has so successfully and imaginatively transcended that its conventions and proprieties are completely irrelevant to him:

> "We are mentally, spiritually intimate, therefore we should be *more or less physically intimate too*—it is more whole" [Birkin tells Gerald].
> "Certainly it is," said Gerald. Then he laughed pleasantly, adding: "It's rather wonderful to me."
> He stretched out his arms handsomely.
> "Yes," said Birkin. "—I don't know why one should have to justify oneself." (*Women in Love*, "Gladiatorial"; my italics)

What is most significant here, it seems to me, is Birkin-Lawrence's assertion that "we should be *more or less* physically intimate"—the emphasis certainly being on "less"; for what Birkin-Lawrence is advocating here, rather than homoeroticism sublimated or otherwise, is the Lawrentian metaphysic of "wholeness" ("it is more whole")—a metaphysic which *always includes the body* in some way (sexual or non-sexual) as a major part of being; but of course, at the same time that Lawrence was advocating his metaphysic of wholeness, he was always attempting to make his own Lawrentian brand of "Platonic" male-male relations attractive to the homosexual elite who practised the actual "blasphemy against love." Conceiving himself to be "the anti-Platonic Plato" (Scherr, *D. H. Lawrence's Response*, p. 91), Lawrence craved the vindication of his "Platonic"-Lawrentian approach to homosexuality which celebrated the male body ("more or less") while deploring actual homosexuality. Indeed, Lawrence gives away the "Platonic" aspect of his anti-homosexual, metaphysical strategy in "Gladiatorial" by the very next statement Birkin makes to Gerald; after his (Birkin's) abjuration of "homosexual panic" ("I don't know why one should have to justify oneself"), Birkin tells Gerald:

> "I think also that you are beautiful," said Birkin to Gerald, "and that is enjoyable too. One should enjoy what is given."
> "You think I am beautiful—how do you mean, physically?" asked Gerald, his eyes glistening.
> "Yes. You have a northern kind of beauty, like light refracted from snow—and a beautiful plastic form. Yes, that is there to enjoy as well. We should enjoy everything."

Birkin tells Gerald that he is "beautiful," "physically" beautiful—but it is obvious from what Birkin says immediately afterward that what he really means is that Gerald is *metaphysically beautiful* ("You have a northern kind of beauty"), with "a northern kind of beauty"—this "northern kind of beauty," we know, from the chapter of *Women in Love* immediately preceding "Gladiatorial" (Chapter XIX, "Moony"), is an emblem of "The white races" and "snow-abstract annihilation":

> The white races, having the arctic north behind them, the vast abstraction of ice and snow, would fulfil a mystery of ice-destructive knowledge, snow-abstract annihilation....
> Birkin thought of Gerald. He was one of these strange white wonderful demons from the north, fulfilled in the destructive frost-mystery. And was he fated to pass away in this knowledge, this one process of frost-knowledge, death by perfect cold? Was he a messenger, an omen of the universal dissolution into whiteness and snow? (*Women in Love*, Chapter XIX, "Moony")

Like a Platonic philosopher, Birkin-Lawrence subordinates Gerald's physical characteristics to his (Birkin-Lawrence's) metaphysical vision.

Thus Gerald's "beauty," rather than being sexy, is symbolic—symbolic of the beauty of a certain phase of "The white races" and their civilization in danger of being destroyed via "a process of frost-knowledge, death by perfect cold," "dissolution into whiteness and snow." If, as one critic states,

> Gerald is the dazzling dead end of a culture whose roots are Grecian (Chamberlain 414),

then Birkin-Lawrence aspires to save that culture first of all by saving Gerald via a revision of "Grecian"-"Platonic" homoeroticism, homoeroticism which in Lawrence's day had greatly degenerated from that of Plato's age, thanks to the modern homosexual intelligentsia such as the promiscuous John Maynard Keynes (see Skidelsky, *John Maynard Keynes: Hopes Betrayed*, p. 204)—homosexuality which Lawrence-Birkin wished to totally transform and eliminate so as to serve his (Lawrence's) agenda as priest of heterosexual love; but first Lawrence-Birkin would need the very allegiance of Gerald, an allegiance which he attempts to obtain in one of the late chapters of the novel (Chapter XXV, "Marriage or Not"). Having already achieved his triumph with Ursula in "Excurse" (Chapter XXIII), Lawrence-Birkin turns his strategy on Gerald, trying to win him over as an ally in his (Birkin-Lawrence's) quest for "a greater power of individuality" (in Birkin's case) and supreme poetic strength (in Lawrence's):

> "In fact," said Birkin, "because the relation between man and woman is made the supreme and exclusive relationship, that's where all the tightness and meanness and insufficiency comes in."
>
> "Yes, I believe you," said Gerald.
>
> "You've got to take down the love-and-marriage ideal from its pedestal. We want something broader.—I believe in the *additional* perfect relationship between man and man—additional to marriage."
>
> "I can never see how they can be the same," said Gerald.
>
> "Not the same—but equally important, equally creative, equally sacred, if you like."
>
> Gerald moved uneasily.—"You know, I can't feel that," said he. "Surely there can never be anything as strong between man and man as sex love is between man and woman. Nature doesn't provide the basis."
>
> "Well, of course, I think she does. And I don't think we shall ever be happy till we establish ourselves on this basis. You've got to get rid of the *exclusiveness* of married love. And you've got to

> admit the unadmitted love of man for man. It makes for a greater freedom for everybody, a greater power of individuality both in men and women." (*Women in Love*, Chapter XXV, "Marriage or Not")

"A greater power of individuality": this is indeed what Birkin aspires to in *Women in Love*—a "power of individuality" that he wishes to enhance even in the midst of his impending marriage to Ursula. Birkin's valorization of "a greater power of individuality" is of course Lawrence's own; as Lawrence declared, in a letter of his *Women in Love* period:

> I do esteem individual liberty above everything. What is a nation for, but to secure the maximum of liberty to every individual. (D. H. Lawrence letter to Thomas Dunlop, 12 July 1916)

But of course, for Lawrence, alienated from the English "nation" which had condemned his *Rainbow* and his individualism, "individual liberty"—"the maximum of liberty to every individual"—can only be "secure[d]" in the private realm rather than the public, in the private realm of intimate relationships on the one hand and imaginative creation on the other; thus, when Lawrence, in the midst of his *Women in Love* period (1918), says that

> The love between man and woman is the greatest and most complete passion the world will ever see ("Love," *English Review*, January 1918),

he is staking his unique claim to poetic strength and poetic immortality as the master of all writers on that subject ("The love between man and woman") by virtue of what he feels is his authority on that theme as a result of his experiences with Frieda and other women; that is to say, he is aggrandizing himself as a great creative writer on the basis of his private domain—a private sexual domain which has greatly contributed to his public artistic domain as novelist of the male-female sexual emotions; yet, to "secure" his position of public poetic strength and immortality, Lawrence needs public support—support which he could not get in the realm of reality, but which he could get in the domain of his own imagination—an imagination whose claim to poetic immortality superseded everything—even the supreme Lawrentian theme of male-female relationship; so, when Birkin says to Gerald that "the relation between man and woman" has got to be "take[n] down...from its pedestal," he is not actually contradicting Lawrence's statement that

"The love between man and woman is the greatest and most complete passion the world will ever see," but rather is saying that the male-female relation needs to be of service to "something broader"—that "something broader" being in fact Lawrence's claim to poetic strength and immortality; a claim for which Lawrence also needs the support of men; and that is where "the *additional* perfect relationship between man and man—additional to marriage" comes in; for it is only with the support of the world of men that Lawrence can achieve poetic immortality—and, if he does not have that support in the real world, at least he could in "The world of my novel":

> I know it is true, the book [*Women in Love*]. And it is another world, in which I can live apart from this foul world which I will not accept or acknowledge or even enter. The world of my novel [*Women in Love*] is big and fearless—yes, I love it, and love it passionately. (D. H. Lawrence letter to Ottoline Morrell, 3 October 1916)

Of course, for Lawrence, one aspect of "this foul world" was homosexuality, about which he had indeed written to Lady Ottoline Morrell (in late March 1915), in a letter in which he in fact attacked her "generous" attitude towards homosexuality, and for his own part attacked homosexuality as "evil" and rat-like:

> The feeling that comes out of your letter is like a scent of flowers, so generous and reassuring. It is no good now, thinking that to understand a [homosexual] man from his own point of view is to be happy about him. I can imagine the mind of a rat, as it slithers along in the dark, pointing its sharp nose. But I can never feel happy about it, I must always want to kill it. It contains a principle of evil. There *is* a principle of evil. Let us acknowledge it once and for all. I saw it so plainly in [the homosexual] Keynes at Cambridge, it [homosexuality] made me sick. I am sick with the knowledge of the prevalence of evil [homosexuality], as if it were some insidious disease. (D. H. Lawrence letter to Ottoline Morrell, 24 March 1915)

Lawrence, in the "big and fearless" "world of my novel" *Women in Love*, "can live apart" from "this foul world" and—in his imagination, at any rate—can "kill" "evil," rat-like homosexuality with a strategy that enlists the aid of men like Gerald Crich, whom he must convince that there can be "a perfect relationship between man and man," a relationship which is not "evil," not "some insidious disease," but on the contrary is a natural way of fighting the "disease"; a way which will at the same time help guarantee Lawrence's poetic immortality.

What "natural" way is this? While Gerald tells Birkin that "there can never be anything as strong between man and man as sex love is between man and woman. Nature doesn't provide the basis," Birkin-Lawrence can indeed tell us what is "as strong between man and man as sex love is between man and woman," and how this is based in "Nature."

Part of the answer to Gerald's question about what is "as strong between man and man as sex love is between man and woman" can be found in the "Epilogue" to Lawrence's metaphysical *Movements in European History*. Here Lawrence posits the existence of *natural* power—"nature power" which is possessed by only a chosen few who are "responsible...to God":

> And power, true nature power, *does* come from God. That is, it is either born inside a man, or nothing can give it him....
>
> Now we begin to understand the old motto, *noblesse oblige*. *Noblesse* means, having the gift of power, the natural or sacred power. And having such power obliges a man to act with fearlessness and generosity, responsible for his acts to God....
>
> Some men must be noble, or life is an ash-heap. There *is* natural nobility, given by God or the Unknown, and far beyond commonsense. And towards this natural nobility we must live.
>
> The simple man, whose best self, his noble self, is nearly all the time puzzled, dumb, and helpless, has still the power to recognise the man in whom the noble self is powerful and articulate. To this man he must pledge himself. That is the only way....
>
> This is our job then, our uncommonsense: to recognise the spark of *noblesse* inside us, and let it make us. To recognise the spark of *noblesse* in one another, and add our sparks together, to a flame. And to recognise the men who have stars, not mere sparks of nobility in their souls, and to choose these for leaders....(*Movements in European History*, "Epilogue")

"[P]ower, true nature power," which "come[s] from God," provides the basis for what is "as strong between man and man as sex love is between man and woman," says Lawrence; it is this "nature power"—"the gift of power, the natural or sacred power"—which Birkin-Lawrence believes himself to be endowed with; thus Lawrence-Birkin believes himself "oblige[d] to act with fearlessness and generosity, responsible for his acts to God"—"God" Who is evidently opposed to homosexuality: this, it seems to me, is one way of reading Lawrence-Birkin's concluding meditations in "Exeunt" (Chapter XXXII):

> God can do without man. God could do without the ichthyosauri and the mastodon. These monsters failed creatively to develop, so God, the creative mystery, dispensed with them. In the same way the mystery could dispense with man, should he too fail creatively to change and develop. The eternal creative mystery could dispose of man, and replace him with a finer created being....
>
> It was very consoling to Birkin, to think this. If humanity ran into a cul de sac, and expended itself, the timeless creative mystery would bring forth some other being, finer, more wonderful, some new, more lovely race, to carry on the embodiment of creation. The game was never up. The mystery of creation was fathomless, infallible, inexhaustible forever. Races came and went, species passed away, but ever new species arose, more lovely, or equally lovely, always surpassing wonder. The fountain-head was incorruptible and unsearchable. It had no limits. It could bring forth miracles, create utter new races and new species, in its own hour, new forms of consciousness, new forms of body, new units of being. To be man was as nothing compared to the possibilities of the creative mystery. To have one's pulse beating direct from the mystery, this was perfection, unutterable satisfaction....

As one who has "the gift of power, the natural or sacred power" that "*does* come from God," together with "natural nobility, given by God," Lawrence feels that it is his *noblesse oblige* duty to champion God's "creative mystery" against the "triumphant decay" brought about by "the men loving men" (as Lawrence explained in his letter of 19 April 1915 to David Garnett)—this "triumphant decay" inevitably will lead to "a cul de sac" for humanity, says Lawrence, unless the mass of "simple" men "recognise the man in whom the noble self is powerful and articulate": that "man" being, of course, the "noble,...powerful and articulate" D. H. Lawrence, who by the time of his *Women in Love* period had become unshakably convinced of his greatness, his "peerlessness":

> Where are my peers? I acknowledge no more than five or six—not so many—in the world. (D. H. Lawrence letter to Bertrand Russell, 2 June 1915)

Surely the "peerless" Lawrence conceived himself to be "the man in whom the noble self is powerful and articulate." According to Lawrence's imaginative conception, then, the mass of "simple" men "must pledge [themselves]" to "the man in whom the noble self is powerful and articulate"—that is, to D. H. Lawrence himself: "That is the only way" to save Western civilization from a decadent state of affairs in which "life is an ash-heap"—"an ash-heap" characterized by homosexuality, among other ignoble, "rat-like" phenomena which, in Lawrence's vision, must be transformed/eliminated. In Lawrence's imaginative-phenomenological vision, this is the job of Lawrence the leader, once the mass majority of "simple" men "recognise the men who have *stars*, not mere sparks of nobility in their souls, and...choose these for leaders" (my italics); and Lawrence in his metaphysical *Movements* concludes by exhorting his readers to

> follow only the leader who is a star of the new, *natural noblesse* [Lawrence's italics]. (*Movements*, "Epilogue")

Thus Lawrence's "love of man for man" has its "natural" basis in the *natural noblesse* of "the leader," the greater man, the "star" who is to be followed by other, lesser men who are full of love and obedience—especially obedience:

> there will be profound, profound obedience..., obedience to the incalculable power-urge. And men must submit to the greater soul in a man, for their guidance....All men say, they want a leader. Then let them in their souls *submit* to some greater soul than theirs....It's the deep, fathomless submission to the heroic soul in a greater man....it isn't love. It is life-submission. (*Aaron's Rod*, Chapter XXI, "Words")

In *Aaron's Rod*, written shortly after *Women in Love*, Lawrence makes it clear that Birkin may have been a bit disingenuous when he spoke to Gerald about "love of man for man"; evidently Lawrence-Birkin was more interested in power over men than in the "love of man for man": for power would enable Lawrence to create a new world, with Lawrence—in his imagination, at least—the leader, the "star" in that endeavor, an endeavor to be undertaken by heterosexually fulfilled Lawrentian men "for life's sake":

> Leaders—this is what mankind is craving for.
> But men must be prepared to obey, body and soul, once they have chosen the leader. And let them choose the leader for life's sake only....
> ...Men, being themselves made new after the act of coition, wish to make the world new....[These Lawrentian men] are bent

> on the same activity,...to be busy making a new world. (*Fantasia of the Unconscious*, pp. 124, 143)

Thus, according to Lawrence, the basis of what is "as strong between man and man as sex love is between man and woman" consists of two main components: (1) the noble leader, the "star" and (2) the association between leader and followers in service of "making a new world." Clearly homosexuals are not included in the vanguard of the Lawrentian "new world"; indeed, the homosexuals in the new Lawrentian world are evidently supposed to undergo a great change of identity—this change is adumbrated, it seems to me, in the example of Loerke in *Women in Love*.

Lawrence's final action on Loerke in *Women in Love* indeed demonstrates that Lawrence in *Women in Love* was finding a way to eliminate homosexuality as a viable mode of behavior for his characters and in his phenomenological world; indeed, Lawrence in *Women in Love* went far towards poetically constructing homosexuality as a synecdoche for all the disintegrative, "end-of-the-world" forces operating in the modern world; as Lawrence explains about "The book,"

> *Women in Love*. The book frightens me: it is so end-of-the-world. But it is, it must be, the beginning of a new world too. (D. H. Lawrence letter to Catherine Carswell, 7 November 1916)

In *Women in Love* the "end-of-the-world" motif is masterfully and synecdochically delineated in the character of Loerke, himself a synecdochic character; as one Lawrence scholar notes:

> Loerke represents a case history of all the standard perversions (Doherty 1996, 151)

—with Loerke's primary "standard perversion" being homosexuality; yet the fact is that, as *Women in Love* moves on, Loerke seems to become less "perverse"; indeed, he may even be (albeit tentatively) a small part of "the beginning of a new world" which Lawrence believed that *Women in Love* "is" and "must be" in addition to its "end-of-the-world" aspect. As *Women in Love* moves towards its memorable conclusion, Lawrence suddenly makes Loerke an exemplar of heterosexual desire and expertise:

> Loerke was waiting for her [Gudrun] now. The little artist, isolated in his own complete envelope, felt that here at last was a woman from whom he could get something. He was uneasy all the while, waiting to talk with her, subtly contriving to be near her. Her pres-

> ence filled him with keenness and excitement, he gravitated cunningly towards her, as if she had some unseen force of attraction.
> He was not in the least doubtful of himself, as regards Gerald. Gerald was one of the outsiders. Loerke only hated him for being rich and proud and of fine appearance. All these things, however, riches, pride of social standing, handsome physique, were externals. When it came to the relation with a woman such as Gudrun, he, Loerke, had an approach and a power that Gerald never dreamed of.
> How should Gerald hope to satisfy a woman of Gudrun's calibre? Did he think that pride or masterful will or physical strength would help him? Loerke knew a secret beyond these things. The greatest power is the one that is subtle and adjusts itself, not the one which blindly attacks. And he, Loerke, had understanding where Gerald was a calf. He, Loerke, could penetrate into depths far out of Gerald's knowledge, Gerald was left behind like a postulant in the ante-room of this temple of mysteries, this woman. But he, Loerke, could he not penetrate into the inner darkness, find the spirit of the woman in its inner recess, and wrestle with it there, the central serpent that is coiled at the core of life. (Pp. 450-451)

Now that Loerke has found the right woman ("here at last was a woman from whom he could get something"), Lawrence tells us, he (Loerke) is veritably obsessed with her ("Her presence filled him with keenness and excitement, he gravitated...towards her, as if she had some unseen force of attraction"); he is full of heterosexual desire for her, she has overwhelmed him just as she had overwhelmed Gerald, whom he (Loerke), in standard heterosexual fashion, now sees as his rival: "He [Loerke] was not in the least doubtful of himself as regards Gerald....Loerke only hated him [Gerald]....When it came to the relation with a woman such as Gudrun, he, Loerke, had an approach and a power that Gerald never dreamed of." Indeed, Loerke clearly views himself as far more heterosexually suitable for Gudrun than Gerald is; and Lawrence evidently agrees that, "When it came to the relation with a woman such as Gudrun, he, Loerke, had an approach and a power that Gerald never dreamed of." Lawrence does not explicitly state what this great Loerkian "approach" and "power" in relation to "a woman such as Gudrun" is; but nevertheless, judging from the recent remarks of some feminist Lawrentian critics, Loerke's heterosexual future with Gudrun is at least quite plausible. As one feminist critic "rethinking Lawrence" recently remarked: "Lawrence always gives the chance of new life"

(Davis 182)—and in *Women in Love*, it seems to me, a case can be made that Lawrence is "giv[ing] the chance of new life" to Loerke, in a sense, by sending him off with Gudrun on a potentially heterosexual life. This possibility becomes even more plausible when we consider the recent observations of one feminist Lawrentian in relation to Loerke and Gudrun:

> Her [i.e., Gudrun's] story ends on an altogether more intriguing note [than Ursula's], as she [Gudrun] departs with her fellow artist Loerke—a man whose sexual presence creates a fascination....(Barron 14)

—"a fascination" that indeed makes it possible for Loerke to achieve validity in the heterosexual realm; this "fascination" involves Loerke's ability to "penetrate into depths far out of Gerald's knowledge,...in...this temple of mysteries, this woman [Gudrun]....he, Loerke, could...penetrate into the inner darkness, find the spirit of the woman in its inner recess, and wrestle with it there"; whatever this penetration into "the inner darkness...of the woman" may be, it is essentially an antisocial activity:

> What was it, after all, that a woman wanted? Was it mere social effect, fulfilment of ambition in the social world, in the community of mankind? Was it even a union in love and..."goodness"? Who but a fool would accept this of Gudrun? This was but the street view of her wants. Cross the threshold, and you found her completely, completely cynical about the social world and its advantages. Once inside the house of her soul, and there was a pungent atmosphere of corrosion, an inflamed darkness of sensation, and a vivid, subtle, critical consciousness, that saw the world distorted, horrific. (451)

Indeed, both Gudrun and Loerke "saw the world distorted, horrific"; this is a part of the "end-of-the-world" aspect of *Women in Love*. In their antisocial outlook, Loerke and Gudrun envision the "end of the world":

> As for the future, that they never mentioned except one laughed out some mocking dream of the destruction of the world by a ridiculous catastrophe of man's invention: a man invented such a perfect explosive that it blew the earth in two, and the two halves set off in different directions through space, to the dismay of the inhabitants: or else the people of the world divided into two halves, and each half decided *it* was perfect and right, the other half was wrong and must be destroyed; so another end of the world. Or else, Loerke's dream of fear, the world went cold, and snow fell

> everywhere, and only white creatures, polar-bears, white foxes, and men like awful white snow-birds, persisted in ice cruelty. (453)

The "end of the world" aspect of *Women in Love* as delineated in the Loerke-Gudrun conversations is related only to "our" Western civilization which Lawrence wished to save in his imagination; "Loerke's dream of fear," characterized by a state in which "the world went cold, and snow fell everywhere," culminating in "ice cruelty," uniquely pertains to the "mystery of ice-destructive knowledge, snow-abstract annihilation" portrayed much earlier in *Women in Love* in Birkin's vision in "Moony":

> It ["the end of the world"] would be done differently by the white races. The white races, having the arctic north behind them, the vast abstraction of ice and snow, would fulfil a mystery of ice-destructive knowledge, snow-abstract annihilation....
>
> Was this then all that remained? Was there left now nothing but to break off from the happy creative being, was the time up? Is our day of creative life finished? . . .
>
> Birkin thought of Gerald. He was one of these strange white wonderful demons from the north, fulfilled in the destructive frost-mystery. And was he fated to pass away in this knowledge, this one process of frost-knowledge, death by perfect cold? (254)

In his "dream of fear," Loerke evidently shares Lawrence-Birkin's concern that Western civilization will die a "death by perfect cold" characterized by "ice cruelty" and "snow-abstract annihilation"; and Loerke evidently is better suited to deal with this crisis than is Gerald, who is "fated to pass away" in this situation; indeed, Loerke, according to Lawrence at this point, is Gerald's superior even in male-female relationships, for he with his superior "understanding" of Gudrun can "wrestle" with her "spirit...in its inner recess." Gudrun's "spirit," "the house of her soul," is characterized by "a pungent atmosphere of corrosion, an inflamed darkness of sensation . . ."; but of course in *Women in Love* nobody is perfect.

In view of Gudrun's rather unwholesome "soul," Loerke for all his faults is better qualified to deal with her than Gerald is, for Gerald can only provide the "sheer blind force of passion," while Loerke can give her new "thrills":

> What then, what next? Was it sheer blind force of passion that would satisfy her [Gudrun] now? Not this, but the subtle thrills of extreme sensation in reduction. It was an unbroken will [i.e.,

> Loerke's] reacting against her unbroken will in a myriad subtle thrills of reduction, the last subtle activities of analysis and breaking-down carried out in the darkness of her, whilst the outside form, the individual, was utterly unchanged, even sentimental in its poses. (451)

The new "thrills" that Gudrun looks forward to experiencing with Loerke are "subtle" and "sensation[al]," rooted in the battle of "unbroken will[s]" and characterized by "the last subtle activities of analysis and breaking down."

In his remarkable letter of 22 November 1915 to Heseltine, written shortly before his *Women in Love* period, Lawrence asserts that "the great reducing, analytic...process" must come to an end, "Because now, reduction...has reached the point where it...can only produce sensationalism." This "sensationalism," says Lawrence, is part and parcel of "this great flux of disintegration, further analysis, self-analysis." Lawrence's letter to Heseltine, it seems to me, provides an excellent gloss on what is to happen between Loerke and Gudrun at this point in *Women in Love*: they are to experience together "the great reducing, analytic...process" (to quote Lawrence's letter), the "subtle thrills of extreme sensation in reduction," "subtle thrills of reduction, the last subtle activities of analysis" (*Women in Love*, Chapter XXXI, "Snowed Up," p. 451) going on in Gudrun with Loerke as master "craftsman":

> it was time for her [Gudrun] now to pass over to...the final craftsman [Loerke]. (p. 452)

But here in *Women in Love* this "reducing, analytic...process" goes on in the male-female relation of Gudrun and Loerke, while in his letter to Heseltine, Lawrence asserted that "the reduction process" is synonymous with "homosexuality": "In physical life, it is homosexuality, the reduction process" (D. H. Lawrence letter to Heseltine, 22 November 1915)—a process which, "[if] it continues," will cause "our phase, our era" to pass "swiftly into oblivion"—so Lawrence said in November 1915; but, by the time of the height of his *Women in Love* period, when he was writing the last chapters of his "end-of-the-world" work, Lawrence evidently believed that the "reducing, analytic...process," with its "conscious knowledge of the component parts" (D. H. Lawrence letter to Heseltine, 22 November 1915), can take place in heterosexual relationships as well. Thus Lawrence presents the Loerke-Gudrun relation as synecdochic of all passional relationships in which the "analytic process" and "conscious knowledge" are insalubriously predominant. Yet, for all the cerebral, "analytic" quality of the Loerke-Gudrun relationship, Loerke and Gudrun seem to have a future together:

> And all the while they two [Gudrun and Loerke] were hovering, hesitating round the flame of some invisible declaration. He [Loerke] wanted it, but was held back by some inevitable reluctance. She [Gudrun] wanted it also, but she wanted to put it off, to put it off indefinitely. (p. 454)

But the fact is that Loerke does indeed make his "declaration" to Gudrun, praising her as "remarkable" and "extraordinary":

> You, for your part—you know, you are a remarkable woman [Loerke tells Gudrun]....Why deny it—why make any question of it? You are an extraordinary woman, why should you follow the ordinary course, the ordinary life? (p. 457)

As "an extraordinary woman," Gudrun is the proper mate for him, Loerke concludes, finally inviting her to go with him and be his mistress:

> But come to Dresden. I have a studio there—I can give you work—Oh, that would be easy enough....I believe in you. Come to Dresden....(p. 458)

"Believing" in Gudrun, Loerke here is extremely reminiscent of Birkin in relation to Ursula some three hundred pages earlier in the novel:

> "But it is because you love me, that you want me?" she [Ursula] persisted.
> "No it isn't. It is because I believe in you...." [Birkin tells Ursula]. (*Women in Love*, Chapter XIII, "Mino," p. 147)

In this same "Mino" chapter Birkin, in his "declaration" to Ursula, states that

> There is a final me which is stark and impersonal and beyond responsibility. So there is a final you. And it is there I would want to meet you—not in the emotional, loving plane—but there beyond....There we are two stark, unknown beings, two utterly strange creatures, I would want to approach you, and you me....(p. 146)

—and, towards the end of *Women in Love*, Loerke similarly tells Gudrun:

> But it is the *me*—it is the *me* that is looking for a mistress, and my *me* is waiting for the *thee* of the mistress, for the match to my par-

> ticular intelligence..... (*Women in Love*, Chapter XXXI, "Snowed Up," p. 459)

Both Birkin and Loerke evidently believe in the uniqueness of themselves and of their mates; Birkin believes he has an ultimate self, "a final me," in the "beyond," and that Ursula likewise possesses this finality of being ("a final you"); similarly, Loerke believes that he has a unique "me" that is searching for "a mistress," a unique woman who is "the match to my particular intelligence" (p. 459). In their emphasis on the unique nature of their mates and themselves, Loerke and Birkin are indeed echoing the Lawrentian valorization of monogamy in *Fantasia of the Unconscious* (written soon after the publication of *Women in Love*):

> though we have a potential dynamic sexual connection, we men, with almost every woman, yet the great outstanding fact of the individuality even of the blood makes us need a corresponding individuality in the woman we are to embrace. The more individual the man or woman, the more unsatisfactory is a non-individual connection: promiscuity. The more individual, the more does our blood cry out for its own specific answer, an individual woman, blood-polarized with us. (*Fantasia of the Unconscious*, "Sleep and Dreams," p. 203)

Like Lawrence in *Fantasia of the Unconscious*, both Loerke and Birkin take pride in "the great outstanding fact of [their] individuality," "individuality" which "makes [them] need a corresponding individuality" in their mates. Both Birkin and Loerke, being true individuals, need "an individual woman, blood-polarized with us"; Birkin has surely found that woman in Ursula, and Loerke evidently aspires to attain the same sort of "individual" relationship with Gudrun. Indeed, Loerke evidently believes that Gudrun is his "fate":

> "Do you know," he [Loerke] said, suddenly looking at her [Gudrun] with dark, self-important, prophetic eyes, "your fate and mine, they will run together, till—" and he broke off in a little grimace.
> "Till when?" she [Gudrun] asked, blenched, her lips going white. She was terribly susceptible to these evil prognostications. But he only shook his head.
> "I don't know," he said, "I don't know." (pp. 459-460)

With his "self-important" and "prophetic" declarations to Gudrun concerning "your fate and mine...run[ning] together," Loerke here is extremely reminiscent of Birkin in relation to Ursula much earlier in the book:

> She [Ursula] was rich, full of dangerous power. She was like a strange unconscious bud of powerful womanhood. He [Birkin] was unconsciously drawn to her. She was his future. (p. 92)

But Birkin is absolutely sure of "his future" with Ursula:

> You are all women to me....you and I are eternal (*Women in Love*, Chapter XXXII, "Exeunt," p. 481),

Birkin tells Ursula on the very last page of the novel; Loerke, on the other hand, tells Gudrun, "I don't know, I don't know" (p. 460) when she asks him about the duration of their "fate...together." Thus Loerke can easily be seen as a kind of Birkin manqué, longing for a stable relationship with a woman who is "the match to my particular intelligence"—but incapable of attaining that relationship. Yet finally it must be concluded that Loerke's "fate" with Gudrun, his "future" with her, is to be a *heterosexual* one, even though most likely not attaining the salubrious normative character of the Ursula-Birkin connexion. Indeed, the Loerke-Gudrun relation at this stage may in fact partake of that non-phallic "polymorphous perverse" character deplored by Lawrence, Fiedler and Trilling; as the novel nears its end, Gudrun does in fact realize that she is bored by mature genital heterosexuality:

> He [Gerald] bores me [Gudrun says to herself]....His maleness bores me. Nothing is so boring as the phallus, so inherently stupid and stupidly conceited. Really, the fathomless conceit of these men, it is ridiculous—the little strutters.
> They are all alike. Look at Birkin. Built out of the limitation of conceit they are, and nothing else. Really, nothing but their ridiculous limitation and intrinsic insignificance could make them so conceited.
> As for Loerke, there is a thousand times more in him than in a Gerald. (*Women in Love*, Chapter XXXI, "Snowed Up," p. 463)

"Bored" by "the phallus," Gudrun evidently is in the mood for a mode of sexuality in which the "conceited" phallus is not predominant—and in this circumstance she believes that Loerke is the ideal mate for her: "As for Loerke, there is a thousand times more in him than in a Gerald"—"a thousand times more" varieties of "bodies and pleasures" (*History* 159) perhaps, to use the Foucaultian phrase for "polymorphous perversity." Loerke, evidently, is "not stiff with conceit of his own maleness"—that is to say, it seems to me, that Loerke's wonted orientation to sex is not "stiff" or "phallic," unlike that of the "conceited" Gerald and Birkin; but, despite (or perhaps because of) Loerke's lack of the "stiff," "phallic" character, he nevertheless possesses a "sexual...fascination" (Barron 14) for Gudrun—a "fascination" which, while initially it may mainly lead to "polymorphous perverse" activities, can conceivably have a more salubrious ultimate result. In his short but important study of Lawrence, G. Wilson Knight concludes that

> In his [Lawrence's] more imaginative...excursions he is trying to *blast through degradation to a new health* (Knight 408; italics mine)

—and it seems to me that this "blast[ing] through degradation to a new health" is what Lawrence would have be the *telos* of the Loerke-Gudrun relation; as for what sort of non-phallic "polymorphous" pleasures Loerke may have in store for Gudrun, Foucault himself may be able to tell us about them:

> S/M is...the real creation of new possibilities of pleasure....S/M [practitioners]...are inventing new possibilities of pleasure with strange parts of their body—through the eroticization of the body....The idea that bodily pleasure should always come from sexual pleasure, and the idea that sexual pleasure is the root of *all* our possible pleasure—I think *that's* something quite wrong. These [non-phallic S/M] practices are insisting that we can produce pleasure with very odd things, very strange parts of our bodies, in very unusual situations, and so on. (Foucault interview, quoted in Halperin, *Saint Foucault*, pp. 87-88)

Foucault goes on to be a bit more explicit about "the new possibilities of pleasure":

> Physical practices of the fist-fucking sort are practices that one can call devirilized, that is desexed [i.e., degenitalized]....
> ...[These practices are not examples of] phallocratism, of machismo, but rather...make one's body into the site of production of extraordinarily *polymorphous pleasures*, pleasures that at the same time are detached from the valorization of the genitals and especially of the male genitals. (Ibid., pp. 89-90; italics mine)

While "fist-fucking" most likely does not take place between Loerke and Gudrun in *Women in Love*, there is great evidence of Loerke's practise of "S/M" (sado-masochism) in the "Snow" chapter of *Women in Love*

(Chapter XXX); in "Snow" Loerke's "S/M" (sado-masochistic) tendencies are indicated in his "statuette...of a naked girl, small, finely made, sitting on a great naked horse. The girl was young and tender, a mere bud. She was sitting sideways on the horse, her face in her hands, as if in shame and grief, in a little abandon" (429); Loerke briefly discusses his relation with the girl, "his mistress" (432):

> "What was her name?" Gudrun asked Loerke.
> "Annette von Weck," Loerke replied, reminiscent. "Ja, sie war hübsch. She was pretty—but she was tiresome. She was a nuisance—not for a minute would she keep still—not until I'd slapped her hard and made her cry—then she'd sit for five minutes."
> He was thinking over the work, his work, the all-important to him.
> "Did you really slap her?" asked Gudrun, coolly. He glanced back at her, reading her challenge.
> "Yes, I did," he said, nonchalant, "harder than I have ever beat anything in my life.—I had to, I had to.—It was the only way I got the work done." (433)

Thus, like the Foucaultian valorization of "S/M" in general and "fistfucking" in particular, the Loerkian sexual-aesthetic practise with his model-mistress also valorizes the production of "pleasure...in very unusual situations," "situations" which indeed are "devirilized,...degenitalized," totally "detached from the valorization...of the male genitals" and instead rooted in the valorization of the "work of art"—the "work of art," which

> has nothing to do with anything but itself, it has no relation with the everyday world of this and the other, there is no connection between them, absolutely none, they are two different and distinct planes of existence, and to translate one into the other is worse than foolish, it is a darkening of all counsel, a making confusion everywhere. Do you see, you *must not* confuse the relative world of action, with the absolute world of art. That you *must not do* [Loerke tells Ursula]. (*Women in Love*, pp. 430-431)

Thus Loerke's non-phallic "S/M," rather than having anything to do with "the everyday world" of "[phallic-genital] action," is an "artistic" practise connected to his own somewhat warped "world of art"—a "world" which he shares with Gudrun.

What Gudrun and Loerke also share together is "a curious game":

> They had a curious game with each other, Gudrun and Loerke, of infinite suggestivity, strange and leering, as if they had some eso-

teric understanding of life, that they alone were initiated into the fearful central secrets, that the world dared not know....The whole game was one of subtle inter-suggestivity, and they wanted to keep it on the plane of suggestion. From their verbal and physical *nuances* they got the highest satisfaction in the nerves, from a queer interchange of half-suggested ideas, looks, expressions and gestures....(448)

Gudrun and Loerke's "curious game,...strange and leering" seems to me to be rather reminiscent of the Foucaultian game of "S/M":

> The S/M game is very interesting because it is a strategic relation, but it is always fluid. Of course, there are roles, but everybody knows very well that these roles can be reversed. Sometimes the scene begins with the master and slave, and at the end the slave has become the master. Or, even when the roles are stabilized, you know very well that it is always a game....(Foucault interview, quoted in Miller, *Passion*, p. 263)

Gudrun, of course, has already experienced "the master and slave" relation with Gerald, in which "at the end the slave [i.e., Gudrun] has become the master"; with Loerke, however, the "game" is finally more "interesting," more "strategic," more "fluid" in view of the fact that Gudrun and Loerke with their aesthetic-cerebral propensities are quite evenly matched.

In their aesthetic-cerebral enthusiasm Loerke and Gudrun enjoy a "game" of "subtle lusts" (448), "lusts" which would culminate (for Gudrun) in

> a further, slow, exquisite experience to reap, unthinkable subtleties of sensation to know, before she [Gudrun] was finished.
> Of the last series of subtleties Gerald was not capable. He could not touch the quick of her. But...the fine, insinuating blade of Loerke's insect-like comprehension could....[I]t was time for her now to pass over to the other, the creature, the final craftsman....Loerke, in his innermost soul, was detached from everything, for him there was neither heaven nor earth nor hell. He admitted no allegiance, he gave no adherence anywhere. He was single and, by abstraction from the rest, absolute in himself. (452)

Like a Foucaultian "S/M" practitioner, Loerke can provide Gudrun with "unthinkable subtleties of sensation to know"—the verb "know" emphasizing the conscious, sensational, "non-phallic" nature of the experience. Lawrence obviously does not have the greatest admiration for Loerke; he (Lawrence) is ambivalent: Loerke is "insect-like," "the creature," but also a kind of nonpareil, "the final craftsman." As "the final craftsman," Loerke is privileged by Lawrence as the one being uniquely capable of "penetrating" Gudrun, influencing Gudrun in such a way as to make her ready for a new psychosexual realm of "unthinkable subtleties of sensation" to which Loerke will "finally" introduce her, a new mode of sexual experience—partially Foucaultian and decadent perhaps, it is true, but "finally," ultimately, potentially leading to a new life, a kind of rebirth for Gudrun and Loerke, after their "death":

> She [Gudrun] felt an approaching release, a new fountain of life rising up in her [on the eve of leaving with Loerke for Dresden]....She felt a new lease of life was come upon her, and she was happy like a child, very attractive and beautiful to everybody, with her soft, luxuriant figure and her happiness. Yet underneath was death itself....
>
> ...Anything might come to pass on the morrow. And today was the white, snowy, iridescent threshold of all possibility. All possibility—that was a charm to her, the lovely, iridescent, indefinite charm—pure illusion. All possibility—because death was inevitable, and *nothing* was possible but death. (467-468)

Lawrence tells us that Gudrun feels she is experiencing "a new lease of life" but the fact is that "underneath" all Gudrun's lively happiness and beauty is "death itself"; furthermore, Lawrence tells us, Gudrun's feeling of "All possibility"—"Anything might come to pass on the morrow"—is in truth "pure illusion" in view of the fact that "death was inevitable, and *nothing* was possible but death"; yet Lawrence's psychic-metaphysical vision here is "finally" not so pessimistic as it at first appears; an excellent gloss on Lawrence's "death" statements of this period is provided by his essay "The Reality of Peace," written at the height of his *Women in Love* period: here Lawrence declares that

> we must all die....We have always the door of death in front of us, and, howsoever our track winds and travels, it comes to that door at last. We *must* die within an allotted term; there is not the least atom of choice allowed us in this. ("Reality," p. 31)

Thus Lawrence during his *Women in Love* period, the period of World War I, was keenly aware of the omnipresence of death for all of "us"; Gudrun surely is no exception to this fate; and, indeed, in the initiatory stages of her relation with Loerke, "the final craftsman," she will most likely experience a kind of "subtle" death, leading conceivably to rebirth.

Of course, in all this Loerke's homosexuality is completely forgotten, a thing of the past, as it should be according to the Lawrentian scheme of things if psychic-ontological renewal is conceivably to take place; and indeed, for the Lawrence of the *Women in Love* period, such "renewal" was surely to be looked forward to; for as one major biographer of Lawrence in his *Women in Love* period explains, discussing Lawrence in 1917:

> In the depths of both his misfortune and the war, Lawrence the religious man is all the more passionately convinced that the impulse of renewal will always come....(Kinkead-Weekes 1996, 369)

Kinkead-Weekes is surely right when he speaks of "Lawrence the religious man...passionately convinced that the impulse of renewal will always come"; furthermore, for the Lawrence of *Women in Love*, this "impulse of renewal" can even come for ex-homosexuals such as Loerke. Indeed, we can certainly say that Lawrence in *Women in Love*, in the best Christ-like "Salvator Mundi" tradition, forgives his enemy Loerke-Foucault and converts him at the same time. Thus we find that, towards the very end of *Women in Love*, Loerke actually saves Gudrun from the death by strangulation that Gerald nearly inflicts upon her:

> He [Gerald] took the throat of Gudrun between his hands, that were hard and indomitably powerful. And her throat was beautifully, so beautifully soft. Save that, within, he could feel the slippery chords of her life. And this he crushed, this he could crush. What bliss! Oh what bliss, at last, what satisfaction, at last! The pure zest of satisfaction filled his soul....What a fulfilment, what a satisfaction! How good this was, oh how good it was, what a god-given gratification, at last! He was unconscious of her fighting and struggling. That struggling was her reciprocal lustful passion in this embrace, the more violent it became, the greater the frenzy of delight, till the zenith was reached, the crisis, the struggle was overborne, her movement became softer, appeased.
>
> Loerke roused himself on the snow, too dazed and hurt to get up. Only his eyes were conscious.
>
> "Monsieur!" he said, in his thin, roused voice: "Quand vous aurez fini—"
>
> A revulsion of contempt and disgust came over Gerald's soul. The disgust went to the very bottom of him, a nausea. Ah, what

was he doing, to what depths was he letting himself go! As if he cared about her enough to kill her, to have her life on his hands!

A weakness ran over his body, a terrible relaxing, a thaw, a decay of strength. Without knowing, he had let go his grip, and Gudrun had fallen to her knees....(471-472)

Here in this scene it finally (and ironically) appears that Loerke, for all the "overwhelmingly pathological subjectivity" (Doherty 151) he has been identified with throughout the novel, is ultimately more psychosexually healthy than the murderous sado-masochist Gerald, whom Loerke's ironic wit ("Quand vous aurez fini—") deters from murdering Gudrun. Of course, Gerald dies, but Loerke and Gudrun live, and, in the final chapter of the novel (indeed, on the final page)—with its characteristically Lawrentian open-ended quality—we learn simply that

> Gudrun went [with Loerke] to Dresden. She wrote no particulars of herself [to Ursula]. (481)

Thus Loerke and Gudrun evidently will live together in Dresden—and at this point in my monograph it is appropriate for me to make some "final" concluding remarks on Loerke, remarks which go against the tide of the predominant discourse concerning Loerke today.

While major queer theorists today would like to finally define (and valorize) Loerke as "a faggot" (Craft 179), the fact is that it seems fairly safe to say that a good case can be made that, in view of the fact that

> [*Women in Love* is] an assertion of the possibility of rebirth and resurrection from apparent deathliness (Kinkead-Weekes 1996, 712),

it is likely that, as one major Lawrentian critic surmises,

> Gudrun and Loerke...*survive* (Williams 1963, 648; italics mine)

—"survive" indeed, it seems to me, as a heterosexual couple whose future, though uncertain, can conceivably be a salubrious one in which both Loerke and Gudrun attain a kind of self-realization, a

> *building of the self*...which flourishes according to its own autonomous nature....(Scruton 299; italics mine)

—for, as Lawrence himself states,

> The final aim of every living thing, creature, or being is the full *achievement of itself* (*Phoenix* 403; my italics)

—and furthermore, in striving to attain this aim of "full achievement" of self,

> men and women need one another....
> We have our very individuality in relationship....A skylark that was alone on an island would be songless and meaningless, his individuality gone, running about like a mouse in the grass. But if there were one female with him, it would lift him singing into the air, and restore him his real individuality.
> And so with men and women. It is in relationship to one another that they have their true individuality and their distinct being: in contact, not out of contact. This is sex....It is a living contact, give and take: the great and subtle relationship of men and women, man and woman. In this and through this we become real individuals, without it, without the real contact, we remain more or less nonentities....
> But the relationship of man to woman is the central fact in actual human life....
> A young man said to me the other day, rather sneeringly, "I'm afraid I can't believe in the regeneration of England by sex." I said to him: "I'm sure you can't." He was trying to inform me that he was above such trash as sex, and such commonplace as women. He was the usual vitally below par, hollow, and egoistic young man....(*Phoenix* 188, 190-191, 193)

Like the skylark, Lawrence surely needed a "female with him," as mate and subject, for him to "sing" his song as a great creative writer of "real individuality," "distinct being," poetic strength and uniqueness, "in contact" with "the great and subtle relationship of men and women, man and woman," which was his grand, outstanding theme: in writing about this "relationship," "the central fact in actual life," so masterfully, Lawrence could magnificently avoid the fate of "nonentity" by attaining poetic immortality as the poet-priest of Western civilization's "regeneration...by sex"; yet, as Lawrence well knew, his aspirations to "spontaneous-creative fullness of being" (*Psychoanalysis and the Unconscious*, p. 48) and "poetic immortality" (Bloom, *Map of Misreading*, p. 186) through preaching and portraying "the regeneration of England by sex" could indeed be frustrated by the "vitally below par, hollow, and egoistic" who are legion—especially today, especially in academia, where such disciples of Foucault as Leo Bersani attack "authoritative selfhood" (Bersani, *Culture*, p. 3)—"authority in the self with respect to both the inner and the outer worlds" (ibid.)—and instead valorize "The aesthetic of narcissism" as part of his "general ethical-erotic project" (ibid.); Bersani's privileged "narcissism" is

> a self-*jouissance* that dissolves the person [i.e., self] and thereby, at least temporarily, erases the sacrosanct value of selfhood (Bersani, *Culture*, pp. 3-4)

—and, furthermore, this self-dissolving "narcissism" of Bersani's is rooted in the representational reality of (as one homosexual scholar puts it)

> gay men as narcissists addicted to pleasure (Edelman 105),

with "narcissism," "pleasure," and self-dissolution all operating together in "the gay subject" (Edelman 112). In contradistinction to "the gay subject," Lawrence embodies (to use Edelman's phrase)

> the active, penetrative relation of the (straight, male) subject [i.e. self] to the world (Edelman 106)

—for, as Eugene Goodheart recently (and half rightly) observed,

> Lawrence...desire[d]...an absolute self, radically other, free of all constraints, beyond comparison, alone....(*Desire*, p. 78)

But the fact is that what Goodheart calls the "absolute self,...beyond comparison, alone," could more accurately be called "the poetic self" (Bloom, *Anxiety*, p. 121) of the "strong poet" (Bloom, *Anxiety*, p. 5) whom Harold Bloom tells us must

> be assured that *he* is unique and irreplaceable (*Anxiety* 63)

for

> a poet's stance, his Word, his imaginative identity, his whole being, *must* be unique to him, and remain unique, or he will perish, as a poet, if ever even he has managed his rebirth into poetic incarnation. (Bloom, *Anxiety*, p. 71)

Lawrence, with his "poetic incarnation" as "priest of [heterosexual] love" who at the same time privileges "real individuality" (*Phoenix* 191), is *au fond* anathema to Foucault, Foucault's followers, and virtually all the rest of the left-wing intelligentsia; indeed, Lawrence's aspiration to "penetrate" Western civilization and assure his poetic immortality is even today surely placed in some jeopardy by this very powerful intellectual-academic elite; for, even if Lawrence-Christ forgives and "saves" Loerke-Foucault, Foucault and his followers and others, with their various sexual-social-political agendas, find it undesirable to "forgive"

Lawrence for his "heterosexism" and "individuality" (as we will see in the concluding sections of this monograph); and this situation is indeed "a matter of life and death" for Lawrence's poetic immortality—and for all true Lawrentians as well.

WORKS CITED

Adelman, Gary. *Snow of Fire: Symbolic Meaning in "The Rainbow" and "Women in Love."* New York: Garland, 1991.

Barron, Janet. "Equality Puzzle: Lawrence and Feminism." In *Rethinking Lawrence.* Ed. Keith Brown. Philadephia: Open University Press, 1990.

Bersani, Leo. *The Culture of Redemption.* Cambridge: Harvard University Press, 1990.

Bersani, Leo. *Homos.* Cambridge: Harvard University Press, 1995.

Black, Michael. *D. H. Lawrence: The Early Fiction: A Commentary.* London: Macmillan, 1986.

Bloom, Harold. *A Map of Misreading.* New York: Oxford University Press, 1975.

Bloom, Harold. *The Anxiety of Influence: A Theory of Poetry.* New York: Oxford University Press, 1973.

Brown, Norman O. *Life Against Death: The Psychoanalytical Meaning of History.* Middletown: Wesleyan University Press, 1959.

Carpenter, Edward. *Selected Writings: Volume 1: Sex.* London: GMP, 1984.

Carroll, Joseph. *Evolution and Literary Theory.* Columbia: University of Missouri Press, 1995.

Chamberlain, Robert L. "Pussum, Minette, and the Afro-Nordic Symbol in Lawrence's *Women in Love.*" *PMLA* 78 (1963): 407–416.

Clark, L. D. *The Minoan Distance: The Symbolism of Travel in D. H. Lawrence.* Tucson: University of Arizona Press, 1980.

Clarke, Colin, ed. *D. H. Lawrence: "The Rainbow" and "Women in Love": A Casebook.* London: Macmillan, 1969.

Craft, Christopher. *Another Kind of Love: Male Homosexual Desire in English Discourse, 1850–1920.* Berkeley: University of California Press, 1994.

Cruikshank, Margaret. *The Gay and Lesbian Liberation Movement.* New York: Routledge, 1992.

Davis, Jane. "Envoi: the genie in the second-hand shop." In *Rethinking Lawrence.* Ed. Keith Brown. Milton Keynes: Open University Press, 1990.

Delany, Paul. *D. H. Lawrence's Nightmare: The Writer and His Circle in the Years of the Great War.* New York: Basic Books, 1978.

Delavenay, Emile. *D. H. Lawrence and Edward Carpenter: A Study in Edwardian Transition.* New York: Taplinger, 1971.

Doherty, Gerald. "*Ars Erotica* or *Scientia Sexualis?*: Narrative Vicissitudes in D. H. Lawrence's *Women in Love.*" *Journal of Narrative Technique* 26 (1996): 137–157.

Dollimore, Jonathan. *Death, Desire and Loss in Western Culture.* New York: Routledge, 1998.

Donaldson, George. "'Men in Love'? D. H. Lawrence, Rupert Birkin and Gerald Crich." In *D. H. Lawrence: Centenary Essays.* Ed. Mara Kalnins. Bristol: Bristol Classical Press, 1986.

Edelman, Lee. *Homographesis: Essays in Gay Literary and Cultural Theory.* New York: Routledge, 1994.

Ellis, Havelock. *Studies in the Psychology of Sex, Volume II, Sexual Inversion.* Philadelphia: F. A. Davis Co., 1915.

Feuerlicht, Ignace. "Thomas Mann and Homoeroticism." *Germanic Review* 57 (1982): 89–97.

Fiedler, Leslie. *Love and Death in the American Novel.* New York: Doubleday, Anchor Books, 1992.

Fiedler, Leslie. *Waiting for the End.* New York: Stein and Day, 1964.

Fiedler, Leslie. *No! In Thunder: Essays on Myth and Literature.* Boston: Beacon Press, 1960.

Ford, George H. "Introductory Note to D. H. Lawrence's Prologue to *Women in Love.*" In Clarke, pp. 35–42.

Furbank, P. N. *E. M. Forster: A Life: Volume Two.* London: Secker & Warburg, 1978.

Goodheart, Eugene. *The Utopian Vision of D. H. Lawrence.* Chicago: University of Chicago Press, 1963.

Goodheart, Eugene. *Culture and the Radical Conscience.* Cambridge: Harvard University Press, 1973.

Goodheart, Eugene. *Pieces of Resistance.* Cambridge: Cambridge University Press, 1987.

Goodheart, Eugene. *Desire and Its Discontents.* New York: Columbia University Press, 1991.

Gould, Eric. *Mythical Intentions in Modern Literature.* Princeton: Princeton University Press, 1981.

Halperin, David M. *Saint Foucault: Towards a Gay Hagiography.* New York: Oxford University Press, 1995.

Heilbut, Anthony. *Thomas Mann: Eros and Literature.* New York: Knopf, 1996.

Holroyd, Michael. *Lytton Strachey: The New Biography.* New York: Farrar, Straus and Giroux, 1995.

Ingersoll, Earl. "Lawrence and Gender." *D. H. Lawrence Review* 25 (1993-1994): 149–157.

Jay, Karla. "Lesbian Modernism: (Trans)Forming the (C)anon." In *Professions of Desire: Lesbian and Gay Studies in Literature.* Ed. George E. Haggerty and Bonnie Zimmerman. New York: Modern Language Association of America, 1995.

Kermode, Frank. *D. H. Lawrence.* New York: Viking, 1973.

Kinkead-Weekes, Mark. *D. H. Lawrence: Triumph to Exile.* Cambridge: Cambridge University Press, 1996.

Knight, G. Wilson. "Lawrence, Joyce and Powys." *Essays in Criticism* 11 (1961): 403–417.

Lawrence, D. H. *The Prussian Officer and Other Stories.* Ed. John Worthen. Cambridge: Cambridge University Press, 1983.

Lawrence, D. H. *Sons and Lovers.* Ed. Carl Baron. Cambridge: Cambridge University Press, 1992.

Lawrence, D. H. "Love." In *Reflections on the Death of a Porcupine and Other Essays.*

Ed. Michael Herbert. Cambridge: Cambridge University Press, 1988.

Lawrence, D. H. *Women in Love.* Ed. David Farmer, Lindeth Vasey and John Worthen. Cambridge: Cambridge University Press, 1987.

Lawrence, D. H. "Prologue to *Women in Love.*" In *Women in Love.*

Lawrence, D. H. "The Crown." In *"Reflections on the Death of a Porcupine" and Other Essays.* Ed. Michael Herbert. Cambridge: Cambridge University Press, 1988.

Lawrence, D. H. *Movements in European History.* Ed. Philip Crumpton. Cambridge: Cambridge University Press, 1989.

Lawrence, D. H. "The Reality of Peace." In *Reflections on the Death of a Porcupine and Other Essays.* Ed. Michael Herbert. Cambridge: Cambridge University Press, 1988.

Lawrence, D. H. *The Letters of D. H. Lawrence: Volume II: June 1913-October 1916.* Ed. George J. Zytaruk. Cambridge: Cambridge University Press, 1981.

Lawrence, D. H. *The Letters of D. H. Lawrence: Volume III: October 1916-June 1921.* Ed. James T. Boulton and Andrew Robertson. Cambridge: Cambridge University Press, 1984.

Lawrence, D. H. *Psychoanalysis and the Unconscious* and *Fantasia of the Unconscious.* New York: Viking, 1960.

Lyotard, Jean-Francois. *The Postmodern Condition.* Minneapolis: University of Minnesota Press, 1984.

Maddox, Brenda. *The Married Man: A Life of D. H. Lawrence.* London: Sinclair-Stevenson, 1994.

Martin, Robert K. *Hero, Captain, and Stranger: Male Friendship, Social Critique, and Literary Form in the Sea Novels of Herman Melville.* Chapel Hill: University of North Carolina Press, 1986.

Miller, James. *The Passion of Michel Foucault.* New York: Simon & Schuster, 1993.

Price, Martin. "The Sublime Poem: Pictures and Powers." *Yale Review* 58 (1968): 194–213.

Readings, Bill. *Introducing Lyotard: Art and Politics.* New York: Routledge, 1991.

Sale, Roger. "D. H. Lawrence, 1912–1916." *Massachusetts Review* 6 (1965): 467–480.

Sale, Roger. *Modern Heroism: Essays on D. H. Lawrence, William Empson, and J. R. R. Tolkien.* Berkeley: University of California Press, 1973.

Scherr, Barry J. *D. H. Lawrence's Response to Plato: A Bloomian Interpretation.* New York: Peter Lang, 1996.

Scruton, Roger. *Sexual Desire: A Moral Philosophy of the Erotic.* New York: The Free Press, 1986.

Sedgwick, Eve Kosofsky. *Between Men: English Literature and Male Homosocial Desire.* New York: Columbia University Press, 1985.

Smith, Barry. *Peter Warlock: The Life of Philip Heseltine.* Oxford: Oxford University Press, 1994.

Spilka, Mark. "Lawrence's Quarrel with Tenderness." *Critical Quarterly* 9 (1967): 363–377.

Weeks, Jeffrey. *Sex, Politics and Society.* London: Longman, 1981.

Weiskel, Thomas. *The Romantic Sublime: Studies in the Structure and Psychology of Transcendence.* Baltimore: Johns Hopkins University Press, 1976.

Williams, Raymond. "Tolstoy, Lawrence, and Tragedy." *Kenyon Review* 25 (1963): 633–650.

CHAPTER FOUR

Sex, Selfhood, Literature and Politics
The Left-Wing Attack on D. H. Lawrence (Part One)

Recently one major left-wing literary-"cultural" critic described D. H. Lawrence as "This increasingly disregarded and often despised writer" (Dollimore, *Sexual Dissidence*, p. 268). But who is Jonathan Dollimore, and why is he saying such nasty things about D. H. Lawrence?

Dollimore first discusses Lawrence in his dissertation, *Radical Tragedy*, completed in 1982 and published in 1984. In his section on Lawrence, "Lawrence, Leavis and Individualism," Dollimore attacks Lawrence as having "a dislike of...democratic humanitarian philosophy" (*Radical Tragedy*, p. 265). Dollimore goes on to deplore "[Lawrence's] uncompromising individualism," "Lawrence's belief in the creative reality of individuality" (*Radical Tragedy*, p. 265). According to Dollimore, Lawrence's valorization of individuality militates against "the supposedly disintegrative forces in the modern world" and "especially their [deleterious] effects upon selfhood" (*Radical Tragedy*, p. 266); it is for this reason that Dollimore so dislikes Lawrence.

But why should Dollimore dislike Lawrence for fighting against the disintegration of the self? Part of the answer to that question can be found in Dollimore's next work, *Political Shakespeare* (1985); here Dollimore proudly asserts his "commitment to the transformation of a social order which exploits people on grounds of race, gender and class" (*Political Shakespeare*, p. viii). In other words, Dollimore is a politically correct, left-wing literary-cultural critic whose main concern is not the artistic-creative power of the individual but rather the socio-political power (or lack of it) of the group.

Indeed, it is inevitable that the left-wing Dollimore enthusiastically embrace Gay (Queer) Theory; he can easily appropriate the gays as an oppressed group:

> For homosexuals more than most, the search for sexual freedom...has been inseparable from a repudiation of the "Western" culture responsible for their repression and oppression. For some [homosexuals],...this entailed not just the rejection of a repressive social order, but a disidentification from it requiring nothing less than the relinquishing of the self as hitherto constituted and inhabited by that order. In other words, precisely because of the Western integration of subjectivity and sexuality, deviant desire becomes also a refusal of certain kinds of subjectivity. (*Sexual Dissidence*, p. 339)

For Dollimore the left-wing critic, homosexuals are ideal candidates for advocacy, with their "repudiation" of "repressive," "oppressive" Western culture; Dollimore seems to be especially happy about the homosexuals' "relinquishing of the self as hitherto constituted and inhabited by that ["Western" social] order."

Dollimore deplores "the Western integration of subjectivity and sexuality"—but why? What is so bad about the nexus between "subjectivity and sexuality"? Leo Bersani, who is himself gay as well as a major literary-cultural critic-theorist, attacks

> the sacrosanct value of selfhood, a value that accounts for human beings' extraordinary willingness to kill in order to protect the seriousness of their statements. The self is a practical convenience; promoted to the status of an ethical ideal, it is a sanction for violence....[Homo]sexuality...[is] our primary hygienic practice of nonviolence. Gay men's "obsession" with sex...should be celebrated...because it never stops re-presenting the internalized phallic male as an infinitely loved object of sacrifice. (Bersani, *October* 43 (1987), p. 222)

Bersani's weird, complex remarks above can indeed be used to gloss Dollimore's remarks on "the Western integration of subjectivity and sexuality." According to Bersani, "selfhood" (or "subjectivity") has been privileged by the (white male heterosexual) subject to such an extent that it has been responsible for extreme violence, the violence of intolerance against the other in general and the homosexual in particular. Bersani deplores what he calls

> the masculine ideal...of proud subjectivity (p. 222)

—an "ideal" which he opposes with his own weird ideal of "the rectum" which he celebrates; indeed, the very name of Bersani's article—"Is the Rectum a Grave?"—indicates the supreme importance to Bersani of the homosexual rectum as the solution to the West's "integration of subjectivity and sexuality"; Bersani proudly maintains that

> the [homosexual] rectum is the grave in which the masculine ideal...of proud subjectivity is buried,...[and] it should be celebrated for its very potential for death (p. 222)

—"the death," that is, of "proud ["Western" male heterosexual] subjectivity."

It is, of course, important to note that Bersani wrote his article in 1987, when AIDS was already a major fact of (homosexual) life and death; Bersani emphasizes that the "very potential for [the] death" of "proud subjectivity" in the homosexual rectum goes hand in hand with "the certainty of biological death":

> the rectum is the grave in which the masculine ideal...of proud subjectivity is buried,...[and] it should be celebrated for its very potential for death. Tragically, AIDS has literalized that potential [for death] as the certainty of biological death, and has therefore reinforced the heterosexual association of anal sex with...self-annihilation....(p. 222)

Decrying "the masculine ideal...of proud subjectivity," Bersani is proud that homosexuality has the potential to cause the "death" of that subjectivity; yet Bersani grieves over the fact that the figurative—and, according to Bersani, beneficial—"self-annihilation" of homosexuality is surely accompanied by "the certainty of biological death"; "death of the self" in homosexuality is literal as well as figurative, physical as well as psychological, bodily as well as ontological.

But Bersani would have it that the "death of self" which homosexuality entails is a definitely good thing; indeed, he sees homosexuality as morally superior by far to heterosexuality in general and Lawrentian heterosexuality in particular—the fact is that Bersani privileges promiscuous homosexuality over Lawrentian heterosexual "love battle"[1]:

> Far from apologizing for their promiscuity as a failure to maintain a loving relationship, far from welcoming the return to monogamy as a beneficent consequence of the horror of AIDS, gay men should ceaselessly lament the practical necessity, now, of such relationships, should resist being drawn into mimicking *the unrelenting [Lawrentian] warfare between men and women, which nothing has ever changed*. (Bersani, p. 218; italics mine)

Thus for Bersani, homosexuals should be proud that, with "their promiscuity" and aversion to monogamy, they have avoided what (according to Bersani) is the heterosexual reality of "unrelenting warfare between men and women, which nothing has ever changed": in other words, promiscuous homosexuality is morally superior to warlike heterosexuality with its emphasis on "proud subjectivity."

One major advocate of "the masculine ideal...of proud subjectivity" in heterosex is of course D. H. Lawrence, and for this he is hated by left-wing queer theorists such as Dollimore, who states that

> Lawrence audaciously sexualizes Western metaphysics....The emphasis [in Lawrence's metaphysic] falls repeatedly on the individual, the self which is a law unto itself. (*Sexual Dissidence*, p. 269)

The left-wing Dollimore abhors Lawrence's "emphasis...on the individual, the self which is a law unto itself"; Dollimore prefers "The Decentred Subject":

> When Lawrence elaborates his philosophy of individualism he reminds us of the derivation of 'individual': that which is not divided, not divisible....Materialist [i.e., Marxist] analysis tends to avoid the term ['individual'] for just those reasons which led Lawrence to embrace it, preferring instead 'subject.' Because informed by contradictory social and ideological processes, the subject is never an indivisible unity, never an autonomous, self-determining centre of consciousness. (*Radical Tragedy*, p. 269)

One important reason why left-wing critics like Dollimore privilege the weak, non-autonomous "subject" over the strong, "indivisible," "autonomous," unified, centered, "self-determining" "individual" is cited by one Marxist critic writing on Lawrence:

> Marx and Engels argue that contemporary identity is thoroughly ideological and class-bound. What is designated by that apparently ahistorical and classless abstraction, the 'individual', is in fact 'no other person than the bourgeois, than the middle-class owner

of property', a person who must be 'swept out of the way, and made impossible.' (Jim Reilly, "D. H. Lawrence: Cliques and Consciousness," *The British Critical Tradition: A Re-evaluation*, p. 112; quote from Marx, *Karl Marx: Selected Writings*, ed. McLellan, p. 233)

For the left-wing, "the individual" is synonymous with "the bourgeois"; furthermore, according to the Marxist,

> the individual...[is characterized by]...narrow self-seeking...(Engels, *Condition of the Working Class*, quoted in *British Critical Tradition*, p. 113)

—"self-seeking" which is antithetical to "the positive...ideal" that the left-wing aspires to achieve. With "The Decentred Subject," Dollimore believes that we can achieve

> the positive sense of *the ideal* [my italics] . . .—["the ideal" being defined as] that which in virtue of its present unreality affirms known potentialities from within existing, stultifying, social realities. (*Radical Tragedy*, p. 271)

According to Dollimore, "a vision of decentred subjectivity," together with "a critique of existing ["stultifying"] social realities," will result in

> not essence but potential, not the human condition but cultural difference [i.e., "diversity," "multi-culturalism"], not destiny but *collectively* identified goals (*Radical Tragedy*, p. 271; my italics)

—and of course it is Dollimore's "collectively" that finds Lawrence's "individuality" so repulsive.

But Lawrence of course can be used to turn the tables on the left-wing "positive...ideal" attack on the individual. First of all, the Lawrentian individual, far from being an instance of "the bourgeois," is an exemplar of "the religious":

> man, at his highest, is an individual, single, isolate, alone, in direct communication with the unknown God, which prompts within him....(*Kangaroo*, Chapter 16)

Striving for "direct communication with the unknown God," the Lawrentian individual is completely uninterested in being "the middle-class owner of property"; on the contrary:

> The human individual is...always changing....But in his essential core he is naive, and money does not touch him. Money, of

> course, with every man living goes a long way. With the alive human being it may go as far as his penultimate feeling. But in the last naked him it does not enter. ("John Galsworthy")

Far from being "self-seeking," the Lawrentian individual is God-seeking, life-seeking. Seeking God and Life, Lawrence was no "bourgeois."

The Lawrentian God is delineated by Lawrence, appropriately enough, in the last thing he ever wrote:

> God, Almighty God. We have to square ourselves with the very words. And to do so, we must...give them back—Almighty God—the old vital meaning: strength and glory and honour and might and beauty and wisdom. These are the continual attributes of Almighty God, in the far past. And the same today, the god who enters us and imbues us with his strength and glory and might and honour and beauty and wisdom, this is a god we are eager to worship....Almighty God, the God of strength and glory and might and wisdom:...vital and magnificent God....the God of Life....(*Phoenix* 396)

Thus Lawrence's selfhood is "religious" in nature; his is a self that seeks from God—not from the socioeconomic complex—"strength and glory and might and honour and beauty and wisdom,...the God of Life"—and indeed Lawrence is a revolutionary of "Life":

> It's time there was an *enormous* revolution—not to install soviets, but to give life itself a chance....We want a revolution not in the name of money or work or any of that, but of life—and let money and work be as casual in human life as they are in a bird's life, damn it all....you've got to smash money and this beastly *possessive* spirit. I get more revolutionary every minute, but for *life's* sake. The dead materialism of Marx socialism and soviets seems to me no better than what we've got. What we want is life....(D. H. Lawrence letter to Charles Wilson, 28 December 1928)

But what is Lawrence's definition of "life"? The Lawrentian vision of life is lucidly delineated in *Apocalypse*, which Lawrence finished only a few weeks before his death; in *Apocalypse* Lawrence concludes that

> What man most passionately wants is his living wholeness....Man wants his physical fulfilment first and foremost, since now, once and once only, he is in the flesh and potent. For man, the vast marvel is to be alive. For man, as for flower and beast and bird, the supreme triumph is to be most vividly, most perfectly alive. Whatever the unborn and the dead may know, they cannot know

D. H. LAWRENCE TODAY

> the beauty, the marvel of being alive in the flesh....[T]he magnificent here and now of life in the flesh is ours, and ours alone, and ours only for a time. We ought to dance with rapture that we should be alive and in the flesh, and part of the living, incarnate cosmos....
>
> What we want is to destroy our false, inorganic connections, especially those related to money, and re-establish the living organic connections, with the cosmos, the sun and earth, with mankind and nation and family. Start with the sun, and the rest will slowly, slowly happen. (*Apocalypse*, XXIII)

Thus for Lawrence, "life" and "individuality" is anything but a "bourgeois" matter of "money" and "false connections"; rather, it is a matter of "living wholeness," "physical fulfilment," "being alive in the flesh"; "life in the flesh"—not in the capitalist system—is what Lawrence emphasizes: he speaks of "living" man in relation to "flower and beast and bird," not in relation to socioeconomic-political power: the Lawrentian "living" human individual is "potent" "in the flesh", not in possessions and property: indeed, during the *Apocalypse* period (1929-1930) Lawrence makes it clear that he does not like "the bourgeoisie" any better than he likes "Marx socialism and soviets":

> It is a pity that the bourgeoisie, with their greedy dead materialism, have made morality and family and affection and trust all suspicious and repulsive. (D. H. Lawrence letter to Jehanne Moulaert, 26 October 1929)

Thus it is evident that Lawrence found both "Marx socialism" and "the bourgeoisie" to be guilty of "dead materialism": indeed, Lawrence uses the identical phrase—"dead materialism"—to describe "the bourgeoisie" as well as "Marx socialism and soviets." Why then do left-wing critics today have such hostility towards Lawrence?

To answer this question, it is helpful to begin by looking at another Lawrence letter:

> One has to be an absolute individual, separate as a seed fallen out of the pod....Takes some risking....Son todos acobardados. (D. H. Lawrence letter to John Middleton Murry, 17 September 1923)

"Absolute," "individual": these two words and the concepts they represent are anathemas in today's "postmodern" world; one major left-wing critic, Fredric Jameson, notes that we need to...explain why classical modernism is a thing of the past and why post-modernism should have taken its place. (Jameson, *The Anti-Aesthetic*, p. 114)

According to Jameson, this can be explained by the phenomenon of

the "death of the subject" or, to say it in more conventional language, the end of individualism as such. The great modernisms were...predicated on the invention of a personal, private style, as unmistakable as your fingerprint, as incomparable as your own body. But this means that the modernist aesthetic is in some way organically linked to the conception of a unique self and private identity, a unique personality and individuality, which can be expected to generate its own unique vision of the world and to forge its own unique, unmistakable style.

Yet today,...[cultural theorists] are all exploring the notion that that kind of individualism and personal identity is a thing of the past; that the old individual or individualist subject is "dead"; and that one might even describe the concept of the unique individual and the theoretical basis of individualism as ideological....(Jameson, *The Anti-Aesthetic*, pp. 114-115)

Judging from Jameson's incessant and intense repetition of terms like "private" and "unique"—"personal, private style," "unique self," "private identity," "unique personality and individuality," "unique vision of the world," "unique, unmistakable style," "individualism and personal identity," "old individual or individualist subject," "the unique individual"—I would say that Jameson seems to agree with the Lawrentian valorization of individuality:

It seems as though one of the conditions of life is, that life shall continually and progressively differentiate itself, almost as though this differentiation were a Purpose. Life starts crude and unspecified, a great Mass. And it proceeds to evolve out of that mass ever more distinct and definite particular forms, an ever-multiplying number of separate species and orders, as if it were working always to the production of the infinite number of perfect individuals, the individual so thorough that he should have nothing in common with any other individual....

Man's consciousness, that is, his mind, his knowledge, is his greater manifestation of individuality....

And the more that I am driven from admixture, the more I am singled out into utter individuality, the more this intrinsic me rejoices....

Now one craves that his life should be more individual, that I and you and my neighbour should each be distinct in clarity from

> each other, perfectly distinct from the general mass. Then it would be a melody if I walked down the road; if I stood with my neighbour, it would be a pure harmony. (D. H. Lawrence, *Study of Thomas Hardy*, Chapter V)

Lawrence's valorization of "utter individuality" and its joy evidently made a great impression on Jameson; at about the same time as his essay in *The Anti-Aesthetic* (early 1980s), Jameson wrote another essay on modernism and post-modernism in which he definitively and authoritatively identifies Lawrence as being (for Jameson) the supreme exemplar of the modernist "unique self,...unique personality and individuality" with a "unique vision of the world":

> religion and modernism replace dead or false images (systems of representation) with others more lively and authentic. This description of classical modernism as "religion of art" is justified...by the aesthetic reception and experience of the works themselves. At its most vital, the experience of modernism was not one of a single historical movement or process, but of a "shock of discovery," a commitment and an adherence to its individual forms through a series of "religious conversions." One did not simply read *D. H. Lawrence* or Rilke, see Jean Renoir or Hitchcock, or listen to Stravinsky as distinct manifestations of what we now term modernism. Rather one read all the works of a particular writer, learned a style and a phenomenological world. *D. H. Lawrence became an absolute, a complete and systematic world view, to which one was converted*....The crisis of modernism as such came, then, when suddenly it became clear that "D. H. Lawrence" was not an absolute after all, not the final achieved figuration of the truth of the world, but only one art-language among others, only one shelf of works in a whole dizzying library. (Fredric Jameson, *October* 17 [Summer 1981]: 113; my italics)

Apparently Jameson at one time in his life knew the feeling of viewing "D. H. Lawrence [as] an absolute, a complete and systematic world view, to which one was converted"—in any event, he evidently was tempted to feel that way and seems to have devoted much time and energy to exorcising the demon of Lawrence: how else can we explain the bitter intensity of his remarks on Lawrence and his (Jameson's) depiction of a cultural scene in which "the crisis of modernism" was caused by the disillusionment that followed the sudden realization that "'D. H. Lawrence' was not an absolute after all, not the final achieved figuration of the truth of the world." According to

Jameson, this realization—"that 'D. H. Lawrence' was not an absolute after all"—led to

> the shame and guilt of cultural intellectuals,...and the abandonment of culture altogether for immediate political activity. (Ibid.)

In other words, according to Jameson, "cultural intellectuals," discovering to their horror that D. H. Lawrence could not provide them with "the final achieved figuration of the truth of the world," felt "shame and guilt" and instead turned to "immediate political activity" to give meaning to their lives.

It seems to me that Jameson's myth of "cultural intellectuals" becoming "political" is pathetic and contemptible: owing to their "shame and guilt" these "political" intellectuals—Jameson himself, Edward Said, Henry Louis Gates, Cornel West, bell hooks, and of course Terry Eagleton and Stanley Fish, among many others—are making six-figure salaries at the most powerful posts at the most powerful intellectual establishments in the Western "cultural-intellectual" world. Their "political activity" is bogus and opportunistic posturing and playacting—playacting reminiscent of the practise of "carnival":

> There were two reasons why the fizzy, dizzy carnival spirit did not necessarily undermine authority. First of all, *it was licensed or sanctioned by the authorities themselves.*...Second, although the world might appear to be turned upside down during the carnival season, the fact that Kings and Queens were chosen and crowned actually reaffirmed the status quo. (Roger Sales, *English Literature in History*, p. 169; italics mine)

The left-wing "political-cultural" academic "carnival" is clearly "licensed or sanctioned by the authorities themselves," for of course the fact is that

> the public..., directly or indirectly, pays the six-figure salaries commanded by these illustrious radical ideologues....(*New Criterion*, November 1991, p. 1)

—"radical ideologues" who

> have very little dogma and discipline beyond cultivating their own success....(William Kerrigan, *Raritan*, Spring 1995, p. 161)

Thus, in accordance with the "carnival spirit," the left-wing critics are not only "sanctioned by the authorities themselves," but also have "reaffirmed the status quo" by "the fact that Kings and Queens

[are] chosen and crowned" by these left-wing critics: these "Kings and Queens" being the "Kings and Queens" of academe; as Roger Kimball ironically describes the situation of Fredric Jameson himself:

> Among the stars twinkling in the academic firmament these days, none twinkles more formidably than the Marxist literary critic Fredric Jameson. Having taught at Harvard, Yale, and at various campuses of the University of California, Professor Jameson is now ensconced at Duke University—that favored perch for so many academic twinklers today—where he is William A. Lane Professor of Comparative Literature and Director of the Graduate Program in Literature as well as the Duke Center for Critical Theory. (Roger Kimball, "Fredric Jameson's laments," *New Criterion*, June 1991, p. 9)

Moreover, Kimball goes on to mention

> Terry Eagleton, the British literary critic who is Professor Jameson's chief rival for the title of "most important Marxist critic now writing" (Ibid., p. 11).

Thus it is evident that, in true "status quo" fashion, Jameson and Eagleton are "stars," the "Kings" of the academic-literary-theoretical establishment; indeed, even a younger left-wing critic must admit that

> Jameson...remains indebted to...the overall academic master code, which entices even a writer of his range and ambition to out-theorize other theorists and, by outflanking their less "dialectical" positions, to entrench himself more deeply in the game of academic rank. (Jim Merod, *Political Responsibility of the Critic*, pp. 132-133)

But to be a "King" "theorist" in "the game of academic rank" is one thing—to be a real "revolutionary" is surely another. Recently one young left-wing critic pathetically tried to idealize Jameson and the other members of "the postmodern literary left":

> The postmodern literary left can be loosely defined as those writers who reexamine the relation of art to radical politics within the problematics generated by contemporary theory. These writers have come to politics through their original engagement with literature and are heirs to the tradition (from Blake and Shelley...) that art can foster and guide the revolution. (John McGowan, *Postmodernism and its Critics*, p. 145)

But a more accurate assessment of "The postmodern literary left" was recently provided by Harold Fromm, who deplores the "pseudorevolutionary virtue" of the left-wing literary-theoretical-academic establishment; Fromm asserts that "the revolutionary aura [of the left-wing critics] is almost entirely specious—the real agenda being power and success in the academy" (*Academic Capitalism and Literary Value*, p. ix); and Fromm concludes that

> most academic "production"...must be considered as just one form of industry among others, with self-interest, success and profit as the final goals—in sum, as academic capitalism. (Fromm, p. 10)

And Fromm adds that

> many critics and theorists, more interested in political goals than intellectual activity or aesthetic response, malappropriate literary works towards these [political] ends. What is so curious about this development is that the political goals themselves are likely to be purely theoretical, because the real aim [of these left-wing "political intellectuals"] is personal success and power, not genuine ethical reform in the world. *Very few risks are taken* that might jeopardize a rising academic career. (Fromm, p. 10; italics mine)

At this point it seems to me to be quite helpful to look once more at Lawrence's letter on being "an absolute individual":

> One has to be an absolute individual, separate as a seed fallen out of the pod....Takes some risking....Son todos acobardados. (D. H. Lawrence letter to Murry, 17 September 1923)

"Son todos acobardados." "They are all frightened." In Lawrence's view, those who will not be "absolute individual[s]" are "all frightened": they will not take risks, just as the politically correct left-wing critics of today take "very few risks...that might jeopardize a rising academic career" (Fromm, p. 10). "They are all frightened"—but of what? Let us take the case of Jameson and Eagleton: an interesting case indeed; for it seems to me that these two would-be "revolutionaries" are quite frightened of realizing the bogusness of their claims to that title—and consequently they hate and fear the true "revolutionary," the true "transgressor," D. H. Lawrence: indeed, their ostensible hatred and fear of Lawrence is a major part of their strategy for dealing with what I would call their "anxiety of integrity"—which involves their own lack of integrity: rather than realize and admit that they are phoneys, they profess their "revolutionary" left-wing bona fides, identity and selfhood while at the same time indeed denying that such a thing as selfhood and identity exists. A major part of their strategy—conscious or unconscious—in recent years has in fact come to be their mutual coded denial of D. H. Lawrence.

In 1991, Jameson, at his peak with *Postmodernism*, celebrates the postmodernist "extinction" of Lawrentian "charisma," "romantic values," individuality and prophetic power—without even once mentioning Lawrence:

> something...needs to be said to discourage the view that, from the hindsight of postmodern fashion and commerciality, modernism was still a time of giants and legendary powers no longer available to us....[T]he poststructuralist motif of the "death of the subject"...signals the end of...inner-directed individualism, with its "charisma" and its accompanying categorical panoply of quaint romantic values such as that of the "genius" in the first place. Seen thus, the extinction of the "great moderns" is not necessarily an occasion for pathos. Our social order is richer in information and more literate [?!], and socially...more "democratic" in the sense of the universalization of wage labor...: the new order no longer needs prophets and seers of the high modernist and charismatic type [obviously a reference to D. H. Lawrence], whether among its cultural producers or its politicians....(*Postmodernism*, pp. 305-306)

Wishing to forget that "modernism was...a time of giants and legendary powers no longer available to us," Jameson here seems to celebrate the "death of the subject," the death of "charisma" and "romantic values"—"romantic values" involving "genius" and "prophets and seers of the high modernist and charismatic type"—clearly a reference to that supreme "prophet" of the "high modernist" period, D. H. Lawrence. Jameson goes on gladly to declare that

> such [high modernist-charismatic] figures [as D. H. Lawrence, no doubt] no longer hold any charm or magic for the subjects of a corporate, collectivized, post-individualistic age; in that case, goodbye to them [e.g., D. H. Lawrence] without regrets....: woe to the country that needs geniuses [such as Lawrence], prophets [such as Lawrence], Great Writers [such as Lawrence],...! (*Postmodernism*, p. 306)

According to Jameson here, no happy country "needs geniuses, prophets, Great Writers" (*Postmodernism*, p. 306)—good riddance to them, Jameson here asserts; yet a few pages later Jameson contradicts himself: he expresses admiration for "high modernism":

> High modernism does not express those [left-wing] values as such; rather it [i.e., high modernism] emerges in a space opened by them [i.e., left-wing values], and its [i.e., high modernism's] formal values of the New and of innovation, along with its Utopian sense of the transfiguration of the self and the world, are, in ways that remain to be explored, very much to be seen as echoes and resonances of the hopes and optimism of that great period dominated by the Second International. (*Postmodernism*, pp. 312-313)

Here Jameson praises high modernism's "formal values of the New and of innovation, along with its Utopian sense of the transfiguration of the self and the world"; but Jameson weirdly avers that the achievements and characteristics of high modernism should be credited to "the hopes and optimism of that great period dominated by the Second International [an international socialist organization]." And Jameson's supreme example of the high modernist "Utopian sense of the transformation of the self and the world" is none other than D. H. Lawrence himself:

> something...fundamental can be argued from the spirit of the [high modernist] works themselves, and in particular from a renewed scrutiny of the same high-modernist celebration of the self that the anti-political critics adduced to support a notion of the modernists' subjectivism....I want...to propose...that modernism's introspective probing of the deeper impulses of consciousness...was always accompanied by a Utopian sense of the impending transformation or transfiguration of the "self" in question....D. H. Lawrence is filled with intimations of this momentous new sea change from which new people are sure to emerge. What we now have to grasp is that those feelings, expressed in connection with the self, could only come into being in correlation with a similar feeling about society and the object world itself. It is because that object world, in the throes of industrialization and modernization, seems to tremble at the brink of an equally momentous and even Utopian transformation that the "self" can also be felt to be on the point of change....(*Postmodernism*, p. 312)

Thus here Jameson wants to have his cake and eat it too: not only does he want to depreciate Modernism (which Jameson does not capitalize), but also Jameson wants to praise Modernism in such a way as to (mistakenly) trace Modernism's "values" and "sense" to "the Second International." According to Jameson here, the "high-modernist celebration of the self" as exemplified by Lawrence in particular—this Lawrentian "celebration of the self...could only come into being in correlation with a similar feeling about society and the object world itself"—"that object world" which, according to Jameson, "seem[ed] to tremble at the brink of...[a] Utopian transformation"—thus, here Jameson would have it that the "object world" deserves credit for the Lawrentian-Modernist "celebration of the self."

But is this the case with the Lawrentian "celebration of the self"? Does Lawrence believe that the "transfiguration of the self" goes hand in hand with the "Utopian transformation" of "the object world itself"? To answer this question, let us look at Lawrence's classic scene of "transfiguration of the self," presented in the famous "Excurse" chapter of *Women in Love*; in this scene of "transfiguration of the self," Lawrence tells us,

> the world was under a strange ban, a new mystery had supervened.

For Lawrence in "Excurse," the "transfiguration of the self" occurs only when "the object world itself" (to use Jameson's phrase)—the *known* world—is "under a strange ban," replaced by "a new mystery"—the *unknown* world; it is in this "world" that the self-transfiguration of Ursula and Birkin in *Women in Love* takes place:

> This was *no actual world*....The world had become unreal. She [Ursula] herself was a strange, transcendent reality....[S]he saw a strange creature from another world, in him [Birkin].

The "object world" has no place in the Lawrentian transfiguration of the self; on the other hand, "the object world itself" means a great deal to the left-wing critics such as Jameson—indeed, Ursula's statement about Hermione in the "Excurse" chapter of *Women in Love* can certainly be applied to the left-wing literary-cultural critics:

> she is such a materialist....What does she work out to, in the end, with all her social passion....Social passion—what social passion has she?—show it me!—where is it? She wants petty, immediate *power*,...that is all.

Probably the most outstanding example of "petty, immediate power" in academe's literary-critical-theoretical circles is Terry Eagleton, Warton Professor at Oxford University, who in his recent inaugural lecture (27 November 1992) makes it clear that he feels his position is full of fun and power:

> being a professor is better than having a job,

he jokes happily; but at the same time Eagleton is evidently haunted by his memory of the great Lawrentian F. R. Leavis, whom Eagleton has written about and attacked since the beginning of his (Eagleton's) career some thirty years ago (see Scherr, "Eagleton's Flight"). Yet, at the same time that Eagleton is haunted by Leavis even at the moment of his (Eagleton's) greatest political power as Warton Professor at Oxford, Eagleton here in his inaugural lecture can at least mention Leavis by name:

> it was characteristic of the *Leavisian* ideology of English...to discern a peculiarly intimate relation between a certain richly resourceful use of the national language, and a certain uniquely English mode of experiencing....(italics mine)

Attacking "the Leavisian ideology of English" for its privileging "a certain uniquely English mode of experiencing" and the "richly resourceful use of the [English] language" by its greatest writers, Eagleton at least identifies Leavis by name in his attack; but as Eagleton goes on viciously to attack Lawrence, he is apparently so overawed by Lawrence—or so eager to repress the power and memory of Lawrence upon him—that he (Eagleton) cannot even bring himself to mention Lawrence by name:

> the language of muscularity and robustness, of the sinewy and the vigorous, of moral maturity and phallocentric fullness, all of which were found exemplified in perhaps *the most pathologically sexist author that the modern English canon—no slouch at such selections—has managed to produce*

—"the most pathologically sexist author that the modern English canon...has managed to produce" obviously being none other than D. H. Lawrence himself.

But why does Eagleton feel the need to elide the name of D. H. Lawrence in his very attack on him? To answer this question it is helpful to look at one of Eagleton's concluding statements in his lecture:

> It is not the question of whether Alice Walker is greater than Thomas Mann that Washington is weighing up; it is weighing up whether the devastation wreaked by the collapse of the Soviet bloc will permit it [Washington] easy pickings, or unleash forces that might dangerously destabilize its global rule.

Here it seems to me that Eagleton is suffering from the anxiety of integrity: he psychically defends himself against recognizing that he is more interested in "petty [political] power" than in literature, culture or revolution; he seems to fantasize about being in the power precincts of "Washington"—perhaps as an adviser to President Clinton or Hillary (they had just won the 1992 election a few days before Eagleton's lecture); indeed, in his personality Eagleton may be quite similar to Clinton.

Indeed, in 1985, when Eagleton was in the process of reaching his academic-political power peak, one of his left-wing "comrades" complained about

> Eagleton's own *anxieties* in his fluctuations (Richard Aczel, "Eagleton and English," *New Left Review*, no. 154, November/December 1985, p. 120; italics mine)

—"fluctuations" reminiscent, it would seem to me, of a Bill Clinton-like politician; Aczel sardonically informs us:

> If Eagleton can confidently deny the existence of literature in *Literary Theory*, his equally confident description of such a denial as "mad idealism or sentimental demagogy," in a paper presented and distributed among participants at a "Literature, Teaching, Politics" conference can presumably be justified in purely pragmatic terms. The cause of human emancipation dictates the presentation of one argument to the converted (a socialist conference) and its complete opposite to the sceptical laity (the readership of Basil Blackwell publications). ("Eagleton and English," p. 120)

In other words, Eagleton, a "political" phoney lacking integrity, tells his (rather unsophisticated) reading public that "literature" does not exist—tells them this so that they will not privilege great literary figures like Lawrence and Leavis over mediocre Eagleton himself (see Scherr, "Eagleton's Flight")—while in private he (Eagleton) tells his "comrades" that that very same denial of the existence of literature is nothing more than "mad idealism or sentimental demagogy." Will the real Terry Eagleton please stand up? His "comrade" Aczel must wonder—and so do we.

Significantly enough, Aczel is also extremely confused and upset by what he considers to be Eagleton's obsession with Leavis:

> Why...this repeated resurrection of Leavis?

Aczel naively asks ("Eagleton and English," p. 114). The answer to this question is that, for Eagleton with his anxiety of integrity, Leavis in his passion and integrity will never die; and the same of course is true—even more so—of Lawrence. Eagleton himself of course, is far from certain of his own "integrity"—or "immortality":

> If "literary criticism" is to be one day justified at the judgement seat of history—if we will be able to claim that it played a bit part in the averting of fascism or nuclear holocaust...(*Against the Grain*, p. 66)

Eagleton's uncertainty is evident in those "ifs"; he goes on to say that his "comrade"

> [Fredric] Jameson may have the oppressive pleasure of knowing that he is one of the forlornly few names we [left-wing critics] will stammeringly evoke [if literary criticism "is...one day justified"]....(Ibid.)

But of course Jameson himself is uncertain of his own integrity or immortality; reaching his peak with *Postmodernism* in 1991, Jameson admits in that book that many people believe that he,

> having "become" a postmodernist I must have ceased to be a Marxist....(*Postmodernism*, "Conclusion: Chapter 10, Secondary Elaborations," p. 298)

—and Jameson himself confesses that

> I write as a relatively enthusiastic *consumer* of postmodernism....(Ibid.; italics mine)

Thus we have Eagleton with his longings for political power in Clinton's Washington, and Jameson with his enthusiastic consumerism; in stark contrast to these left-wing revolutionary wannabees is the supreme example of D. H. Lawrence, who forthrightly asserts what "revolutionary" activity he is about:

> I always labour at the same thing, to make the sex relation valid and precious, instead of shameful. (D. H. Lawrence letter to Nancy Pearn, 12 April 1927)

Furthermore, Lawrence enjoyed extreme certainty about his own "immortality": "I shall change the world for the next thousand years," Lawrence told his wife Frieda and her daughter Barbara Weekley in the late 1920s (Nehls, *D. H. Lawrence: A Composite Biog-*

raphy, Volume I, p. 162). And Lawrence's certainty permeates his great works—his major novels, poems, essays and letters; a certainty that is lacking in Jameson, Eagleton and the like. It is really no wonder then, that in their envy and resentment of "revolutionary" D. H. Lawrence, who shows them up for the phoneys that they are, Jameson and Eagleton denounce Lawrence, Jameson attacking Lawrence's "charisma" and Eagleton attacking Lawrence's "sexism."

In contradistinction to Jameson and Eagleton is Lionel Trilling, reputed to be the literary critic whose "cultural criticism gives us more to think about than that of any other American of his generation" (Mark Krupnick, *Lionel Trilling and the Fate of Cultural Criticism*, p. 170). Trilling, even as early as 1930 (when he was twenty-five years old), recognized that Lawrence is the true revolutionary:

> For us Lawrence's deepest significance must be as a poet of rebellious social theory....If there is one surely connecting thread running through all Lawrence's work, it is the thread of social interest. He did indeed repudiate our system as a way of life for himself. As a form of treacherous injustice, he kept it within constant reach of his castigating rod. (Lionel Trilling, "D. H. Lawrence: A Neglected Aspect" [1930], in *Speaking of Literature and Society*, pp. 37-38)

For Trilling, Lawrence is the prophet of social reality:

> He [Lawrence] himself used his immense artistic gift never as a thing in itself but as an instrument to reproduce the flux and plasm of life. But it is not with any simple-hearted artist-joy that he concerned himself with this flux and plasm of life. He wrote of it frightened and angered by its misery. With a hard-headed commonsense he...struck square into the middle of the cause of all misery—the social order. (Ibid., pp. 38-39)

In Lawrence's fight against "the social order," Trilling astutely perceives, Lawrence's main weapon is "Sex":

> Lawrence's revolt was against...dehumanization, against the forces which had split the individual..., and had set him into merely mental life. Sex was Lawrence's carryall for the weapons of this revolt....[Sex is Lawrence's way] to bring about liberation and fullness of life. Lawrence was seeking a symbol to express the salutariness of unrestrained contact with some sentient thing and in sex he found the symbol that was at once deepest and most universal. (Ibid., pp. 39-40)

According to Trilling, Lawrence as sexual-social prophet-revolutionary reached his peak in *Lady Chatterley's Lover*:

> the social implications [in Lawrence's work] grow, until in *Lady Chatterley's Lover* they flower into explicitness, and passages of social theory intertwine with passages of sexual practice. (Ibid., p. 40)

As a young Lawrentian, Lionel Trilling has great enthusiasm for Lawrence as social theorist, sexual prophet, and "poet of social theory." Trilling sees how Lawrentian thought (as expressed in *Fantasia of the Unconscious*, for instance) emphasizes

> the "dark" forces, self-assertion, masterfulness, pride and joy (Ibid., p. 40)

—and Trilling shares Lawrence's belief that

> democracy and capitalistic industrialism must of their own necessity bring about the atrophy of the "dark" centers. These [democratic-capitalist-industrialist] agencies cannot exist together with the virtues of pride and *self-integration* [italics mine]. [The capitalistic-democratic] virtues must be those of...idealism, benevolence, dutiful submission—and these [virtues] the rapacity of the modern politico-economic system succeeds in enforcing where Christianity failed. From the defeat of the virtues of the lower centers...comes the messy sterility of modern life. (Ibid., p. 41)

Like Lawrence, Trilling deplores "the spiritual bullying which lies hidden in our notion of love, in our idealism, in our social benevolence" (Ibid.)—all of which are opposed to "the self-integrating 'dark' forces" (Ibid.) that Trilling as well as Lawrence privileges. These "self-integrating 'dark' forces," Trilling tells us, must fight against

> The flat staleness of life, the loss of savor, the inability to feel in the body and in the nerves an irrefutable reason for living....(Ibid.)

According to Trilling, only Lawrence is fully aware, "downright" and "simple-spoken" about the cause of life's "staleness" today:

> No one has said as he [Lawrence] says: we are miserable and full of spleen because...our system has taken from us the body and its joy and knowledge. (Ibid.)

Thus, like Lawrence, Trilling emphasizes self-integration and the phenomenon of "Sex" ("the body and its joy and knowledge") as forces against "our system." Surely Trilling's affirmation of self-integration goes hand in hand with his valorization of Lawrence; indeed, Trilling's wife recently revealed that D. H. Lawrence was in fact Lionel Trilling's ego-ideal; she tells us that

> The failure to make his career as a novelist may not have wholly accounted for the feeling of failure which shadowed Lionel's life even at its most successful. Yet surely it was his sense of having been denied the inner freedom which he supposes might have allowed him to be a novelist which constituted his persisting emotion of deprivation....On 3 July 1961 he records: "Death of Ernest Hemingway. Except Lawrence's 32 years ago, no writer's death has moved me as much—...." That the literary career of D. H. Lawrence might represent for Lionel the career which he had himself failed to achieve is not hard for us to understand....(Diana Trilling, *The Beginning of the Journey*, p. 371)

Unlike left-wing Eagleton and Jameson who seek to deflate Lawrence's "charisma" and celebration of "Sex," Lionel Trilling recognized—and indeed was awed by—Lawrence's greatness and "inner freedom"; the ostensible complacency of the left-wing Jameson and Eagleton in relation to great writers and great literature would have been deplored by Trilling, whose intense quest for self-integration is manifested even in his last major work, *Sincerity and Authenticity* (1970); here Trilling celebrates

> such energy as contrives that the center [of the self] shall hold, that the circumference of the self keep unbroken, that the person be an integer, impenetrable, perdurable, and autonomous in being....(*Sincerity and Authenticity*, p. 99)

Indeed, it is the integrated and integral self, the centered self, the autonomous self that Trilling deems "the opposing self"; as Trilling explains in his classic work of that name, "the opposing self" is

> the self that opposes circumstance, the self that is imagination and desire....(*The Opposing Self* [New York: Viking, 1955], p. 41)

"The opposing self," Trilling tells us, is "the self confronting hostile or painful circumstances" (Ibid., p. 42) with the power of "imagination and desire." With its "imagination and desire," Trilling's "opposing self" is indeed the Lawrentian self, "the self in its health and validity" (Ibid., p. 39)—and with its "health and validity" and "desire" it is, of course, a "heterosexual" self.

NOTE

1. See Barry J. Scherr, "Lawrence, Keats and *Tender Is the Night*: Loss of Self and 'Love Battle' Motifs," *Recovering Literature* 14 (1986).

WORKS CITED

Aczel, Richard. "Eagleton and English." *New Left Review* 154 (November/December 1985): 113-123.

Bersani, Leo. "Is the Rectum a Grave?" *October* 43 (1987): 197-222.

Dollimore, Jonathan. *Political Shakespeare*. Manchester: Manchester University Press, 1985.

Dollimore, Jonathan. *Radical Tragedy*. Brighton: Harvester Press, 1984.

Dollimore, Jonathan. *Sexual Dissidence*. Oxford: Clarendon Press, 1991.

Eagleton, Terry. "The Crisis of Contemporary Culture," "An inaugural lecture as Thomas Warton Professor of English Literature delivered in the Examination Schools, Oxford on 27 November 1992." *New Left Review* 196 (November/December 1992): 29-41.

Eagleton, Terry. *Against the Grain*. London: Verso, 1986.

Fromm, Harold. *Academic Capitalism and Literary Value*. Athens: University of Georgia Press, 1991.

Jameson, Fredric. "Postmodernism and Consumer Society." *The Anti-Aesthetic: Essays on Postmodern Culture*. Ed. Hal Foster. Port Townsend, Washington: Bay Press, 1983.

Jameson, Fredric. *Postmodernism*. Durham: Duke University Press, 1991.

Jameson, Fredric. "'In the Destructive Element Immerse.'" *October* 17 (Summer 1981): 99-118.

Kerrigan, William. "Modernism Muddled." *Raritan* 14 (Spring 1995): 153-162.

Kimball. Roger. "Fredric Jameson's Laments." *The New Criterion* June 1991: 9-16.

Krupnick, Mark. *Lionel Trilling and the Fate of Cultural Criticism*. Evanston: Northwestern University Press, 1986.

Lawrence, D. H. "John Galsworthy." *Phoenix: The Posthumous Papers of D. H. Lawrence*. Ed. Edward D. McDonald. New York: Viking, 1936.

Lawrence, D. H. *Kangaroo*. New York: Thomas Seltzer, 1923.

Lawrence, D. H. *Apocalypse*. New York: Viking, 1966.

Lawrence, D. H. *The Letters of D. H. Lawrence*. Ed. Aldous Huxley. New York: Viking, 1932.

Lawrence, D. H. *Women in Love.* New York: Viking, 1960.

Lawrence, D. H. "Study of Thomas Hardy." *Phoenix: The Posthumous Papers of D. H. Lawrence.* Ed. Edward D. McDonald. New York: Viking, 1936.

McGowan, John. *Postmodernism and Its Critics.* Ithaca: Cornell University Press, 1991.

Merod, Jim. *The Political Responsibility of the Critic.* Ithaca: Cornell University Press, 1987.

Reilly, Jim. "D. H. Lawrence: Cliques and Consciousness." *The British Critical Tradition: A Re-evaluation.* Ed. Gary Day. New York: St. Martin's Press, 1993.

Sales, Roger. *English Literature in History.* New York: St. Martin's Press, 1983.

Scherr, Barry J. "Eagleton's Flight from Lawrence and Leavis." *Recovering Literature* 22 (1995): 35-56.

Trilling, Diana. *The Beginning of the Journey.* New York: Harcourt Brace, 1993.

Trilling, Lionel. *Sincerity and Authenticity.* Cambridge: Harvard University Press, 1971.

Trilling, Lionel. "D. H. Lawrence: A Neglected Aspect." *Speaking of Literature and Society.* Ed. Diana Trilling. New York: Harcourt Brace Jovanovich, 1980.

Trilling, Lionel. *The Opposing Self.* New York: Viking, 1955..

CHAPTER FIVE

Sex, Selfhood, Literature and Politics
The Left-Wing Attack on D. H. Lawrence (Part Two)

But why say that the "healthy" self is a "heterosexual" self? Are we being homophobic here? Far from it; for of course the fact is that the set of homosexual intellectuals (i.e., intellectuals who are also homosexual) has essentially always depreciated the phenomenon of the self: Michel Foucault himself, whom homosexual intellectual Leo Bersani praises as "The Gay Daddy" (Bersani, *Homos*, p. 77), defines the individual self as a mere "effect" and "vehicle" of sociopolitical "power":

> The individual is an effect of [sociopolitical] power, and at the same time...it is the element of its articulation. The individual which power has constituted is at the same time its vehicle. (Foucault, *Power/Knowledge*, p. 98)

Left-wing homosexual intellectual Roland Barthes celebrates the decentered self where there is

> a dispersion of energy in which there remains neither a central core nor a structure of meaning:...I am dispersed. (Quoted in Dollimore, *Radical Tragedy*, p. 270)

Thus neither Foucault nor Barthes takes much stock in the integrated, powerful, "healthy" self. Barthes' self has "neither a central core nor a structure of meaning"; as for Foucault,

> Foucault's vision of individuals...as the product of the social powers that dominate them (Seigel, "Foucault," *Journal of the History of Ideas* 51 [1990]: 274)

is, it seems to me, both uninspiring and un-Lawrentian.

Foucault is even more un-Lawrentian when it comes to the subject of sex. Indeed, Foucault makes no secret of his anti-Lawrentian stance; in his famous *The History of Sexuality: An Introduction*, Foucault makes fun of Lawrence's "concern" about sex:

> Perhaps one day people will wonder at [Lawrence's concern about sex]. They will not be able to understand how a civilization so intent on developing enormous instruments of production and destruction found the time and the infinite patience to inquire so anxiously concerning the actual state of sex; people will smile perhaps when they recall that here were men—meaning ourselves—who believed that therein [i.e., in sex] resided a truth every bit as precious as the one they had already demanded from the earth, the stars, and the pure forms of their thought; people will be surprised at the eagerness with which we went about pretending to rouse from its slumber a sexuality which everything—our discourses, our customs, our regulations, our knowledge—was busy producing in the light of day and broadcasting to noisy accompaniment. And people will ask themselves why we were so bent on ending the rule of silence regarding what was the noisiest of our preoccupations. (*The History of Sexuality: An Introduction*, pp. 157-158)

Here Foucault ridicules the Lawrentian concern with sex, "the actual state of sex"—the Lawrentian belief that in sex "resided a truth" that was supremely "precious": all this concern, according to Foucault, is just nothing more than a lot of "noise"—"noise" produced by "everything—our discourses, our customs, our institutions, our regulations, our knowledges." (Clearly Foucault's "everything" is a lot less sexy than Lawrence's "noise.")

Lawrence's foolish "noise," according to Foucault, is found in statements such as this one, from Lawrence's character Kate in *The Plumed Serpent*:

> How wonderful sex can be, when men keep it powerful and sacred, and it fills the world! like sunshine through and through one! (Quoted in *History of Sexuality: An Introduction*, p. 157)

For Lawrence, sex can be "wonderful," "powerful," "sacred"; for Foucault,

> sex is boring (*The Foucault Reader*, p. 340)

Foucault made that statement in April 1983, a few months before his death from AIDS in 1984. Indeed, even in *The History of Sexuality* (1976), Foucault makes clear that he valorizes "a nonsexual economy of pleasure" (Harpham, *Ascetic Imperative*, p. 232):

> sex is...historically subordinate to a larger deployment of sexuality that interprets, controls, normalizes, and disciplines; resistance to this deployment now must rally around *bodies and pleasures, not sex.* (Ibid; italics mine)

Thus, for Foucault, apparently "sex" is antithetical to "bodies and pleasures." Foucault apparently believes that "sex," through its subordination to the "deployment of sexuality," is "boring," a phenomenon that is under control of the "social body" (i.e., the inherent power mechanism of society) and thus cannot be a site of "resistance" to established society. As Bersani recently explained:

> It is the original thesis of his [Foucault's] *History [of Sexuality]* that power in our societies functions primarily not by repressing spontaneous sexual drives but by producing multiple sexualities, and that through the classification, distribution, and moral rating of those sexualities the individuals practicing them can be approved, treated, marginalized, sequestered, disciplined, or normalized. (Bersani, *Homos*, p. 81)

Rather than being a source of freedom and liberation, sex for Foucault—thanks to "the deployment of sexuality" which "has its reason for being...in proliferating, innovating, annexing, creating and penetrating bodies in an increasingly detailed way, and in controlling populations in an increasingly comprehensive way" (*The History of Sexuality: An Introduction*, p. 107)—sex is utilized, exploited by "recent devices of power," in an "arrangement"—an "arrangement" which

> has been linked from the outset with an intensification of the body—with its exploitation as an object of knowledge and an element in relations of power. (Ibid.)

Exploiting the body as an object in the Foucaultian knowledge-power configuration, the deployment of sexuality (according to Foucault) manages to be "a means of social control and political subjugation" (Ibid., p. 123). This "political ordering of life" (Ibid.) goes hand in hand with what Foucault calls "bio-power,"

> methods of power and knowledge [which] assumed responsibility for the life processes and undertook to control and modify them [the life processes]. (Ibid., p. 142)

This scientific-political bio-power

> brought life and its mechanisms into the realm of explicit calculations and made knowledge-power an agent of transformation of human life [in the Western world]. (Ibid., p. 143)

"[L]ife and its mechanisms," "explicit calculations": Foucault's language is not very Lawrentian—neither is Foucault's assessment of the role of sex in "human life": according to Foucault,

> Sex...was employed as a standard for the disciplines and as a basis for regulations. This is why in the nineteenth century sexuality was sought out in the smallest details of individual existences; it was tracked down in behavior, pursued in dreams; it was suspected of underlying the least follies, it was tracked back into the earliest years of childhood; it became the stamp of individuality—at the same time what enabled one to analyze the latter and what made it possible to master it. (Ibid., p. 146)

According to Foucault, sex was simply a mechanism, a device by means of which the power-knowledge establishment of the state-society could manipulate and master "individuality" via

> this *technology* of sex (Ibid.; my italics)

which is

> a whole series of different tactics that combined in varying proportions the objective of disciplining the body and that of regulating populations. (Ibid.)

Thus the purpose of sex for the "knowledge-power" society is to be "organized," "managed," "invested" by "the mechanisms of power,"—"mechanisms" which simultaneously exploit, aid, and control the body:

> the mechanisms of power are addressed to the body, to life, to what causes it to proliferate, to what reinforces the species, its stamina, its ability to dominate, or its capacity for being used. (Ibid., p. 147)

So, according to Foucault, sex came under the control of "Power":

> Power delineated it, aroused it, and employed it....[S]exuality, far from being repressed in the [late nineteenth century] society..., on the contrary was constantly aroused....[S]exuality was on the side of the norm, knowledge, life, meaning, the disciplines, and regulations. (Ibid., p. 148)

In other words, "Power" gives "sexuality" its incitement, meaning, importance and management: "power mechanisms aimed at controlling and administering the everyday life of sexuality" (Ibid., p. 150). According to Foucault, "the modern technologies of power...take life as their objective" (Ibid., p. 152)—*sex life* in particular; indeed, it is "Power" that has made sex the all-important idea, the

> idea that there exists something other than bodies, organs,...sensations and pleasures; something else and something more, with intrinsic properties and laws of its own: "sex." (Ibid., pp. 152-153)

But Foucault says that "sex" is simply a "notion" that was established by "the deployment of sexuality, with its different strategies" (Ibid., p. 154); but the "notion" of "sex," says Foucault, generated a "theory"; and

> The theory thus generated performed a certain number of functions that made it indispensable. First, the notion of "sex" made it possible to group together, in an artificial unity, anatomical elements, biological functions, conducts, sensations, and pleasures, and it enabled one to make use of this fictitious unity as a causal principle, an omnipresent meaning, a secret to be discovered everywhere: sex was thus able to function as a unique signifier and as a universal signified. (Ibid., p. 154)

"Unique" "sex", says Foucault, was manipulated by "power" in such a way as to deceive individuals by means of making "sex" appear far more powerful than it really was/is:

> the notion of sex brought about a fundamental reversal; it made it possible to invert the representation of the relationships of power to sexuality, causing the latter to appear, not in its essential and positive relation to power, but as being rooted in a specific and irreducible urgency which power tries as best it can to dominate....(Ibid., p. 155)

While (according to Foucault) the fact is that sex is simply part and parcel of "power" (i.e., "sex" has an "essential and positive relation to power"), "the notion of sex" makes sex "appear...as being rooted in a specific and irreducible urgency which power tries...to dominate." But "sex," says Foucault, is not opposed to "power"; nor is sex (says Foucault) "a unique signifier" or "a universal signified": "Sex...appears to dominate us," but it is really only one element in "the deployment of sexuality":

> Sex—that agency which appears to dominate us and that secret which seems to underlie all that we are, that point which enthralls us through the power it manifests and the meaning it conceals, and which we ask to reveal what we are and to free us from what defines us—is doubtless but an ideal point made necessary by the deployment of sexuality and its operation. We must not make the mistake of thinking that sex is an autonomous agency....On the contrary, sex is the most speculative, most ideal, and most internal element in a deployment of sexuality organized by power in its grip on bodies and their materiality, their forces, energies, sensations, and pleasures. (Ibid., p. 155)

According to Foucault, sex only seems ("appears") to "dominate" and "enthrall" us; sex only seems to have the power "to free us": the fact (according to Foucault) is that sex is just "an ideal point made necessary by the deployment of sexuality"—"the deployment of sexuality" which itself is also just an instrument "organized by power in its grip on bodies and . . .their forces, energies, sensations, and pleasures." Foucault derides

> the importance we ascribe to it [sex], the reverential fear with which we surround it [sex], the care we take to know it [sex]. (Ibid., p. 156)

Foucault goes on to attack

> the fact that over the centuries it [sex] has become more important than our soul, more important almost than our life....The Faustian pact, whose temptation has been instilled in us by the deployment of sexuality, is now as follows: to exchange life in its entirety for sex itself....Sex is worth dying for. (Ibid., p. 156)

No fan of "sex," Foucault deplores the "importance" of sex, "the reverential fear" inspired by sex, and "the Faustian pact" according to which "Sex is worth dying for."

Reverence for sex, an intense sense of the importance of sex, the sense that "Sex is worth dying for": these are indeed Lawrentian characteristics that Foucault attacks. In an essay of his *Lady Chatterley's Lover* period (1928), for instance, Lawrence passionately declares that

> sex and beauty are one thing, like flame and fire. If you hate sex you hate beauty. If you love *living* beauty, you have a reverence for sex....[To] love living beauty you must have a reverence for sex. ("Sex versus Loveliness")

Furthermore, in his famous essay "A Propos of *Lady Chatterley's Lover*," Lawrence states that we must have

> a proper reverence for sex...

—a Lawrentian "reverence for sex" which is antithetical to Foucault; a Lawrentian reverence of which Foucault was well aware: for of course Foucault quotes from "A Propos of *Lady Chatterley's Lover*" in his important conclusion to *The History of Sexuality: An Introduction*; here Foucault makes it clear that Lawrence is the supreme cultural figure involved in the valorization of sex. Immediately before quoting from Lawrence's celebration and valorization of sex in *The Plumed Serpent*, Foucault asserts that the fact is that it is "power" through "the deployment of sexuality" which gives "sex" an importance it certainly does not deserve:

> the deployment of sexuality permits the techniques of power to invest life....
>
> By creating the imaginary element that is "sex," the deployment of sexuality established one of its most essential internal operating principles: the desire for sex—the desire to have it, to have access to it, to discover it, to liberate it, to articulate it in discourse, to formulate it in truth. It constituted "sex" itself as something desirable. And it is this desirability of sex...that makes us think we are affirming the rights of our sex against all power, when in fact we are fastened to the deployment of sexuality that has lifted up from deep within us a sort of mirage in which we think we see ourselves reflected—the *dark* shimmer of sex. (Ibid., pp. 156-157; my italics)

Foucault's mention of "the dark" in relation to "sex," it seems to me, is a definite reference to Lawrence (see Scherr). Throughout most of the major novels (*Sons and Lovers*, *The Rainbow*, *Women in Love*), Lawrence refers to "the dark fire" of sex, the "dark flood" of sex, the "fecund darkness" of sex; thus, in mocking "the dark shimmer of sex" as a mere mirage created by "the deployment of sexuality" that "makes us think we are affirming the rights of our sex against all power, when in fact we are fastened to the deployment of sexuality," Foucault derides Lawrence's reputation as sexual revolutionary, asserting that the Lawrentian "affirming the rights of our sex against all power" is really merely an instrument of power's "deployment of sexuality" and its deceiving "us" by making "us...think we see ourselves reflected...[in] the dark [Lawrentian] shimmer of sex" which is just "a sort of mirage" or illusion.

Foucault goes on then to quote Lawrence's *The Plumed Serpent* on "how wonderful sex can be" (Ibid., p. 157)—and then Foucault immediately proceeds to offer his own (now orthodox) theory of "sex" as simply a social construct which is "historically subordinate to sexuality":

> "sex" is historically subordinate to sexuality....sexuality is a very real historical formation; it is what gave rise to the notion of sex....We must not think that by saying yes to sex, one says no to power; on the contrary, one tracks along the course laid out by the general deployment of sexuality. It is the agency of sex we must break away from, if we aim—through a tactical reversal of the various mechanisms of sexuality—to counter the grips of power with the claims of bodies, pleasures, and knowledges, in their multiplicity and their possibility of resistance. The rallying point for the counterattack against the deployment of sexuality ought not to be sex-desire, but bodies and pleasures. (Ibid., p. 157)

In other words, by giving "sexuality" priority over "sex," Foucault thinks that he is demystifying the Lawrentian notion of sex and the power of sex—the revolutionary power of sex in particular (see Trilling on Lawrence). Foucault is thinking/speaking of Lawrence when Foucault speaks of those who "think that by saying yes to sex, one says no to power"—this "saying yes to sex," according to Foucault, is in fact the *conventional* way to be (says Foucault)—i.e., in accordance with "the course laid out by the general deployment of sexuality." Thus, for Foucault, Lawrence would seem to offer precisely the wrong "strategy" for "counter[ing]...power": Lawrentian "sex" and "sex-desire" plays right into the hands of "civilization" (p. 157) and "the power mechanisms of sexuality" (p. 158), says Foucault. But if Lawrence is so wrong according to Foucault, what is Foucault's "sexual" solution?

Foucault says that "It is...sex that we must break away from" (p. 157)—and in place of "sex" there should be "the claims of bodies, pleasures, and knowledges, in their...possibility of resistance" to "power." Foucault goes on briefly to quote Lawrence again, as if to remind his (Foucault's) readers of the kind of "sex" he (Foucault) is fighting against with his concept of "bodies and pleasures" (p. 157); and then, pretending to superior wisdom, Foucault concludes that "power" has tricked us all into loving sex:

> We are often reminded of the countless procedures which Christianity once employed to make us detest the body; but let us ponder all the ruses that were employed for centuries to make us love sex, to make the knowledge of it desirable and everything said about it precious. (p. 159)

For Foucault, "sex" does not "liberate" us; rather, we must be liberated from sex—liberated from sex by "a different economy of bodies and pleasures":

> one day, perhaps, in a different economy of bodies and pleasures, people will no longer quite understand how the ruses of sexuality, and the power that sustains its organization, were able to subject us to that austere monarchy of sex....(p. 159)

For Foucault, Lawrentian "sex" is an "austere monarchy" bringing neither pleasure nor power to people; this "austere monarchy of sex," says Foucault, must be resisted by "bodies and pleasures." But what does Foucault mean by "bodies and pleasures" and "a different economy of bodies and pleasures"? One student of Foucault concludes that

> I can form no concrete picture of what resistance to the deployment of sexuality in the regime of bio-power in the name of the body and its pleasures would be like. (Nancy Fraser, "Foucault's Body-Language," *Salmagundi* 61 [1983]: 66)

But recently Foucault scholars have figured out that what Foucault means by "bodies and pleasures" is nothing other than "S/M":

> S/M is...the real creation of new possibilities of pleasure....[Through S/M, people] are inventing new possibilities of pleasure with strange parts of their body—through the eroticization of the body. I think it's a kind of creation, a creative enterprise, which has as one of its main features what I call the desexualization of pleasure. The idea that bodily pleasure should always come from sexual pleasure, and the idea that sexual pleasure is the root of *all* our possible pleasure—I think *that's* some-

> thing quite wrong. (Foucault, quoted in Miller, *Passion of Michel Foucault*, p. 263)

Foucaultian "bodies and pleasures" has radical implications for the phenomenon of selfhood; Foucault tells us that "sexuality" should function in such a way that sexuality becomes an affirmation of "non-identity":

> I think it is politically important that sexuality be able to function the way it does in the [homosexual-S/M] saunas, where, without [having to submit to] the condition of being *imprisoned in one's own identity*, in one's own past, in one's own face, one can meet people who are to you what one is to them: nothing else but *bodies* with which combinations, fabrications of *pleasure* will be possible. These places afford an exceptional possibility of *desubjectivization*, of desubjection,...[Anonymity is important] because of the *intensity* of the *pleasure* that follows from it. It's not the affirmation of identity that's important, it's the affirmation of *non-identity*....It's an important experience in which one invents...*pleasures* which one fabricates together [with others]. (Foucault, quoted in Halperin, *Saint Foucault*, p. 94; italics mine)

Here Foucault valorizes both S/M and promiscuity in the homosexual saunas as ways to "desubjectivization" and "the affirmation of non-identity": through promiscuity—treating people as "nothing else but bodies with which combinations, fabrications of pleasure will be possible"—these people ("bodies") achieve "non-identity"; apparently for Foucault this "non-identity" is a desirable goal. D. H. Lawrence, on the other hand, privileges heterosexuality, individuality, monogamy:

> No getting away from the fact that the blood of woman is dynamically polarized in opposition, or in difference to the blood of man. The crisis of their contact in sex connection is the moment of establishment of a new flashing circuit throughout the whole sea: the dark, burning red waters of our under-world rocking in a new dynamic rhythm in each of us. And then in the second place, the blood of an individual is his *own* blood. That is, it is individual. And though we have a potential dynamic sexual connection, we men, with almost every woman, yet the great outstanding fact of the individuality even of the blood makes us need a corresponding individuality in the woman we are to embrace. The more individual the man or woman, the more unsatisfactory is a non-individual connection: promiscuity. The more individual, the more does our blood cry out for its own specific answer, an

> individual woman, blood-polarized with us. (D. H. Lawrence, "Sleep and Dreams," Chapter XIV, *Fantasia of the Unconscious*, p. 203)

Valorizing the "dynamic" male-female relationship rooted "in difference," Lawrence concludes that "[t]he crisis of their [man and woman] contact in sex connection" causes the "establishment of...a new dynamic rhythm" in them, the *individual* man and woman, each of whom has their own "individual...blood"—"blood" for Lawrence signifying the living essence of the individual being:

> One lives, knows, and has one's being in the blood....(D. H. Lawrence letter to Bertrand Russell, 8 December 1915)

—and this "fact" of the individual "blood" of the individual man and woman makes "a non-individual connection"—i.e., "promiscuity"—very "unsatisfactory" for the most highly developed, supremely individual human beings; for, says Lawrence, the most individual man's most individual "blood" (or essence) will "cry out for...an individual woman, blood-polarized with us."

While Lawrence prizes the supremely heterosexual, supremely individualized self in relationship, Foucault valorizes his goal of "inventing oneself" through *homosexual S/M* activities—"inventing oneself" in such a way that one indeed destroys the Lawrentian virile-sexual self (with its "phallocratism") and indeed creates a "devirilized,...desexed" self:

> Physical practices of the fist-fucking sort are practices that one can call devirilized, that is desexed [i.e., degenitalized]. They are in effect extraordinary counterfeit pleasures which one achieves by means of various devices, signs, symbols, or drugs....
>
> What these signs and symbols of masculinity are for is not to go back to something that would be on the order of phallocratism,...but rather to invent oneself, to make one's body into the site of production of extraordinarily polymorphous pleasures, pleasures that at the same time are detached from the valorization of the genitals and especially of the male genitals. After all, the point is to detach oneself from this virile form of obligatory pleasure—namely orgasm, orgasm in the ejaculatory sense, in the masculine sense of the term. (Foucault, quoted in Halperin, *Saint Foucault*, pp. 89-90)

Foucault valorizes "devirilized" "fist-fucking" because it is antithetical to "phallocratism" and "this virile form of obligatory pleasure, namely orgasm, orgasm in the ejaculatory sense, in the masculine sense of the term"; Lawrence, on the other hand, cherishes his phallus and his orgasm:

> The phallus is a column of blood that fills the valley of blood of a woman. The great river of male blood touches to its depths the great river of female blood [during sex]....It [sex in marriage] is the deepest of all communions, as all the religions, in practice, know. And it [sex in marriage] is one of the greatest mysteries, in fact, the greatest,...the supreme achievement...[is] mystic marriage.
>
> And this is the meaning of the sexual act: this Communion....This is marriage,...this communion of the two bloodstreams....
>
> Two rivers of blood, are man and wife, two distinct eternal streams, that have the power of touching and communing and so renewing, making new one another....And the phallus is the connecting-link between the two rivers, that establishes the two streams in a oneness....And this, this oneness gradually accomplished throughout a life-time in twoness, is the highest achievement of time or eternity. From it all things human spring, children and beauty and well-made things: all the true creations of humanity. And all we know of the will of God is that He wishes this, this oneness, to take place, fulfilled over a lifetime....("A Propos of *Lady Chatterley's Lover*," *Phoenix II*, pp. 505-506)

For Lawrence, "the phallus" is "the connecting-link" that makes possible "the deepest of all communions,...the supreme achievement" of "mystic marriage," "[the] Communion of the two blood-streams," male and female, "man and wife, two distinct eternal streams, that have the power of touching and communing, and so renewing, making new one another...."

Thus for Lawrence the phallus deserves credit for the "touching and communing and so renewing" that takes place in the male and female during Lawrentian sex—reverent, marital, monogamous sex ("this oneness gradually accomplished throughout a life-time in twoness"); in addition to the phallus Lawrence privileges marriage, monogamy and sex: sex, according to Lawrence, is the royal road to renewal of the individual human being through "the power of touching and communing." Through touching, communing and renewal of being, says Lawrence, comes our "phallic" future:

> the bridge to the future is the phallus....

> For the new impulse to life will never come without blood-contact; the true, positive blood-contact....And the essential blood-contact is between man and woman, always has been so, always will be. The contact of positive sex.
> If England is to be regenerated...then it will be by the arising of a new blood-contact, a new touch, and a new marriage. It will be a phallic...regeneration. For the phallus is only the great old symbol of godly vitality in a man, and of immediate contact. (Ibid., p. 508)

For Lawrence the phallus and heterosexuality are the way to "renewal" and "regeneration" for the individual man and woman and for the entire civilization as well; Foucault, on the other hand, deplores "phallocratism," finds that "sex is boring," and opts for "pleasure":

> It is very interesting to note that for centuries people...have always spoken about desire, and never about pleasure. "We have to liberate our desire," they say. No! We have to create new pleasure. And then maybe desire will follow. (Michel Foucault, quoted in *Saint Foucault*, p. 93)

But was Foucault really so enthusiastic about "pleasure" after all? In a confessional interview a few months before his death, Foucault admits that

> I have real difficulty in experiencing pleasure....Because I think that the kind of pleasure I would consider as the *real* pleasure would be so deep, so intense, so overwhelming that I couldn't survive it. I would die...A pleasure must be something incredibly intense. (Foucault, "The Minimalist Self," quoted in Macey, *The Lives of Michel Foucault*, p. 373)

Thus it is evident that Foucault with his fear of the "intense" and the "overwhelming," is actually afraid of "the *real* pleasure"; accordingly, Foucault's "desexualization" of pleasure can surely be seen as a *de-intensification* of pleasure; similarly, Foucault's assertion that "sex is boring" can certainly be seen as a defense against his fear of being "overwhelmed" by sex; and, finally, Foucault's attack on "phallocratic" orgasm—"this virile form of obligatory pleasure—namely orgasm, orgasm in the ejaculatory sense, in the masculine sense of the term"—Foucault's attack may indeed be seen as Foucault's means of "detach[ing] [him]self" from "pleasure."

With his fear of "pleasure" and the "intense," Foucault is surely no Lawrentian. Lawrence of course privileges "pleasure" in "sex":

> The quiver was going through the man's body, as the stream of consciousness...turn[ed] downwards. And he was helpless, as the penis in slow soft undulations filled and surged and rose up, and grew hard, standing there hard and overweening, in its curious towering fashion. The woman too trembled a little as she watched. "There! Take him, then! He's thine," said the man.
> And she quivered, and her own mind melted out. Sharp soft waves of unspeakable *pleasure* washed over her as he entered her, and started the curious molten thrilling that spread and spread till she was carried away with the last blind flush of extremity. (*Lady Chatterley's Lover*, Chapter XIV; italics mine)

Thus for Lawrence "unspeakable pleasure" is valorized as the beneficial effect of the "mind['s] melt[ing] out" during "sex": "the stream of consciousness...turn[ing] downwards" results in penile erection for "the man" and "unspeakable pleasure" for male and female who let themselves be moved by "The [sexual] quiver" in all its intensity; as for Lawrence's intensity, poet Robert Creeley recently stated:

> [N]o [other] writer I'm aware of has ever been able to convey as *intense* feelings as he [Lawrence]. (Robert Creeley, quoted in *Legacy of D. H. Lawrence: New Essays*, p. 133; my italics)

And of course F. R. Leavis valorizes "Lawrence's intense apprehension of...life," "the intensity...of the [Lawrentian] intuition," "[Lawrence's] poetic intensity," and "[Lawrence's] disturbing intensity" (F. R. Leavis, "Lawrence and Tradition," Chapter III, *D. H. Lawrence: Novelist*)

Meanwhile, Foucault longs for the Lawrentian "pleasure" and "intensity" even as he fears it: in 1983, in the midst of the early stages of the AIDS epidemic, Foucault told another homosexual intellectual, D. A. Miller of Berkeley, that he (Foucault) was not afraid of AIDS:

> "To die for the love of boys: What could be more beautiful?" (Quoted in *Passion of Michel Foucault*, p. 350)

Foucault said to Miller, in terms reminiscent of Lawrence-Mellors' words to Lady Chatterley:

> "I could die for the touch of a woman like thee" (*Lady Chatterley's Lover*, Chapter Ten)

—words which indicate that Lawrence-Mellors is willing to die for "the touch of a woman" in the same way that Foucault is willing to die for "the love of boys"; words which can help make the case that Foucault aspired to be a kind of homosexual-pedophile version of the Lawrentian heterosexual hero. There is, indeed, something poignant in Foucault's sentimental longing for and weird idealization of "the love of boys"—especially in view of the fact that Foucault evidently never attained the "pleasure" he yearned for, even though he did indeed die (from AIDS) for it: in the same period of his life during which he valorized "the love of boys"—and during which he was already (unknowingly) dying of AIDS, Foucault told an interviewer that

> I think that pleasure is a very difficult behavior. It's not as simple as that to enjoy one's self. And I must say that's my dream. I would like and I hope I'll die from an overdose of pleasure of any kind. Because I think it's really difficult and I always have the feeling that I do not feel *the* pleasure, the complete total pleasure and, for me, it's related to death. Because I think that the kind of pleasure I would consider as *the* real pleasure would be so deep, so intense, so overwhelming that I couldn't survive it. I would die. (Quoted in Miller, *Passion of Michel Foucault*, p. 306)

It is no wonder, then, that Foucault, having failed to attain "*the* pleasure" to which he aspired, can state that "we are all living more or less in a state of sexual misery" in "[the] dreary desert of sexuality" ("Power and Sex," in Michel Foucault, *Politics, Philosophy, Culture*); Lawrence, on the other hand, finds sex to be, not a source of misery, but of happiness and healing:

> "It heals it all up, that I can go into thee. I love thee that tha opened to me. I love thee that I came into thee like that." (*Lady Chatterley's Lover*, Chapter Twelve)
>
> She looked in his face anxiously. It was thin, and the cheekbones showed. But his eyes smiled at her, and she felt at home with him. There it was: suddenly, the tension of keeping up her appearances fell from her. Something flowed out of him physically, that made her feel inwardly at ease and happy, at home. With a woman's now alert instinct for happiness, she registered it at once. "I'm *happy* when he's there!" Not all the sunshine of Venice had given her this inward expansion and warmth. (*Lady Chatterley's Lover*, Chapter Eighteen; italics mine)

And of course there is the Lawrentian "pleasure":

> Then with a quiver of exquisite pleasure he touched the warm soft body, and touched her navel for a moment in a kiss. And he had to come into her at once....(*Lady Chatterley's Lover*, Chapter Ten)

Failing to attain Lawrentian healing, happiness and pleasure through sex, Foucault and his homosexual followers offer, in place of Lawrentian sexual joy, a kind of perverse sexual originality: it is as if gay theorist-activists think that they must parade their erotic "originality" in order to compensate for their sexual-passional-"Lawrentian" inadequacy; thus the ardent Foucauldian David Halperin praises

> his [Foucault's] claim that what gay men of his era were up to was "the real creation of new possibilities of pleasure, which people had no idea about previously," [a claim which] is amply borne out by the example of fist-fucking. For whatever else one might say about fist-fucking, there is no doubt about the fact that it *is*, historically speaking, a new pleasure. According to one expert writing in 1983, for example, fist-fucking "may be the only sexual practice invented in the twentieth century" (or, to be more precise, it *was* the only such practice invented in the twentieth century until the fin-de-siecle discoveries of phone sex and fax sex). (*Saint Foucault*, p. 92)

Evidently afflicted with a kind of "anxiety of influence" and "anxiety of intensity" in relation to Lawrentian "pleasure," Foucauldians must convince themselves that they are involved in "the real creation of new *possibilities* of pleasure"—"possibilities of pleasure," not "*real* pleasure"; indeed, it seems to me that, where "the *real* pleasure" is concerned, D. H. Lawrence, the great advocate and delineator of "the *real* [heterosexual] pleasure" in *Lady Chatterley's Lover* and elsewhere, is in fact the great precursor, the authentic exemplar of "bodily consciousness" and "pleasure" in relation to whom the Foucauldian gay theorists are anxiety-plagued, intensity-deficient mockeries. One Foucault scholar tells us about

> fist-fucking—the gentle insertion of one person's hand and forearm up another person's ass. It is an act of corporeal acrobatics that, in the words of one expert, requires "seducing one of the jumpiest and tightest muscles in the body." A long and elaborate ritual is necessary to perform the act at all, beginning with a douche and manicure, continuing with the slow, gradual introduction of first fingers, then the hand, and eventually the arm, lubricated by vast quantities of Crisco....
>
> ...fist-fucking was something new—a practice that neither

> Sade nor Sacher-Masoch had ever dreamed of. It was also, like a number of other S/M techniques, a practice that was, for many, all foreplay and no climax: its pleasures stopped short of orgasm. (Miller, *Passion of Michel Foucault*, pp. 266-267)

Indeed, one expert on fist-fucking explains that

> Many participants [in fist-fucking] aren't interested in coming. It's much more of a mind space between two people. (Geoff Mains, *Urban Aboriginals*, quoted in Miller, *Passion of Michel Foucault*, p. 267)

This Foucaultian practice of fist-fucking, which is evidently constitutive of "a mind space between two people," certainly demonstrates that the much-ballyhooed Foucaultian "pleasure" may most likely be essentially just another more sensational, more modern (or postmodern) manifestation of the "mental consciousness" that Lawrence so inveighed against. Indeed, Lawrence tells us that

> Sex is not *living* till it is *unconscious*: and it never becomes unconscious by *attending to* sex. (D. H. Lawrence letter to H. O. Meredith, 2 November 1915; my italics)

Certainly fist-fucking, with its "long and elaborate ritual," and its "mind space," is full of "attending to," and is neither "unconscious" nor "living": if it is "dead" then, how can it be a genuine and effective form of "resistance," of "sexual dissidence," of "transgression" and "subversion"?

"Resistance," "sexual dissidence," "transgression," "subversion": these are some of left-wing literary critic Jonathan Dollimore's favorite words. Dollimore avers

> the connection between political and sexual subversion (*Sexual Dissidence*, p. 240)

—yet surely Lawrentian "sexual subversion" is far more vital and alive than Foucaultian fist-fucking; yet it seems to me that there is an even more important point to be made here: by equating the political and the sexual, the left-wing critic, the Foucaultian critic, it seems to me, is essentially belittling sex, minimizing sex, domesticating sex, trying to deprive sex of its magical, mystical, "Lawrentian" element.

But why should these left-wing critics want to do this to sex? Lawrence himself can surely give us the answer:

> ...there are the *extremely conscious men* of *strong will* and traditional *social* habit. These men...are merely *automatic*. They are all for criticism of the condition of affairs, they are *the most advanced minds*. They never speak for themselves, but *always for the oppressed*; but *most of all against the repressors*. To these men the world is full of monsters, little monsters, who must be attacked at all costs.
>
> These *blameless men* engaged in attacking the little monsters of their day are the purest type of *disintegrators*. They have *reduced their own instinctive, sensuous self* to a viscous *mass*, their *minds triumph*, dry and scaly and brittle, the very-dry essence of corruption, engaged for ever in destruction, denial, negation, reduction. They have become purely instrumental, *they have ceased to have a self at all*. Like some extreme instrumental insects, they run brittly hither and thither, at their *tiny work of breaking down*, breaking down blindly and brittly the vast organic mass before them.
>
> But they are the very soul of the null envelope. This is the spirit of the null envelope itself,...purely instrumental, *without self*....They are the workers of pure nullity, within the envelope of nullity.
>
> These are our *most advanced minds*, crying for peace and universal brotherhood. For peace and universal brotherhood are indeed complete amorphous nullity within the envelope, within the fixed, accomplished form. (*Reflections on the Death of a Porcupine*, pp. 473-474; italics mine)

These hyper-political left-wing critics, Lawrence tells us, are "extremely conscious," full of "strong will and traditional social habit"—the "traditional social habit" which seeks to make superficial laws to have power over the social "shell" without changing and vitalizing the inner being of society and making real vital change. These "automatic" left-wing critics, full of "mental-consciousness" ("the most advanced minds"), have no inner being of their own; as Lawrence tells us:

> we have forgotten ourselves. We are Hamlet without the Prince of Denmark. We cannot *be*. "To be or not to be"—it is the question with us now....And nearly every Englishman says "Not to be." So he goes in for Humanitarianism and suchlike forms of not-being (D. H. Lawrence letter to Ernest Collings, 17 January 1913)

—and these "Humanitarian" left-wing critics "never speak for themselves, but always for the oppressed"—for the gays, for the blacks, for the feminists, etc., etc.—"but *most of all against the repressors*" (my italics)—and indeed, today, for the left-wing cultural critic, D. H. Lawrence is one of "the repressors," one of the "monsters...who must be attacked at all costs." Thus Dollimore vehemently refers to Lawrence as "This...despised writer"; and Eagleton attacks Lawrence as "the most pathologically sexist author." These left-wing critics with their moral pretensions ("blameless men," Lawrence sarcastically calls them) are "the purest type of disintegrators"—and, indeed, Dollimore, for example, valorizes

> the disintegration of [the] existing order (*Sexual Dissidence*, p. 88)

—and, like his left-wing master Terry Eagleton (see Scherr), Dollimore loves "contradictions":

> In a revolutionary conjuncture contradictions may contribute to the disintegration of an existing order...through terrible suffering, victimization, and struggle. That has to be said. In a non-revolutionary conjuncture contradictions render social processes the site of contest, struggle, and change. And, again, suffering, victimization, and struggle....In short: change, contest, and struggle are in part made possible by contradiction. But also suffering, victimization, and struggle. (*Sexual Dissidence*, p. 88)

But why all this left-wing interest in "disintegration," "suffering," "victimization" of others? The reason for this left-wing passion "for the oppressed; but most of all against the repressors," it seems to me, is that (as Lawrence says) these left-wingers have destroyed "their own instinctive, sensuous self" and rather than strive for any kind of genuine self-fulfillment they put all their passion into "pity" for "the oppressed"; as Lawrence explains:

> Let us only have had enough of pity: pity that stands before the glass and weeps for ever over the sight of its own tears. This is what we have made of Christ's Commandment: "Thou shalt love thy neighbour as thyself"—a mirror for the tears of self-pity. How do we love our neighbour? By taking to heart his poverty, his small wage, and the attendant evils thereof. And is that how we love our neighbour as *ourselves*? Do I, then, think of myself as a moneyed thing enjoying advantages, or a non-moneyed thing suffering from disadvantages? Evidently I do. Then why the tears? They must rise from the inborn knowledge that neither money nor non-money, advantages or disadvantages, matter supremely....I am weeping over my denied self. And I am very sorry for myself, held in the

> grip of some stronger force. Where can I find an image of myself? Ah, in the poor, in my poor neighbour labouring in the grip of an unjust system of capitalism. Let me look at him, let my heart be wrung, let me give myself to his service. Poor fellow, poor image, he is so badly off. Alas and alas, I do love my neighbour as myself: I am as anxious about his pecuniary welfare as I am about myself. I am so sorry for him, the poor X. He is a man like me. So I lie to myself and to him. For I do not care about him and his poverty: I care about my own unsatisfied soul. But I sidetrack to him, my poor neighbour, to vent on him my self-pity....
>
> He who would save his life must lose it....Certainly let him cast it upon the waters....[W]hen he reaches the shore, when he has traversed his known and come to the beach to meet the unknown, he must strip himself naked and plunge in, and pass out: if he dare. And the rest of his life he will be a stirring at the unknown, cast out upon the waters. But if he dare not plunge in, if he dare not take off his clothes and give himself naked to the flood, then let him prowl in rotten safety, weeping for pity of those he imagines worse off than himself. He dare not weep aloud for his own cowardice. And weep he must. So he will find him objects of pity. (*Study of Thomas Hardy*, Chapter 2)

Like a Biblical prophet, Lawrence here denounces the moral-ontological bankruptcy of "pity," which is really (Lawrence tells us) only displaced "self-pity"; this displaced "self-pity" is characteristic of the left-wing sociopolitical elites ("limousine liberals" we call them today), who, despite their socioeconomic "advantages," feel very sorry for themselves because they lack the emotional courage and inner strength to "meet the unknown" and discover/develop their true selves to the point of Lawrentian "spontaneous-creative fullness of being" (to use Lawrence's phrase in *Psychoanalysis and the Unconscious*); instead of internal strength of self these left-wing "disintegrators" find and develop their external sociopolitical strength by using their great mental consciousness ("they are the most advanced minds") to "speak...for the oppressed"; at the same time that they "speak...for the oppressed," these "blameless" left-wing thinkers—attacking "monsters" such as Lawrence—have also attacked and "reduced their own instinctive, sensuous self," this reduction of their "instinctive, sensuous self" leading them (the left-wing thinkers) to a state of affairs where "they have ceased to have a self at all."

With his unique insight Lawrence realizes that the fact that these left-wing political activists are "without self," "have ceased to have a self at all," is intimately related to the fact that "they have reduced their own instinctive, sensuous self to a viscous mass"—as Foucault and his followers have. Thus the privileging of the political over the sexual that is characteristic of the left-wing (Eagleton, Dollimore, Foucault, etc.) is deeply related to the fact that their "instinctive self" is "reduced" (i.e., disintegrated) and "viscous" (i.e., sticky, devoid of individuality); accordingly "they have ceased to have a self at all"; thus left-wing gay critic Leo Bersani valorizes

> the self-shattering which may be the secret reason for S/M...(Bersani, *Homos*, p. 94)

According to Bersani, in S/M's

> self-shattering, the ego renounces its power over the world....Through pain, S/M dramatizes (melodramatizes) the potential ecstasy in both a hyperbolic sense of self [in sadism] and the self's renunciation of its claims on the world [in masochism]. (*Homos*, pp. 94-95)

Bersani posits

> the jouissance of self-loss (*Homos*, p. 96)

and goes on to assert that

> S/M strips away defenses against *the joy of self-dissolution* (*Homos*, pp. 96-97; italics mine)

In contradistinction to Bersani's "joy of self-dissolution" and "jouissance of self-loss" is Lawrence's paradisal "way of freedom":

> There was another way, the way of freedom. There was the Paradisal entry into pure, single being, the individual soul [i.e., the individual self] taking precedence..., stronger than any pangs of emotion, a lovely state of free proud singleness, which accepts the obligation of the permanent connection with others, and with the other, submits to the yoke and leash of love, but never forfeits its own proud individual singleness, *even while it loves and yields.* (*Women in Love*, Chapter XIX, "Moony"; italics mine)

Here Lawrence-Birkin posits "the way of freedom" with its joyful ("Paradisal") achievement of maximum selfhood and individuality ("pure, single being")—an achievement in which "the individual soul" is privileged over "any pangs of emotion": thus the individual self ("soul") is "free," "proud," "single,"—yet at the same time it (the self) is certainly supremely capable of "lov[ing] and yield[ing]" without losing "its own proud individual singleness": thus there is love without the self-loss and self-dissolution that Bersani valorizes—indeed, Lawrence-Birkin makes it clear that

> One might abandon oneself utterly to the *moment*, but not to any other being. (*Women in Love*, Chapter XXIII, "Excurse")

Thus the Lawrentian self can abandon itself temporarily to "the *moment*" of passion, but will not abandon itself to the dubious joys of "self-loss" and "self-dissolution."

While the Lawrentian self, as Robert Langbaum notes, is "strong" and at the same time "open to connections" (*Mysteries of Identity*, p. 7), the left-wing self is extremely weak—and the left wing valorizes this weakness: left-wing Dollimore praises the homosexual self as a "decentered," "dispersed" self that is incapable of "phallocentric," "subjective depth" (*Sexual Dissidence*, p. 15)—and Dollimore, in his discussion and valorization of the most chic homosexual of all, Oscar Wilde, praises homosexual "transgression" ("deviant desire"):

> deviant desire [i.e., homosexuality], rather than creating a new *integrity of self*, actually *decentres or disperses the self*....(*Sexual Dissidence*, p. 14; italics mine)

Thus it is evident that, with their "instinctive, sexual self" reduced, broken down, "dispersed," the left-wing critics, as "their minds triumph," have no self at all, and, being "without self," they find their only deep satisfaction in the pursuit of socioeconomic-political power—which, as Lawrence has shown us many times (in Gerald Crich of *Women in Love*, Clifford Chatterley of *Lady Chatterley's Lover*, Rico of *St. Mawr*, among others), does not require a deep or authentic sense of self. Thus the left-wing cultural-literary critic's obsession with power and the *resistance* to power (i.e., counter-power, just another mode or form of power) is a result of their sensual-ontological failure (in the Lawrentian sense)—a failure which is manifested, for example, in Terry Eagleton's valorization of the socio-political body and elimination of the Lawrentian-physical body:

> The discourse of the body is not a matter of Lawrentian ganglions and suave loins of darkness, but a *politics* of the body, a rediscovery of its sociality through an awareness of the forces which con-

trol and subordinate it. (Terry Eagleton, *Literary Theory*, "Conclusion: Political Criticism," p. 215)

Indeed, today Eagleton, even though the head of Oxford's English department, is evidently not interested in "English" at all, but in "active political struggle":

> forms of consciousness may be transformed almost literally overnight,...in active political struggle. This is...an empirical fact. When men and women engaged in quite modest, local forms of political resistance find themselves brought by the inner momentum of such conflicts into direct confrontation with the power of the state, it is *possible* that their political consciousness *may be* definitively, irreversibly altered. (Eagleton, *Ideology: An Introduction*, pp. 223-224; my italics)

No longer interested in literature, Eagleton today from his catbird's seat at Oxford makes vague pronouncements about "local forms of political resistance" and "direct confrontation with the power of the state" that *may possibly*—just *possibly*, mind you—cause "men and women" to have their "political consciousness...definitively, irreversibly altered"; Eagleton himself does not seem to believe what he says about the efficacy of "direct confrontation with the power of the state" to bring about a change in the "political consciousness" of those "engaged" persons who are involved "in active political struggle"—and certainly Eagleton himself does not seem to have suffered from or participated in any "active political struggle" worthy of the name. Yet Eagleton, like other left-wing critics (e.g., Jonathan Dollimore), pays passionate homage to those people "engaged in quite modest, local forms of political *resistance*"—"resistance" being the key, Foucaultian term: for these armchair revolutionaries, these left-wing literary-cultural critics have come to valorize the "local...political resistance" of the homosexual(s)—especially since AIDS—and this valorization of the homosexual as the ideal practitioner of "resistance" and "transgression" has been accompanied by great admiration for the "selflessness" of the homosexual (regardless of the causes/origins of this "selflessness" in S/M or whatever); for

> "the death of the subject" [i.e., "the death of the self"] enters popular discourse most directly through the various challenges posed to the identification of subjectivity as such with the particular subject-position associated with *straight, white, middle-class men*. (Edelman, *Homographesis*, p. 96; my italics)

Thus the self in its subjective power is essentially identified with "straight, white, middle-class men"—the villains, according to left-wing ideology; and, by opposing these masculine-heterosexual-white "villains"—"villains" who (according to left wingers) dominate Western civilization—the homosexual in general and the gay AIDS activist in particular are doing their part to

> produce an oppositional political discourse that has the potential, in its necessary struggle against both the officially sanctioned representations of the [AIDS] epidemic and their intended constitution of a "normal" or "healthy" subjectivity [i.e., selfhood], to naturalize and reposition certain aspects of the ideological structures that inform and produce those noxious representations and those oppressive subjectivities in the first place. (*Homographesis*, p. 97)

The ultimate goal of these gay AIDS activists, if we are to believe one major gay critic, is "The Last Gasp of the White Male Heterosexuals" (*Homographesis*, p. 100), which means

> the imminent end of an empire, the demise of the imperial subject secure in his centrality to, his identification with, history and civilization (*Homographesis*, p. 100)

—that "empire" being essentially the "capitalist"-"sexist" "empire" so detested by (heterosexual) Eagleton and (homosexual) Edelman alike; that "imperial subject" being none other than the white male heterosexual so valorized in the work of D. H. Lawrence.

Lawrence's valorization of the heterosexual male subject goes hand in hand with his emphasis on the self. In one of his last essays, "We Need One Another," Lawrence avers that "men and women need one another" at the same time that

> We are all individualists: we are all egoists: we all believe intensely in freedom, our own at all events. We all want to be absolute, and sufficient unto ourselves. And it is a great blow to our self-esteem that we simply *need* another human being

for

> everything, even individuality itself, depends on relationship....
> We have our very individuality in relationship. Let us swallow this important and prickly fact....It is in the living touch between us and other people, other lives, other phenomena that we move and have our being....Our individuality means nothing.

> A skylark that was alone on an island would be songless and meaningless, his individuality gone, running about like a mouse in the grass. But if there were one female with him, it would lift him singing into the air, and restore him his real individuality.
>
> And so with men and women. It is in relationship to one another that they have their true individuality and their distinct being [i.e., their selfhood]; in contact, not out of contact. This is sex....It is a living contact, give and take: the great and subtle relationship of men and women, man and woman. In this and through this we become real individuals, without it, without the real contact, we remain more or less nonentities.

Thus Lawrence, by valorizing selfhood, "real individuality," and "being,"—and by postulating "sex" as the royal road to the attainment of these Lawrentian goals—is hated by the left wing: they consider Lawrence to be the antithesis of their values and virtues. But what are their values and virtues? With their "selflessness," their lack of "instinctive, sensuous self," their lust for "disintegration" and for power in academia, these anti-Lawrentian left-wing literary-cultural critics are evidently afflicted with what Lawrence calls "psychic starvation":

> Man doth not live by bread alone. It is time we made haste to settle the bread question, which after all is only the ABC of social economies, and proceeded to devote our attention to this much more profound and vital question: how to establish and maintain the circuit of vital polarity from which the psyche actually develops, as the body develops from the circuit of alimentation and respiration. We have reached the stage where we can settle the alimentation and respiration problems almost offhand. But woe betide us, the unspeakable agony we suffer from the failure to establish and maintain the vital circuits between ourselves and the effectual correspondent, the other human being, other human beings, and all the extraneous universe. The tortures of psychic starvation which civilized people proceed to suffer, once they have solved for themselves the bread-and-butter problems of alimentation, will not bear thought. Delicate, creative desire, sending forth its fine vibrations in search of the true pole of magnetic rest in another human being or beings, how it is thwarted, insulated by a whole set of india-rubber ideas and ideals and conventions, till every form of perversion and death-desire sets in! (*Psychoanalysis and the Unconscious*, Chapter VI)

With their "psychic starvation," their lack of "creative desire," these anti-Lawrentian literary-cultural critics have only their left-wing "india-rubber ideas and ideals and conventions" which promote "every form of perversion and death-desire"—and chief among these "perverted" left-wing "death-desire[s]" is the desire for "the death of the subject"; and, indeed, with "the death of the subject," the death of "desire" itself, as it (desire) is defeated by the left wing critics' favorite phenomenon, "History": "Always historicize!" commands Jameson at the very beginning of his left-wing classic *The Political Unconscious* ("Preface," p.9), as he goes on to assert "the primacy of History itself" ("Preface," p. 14); as for Jameson's "History,"

> History is what hurts, it is what refuses desire and sets inexorable limits to individual as well as collective praxis.... (*Political Unconscious*, p. 102)

As the proponents of "History," the enemy of "desire," Jameson, Eagleton, Dollimore and the rest must perforce fight against D. H. Lawrence, who even today is celebrated (by the right wing!) as

> our supreme genius in the depiction of the relationships between men and women...(Paul Dean, "D. H. Lawrence in love," *The New Criterion*, February 1995, p. 23)

Indeed, Lawrence can be seen as an obstacle to the power of Jameson's "History"; as Denis Donoghue notes,

> Lawrence is primarily concerned with...reality, the sense in which it is before and after history, and often confounding history. (*Thieves of Fire*, p. 121)

The Lawrentian "reality" which is "before and after history, and often confounding history" is the reality of Lawrentian desire itself—desire which is characterized by

> the living presence that all ideals deny. (Gerald J. Butler, *Recovering Literature*, Volume 15, Summer, 1987, p. 17)

The left-wing idealist literary-cultural critics, in denying "the living presence" of individuality, sex and selfhood, must as a matter of course deny "the living presence" of Lawrence as well; this left-wing denial of Lawrence is indeed a great loss, for, as F. R. Leavis states,

> the insight, the wisdom, the revived and re-educated feeling for health, that Lawrence brings are what, as our civilization goes, we desperately need. (Leavis, *D. H. Lawrence: Novelist*, "Introduction")

But "what...our civilization...desperately need[s]" is certainly not what is needed by "the System," "the System" whose

> rulers or leaders of states, churches, or any other institutions...say high sentiments are good because, so long as people hold them, people are, as individuals, blind to even their most elemental impulses, wishes and needs. In other words, high sentiments justify the rulers or leaders in exploiting us as individuals...for the survival, *not of our individual selves* but of a social or political or religious system. (Wayne Burns, *The Vanishing Individual*, p. 22)

For the left-wing "leaders" of academic "institutions"—Eagleton, Jameson, Foucault, etc.—the "high sentiments" of neo-Marxism, feminism, "diversity" (e.g., gay affirmation, reverse discrimination, multi-culturalism) go hand in glove with the way in which

> the System is pressuring all of society, all of mankind, into a state of mass conformity bordering on mass neurosis in which individual deviations from the System's norm have to be stamped out at any cost. (Wayne Burns, *The Vanishing Individual*, p. 55)

This "System" based on "high sentiments" and "mass conformity" made it easily possible for a black man to get away with murdering a white woman (and white Jewish man) once the System's pieties about "racism" were manipulated by his black lawyer in such a way that "individual deviations from the System's norm"—the norm that "racism" makes it permissible for blacks to commit any crime they desire and be found "not guilty"—were not even attempted by the white members of the jury, and instead "jury nullification" of justice prevailed. Similarly, the academic System's pieties about the "evil" Lawrentian white heterosexual male, with his "centered" self, his "pleasure," his "desire," and his individuality, make it virtually inevitable that Lawrence will be "increasingly disregarded and often despised" (Dollimore 268) by the left-wing academic elite. Yet perhaps this is to the good, for, as Jerry Zaslove states:

> Although D. H. Lawrence occupies a unique place in twentieth century English literature, his reputation...must nevertheless be insecure if the inner nature of his critical vision is to be understood. ("Introduction" to Gerald J. Butler, *This Is Carbon*)

And surely, as long as the academic-intellectual establishment continues to be dominated by the current "ideologized, spectacular intellectual culture with its mock left-wing jargons" (Zaslove viii), it is extremely unlikely that Lawrence's "reputation" will improve.

WORKS CITED

Bersani, Leo. *Homos*. Cambridge: Harvard University Press, 1995.
Burns, Wayne. *The Vanishing Individual. Recovering Literature* 21 (1995).
Butler, Gerald J. *This Is Carbon*. Seattle: Genitron Press, 1986.
Dean, Paul. "D. H. Lawrence in love." *The New Criterion*, February 1995: 17-23.
Dollimore, Jonathan. *Radical Tragedy*. Brighton: Harvester Press, 1984.
Dollimore, Jonathan. *Sexual Dissidence*. Oxford: Clarendon Press, 1991.
Donoghue, Denis. *Thieves of Fire*. London: Faber and Faber, 1973.
Eagleton, Terry. *Literary Theory: An Introduction*. Oxford: Basil Blackwell, 1983.
Eagleton, Terry. *Ideology: An Introduction*. London: Verso, 1991.
Edelman, Lee. *Homographesis: Essays in Gay Literary and Cultural Theory*. New York: Routledge, 1994.
Foucault, Michel. *The History of Sexuality: An Introduction*. New York: Random House, 1978.
Foucault, Michel. *The Foucault Reader*. Ed. Paul Rabinow. New York: Pantheon, 1984.
Foucault, Michel. *Politics, Philosophy, Culture*. Ed. Lawrence D. Kritzman. New York: Routledge, 1988.
Foucault, Michel. *Power/Knowledge: Selected Interviews and Other Writings 1972-1977*. New York: Pantheon, 1980.
Fraser, Nancy. "Foucault's Body Language." *Salmagundi* 61 (1983): 55-70.
Halperin, David. *Saint Foucault*. New York: Oxford University Press, 1995.
Harpham, Geoffrey Galt. *The Ascetic Imperative in Culture and Criticism*. Chicago: University of Chicago Press, 1987.
Jameson, Fredric. *The Political Unconscious*. Ithaca: Cornell University Press, 1981.
Langbaum, Robert. *The Mysteries of Identity: A Theme in Modern Literature*. New York: Oxford University Press, 1977.
Lawrence, D. H. *Reflections on the Death of a Porcupine and Other Essays*. Ed. Michael Herbert. Cambridge: Cambridge University Press, 1988.
Lawrence, D. H. "Sex versus Loveliness." *Phoenix II: Uncollected, Unpublished, and Other Prose Works by D. H. Lawrence*. Ed. Warren Roberts and Harry T. Moore. New York: Viking, 1970.

Lawrence, D. H. Lawrence. "A Propos of *Lady Chatterley's Lover.*" *Phoenix II.* Ed. Roberts and Moore. New York: Viking, 1970.

Lawrence, D. H. *Women in Love.* New York: Viking, 1960.

Lawrence, D. H. "Study of Thomas Hardy." *Phoenix: The Posthumous Papers of D. H. Lawrence.* Ed. Edward D. McDonald. New York: Viking, 1936.

Lawrence, D. H. "We Need One Another." *Phoenix: The Posthumous Papers of D. H. Lawrence.* Ed. Edward D. McDonald. New York: Viking, 1936.

Lawrence, D. H. *Lady Chatterley's Lover.* New York: Grove Press, 1962.

Lawrence, D. H. *Psychoanalysis and the Unconscious & Fantasia of the Unconscious.* New York: Viking, 1960.

Lawrence, D. H. *The Letters of D. H. Lawrence.* Ed. Aldous Huxley. New York: Viking, 1932.

Lawrence, D. H. *The Letters of D. H. Lawrence: Volume II, June 1913- October 1916.* Ed. George J. Zytaruk. Cambridge: Cambridge University Press, 1981.

Leavis, F. R. *D. H. Lawrence: Novelist.* New York: Simon & Schuster, 1969.

Macey, David. *The Lives of Michel Foucault.* New York: Pantheon, 1993.

Miller, James. *The Passion of Michel Foucault.* New York: Simon & Schuster, 1993.

Scherr, Barry J. "The 'Dark Fire of Desire' in D. H. Lawrence's *Sons and Lovers.*" *Recovering Literature* 16 (1988): 37-67.

Scherr, Barry J. "Lawrence's Dark Flood." *Paunch* 63-64 (December 1990): 209-246.

Scherr, Barry J. "D. H. Lawrence's Darkness." *Recovering Literature* 18 (1991): 8-40.

Scherr, Barry J. "Eagleton's Flight from Lawrence and Leavis." *Recovering Literature* 22 (1995): 35-56.

Seigel, Jerrold. "Avoiding the Subject: A Foucaultian Itinerary."*Journal of the History of Ideas* 51 (1990): 273-299.

Trilling, Lionel. "D. H. Lawrence: A Neglected Aspect." *Speaking of Literature and Society.* Ed. Diana Trilling. New York: Harcourt Brace Jovanovich, 1980.

CHAPTER SIX

Conclusion

Lawrence's "Poetic Immortality" Today

Lawrence in his last years evidently lost interest in the subject of homosexuality in general and in "saving" homosexuals from their "blasphemy against love" (*Letters II* 321) in particular; nevertheless, Lawrence's aspiration to poetic immortality remained undaunted and undimmed: only his strategy for attaining it had changed somewhat, as we shall see.

Lawrence's new attitude toward homosexuality can be seen in his letter of 13 July 1927 to Dr. Trigant Burrow, an American psychiatrist; in his letter Lawrence makes a brief, facetious reference to homosexuality:

> I'll try and find your paper on the "Genesis and Meaning of Homosexuality"—you should have said "Genesis and Exodus."

Here Lawrence is evidently expressing his jocularity in relation to the issue and analysis of homosexuality; furthermore, he is expressing his hope that homosexuality, regardless of its origin ("Genesis"), will someday disappear, depart, leave (i.e., have an "Exodus"). Thus Lawrence at this stage of his aspiration to poetic strength and poetic immortality did not feel that it was essential for him to deal with, solve, "save" the subject of homosexuality in order to assure his poetic immortality. Indeed, Lawrence's strategy for attaining poetic immortality at this point definitely did not include dealing with homosexuality; for in the last few years of Lawrence's life—his

Lady Chatterley's Lover period—Lawrence in his quest for poetic immortality underwent what Bloomian literary theory calls "*Askesis*,...a [psychic-poetic] movement...[in which the strong poet] yields up part of his own human and imaginative endowment" (Bloom, *Anxiety*, p. 15) in order that he may attain poetic immortality; Lawrence's "*askesis*, a self-curtailment which seeks transformation at the expense of narrowing the creative circumference" (*Anxiety*, p. 119) of the potentially strong poet, is brilliantly manifested in *Lady Chatterley's Lover*, where Lawrence enacts "a curtailment, a sacrifice of some part of himself whose absence will individuate him more, as a poet" (*Anxiety*, p. 121)—and part of Lawrence's "curtailment" of "his own human and imaginative endowment" was the cessation of his "human and imaginative" aspiration to "save" homosexuals; during his *Lady Chatterley's Lover* period, Lawrence's exclusive preoccupation was the male-female "sex relation"; indeed, he even seemed to forget that he had ever been interested in anything other than the male-female sexual relationship: in April 1927, in the very midst of his *Lady Chatterley's Lover* period, and shortly before his jocular remarks on "Genesis and Exodus" of "Homosexuality" to Trigant Burrow, Lawrence proudly declared that

> I'm in a quandary about my novel, *Lady Chatterley's Lover*. It's what the world would call very improper. But you know it's not really improper—I always labour at the same thing, to make the sex relation valid and precious, instead of shameful. (D. H. Lawrence letter to Nancy Pearn, 12 April 1927)

"To make the sex relation valid and precious, instead of shameful": this is Lawrence's great aim and aspiration, the attainment of which is part and parcel of his achievement of "poetic immortality"; and, evidently, Lawrence has succeeded in making his name synonymous with making "heterosex" a "valid and precious" phenomenon—as one scholar of the philosophy of sex recently commented:

> D. H. Lawrence may have gone in a bit over his head, so to speak, but at least he was clear in his blasphemous piety about the unappreciated significance, the wonder of heterosex. (Solomon, "Heterosex," p. 206)

In contradistinction to Lawrence's "blasphemous piety about...the wonder of heterosex" is the "blasphemy against love," homosexuality, which nowadays is the site of far more "cultural" attention and "intellectual" excitement than "heterosex" is:

> In the excitement, confusion, liberation, oral and moral indignation inspired by the rediscovery of homosexual love and legitimacy, heterosex has been somewhat left behind. Adam and Eve become a tired paradigm, a fashion too established and too familiar to inspire philosophical speculation and excitement. (Solomon, "Heterosex," p. 205)

For Lawrence, on the other hand, all the "excitement" is to be found in "shocking" heterosexuality, while homosexuality essentially is unexciting, indeed "damp"; in a letter written at the height of his *Lady Chatterley's Lover* period, Lawrence forthrightly declares:

> Andre Gide's *Corydon*...is a damp little production....
> ...And moreover I've got on my conscience a novel I wrote, and which is much too shocking...for any publisher. Says shit! and fuck! in so many syllables....But it's a good novel—love, as usual—and very nice too, but says all the things it shouldn't say....(D. H. Lawrence letter to Beatrice Campbell, 3 February 1928)

Famed gay writer and Nobel Prize winner Andre Gide's *Corydon*, an impassioned defense of homosexuality, was recently praised by one major left-wing scholar of gay theory:

> In 1924 he [Gide] published *Corydon*, a courageous defense of homosexuality which he declared to be his most important book....In *Corydon* he did not just demand tolerance for homosexuality but also insisted that, far from being contrary to nature, it was intrinsically natural; that heterosexuality prevails merely because of convention; that historically homosexuality is associated with great artistic and intellectual achievement while heterosexuality is indicative of decadence. About some of these provocative and suspect claims I would only observe that the fury they have generated in commentators is as significant as, and related to, Gide's reasons for making them in the first place. Gide was exactly right when he said: "we are accepted if we are plaintive; but if we cease to be pitiable we are at once accused of arrogance." (Dollimore 1991, 12).

But Lawrence's response to Gide's *Corydon*, far from being one of "fury," is indeed one of bored contempt: for Lawrence, Gidean "homosex" is dull and lifeless, a flaccid penis ("damp" and "little"); Lawrentian heterosex, on the other hand, is "shocking," excitingly unconventional and transgressive, for his "heterosexy" novel *Lady Chatterley's Lover* ("love as usual") "says all the things it shouldn't say"—and in the process of "say[ing] all the things it shouldn't say"

Lady Chatterley guarantees Lawrence's priority and poetic immortality; for, as Eric Bentley tersely remarked,

> heterosexual intercourse couldn't be glamorized until the 1920's and even then only in a banned book—*Lady Chatterley* (Bentley 131)

—and thus, by being *the first* to "glamorize" heterosex Lawrence assured his originality, uniqueness, "priority"—all elements of poetic immortality. Defining "priority," Harold Bloom tells us that

> the commodity in which poets deal, their authority, their property, turns upon priority. They own, they are, what they become first in naming. (Bloom, *Anxiety*, p. 64)

"First in naming" the "glamorous" nature of "heterosexual intercourse," Lawrence the author of *Lady Chatterley* even today is portrayed as having a "flagrantly heterosexual, oppressively phallic image" (Parkes 1996, 111)—an image for which "Lawrence" has certainly suffered in these politically correct times. For Lawrence's presentment of the "true glamour" of heterosex (Bentley 130) runs counter to the academic-intellectual elite headed by Terry Eagleton and Eve Kosofsky Sedgwick, among others, whose ideology is antithetical to

> his [Lawrence's] own visceral,...economically blind account of a world in which every issue for every inhabitant revolved around bourgeois sexual prohibition and the worship or subversion of the phallus. (Sedgwick, *Between Men*, p. 215)

Feminist-gay theorist Sedgwick cannot relate to the "visceral" D. H. Lawrence; according to Sedgwick, Lawrence is inexcusably oblivious of political economy (i.e., he is "economically blind"): all Lawrence cares about, Sedgwick complains, is the "sexual," "the phallus"; and Sedgwick's priggish, politically correct kvetching here can perhaps best be answered by Lawrence himself, in his own sardonic remark about the possibility of getting *Lady Chatterley's Lover* published; he wrote to his publisher:

> I've been thinking about *Lady Chatterley's Lover* and think I'll get him typed in London before long, and let you have a copy, so that you can see how possible or impossible he is. But there is much more latitude these days, and *a man dare possibly possess a penis*. (D. H. Lawrence letter to Martin Secker, 29 April 1927; my italics)

But Eve Kosofsky Sedgwick evidently disagrees; indeed, her reductive ridicule of Lawrence's world view as one "in which every issue for every inhabitant revolved around bourgeois sexual prohibition and the worship or subversion of the phallus" is extremely reminiscent of the "gutter paper" (Kinkead-Weekes 1996, 672) *John Bull*'s attack on Lawrence some sixty years before Sedgwick's:

> Unfortunately for literature as for himself, Mr. Lawrence has a diseased mind. He is obsessed by sex. We are not aware that he has written any book during his career that has not over-emphasized this side of life.
>   Now, since he has failed to conquer his obsession, the obsession has conquered him. He can write about nothing else, apparently. ("Famous Novelist's Shameful Book: A Landmark in Evil," *John Bull*, 20 October 1928, in Draper, p. 278)

Like Eve Kosofsky Sedgwick, *John Bull* deplores Lawrence's "obsession" with (hetero)sex; but, unlike *John Bull*, Sedgwick herself has her own approbatory "obsession" with one of the "sexualities"—homosexuality:

> It *feels* queer, and good—I'm sure I wasn't the only one at the [1992 gay pride] march to have this sensation—when the wave of a broadly based public movement somehow overtakes…the little, stubborn current of an individual narrative or obsession, an individual wellspring of narrow, desiring cathexis and cognition. (*Tendencies*, p. xi)

Valorizing "the wave of a broadly based public movement," Sedgwick decries "the little, stubborn current" of "an individual" emotion and passion, which she characterizes as "little," "stubborn," "narrow" and "desiring"—all evidently derogatory terms in Sedgwick's lexicon. Clearly Eve Kosofsky Sedgwick, with her privileging of politically correct "public movement[s]" over individual desire and passion, is antithetical to Lawrence, with his valorization of "the sexual individual" (D. H. Lawrence letter to Trigant Burrow, 13 July 1927)—"the sexual individual" whose mind must experience Lawrentian liberation:

> The mind has an old grovelling fear of the body and the body's potencies. It is the mind we have to liberate….("A Propos of *Lady Chatterley's Lover*")

Aspiring to liberate "the sexual individual" mind and so reach "the deeper sex of the real individual" (ibid.), Lawrence saw this Lawrentian liberation as the way for "the living self" to attain "fullness of being"—and for Lawrence himself to attain the status of "saviour":

> Each human self is single...and unique....Each self is unique, and therefore incomparable....The living self has one purpose only: to come to its own fullness of being, as a tree comes into full blossom, or a bird into spring beauty, or a tiger into lustre ("Democracy," *Phoenix* 714)

—or a D. H. Lawrence into "poetic immortality": for what Lawrence wanted for himself—uniqueness, individuality, "fullness of being"—he indeed wanted, *mutatis mutandis*, for all human beings—human beings who, in consequence of following the Lawrentian way to "new connection," greater "life," would perforce make Lawrence "an aristocrat," "a saviour":

> If a man, whether by thought or action, makes *life* he is an aristocrat....Man's life consists in a connection with all things in the universe. Whoever can establish, or initiate, a new connection between mankind and the circumambient universe is, in his own degree, a saviour. ("Aristocracy," *Phoenix II* 477-478)

As "saviour," Lawrence "initiate[s]...a new connection between mankind and the circumambient universe" in the realm of sex (heterosex, that is); he "establish[es]...a new connection" between "thought and action, word and deed" in the sexual domain:

> In the past, man was too weak-minded, or crude-minded to contemplate his own physical body and physical functions, without getting all messed up with physical reactions that overpowered him. It is no longer so. Culture and civilisation have taught us to separate the word from the deed, the thought from the act or the physical reaction. We now know that the act does not necessarily follow on the thought. In fact, thought and action, word and deed are two separate forms of consciousness, two separate lives which we lead. We need...to keep a connection. But while we think we do not act, and while we act we do not think. The great necessity is that we should act according to our thoughts, and think according to our acts. But while we are in thought we cannot really act, and while we are in action we cannot really think. The two conditions, of thought and action, are mutually exclusive. Yet they should be related in harmony.
>
> And this is the real point of this book [*Lady Chatterley's Lover*]. I want men and women to be able to *think* sex, fully, completely, honestly, and cleanly....Years of honest thought of sex, and

> years of struggling action in sex will bring us at last to where we want to get, to our real and accomplished chastity, our completeness, when our sexual act and our sexual thought are in harmony, and the one does not interfere with the other. ("A Propos of *Lady Chatterley's Lover*")

According to Lawrence, up until his poetic intervention human beings were incapable of contemplating their "physical body and physical functions" without being overwhelmed by "physical reactions"; now, according to Lawrence, with the advent of *Lady Chatterley's Lover*, it has been demonstrated that it is possible to *think* about sex (i.e., by reading and contemplating *Lady Chatterley's Lover*) without "the act [of sex]...necessarily follow[ing] on the thought." Up to now, Lawrence tells us, humanity in sex did not "act according to [their] thoughts, and think according to [their] acts": there was no "harmony" between "thought" and "act" in the sexual realm. But Lawrence as "saviour" makes the new connection between "our sexual act and our sexual thought," places them "in harmony," which leads to "our completeness"—a "completeness" which Western civilization ("we") will enjoy when "we...catch up":

> Now we have to catch up, and make a balance between the consciousness of sex and the act of sex, the thoughtful consciousness of the body's sensations and experiences, and these sensations and experiences themselves. Balance up the consciousness of the act, and the act itself. Get the two in harmony. It means having a proper reverence for sex, and a proper awe of the body's strange experiences. ("A Propos of *Lady Chatterley's Lover*")

By connecting "the consciousness of sex" with "the act of sex," a Lawrentian "harmony" is enacted, the result of which is a veritably religious appreciation of the cosmic nature of sex: "a proper reverence for sex, and a proper awe of the body's strange experiences" in sex.

"Reverence," "awe": these emotions towards heterosex are at the root of the Lawrentian "connection with...the universe"; a connection based on the Lawrentian premise that "Life is only bearable when the mind and the body are in harmony, and there is a *natural* balance between the two, and each has a *natural* respect for the other."

Lawrence's emphasis on the "natural"—"*natural* balance," "*natural* respect"—is a mainstay of his role as "saviour"; it is

> The body...in its spontaneous *natural* self (ibid.; italics mine)

which Lawrence aspires to save from being "dead or paralysed" (ibid.). To save "the body...in its spontaneous natural self" Lawrence vividly "initiate[s]...a new connection between mankind and the circumambient universe" pertaining to the "real" sexual relation,

> the real sex in a man, that has the rhythm of the seasons and the years, the crisis of the winter solstice and the passion of Easter....[,] the profound, rhythmic sex of a man's inward life....("A Propos of *Lady Chatterley's Lover*")

Thus, making "real" the "connection" between "real sex" and the natural rhythms of "the circumambient universe," Lawrence indeed presents himself as the "saviour" of "sex and marriage":

> Now this question of sex and marriage is of paramount importance....
>
> ...the Church is established upon the element of *union* in mankind. And the first element of union in the Christian world is the marriage-tie. The marriage-tie, the marriage bond,...is the fundamental connecting link in Christian society. Break it, and you will have to go back to the overwhelming dominance of the State, which existed before the Christian era. The Roman State was all-powerful....It was the same in Greece....
>
> Now the question is, do we want to go back, or forward [i.e., the modern "Soviet State"], to any of these forms of State control? Do we want to be like the Romans...?...Do we want to be bullied by a Soviet?
>
> For my part, I have to say No! every time. And having said it, we have to come back and consider the famous saying, that perhaps the greatest contribution to the social life of man made by Christianity is—marriage. Christianity brought marriage into the world: marriage as we know it....Christianity made marriage in some respects inviolate, not to be violated by the State. It is marriage, perhaps, which has given man the best of his freedom, given him his little kingdom of his own within the big kingdom of the State, given him his foothold of independence on which to stand and resist an unjust State. Man and wife, a king and queen with one or two subjects, and a few square yards of territory of their own: this, really, is marriage. It is a true freedom because it is a true fulfilment, for man, woman, and children.
>
> Do we then want to break marriage? If we do break it, it means we all fall to a far greater extent under the direct sway of the State. Do we want to fall under the direct sway of the State, any State? For my part, I don't. ("A Propos of *Lady Chatterley's Lover*")

Appropriating "Christianity" as an aid to his status as "saviour" of Western civilization, Lawrence seizes upon "this question of sex and marriage" as the ultimate issue for humanity—an issue the importance of which, according to Lawrence, was first premised thousands of years ago, by the Christian Church, in "the Christian world"; evidently disregarding the "love battle" aspect of marriage that he so uniquely and unsurpassedly delineates (see Scherr, 1986 and 1994), Lawrence at this stage of his strategy for assuring his "poetic immortality" now presents marriage as the supreme emblem of *union* in mankind." Postulating "the marriage-tie, the marriage bond" as "the fundamental connecting link in Christian society," Lawrence makes it clear that the Lawrentian vision has no meaningful place in it for homosexuality; furthermore, *pace* Foucault and his left-wing followers who posit and decry the existence of "heterosexual tyranny" (Dollimore 59), Lawrence decisively and authoritatively states that hetero-marriage is the only obstacle in the way of "the overwhelming dominance of the State." Thus, by vigorously advocating and delineating the connection between marriage and freedom, Lawrence explains, he is indeed acting as the "saviour" of "the best of [humankind's] freedom,…a true freedom"—a "freedom" which makes it possible for man "to stand and *resist* an unjust State" (italics mine). Thus, some fifty years before Foucault, Lawrence is talking about "resistance"—but "resistance," not in the context of Foucaultian homosexual-S/M "bodies and pleasures" (Foucault, *History*, p. 157) in which

> Fist-fucking and sado-masochism appear…as utopian political practices,…a means of *resistance* (Halperin, *Saint Foucault*, p. 97; italics mine)

—but rather in the Lawrentian heterosexual-marital context of hetero-marriage,

> marriage…, a sacrament of *man and woman* united in the sex communion, and never to be separated, except by death. And even when separated by death, still not freed from the marriage. Marriage, as far as the individual went, eternal. Marriage, making one complete body out of two incomplete ones, and providing for the complex development of the man's soul and the woman's soul in unison, throughout a life-time. ("A Propos of *Lady Chatterley's Lover*"; italics mine)

Lawrence's paean to hetero-marriage is part and parcel of his emphasis on "spontaneous-creative fullness of being" (*Psychoanalysis and the*

Unconscious, p. 48) in the individual man and woman; for, according to Lawrence, "Marriage...[provides] for the complex development of the man's soul and the woman's soul in unison, throughout a life-time": without the "unison" of marriage, the maximum "complex development" of the individual man and woman would not take place. It is only through hetero-marriage, Lawrence declares,

> Marriage sacred and inviolable, the great way of earthly fulfilment for man and woman, in unison...("A Propos of *Lady Chatterley's Lover"*)

that Lawrentian "spontaneous-creative fullness of being" can be realized.

With marriage as "the great way of earthly fulfilment for man and woman," Lawrence as the great advocate of marriage becomes the earthly "saviour" of humanity, making even the Catholic Church a mere adjunct to his aspirations toward "poetic immortality" and "saviourhood":

> I see the soul as something which must be developed and fulfilled throughout a life-time, sustained and nourished, developed and further fulfilled, to the very end....
> Then I realise that marriage...is essential, and that the old Church knew best the enduring needs of man....The Church established marriage for life, for the fulfilment of the soul during life, not postponing it [i.e., "the fulfilment of the soul"] till the after-death. (Ibid.)

Thus, for Lawrence, "the soul" is an ontological entity that reaches complete development and fulfillment, not in the afterlife (what Lawrence calls "the after-death"), but rather "throughout a life-time" here on earth; and, according to Lawrence, this "soul"-fulfillment ("fulfilment of the soul") can only be attained through the religious ("sacred") way of Lawrentian "Marriage sacred and inviolable," an experience which (according to Lawrence) is a supreme part of "The rhythm of life":

> The old Church knew that life is here our portion, to be lived, to be lived in fulfilment....The rhythm of life itself was preserved by the Church hour by hour, day by day, season by season, year by year, epoch by epoch, down among the people....It is the rhythm of the daily sun. We feel it in the festivals, the processions, Christmas, the Three Kings, Easter, Pentecost, St. John's Day, All

> Saints, All Souls. This is the wheeling of the year, the movement of the sun through solstice and equinox, the coming of the seasons, the going of the seasons. And it is the inward rhythm of man and woman too, the sadness of Lent, the delight of Easter, the wonder of Pentecost, the fires of St. John, the candles on the graves of All Souls, the lit-up tree of Christmas, all representing kindled rhythmic emotions in the souls of men and women. And men experience the great rhythm of emotion man-wise, women experience it woman-wise, and in the unison of men and women it [i.e., "The rhythm of life itself," "the great rhythm of emotion"] is complete. ("A Propos of *Lady Chatterley's Lover*")

Here Lawrence establishes the "vital" "new connection" ("Aristocracy," *Phoenix II*) between "The rhythm of life itself" and "the inward rhythm of man and woman," man and woman whose "unison" makes the consummation of "The rhythm of life itself," together with the culmination of "the great rhythm of emotion"— an emotional rhythm that supremely manifests itself in "the rhythm of marriage":

> God created the universe new every day:...to the living, emotional soul, this is true. Every dawn dawns upon an entirely new universe....And the soul of man and the soul of woman is new in the same way, with the infinite delight of life and the ever-newness of life. So a man and a woman are new to one another throughout a life-time, in the rhythm of marriage that matches the rhythm of the year. ("A Propos of *Lady Chatterley's Lover*")

"The rhythm of marriage," according to Lawrence, is the supreme connection that humanity is capable of attaining with "the universe" that "God created"—a universe the "newness" of which is connected with the "newness" a man and woman have for one another in the natural "rhythm of marriage that matches the rhythm of the year." For Lawrence, "a man and a woman"—"Sex"—is the most poignant manifestation of "ever-newness" "in the universe":

> Sex is the balance of male and female in the universe, the attraction, the repulsion, the transit of neutrality, the new attraction, the new repulsion, always different, *always new*....Sex goes through the rhythm of the year, in man and woman, ceaselessly changing: the rhythm of the sun in his relation to the earth. Oh, what a catastrophe for man when he cut himself off from the rhythm of the year, from his unison with the sun and the earth. Oh, what catastrophe, what a maiming of love when it was made a...merely per-

> sonal feeling, taken away from the rising and the setting of the sun, and cut off from the magic connection of the solstice and the equinox! This is what is the matter with us. We are bleeding at the roots, because we are cut off from the earth and sun and stars, and love is a grinning mockery, because, poor blossom, we plucked it from its stem on the tree of Life, and expected it to keep on blooming in our civilized vase on the table. (Ibid.)

Here Lawrence valorizes and defines "Sex" as "the balance of male and female in the universe,...always different, always new," with "the infinite delight of life and the ever-newness of life" being manifested in sex in a natural "rhythm of the year, in man and woman, ceaselessly changing," like "the rhythm of the sun in his relation to the earth." But this supremely natural, ever-new, vital "rhythm of life itself" in "Sex" is characteristic only of the uniquely Lawrentian "Sex": for, according to Lawrence, man today for the most part is "cut...off from the rhythm of the year, from his unison with the sun and the earth"; furthermore, as a result of man's state of being "cut off" from nature ("the sun and the earth"), man's ability to love is maimed inasmuch as human love today has been "taken away from the rising and the setting of the sun, and cut off from the magic connection" with nature ("the solstice and the equinox"); because man today is cut off from nature—"cut off from the earth and sun and stars"—modern love is a "mockery," unnatural like a "poor blossom" that has been taken out of its natural, vital state ("plucked...from its stem on the tree of Life") and placed "in our civilized vase on the table." Lawrence makes it clear that, for him, hetero-married love is all-important—but only if it is rooted in nature:

> Marriage is the clue to human life, but there is no marriage apart from the wheeling sun and the nodding earth, from the straying of the planets and the magnificence of the fixed stars. ("A Propos of *Lady Chatterley's Lover*")

In illuminating the vital connection between human sexual love and natural-cosmic phenomena ("the wheeling sun," "the nodding earth," "the straying of the planets," "the fixed stars"), Lawrence once more succeeds in portraying himself as having attained "saviour" status; indeed, Lawrence actually appropriates Jesus himself to his (Lawrence's) quest for "saviour" status and "poetic immortality" by means of Lawrentian "phallic" marriage,

> marriage, the mystery of marriage, marriage which fulfils itself here, in this life. We may well believe that in heaven there is no marrying or giving in marriage. All this has to be fulfilled here, and if it is not fulfilled here, it will never be fulfilled. The great saints only live, even Jesus only lives to add a new fulfilment and a new beauty to the permanent sacrament of marriage. ("A Propos of *Lady Chatterley's Lover*")

Thus Lawrence in his quest for saviourhood and poetic immortality goes so far as to pronounce that "the mystery of marriage"—specifically, *Lawrentian* marriage—is so all-important that the ultimate purpose of Christianity in general and Jesus in particular is to advance the cause of Lawrentian hetero-marriage: "The great saints only live, *even Jesus only lives* to add a new fulfilment and a new beauty to the permanent sacrament of marriage." In his supreme solipsism—the "triumphant solipsism" (Bloom *Map* 9) of the supremely strong poet—Lawrence easily misreads and distorts the meaning of Christianity and Jesus to make them serve the Lawrentian purpose of "new fulfilment" and "new beauty" through "marriage"—specifically, uniquely Lawrentian marriage—marriage which is "basically and permanently phallic":

> But...marriage is no marriage that is not basically and permanently phallic, and that is not linked up with the sun and the earth, the moon and the fixed stars and the planets, in the rhythm of days, in the rhythm of months, in the rhythm of quarters, of years, of decades and of centuries. (Ibid.)

By valorizing and defining "phallic marriage," Lawrence as "saviour" initiates a new "mankind"-"circumambient universe" "connection" (*Phoenix II* 478) between the erect penis ("phallus"), genuine marriage (i.e., "phallic" marriage: "marriage is no marriage that is not basically and permanently phallic"), and the cosmos; indeed, for "saviour" Lawrence, the genuine marriage needs not only the "phallic" connection but also the connection with the universe, "the sun and the earth, the moon and the fixed stars and the planets." Indeed, Lawrentian "phallic" marriage is profoundly rooted in Lawrence's *cosmic* belief in "the phallus":

> I [have]...positive belief, that the phallus is a great sacred image: it represents a deep, deep life which has been denied in us, and still is denied....One can still believe. And with the [phallus], and belief

> in the mystery behind it, goes beauty. (D. H. Lawrence letter to E. H. Brewster, 27 February 1927)

As the "One [who] can still believe" in "the phallus" as "a great sacred image," Lawrence the "saviour" endeavors uniquely to rescue the "deep, deep life which has been denied in us, and still is denied"; thus here Lawrence declares himself to be capable of taking the unique, unprecedented action of bringing to "us" (i.e., Western civilization) the "deep, deep life" of genuine, natural, "sacred" sex vitality, its "mystery" and "beauty," as symbolized by and embodied in the phallus: this Lawrence proceeds to do in his "declaration of the phallic reality"—namely, *Lady Chatterley's Lover*:

> As for my novel, *Lady Chatterley's Lover*...It's the most improper novel ever written....It's a declaration of the phallic reality. (D. H. Lawrence letter to Koteliansky, 23 December 1927)

In a civilization which has for so long "denied" the "deep, deep life" of "the phallic reality," Lawrence the "saviour" knew that, even though

> mine is the truly moral and religious position (D. H. Lawrence letter to Nellie Morrison, 8 January 1928),

his *Lady Chatterley's Lover*, with its "phallic reality," would still be regarded as "the most improper novel ever written"; but, Lawrence insists,

> Of course the book [*Lady Chatterley's Lover*] isn't improper: but it *is* phallic....And the phallic reality is what one must fight for. (D. H. Lawrence letter to Edward McDonald, 9 March 1928)

Fighting for "the phallic reality," Lawrence as "saviour" sees himself as fighting to make a better world with his "phallic novel":

> It [*Lady Chatterley's Lover*] is frankly and faithfully a phallic novel, but tender and delicate, as I believe in it: and as I believe is necessary for us to become. It'll infuriate *mean* people: but it will surely soothe decent ones. (D. H. Lawrence letter to Mabel Dodge Luhan, 13 March 1928)

Lawrence the "saviour" goes on to explain that his "phallic novel" can save the world from "going crazy":

> *Lady Chatterley's Lover*...It's a phallic novel, frankly: but tender and delicate. And I believe in it. I believe the world is going crazy for lack of the real phallic feeling and consciousness—which is

more than mere sex. Sex can be any sort of cerebral reaction, mere cerebration transferred to the sexual centres. But the phallic reality is another reality. (D. H. Lawrence letter to Christine Hughes, 13 March 1928)

With the "tender and delicate" quality lacking in "us," Lawrence aspires to save "us" by helping us to become "tender and delicate" by means of his "sooth[ing]" "phallic novel" *Lady Chatterley's Lover*, which is itself indeed "tender and delicate" even while "the world is going crazy for lack of the real phallic feeling and consciousness": "the real phallic feeling and consciousness" with all of its "tender and delicate" character—the character of quintessentially Lawrentian sex, which is "more than mere sex." For Lawrence, "mere sex" has too much of a "cerebral" taint to make it the "saving" force that "saviour" Lawrence's "phallic reality" is:

> [*Lady Chatterley's Lover*] is a phallic novel, but tender and delicate....I do believe the phallic reality is *good and healing*, in a world going insane. I believe the phallic consciousness makes us gentle and really human hence my novel....(D. H. Lawrence letter to Alice Henderson, 13 March 1928; italics mine)

Connecting Lawrentian "phallic" sex with sanity, Lawrence in his *Lady Chatterley's Lover* period (1927-1929) sees himself as saving the world, "healing...a world going insane"—"healing" this "crazy" world by "mak[ing] us gentle and really human" through bringing us the Lawrentian good news about "the phallic reality" for which he is ready to fight:

> one has to fight....I feel one still has to fight for the phallic reality, as against the non-phallic cerebration unrealities. (D. H. Lawrence letter to W. Bynner, 13 March 1928)

Thus the Lawrentian "phallic reality," standing in contradistinction to "the non-phallic cerebration unrealities," is a natural, uncerebral way of sexual being:

> You know I believe in the phallic reality, and the phallic consciousness: as distinct from our irritable cerebral consciousness of today. That's why I do the book [*Lady Chatterley's Lover*]—and it's not just *sex*. Sex alas is one of the worst phenomena of today: all cerebral reaction, the whole thing worked from mental processes and itch, and not a bit of the real phallic insouciance and spontaneity. But in my novel [*Lady Chatterley's Lover*] there is. (D. H. Lawrence letter to George Conway, 15 March 1928)

Thus, while Lawrentian "phallic" sex is natural, full of "insouciance and spontaneity," the "sex" he is fighting against is evidently a social-cultural construct of "our irritable cerebral consciousness of today," a "cerebral consciousness" which makes "*sex*...all cerebral reaction, the whole thing worked from mental processes,"—"mental processes" which are merely shallow when compared to the Lawrentian "phallic consciousness":

> Phallic consciousness is so much deeper than what we call sex. I don't call my novel [*Lady Chatterley's Lover*] a sex novel: It's a phallic novel. (D. H. Lawrence letter to Trigant Burrow, 15 March 1928)

By initiating—indeed, creating—the imaginative-conceptual reality of "the phallic consciousness," Lawrence the "saviour" could transcend the mundane "mere sex" of his own day; he could look down upon "the irritable cerebral consciousness"; he could immerse his creative imagination and his saviourship in the healing "phallic reality":

> I believe in the phallic consciousness, as against the irritable cerebral consciousness we're afflicted with....Sex is a thing that exists in the head, its reactions are cerebral, and its processes mental. Whereas the phallic reality is warm and spontaneous....(D. H. Lawrence letter to Curtis Brown, 15 March 1928)

Thus for Lawrence the "warm and spontaneous" nature of his "phallic reality" and his "phallic consciousness" is essential to his identity as "saviour" of Western civilization and attainer of "poetic immortality":

> the phallic consciousness...is the source of all real beauty, and all real gentleness. And these are the two things, tenderness and beauty, which will save us from horrors....[T]he phallic consciousness...is not the cerebral sex-consciousness, but something really deeper, and the root of poetry, lived or sung. (D. H. Lawrence letter to Harriet Monroe, 15 March 1928)

Here Lawrence declares that the source of his poetic strength and inspiration, "the root of [his] poetry, lived or sung," the fountainhead of the "tenderness and beauty" of his *Lady Chatterley's Lover*, is "the phallic consciousness"; furthermore, Lawrence the saviour explicitly states that his "phallic consciousness,...the source of all real beauty, and all real gentleness," is the saving consciousness which will "save" Western civilization ("us") from the "horrors" of self-destruction, if we have the courage to embrace and advocate this Lawrentian "phallic consciousness," which, for Lawrence, is "the root of poetry, lived or sung"—in particular, the root of *Lady Chatterley's Lover*, which Lawrence describes as

> a phallic novel: a delicate and tender phallic novel....
> It [*Lady Chatterley's Lover*] is strictly a novel of the phallic consciousness as against the mental consciousness of today. For some things, you will probably dislike it: because you are still squeamish, and scared of the phallic reality. *It is perfectly wholesome and normal, and man and a woman.* (D. H. Lawrence letter to Rolf Gardiner, 17 March 1928; italics mine)

Regarding himself as infinitely superior to such "squeamish" friends as Rolf Gardiner, Lawrence the "phallic" "saviour" is certainly not "scared of the phallic reality" which he has indeed named and discovered at the same time; furthermore, "phallic" Lawrence can indeed maintain that his attainment of "saviour" greatness and poetic immortality lies in his apotheosizing of the "perfectly wholesome and normal"—that "perfectly wholesome and normal," that is to say, which is Lawrentian heterosex ("man and a woman"). By equating the "perfectly wholesome and normal" with "man and a woman," Lawrence the heterosex saviour makes himself easily vulnerable to being labelled and condemned by today's politically correct academicians as "blindingly heterosexist" (Dollimore 275)—but Lawrence himself would surely agree that this is a small price to pay for "poetic immortality." Indeed, Lawrence in his *Lady Chatterley's Lover* period was in fact more than ready to be ostracized, made a pariah, "set apart":

> what I believe in is the true phallic consciousness....the book [*Lady Chatterley's Lover*] must be read—it's a bomb, but to the living, a flood of urge....This is where I throw a straight bomb at the skull of idealistic Mammon. And of course it [*Lady Chatterley's Lover*] will in a way set me apart even more definitely than I am already set apart. It's destiny. (D. H. Lawrence letter to Rolf Gardiner, 17 March 1928)

Thus Lawrence in his *Lady Chatterley's Lover* period feels just fine about being definitely, distinctively, decisively "set apart" from virtually all other major writers and thinkers of his civilization—as the salvific apostle of "the true phallic consciousness," Lawrence could see no other "destiny" for himself and his *Lady Chatterley's Lover*, a book which "must be read" so that it may minister to "the living" as a revivifying "flood of urge" while at the same time being "a bomb" against the evil power of "idealistic Mammon," the false god in opposition to "the true phallic consciousness" in which Lawrence believes, and the advocacy of which sets Lawrence apart, assuring his uniqueness, poetic strength and immortality in a world dominated by "this perpetual state of funk" (D. H. Lawrence letter to Laurence Polinger, 17 March 1928), an erotophobic state which Lawrence aims to make "us" overcome:

> We are just human beings with living sex. We are all right, if we had not this unaccountable and disastrous *fear* of sex....
>
> Accept the sexual, physical being of yourself, and of every other creature. Don't be afraid of it....[W]hen men and women are physically cut off, they become at last dangerous, bullying, cruel. Conquer the fear of sex, and restore the natural flow....If you don't, if you don't put back a bit of the old warmth into life, there is savage disaster ahead. (D. H. Lawrence, "The State of Funk," *Phoenix II*, pp. 568, 570)

As the champion of "living sex," Lawrence deplores "this unaccountable and disastrous *fear* of sex," a fear that he hopes to cure "us" of with works such as *Lady Chatterley's Lover*, works which will make us "all right" by making us "Accept the sexual" by getting rid of "the fear of sex" and replacing this fear with "the natural flow"—"the natural flow" which involves "[the] normal," "the phallic," "[the] wholesome and natural":

> My novel [*Lady Chatterley's Lover*] is perfectly normal, and the phallic part of it is, or should be, part of every man's life, and every woman's....I defy any human being to find my novel anything but wholesome and natural. (D. H. Lawrence letter to Laurence Pollinger, 17 March 1928)

Valorizing the "normal," "the phallic," the "wholesome and natural," Lawrence stands in direct opposition to the gay-lesbian-social constructionist set that dominates academia today. As one major Ivy League gay-lesbian scholar of social constructionism explains, social constructionism is the opponent of essentialism, especially with regard to "the issue of the relation between the social and the natural":

> Essentialists and constructionists are most polarized around the issue of the relation between the social and the natural. For the

> essentialist, the natural provides the raw material and determinative starting point for the practices and laws of the social. For example, sexual difference (the division into "male" and "female") is taken as prior to social differences which are presumed to be mapped on to, *a posteriori*, the biological subject. For the constructionist, the natural is itself posited as a construction of the social. In this view, sexual difference is discursively produced, elaborated as an effect of the social....Thus while the essentialist holds that the natural is *repressed* by the social, the constructionist maintains that the natural is *produced* by the social. (Fuss, *Essentially Speaking*, p. 3)

Thus Lawrence aspires to liberate in "us" the very "*natural* flow" (my italics) whose existence the gay-lesbian social constructionist would indeed deny. For Lawrence, of course, this "wholesome and normal" "natural flow" is synonymous with "man and a woman"; for the social constructionist, "man" and "woman" do not even exist "naturally," but only "politically": one major French lesbian social-constructionist insists that

> the categories "man" and "woman"...are political categories and not natural givens. (Wittig, *Straight Mind*, pp. 13-14)

Thus for the social constructionist, "man" and "woman" are creations of "the political," not of "the natural"; indeed, Lawrentian "nature" itself does not even exist, according to lesbian social-constructionist theorist Monique Wittig, who complacently states that

> it has been accepted in recent years that there is no such thing as nature, that everything is culture....(*Straight Mind*, p. 27)

The concept of "the natural" is anathema to the gay-lesbian theorist for the very reason that even today, as Jonathan Dollimore sympathetically observes,

> there persists the use of homosexuality as a symbol of evil and/or the quintessentially unnatural. (Dollimore 47)

In a society that denies the existence of "the natural," then, there is obviously no way that lesbianism-homosexuality can be condemned as "unnatural"; thus a major goal of the gay-lesbian sociocultural-political agenda is, as sympathizing left-winger Jonathan Dollimore explains, to discredit

> a system of "natural" sexual difference which produces woman [and man] and must be abolished. (Dollimore 60)

Decrying "'natural' sexual difference," leftist-gay theory deplores D. H. Lawrence, the supreme champion of "the natural"; as F. R. Leavis significantly noted some seven decades ago, Lawrence stands for

> a human naturalness, inevitable, and more than humanly sanctioned (Leavis, "Reminiscences of D. H. Lawrence," *Scrutiny* 1 [1932]: 190)

—"a human naturalness" which is surely contra Wittig, Fuss and their Foucaultian ilk. Furthermore, according to Leavis some seventy years ago, Lawrence is the supreme exemplar of "the normal":

> Lawrence shows himself normal, central and sane to the point of genius. (Leavis, "D. H. Lawrence and Professor Irving Babbitt," *Scrutiny* 1 [1932]: 275)

Indeed, according to Leavis, Lawrence

> may be said to represent,...in an age that has lost the sense of it, *human normality*, as only great genius could. (Leavis, "D. H. Lawrence and Irving Babbitt," *Scrutiny* [1932]: 279; italics mine)

Lawrence, too, of course valorized "the normal," praising the "perfectly wholesome and normal, and man and a woman" nature of his work in general ("I always labour at the same thing, to make the sex relation valid and precious") and of *Lady Chatterley's Lover* in particular; but it is this very Lawrentian valorization of the "wholesome," "natural," "normal," "valid," "precious" "[hetero]sex relation" that goes against the grain of such powerful academicians as famed lesbian theorist Judith Butler of UC-Berkeley, who bitterly confesses that the concept of "human normality"—as embodied in the priority of "natural" heterosex—caused her great and lengthy suffering:

> As a young [lesbian] person, I suffered for a long time, and I suspect many [homosexual] people have, from being told, explicitly or implicitly, that what I "am" is a copy, an imitation, a derivative example, a shadow of the real. Compulsory heterosexuality sets itself up as the original, the true, the authentic; the norm that determines the real implies that being "lesbian" is always a kind of miming, a vain effort to participate in the phantasmatic plenitude of *naturalized heterosexuality* which will always and only fail. (Butler, "Imitation," in Fuss 1991, 20-21; italics mine)

Thus Butler bitterly believes that she has been a suffering lesbian victim of heterosexuality's judgment that she as a lesbian is merely "a derivative example...of the real"—"the real" being heterosex, of which lesbianism is "an imitation...which will always and only fail." In a strategic attempt to circumvent the "priority" of "naturalized heterosexuality"—the status of heterosex as "the original, the true, the authentic" sex, the "normal" sex, the "real" sex—the affronted Butler desires "to call into question the claims of heterosexual priority" ("Imitation," p. 17) by

> depriving the naturalizing narratives of compulsory heterosexuality of their central protagonists: "man" and "woman." (Butler, *Gender Trouble*, p. 146)

For Western civilization, of course, one of the greatest creators of "naturalizing narratives of compulsory heterosexuality" has surely been D. H. Lawrence, whose entire vision is based on his "central protagonists: 'man' and 'woman'" engaged in the communion of "blood-marriage":

> Marriage is no marriage that is not a correspondence of blood. For the blood is the substance of the soul, and of the deepest consciousness. It is by blood that we are: and it is by the heart and the liver that we live and move and have our being. In the blood, knowing and being, or feeling, are one and undivided: no serpent and no apple has caused a split. So that only when the conjunction is of the blood, is marriage truly marriage. The blood of man and the blood of woman are two eternally different streams, that can never be mingled....But therefore they are the two rivers that encircle the whole of life, and in marriage the circle is complete, and in sex the two rivers touch and renew one another, without ever commingling or confusing. We know it. The phallus is a column of blood that fills the valley of blood of a woman. The great river of male blood touches to its depths the great river of female blood—yet neither breaks its bounds. It is the deepest of all communions, as all the religions, in practice, know. And it is one of the greatest mysteries, in fact, the greatest,...the supreme achievement of the mystic marriage. ("A Propos of *Lady Chatterley's Lover*")

For Lawrence, "marriage" must be "a correspondence of blood," "blood" for Lawrence being synonymous with "the substance of the soul, and of the deepest consciousness"; indeed, when he was at the very height of his powers, during his *Rainbow-Women in Love* period, Lawrence had of course explicitly posited the existence of the supremely deep "blood consciousness" and its origins in heterosex:

> there is a blood-consciousness which exists in us independently of the ordinary mental consciousness....There is the blood-consciousness, with the sexual connection....One lives, knows, and has one's being in the blood, without any reference to nerves and brain....[W]hen I take a woman, then...my blood-knowing is overwhelming. There is a transmission...between her blood and mine, in the act of [heterosexual] connection....(D. H. Lawrence letter to Bertrand Russell, 8 December 1915)

—and, similarly, during his *Lady Chatterley's Lover* period, Lawrence has his valorized "protagonists," "male" and "female," engaged in a "blood-relation" in which "In the blood, knowing and being, or feeling, are one and undivided" due to the fact that "no serpent and no apple"—that is to say, no "mental consciousness"—has impacted this relation between "knowing and being, or feeling": no deleterious cerebral ("mental") "split" between "knowing" and "feeling" happens in a "blood marriage," the "marriage [that is] truly marriage" and that involves the "eternally different" Lawrentian "protagonists," "man" and "woman," with their "two eternally different [blood] streams" which encompass "the whole of life"; this Lawrentian "blood marriage" is indeed the ultimate manifestation and consummation of "the whole of life," life's completion in "touch" and "renew[al]" "in sex"—the unique Lawrentian heterosex that takes place "in marriage." The unique Lawrentian heterosex that takes place in unique Lawrentian "marriage" is indeed valorized by Lawrence as "the deepest of all communions, as all the religions...know"; indeed, the entire phenomenon of "the supreme achievement" of Lawrentian "mystic marriage" is valorized by Lawrence as "the greatest" of the Lawrentian "religious" "mysteries"; and surely Lawrence's supreme appreciation of "the mystic marriage" of heterosex is rooted in Lawrence's "magnificent" "religious sense"; as F. R. Leavis eloquently noted some seventy years ago:

> Lawrence...was, as he says again and again, essentially religious....And it is Lawrence's greatness that he convinces us of his actually believing in something "beyond his fellow-men." He alone cannot give us the religion for which the human spirit withers, but the fact that he lived and was so is a highly valuable fact....Lawrence's preoccupation with sex was religious....

> Lawrence..., more than anyone else in our time, makes it possible to cherish some faith in the future of humanity. If the religious sense that he represents so magnificently cannot be generally recovered it is difficult to think with hope of the future....(F. R. Leavis, *For Continuity*, pp. 155-158)

Thus "Lawrence's greatness" is rooted in his "essentially religious" nature—as Lawrence himself fully realized, even as a young man:

> primarily I am a passionately religious man, and my novels must be written from the depth of my religious experience. (D. H. Lawrence letter to Edward Garnett, 22 April 1914)

As "a passionately religious man," whose "novels must be written from the depth of my religious experience," Lawrence is obviously anathema to the politically correct forces that dominate current "intellectual" life; for Lawrence's "religious sense" is certainly not welcome today—especially in academia; as Robert Bork recently observed:

> The inner need for pervasive meaning was satisfied through most of history in Western civilization by religion. But as religious faith began a retreat, beginning in the eighteenth century and proceeding apace in the nineteenth and twentieth, the intellectual's need for meaning did not decline but remained urgent. Now, however, meaning must be found in a secular belief system. It is difficult to think of anything that would fit this specification for most intellectuals other than politics....To be a civil religion, however, this politics...must be a politics of ideology.
>
> In our time that means left-wing politics, which offers a comprehensive world view and a promise of ultimate salvation in a utopia that conventional politics cannot offer....Not only communism but fascism and Naziism were faith systems of the Left, offering transcendental meaning to their adherents. (Bork 85)

Lawrence's "belief system"—involving belief in the sexual sublime, "blood consciousness," and of course his own poetic immortality—has certainly raised the hackles of liberal Ivy League pseudo-Lawrentians such as Daniel R. Schwarz, who patronizingly describes Lawrence's "value":

> [During his *Rainbow-Women in Love* period] he [Lawrence]...[is] seeing himself as a prophetic *Ubermensch*....[But] it is very difficult to take Lawrence very seriously either as a political or moral philosopher or as a psychologist. He is to be valued because he invented a language and a fictional form to render our unconscious, biological, physiological, sexual, and passionate feelings—or, at

> least he made vast strides towards rendering those inarticulate aspects of ourselves. Do we not value Lawrence because within his best fiction and poetry his *performances* of the aforementioned aspects of human life touch our suppressed, inarticulate, and dimly acknowledged passions and feelings? (Schwarz 1989, 192-193)

But, whatever slight enthusiasm Schwarz may have for Lawrence's rendering of "our...feelings," Schwarz shows far more vehement passion and feeling in his politically correct denunciation of D. H. Lawrence:

> I have always been troubled by Lawrence's misanthropy, anti-Semitism, and penchant for violent political solutions....I believe that Lawrence veers into a sociopathic fascist vision where self-proclaimed *Ubermenschem* are allowed to let their atavistic psyches roam free. (Schwarz 1989, 207)

Here Schwarz is certainly being reductive, simplistic and unfair in his approach to Lawrence; as my monograph has hopefully shown, for example, Lawrence's "anti-Semitism" is nothing of the sort: to call it that is to misread Lawrence to the point of making a politically correct mockery of literary interpretation; indeed, it seems to me that all of Schwarz's attack on Lawrence—"Lawrence's misanthropy, anti-Semitism,...penchant for violent political solutions,...sociopathic fascist vision"—is the attack of a well-intentioned literary critic who has let himself be overwhelmed by sociopolitical considerations and who has failed to appreciate the role of Lawrence's overriding quest for poetic immortality in Lawrence's "sociopathic...vision"—which is in fact not "sociopathic" at all, but rather the vision of a supremely strong poet in his creative imagination and great uniqueness. With his overemphasis on politics, Schwarz believes that "Literature written at the political edge reminds us of what literature has always been about: urgency, commitment, tension, and feeling" (Schwarz 1992, 152); evidently Schwarz does not appreciate the "urgency" of Lawrence's struggle for poetic immortality—an "urgency" rooted, not in "the political," but rather in what Harold Bloom calls "strangeness":

> I have tried to confront greatness directly: to ask what makes the author and the works canonical. The answer...has turned out to be strangeness, a mode of originality that...cannot be assimilated....

> One mark of an originality that can win canonical status for a literary work is a strangeness that we...never altogether assimilate....
>
> ...the tang of originality must always hover in an inaugural aspect of any work that incontestably wins the agon with tradition and joins the Canon. Our educational institutions are thronged these days by idealistic resenters who denounce competition in literature as in life, but the aesthetic and the agonistic are one....(Bloom, *Western Canon*, pp. 2-3, 4, 6)

One major component of Lawrence's "greatness," "strangeness," and "originality" is his advocacy of "the phallic reality"—particularly in *Lady Chatterley's Lover*:

> It [*Lady Chatterley's Lover*] is really a novel contrasting the mental consciousness with the phallic consciousness....It is quite true, sex today is all mental; intellectual reactions reflected down on to physical processes: and that is repulsive....But the phallic reality is a free consciousness and a vital impulse, and is *the great and saving reality*. (D. H. Lawrence letter to Max Mohr, 22 March 1928; italics mine)

Lawrence's "saving reality" once again guarantees his "saviour" status and his poetic immortality—both of which are located in the religious-"spiritual" realm rather than in the "political" realm; as Lawrence scholar Mara Kalnins notes:

> Lawrence's view of man...is not political but spiritual, not a denial of men's individuality but a confirmation of it based on an acceptance of the innate and inexplicable differences between men. (Kalnins 23)

The "saving reality" of Lawrence's "religion" is rooted in "saying...natural things" (D. H. Lawrence letter to Aldous Huxley, 2 April 1928) in *Lady Chatterley's Lover* and elsewhere; the "saving reality" of Schwarz and other politically correct "anti-Lawrence Lawrentians" is rooted in

> the Holy Trinity of "race, gender and class"...(*New Criterion*, February 1997, p. 2)

—indeed, as one conservative cultural critic observes,

> In English departments, "race, gender and class" have taken center stage, while questions of literary merit have been rendered illegitimate—"marginalized," in the current discourse. (Seaton 4)

Thus Daniel R. Schwarz proudly announces that "in my [English] department [at Cornell], we just voted a concentration in gay, bisexual, and lesbian studies" (Schwarz 1992, 155); in the same vein, Schwarz praises "the power and eloquence of...Kate Millett" (Schwarz 1992, 160)—Kate Millett, the famed gay-lesbian critic and author of the "atrocious" *Sexual Politics*: as Camille Paglia recently noted,

> Kate Millett's *Sexual Politics* (1970)...reduced complex artworks to their political content and attacked famous male artists and authors for their alleged sexism. That atrocious book...[is] responsible for the current eclipse of D. H. Lawrence...in the college curriculum....(Paglia, "Academic Feminists Must Begin to Fulfill Their Noble, Animating Ideal," *Chronicle of Higher Education*, July 25, 1997, p. B4)

There is no time here to deal with Kate Millett in this particular monograph, especially when Peter Balbert's pioneering study *D. H. Lawrence and the Phallic Imagination* does so at length; but the fact that a respectable Ivy League "Lawrentian" like Schwarz can have such admiration for Lawrence hater Kate Millett indicates that it may indeed be an understatement to say that

> Today the novels of D. H. Lawrence occupy a more tenuous position in the canon of English literature than they did a generation ago. (Pecora, *Columbia History of the British Novel*, p. 728)

Yet at the same time that she realizes Lawrence's dire situation at this juncture, Camille Paglia believes that this is no time for inactive despair: she tells us that today

> The situation with Lawrence is...extreme. As far as women's studies is concerned, he has ceased to exist....
> ...theory has supplanted literature, and criticism has degenerated into moralistic text-trashing. Those who love Lawrence...must speak. (Paglia, *Vamps*, pp. 328-329)

One strategy recently practised by "Those who love Lawrence" is to recognize the political realities of the academy and cater to them in an attempt to improve Lawrence's status "in the academy"; one of these "politically correct" realities was recently described by gay critic-theorist Tim Dean:

> just as *queer* is becoming the most fashionable label to wear in certain circles, so *homophobic* is one of the most damning. By now

the charge of homophobia has acquired a debate-halting force in
the academy, to a point where homophobia panic (the liberal's fear
of being considered homophobic) has replaced homosexual panic
(the putatively straight man's fear of being considered homosexual). (Tim Dean, "On the Eve of a Queer Future," *Raritan*, Summer 1995, pp. 118-119)

As Tim Dean notes, homosexuality is privileged "in the academy," while there is at the same time a kind of witch-hunt going on there for "homophobes"; in the midst of this McCarthyesque, pro-homosexual, left-wing atmosphere in academia, well-meaning Lawrentians intend to help his position (and, perhaps, their own) by portraying him as being more tolerant of homosexuality than he in fact was—and by portraying themselves as being downright sympathetic to it; thus Mark Kinkead-Weekes, in his magisterial biography of Lawrence during his *Rainbow-Women in Love* period, asserts that

> [I]f he [Lawrence] had desired and sought homosexual fulfilment, it would not have been furtively—and it would certainly have had a marked effect on him and his work.
>
> This is a question of character and integrity, not of morals or judgment of sexual preference. It is possible to charge the Lawrence of 1917 (should anyone so wish) with failing to imagine how fulfilled homosexuality might be fully as creative of rich new life as fulfilled heterosexuality. And it is possible to accuse him, contrariwise, of admitting and justifying homosexual impulses...that (in someone's own view) he ought to have repressed altogether because they are disgusting. What [is]...impossible is to [validly] charge him [Lawrence] with being "a homosexual" who would not admit his true nature, or one who after furtive acts concealed himself in a lifelong hypocrisy....
>
> In fact our culture is seriously at fault in having no language for the whole spectrum of possibility and satisfaction that lies between the admission of sexual attractiveness between men, and the fulfilment of sexual desire in acts of sodomy and mutual masturbation. The word "homosexual"—especially if opposed to "heterosexual" as though these were categorically exclusive—is of confusing span, and hence intolerable crudity. In many of the world's cultures male friendship is expressed physically, quite naturally. Men touch each other, put their arms around each other, kiss each other, admire and love each other, without any sense that their behaviour is incongruous with their relations with women.

> Yet our culture apparently finds it necessary to label someone as "*a* homosexual" as *categorically opposed* to "*a* heterosexual," and to find in any sexual attraction between men the evidence of categoric "homosexual" preference. Lawrence himself seems far wiser, more honest, and more humane, though he was so much a child of his Englishness as to have been probably rather physically inhibited than otherwise in his relations with other men. It is only after the wrestling match that Birkin can tell Gerald he is beautiful....One rather hopes that, after some bout of work in the fields, it got as close as that with [Lawrence and his farmer friend] William Henry. (Mark Kinkead-Weekes, *D. H. Lawrence: Triumph to Exile*, pp. 380-381)

Mark Kinkead-Weekes evidently wants to have his cake and eat it too: first of all, he admits that all the evidence indicates that "the Lawrence of 1917" had not "desired and sought homosexual fulfilment"—it would have had "a marked effect on him and his work" if he had, and there is indeed an essential continuity in Lawrence and his work from the beginning through *Lady Chatterley's Lover* and beyond to the end; yet, at the same time that Kinkead-Weekes admits that Lawrence did not desire and seek "homosexual fulfilment," Kinkead-Weekes indeed seems apologetic about that fact, and evidently tries to make up for Lawrence's lack of homosexuality by presenting his (Kinkead-Weekes') own critique of "our culture" and how it is "at fault in having no language for the whole spectrum of possibility and satisfaction that lies between the admission of sexual attractiveness between men, and the fulfilment of sexual desire in acts of sodomy and mutual masturbation": in other words, Kinkead-Weekes more or less presents himself as extremely sympathetic to a kind of quasi-homosexuality which in fact has nothing to do with Lawrentian touch between men—touch which is rooted in Lawrence's "religious"-Biblical bent and in his "political"-strategic aspiration to wean practising homosexuals away from their "blasphemy against love" (as the present monograph has strongly suggested). Indeed, Mark Kinkead-Weekes' apparent advocacy of this quasi-homosexuality suggests that he himself may have been reading too much (or been too influenced by) Michel Foucault; the Foucaultian taint in Kinkead-Weekes' magisterial biography can be seen to appear, it seems to me, in his ostentatious mention of "homosexual" and "heterosexual" as "categories"—a rubric straight out of Foucault. Further evidence of Kinkead-Weekes' work being slightly blemished by trendiness is his "politically correct" regret that "Lawrence...[was] probably rather physically inhibited than otherwise in his relations with other men"—that is to say, Lawrence was less "homoerotic" than Kinkead-Weekes had hoped him to be; yet Kinkead-Weekes concludes with the fervent hope that Lawrence "got as close...with William Henry" as Birkin got with Gerald in *Women in Love* (with "work in the fields" having to substitute for nude wrestling in Kinkead-Weekes' scenario).

Yet, whatever the few weaknesses of Mark Kinkead-Weekes' important biography of Lawrence, Mark Kinkead-Weekes is certainly one of the major Lawrentians of our day; indeed, Kinkead-Weekes, in some recent remarks on Lawrence, provides us with a key to finding new approaches to Lawrence: in a discussion of "D. H. Lawrence's Writing Life," Kinkead-Weekes gives us some important advice on how to "understand" Lawrence:

> Lawrence was first and foremost a *writer*—the greatest English writer of this century—and moreover a writer whose work came directly out of his life-experience....His writing was his most intense way both of living and of grappling with his problems—and I don't think we shall ever understand him unless we try to look over his shoulder, and discover how, and why, he came to write as he did, and how his work both came out of, and sought to comprehend, what was happening to the living man. That of course is no easy task. (*Beyond Gossip: D. H. Lawrence's Writing Life*, pp. 5-6)

Thus Kinkead-Weekes advises us that the way to "understand" Lawrence is by "try[ing] to look over his shoulder, and discover how, and why, he came to write as he did, and how his work both came out of, and sought to comprehend, what was happening to the living man." One major aspect of "the living man" Lawrence is surely found in the fact that Lawrence was "homo religiosus" (Schneider 131)—"religious man" whose

> conviction that he has a covenant with God...gives him [Lawrence] a...[supreme] strength and courage....(Schneider, *Consciousness of D. H. Lawrence*, p. 131)

As "homo religiosus," one Lawrence scholar explains,

> he [Lawrence during his *Rainbow-Women in Love* period and after] had to create the new heaven and earth in *fact*—in the building of a new religious society. (Schneider 87)

The basis of that Lawrentian "religious society" leads us to the other all-important aspect of "the living man" Lawrence—an aspect of "the living man" Lawrence that is surely evident in the very title of a recent biography, *The Married Man: A Life of D. H. Lawrence* by Brenda Maddox. Thus "the living man" Lawrence includes "The Married Man" Lawrence and "The Religious Man" Lawrence, both of whom come together to create the conception of the Lawrentian "religion of marriage"; this Lawrentian "religion of marriage," Lawrence explains, involves "communion" between the "two distinct eternal [blood-] streams" of "man and wife":

> And this is the meaning of the sexual act:...This is marriage,...this communion of the two blood-streams [male and female], this, and nothing else: as all the religions know.
>   Two rivers of blood, are man and wife, two distinct eternal streams, that have the power of touching and communing and so renewing, making new one another....And the phallus is the connecting link between the two rivers, that establishes the two streams in a oneness, and gives out of their duality a single circuit, forever. And this, this oneness gradually accomplished throughout a life-time in twoness, is the highest achievement of time or eternity. From it all things human spring, children and beauty and well-made things, all the true creations of humanity. And all we know of the will of God is that He wishes this, this oneness, to take place, fulfilled over a life-time, this oneness within the great dual blood-stream of humanity. ("A Propos of *Lady Chatterley's Lover*")

As religious "communion," Lawrentian marriage is "eternal," with the Lawrentian phallus establishing connection "forever" between the male and female "rivers of blood"; this Lawrentian connection "is the highest achievement of time or eternity" according to Lawrence, who of course is indeed asserting his own poetic immortality in his own poetic "highest achievement" which is of course grounded in his depiction of "man and wife" in his works, works which spring from "this oneness [between man and wife]"—"oneness" which leads to "children and beauty and well-made things, all the true creations of humanity" in general and of D. H. Lawrence in particular—D. H. Lawrence whose "creations" are inspired by "the will of God,"—"God" who "wishes this, this oneness [between "man and wife"], to take place"—as does D. H. Lawrence, who surely wishes to "be at one with God," "God" for Lawrence being synonymous with "the strength and glory of being alive, today, yesterday, and even forever":

> We want God? Well, there is God. He doesn't go away just because we tell him to. God makes the universe afresh every day, and if we refuse to be made afresh, that is our look-out....
>
> ...God, who is the strength and glory of being alive, today, yesterday, and even forever. I don't know anything else about God, except he is...the strength and glory of being alive, and that I live in his cosmos.
>
> And wherever I am and whatever I am, I want to be at one with God and with his living cosmos. I want to live with the rhythm of the sun and the earth, and the pale-threading rhythm of the moon. I want someone to teach me the rhythm of the year of the stars, and the erratic rhythm of the planets. I want a woman to go through the rhythm of life with me. Even my reason tells me there is a great creative urge, stronger even than death. And my feelings tell me there is God, who dances in the midst of space in delight, and who pauses sometimes in the vast, vast wonder of it all, and who is sometimes angry, cheated. And even my reason tells me that the creative urge touches me with renewal....[M]y feelings tell me that the same thing that holds me alive, holds me to God, holds me to the woman, holds me to hope....("A Propos of *Lady Chatterley's Lover*, MSII," in Squires, ed., *Lady Chatterley's Lover*, p. 371)

Lawrence's "hope" in fact is the hope of the Lawrence who is beyond "Lawrence the Married Man" and "Lawrence the Religious Man": it is the hope of Lawrence the great creative writer striving for poetic immortality; in that quest for poetic immortality, Lawrence "want[s] God" to imbue him with "the strength and glory of being alive, today, yesterday, and *even forever*": the "strength and glory," that is, of "poetic immortality" ("being alive...even forever"); thus we can indeed see that the "religious" Lawrence loves God and "want[s] to be at one with God and with his living cosmos"—a "living cosmos" in which Lawrence aspires to be included as "a creature" of "the living God":

> All that matters is to be at one with the living God
> to be a creature in the house of the God of Life.
> ("Pax," *Last Poems*)

As "a creature in the house of the God of Life," Lawrence prays to the all-powerful "living God" to give him (Lawrence) his own unique power:

> For thine is the kingdom
> the power, and the glory....
>
> Give me, Oh give me...
> my kingdom, my power, and my glory.
>
> All things that turn to thee
> have their kingdom, their power, and their glory.
>
> Like the kingdom of the nightingale at twilight
> whose power and glory I have often heard and felt.
>
> Like the kingdom of the fox in the dark
> yapping in his power and his glory
> which is death to the goose.
>
> Like the power and the glory of the goose in the mist
> honking over the lake.
>
> And I, a naked man, calling
> calling to thee for my mana,
> my kingdom, my power, and my glory.
> ("Lord's Prayer," *Last Poems*)

Feeling himself to be "at one with the living God," Lawrence has no reservations about asking God to "Give me...my kingdom, my power, and my glory"—Lawrence's would-be "kingdom,...power,... and glory" essentially consisting of the reality of Lawrence's achievement of "poetic immortality": "poetic immortality" which will provide him with the complete achievement of his self, the total fulfillment of his potential as a "singer" ("poet"): just as the nightingale achieves himself in his song, the fox in his "yapping" and the goose in his "honking,"—so Lawrence hopes to attain "my kingdom, my power, and my glory" by means of his "song," his creative writing, which in its power is the basis of Lawrence's claim to "my mana," "mana" being "impersonal supernatural force or power that may be concentrated in objects or persons and that may be inherited, acquired, or conferred" (Webster's Third International). Fervently acknowledging "the kingdom/ the power, and the glory" of God, Lawrence, as one of the "things that turn to thee [God]," beseeches God to give him "my mana,/ my kingdom, my power and my glory"; thus Lawrence, in gaining "my mana" from God, indeed achieves the "transcendental meaning," the "ultimate salvation," and the "inner...pervasive meaning" that today's "people...[of] ideas" seek in "a politics of ideology" (Bork 84-85). Unlike today's "men of ideas," Lawrence attains his "mana" as "a naked man"—that is to say, as an Adamic, heterosexual man who "want[s] a woman to go through the rhythm of life with me"; this woman will, hopefully, aid him in the attainment of his consummation in "a great creative urge, *stronger even than death*"—the "creative urge" of "poetic immortality" which with God's help Lawrence will achieve: this "creative urge" results in Lawrence's being "touch[ed]...with renewal": the "glory"-filled "renewal" of the poetic immortality he achieves; thus poetic immortality "holds [Lawrence] alive" in the "hope" that, thanks to God and to "the woman," he (Lawrence) will have "the strength and glory of being alive,...even forever" as the "priest of love," the great sexual liberator, the brave rebel; even the left-wing, anti-Leavis critic David Simpson recently praised "the emotionally demanding vitalism of D. H. Lawrence" (Simpson 254) and noted that

> from my own schoolboy days [1970s at Cambridge] I well remember the forceful example of teachers for whom all literature led to Lawrence, and to an ideal freedom from inhibition, whether sexual or social (Simpson 254)

—and even the liberal Lawrentian Eugene Goodheart lauds

> the audacious authority of Lawrence's work, its subversive message (Goodheart 1991, "Censorship," p. 238)

and concludes that

> Any intelligent reader of Lawrence, of course, knows that he was an embattled writer, that his is a transgressive imagination, constantly challenging cultural taboos. (Goodheart 1991, "Censorship," p. 237)

Thus one would surely think that Lawrence's standing as "emotionally demanding" champion of "freedom from inhibition, whether sexual or social," his "transgressive imagination, constantly challenging cultural taboos," his "audacious authority" and "subversive message" would guarantee Lawrence's popularity with the so-called adversary culture that today dominates academia; but this is not the case; for the fact is that the academic elite today are not interested in Lawrence's "emotionally demanding" sexual-religious vision; indeed, the "adversary culture" of today is not interested in sexual liberation—and this has been bad for Lawrence's reputation; as Lawrentian Keith Sagar recently noted, reminiscing about Lawrence's status "in the golden age of the fifties and sixties" (Sagar 1992, 32):

> When I began to write criticism of Lawrence in the fifties, in the heyday of Dr. Leavis,...[w]e were all genuinely excited by Lawrence, who spoke directly to us about our most urgent concerns....
>
> [But today our] problem is that the younger people to whom we would like to speak, both as critics and as teachers, can no longer be assumed to share our assumptions about Lawrence, especially those of us whose assumptions were formed in the golden age of the fifties and sixties. The world has moved on a long way since then. Some of Lawrence's battles have been permanently won, some perhaps permanently lost.
>
> Of course, each of us found different things to admire in Lawrence; but one thing we all admired was the refreshing sanity of his attitude to sex—his willingness to speak frankly about it so that it was no longer a dirty little secret, and his insistence that good sex was one of the best things in life. And if our own sex lives, when we finally managed to have any, did not quite match up with those of Lawrence's characters, we assumed that we were inadequate people who could hardly expect the rewards of the all-or-nothing Lawrentian hero.
>
> Now, with the advantage of hindsight, we can see that we made too much of sex in Lawrence. It was partly his own fault—he did call himself a Priest of Love. But we only partly understood what he was saying about sex (ignoring, for example, the religious implications of the word "priest")....
>
> Lawrence contributed a good deal to the revolution of the sixties, and was one of its gurus. When the dust settled, sex ceased, in the seventies, to be the all-important matter it had been. But the teachers of my generation were still teaching Lawrence as though we expected our students to be just as excited by Lawrence on sex as we had been in the fifties. Our students found it hard to see what all the fuss was about. (Sagar 1992, 31-32)

Lawrence scholars during "the golden age of the fifties and sixties"—the age of Leavis, Fiedler and Trilling—"all admired...his [Lawrence's] attitude to sex,...his [Lawrence's] insistence that good sex was one of the best things in life"; but today the left-wing academic-intellectual elite "find[s] it hard to see what all the fuss [is] about" as far as Lawrentian sex is concerned. The supreme representative of this anti-Lawrentian attitude to sex is of course Michel Foucault, who concludes that "one day people will wonder at [Lawrence's "fuss" about sex]....[P]eople will smile...when they recall that here were men [e.g., Lawrence]...who believed that [in sex]...resided a truth every bit as precious as the one they had already demanded from the earth, the stars, and the pure forms of their thought" (*History* 157-158). We now know that it should not surprise us that Foucault should feel this way, in view of Foucault's late confession that "sex is boring" (*Foucault Reader* 340); furthermore, we have Foucault's disciple Leo Bersani to let us know (in his famous essay "Is the Rectum a Grave?") that

> There is a big secret about sex: most people don't like it. (Bersani, "Rectum," p. 197)

It is of course very evident that Bersani himself does not like sex—at least not Lawrentian, heterosexual sex; instead, Bersani privileges "a certain [Foucaultian] refusal of sex as we know it":

> The immense body of contemporary discourse that argues for a radically revised imagination of the body's capacity for pleasure—a discursive project to which Foucault...belong[s]—has as its very condition of possibility a certain refusal of sex as we know it....(Bersani, "Rectum," p. 215)

In his "radically revised imagination of the body's capacity for pleasure," Bersani valorizes, not "sex as we know it," but rather

> sex as self-abolition (Bersani, "Rectum," p. 218),

"self-abolition" which is antithetical to "Phallocentrism": deploring "phallocentrism," Bersani privileges the

> strong appeal of powerlessness, of the loss of control. Phallocentrism is...above all the denial of the *value* of powerlessness....I don't mean the value of gentleness, or nonaggressiveness, or even of passivity, but rather of a more radical disintegration and humiliation of the self. (Bersani, "Rectum," p. 217)

Advocating the "radical disintegration and humiliation of the self," Bersani valorizes masochism, defining "the sexual" as

> the *jouissance* of exploded limits,...the *ecstatic suffering* [italics mine] into which the human organism momentarily plunges when it is "pressed" beyond a certain threshold of endurance. Sexuality...may be a tautology for masochism. (Bersani, "Rectum," p. 217)

Equating the joy of sex with the "jouissance" of "masochism" and its "ecstatic suffering," Bersani argues that the "self-shattering...self-debasement...[of] masochism" (p. 217) is the solution to the "inglorious" (p. 216) "phallocentric" self:

> the ["phallocentric"] self which the [Foucaultian-Bersanian] sexual shatters provides the basis on which sexuality is associated with power. It is possible to think of the sexual as, precisely, moving between a hyperbolic sense of self and a loss of all consciousness of self. But sex as self-hyperbole is...a repression of sex as self-abolition. It inaccurately replicates self-shattering as self-swelling, as psychic tumescence. If, as these words suggest, men are especially apt to "choose" this version of sexual pleasure, because their sexual equipment appears to invite by analogy, or at least to facilitate, the phallicizing of the ego, neither sex has exclusive rights to the practice of sex as self-hyperbole. For it is...primarily *the degeneration of the sexual into a relationship that condemns sexuality to becoming a struggle for power*. As soon as persons are posited, the war begins. It is the self that swells with excitement at the idea of being on top, the self that makes of the inevitable play of thrusts and relinquishments in sex an argument for the natural authority of one sex over the other. (Bersani, "Rectum," p. 218)

Bersani decries "sex as self-hyperbole" as bogus heterosexist-phallocentric "repression" of the true character of sex: "sex as self-abolition"; according to Bersani, "sex as self-abolition," with its "self-shattering," is what *real* sex is all about: the heterosexist "self-swelling" and "psychic tumescence" of heterosex, says Bersani, is simply a cover-up—and, according to Bersani, it is a cover-up which is violent, warlike and unwholesome, rooted in selfishness and powerseeking; for, according to Bersani, heterosex, with its tendency to result in serious relationships rather than in the "promiscuity" characteristic of homosex (Bersani, p. 218), is noxious since "the degeneration of the sexual into a relationship [in heterosex]" is odious in view of the fact that this heterosex "relationship" (as opposed to homosex promiscuity) leads ("condemns") "sexuality to becoming a struggle for power"—"a struggle for power" that is caused by "persons" being "posited" in contrast to the anonymous promiscuous homosex which Bersani idealizes and valorizes: "As soon as persons [selves] are posited, the war begins. It is the self" that is responsible for what Bersani calls "the unrelenting warfare between men and women, which nothing has ever changed" (Bersani, "Rectum," p. 218).

It seems to me ironic and deeply absurd that Bersani should evidently claim to have expertise and authority on the subject of normative heterosexual relationships, "men and women"; for the fact is that Bersani's main interest is not "the unrelenting warfare between men and women" in their incorrigible "practice of sex as self-hyperbole" which "condemns sexuality to becoming a struggle for power"—no, Bersani's main interest is actually

> the primacy of [homosexual] masochism (*Homos*, p. 95),

—"masochism" for Bersani being supremely praiseworthy in its "passion for pleasure":

> If there is anything that needs to be accounted for in masochism, it is not a supposed identity of pain and pleasure, but rather a passion for pleasure so intense that extreme pain is momentarily tolerated (rather than loved for its own sake) as necessary to bring the masochist to that biochemical threshold where painful stimuli begin to produce pleasurable internal [biochemical] substances. Masochism would, then, be an extreme hedonistic discipline. (*Homos*, pp. 93-94)

Furthermore, in Bersani's valorization of "masochism," "masochism" is not only the ultimate "hedonistic discipline" in the service of "a passion for pleasure"—it is also morally superior to other sex practises—for, in masochism according to Bersani, masochism has

> the unexpected—and *politically salutary*—consequence of enacting the appeal of renunciation. The most radical function of [masochism]...lies...in the shocking revelation that, for the sake of that [masochistic-erotic] stimulation, human beings may be willing to give up control over their environment. (*Homos*, p. 95; italics mine)

Thus the left-wing-homosexual-masochist-intellectual Bersani privileges masochism for its valorizing of "The appeal of powerlessness" (*Homos*, p. 95)—"The appeal of powerlessness" in homosexual masochism being for Bersani evidence in support of his contention that "inherent in the very exercise of power is the temptation of its renunciation" (*Homos*, p. 96)—renunciation "for the sake of pleasure" (*Homos*, p. 99); this "renunciation," in Bersani's view, can aspire to the heights of political correctness, with "Masochistic jouissance" potentially being "a political corrective to the *sadistic use of power*" (italics mine; Bersani does not explain what he means by this phrase), with "the self-shattering" of "Masochistic jouissance" a truly salubrious (in Bersani's view) socio-political phenomenon (that "makes the subject unfindable as an object of discipline"—or as anything else, for that matter). Thus, Bersani concludes, "masochistic surrender [can] operate as effective (even powerful) resistance to coercive [political] designs" (*Homos*, p. 99).

Those of us who have become conversant with left-wing critical theory should not be too surprised at Bersani's valorization of masochism, for left-wing literary-cultural critics have recently privileged what they call "the masochist's reformist and judicial impulse" (Frost 238) as a matter of course, lauding the masochist as "social reformer":

> The social reformer and the masochist share a common goal of exposing and realigning distributions of power. (Laura Frost, "Masochism and Social Reform," *Sex Positives?*, p. 238)

Thus "the masochist," for all his apparent psychopathology and insalubriousness, is to be praised (according to the left wing) for his "goal of exposing and realigning distributions of power." Surprisingly enough, this nexus between "the [left-wing] social reformer and the masochist" brings us back at last to Lawrence himself, who in the last days of his *Lady Chatterley's Lover* period voiced some remarkable insights concerning the connexion between the left wing "social reformer" and the masochist "death of all joy": in a recently published letter, Lawrence observes that

> the very nastiest attacks on me in the papers come from the socialists....The socialist always kills the man, in a man....What I care about, in a man, is the man, not the socialist. And that very capacity for joy, for real *fun*, that I care about. Becoming self-conscious kills joy and fun only because we don't become genuinely aware of ourselves, right through. We stop short, and substitute a narcissus image, and *that* is the real death of all joy. The bane of socialists is that they are half-self-conscious, and for the other half

> substitute a narcissus image of their own perfect rightness etc, which is hell. (D. H. Lawrence letter to P. R. Stephensen, 5 September 1929)

Concluding that his "nastiest" enemies are "the socialists," Lawrence avers that the left-wing way inexorably has an emasculating effect on its members—it "always kills the man, in a man," making the left-wing man incapable of having "that very capacity for joy, for real *fun*" that means so much to Lawrence in his *Lady Chatterley's Lover* period; indeed, the "joy" of sex is surely manifest in many of the lovemaking scenes in *Lady Chatterley*:

> He put his face down and rubbed his cheek against her belly and against her thighs, again and again. And again she wondered a little over the sort of *rapture* it was to him. She did not understand the beauty he found in her, through touch upon her living secret body,...the ecstasy of [sexual] beauty. (*Lady Chatterley's Lover*, Chapter X; italics mine)

In addition to *Lady Chatterley's Lover*'s "joy" of sex, there is also the "real *fun*" of such scenes as those in which Mellors addresses his penis, "John Thomas":

> The man [Mellors] looked down in silence at the tense phallos [his own]...."Ay!" he said at last, in a little voice. "Ay ma lad! tha'rt theer right enough. Yi, tha mun rear thy head! Theer on thy own, eh? an' ta'es no count o' nob'dy! Tha ma'es nowt o'me, John Thomas. Art boss? of me? Eh well, tha'rt more cocky than me, an' tha says less. John Thomas! Dost want *her*! Dost want my lady Jane? Tha's dipped me in again, tha hast. Ay, an' tha comes up smilin'...." (*Lady Chatterley's Lover*, Chapter XIV)

Indeed, the authoritative Oxford don John Bayley states that

> *Lady Chatterley's Lover* was inspired above all by Lawrence's sense of comedy:...sexual liberation [for Lawrence] was above all a question of being joyous and amused by life. (Bayley, *Lawrence and comedy*, p. 206)

Instead of the "joy," the "ecstasy," the "rapture" and "real *fun*" of life and sex, Lawrence tells us, the political left wing has the anti-joy self-consciousness that Lawrence decries,—the self-consciousness which "kills joy and fun" by occluding *genuine* self-awareness and replacing genuine self-awareness with "a narcissus image" which is "the real death of all joy." For the political left this "narcissus image" is rooted in the egregious self-righteousness that is their trademark: the left wing's "narcissus image of their own perfect rightness etc" is an extreme example of the empty "mental-spiritual" idealism that Lawrence defines as "hell."

With their self-consciousness and their "narcissus image of their own perfect rightness" which they substitute for genuine self-awareness, the left wing in academe have made a "hell" for themselves as they lose the capacity for joy and replace it with the obsession of political correctness—as manifested, for example, in Terry Eagleton's sterile, politically correct discussion of "the body"—or rather, "the discourse of the body"—in his trendy vade mecum *Literary Theory*:

> In any politics which puts identity and relationship centrally at stake, renewing attention to lived experience and the discourse of the body, culture does not need to argue its way to political relevance. Indeed one of the achievements of the women's movement has been to redeem such phrases as "lived experience" and "the discourse of the body" from the empiricist connotations with which much literary theory has invested them. "Experience" need now no longer signify an appeal away from power-systems and social relations to the privileged certainties of the private, for feminism recognizes no such distinctions between questions of the human subject and questions of political struggle. The discourse of the body is not a matter of Lawrentian ganglions and suave loins of darkness, but a *politics* of the body, a rediscovery of its sociality through an awareness of the forces which control and subordinate it. (*Literary Theory*, "Conclusion: Political Criticism")

Like the left-wing homosexualt Foucault, the left-wing heterosexual Eagleton evidently finds that "sex is boring" (*Foucault Reader* 340)—he privileges "politics...[and] power systems and social relations" over "the private," the Lawrentian realm of intimate heterosexual relations; rather than the Lawrentian "joy" of the body, Eagleton valorizes a sterile "*politics* of the body." Furthermore, in Eagleton's theory the body is seen, not as the site of Lawrentian pleasure and glory, but rather as the site of victimization (the body, according to Eagleton, being dominated by "the forces which control and subordinate it"); we cannot imagine an Eagleton woman saying along with Lady Chatterley that "I love it!"—"it!" being her body—and declaring

> Give me the body. I believe the life of the body is a greater reality than the life of the mind: when the body is really wakened to life. (*Lady Chatterley's Lover*, Chapter XVI)

Eagleton of course values "the life of the mind," the "political" mind, far more than he does "the life of the body," the "Lawrentian" body—perhaps because his (Eagleton's) body has not been "really wakened to life"; in any event, Eagleton evidently gets a real thrill out of contemplating "global political power":

> "culture" itself,...in moving beyond the isolated work of art into the arenas of language, lifestyle, social value, group identity, inevitably intersects with questions of global political power. (Eagleton, *Literary Theory*, "Afterword," p. 204; italics mine)

It is "global political power," not the "work of art," that is Eagleton's chief preoccupation; and this is true of virtually all left-wing, "politically correct" critics and theorists—the critics and theorists that dominate academia; these theorists would agree with Hunter S. Thompson that politics is "better than sex" (Hunter S. Thompson, *Better Than Sex: Confessions of a Political Junkie*). Indeed, Eagleton's influential left-wing devaluation of Lawrentian sex leads to such statements as these made recently by a neophyte Lawrence critic who complains that

> what happens constantly in Lawrence studies is that.... sex...distracts from what...is actually the deeper subject, namely language (Becket 155)

and who asserts that

> the real subject [in Lawrence] is not...sex. (Becket 167)

Of course Lawrence himself certainly would not agree with Professor Becket's assessment:

> I'll do *my life work*, sticking up for *the love between man and woman*....I shall *always* be a priest of [heterosexual] love....(D. H. Lawrence letter to Sallie Hopkin, 25 December 1912; italics mine)

> I *always* labour at the same thing, to make the sex relation valid and precious....(D. H. Lawrence letter to Nancy Pearn, 12 April 1927; italics mine)

"Sticking up for the love between man and woman" is Lawrence's "life work"—the main basis of his claim to "poetic immortality." Indeed, D. H. Lawrence without "the real subject" of "sex" is like *Hamlet* without the Prince; yet Professor Becket's privileging of "language" over "sex" is part and parcel of the Foucaultian left-wing social constructionist theory according to which

> Sexuality must not be thought of as a kind of natural given....It ["Sexuality"] is the name that can be given to a [socio-]historical construct: not a furtive reality that is difficult to grasp, but a great surface network in which the stimulation of bodies, the intensification of pleasures, *the incitement to discourse*, the formation of special knowledges, the strengthening of controls and resistances, are linked to one another....(Foucault *History* 105-106; italics mine)

The Foucaultian "incitement to discourse" is of a piece with the left-wing insistence that

> the category of sex and its derivatives—e.g. gender, sexual difference, "woman" and "man"—have no natural or biological reality. They are all ideological [social] constructs, effects of an oppressive discourse of heterosexuality. (Dollimore, *Sexual Dissidence*, pp. 58-59)

A left-wing Foucaultian social constructionist herself, the "Lawrentian" Fiona Becket denies Lawrence's "incorrigible biologism" (Butler, *This is Carbon*, p. 31) and even (mistakenly) claims that Lawrence himself is a social constructionist:

> His [Lawrence's] interest...is on love as a cultural construct and one that is constructed *in* language. (Becket 159)

Becket evidently shares the Foucaultian "belief that it is through discourse that our relation to reality is organised—...[that is to say,] language structures the real" (Weeks, *Against Nature*, p. 27); she also evidently shares some left-wing Eagletonian beliefs:

> "Love" is...culturally constructed as problematic, founded as it seems to be on a proliferating ground of oppositions and *contradictions* (Becket 160; italics mine)

The influence of Eagleton is evident in Becket's emphasis on "contradictions" (see Scherr, "Eagleton's Flight")—and, later, in her emphasis on "sexuality [*not* biological sex], gender and the heterosexist paradigm" (Becket 185), she shows the politically correct influence of Eagleton and Michel Foucault as well—a left-wing influence which is the product of

> [t]he notion that politics is a necessary means of finding meaning in personal life....[This notion] necessarily leads to the politicization of all areas of life and culture, summed up in the phrase used by feminists and others that "the personal is political and the polit-

> ical is personal." Politics is always and inevitably about power. Personal relations are, therefore, inevitably power relationships. The radical feminist branch of modern liberalism, to take one example, sees all male-female interactions, including marriage, as power relationships....(Bork 29)

Reducing "personal relations" to "power relationships," the left wing in academia and elsewhere inevitably finds repugnant the Lawrentian emphasis on "the personal," the "feelings and emotions": phenomena which are antithetical to the left-wing ("bolshevist") mentality—as Lawrence astutely observed some seven decades ago:

> Bolshevism...is just a superlative hatred of the thing they call the bourgeois....Feelings and emotions...are so decidedly bourgeois that you [i.e., the left-wing, "bolshevists"] have to invent a man without them. Then the individual, especially the *personal* man, is bourgeois: so he must be suppressed. (*Lady Chatterley's Lover*, Chapter IV)

Thus for Lawrence the left-wing mentality ("Bolshevism") is so averse to "feelings and emotions" that it finds it necessary to "invent" a feelingless, emotionless man—a man who is not "personal." The above statement quoted from *Lady Chatterley's Lover* is made by a minor character in the book, of course, but the sentiment expressed is extremely reminiscent of Lawrence's remarks in the letter of his *Lady Chatterley's Lover* period (5 September 1929 to P. R. Stephensen) in which he asserts that "The socialist always kills the man, in a man." But left-wing academia does not agree with Lawrence's privileging of emotional, feeling relationships; left-of-center "Lawrentian" Peter Scheckner complains that:

> In *Lady Chatterley's Lover*,...Lawrence magnified sexual relations and minimize[d] the [sociohistorical] conditions....[T]he novel [*Lady Chatterley's Lover*] is dominated by...a relationship [Mellors and Lady Chatterley] that is romanticized to the point that everyone and everything else in society is eclipsed. The rich tapestry of history, social struggle, and the interdependence of the public and private sectors is greatly diminished. Mellors relates to no one except Constance. (Scheckner 161)

In opposition to the Lawrentian "magnification" and glorification of "sexual relationships" left-wing academia offers a vague, intellectually-morally-emotionally bankrupt, politically correct idealism that is merely a camouflage for mediocre left-wing academia's vehement self-aggrandizement and sanctimonious self-congratulation, as left-wing English professors praise themselves (indeed, without irony) for their "focus...on the trinity of gender, race, and class":

> Contemporary focus in English departments on the trinity of gender, race, and class is relentlessly driven by a fundamental concern for justice. This engine moves the most exciting criticism today in the direction of advocacy and transformation....The [left-wing] poststructuralist agenda—whether it be the new historicist concern about the workings of power camouflaged by rhetoric of "truth" or virtue," the feminist exposure of millenia of patriarchal domination, or the Marxist unmasking of class hegemony—ultimately conveys in all its forms a crusade meant to right historical wrongs, to reinstate marginalized groups. (Born, *The Birth of Liberal Guilt*, p. 4)

The left wing in academia pretends to moral-ethical superiority in its ostensible "fundamental concern for justice" and its supposed "crusade meant to right historical wrongs, to reinstate marginalized groups"; but, as one moderate-liberal Lawrentian concludes,

> The laudatory idealistic defense of historical victims and the assault on historical oppressors sometimes degenerates into an intellectually stifling atmosphere of judgmental self-righteousness which makes open discussion and disagreement at best vexed. At worst, those who deconstruct the tacit binaries of power are themselves assuming power and in danger of disenfranchising others. (Parker, *Ethics*, p. 196)

The truth of Parker's remark about "disenfranchising others" can be testified to by any one of the myriad white male heterosexual victims of "reverse discrimination" (racial/gender preferences, "affirmative action"); indeed, the power of the reverse discrimination-PC (political correctness) regime in left-wing "literary-critical" academia was flagrantly demonstrated recently by the awarding of the Nobel Prize in Literature to Toni Morrison—as the *New Criterion* astutely observed:

> Morrison has made a magnificent literary career out of left-wing sermonizing and sentimentality....Being (a) black, (b) female, and (c) a paid-up late-twentieth century subscriber to academic political correctness, she plays the race-n'gender card wherever it can be played—which, in the world according to Morrison, is well-nigh everywhere. Heaving leftward paid off mightily for...[Morrison]. Morrison...has been showered with all matter of literary honors

> and awards. She scooped up the Pulitzer Prize in 1988 for her novel *Beloved* and—just this fall [1993]—she found herself the recipient...of that nonpareil of laurel-crowns, the Nobel Prize in Literature.
>
> The Nobel Prize? Toni Morrison and the Nobel Prize in Literature?...We knew it could only be a matter of time before someone of Morrison's indisputable qualifications came to the attention of the Swedish Academy—someone, that is to say, who is (a) black, (b) female, and (c) a paid-up late-twentieth-century subscriber to academic political correctness....(Kramer, *New Criterion*, January 1994, pp. 1-2)

My mention of Toni Morrison at this point is anything but accidental; for the fact is that Morrison is indeed the most egregious example of the current situation in literary-critical academia whereby a mediocre yet politically correct, "reverse racist," "reverse sexist" writer ends up receiving more attention from literary-academic "scholars" than does...—D. H. Lawrence! The shocking fact is that the 1994 MLA Bibliography records eighty-three items about Toni Morrison, and only sixty-two items about D. H. Lawrence; similarly, the 1995 MLA Bibliography shows sixty items on Morrison, and only thirty-eight items on Lawrence—thus, judging from these most recent bibliographies there has been over forty percent more literary-academic scholarship published on Toni Morrison than on D. H. Lawrence: a truly sad state of affairs, and evidence that the political-academic-literary establishment does indeed reward "the mediocrities who do as the ruling classes tell them" (Ellis, *Literature Lost*, p. 53)—among these mediocrities being both Toni Morrison and Maya Angelou, both of whom—along with their politically correct race-gender "conventional pieties" (Ellis 48)—have been catered to by, and aligned with the Clinton White House, which thrives on the power it derives from "group grievances" (Ellis 50) and identity politics (based mainly on race, gender, and sexual orientation) which are so popular in academia, Hollywood, and other cultural elite left-wing centers, the inhabitants of which are frequently invited to the Clinton White House. (Can anybody imagine D. H. Lawrence ever being invited to the White House?)

Lawrence himself of course was painfully aware of his own genuinely subversive nature—as the author of *Lady Chatterley's Lover*, for instance:

> Then lately they have been making a great fuss over *Lady C.*— Scotland Yard holding it up—visiting my agents—sort of threat-

> ening criminal proceedings....Really, why does one write!—or why does one write the things I write? I suppose it's destiny, but on the whole, an unkind one. Those precious young people who are supposed to admire one so much never stand up and give one a bit of backing. I believe they'd see me thrown into prison for life, and never lift a finger. What a spunkless world! (D. H. Lawrence letter to Ottoline Morrell, 5 February 1929)

Embattled and alone in "a spunkless world," Lawrence the genuine revolutionary ("We want a revolution...in the name of...life"; D. H. Lawrence letter to Charles Wilson, 28 December 1928) could easily see himself being "thrown into prison"—something that would certainly not happen to "the mediocrities who do as the ruling classes tell them"—mediocrities like Morrison, Angelou, and Henry Louis Gates, "Harvard Professor of English and Afro-American Studies," who cannot tell the difference between Robert Burns and William Shakespeare (See Mark Steyn, "Present-tense culture," *New Criterion*, April 1997, p. 14). The African-American, Marxist, and Gay-Lesbian "subversives" and "victims" of today are rewarded in the Establishment-academy with six-figure salaries; but the Lawrence of *Lady Chatterley's Lover*—the true revolutionary "subversive"— knew that

> they [the Establishment] take the whole thing *Lady C.* as anti-bourgeois and subversive (D. H. Lawrence letter to Jean Watson, 16 November 1929)

—but he (Lawrence) would nonetheless fight the Establishment, fight the Establishment in the name of "life":

> If one is a man, one must fight, and slap back at one's enemies, because they are the enemies of life....(D. H. Lawrence letter to Brewster, 7 February 1929)

As "a man," Lawrence felt that the test of manhood was to fight for life against "the enemies of life." But unfortunately, today the Lawrentian realities of "life" and "manhood" are held in disrepute by many intellectuals—thanks to left-wing academe; Terry Eagleton, in his popular and influential textbook *Literary Theory*, spitefully pokes fun at Lawrentian "Life":

> For D. H. Lawrence, emotions, "personality" and the "ego" were equally discredited, and must give way to the ruthlessly impersonal force of spontaneous-creative Life....

> ...[Leavis' Lawrentian literary journal] *Scrutiny*...[was] concerned...with the unique value of the individual and the creative realm of the interpersonal. These values could be summarized as "Life," a word which *Scrutiny* made a virtue out of not being able to define. If you asked for some reasoned theoretical statement of their case, you had thereby demonstrated that you were in the outer darkness: either you felt Life or you did not. Great literature was a literature reverently open to Life, and what Life was could be demonstrated by great literature. The case was circular, intuitive, and proof against all argument, reflecting the enclosed coterie of the [Lawrentian] Leavisites themselves. It was not clear what side Life put you on in the General Strike, or whether celebrating its vibrant presence in poetry was compatible with endorsing mass unemployment. If Life was creatively at work anywhere then it was in the writings of D. H. Lawrence, whom Leavis championed from an early date; yet "spontaneous-creative life" in Lawrence seemed happily to co-exist with the most virulent sexism, racism and authoritarianism....(*Literary Theory*, "The Rise of English")

The best of "the mediocrities who do as the ruling classes tell them," Eagleton of academic establishment Oxford at least does Lawrence the service of recognizing Lawrence's (and Leavis') supreme importance—but of course Eagleton, with his own trendiness and superficiality and lack of intensity, completely misreads Lawrence (see Scherr, "Eagleton's Flight"), failing to perceive that Lawrentian "spontaneous-creative Life" is a way to attain genuine intensity of the "emotions"—an intensity which for Lawrence is essentially religious:

> Whenever the soul is moved to a certain fullness of experience, that is religion. Every sincere and *genuine* [italics mine] feeling is a religious feeling.... Everything that puts us into connection, into vivid touch, is religious....[Everything that]...puts us curiously into touch with life...achieves thereby certain religious feeling, and gives a certain religious experience....Once you have a real glimpse of religion, you realise that all that is *truly* felt, every feeling that is felt in true relation, every vivid feeling of connection, is religious,...and the only irreligious thing is the death of feeling, the causing of nullity; the frictional irritation which, carried far, tends to nullity. (*Apocalypse*, Fragment 1, p. 155)

The Lawrentian "soul" (i.e., self), capable of attaining "a certain *fullness of experience*," is the "religious" self; this Lawrentian "religious" self is able to fully experience "sincere and genuine feeling"; and "genuine feeling is a religious feeling"; but most people are incapable of "genuine," "religious" feeling—most people are incapable of "achiev[ing] a state of feeling which...is religious," for most people cannot come "into connection, into vivid touch...with life": the "vivid...touch with life" that leads to "religious feeling" and "religious experience," for "all that is *truly* felt...is religious"—and far too many people are incapable of *true*, "religious" feeling; furthermore, these same people are incapable of responding to literature:

> The man who has lost his religious response *cannot* respond to literature or to any form of art, fully: because the call of every work of art, spiritual or physical, is religious, and demands a religious response. (*Apocalypse*, Fragment 1, p. 155)

It is this "religious response"—"religious response" rooted in "fullness of experience" and "sincere and genuine feeling"—which Eagleton and his ephebes are incapable of manifesting. Thus, deriding the "religious sense" Eagleton valorizes

> the "taken-for-granted" post-atheism of Marx

which says that

> God is truly dead....(*Criticism and Ideology*, Chapter 1, "Mutations of Critical Ideology")

—and, for Eagleton, this is good news, since (according to Eagleton)

> The death of God is the death of the [capitalist-ideological] superstructure.... (*Ideology of the Aesthetic*, p. 258)

Denying God ("God is absent" [*Marxism* 33]), attacking "reactionary Christian moralism" (*Marxism* 42), Eagleton, in his lack of "religious sense" and his "lost...religious response," "*cannot* respond to literature" (as Lawrence could have predicted); and finally Eagleton indeed denies and attacks literature:

> Anything can be literature, and anything which is regarded as unalterably and unquestionably literature—Shakespeare, for example—can cease to be literature....Literature, in the sense of a set of works of assured and unalterable value, distinguished by certain shared inherent properties, does not exist....
> ...There is no such thing as a literary work or tradition which is valuable *in itself*, regardless of what anyone might have said or come to say about it. "Value"...means whatever is valued by cer-

tain people in specific situations, according to particular criteria and in the light of given purposes. It is thus quite possible that, given a deep enough transformation of our history, we may in the future produce a society which is unable to get anything at all out of Shakespeare. His works might simply seem desperately alien....In such a situation, Shakespeare would be no more valuable than much present-day graffiti. And though many people would consider such a social condition tragically impoverished, it seems to me dogmatic not to entertain the possibility that it might arise rather from a general human enrichment. (*Literary Theory*, "Introduction: What is Literature?")

Denigrating literature ("Anything can be literature"), denying literature ("Literature...does not exist"), Eagleton evidently looks forward to the day when even Shakespeare will no longer be considered literature,—for Eagleton in his lack of vital "religious" connection with literature can indeed see as salubrious a "situation" in which "Shakespeare would be no more valuable than...graffiti." Thus it is no wonder that Eagleton in his failure of "religious response" to literature in general—and to Lawrence in particular—shows in his obnoxious remarks on Lawrence the results of "the death of feeling," "the frictional irritation which...tends to nullity"—with Eagleton's "nullity" resulting in irresponsible, meaningless and unsupported accusations against Lawrence, charging Lawrence with "the most virulent sexism, racism and authoritarianism" (*Literary Theory*, Chapter 1, "The Rise of English"). It is time for Lawrentians to face the left wing's bogus attacks on Lawrence—and it seems to me that the best way to do this is by emphasizing and delineating the "religious"-"political" Lawrence (as I have attempted to do in the present work) in such a way as to demonstrate both the essential sublimity of his intentions and aspirations (that is to say, he wanted to save the world as well as to save himself, "himself" being his poetic self striving to attain "poetic immortality") and the extraordinary manner in which the "religious" "saviour"-prophet Lawrence works in tandem with the "political" novelist-poet-essayist Lawrence who uses his writings to achieve his aesthetic-philosophicoreligious agendas—agendas which surely transcend the vulgar "sexism, racism and authoritarianism" accusations that Eagleton vehemently (and unsupportedly and unconvincingly) hurls at Lawrence. (In this day and age, common *politicians*, from Jesse Jackson to Jesse Helms, from David Dinkins to David Duke, have been accused of "racism"—doesn't a great creative artist like David Herbert Lawrence deserve better?) Thus, in an essay to redress the balance in Lawrence's favor, I hopefully demonstrate in detail early in this study that Lawrence, far from being guilty of vulgar "racism" (i.e., anti-Semitism), actually in a very real sense aspired to be "Jewish" as part of his quest for poetic immortality. Indeed, Lawrence as "Jew" is (as I hope I have demonstrated earlier in this work) a fine and likely scenario; for

> As Thorstein Veblen noted, the "intellectual preeminence" of Jews derives from their marginal status as a rootless people with a wandering curiosity, uninhibited by existing conventions, and thus always in "the vanguard of inquiry." (Diggins, *Promise*, p. 382)

Like the Jews, Lawrence is "intellectually preeminent," yet "marginal" and "rootless" and "uninhibited" and "wandering"—indeed, Lawrence himself refers to himself as "wandering Jew":

> I am turned into a wandering Jew, my feet itch, and a seat burns my posterior if I sit too long. (D. H. Lawrence letter to Irene Whittley, 18 December 1919)

But probably most important to Lawrence's "Jewishness" is his enthusiasm for the Jewish "One God":

> The Jews did a wonderful thing when they focused the whole religious feeling of man upon One God. (*Apocalypse* 156)

Full of enthusiasm for the "One God," Lawrence stands in contradistinction to the cultural-theorist left wing; instead of God, the left wing has "Historicism"; as Eugene Goodheart explains:

> Historicism is inimical to the individual will, or rather it transforms intention into an instrument of forces always greater than itself. And it does so with a certain pleasure, for "history" (or the historicist's version of history) is a sort of God. (Goodheart, "Censorship," *Representing Modernist Texts*, p. 239)

Lawrence reveres the "One God"; left-wing literary critics, on the other hand, find "God's death" (Born, *Birth*, p. 5) to be a definitely good thing, leading to left-wing social-political activism which (according to the left) is "a crusade meant to right historical wrongs, to reinstate marginalized groups" (Born, *Birth*, p. 4)—thus "the death of God" (Born, *Birth*, pp. 17, 18) is an unmixed blessing for left-wing critical theorists, for, according to them, "the death of God" leads to "ethical criteria of justice, fairness, and access to power"

(Born, *Birth*, p. 173) as left-wing man (and woman) takes God's place in the moral-ethical universe of "the post-theistic liberal [left-wing] conscience" (Born, *Birth*, p. 5)—in other words, "God's Death and the Moral Imperative" (Born, *Birth*, p. 18) go hand in hand in left-wing literary-critical theory—with "the Moral Imperative" to be dictated, these days, by the likes of Bill and Hillary Clinton, Al Gore, Jesse Jackson, Al Sharpton, Oprah Winfrey, etc.

But what of the proud left-wing claim that "the death of God" leads to "the birth of liberal guilt"—"guilt" which leads to various politically correct schemes to advance "social justice" (Born, *Birth*, p. 122) agendas and promote "the attempt to fuse private and public virtue" (Ibid. 122); interestingly enough, Lawrence himself with his unique sagacity demystifies the self-righteous left-wing social reformers as "liars," egotistic ciphers, "fine cabbages" who through their self-centered quest for "social justice" hanker to attain a kind of bogus immortality:

> The soul does not come into being at birth. The soul comes into being in the midst of life....
> It is absurd to talk about all men being immortal, all having souls. Very few men have being at all. They perish utterly, as individuals....Most men are just transitory natural phenomena. Whether they live or die does not matter: except in so far as every failure in the part is a failure in the whole. Their death is of no more matter than the cutting of a cabbage in the garden, an act utterly apart from grace. (*The Crown*, "The Flux of Corruption")

According to Lawrence, the existence of "the soul" in human beings cannot be taken for granted (we are not endowed with souls "at birth")—the soul can only be achieved "in the midst of life" by one's special efforts—and only a few extraordinary people are able to achieve souls and be "immortal" ("It is absurd to talk about all men being immortal, all having souls"), since "Very few men have being at all," "being" for Lawrence here being synonymous with individuality ("men" as "individuals"). Because Lawrentian men have true individuality, true "being," they are capable of "being immortal," of "having souls"; but most non-Lawrentian men have no individuality and therefore no "being," no "soul": these non-Lawrentian men, without individuality or "being" or "soul," are simply "cabbages" whose death does not matter for they are "utterly apart from grace." These willful, egotistic, non-Lawrentian men

> assert themselves as important, as absolute mortals. They are just liars....
>
> They are all just fat lies, these people, these many people, these *mortals* [my italics]. They are innumerable cabbages in the regulated cabbage plot. And our great men are no more than Mrs. Wiggs of the Cabbage Patch. (Ibid.)

The left-wing social reformers, even though they "assert themselves as important," are in fact "just liars": they are really merely "these mortals" who can never attain Lawrentian immortality, for they lack Lawrentian individuality, being and "soul," even if they are so-called great men; indeed, these "great men" are neither great nor men in Lawrence's view: in their absence of being they can attain neither greatness nor manhood: for Lawrence, "our great men" are simply tantamount to "Mrs. Wiggs of the Cabbage Patch"—that is to say, they are merely superior ("fine") cabbages:

> [T]his is the state of man, when he falls into self-sufficiency, and asserts that his self-conscious ego is It. He falls into the condition of fine cabbages. (Ibid.)

One of the major pseudo-"great men" ("fine cabbages") whom Lawrence decries is surely the American President Woodrow Wilson, whose "self-conscious ego" ("egoistic *will*") is deplored by Lawrence as selfish and duplicitous:

> it seems much easier to summon up energy for some egoistic or mercenary purpose, particularly for the enforcing of the egoistic *will*, than for a good purpose....[T]he charlatan and the witch and the fakir can summon up a lot of energy just for their own ends. I'm surprised what a lot of that there is in the world—especially in the business world—a fakir-like energised charlatanry, consciously self-energised. I believe Henry Ford and President Wilson were that way....(D. H. Lawrence letter to Earl Brewster, 22 August 1927)

Full of "self-sufficiency" and the belief that "his self-conscious ego is It," the ostensibly well-intentioned liberal Woodrow Wilson, like the "mercenary" industrialist Henry Ford, is *au fond* concerned only with "the enforcing of [his] egoistic *will*," "[his] egoistic...purpose,"—and, like other left-wing thinkers, Wilson would be one that "always kills the man, in a man" (D. H. Lawrence letter to Stephensen, 5 September 1929)—all for the sake of left-wing ideals; as Lawrence explains it in his brilliant *Fantasia*:

> Our leaders have not loved men: they have loved ideas, and have been willing to sacrifice passionate men on the altars of the blood-drinking, ever-ash-thirsty ideal. Has President Wilson, or Karl Marx, or Bernard Shaw ever felt one hot blood-pulse of love for the working man, the half-conscious, deluded working man? Never. Each of these [left-wing] leaders has wanted to abstract him away from his own *blood and being*, into some foul...abstraction of a man. (*Fantasia*, "The Birth of Sex"; my italics)

Left-wing leaders such as Wilson and Marx, Lawrence tells us, are just ideologues who "have loved ideas" rather than people; they have especially loved their left-wing "blood-drinking...ideal[s]" and abstractions; indeed, in their enthusiasm for "foul abstraction" these left-wing leaders even want to "abstract" working people from their own "blood and being," destroying their concrete, flesh-and-blood quality ("blood") and individual potentiality ("being"), and turning them into bloodless ideological abstractions. Thus Lawrence sees and abhors the "energised charlatanry" of "egoistic" left-wing ideologues, and deftly impugns the motives of these "great men" who see people only as ideological objects. Ridiculing the pseudo-"great men" such as Wilson and Marx, Lawrence certainly consigns them to the category of "fine cabbages" that want to help other cabbages— or, rather, "other people":

> Long ago [Lawrence sardonically states] we agreed that we had fulfilled all purpose and that our only business was to look after other people. We said: "It is marvellous, we are really complete." If the regulation cabbage, hidebound and solid, could walk about on his stalk, he would be very much as we are. He would think of himself as we think of ourselves, he would talk as *we* talk, of the public good....
>
> Then he would say: "I must do something." Looking round, he would see little dwindly cabbages struggling in the patch, and would say: "So much injustice, so much suffering and poverty in the world, it cannot be." Then he would set forth to make dwindly cabbages into proper, fine cabbages. So he would be a reformer.
>
> He would kick, kick, kick against the conditions which make some cabbages poor and dwindly, most cabbages poorer and more dwindly than himself....
>
> Let no one suffer, they [the social reformers] have said. No mouse shall be caught by a cat, no mouse. It is a transgression. Every mouse shall become a pet, and every cat shall lap milk in peace, from the saucer of utter benevolence.

> This is the millenium, the golden age that is to be, when all shall be domesticated, and the lion and the leopard and the hawk shall come to our door to lap milk and to peck the crumbs, and no sound shall be heard but the lowing of fat cows and the baa-ing of fat sheep.
> This is the Green Age that is to be, the age of the perfect cabbage. This was our hope and our fulfilment, for this, in this hope, we lived and we died.
> So the virtuous, public-spirited ones have suffered bitterly from the aspect of their myriad more-or-less blighted neighbours, whom they love as themselves. They [the left-wing social reformers] have lived and died to right the wrong conditions of social injustice. (*The Crown*, "The Flux of Corruption")

Sardonically mimicking the socio-political voice of the left-wing social reformers who complacently believe that "our only business [is] to look after other people," Lawrence derides these shallow left wingers for their smug belief that "we are really complete"; according to Lawrence, these left-wing social reformers are so satisfied with their own ontological development ("we had fulfilled all purpose") that they believe there is nothing left to do for their being as individuals: in view of their being so "really complete," all these left-wing social reformers need to think about (or so they say) is "the public good"—"the public good" essentially being the welfare of the "little dwindling cabbages struggling in the patch": in other words, for Lawrence these left-wing social reformers reduce human beings to "little dwindly cabbages" who must be ministered to by the "fine cabbages" ("fine cabbages" being left-wing elite leaders; in our day, the best example of these "fine cabbages" would of course be the Kennedys). These "fine cabbage" left-wing social reformers decry "So much injustice, so much suffering and poverty in the world"—and proceed to make things worse by playing God and violating the order of Nature as they "set forth to make dwindly cabbages into proper, fine cabbages"; these left-wing elite "fine cabbages" would have themselves "be...reformers" that "kick against the conditions which make some cabbages poor and dwindly, most cabbages poorer and more dwindly than [themselves]"—even though, as we know today after some forty years of "Great Society" programs, the social reformers are "but...kicking against the pricks" (ibid.) and failing to make the "poor and dwindly cabbages" any less "poor and dwindly" (as we know from increasing rates of inner city poverty, illiteracy, illegitimacy, ignorance, crime, drug abuse, child abuse, etc.); yet what really matters to these "fine cabbage" social reformers is their own hubristic self-gratification as they set forth their fairy-tale, sanctimonious vision of an unnatural world in which "no one [will] suffer….No mouse shall be caught by a cat….It is a transgression. Every mouse shall become a pet, and every cat shall lap milk in peace, from the saucer of utter benevolence"—"utter benevolence" which today results in such injustices as reverse discrimination—particularly in academia, where unqualified "poor and dwindly cabbages" (i.e., "oppressed minorities") are rewarded solely on the basis of their race and gender, while qualified "cats" (i.e., intellectually gifted white, heterosexual, "traditional," politically incorrect males) are made to flounder on the margins as punishment for their "oppressor" status; all this being part and parcel of the left-wing "millenium," in which individuality, uniqueness, and creative ability are eliminated ("all shall be domesticated"): this is the left-wing "millenium" which Lawrence indeed demystifies and decries. Sardonically designating the utopian left-wing "golden age" of the future ("the millenium, the golden age that is to be") as "The Green Age that is to be, the age of the perfect cabbage," Lawrence sees how the left-wing "fine cabbage" blueprint for the future makes for the annihilation of all flesh-and-blood individuality and passion. Noting the monomaniacal fanaticism with which the extreme left wingers pursue their "Green Age" agenda of turning human beings into vegetables ("perfect cabbage[s]"), Lawrence proceeds to mimic the ardent, indeed obsessive, revolutionary voice of the "fine cabbage" left wingers: "This ["Green Age…, the age of the perfect cabbage"] was our hope and our fulfilment, for this, in this hope, we lived and we died"; but Lawrence has no sympathy for these left-wing "virtuous, public-spirited ones" who (Lawrence sarcastically notes) "have suffered bitterly from the aspect of their myriad more-or-less blighted neighbours, whom they love as themselves"; supposedly, the "fine cabbage" left-wing social reformers "have lived and died to right the wrong conditions of social injustice"—but Lawrence brilliantly demystifies (and de-idealizes) the motivation of these "virtuous, public-spirited ones," who in our day include (among others) Kennedy and Clinton and (indeed) Martin Luther King—all in fact self-indulgent, narcissistic, hedonistic (i.e., womanizing) elitists whose "humanitarianism" is the product of their "self-consciousness" and "corruption," which is in fact their corrupt, egocentric "desire for immortality"; as Lawrence remarkably explains:

> The most unselfish, the most humanitarian of us all, he is the *hollowest* and fullest of rottenness. The more rotten we become, the more insistent and insane becomes our desire to ameliorate the conditions of our poorer, and maybe healthier neighbours.
>
> Fools, vile fools! Why cannot we acknowledge and admit the horrible pulse and thresh of corruption within us. What *is* this self-consciousness that palpitates within us like a disease? What is it that threshes and threshes within us, drives us mad if we see a cat catch a sparrow?
>
> We dare not know. Oh, we are convulsed with shame long before we come to the point. It is indecent beyond endurance to think of it.
>
> Yet here let it be told. It was the living desire for immortality, for *being*, which urged us ceaselessly. It [i.e., the desire for immortality] was the bud within the ["fine," left-wing] cabbage, threshing, threshing, threshing. (*The Crown*, "The Flux of Corruption"; first italics mine, later italics Lawrence's)

According to Lawrence, "the most humanitarian of us all" is in fact "the hollowest," the most egregiously lacking in uniqueness, in individuality, in "being"; these humanitarians are in fact the "fullest of rottenness"—and in their hollowness (i.e., their lack of genuine individuality and "being") and their rottenness (i.e., their anti-life, anti-Lawrentian character), they frantically ("insistent[ly]," "insane[ly]") feel the left-wing extremist "desire to ameliorate the conditions of [their] poorer, and...healthier neighbours"; thus, Lawrence would say, the dogged ideological efforts of today's Big Government left wingers like (say) Teddy Kennedy, are a device to cover up the essential lack of being, the "hollowness," and the veritable decadence, psychic-ontological-moral decadence, the "rottenness," of these pompous left-wing liberals who in intrusive Big Government guise interfere in the lives of their "healthier neighbours" by telling them how to live, how to think, how to spend their money. But the "horrible" truth about these rich, elitist left wingers is that their "desire to ameliorate the conditions of...[their] neighbours" is rooted in the "self-consciousness" of their obsessive, shameful "desire for immortality"—"immortality" which these political left wingers can never attain because they do not have within them the individuality, the "being," that is the *sine qua non* for genuine, Lawrentian "immortality"; instead, they merely possess "self-conscious," "assertive egos" that "extinguished any shoot of tender immortality" in them (ibid.)—and consequently, instead of attaining genuine "living...immortality," they (the "humanitarians") attain "the fixed will of the temporal form" which "triumphed in assertion" (ibid.), an "assertion" of the "false absolute self," the "self-conscious ego" (ibid.) that is antithetical to the genuine "immortality"—immortality which Lawrence is capable of attaining thanks to his transcendental belief in "the unseen goodness" (*The Crown*, "The Nupitals of Death and the Attendant Vulture") rather than in "the egoistic will" (ibid.); it is this "unseen goodness" which Lawrence credits with "saving" him:

> The soul is still alive, while it has passion: any sort of passion, even for the brush with death....And in the brush with death it may be released again into positive life. A man may be sufficiently released by a fall on the rope and the dangling for a few minutes of agony, in space. That may finally reduce his soul to its elements, set it free and child-like, and break down that egoistic entity which had developed upon it from the past. The near touch of death may be a release into life; if only it will break the egoistic will, and release that other flow.
>
> But if a man, having fallen very near to death, gets up at length and says: I did it! It's my triumph! I beat the mountains that time!—then, of course, his ego has only pulled itself in triumph out of the menace, and the individual will go on more egoistic and barrenly complacent.
>
> If a man says: "I fell! But the unseen goodness helped me, when I struggled for life, and so I was saved,"—then this man will go on in life unimprisoned, the channels of his heart open, and passion still flowing through him....
>
> There must be a certain faith. And that means, an ultimate reliance on that which is beyond our will, and not contained in our ego. (Ibid.)

Thus Lawrence's "soul" is "still alive"; indeed, Lawrence's soul is "saved," full of "positive life," because, rather than relying on his "egoistic entity," his "egoistic will," for assistance in his quest for "immortality," for ultimate triumph in *his* "brush with death," Lawrence prays and is grateful to "the unseen goodness" for saving him in his struggle for life, "and so I was saved,"—saved for the greatness of poetic immortality. Unlike the left-wing "humanitarians," full of "egoistic will," Lawrence believes in, has "an ultimate reliance" on, "the unseen goodness," which is "beyond our will, and not contained in our ego." This "unseen goodness," this "beyond," is none other than God—it is God that Lawrence needs for "immortality":

> Without God, without some sort of immortality,...we are nothing....
> My immortality is not from the beginning, in my endless ancestry. Nor is it on ahead in life everlasting. My life comes to me from the great Creator, the Beginner....
> I am not immortal till I have achieved immortality. And immortality is not a question of time, of everlasting life. It is a question of consummate being. Most men die and perish away, unconsummated, unachieved. It is not easy to achieve immortality, to win a consummate being. It is *supremely* difficult. It means undaunted suffering and undaunted enjoyment, both. And when a man has reached his ultimate of enjoyment and his ultimate of suffering, *both*,...then he is made absolute....Then he is immortal. It is not a question of time. It is a question of being. It is not a question of submission, submitting to the divine grace: it is a question of submitting to the divine grace, in suffering and self-obliteration, *and* it is a question of conquering by divine grace, as the tiger leaps on the trembling deer, in utter satisfaction of the Self, in complete fulfilment of desire. The fulfilment is dual. And having known the dual fulfilment, then within the fulfilled soul is established the divine relation,...the soul has achieved immortality, it has attained to absolute being. (*The Crown*, "To Be, and to Be Different"; first italics mine; second italics Lawrence's; third italics mine)

For Lawrence, then, God is indeed essential ("Without God,...we are nothing"), as is "immortality" ("without some sort of immortality,...we are nothing")—but in this of course Lawrence is certainly exceptional, in view of the fact that "Not many people are anything at all....Essentially, they don't exist, they aren't there" (*Women in Love*, Chapter II, "Shortlands") and "I never yet met a man who was anything but what he had been *told* to be" (as Lawrence bitterly concludes in the last paragraph of *The Crown*). Yet, undaunted, Lawrence confidently seeks his "immortality," secure in the belief that "My life comes to me from the great Creator" (that is to say, from *God*); furthermore, Lawrence is sure that, in view of the fact that he must *achieve* his "immortality," he can manage this feat by dint of "win[ning] a consummate being" by means of "undaunted suffering and undaunted enjoyment, both"—that is to say, by living a "supremely" intense life, a life in which he attains "his ultimate of enjoyment and his ultimate of suffering, *both*....Then he is immortal." Yet Lawrence is certain that in order to achieve this supreme intensity he must have a supremely intense, supremely creative interactive relation to God, to "the divine grace"—a relation in which he (Lawrence) can at one and the same time submit to "the divine grace" *and* gain power from "the divine grace,"—power which may then be used for "conquering by divine grace,...in the utter satisfaction of the Self, in complete *fulfilment of desire*"—the desire for "poetic immortality"; for Lawrence, the "utter satisfaction of the Self" that is attained in "poetic immortality" is tantamount to the "Heaven" of Lawrentian "manhood":

> *Heaven* lies about us in our *consummation of manhood*, if we are men. If we are men, *we attain to heaven* in our *achieved manhood*, our flowering maturity. ("Reality of Peace," III; my italics)

Thus, once Lawrence, with the help of God ("the divine grace"), attains his "consummation of manhood," his "utter satisfaction of the Self" as a result of his achievement of the supreme individuality and uniqueness that is part and parcel of "poetic immortality," he (Lawrence) "attain[s] to heaven in [his] achieved manhood, [his] flowering maturity"; "divine grace," "consummation of manhood," "satisfaction of the Self": these are among the supreme Lawrentian values; yet today these values resonate not at all among the intellectual-cultural-power elites: "the divine grace" is replaced by "the death of God," with God Himself being replaced by "irresistible," "charismatic" left-wing celebrities (Kennedy, Clinton, King, Oprah Winfrey, Jesse Jackson) and their bogus "moral authority" (political correctness having replaced religion); as for "our consummation of manhood," Leslie Fiedler prophetically declared some thirty-five years ago that

> There *is* a weariness in the West which undercuts the struggle between socialism and capitalism, democracy and autocracy; a weariness with humanism itself which underlies all the movements of our world, *a weariness with the striving to be men*. (Leslie Fiedler, *Waiting for the End*, p. 168; first italics Fiedler's; second italics mine)

Weary with the struggle for "manhood," the West today via its left-wing academics decries "achieved manhood" as "heterosexual arrogance" (Clarke 1996, 84), "extreme masculinism" (Clarke 1998, 244) and "masculinist patriarchalism" (Clarke 1998, 245); furthermore, the most powerful man in the West—indeed, in the entire world—is not considered a "man" even by his most sympathetic critics; recently one ardent Bill Clinton supporter was forced to admit that

> Clinton...[is] both man and boy....
> ...[Clinton's] refusal to own up to bad behavior...is boyish stuff....A man understands that there comes a time when you simply have to take responsibility for your behavior. For Clinton, that time never comes....
> In the end, there is but one thing to say about this sort of behavior: It is not manly....(Richard Cohen, "Would Clinton Leave the Scene of an Accident?" *New York Post*, February 18, 1998, p. 25)

With his failure to take responsibility for his behavior, Bill Clinton is surely "not manly"—furthermore, he is not Lawrentian, for Lawrence emphatically declares that

> More and more I admire...true classic dignity and *self responsibility*. (D. H. Lawrence letter to Lady Ottoline Morrell, 7 April 1916; italics mine)

Thus the Lawrentian Birkin, in his ultimate sexual relations (perhaps anal) with Ursula towards the end of *Women in Love*, manifests the "self responsibility" valorized by Lawrence:

> Birkin...seemed [to Ursula] to have turned into something wicked and flickering, mocking, suggestive, quite impossible. Ursula was frightened of him, and fascinated....For a moment she revolted....She would break the spell. But before the resolution had formed she had submitted again....He knew all the time what he was doing, she could see it in his smiling, concentrated eyes. It was *his responsibility*, she would leave it to him....
> ...And she gave way, he might do as he would. His licentiousness was repulsively attractive. But he was *self-responsible*, she would see what it was. (*Women in Love*, Chapter XXX, "Snow"; italics mine)

Full of "self-responsibility" in his sexual relations with Ursula, the Lawrentian Rupert Birkin is a far cry from the American President

Clinton, who indeed evidently possesses no selfhood whatsoever; as one Clinton observer recently noted:

> this President [Clinton] is not a damaged self. He is someone with no self at all. This is what distinguishes him, both from Nixon, and from normal people....
>
> ...This explains why his [Clinton's] lies are not lies as others understand the term. The President means everything he says at the moment he says it, and because no thing or moment is connected to any other [since he has no self], everything he says is sincere. Some part of Richard Nixon knew he was a crook, even as he denied it. Since there is no other part of President Clinton besides the part that is speaking, there is no deception, and no guilt. (Richard Brookhiser, "Clinton & Nixon," *National Review*, February 23, 1998, pp. 42-43)

Indeed, since he lacks any sense of self, Clinton is even incapable of Lawrentian self-aggrandizing "heterosexual arrogance," as he (Clinton) denies "hav[ing] sexual relations with that woman"—or any other woman, for that matter, these days (February 1998). But Clinton's "selfless," hypocritical, politically correct failure to stand up for "heterosexual arrogance" (even his own) is surely in accord with those left-wing "Lawrentians" who valorize

> diverse sexualities..., sexual diversity and difference (Kelsey 176)

—and accordingly attack Lawrentian "heterosexual arrogance" as

> the signifying force that prevents...a full dialogical expression of polymorphous desire (Kelsey 180)

—"polymorphous desire" being privileged by these left-wing Lawrence critics over what they hostilely and condescendingly refer to as "heterosexual morality" (Kelsey 183, 185).

Lawrence of course makes "heterosexual morality" exciting and meaningful ("And the great living experience for every man is the adventure into the woman.... The man embraces in the woman all that is not himself, and from that one resultant, from that embrace, comes every new action" [D. H. Lawrence letter to Bertrand Russell, 24 February 1915]); at the same time Lawrence decries homosexuality as the "blasphemy against love" (D. H. Lawrence letter to David Garnett, 19 April 1915); for this Lawrentian valorization of heterosex and condemnation of homosex, Lawrence today is vilified by influential, trendy, extremist queer theorists as a heterosexist guilty of "a murderous homophobia of genocidal scope" (Stephen Barber, *Novel Gazing: Queer Readings in Fiction*, p. 418). But in fact if these politically correct, politically obsessed critics could get beyond *their* prejudices, they would realize that what Lawrence really wants is a better life for everybody; as Lawrence himself explains in one of his last essays:

> There is a great change coming, bound to come....If we are intelligent, alert and undaunted, then life will be much better, more generous, more spontaneous, more vital, less basely materialistic. If we fall into a state of funk, impotence and persecution, then things may be very much worse for us than they are now. It is up to us. It is up to men to be men. ("State of Funk")

Thus for Lawrence it is imperative that "men...be men" so that "life will be much better, more generous, more spontaneous, more vital, less basely materialistic"; yet, as Leslie Fiedler presciently noted, "in the West...[there is] a weariness with the striving to be men"; indeed, today "man" has in fact been replaced by the politically correct categories of "race, class, and gender": for the politically correct left-wing cultural elite, "man" no longer possesses individuality, selfhood or uniqueness, but is rather merely a member of some sociopolitical group ("oppressed" or "oppressor," as the case may be); furthermore, the most culturally influential left-wing intellectuals of our day deny even the actual existence of "man": Foucault himself of course postulates, in addition to "the death of God," the death of "man":

> In our day,...it is not so much the absence or the death of God that is affirmed as the end of man....since he [man] has killed God, it is he himself who must answer for his own finitude; but since it is in the death of God that he speaks, thinks, and exists, his murder itself is doomed to die; new gods, the same gods, are already swelling the future Ocean; man will disappear. (*Order of Things*, p. 385)

As one Foucault scholar explains: "For Foucault,...the death of man [means that]...the noble notion of an autonomous subject has been rendered untenable by the discoveries of [left-wing] psychoanalysis, linguistics and Marxism....[Foucault] is appropriating a bleakly Nietzschean vision of a post-theological world in which a divinely guaranteed notion of man is being called into question" (Macey 90). Thus for Foucault and his myriad followers, "the death of God" and "the death of man" go hand in hand. This state of affairs, it seems to me, has extremely serious ramifications for the reputation of D. H. Lawrence; for, in this our "post-theological world" (at least in academe), with the hegemony of the nihilist cultural elitist left wing for whom political correctness serves as the new "theology" in the academy, "[Lawrence's] innately religious vision and search,...[his] endemic moral strength" (Panichas 79) make him even more dangerous and hateful to the atheistic left wing (whose main "religion" is "diversity," "tolerance" of "alternative lifestyles," and privileging of non-Western cultures ["multi-culturalism"]) than he ever was to the ultra-conservative Eliotic right wing some seven decades ago.

Leavis successfully fought for Lawrence against the forces of the ultraconservative Eliotic right; today it remains for a new Leavisite-Lawrentian to lead the fight for Lawrence against the many-headed hydra of the left. The anti-Lawrence left, indeed, possesses rather less "vital intelligence" (to use a Leavis phrase; *D. H. Lawrence: Novelist*, p. 62) and less maturity than the anti-Lawrence Eliotic right of an earlier day; being more narcissistic and even more set in their pieties, the left is evidently even less capable of Leavisite "growing into understanding" about Lawrence; as Leavis declares:

> Lawrence's insight was penetrating and clear, and he was marvellously intelligent, and the worst difficulty we have in coming to terms with his art is that there is resistance in us to what it has to communicate—if only the kind of resistance represented by habit; habit that will not let us see what is there for what it is, or believe that the door is open. And learning to recognize the success and the greatness of [Lawrence's work]—I speak for myself—was not merely a matter of applying one's mind in repeated re-readings and so mastering the methods of the art and the nature of the organization; it was a matter, too, of growing—growing into understanding. (Leavis, *D. H. Lawrence: Novelist*, Chapter One, "Lawrence and Art")

Unfortunately, it seems to me that there is not likely to be much "growing into understanding" regarding Lawrence in this day and age,—a day and age which, far from being "less basely materialistic" as Lawrence hoped it would be ("State of Funk"), has instead reached the stage where it is so "basely materialistic" that even a liberal pundit can sarcastically conclude that

> Perhaps Bill Clinton is the Devil....Certainly, the voters have closed their eyes and made their pact with the Devil: Keep us pros-

> perous and we won't hold you to any special moral or ethical standards. (Maureen Dowd, "Sympathy for the Devil," *New York Times*, March 11, 1998)

In this day and age, when staying "prosperous" takes priority over "moral or ethical standards," D. H. Lawrence and the Lawrentian ethos are bound to be unpopular; Lawrence of course explicitly states that "a deep moral sense" is all-important to him as man, writer, and member of Western civilization: when asked what makes a writer write, Lawrence authoritatively states:

> You don't write for anybody; you rather write from a deep moral sense—for the race, as it were. (Nehls, *D. H. Lawrence, Volume II*, p. 414)

Lawrence aspired to improve the "moral sense" of "the race" (i.e., Western civilization)—particularly he wanted "to make the sex relation valid and precious, instead of shameful" (D. H. Lawrence letter to Nancy Pearn, 12 April 1927); but this Lawrentian aim stands in opposition to today's "baby boomer" mentality that divorces sex from morality: in this day and age the sexual ethos of the elite culture is dominated by

> the central dogma of the baby boomers: the belief that sex, so long as it's consensual, ought never to be subject to moral scrutiny at all....(David Frum, "A Generation on Trial," *Weekly Standard*, Feb. 16, 1998, p. 23)

In contradistinction to the elite left-wing baby boomer culture which believes that "sex...ought never to be subject to moral scrutiny at all,"

> Lawrence...charged [i.e., imbued] the erotic life with morality (D. Trilling 1973, p. 3).

But perhaps most important of all is the Lawrentian "reverence" which goes hand in hand with Lawrentian "morality,"—Lawrentian reverence,

> a presiding reverence in Lawrence's life and art. (Panichas 80)

Indeed, perhaps the most important factor in the decline, in "Western civilization" today, of Lawrentian "morality" and Lawrentian "reverence" for sex in particular ("a proper reverence for sex" [*Phoenix II* 490) and for "life" in general, is the replacement of what

Lawrence in his essay "John Galsworthy" calls "the alive human being" (who is capable of "reverence") by "The social being" who is incapable of "reverence," incapable of "at-oneness with the living universe"; "The social being" who, rather than feeling "reverence" for "the living universe," instead "becomes obsessed with...material assurance":

> While a man remains a man, a true human individual, there is at the core of him a certain innocence or naivete which defies all analysis....[I]n his essential core he is naive, and money does not touch him. Money, of course, with every man living, goes a long way. With the alive human being it may go as far as his penultimate feeling. But in the last, naked him it does not enter.
>
> With the social being, it [money] goes right through the centre, and is the controlling principle, no matter how much he may pretend, nor how much bluff he may put up....
>
> While a man remains a man, before he falls and becomes a social individual, he innocently feels himself altogether within the great continuum of the universe. He is not divided nor cut off. Men may be against him, the tide of affairs may be rising to sweep him away. But he is one with the living continuum of the universe. From this he cannot be swept away. Hamlet and Lear feel it, as does Oedipus or Phaedra. It is the last and deepest feeling that is in a man [or a woman], while he remains a man [or a woman]....It is the essential innocence and naivete of the human being, the sense of being at one with the great universe-continuum of space-time-life, which is vivid in a great man, and a pure nuclear spark in every man who is still free.
>
> But if man loses his mysterious naive assurance, which is his innocence; if he gives *too* much importance to the external objective reality, and so collapses in his natural innocent pride; then he becomes obsessed with the idea of objective or material assurance; he wants to *insure* himself, and perhaps everbody else: universal insurance. The impulse rests on fear. Once the individual loses his naive at-oneness with the living universe, he falls into a state of fear, and tries to insure himself with wealth. If he is an altruist, he wants to insure everybody, and feels it is the tragedy of tragedies if this can't be done. But the whole necessity for thus materially insuring oneself with wealth, money, arises from the state of fear into which a man falls who has lost his at-oneness with the living universe, lost his peculiar nuclear innocence, and fallen into fragmentariness. Money, material salvation is the only salvation. What is salvation is God. Hence money is God [for "the social being"]. ("John Galsworthy")

For the Lawrentian "alive human being" money is not all-important: although it "goes a long way" (i.e., it has its advantages and its influence), money is not ultimately important to "the last, naked [self]" of the Lawrentian "alive human being"; for the anti-Lawrentian "social being," on the other hand, money is "the controlling principle." This situation in which the Lawrentian "alive human being" is ultimately not dominated by money is caused by the fact that the "alive human being" exists in a state of "living" relation to "the great continuum of the universe"—that is, the Lawrentian "human being" "is one with the living continuum of the universe." This Lawrentian sense of reverence for the universe, "the sense of being at one with the great universe-continuum of space-time-life," is lacking in the anti-Lawrentian "social being," who "loses his mysterious naive assurance" and forfeits his "natural innocent pride" by "giv[ing] *too* much importance to the external [i.e., material] reality"; as a consequence of the social being's lack of "mysterious...assurance," he "becomes obsessed" with the anti-Lawrentian, materialistic "material assurance" rooted in money and the sort of security that money may provide so that he can "*insure* himself, and...everybody else: universal insurance"—the "universal insurance," indeed, of the atheistic left-wing "welfare state" with its Big Government and its myriad "safety nets" destroying individuality, self-reliance and indeed reliance upon God (reliance on God and self being replaced by reliance upon the State). Indeed, it seems to me that the Clintons' socialistic universal mandatory health insurance program (pre-November 1994) is rather reminiscent of the "universal insurance" sought by the atheistic, materialistic, anti-cosmic "social being" whom Lawrence deplores. Like (say) the Kennedys, those "social beings" who have lost their "at-oneness with the living universe" and consequently "[fall] into a state of fear,"—these "social beings," to compensate for their anti-cosmic and indeed Godless view of the universe, play God themselves not only by taking to fighting for their own ontological "insur[ance] with wealth" but also by claiming to fight for the "insurance with wealth" of "everybody" else as well—by advocating a socialistic State, the redistribution of income, racial/gender preferences, and so on: all measures conducing to the *material* improvement of favoured groups (blacks, gays, etc.) rather than to the moral-spiritual-ontological improvement of all individuals; this elitist left-wing "social being" privileging of the material over the moral-ontological is inevitable, for (as Lawrence states in his "Galsworthy" essay) "the whole necessity for thus materially insuring oneself with wealth, money, arises from the state of fear into which a man falls who has lost his at-oneness with the living universe,...and fallen into fragmentariness,"—the very fragmentariness of self, it seems to me, that is so valorized by today's left-wing Foucaultian gay theorists such as Bersani, Edelman, and Halperin,— who deplore "male heterosexual identity as the exemplary figure for the [anti-fragmentary] *autonomy and coherence* of the subject as present to himself" (Edelman, *Homographesis*, p. 12; my italics), and indeed celebrate the "jouissance" of (male homosexual) sado-masochistic "self-shattering," "self-annihilation" (Bersani 1987, "Rectum" 222), the antithesis of (male heterosexual) "autonomy and coherence of [the self]"; furthermore, left-wing (pro-queer) Marxist theorists (like Dollimore) valorize self-fragmentation as "the decentring of man" (Dollimore, *Radical Tragedy*, p. 271), a psychic-ontological state in which "[b]ecause informed by contradictory [and fragmentizing] social and ideological processes, the subject [i.e., self] is never an indivisible [i.e., unfragmented] unity, never an autonomous, self-determining centre of consciousness" (*Radical Tragedy*, p. 269). For Dollimore and his ilk, the fragmented human subject/self "does not (cannot) transcend the material forces and relations of production" (Dollimore, *Political Shakespeare*, p. viii); thus the left-wing Dollimorian self, like the anti-Lawrentian "social being," is incapable of transcendence, totally lacking "at-oneness with the living universe," and simply materialistic, finally believing that "Money, material salvation is the only salvation....money is God." A major conservative Lawrentian recently noted that this left-wing "materialism" defines "the liberal ethos" and "the liberal tone":

> the elements of materialism, positivism, and utilitarianism inform the liberal tone—and the liberal ethos....Deeply embedded in the liberal tone, and style, one...finds an instinctive antagonism to the moral sense; to the moral view of the universe as a spiritual cosmos rooted in the principle of unity....(Panichas 98-99)

The Lawrentian George A. Panichas perceives that the left-wing "liberal ethos," with its "instinctive antagonism to the moral sense...[and to] the moral view of the universe as a spiritual cosmos rooted in the principle of unity," is indeed antithetical to the Lawrentian "deep moral sense" as well as to the Lawrentian vision of the cosmos as "the great continuum of the universe," "the living continuum of the universe" ("Galsworthy"); furthermore, the left-wing "social being" fervently opposes Lawrence's "reverent awareness of the idea of the holy" (Panichas 81), as well as "the element of transcendence that informs and defines, giving distinction and recognition to, his [Lawrence's] burden of vision" (Panichas 81). The "vision" of the left-wing "social being," on the other hand, is rooted in "The liberal tone, as it is employed by those who now dominate the academy and high journalism,...[a tone which is] a highly polished and sharpened technique rejecting and supplanting the moral tone that is registered in terms of insight, wisdom, reverence" (Panichas 97).

Instead of being characterized by the "insight, wisdom, [and] reverence" of "the moral tone" (Panichas 97), "the liberal tone" is characterized by "its own self-assertiveness and self-righteousness" (Panichas 98); and "the liberal ethos," ultimately, by its own narcissistic "onanism." As Leslie Fiedler wisely noted some fifty years ago, the "liberal mind" is the elitist, narcissistic, "onanist" "chief enemy of literature today":

> Though not always consciously, I have been searching for strategies to oppose that "scientific [i.e., left-wing, Marxist] criticism whose methods are mining, digging or just plain grubbing," and which assumes that the work of art is essentially a social function or a function of language, amenable to analysis in terms of the currently honorific vocabularies of various sciences....I am opposed to the dogged anti-Romanticism of much contemporary criticism which leads to a contempt for the imagination....
>
> ...[It is essential] to enlist criticism against the chief enemy of literature today, the "liberal" or scientific mind, with its opposition to the frivolous and the tragic, its distrust of such concepts as God, the Devil, Genius and Taste....
>
> In *intent*, the good critic addresses the common reader, not the initiate, and that intent is declared in his language....The primary act of faith which makes criticism possible compels the critic under any circumstances to speak *as if* to men and not to specialists. The compulsory comprehensibility of the critic is not a matter of pandering to indolence, prejudice or ignorance, but of resisting the impulse to talk to himself or a congeries of reason-

> able facsimiles of himself. In an age of...the widespread failure of
> love, it is difficult to be an *amateur*; but at last one remembers that
> the opposite of the *amateur* is the onanist....(Leslie Fiedler,
> "Toward An Amateur Criticism," *Kenyon Review* 12 [1950]: 561-
> 563)

What the young Leslie Fiedler wisely perceived half a century ago is even more true today: the left-wing "social being" literary-cultural critic plays it safe: he/she avoids the genuine individual emotional involvement of the Lawrencean "true human individual,...alive human being" ("John Galsworthy") "amateur" (Fiedler 563) critic—instead, he/she promulgates left-wing politically correct dogmas and bromides that valorize "materialism"; and he/she adopts the "scientific" (i.e., Marxist) stance "which assumes that the work of art is essentially a social function." Fiedler bravely opposes these left-wing Marxist "last-ditch defenders of rationality and the primacy of political fact, intrinsically hostile to...myth and passion" (Fiedler, *Collected Essays, Volume II*, p. 463); he deplores their critical approach, which is characterized by "a contempt for the imagination." This leftwing, "scientific," anti-imagination critic, with his "liberal mind," Leslie Fiedler tells us, is "the chief enemy of literature today," denying "The ultimate and the transcendent dimensions of life and of belief" (Panichas 234), and replacing these "dimensions" with leftwing elitism, elitism according to which the left-wing "social being" literary-cultural critic "speak[s] *as if*...to specialists," "talk[ing] to himself or a congeries of reasonable facsimiles of himself," scorning the need for the critic to be comprehensible to others ("compulsory comprehensibility") besides his own elite, jargon-ridden group. (The Marxist critic Fredric Jameson is famous for his failure to achieve "compulsory comprehensibility" in his work; see *Philosophy and Literature* 19 [1995]: 204 and *Philosophy and Literature* 21 [1997]: 508; in both 1995 and 1997 Jameson was the winner of "The PHILOSOPHY AND LITERATURE Bad Writing Contest.") The left-wing critic's failure to achieve "The compulsory comprehensibility of the critic," Leslie Fiedler explains, is rooted in narcissistic mental masturbation, with the "scientific" left-wing "social being" literary critic being tantamount to "the onanist."

In opposition to this left-wing "social being" sort of critic, this "liberal"-minded critic, this "onanist" critic, is the "amateur" critic, who is like the Lawrencean "alive human being"; he (the "amateur" critic) tells his readers by his "tone" that "the works of art being discussed have really *happened* to [him]..., and have been ingested into the totality of [his] experiences"; significantly enough, D. H. Lawrence crowns Leslie Fiedler's list of the great "amateur critics":

> The voices of "Longinus" or Nietzsche, of Coleridge or D. H. Lawrence,...One feels in their tone and texture an assurance that the works of art being discussed have really *happened* to the men that discuss them, and have been ingested into the totality of their experiences. (Fiedler, "Amateur Criticism," p. 572)

The "voice" of the "amateur critic," whose apotheosis is Lawrence, communicates "an assurance" that the works of art being discussed by the critic "have really *happened*" to the critic in the deepest recesses of his emotional being; indeed, the work of art has been ontologically "ingested" into the living being of the "amateur critic," assimilated into the vital "totality of [his] experiences." Furthermore, just as the Lawrencean "alive human being" is "at one with the great universe-continuum of space-time-life" ("Galsworthy"), so is the "alive human being" "amateur critic" at one with the work of art, as the "amateur critic" in his criticism succeeds in "becoming one with [the work of art], not abstractly, but in [his] living personality" (Fiedler 572). Ultimately, says Leslie Fiedler, the literary criticism of the "amateur critic" with his "living personality" is "testimony,"

> testimony to the possibility of literature being assimilated to the experience of the individual in richness and joy....(Fiedler 572)

Valorizing Lawrencean "richness and joy" as well as the Lawrencean "experience" of the Lawrencean "individual," Leslie Fiedler brings to us the Lawrencean realization that literature (particularly the novel) can greatly enhance the "richness and joy" of the *individual* human life,

> man alive, and live woman (D. H. Lawrence, "Why the Novel Matters")

—but only if the individual man and woman alive realize that

> life itself, and not inert safety, is the reason for living. ("Why the Novel Matters")

In academia today, "inert safety" is synonymous with "an institutionally entrenched orthodoxy...enforced by what has become known as political correctness" (Ellis 11). In today's "literary-cultural criticism," this "inert safety" is certainly manifested in the "scientific," "liberal," left-wing approach that Leslie Fiedler in 1950 decries; the "inert safety" of politically correct "race-class-gender" pieties and obsessions in academia today, when unquestioned "race-class-gender" dogmas certainly have hegemony, makes it extremely unlikely that for the time being the vital passional Lawrentian ethic and reputation, with its emphasis on "the experience of the [intense, "religious"] individual," will achieve predominance in academia's literary-cultural criticism.

Yet of course there was a time when Lawrence's "poetic immortality" achieved considerable recognition and appreciation: the time, indeed, of Fiedler and Leavis, a time when Lawrentian "intensity" and "the individual" and "life" were valorized:

> the intensity of [Lawrence's] intuition expresses itself in an intensity of preoccupation with the individual. No one could have been more profoundly possessed [than Lawrence] by the perception that life is a matter of individual lives, and that except in individual lives there is no life to be interested in or reverent about, and no life to be served. (F. R. Leavis, *D. H. Lawrence: Novelist*, Chapter Three, "Lawrence and Tradition")

Significantly enough, Leavis and Fiedler were both writing about the valorization of the individual in 1950-51, the very beginning of "the Lawrence decade": the decade in which Lawrence attained his greatest stature and critical acclaim, culminating in the 1959 publication of the unexpurgated Grove Press edition of *Lady Chatterley's Lover*. Perhaps if academia can once again appreciate the intensity of the individual—and perhaps if books such as the present volume can "change" a few people's minds—then there might be "a new spring" in Lawrence studies; I am reminded of one of Lawrence's own letters, written during another very despairing time for Western civilization (the period of the Great War):

> I wish there could be a new spring of hope and reality in mankind: I do wish a few people could change, and stand for a fresh and happier world. I suppose it will come, and we shall live through. That is our business, at any rate. We must live through, for the hope of the new summer of the world. (D. H. Lawrence letter to Ernest Collings, 3 March 1917)

Perhaps this study of mine will make "a few people...change"; certainly the time for "the new summer" in Lawrence studies is long overdue.

WORKS CITED

Barber, Stephen. "Lip-Reading: Woolf's Secret Encounters." In *Novel Gazing: Queer Readings in Fiction*. Ed. Eve Kosofsky Sedgwick. Durham: Duke University Press, 1997.

Bayley, John. "Lawrence to Larkin: A changed perspective." In *Lawrence and comedy*. Ed. Paul Eggert and John Worthen. Cambridge: Cambridge University Press, 1996.

Becket, Fiona. *D. H. Lawrence: The Thinker as Poet*. New York: St. Martin's Press, 1997.

Bentley, Eric. "We Are in History." In *Homosexualities and French Literature: Cultural Contexts/Critical Texts*. Ed. George Stambolian and Elaine Marks. Ithaca: Cornell University Press, 1979.

Bloom, Harold. *The Western Canon: The Books and School of the Ages*. New York: Harcourt Brace & Company, 1994.

Bloom, Harold. *A Map of Misreading*. New York: Oxford University Press, 1975.

Bloom, Harold. *The Anxiety of Influence: A Theory of Poetry*. New York: Oxford University Press, 1973.

Born, Daniel. *The Birth of Liberal Guilt in the English Novel*. Chapel Hill: University of North Carolina Press, 1995.

Butler, Judith. *Gender Trouble: Feminism and the Subversion of Identity*. New York: Routledge, 1990.

Butler, Judith. "Imitation and Gender Insubordination." In *Inside/Out: Lesbian Theories, Gay Theories*. Ed. Diana Fuss. New York: Routledge, 1991.

Clarke, Bruce. *Dora Marsden and Early Modernism: Gender, Individualism, Science*. Ann Arbor: University of Michigan Press, 1996.

Diggins, John Patrick. *The Promise of Pragmatism: Modernism and the Crisis of Knowledge and Authority*. Chicago: University of Chicago Press, 1994.

Draper, R. P. *D. H. Lawrence: The Critical Heritage*. New York: Barnes & Noble, 1970.

Eagleton, Terry. *Literary Theory: An Introduction: Second Edition*. Minneapolis: University of Minnesota Press, 1998.

Eagleton, Terry. *Criticism and Ideology: A Study in Marxist Literary Theory*. London: Verso, 1978.

Eagleton, Terry. *The Ideology of the Aesthetic.* Oxford: Blackwell, 1998.

Eagleton, Terry. *Marxism and Literary Criticism.* London: Methuen, 1976.

Fiedler, Leslie. "Toward an Amateur Criticism." *Kenyon Review* 12 (1950): 561–574.

Foucault, Michel. *The Order of Things: An Archaeology of the Human Sciences.* New York: Random House, 1970.

Frost, Laura. "'With This Ring I Thee Own': Masochism and Social Reform in *Ulysses.*" In *Sex Positives?: The Cultural Politics of Dissident Sexualities.* Ed. Thomas Foster, Carol Siegel, and Ellen E. Berry. New York: New York University Press, 1997.

Fuss, Diana. *Essentially Speaking: Feminism, Nature & Difference.* New York: Routledge, 1989.

Goodheart, Eugene. "Censorship and Self-Censorship in the Fiction of D. H. Lawrence." In *Representing Modernist Texts.* Ed. George Bornstein. Ann Arbor: University of Michigan Press, 1991.

Kalnins, Mara. "Introduction" to D. H. Lawrence, *Apocalypse and the Writings on Revelation.* Ed. Mara Kalnins. Cambridge: Cambridge University Press, 1980.

Kinkead-Weekes, Mark. *Beyond Gossip: D. H. Lawrence's Writing Life.* Austin: Harry Ransom Humanities Research Center, The University of Texas at Austin, 1995.

Lawrence, D. H. *Women in Love.* Ed. David Farmer, Lindeth Vasey and John Worthen. Cambridge: Cambridge University Press, 1987.

Lawrence, D. H. *The Letters of D. H. Lawrence: Volume II: June 1913-October 1916.* Ed. George J. Zytaruk. Cambridge: Cambridge University Press, 1981.

Lawrence, D. H. *The Letters of D. H. Lawrence: Volume VI: March 1927-November 1928.* Ed. James T. Boulton, Margaret H. Boulton, and Gerald M. Lacy. Cambridge: Cambridge University Press, 1991.

Lawrence, D. H. *The Letters of D. H. Lawrence: Volume VII: November 1928-February 1930.* Ed. Keith Sagar. Cambridge: Cambridge University Press, 1993.

Lawrence, D. H. *Lady Chatterley's Lover and A Propos of "Lady Chatterley's Lover."* Ed. Michael Squires. Cambridge: Cambridge University Press, 1993.

Lawrence, D. H. "The State of Funk." In *Phoenix II: Uncollected, Unpublished, and Other Prose Works by D. H. Lawrence.* Ed. Warren Roberts and Harry T. Moore. New York: Viking, 1970.

Lawrence, D. H. "Why the Novel Matters." In *Phoenix: The Posthumous Papers of D. H. Lawrence.* Ed. Edward D. McDonald. New York: Viking, 1936.

Paglia, Camille. *Vamps and Tramps.* New York: Vintage, 1994.

Panichas, George A. *The Critic as Conservator: Essays in Literature, Society, and Culture.* Washington, D. C.: Catholic University of America Press, 1992.

Parker, David. *Ethics, Theory, and the Novel.* Cambridge: Cambridge University Press, 1994.

Parkes, Adam. *Modernism and the Theater of Censorship.* New York: Oxford University Press, 1996.

Pecora, Vincent P. "D. H. Lawrence." In *The Columbia History of the British Novel.* Ed. John Richetti. New York: Columbia University Press, 1994.

Sagar, Keith. "Lawrence and the Resurrection of Pan." In *D. H. Lawrence: The Centre and the Circles.* Ed. Peter Preston. Nottingham: D. H. Lawrence Centre, University of Nottingham, 1992.

Scheckner, Peter. *Class, Politics, and the Individual: A Study of the Major Works of D. H. Lawrence.* Rutherford: Fairleigh Dickinson University Press, 1985.

Schneider, Daniel J. *The Consciousness of D. H. Lawrence: An Intellectual Biography.* Lawrence: University Press of Kansas, 1986.

Schwarz, Daniel R. "Canonicity, Culture, and Pluralism: A Humanistic Perspective on Professing English." *Texas Studies in Literature andLanguage* 34 (1992): 149–175.

Schwarz, Daniel R. *The Transformation of the English Novel: 1890–1930.* NewYork: St. Martin's Press, 1989.

Seaton, James. *Cultural Conservatism, Political Liberalism: From Criticism to Cultural Studies.* Ann Arbor: University of Michigan Press, 1996.

Sedgwick, Eve Kosofsky. *Tendencies.* Durham: Duke University Press, 1993.

Simpson, David. "New Brooms at Fawlty Towers: Colin MacCabe and Cambridge English." In *Intellectuals: Aesthetics, Politics, Academics.* Ed. Bruce Robbins. Minneapolis: University of Minnesota Press, 1990.

Solomon, Robert C. "Heterosex." In *Sexuality and Medicine, Volume I: Conceptual Roots.* Ed. Earl E. Shelp. Boston: D. Reidel Publishing Company, 1987.

Trilling, Diana. "Lawrence and the Movements of Modern Culture." In *D. H. Lawrence: Novelist, Poet, Prophet.* Ed. Stephen Spender. London: Weidenfeld and Nicolson, 1973.

Weeks, Jeffrey. *Against Nature: Essays on History, Sexuality and Identity.* London: Rivers Oram Press, 1991.

Wittig, Monique. *The Straight Mind.* Boston: Beacon Press, 1992.

Index

Aaron's Rod, 85, 121-123, 137-138, 299, 306-307
Academic Questions, 4, 52
Aczel, Richard, 335-336
affirmative action, 25-26, 63, 81-82
After the New Criticism, 22
Against the Grain, 336
Angelou, Maya , 417-418
Another Kind of Love, 282
The Anti-Aesthetic, 326-327
Anxiety of Influence, 18-19, 102, 105, 107, 128, 195, 315, 374
Apocalypse and the Writings on Revelation, 98, 104-105, 152, 153, 324-325
   Chapter IV, 86
   Fragment One, 152-153, 163-168, 419-420
Ascetic Imperative, 345
Asquith, Cynthia, 13, 70-71, 101, 208-209, 212, 272
(The) Autobiography of Bertrand Russell, Volume II, 228

Balbert, Peter 398
Barber, Stephen , 434

Barthes, Roland, 343
Bate, W. J., 82-83
Bentley, Eric, 376
Beresford, J. D., 207
Berman, R.A., 11, 22
Bersani, Leo, 88, 200, 314, 315, 320-322, 343-345, 363, 407-410, 439
   on death, 320-322
Best of the Best, 20, 49
Bestiality, 202-203
Between Men, 248, 249, 251, 376
Beyond the Heroic, 57
Birrell, Francis , 193
Birth of Liberal Guilt, 422-423, 416
Black, Michael, 180
"blood-consciousness", 100-101, 139, 198, 236, 263-266, 275, 394
Bloody Crossroads, 76
Bloom, Harold, 18-22, 30-31, 47-53, 65-66, 87-88, 102, 107, 128, 174, 215, 275, 376, 396-397
   Bloomian theory, 18-19, 22, 50, 374
   On Michel Foucault, 21
   on tradition, 87
   triumphant solipsism, 161, 162, 191, 250, 255, 281, 385

Bly, Robert, 79
Bork, Robert, 3-4, 12, 395, 405, 415
Breaking Ranks, 78
Brewster, E. H., 386, 418
The British Critical Tradition: A Re-evaluation, 322-323
Broaddrick, Juanita, 58
Brown, Curtis, 388
Brown, Norman O., 279-280
Burns, Wayne, 369
Burns, Robert, 418
Burrow, Trigant, 373-374, 377, 388
Butler, Judith, 88, 392-393
Butler, Gerald J., 10, 368-369, 414
Bynner, W., 387

Cambridge-Bloomsbury group, 88, 192-205, 215, 247
Cambridge Quarterly "Lawrence and Forster," 30
Campbell, Beatrice, 375
Campbell, Gordon, 30, 274
Cannan, Mary, 186
Carpenter, Edward, 223-224, 228, 232-233, 237, 244-246
Carswell, Catherine, 103, 108, 238-243, 250, 253, 300
"Censorship and Self-Censorship in the Fiction of D. H. Lawrence," 405
Chambers, Jessie, 223
Clayton, Katherine, 208
Clinton, Bill, 15, 46, 51, 53, 54, 55, 57, 63, 72, 83-86, 335, 417, 423, 438
Clinton, Hillary, 37, 46, 71, 335, 423
Collected Essays of Leslie Fiedler, Volume II, 441
Collings, Ernest, 247, 360, 443
Columbia History of the British Novel, 398
Commentary, 25, 51
  "Culture and the Present Moment," 6
Condition of the Working Class, 323
Consequences of Pragmatism, 61, 64

Conway, George, 387
Coombes, Harry, 77
Cooper, Gary, 284
Corydon, 375
Courage of Judgment, 45-47
Craft, Christopher, 32-34, 43, 256, 282-284, 313
Crews, Frederick 4
Crichton, Kyle S., 83
Criticism and Social Change, 25
"The Crown", 199-203, 223, 423-431
Cruikshank, Margaret, 282
Cultural Criticism, 51, 68
Culture and the Radical Conscience, 284-285

D. H. Lawrence: A Composite Biography, Volume II, 83
D. H. Lawrence: A Critical Anthology, 77
D. H. Lawrence and Edward Carpenter, 223
D. H. Lawrence and the Phallic Imagination, 398
"D. H. Lawrence: Cliques and Consciousness," 323
D. H. Lawrence: Life into Art, 61
D. H. Lawrence: Novelist, 4, 14, 43-44, 52, 435
  "Introduction", 368
  "Lawrence and Tradition," Chapter III, 356, 443
D. H. Lawrence's Response to Plato: A Bloomian Interpretation, 19, 293
D. H. Lawrence: The Early Fiction, 180
D. H. Lawrence: The Rainbow and Women in Love: A Casebook, 216
D. H. Lawrence, Volume II, 436
D.H. Lawrence's Nightmare: The Writer and His Circle in the Years of the Great War, 184, 199, 201, 224-225, 227
Daleski, H. M., 98

Dax, Alice, 223
de Beauvoir, Simone, 281
de Lauretis, Teresa, 58-59
Dean, Paul, 368
Dean, Tim, 398-399
Death in Venice, 173-175
Deceived with Kindness: A Story of Bloomsbury, 193
Delany, Paul, 88, 101, 125, 184, 199, 201, 224-225, 227
Delavenay, Emile, 223
"Democracy," 378
  Chapter IV ["Individualism"], 73
Desire and Its Discontents, 281, 285-286, 291
Dickinson, Goldsworthy Lowes, 201
Dictatorship of Virtue, 74-75
Dollimore, Jonathan, 33-37, 41-43, 53, 65, 67, 77-78, 88, 173, 319-323, 343, 359-361, 365, 368-369, 375, 381, 389, 391, 439
"Domestic Violence in 'The White Stocking': A Lawrencean Case Study", 37
Donaldson, George 254
Donoghue, Denis, 6, 368
Dowd, Maureen, 436
Dreiser, Theodore, 2-3
Dunlop, Thomas, 178, 256, 295
Dworkin, Andrea, 58

E. M. Forster: A Life, Volume Two, 183
Eagleton, Terry, 37, 78, 328-330, 333-337, 361, 363-366, 368-369, 376, 412-413, 418-421
"Eagleton and English," 334-336
Eder, David, 15-18
Edmundson, Mark 21, 77
"Education of the People," Chapter IV, 64
Edward Carpenter: Selected Writings, Volume I: Sex, 233
Eliot, T. S., 37, 435
Ellis, David, 30
Ellis, Havelock, 228—234, 236-237

Ellis, John, 3-4, 51, 58, 65, 70, 77, 80-82, 417, 442-443
Engels, Friedrich, 79, 323
English Literature in History, 328
English Review, 295
Epistemology of the Closet, 48, 172, 182, 249, 251-252
Epstein, Joseph, 25
(The) Escaped Cock, 153-163, 166
Essays on Heidegger, 62
Fantasia of the Unconscious, 299-300, 305
  Chapter III, "Plexuses, Planes, and So On", 132
  Chapter IX, "The Birth of Sex," 424-425
  Chapter XI, "The Vicious Circle," 132
  Chapter XIV, "Sleep and Dreams," 306, 352-353
Farmer, David, 260
feminism, 10, 14, 49, 58, 66, 223, 230, 242, 302, 361, 369, 376
Feuerlicht, 173
Fiedler, Leslie, 69, 76, 97-99, 210-211, 277-280, 284, 307, 406, 431, 434, 440-443
Firestone, Shulamith, 7
First Things, 70
Fish, Stanley, 328
fist-fucking, 43, 308-309, 353, 356-359
Fonda, Jane, 12
For Continuity, 12, 394-395
Ford, George H., 215, 238-239
Forster, E. M., 15, 20, 30, 182-186, 196-199, 201, 245-247
  letter to D. H. Lawrence, 30
Foucault, Michel, 21-23, 30-31, 43, 49, 77-78, 88, 291-292, 307, 308-312, 315, 343-359, 363-365, 369, 434, 439
  On death, 356-357
  on individuality, 21-23, 315, 345
  On Lawrence, 344
  On religion, 351, 434-435

On sex, 344-355, 407
The Foucault Reader, 344-345
Fox-Genovese, Elizabeth, 27
Frank, Barney, 53
Fraser, Nancy, 351
Furbank, P. N., 183

Garnett, Angelica, 193
Garnett, David, 192-193, 201, 224, 245, 291, 298, 433
Garnett, Edward, 83, 174
Gates, Henry Louis, 328, 418
The Gay and Lesbian Liberation Movement, 282
Gay Roots, "Bloomsbury: A Gay Perspective," 188
gay theory, 41, 48, 313, 320-321, 358, 375-376, 439
Gertler, Mark, 102-103, 107-108, 119, 222
Gide, Andre, 375
Gilbert, Sandra, 51, 52
Ginzberg, Louis, 133
"Goats and Compasses," 199, 212, 213, 215, 226-227
Goodheart, Eugene, 61-64, 70, 281-282, 284-291, 405
Gore, Al, 423
Grant, Duncan, 193
Gray, Cecil, 199, 212, 226
"Great Society", 46
The Great Tradition, 69
Grosskurth, 228

Halperin, David, 88, 291-292, 308, 352-353, 358, 439
Hardy, G. H., 201
Hart, Jeffrey, 75, 78-79
Hartman, Geoffrey, 128
Havelock Ellis, 228
Hegel Dictionary, 33
Henderson, Alice, 387
Henke, Suzette, 7
Herbert, Michael, 273

Hero, Captain, and Stranger: Male Friendships, Social Critique, and Literary Form in the Sea Novels of Herman Melville, 209
Heseltine, Philip, 197, 219-222, 225-226, 228, 238, 304
Heterosexuality, 23, 30, 32, 35, 54, 58-59, 82, 88, 366, 374-375
  Lawrence on, 13-14, 31-33, 35-36, 45, 52, 55-57, 59, 64-65, 80, 88, 171-319, 339, 352-355, 358, 366-368, 374-377, 405, 407
  morality, 80
History of Sexuality, Volume I: An Introduction, 77, 307, 344-351, 407
Hobman, J. B., 15, 17
Holroyd, Michael, 202
Homographesis, 365, 439
homophobia, 42, 250-251, 343, 399, 433-434
Homos, 200, 343-345, 409-410
homosexual, 14, 20-21, 23, 30, 36, 41-43, 59, 88, 171-365, 375
  and greatness, 171, 198, 228-229, 375
  desire, 42, 283
  Lawrence on, 31-33, 171-319, 373, 375
  narcissistic element in, 172, 198, 267-268
  panic, 248-249, 292-293, 399
  promiscuity, 42-43, 320-322, 352
  "self-loathing", 282
  "sensationalism", 181, 184-185, 198, 273, 304
  violence against, 320-321
Homosocial bonds, 249-252
hooks, bell, 328
Hopkin, Sallie, 14, 206, 223, 237
Hopkin, William E., 223, 244-245
Human Diversity, 63

Ideology: An Introduction, 365

D. H. LAWRENCE TODAY 451

Individuality, 21-24, 26-29, 37, 79-80, 87-88, 319-320, 326, 331, 368-369, 377
   Foucault on individuality, 21-23, 343-346
   Lawrence on, 26-30, 33, 36, 53-55, 65, 73, 74, 199, 227, 250, 252, 255-260, 263, 294-295, 305, 314, 319, 326-327, 331, 352-353, 355, 366-367, 423, 443
Ingersoll, Earl, 5-6, 282
(The) Intermediate Sex, 223, 233
Introducing Lyotard, 280
"Is the Rectum a Grave?", 320-321, 322, 407-409, 439

Jackson, Jesse, 46, 53, 63, 423
Jacoby, Russell, 73-74
Jaffe, Else, 141
James, Henry, 2-3
James Joyce and the Politics of Desire, "Introduction: Defusing the Patriarchal Can(n)on,", 7
Jameson, Fredric, 37, 325-333, 336, 368-369, 441
Jewish Law, 99-100, 102, 106, 107, 109, 110
John Bull, 377
"John Galsworthy", 324, 437-440
John Maynard Keynes: Hopes Betrayed, 294
Joyce, James, 1, 5-8, 52, 66-67, 143-144
Journal of the History of Ideas, 344
Joyce in Context, 6

Kalnins, Mara, 153, 397
Kangaroo, 65, 127, 129-141
   Chapter 7, 132
   Chapter 11, "Willie Struthers and Kangaroo", 65, 133-134
   Chapter 15, 135
   Chapter 17, "Kangaroo is Killed", 136-139
   Chapter 18, "Adieu Australia", 140

Karl Marx: Selected Writings, 322-323
Kennedy, Ted, 12, 13
Kenyon Review, 441, 442
Keynes, John Maynard, 88, 188, 193, 194, 198-202, 208, 247, 294, 296
Kinkead-Weekes, 16, 60, 98, 312-313, 377, 399-401
Knight, G. Wilson, 308
Koteliansky, S. S., 16, 126, 142, 189, 196, 244, 246, 386

Lady Chatterley's Lover, 31, 35, 56-60, 349, 358, 374-376, 386, 387, 388-390, 392, 397, 400, 403, 410-415, 417-418, 443
   Chapter X, 31-32, 57, 356-358
   Chapter XII, 357
   Chapter XIV, 56, 57; 356
   Chapter XVIII, 56, 59-60; 357
Last Poems
   "Pax," 403
   "Lord's Prayer," 404
Lawrence, D. H.
   anti-Semitism, 15, 17, 19-20, 88, 124, 422
   apocalyptic vision, 113-115, 118-119
   as a wandering Jew, 119-171
   as "The Priest of Love", 52, 125, 184, 188, 193-194, 199, 203, 226, 240, 253, 281, 285, 294, 406
   at Cambridge, 187-190, 208, 296
   at Derbyshire, 204-205, 207
   at Mount Sinai, 124
   "Blutbruderschaft" 250-258
   death, 180
   in Australia, 126-131, 134, 136-140, 142
   in Baden-Baden, 123-124
   in Ceylon, 125-126
   in Cornwall, 206-209
   letters to Amy Lowell, 180-181, 251, 253
   letters to Arthur McLeod, 31, 172
   letters to Barbara Low, 188, 212, 247
   letters to Beatrice Campbell, 375

letters to Bertrand Russell, 64, 100-101, 104, 183-186, 187, 188, 198, 236, 263-265, 298, 353
letters to Catherine Carswell, 103, 108, 238-243, 250, 253, 300
letters to Charles Wilson, 29, 418
letters to Cynthia Asquith, 13, 70-71, 208-209, 212, 272
letters to David Garnett, 193-196, 298
letters to Dr. David Eder, 15-18
letters to Dollie Radford, 26-28, 272
letters to Dunlop, 175-176, 178, 256
letters to E. H. Brewster, 386, 418
letters to E.M. Forster, 184
letters to Edward Garnett, 83, 174-175
letters to Edward McDonald, 386
letters to Else Jaffe, 141
letters to Ernest Collings, 247, 360, 443
letters to Gordon Campbell, 30, 274
letters to Harriet Monroe, 141, 196
letters to Henry Savage, 171, 172, 173-174, 179, 229
letters to Hugh Meredith, 197-198, 359
letters to J. B. Pinker, 74, 108, 180, 256
letters to J. D. Beresford, 207
letters to Jean Watson, 418
letters to Jehanne Moulaert, 325
letters to John Middleton Murry, 104, 206, 325
letters to Katherine Clayton, 208
letters to Katherine Mansfield, 198, 203-204, 206
letters to Laurence Polinger, 390
letters to Mark Gertler, 102-103, 105, 107-108, 115, 119, 222
letters to Martin Secker, 376
letters to Mary Cannan, 186
letters to Nancy Pearn, 56, 336, 374
letters to Nellie Morrison, 386
letters to Ottoline Morrell, 31, 64, 85, 103, 189-192, 199, 204, 209, 212, 213, 218-221, 230, 296, 418
letters to Philip Heseltine, 197, 221, 226, 238, 304
letters to Robert Nichols, 197
letters to S. S. Koteliansky, 16, 126, 189, 212, 244, 246, 386
letters to Sallie Hopkin, 14, 206
letters to Sallie Hopkin, 223-224, 237
letters to Thomas Dunlop, 256, 295
letters Dr. Trigant Burrow, 373, 374, 377
letters to William Hopkin, 223, 244-245

Messiah complex, 125, 192, 203, 208, 213, 224, 281, 312, 331
misanthropy, 116, 117, 119, 175, 237, 244
morality, 15, 80, 83, 86, 194, 325, 386, 435-436
  on America, 123, 141-142
  on ancient Greece, 213
  on community, 28-29
  on death, 151-153, 161, 179, 182, 196-197, 219, 240-241, 268, 272, 273-274, 275, 276-277, 311-313
  on Europe, 125-127, 141-142, 181-182, 207, 209, 272
  on heterosexuality, 13-14, 31-33, 35-36, 45, 52, 55-57, 59, 64-65, 80, 88, 171-319, 339, 352-355, 358, 366-368, 374-377, 405, 407
  "vital sex," 183
  on homosexuality, 31-33, 171-319, 373, 375
  redemption of, 203, 208, 212, 224-226, 238, 247, 270-271, 282, 290, 312-313, 373-374
  on "human values", 12
  on individuality, 26-30, 33, 36, 53-55, 65, 73, 74, 199, 227, 250, 252,

255-260, 263, 294-295, 305-306, 314-315, 319, 326-327, 331, 352-353, 354-355, 366-367, 423, 443
  on materialism, 437-438
  on "life values", 11-13
  on marriage, 218, 239-243, 260-263, 267, 284, 295-296, 352, 354, 366-367, 380-395, 402-403
  "ultimate", 241, 243-246
  on *Moby Dick*, 209, 212
  on politics, 8, 85, 285
  "pure relationships", 238-239, 250
  on "pure understanding", 271-276
  on reality, 18, 46, 206, 368
  on religion, 37, 59-61, 63-65, 68-72, 86-87, 97-168, 175, 219, 247, 297-298, 386, 394-395, 397, 400, 401, 402-405, 419-424, 429-431 440, 443, 435, 437
  Christianity, 97-168, 361
  Judaism, 97-168, 422
  on "sensitive man," 199-201, 203-204
  on sex, 5, 8-9, 12-14, 30-33, 37-38, 44-46, 52, 55-57, 59-60, 74, 80, 100-101, 109, 118, 121, 122-123, 130, 133, 150, 153-154, 160-161, 171-319, 336-338, 344, 348-353, 354-358, 359, 361, 364, 366-368, 374-394, 397, 402, 405-407, 410-418, 432-434, 436
  on suicide, 229-230
  on Thomas Mann's *Death in Venice*, 173-174
  on transcendence, 20, 69, 70, 231, 267, 272-274 275-277, 333, 440
  poetic immortality, 28, 50, 55, 87-88, 161, 163, 168, 171-319, 336, 373-376, 378-382, 384, 385, 388-405, 421, 422, 430, 443
  poetic strength, 18, 28, 55, 250-253, 256, 275, 281, 282, 290, 294-296, 373-374, 388-390
Lawrence, Frieda , 13-14, 16-17, 40, 104, 127, 141, 171, 174-175, 187, 191-192, 218-219, 221, 230, 240-241, 251, 253, 295, 336-337, 356
Leavis, F. R., 4-5, 6, 12, 14, 34, 39-41, 42, 43-46, 52, 66, 69-70, 71-72, 75-78, 87, 319, 334, 335-336, 356, 368, 392, 394-395, 405-406, 419, 435, 443
Legacy of D. H. Lawrence: New Essays, 356
Lentricchia, Frank , 22, 23, 25
Letters I, 99, 100
Letters II, 373
Lewiecki-Wilson, 7, 9
  "alternative family forms," 8-9
  On *Women in Love*, 10-11
Lewinsky, Monica, 57
(The) Liberal Imagination, 1-4, 14, 78-79
  "Preface", 12
Life Against Death, 279-280
"*Literature Lost*: Social Agendas and the Corruption of the Humanities", 51, 65, 70, 80-81, 417
Literary Theory, 335, 412-413
  Chapter 1, "The Rise of English", 418-421
  "Conclusion: Political Criticism," 364-365, 412-413
The Lives of Michel Foucault, 355
Love and Death in the American Novel, 210-211, 277-279
Low, Barbara, 188, 212, 247
Lowell, Amy, 180-181, 182, 251-253
Lyotard, Jean-Francois, 280
Lytton Strachey: The New Biography, 201, 202

MLA International Bibliography, 4, 417
1996, 6
(1997), 67
Mac Donald, Heather, 11
Maddox, Brenda, 402
Mains, Geoff, 359

Making It, 75-76
The Man Who Died, 35
Mann, Thomas, 173-175, 177, 334
Mansfield, Katherine, 198, 203-204, 206
(A) Map of Misreading, 87, 102, 174, 215, 217, 250, 275, 385
Martin, Robert K., 20, 209-212
(The) Married Man: A Life of D. H. Lawrence, 225, 402
Marxism, 12, 20, 22, 29, 49, 182, 322-324, 325, 329, 336, 416, 425, 434-441
Massachusetts Review, 268
Masturbation, 185, 186
materialism, 12, 13, 28, 29, 41, 46, 71-72, 207, 434-441
"mature genital sexuality", 277-280
McDonald, Edward, 386
McLeod, Arthur, 31, 172
Melville, Herman, 209-215
"mental-consciousness", 198, 204
Meredith, Hugh, 197, 198, 359
(The) Mid-Century,
 "Love and Death in the American Novel," 278
 "Paradise Reached For," 279
Michel Foucault, *Politics, Philosophy, Culture*
 Power and Sex," 357
Middleton, Richard, 230
Miller, D. A., 356
Miller, James, 77, 310, 352, 357, 359
Millett, Kate, 43, 398
"The Minimalist Self," 355
Moby Dick, 209-215
Modern Age, 24
Modernism, 6, 326-327, 331-333
Monroe, Harriet, 141, 196, 388
Moore, G. E., 201
Moore, Harry T., 52, 221
Morrell, Ottoline, 31, 64, 85, 103, 199, 204, 209, 212-213, 215, 218-221, 227-228, 230, 296, 418

Morrison, Nellie, 386
Morrison, Toni, 4-5, 11, 52, 67, 416-418
Moulaert, Jehanne 325
Movements in European History, 297-299
 "Epilogue", 297, 299
multiculturalism, 27, 41, 49-50, 52, 73, 86-87, 369, 435
Murry, John Middleton, 104, 198, 203-204, 206, 325
Mysteries of Identity, 222, 364
Mythical Intentions in Modern Literature, 281

National Review, 75, 79
Neoconservative Criticism, 75
New Criterion,
 "D. H. Lawrence in love," 368
 "Lionel Trilling in the Classroom," 79
 "Present-tense culture," 418
"New Deal", 46
New Left Review, 335
New Princeton Encyclopedia, 20
New York World, 83
New York Times, 435-436
Novel Gazing: Queer Readings in Fiction, 434
The New Yorker, 41
Newsweek, 49
Nichols, Robert, 197
No! in Thunder, 76, 284
Novel, 44

O'Hara, Daniel T., 22-25, 48, 51
October, 320
Order of Things, 434

Paglia, Camille, 398
Panichas, George A., 34-36, 43-47, 53-54, 83-84, 435, 439-441
Passion of Michel Foucault, 77, 310, 352, 356-357, 359

Pearn, Nancy, 56, 336, 374
Peter Warlock: The Life of Philip Heseltine, 226
Phaedrus, 97
"phallic consciousness, " 35-36, 386-390, 397
Philosophy and Literature, 441
Phoenix, 98-100, 102, 107, 109, 152, 173-174, 313-314, 383, 385
   "Book Review of *Art Nonsense and Other Essays* by Eric Gill," 86, 152, 324
   "Morality and the Novel," 11, 250
Phoenix II,
   "The State of Funk," 11, 390, 434
   "A Propos of *Lady Chatterley's Lover*," 349, 354-355, 377-385, 393, 402-403
Pinker, J. B. , 74, 108, 180, 256
Plato, 19, 87, 97, 172, 197, 201, 210, 233, 292-294
(The) Plumed Serpent, 148-153, 344, 349-350
Podhoretz, Norman, 75-76, 78-79
Polinger, Laurence, 390
political correctness, 3-4, 6, 10, 14-15, 27, 35, 37, 39-43, 47, 49, 50-52, 53, 54, 56, 57, 58-59, 61-63, 65-66, 68-69, 70, 71, 73-75, 77, 80, 82-83, 86-88, 376-377, 389, 398, 401, 412, 413, 414, 415, 416-417, 433, 434-435, 442-443
Political Shakespeare, 319, 439
Poplawski, Paul, 68-69
post-modernism, 326-327, 331, 336
Postmodernism, 331-332, 336
Power/Knowledge, 21, 343
(The) Practice of Love: Lesbian Sexuality and Perverse Desire, 59
Price, Martin, 261, 267
The Priest of Love: A Life of D. H. Lawrence, 52, 221
"(The) Principles of Right," 24
Profscam, 27
"The Prussian Officer", 177-180

Psychoanalysis and the Unconscious, 72, 250, 280, 362, 367-368

Queer Forster, 20
Quest for Rananim, 244

racism, 3, 4, 25, 49, 62, 88, 369, 421
Radford, Dollie, 26, 272
Radical Parody, 22-24, 25, 48, 51
Radical Tragedy, 41, 319, 322, 343, 439
The Rainbow, 28-29, 103-104, 105, 107, 172-175, 205, 206-207, 213, 222, 224, 237, 295, 349, 402
"Rananim", 16, 183, 244-245
Random House Compact Unabridged Dictionary, Special Second Edition, 3, 262
Recovering Literature, 368
Reflections on the Death of a Porcupine and Other Essays, 200, 202, 359-360, 431
   "The Reality of Peace," Chapter II, 272-277, 311
   "The Reality of Peace," Chapter III, 431
Reign of Ideology, 62, 70
Reilly, Jim , 323
Reverent Discipline, 43-44, 46-47
reverse discrimination, 3-4, 24-27, 47, 50-52, 63, 69, 71-73, 75, 81-83, 86, 369, 434
Review of English Studies, 75
Rorty, Richard , 61-64
Rosenbaum, Yankel, 27
Rosenberg, Harold, 41
Ruderman, Judith, 17
Russell, Bertrand , 64, 70-71, 100-101, 103-104, 110, 183-186, 187, 188, 198, 201, 227-228, 236, 263-265, 298, 353, 433
sado-masochism, 21, 23, 43, 291-292, 308-310, 313, 351-353, 356-359, 363, 439
"Sado-Masochistic Studies," 21

Sagar, Keith, 40-41, 60-61, 119, 406
Said, Edward, 328
Saint Foucault, 291-292, 308, 352-353, 355, 358
Sale, Roger, 267-269
Sales, Roger, 328
Salmagundi,
  "Birthing an Ecstatic Anxiety: Harold Bloom's *Western Canon* and its Readers," 48
  "The Claims of a Common Culture: Gender, Race, Class and the Canon," 27
  "Foucault's Body-Language," 351
Savage, Henry, 171, 179, 229-230
social reform, 237
Scherr, Barry J., 9, 19, 32, 44, 50-51, 87-88, 172, 191, 293, 335, 349, 361
Scrutiny, 41, 44, 75
Scruton, Roger, 185, 313
Seaton, James, 68, 397
Secker, Martin, 376
Sedgwick, Eve Kosofsky, 48, 88, 172, 182, 248, 249, 251-252, 376-377
Selected Writings,Volume 1: Sex, 223
Sex, Politics and Society, 224
sexism, 3, 4, 7, 25, 38, 49, 62-63, 78, 88, 361
Sexual Desire: A Moral Philosophy of the Erotic, 185
Sexual Dissidence, 319-320, 322, 359, 361
sexual inversion" 229-231
Sexual Inversion, 225-226, 228, 229-230, 233-234, 236-237
Shakespeare, 47, 418
Shakespeare: The Invention of the Human, 51-52
Sharpton, Al, 63, 423
(The) Signature, 223
Simpson, David, 405
Simpson, O. J., 37, 39
Smith, Barry, 75, 226
social engineering, 24, 47, 424

sodomy, 185, 186, 210, 227
  "higher", 201-202, 205
Sons and Lovers, 100-101, 349
Spilka, Mark, 37-41, 44-46, 161, 269
  "Defending Lawrence", 38-39
  speech to the D. H. Lawrence Society of North America, 38
Spirit of D. H. Lawrence, 29
Starr, Ken, 48
Steyn, Mark, 418
Strachey, Lytton, 88, 198, 201-202, 247
Studies in Classic American Literature, 74, 85, 211
Studies in the Psychology of Sex, 237
Study of Thomas Hardy, 98-102, 106-112, 117, 130, 133-134, 140-141, 161, 180, 183
  Chapter I, 181
  Chapter II, 181-182, 362
  Chapter III, 181
  Chapter V, 326-327
  Chapter VII, "Of Being and Not-Being", 64, 117, 134, 183
  Chapter IX, 227
Symposium, 97

Textual Practice, 42
This Is Carbon, 369
"The Thorn in the Flesh," 180
Thornton, Weldon, 68-69
Thought, Words and Creativity: Art and Thought in Lawrence, 69-70, 71-72, 75-77
Thucydides, 213-215
To The Lighthouse, 66
Trilling, Lionel, 1, 4, 12, 14, 78-79, 278-279, 306, 337-339, 350, 405
  on liberalism, 1-3
  on Virginia Woolf, 6
  review of Brown's *Life Against Death*, 279-280
  review of Fiedler's *Love and Death*, 278
Ulysses, 66, 144

Ulrichs, K. H., 223
Urban Aboriginals, 359
(The) Utopian Vision of D. H. Lawrence, 285

Vamps & Tramps, 398
(The) Vanishing Individual, 369
Vasey, Lindeth, 260

Waiting for the End, 280, 284, 431
Walker, Alice, 334
Watson, Jean, 418
"We Need One Another," 366-367
Webster's Third International Dictionary, 85, 275, 404
Weekley, Barbara, 336-337
Weeks, Jeffrey, 224
West, Cornel, 78, 328
(The) Western Canon, 47-52, 66, 87-88, 396-397
Whitehead, Alfred North, 83
"Why the Novel Matters", 46, 441
Will, George, 3
Wilson, Charles, 29, 418
Wilson, Woodrow, 424, 425
Winfrey, Oprah, 37, 423
Women in Love, 9, 10-11, 13, 26, 28, 31-33, 44-47, 54, 55-57, 60-61, 66, 71-73, 103, 107-120, 172-319, 333, 363-364, 395, 399-401, 402, 430, 432
  Chapter III, "Class-room," 109-110
  Chapter V, "In the Train", 55-57, 243-245
  Chapter VIII, "Breadalby", 246, 254-255
  Chapter XIII, "Mino," 305
  Chapter XIV, "Water-Party", 114-115, 246-247, 265
  Chapter XVI, "Man to Man", 73, 247-258
  Chapter XIX, "Moony", 255, 258-259, 260, 293, 303
  Chapter XX, "Gladiatorial", 260-268, 289-293
  Chapter XXI, "Threshold", 262-263
  Chapter XXIII, "Excurse", 44-45, 74, 111-113, 267, 286-287, 294, 333
  Chapter XXV, "Marriage or Not", 294-295
  Chapter XXVII, "Flitting", 267, 271
  Chapter XXX, "Snow", 270, 308-309
  Chapter XXXI, "Snowed Up", 9-10, 300-313
  Chapter XXXII, "Exeunt", 60-61, 269-270, 298, 307
  "Foreword," 54, 109
  "Prologue", 215-217, 218-225, 227-244
Woolf, Virginia, 5-6, 66-67
World War I, 63, 12, 13, 16, 26, 28, 29, 35-36, 55, 60, 73, 104, 180-181, 200, 208, 244, 272, 274, 311-312, 443
Worthen, John, 260
Writing Against the Family, 8

Year's Work in English Studies, 65

Zaslove, Jerry, 369
Zytaruk, George J., 16, 29, 244